# Politics in the Developing World

*Edited by*

Peter Burnell
and Vicky Randall

OXFORD
UNIVERSITY PRESS

# OXFORD

UNIVERSITY PRESS

Great Clarendon Street, Oxford OX2 6DP

Oxford University Press is a department of the University of Oxford.
It furthers the University's objective of excellence in research, scholarship,
and education by publishing worldwide in

Oxford New York

Auckland Bangkok Buenos Aires Cape Town Chennai
Dar es Salaam Delhi Hong Kong Istanbul Karachi Kolkata
Kuala Lumpur Madrid Melbourne Mexico City Mumbai Nairobi
São Paulo Shanghai Taipei Tokyo Toronto

Oxford is a registered trade mark of Oxford University Press
in the UK and in certain other countries

Published in the United States
by Oxford University Press Inc., New York

A catalogue record for this title is available from the British Library

Library of Congress Cataloging in Publication Data
(Data available)

ISBN-13: 978-0-19-926442-1
ISBN-10: 0–19–926442–2

10 9 8 7 6 5 4 3 2

Typeset by Newgen Imaging Systems (P) Ltd., Chennai, India
Printed and bound in Great Britain on acid-free paper by
Antony Rowe Limited, Chippenham

# Preface

Putting together this volume has been an extremely demanding and time-consuming, though also highly rewarding, experience. Taking advantage of the fact that she is writing this preface, Vicky Randall would like to record that Peter Burnell has been the ideal collaborator, energetic, highly efficient and intellectually discerning and resourceful. We also both want to thank the team at Oxford University Press—Helen Adams, Ruth Anderson and Sue Dempsey—for all their encouragement, guidance and support throughout this exercise.

Peter Burnell
Vicky Randall
July 2004

# Source acknowledgements

The authors and publisher would like to thank the following for permission to reproduce copyright material:

Box 12.4 is an abbreviated version of 'The Democracy Template', reprinted by permission of the publisher from *Aiding Democracy Abroad: The Learning Curve*, Thomas Carothers (Washington DC, Carnegie Endowment for International Peace, 1999) **www.ceip.org**

Chapter 11 by Martin Doornbos is based on his article which first appeared in *Development and Change* (Vol. 33, Number 5, Blackwell Publishing).

The following figures and tables are reproduced by kind permission of World Bank: From *World Development Indicators 2003:* Figure 1, Inequality in selected countries; Figure 3, Total public expenditure as a % of GDP for country groups and selected countries, 2000; Table 1, Extreme poverty, 1990–2015; Table 2 Economic Growth, 1980–2001. Also a small selection of data extracted from *Global Development Finance: Statistical Appendix (2003)*, drawn from Tables A.43 and A.51.

# Contents

## Part One  Approaches and global context

## Part Two  Society and state

## Part Three **State and society**

## Part Four **Policy issues**

## Part Five **Case studies**

# Detailed contents

# List of figures and maps

# List of boxes

# List of tables

# About the contributors

**Tony Addison** is Deputy Director, World Institute for Development Economics Research (United Nations University-WIDER), Helsinki, Finland.

**Peter Burnell** is a Professor in the Department of Politics and International Studies, University of Warwick, UK.

**Thomas M. Callaghy** is Professor of Political Science in the Department of Political Science, University of Pennsylvania, USA.

**Martin Doornbos** is Emeritus Professor of Political Science at the Institute of Social Studies, The Hague, the Netherlands.

**Peter Ferdinand** is a Reader in the Department of Politics and International Studies, University of Warwick, UK.

**Michael Freeman** is a Research Professor in the Department of Government and was formerly Deputy Director of the Human Rights Centre, University of Essex, UK.

**Jeff Haynes** is a Professor in the Department of Law, Governance and International Relations, London Metropolitan University, UK.

**Stephen Hobden** was formerly a lecturer in the Department of International Politics, University of Wales, Aberystwyth, UK.

**Rob Jenkins** is Professor of Political Science, Birkbeck College, University of London, UK.

**Adrian Leftwich** is a Senior Lecturer in the Department of Politics, University of York, UK.

**Marton T. Markovits** is a doctoral candidate in the Department of Political Science, University of Pennsylvania, USA.

**Peter Newell** is a Fellow of the Institute of Development Studies, University of Sussex, UK.

**Marina Ottaway** is Senior Associate in the Democracy and Rule of Law Project, of the Carnegie Endowment for International Peace, Washington, DC, USA.

**Mark Otter** was formerly in the School of Political Science and International Studies at the University of Queensland and is now Manager of International Programs with WWF Australia.

**Jenny Pearce** is Professor of Latin American Politics in the Department of Peace Studies, University of Bradford, UK.

**David Pool** is a Lecturer in the Department of Government, University of Manchester, UK.

**Vicky Randall** is a Professor in the Department of Government, University of Essex, UK.

**Richard Robison** is a Professor of Political Economy at the Institute of Social Studies, The Hague, the Netherlands.

**James R. Scarritt** is Emeritus Professor in the Department of Political Science and Faculty Research Associate in the Institute of Behavioural Science at the University of Colorado at Boulder, USA.

**Andreas Schedler** is a Professor in the Department of Political Studies, Centro de Investigacion y Docencia Economicas, Mexico City, Mexico.

**Robert Schrire** is a Professor and Chair of the Political Studies Department, University of Cape Town, South Africa.

**Peter Siavelis** is an Associate Professor in the Department of Political Science, Wake Forest University, USA.

**Rachel Sieder** is a Senior Lecturer in Politics, Institute of Latin American Studies, School of Advanced Studies, University of London, UK.

**Brian Smith** is Emeritus Professor of Politics, University of Dundee, and Visiting Professor of Politics, University of Exeter, UK.

**Kathleen Staudt** is Professor of Political Science, the University of Texas at El Paso, USA.

**David Taylor** is Vice Provost, Aga Khan University, Karachi, Pakistan.

**Stephen Wright** is Professor, Department of Political Science, Northern Arizona University, USA.

# List of acronyms and abbreviations

| | |
|---|---|
| ACP | Africa-Caribbean-Pacific states |
| AFDL | Alliance des forces démocratiques pour la libération du Congo-Zaire |
| AIDS | acquired immune deficiency syndrome |
| ANC | African National Congress (South Africa) |
| AOSIS | Alliance of Small Island States |
| ASEAN | Association of South-East Asian Nations |
| BJP | Bharatiya Janata Party (India) |
| CACIF | Comité de Asociaciones Comerciales, Industriales y Financieras (Guatemala) |
| CBO | community-based organization |
| CFCs | Chlorofluorocarbons |
| CHOGM | Commonwealth Heads of Government |
| CIA | Central Intelligence Agency (USA) |
| CORFO | Chilean Development Corporation |
| DAC | Development Assistance Committee (of the Organization for Economic Cooperation and Development) |
| DPRK | Democratic People's Republic of Korea |
| DRC | Democratic Republic of the Congo (formerly Zaire) |
| ECOSOC | Economic and Social Council (United Nations) |
| ECOMOG | ECOWAS Monitoring Group |
| ECOWAS | Economic Community of West African States |
| EEZ | exclusive economic zone |
| EPB | Economic Planning Board (South Korea) |
| FDI | foreign direct investment |
| FRG | Frente Republicano Guatemalteco (Guatemala) |
| FSC | Forestry Stewardship Council |
| FIS | Front Islamique du Salut (Algeria) |
| G7 | Group of 7 economic summit |
| G77 | Group of 77 least developed countries |
| GAM | Aceh Freedom Movement |
| GATT | General Agreement on Tariffs and Trade |
| GDP | Gross Domestic Product |
| GEF | Global Environment Facility |
| GMOs | genetically modified organisms |
| HIP(I)C | Heavily Indebted Poor Countries (Initiative) |
| HIV | human immunodeficiency virus |
| IFE | Federal Electoral Institute (Mexico) |
| IFP | Inkatha Freedom Party (South Africa) |
| IMF | International Monetary Fund |
| IPU | Inter-Parliamentary Union |
| ISI | import-substituting industrialization |
| ISO | International Organization for Standardization |
| LDCs | less developed countries |

| | |
|---|---|
| LFO | Legal Framework Order (Pakistan) |
| MAD | Mutually Assured Destruction |
| MAR | Minorities at Risk project |
| MDGs | Millenium Development Goals (of the United Nations) |
| MINUGUA | Misión de las Naciones Unidas en Guatemala |
| MKSS | Mazdoor Kisan Shakti Sangathan (India) |
| MLC | Mouvement pour la libération du Congo |
| MNCs | multinational corporations |
| NAFTA | North American Free Trade Agreement |
| NDA | National Democratic Alliance (India) |
| NEPAD | New Economic Partnership for Africa's Development |
| NGO | non-governmental organization |
| NICs | newly industrialized countries (mainly East Asia) |
| NIE | new institutional economics |
| NIEO | New International Economic Order |
| NSSD | National Strategy for Sustainable Development |
| OECD | Organization for Economic Cooperation and Development |
| OPEC | Organization of Petroleum Exporting Countries |
| PAC | Pan Africanist Congress (South Africa) |
| PFN | Pentecostal Fellowship of Nigeria |
| PKI | Indonesian Communist Party |
| POPs | persistent organic compounds |
| PPC | People's Plan Campaign (India) |
| PPP | Pakistan People's Party |
| PRD | Party of the Democratic Revolution (Mexico) |
| PRI | Institutional Revolutionary Party (Mexico) |
| PRN | National Revolutionary Party (Mexico) |
| PRSPs | Poverty Reduction Strategy Papers |
| RCD | Rassemblement congolaise de la démocratie |
| ROK | Republic of Korea (South Korea) |
| RSS | Rashtriya Swayamsevak Sangh (India) |
| SACP | South African Communist Party |
| SALs | Structural Adjustment Loans |
| SAVAK | Iran Intelligency Agency (Ministry of Security) |
| SIDS | Small Islands Developing States Network |
| SOEs | state-owned enterprises |
| SWAPO | South West Africa People's Organization (Namibia) |
| TERI | Energy and Resources Institute |
| TNCs | transnational corporations |
| TRC | Truth and Reconciliation Commission (South Africa) |
| UDF | United Democratic Front (South Africa) |
| UN | United Nations |
| UNCED | United Nations Conference on Environment and Development (1992) |
| UNCTAD | United Nations Conference on Trade and Development |
| UNDP | United Nations Development Programme |
| UNEP | United Nations Environment Programme |
| UNICEF | United Nations Children's Fund |

| | |
|---|---|
| UP | Uttar Pradesh (India) |
| URNG | Unidad Revolucionaria Nacional Guatemalteca (Guatemala) |
| WSSD | World Summit on Sustainable Development (2002) |
| WWF | World Wide Fund for Nature |
| WTO | World Trade Organization |

# Introduction

*Peter Burnell and Vicky Randall*

**THE** aim of this book is to explore the changing nature of **politics** in the **developing world** in the early years of the twenty-first century. Both 'politics' and the 'developing world' are concepts which require further elaboration and which are discussed more fully below. By politics we mean broadly activities associated with the process and institutions of government, or the state, but in the context of wider power relations and struggles. By the developing world we are primarily referring to those regions which were formerly colonized by Western powers, have been late to industrialize, and sustain high levels of poverty: Africa, Asia, the Caribbean, the Middle East, and South America.

In our analysis of politics in the developing world, the complex and changing nexus between state and society has centre stage. This is because it is the reciprocal interaction of state and society and the influence that each one exerts on the other that most accounts for the distinctive character of developing countries' politics. Needless to say that influence varies in both degree and kind, over time and as between individual states. The book does not set out to present a case for saying the state is now marginal from the political analysis of developing countries nor does it argue that we must 'bring the state back in'. On the contrary it recognizes that issues concerning the state have been, are, and will remain central to the political analysis, notwithstanding important developments—political,

financial, economic, technological, and so on—at the sub-state, regional, and especially global levels that are reshaping the nature, size, and role of individual states.

A book about politics in the developing world is not the same thing as a book about development per se, or development studies. Indeed the book does not have as its objective to give emphasis to the politics *of* development, where that means the political economy of economic growth or of socio-economic change. Certainly there has been a trend in the study of development to comprehend that process in an increasingly holistic sense—one that emphasizes its multifaceted nature and the interconnectedness of the various parts, of which politics provides one very important element. And key relationships between politics and society and between politics and the economy are both explored in the chapters in the book, but without any mission to demonstrate that politics is in some sense the 'master science' which unlocks all other subjects. Instead the consequences that development can have for politics in the developing countries are every bit as much a part of the analysis in this book as the implications that the politics have for development.

A word is also needed explaining the geographical coverage of the book. As related below, the boundaries of the developing world are neither uncontentious nor unchanging. We have already suggested which regions have tended historically to be associated with it. However, this book's coverage, and especially the case studies, does not include all parts of the developing world, primarily for pragmatic reasons. Thus countries like Cuba, Vietnam, and the rest that at one time claimed to be socialist, even Marxist-Leninist, are part of the developing world just as are countries that now defer to capitalism and have a form of political pluralism. They are, however, very much a dwindling band and new recruits now seem unlikely in the post-Soviet, post-cold war environment, where international forces of globalization appear so hostile. They can hardly be considered very representative, and so do not feature among the case study chapters. On the other hand, we have had to follow the conventional view that China, for all its developing world characteristics, is best left out of the analysis. China is unique in many notable respects. It is sufficiently large, complex, and important to warrant studying on its own.

There are other parts of the world, beyond the regions traditionally included, that might now be considered to fall into this developing world category. Although no express reference is made in the book to those elements of the post-communist world, the new European and Central Asian states that formerly belonged to the 'Second World' have many of the characteristics long associated with the developing world. Some of them have come to acquire developing country status, as the Organization for Economic Cooperation and Development's (OECD) Development Assistance Committee (DAC) has made countries like Albania, Armenia, and Turkmenistan eligible for official development assistance. By comparison it styles the post-communist world's more advanced members 'countries in transition', entitled to compete only for a separate, much smaller category of support, called 'official aid'. However, as in the case of China, readers are free to apply the concepts and propositions in this book to an examination of all these other countries if they wish, just as area specialists seeking insights into those countries will find material here that has relevance for their own subject. The same point applies to those particular regions or localities in the more developed countries of the North that seem to share certain 'southern' or 'Third World' characteristics, such as a significant degree of relative economic backwardness and associated deficiencies of social welfare or physical quality of life.

# From 'Third World' to developing world

The developing world has been variously referred to as the 'Third World', the South, and the less developed countries among other titles. The question of the meaningfulness of the 'Third World' as an organizing concept has long been the subject of dispute no less than the term's precise definition or true origins. Successive rationales for marking out a distinct 'Third World' associated this world with a stance of non-alignment towards the capitalist and communist superpowers; with post-colonial status, with dependence on Western capitalism, and with poverty and economic 'backwardness'. Following the collapse of Soviet power, the disappearance of the 'Second World' served to hasten the decline of the 'Third World' as a category name. In keeping with this trend we have preferred to use the term 'developing world' for this book. But whatever term is favoured there has

also been a growing appreciation of the very rich diversity to be found among and within those countries traditionally seen to come under its umbrella.

Some of the differences have always been there, like the enormous range in demographic and territorial size. Even just at the lower end of the scale, the distinction between 'small' and 'micro' states is an ongoing topic for debate. However, the combined total number is believed to account for anywhere between a maximum of 140 and a minimum of fewer than 80—but still representing around 40 per cent—of all developing countries and territories. In contrast, in a regional context some of the larger developing countries can be thought to be approaching almost superpower-like status, notwithstanding their vulnerability to certain major external shocks. Thus a state like India, a nuclear power with a population that exceeds one billion people, has a very strong claim to be admitted to the permanent membership of the United Nations Security Council.

Similarly the developing world has always been noted for its considerable differences in terms of economic dynamism and technological progress, and recent decades have served only to make these contrasts more pronounced. Just as average incomes have been in decline in many parts of Africa in the last two decades so some of the so-called 'tiger' economies in East Asia have become developed countries in all but name. Singapore, for instance, has one of the highest average incomes per head of any country in the world.

Until the 1980s, despite these disparities in size and economic performance, it was possible to argue that most countries in the developing world had in common certain political traits. These included a tendency towards authoritarian rule, whether based on the military or a single ruling party, severe instability and internal conflict, and endemic corruption. More recently political differences that were already there have become much more apparent. We are increasingly aware of the wide disparities in state strength and efficacy. To a considerable extent this recognition owes to growing incidence of state failure, in extreme cases state collapse, that parallel a much larger number of cases where simply the governance capabilities of the state appear to be very weak or are severely constrained. Likewise the politics of ethnic and religious identity have been increasingly in evidence, our perception sharpened, perhaps, by increased interest in possible implications for regional and wider international security interests. But they have been much more visible in some developing regions or countries than others: in Latin America, in particular, they constitute a very minor theme.

In sum we are increasingly conscious of the complexity and diversity of the developing world. The fact that some common features among developing countries such as the colonial experience are now receding into history and some practical manifestations of 'Third World solidarity' like the virtually defunct Non-Aligned Movement have also disappeared, means the numerous differences within the developing world now appear in sharper relief.

# Politics as independent or dependent variable?

Most people, still more so politics students, will have some idea of what is intended by the term 'politics'. Generally political scientists understand politics to refer to activities surrounding the process and institutions of government or the state and that is a focus we share in this book. However, there is another tradition, that some describe as 'sociological' that tends to identify politics with power relationships and structures, including but by no means confined to the state: they include for instance relationships between socio-economic classes and between genders. When studying politics in the developing world, we believe it is particularly important to locate analysis of political processes in their narrower sense within the wider context of social relationships and conflicts. One of the themes and puzzles that pervade this field is the relationship between the more formal aspects of political processes and institutions that may have been to some degree imposed or modelled on Western prototypes, and their 'informal' aspects. For instance, to understand how political parties really work we need to consider not only formal organizational characteristics—rules, authorized decision-making bodies, membership, and so on—but informal hierarchies of power, such as those between patrons and clients, that operate within them.

Despite our insistence on the need to understand politics in this wider power context, this does not mean that we deny what is sometimes referred to as the **'autonomy' of the political**, that is the ability of politics to have independent and significant effects of its own. Thus any account of politics in the developing world that goes beyond the merely descriptive can have one or both of two objectives: to make sense of the politics; to disclose what else the politics itself helps us to understand better. Succinctly, politics can be treated as *explanandum* or *explanans*, and possibly as both.

For some decades there was a large movement in political science to view politics as the dependent variable. Analysts sought to advance our understanding of politics and gain some predictive potential in regard to future political developments by rooting it in some 'more fundamental' aspects of the human condition, sometimes called structural 'conditions'. This was nowhere more evident than in the tendency to argue that the kind of political regime—namely the relationship between rulers and ruled, conventionally depicted somewhere along the continuum from a highly authoritarian to a more liberal democratic polity—is a product largely of economic circumstance. The level of economic achievement, the nature and pace of economic change and the social consequences were all considered highly important. It was not only Marxists who subscribed to broadly this kind of view. But there were also others who sought to explain politics especially in some parts of the developing world more as an outcome of certain cultural conditions or of a matrix of social divisions much more confusing than a simple class-based analysis would allow. These and other inclinations that view politics as contingent are still very much in evidence in contemporary theorizing about politics in the developing world, as several chapters in Parts One and Two of the book will show.

However, over recent decades in political science the larger study of comparative politics and area studies too have increased the weight given to the idea of politics as an independent variable, claiming in principle that politics matters: not only is it affected, but it too can have effects. Mair (1996) has characterized this as a shift from an emphasis on questioning what causes political systems to emerge, take shape, and possibly persist to questions about what outputs and outcomes result from the political processes and how well various political institutions perform. Making sense of the politics now goes beyond just explaining it. It extends also to an investigation of the impact of politics and its consequences, and that includes how political features such as the state are influenced by yet other features that are themselves political, both directly and indirectly through the mediation of intervening variables. For example in an increasing number of places civil society and social movements are coming to play a significant political role.

This move to view politics as at least being semi-autonomous and not just the dependent variable coincides with the rise of new institutionalism in political studies. New institutionalism has been described in a seminal article by March and Olsen (1984: 747) as neither a theory nor a coherent critique of one but instead 'simply an argument that the organisation of political life makes a difference'. The new institutionalism directs us to study political process and political design as much as outcome and the contextual 'conditions'. This is not a completely new mood. As March and Olsen rightly say, historically, political science has emphasized the ways in which political behaviour is embedded in an institutional structure of norms, rules, expectations, and traditions that constrain the free play of individual will. The implications of this approach, as well as the idea that to comprehend politics at its fullest we should trace the meaning political forms and political choices have for wider developmental issues like economic management and welfare concerns, are explored in Parts Three and Four of the book especially. In doing so the chapters provide a bridge to studying the larger phenomenon of human development. Here we take our cue from the United Nations Development Programme where it says its *Human Development Report 2002* is 'first and foremost about the idea that politics is as important to successful development as economics' (UNDP 2002: v). The UNDP's understanding is that human development, an idea that is currently fashionable among many analysts of development, aims to promote the freedom, well-being, and dignity of people everywhere.

# Global trends

Notwithstanding the increasing differentiation within the developing world it is a fact that over the last twenty years or so there has also been a growing convergence, due to the presence of a number of major interconnected trends, political and economic, domestic and international. But these trends, far from reconfirming the more old-fashioned notions of the 'Third World', are instead ensuring that some of the most striking similarities in the developing world today have a very different character from the 'Third World' of old. This point is well worth illustrating before moving on.

One such trend comprises pressures from within and without the societies to adopt the so-called 'Washington consensus' of the Bretton Woods institutions—the International Monetary Fund and World Bank—on economic policy and national economic management. They can be held responsible in part for a near universal movement in the direction of neo-liberalism and marketization. There is an ongoing shift from public ownership and the direct control of economic life by the state towards acceptance and encouragement of the idea of for-profit enterprise and a growing role for non-governmental development organizations. Although proceeding at a different pace in different places and experiencing widely varying degrees of success, the implications of such changes for politics generally and the state specifically are profound. Ultimately the same might become true of the recent signs that a 'post-Washington consensus' giving much higher priority to tackling poverty could be evolving, although it is far too early to judge whether ideas are really changing and how far, let alone to see any sustained shifts in government policies.

If economic liberalization is one prong of a growing convergence among developing countries then pressures towards political liberalization and democratization have been a second and, according to some accounts, symbiotically related development. Again we should not exaggerate the amount of substantive change that has actually taken place. Indeed, after a time in the early 1990s when the 'third wave' of democratization seemed to have unstoppable momentum and some observers talked about the 'end

of history', far more cautious claims are now much in evidence, as the complex reality that contains some significant continuities becomes increasingly apparent. Yet irrespective of how democratic and well governed most developing countries now really are and how many countries possess genuine market economies, pressures to engage with and struggles to adapt or resist aspects of economic liberalization and government reform have been ubiquitous. As these came to be among the prime moving principles of the collective drama of developing countries from the 1980s on, the developing world began to look a very different place from the way the 'Third World' was understood in previous decades.

But underpinning these and other shared developments like the growing salience of environmental issues and discussion of human rights has been the growing impact of globalization. Here globalization is understood at minimum as 'the process of increasing interconnectedness between societies such that events in one part of the world more and more have effects on peoples and societies far away' (Baylis and Smith 2001: 7). Of course the developing countries are touched unevenly and in different ways. But there is a good case for arguing that many of the so called 'dependent countries' of the 'Third World' now see their fortunes influenced increasingly either directly by the forces of globalization—positively or negatively—or indirectly where they are bystanders sharing little in globalization's chief claimed benefits. Yet they are not themselves the drivers of globalization. Theorists of globalization tell us the sites of power are becoming more dispersed and power is leaking away from states, towards an assortment of sub-state, inter-state, supra-state and especially non-state institutions. Hardly any country is immune from this tendency for the borders to be breached, as extra-national forces and outside institutions increasingly make close connections with domestic actors and influence events at levels of society below the central government and beyond the state. Yet there is compelling evidence to suggest that it is centres of power based in or run from North America, Western Europe, and Japan that remain dominant.

Thus while the old order summed up by first, second, and third worlds has disappeared and the international system appears to be edging closer to a more diffuse, somewhat fragmented form of multi-level governance, developing world societies do not share an identical situation to their counterparts in the rich, powerful North. The contrasting claim that in the post-communist era the states system has moved from bipolarity to unipolarity not multipolarity, given the United States' military hegemony, its resurgent unilateralism and, 'post-September 11', its far-reaching foreign political ambitions, is highly significant for developing countries. But if true, that claim far from elevates their position. These and other developments at the international level have undoubted importance for politics in the developing world. At the same time we should remain self-aware and resort to questioning with respect to how we construct our understanding of other and often very different societies. That extends to the analytical frameworks, the explanatory theories, and, most especially, any normative propositions that we choose to employ. We should be continually challenging ourselves to distinguish between, on the one side, what, how, and how far changes are taking place in developing world politics, and on the other side changing understandings that reflect more an evolving situation, fashionable paradigms, and new nostrums in the rest of the world, particularly the most powerful and affluent countries.

# Organization of the book

The book comprises five parts. Part One on analytical approaches and the global context should be read first. The aim of this part is to provide an introduction to general theoretical approaches offering alternative ways of making sense of the politics in the developing world. These simplifying devices enable us to bring some order to a great mass of facts. They are useful both for directing our enquiries and because they provide a lens or set of lenses through which to interpret the empirical information, and suggest explanations for what we find there. Ultimately, the point of theorizing is not simply to explain but to provide a gateway to prediction. And however tenuous are social science's claims to be able to predict with any confidence matters political, the book aims both to assess the present of developing countries in the light of the past and to identify the major political uncertainties facing them in the foreseeable future.

Special attention is given to the international context. The glib conviction that now more than ever all of humanity resides in 'one world' betokens a very real fact of growing interconnectedness and interdependence, however asymmetric, between nations and state as well as non-state actors. The different analytical approaches these chapters offer should not be viewed entirely as mutually exclusive rivals. Each can quite plausibly have something valuable to offer at one and the same time, more especially when applied to different country situations and historical epochs. Readers must form their own judgements about which particular theoretical propositions offer most insight into particular issues and problems or the more general conditions of the politics of developing countries.

Parts Two and Three aim to illuminate the changing nature, role, and situation of the state in relation to key social variables within developing countries. The two parts are a mirror image of one another. Together they explore both how the politics reflects or is affected by social context and how states specifically have responded to the challenges posed by society, and the social effects. Particular attention is given to what this means in terms of the changing use and distribution of political power among state institutions and other actors.

Part Four identifies major policy issues that confront to greater or lesser degree all developing countries. In general terms the issues are not peculiar to the developing world but they do have a special resonance there. And although the issues also belong to the larger discourse on development per se, the chapters in Part Four aim to uncover why and how they become expressly political and to compare different possible political responses and their consequences both for politics and development.

Part Five aims to illustrate in some depth or by what is sometimes called 'thick description' principal themes raised in the earlier parts, so complementing the use there of examples drawn from right across the developing world. Each chapter in Part Five combines two countries chosen both for their intrinsic value and for the contrasts they provide in relation to a larger theme. All major regions are represented. In total the studies once again highlight the great diversity of experience in the developing world; they also demonstrate the benefit to be gained from a detailed historical knowledge of the individual cases. But although the cases differ not least in respect of their relative 'success' or 'failure' regarding development in the widest sense and politics specifically, none of them offers a purely straightforward picture. The case studies should be read in conjunction with the appropriate chapter or chapters from the earlier parts, and are not intended to be read in isolation.

The editors' view is that a final chapter headed Conclusions is not appropriate, in any case unmanageable, and probably undesirable. The chapters each contain their own summaries; such a large collected body of material is not easily reduced without making some arbitrary decisions; and, most importantly, readers should be encouraged to form their own conclusions. It is almost inevitable that readers will differ in terms of the themes, issues, and even the countries or regions they will most want to form conclusions about. And it is in the nature of the subject that there is no single 'right' set of answers that the editors can distil. On the contrary, studying politics in the developing world is so fascinating precisely because it always has given rise to yet more, challenging new questions.

So we finish here by posing some big overarching questions that you might want to keep in mind as you read the chapters. They can be used to help structure the sort of general debate that often takes place towards the end of a course or study programme similar to the ones for which this book is intended. In principle the subject of each and every one of the chapters and all the case studies merit study as individual items. But for courses occupying a more limited number of weeks one possibility is for lectures or presentations by tutors to concentrate on material drawn from Parts One, Two, Three and Four, and for the allotted student reading preparatory to each week to include relevant case study material as well.

- Is politics in the developing world so different from elsewhere that understanding it requires a distinct theoretical framework?

- Is there a theoretical framework adequate for the purpose of comprehending politics in all countries of the developing world?

- Are the main political trends experienced by the developing world in recent decades summed up best by increasing diversity or, alternatively growing convergence?

- In what political respects is the developing world truly developing, and in what respects are significant parts of it not developing?

- What grounds are there for being optimistic or alternatively pessimistic about future politics in the developing world?

- Are the state's role and nature fundamentally changing in the developing world, and if so, in what directions?

- What are the principal forces, domestic or global, creating incentives and pressures for change of the nature and role of the state in the developing world?

- What lessons most relevant to other societies can be learned by studying politics in the developing world?

## WEB LINK

**www.id21.org**  Information for Development in the 21st Century—a searchable online collection of short digests of the latest social and economic research studies across thirty key topics.

# Part One

## Approaches and global context

Politics in the developing world offers an enormously rich and fascinating canvas of material for investigation. If we are to make sense of what we find we must approach the subject in a structured and orderly way, with a clear sense of purpose. That means having an adequate framework, or frameworks, of analysis comprising appropriate concepts lucidly defined together with a set of coherent organizing propositions. Propositions are advanced to explain the political phenomena in terms of their relationship with one another and their relations with other variables—both the influencing factors and the factors that are themselves influenced by, and demonstrate the importance of, politics. This part introduces analytical approaches to the study of politics in the developing world. It sets out to situate that politics within an international and increasingly globalizing environment, as befits the increase of interdependence ('one world') and supraterritoriality that appear so distinctive of modern times. This part has two aims: **first** to identify whether the 'developing world' is a sufficiently distinct entity to warrant its own theory, as we seek to comprehend its politics. It compares the main broad-gauge theoretical frameworks that at different times have been offered for just this very purpose. Do individual theories work better for some cases than for others, across the enormous range from resource-poor micro-states or small states like islands in the Pacific to countries that in a regional context look more like superpowers, such as India, Brazil, or Nigeria? The **second** aim is to show why and in what ways it is becoming increasingly difficult to understand or even just describe politics within developing countries without taking into account influences in the wider international system. These are the inter-state and supra-state influences that originate in economic, financial, diplomatic, cultural, and other forums. Many of these influences can penetrate state borders without having either express consent or tacit approval from government. They collaborate and collide with a variety of intra- and non-state actors, reaching far down to the sub-state and sub-national levels. At the same time developing countries also participate in and seek to influence regional networks and wider international organization, with varying degrees of success (Appendix 2 provides an illustrative list of regional inter-governmental organizations). Thus the place of 'south–south' relations should be compared with 'north–south' relations before and since the end of the cold war. This part helps us to consider the developing world's place within the global system as a whole: such questions as how are far developing country politics conditioned by powerful constraints and pressures originating outside? Are those pressures and constraints and their impact in any sense comparable to 'neo-colonialism' or the imperialism of old? Is power in the developing world now being ceded not so much to governments in the rich world as to a more diffuse and less controllable multi-layered set of global commercial, financial, and economic forces and institutions?

# Analytical approaches to the study of politics in the developing world

*Vicky Randall*

## OVERVIEW

Two contrasting broad approaches long dominated political analysis of developing countries. One was a politics of **modernization** that gave rise to '**political development**' theory, then to revised versions of that approach which stressed the continuing if changing role of tradition, and the need for strong government, respectively. Second was a Marxist-inspired approach that gave rise to **dependency theory** and subsequently to neo-Marxist analysis that focused on the relative autonomy of the state. By the 1980s both approaches were running out of steam but were partially subsumed in **globalization theory** that emphasized the ongoing process, accelerated by developments in communications and the end of the cold war, of global economic integration and its cultural and political ramifications. Nowadays it is difficult to identify a distinct underlying approach to politics in the **developing world**, but perhaps it is unnecessary and in its absence certain key themes and agendas lend a respectable degree of coherence.

# Introduction

This chapter provides an introduction to the main broad analytical approaches or frameworks of interpretation that have been employed in studying **politics** in the developing world. The 'developing world' is clearly a vast field, covering a great number of highly diverse political systems. To varying degrees those seeking to make sense of this field have felt a need for theories or frameworks of analysis to provide them with appropriate concepts or containers of information, and allow comparison and generalization across countries or regions. Some frameworks have been relatively modest or 'middle-range' but others have been much more ambitious in scope and claims. Moreover, despite aspirations to scientific objectivity and rigour they have inevitably reflected the circumstances in which they were formulated—for instance political scientists' underlying values, domestic political pressures and funding inducements, as well as perceived changes in the developing countries themselves. We all need to be aware of these approaches, and the surrounding debates, if we are to read the literature critically and form our own views.

We begin with what can be called the politics of modernization, emerging in the United States in the 1950s. This approach, including political development theory and its various 'revisions', operated from a mainstream, liberal, or, to its left critics, pro-capitalist perspective. The second and opposed approach, stemming from a critical, Marxist-inspired perspective, has taken the form first of **dependency theory** and then of a more state-focused Marxist approach. More recently the dominant though by no means unchallenged paradigm has been globalization theory, to some degree incorporating elements of both developmentalist and dependency perspectives. Globalization theory, however, has also served to problematize politics in the developing world as a coherent field, partly because it tends to undermine the premise of a distinct developing world. For this and other reasons, some have suggested that the field is currently in crisis. The latter part of this chapter considers how far a distinctive and coherent approach to politics in the developing world is still discernible in the present day, and also asks whether such an approach would be desirable.

# 'Politics' and the 'developing world'

Before considering the three main approaches themselves, we need briefly to revisit the notions of 'developing world' on the one hand and 'politics' on the other. This is because to understand and assess the approaches we need some idea of what it is that such analysis is supposed to make intelligible or explain. As noted in the introduction, the term 'developing world' has conventionally referred to the predominantly post-colonial regions of Africa, Asia, Latin America and the Caribbean, and the Middle East, perceived to be poorer, less economically advanced, and less 'modern' than the developed world. 'Developing world' is preferred to 'Third World', because that latter term carries some particular historical connotations that make it especially problematic.

But even when we use the less problematic 'developing world', there have always been questions about what makes such a concept meaningful. What exactly are the defining features that these countries have in common and that distinguish them from the 'developed world', both generally and in terms of their politics? Are such common features more important than their differences? These questions, becoming more pressing as the differences have grown, have clear implications for both the need and the possibility for some kind of general approach to understanding and analysing them.

Similarly, 'politics' is a highly contested notion. Politics on one understanding is a kind of activity associated with the process of government, and in modern settings also linked with the 'public' sphere. On another understanding it is about 'power' relations and struggles not necessarily confined to the process of government or restricted to the public domain. This volume takes the view that neither perspective on its own is sufficient, in general but particularly in a developing world context. Our preferred focus is on state–society relations and seeks to investigate both central governmental processes and power relations within society, and how they interact. One question to be asked about the various approaches to studying politics in developing countries, surveyed below, is how far they enable us to do this.

A further important question concerns the **autonomy of politics**: how far is politics as a level or sphere of social life determined by economic and/or social/cultural dimensions of society and how far

does it independently impact on those dimensions? Is the autonomy of politics itself variable? The different approaches to be considered all address this question, more or less explicitly, but arrive at very different conclusions.

## Key points

- Awareness of the main analytical approaches enables students to be more critical.

- The expression 'developing world' is preferable to 'Third World' but the diversity of countries included still makes generalization problematic.

- Studying politics in developing countries means investigating both central government processes and power relations in society, and their interaction.

- A further important question concerns the relative autonomy of politics.

# Dominant approaches

It must be stressed that approaches to the study of politics in this vast swathe of the world's countries have in practice been extremely diverse. Most of the analytic toolkit of political science has been applied at one time or another. This includes statistical analysis, **rational choice theory**, and **discourse theory**. On the other hand many country-based studies have not been explicitly theoretical at all. Nonetheless it is possible to argue that most studies of politics in developing countries have been informed to some degree by one or other of three main dominant approaches.

## The politics of modernization

The emergence of the 'politics of modernization' approach reflected both changing international political circumstances and developments within social science and specifically within political science. Out of the Second World War a new world was

born in which first two superpowers, the United States and the Soviet Union, confronted one another and, secondly, a process of decolonization was set in train leaving a succession of constitutionally independent states. Soon the two powers were vying for influence in these states. Within the United States, social scientists, and increasingly political scientists, were encouraged to study them.

However, the field of comparative politics at that time was ill-equipped to do so. It was (i) highly parochial—focused on a narrow range of Western countries, (ii) typically concerned with the legal and historical development of governing institutions, and (iii) not systematically comparative at all. Responding to this new challenge, comparative politics drew on two developments in the social sciences. First, the 'behavioural revolution' encouraged a more 'scientific' approach that sought to build general social theories and test them empirically. Second, especially in sociology but also in economics, interest was growing in tracing and modelling processes of 'modernization'. Sociology has from its inception been concerned with the impact of industrialization on pre-industrial society, and modernization theory was able to draw on the insights of its founding fathers, including Spencer (1829–1903), Durkheim (1858–1917), and Weber (1864–1920). Modernization theory took different forms: some concentrated on the process of increasing 'structural' or institutional differentiation, others on the psychological or cultural prerequisites. There was, however, a prevalent assumption that the process of modernization experienced in the West provided a valuable guide to what to expect in the developing world.

## Political development theory

In this context interest grew in elaborating a specific concept and theory of political development. A significant step was the setting up by the American Social Science Research Council in 1954 of a Committee of Comparative Politics, chaired by Gabriel Almond. The intention was to promote both case studies of politics in developing countries and more general debate that could produce a framework for comparative political analysis. For over a decade this Committee and the funds at its disposal strongly influenced the emerging field of study. Whilst no one framework of analysis dominated, the one initially proposed and subsequently developed by Almond himself was both influential and highly representative.

Almond developed a structural-functional approach to compare politics in different countries and as a basis for his concept of political development. Two immediate sources of his model were: the framework devised by behavioural political scientist David Easton (1965), based on an engineering system, for analysing political systems in terms of inputs, outputs, and feedback loops; second, the 'structural-functionalism' of sociologist Talcott Parsons (1960), who argued that increased complexity of social structures was linked to improved performance of necessary social system functions. Parsons also developed the concept of 'pattern variables', referring to the more modern or traditional styles in which social actors performed their roles. For instance achievement (merit) was contrasted with ascription (the status awarded at birth) as the basis for evaluating someone's social status.

Almond's model, modified over time (see Box 1.1), began by building on Easton's 'inputs' and 'outputs' to distinguish a series of political functions and then examining their relationship, following Parsons, with particular structures or institutions. There were four input functions—political socialization (instilling attitudes towards the political system), political recruitment, and the 'articulation' and 'aggregation' of interests (demands). On the output side three functions were identified—rule-making, rule implementation, and rule adjudication—and there was a more pervasive function of political communication.

Almond originally suggested that political development could be understood as the process through which these functions were increasingly associated with specialized structures—parties for interest aggregation, legislatures for rule-making, and so on—and with the emergence of modern styles of politics, based on Parsons's pattern variables described above. Later (1960) he identified five political system 'capabilities' (extractive, regulative, distributive, symbolic, and responsive), which were expected to grow as structures became more specialized and political styles more modern. These capabilities in turn would help the system to deal with four main problems (some writers later referred to these as 'crises')—of state-building (with the focus on state structures), nation-building (focusing on cultural integration), participation, and distribution.

Almond's approach has been extensively and justly criticized, although it must be said that political scientists continue to use many of the concepts he developed, for instance state-building (see Chapter 10) and nation-building. Although he sought, through identifying general political functions, to get away from specific political systems and thereby facilitate comparison, in practice these functions clearly derived from American political experience and did very little to illuminate the case studies they were applied to. Criticisms levelled against Almond's scheme, that it was unilinear (assuming one general direction of change), teleological (holding out the goal of a modern, most of the time a

## Box 1.1 Almond's framework for comparative analysis

**Political system**

INPUT FUNCTIONS **and typical associated structures**

OUTPUT FUNCTIONS **and typical associated structures**

**Political socialization** (family, schools, religious bodies, parties etc)

**Rule-making** (legislatures)

**Political recruitment** (parties)

**Rule implementation** (bureaucracies)

**Interest articulation** (interest groups)

**Rule adjudication** (judicial system)

**Interest aggregation** (parties)

**Political communication**

Political systems develop *five capabilities*:
- extractive (drawing material and human resources from environment)
- regulative (exercising control over individual and group behaviour)
- distributive (allocation of different kinds of 'good' to social groups)
- symbolic (flow of effective symbols, e.g. flags, statues, ceremony)
- responsive (responsiveness of inputs to outputs)

These help them to face *four kinds of problem*:
- state-building (need to build structures to penetrate society)
- nation-building (need to build culture of loyalty and commitment)
- participation (pressure from groups to participate in decision-making)
- distribution (pressure for redistribution or welfare)

(Almond and Powell 1966)

---

liberal-democratic, polity), and ethnocentric, were also made of other attempts to conceptualize political development, with the added observation that they were extremely diverse, demonstrating a lack of consensus on what political development actually was. In one famous study, Pye (1966) identified ten different understandings of political development, although he argued that these could be reduced to three main themes: a concern, even if only at the level of rhetoric with equality; growing political system capability; and increasing differentiation of political roles and structures.

Political development theory, in this form, was in decline by the late 1960s, not least because supporting funding was drying up. But it has not entirely disappeared and in particular one can argue that many of its central themes have been taken up in the literature emerging from the 1980s about democratization. In addition, in a recent paper that is provoking much discussion Moore (2000) has revived the term 'political development' but in the specific sense of the development of an effective, and

responsive, state. Before leaving political development theory, though, two further developments should be noted.

## Modernization revisionism

One strand of criticism of political development theory—**modernization revisionism**—centred on its oversimplified notions of tradition, modernity, and their interrelationship. Taking up arguments voiced by social anthropologists against modernization theory, some political scientists questioned what they perceived as an assumption that political modernization would eliminate 'traditional' elements of politics such as caste and ethnicity (the topic of religion was largely ignored until the 1980s—see Chapter 6). Instead they suggested that aspects of political modernization could positively invigorate these traditional elements, albeit in a changed form, and also that these elements would invariably influence in some measure the form and pace of political

## Box 1.2  Patron–client relations (selected quotations)

An anthropological account of a traditional patron–client relationship between landlord and sharecropper:

A peasant might approach the landlord to ask a favour, perhaps a loan of money or help in some trouble with the law, or the landlord might offer his aid knowing of a problem. If the favour were granted or accepted, further favours were likely to be asked or offered at some later time. The peasant would reciprocate—at a time and in a context different from that of the acceptance of the favour in order to de-emphasize the material self-interest of the reciprocative action—by bringing the landlord especially choice offerings from the farm produce or by sending some members of the peasant family to perform services in the landlord's home, or refraining from cheating the landlord, or merely by speaking well of him in public and professing devotion to him.

(Silverman 1977: 296)

Patron–client relationships in Mexican party politics:

Given PRI monopolization of public office, for much of the post-revolutionary period the most important actors in the competition for elected and appointed positions have been political *camarillas* within the ruling elite. Camarillas are vertical groupings of patron–client relationships, linked at the top of the pyramid to the incumbent president. These networks are assembled by individual politicians and bureaucrats over a long period of time and reflect the alliance-building skill and family connections of the patron at the apex.

(Craig and Cornelius 1995: 259–60)

Neopatrimonialism in Africa:

The institutional hallmark of politics in the ancient regimes of postcolonial Africa was neopatrimonialism . . . Neopatrimonial strongmen all relied on the award of personal favours. Within the state, these favours typically took the form of public sector jobs; within society, the distribution of public resources through licences, contracts and projects. In return for material rewards, clients mobilized political support and referred all decisions upward in mark of loyalty to patrons. This happened at every level; at the top, the ruler's faithful political aristocracy was rewarded with prebendal control of public offices, monopoly rents, and the possibility of creating its own clientelist networks.

(Bratton and van de Walle 1997: 61, 65–6)

change. This perspective also drew attention to the role of 'traditional' patron–client relationships within seemingly modern political parties and bureaucracies, an extremely important insight with continuing relevance (see Box 1.2). Despite further criticisms that have been made of modernization revisionism in its turn, this perspective has greatly enhanced our understanding of political processes in the developing world.

## Politics of order

There is some disagreement as to how far the second development, referred to here as the **'politics of order'** thesis, was essentially part of the political development approach or represented a break with it. On the one hand, critics on the left have seen it as informed by the same underlying concern to promote forms of politics compatible with capitalist interests: in Cammack's words (1997: 13) 'the project at the heart of political development theory was the establishment across the developing world of stable capitalist regimes'. Even Almond himself has retrospectively argued for continuity (1987), claiming that much of the scepticism and pessimism to be found in the strong government perspective existed within political development theory from the start. On the other, its leading exponent, Samuel Huntington, launched a scathing attack on political development theory (1971) for its unrealistic optimism, suggesting that rather than political development it might be more relevant to talk about political decay.

Huntington criticized what he saw as a mistaken assumption in political development theory that in developing societies, economic growth would lead to social change (greater social pluralism, higher literacy rates, and so on) supportive of liberal democracy. Instead rapid economic growth from low initial levels could be profoundly destabilizing, generating social dislocation and frustration that could convert into excessive pressures on fragile political institutions. In this context he maintained that what mattered was not what form of government existed (whether democratic or communist) but the degree of government. Huntington's search for the sources of strong government in developing societies led him to reassess the political role of the military, arguing that military rule could provide stability and direction in countries at an early stage of development, although he saw strong ruling political parties, whether in one-party or multi-party systems, as the best means of providing **legitimacy** and coherence for government.

Critics charged Huntington and others preoccupied with the politics of order and strong government with being apologists for authoritarian rule and inherently conservative, and for projecting domestic US concerns about increasing political instability (student and black protest; opposition to the Vietnam war). But it must also be said that this perspective injected a welcome dose of realism into the discussion; political development on Almond-type lines was just not happening. Secondly it drew attention to the ability of political institutions not just to reflect economic and social development but themselves to make an active difference, that is, to the 'relative autonomy of the political'.

## Marxist-inspired approaches

The second main category of approaches to be examined stems from a broadly Marxist perspective. As such it has opposed the politics of modernization school which it sees as driven by bourgeois or capitalist interests, and has stressed the determining role of processes of economic production and/or exchange and the social class relationships embedded in them. In fact dependency theory, which emerged in the late 1960s, was primarily concerned to refute models of economic development and also modernization theory; its implications for politics, at least in the narrower governmental sense, were almost incidental although it had considerable impact on the study of politics in the developing world.

One main reason was that it drew attention to a serious shortcoming of all forms of political development theory, their near total neglect of the international

context and implied assumption that politics in developing countries was shaped by purely domestic forces. Dependency theory originated in South America and reflected that continent's experience but was quickly applied to other parts of the developing world. It has taken numerous forms but will be briefly illustrated here through the arguments of a leading exponent, Gunder Frank (see also Chapters 2 and 4).

Frank (1969) maintained that the developing world had been increasingly incorporated into the capitalist world economy from the sixteenth century onwards. In fact development of the developed world (known as the metropolis or core) was premised upon '**underdevelopment**' of the developing world (known as satellite economies or the periphery); development and underdevelopment were two sides of the same coin. Despite formal political independence former colonies remained essentially dependent because the metropolis was able to extract most of their economic surplus through different kinds of monopoly. Even when such economies appeared to be developing, this was only dependent and distorted development. Frank argued that the only way a satellite economy could end this dependence was to drastically reduce ties with the metropolis; later he recognized that even this was not really an option.

Whilst for a time dependency theory was extremely influential, it was also increasingly and justly criticized for the crude generalization and determinism of its economic analysis. Not all versions were quite as deterministic as Frank's. Wallerstein recognized a 'semi-periphery' of countries like the East Asian 'tigers' which over time had been able to improve their position within the overall 'world system', and by their example offered others on the periphery the hope of doing so too (Wallerstein 1979). Cardoso (1973) used the case of Brazil to argue that there could be meaningful 'associated dependent development'. By the 1980s, because of its weakness as economic theory but also because of the growing ascendancy of **neo-liberal** economic doctrine and developments in the world economy that appeared to contradict it, dependency theory was losing currency. Yet ironically the emerging 'debt crisis' of that same decade and imposition of **structural adjustment** requirements (see Chapter 2) has seemed one of its best illustrations.

What did dependency theory have to say about politics in developing countries? Frank tended to minimize the independent effects of politics. He argued that both the state and the national political elite in such countries were identified with the 'comprador' economic class which served as the local agent of metropolitan capital and consequently had a vested interest in the status quo. The only real possibility of change would be a revolution of those at the end of the chain of exploitation—the peasantry and urban poor—who had nothing to lose. Short of that, the different forms of politics, contests between political parties and so forth, had little significance. Again there were some variations in this position. Wallerstein had more to say about politics and a less reductionist view of the state but still ultimately saw strong states as a feature of the developed world and reinforcing capitalist interests. Even more exceptional were Cardoso and Faletto (1979), who used a comparison of Argentina and Brazil, two countries where 'associated dependent development' had been possible, to develop a complex political analysis. This showed two things. First, politics is not simply about external processes of domination but also involved national processes of reconciling and incorporating newly mobilized social groups. Second, the actual content of domestic politics differed from one developing country to another, reflecting differing resource bases and levels of foreign intervention.

With the possible exception of Cardoso and Faletto, dependency theory shed little direct light on the political process as such within developing countries (Smith 1979). Its real contributions were to insist on the intimate link between politics and economics, which had been largely neglected in the politics of modernization literature, and to demonstrate that the domestic politics of developing countries was incomprehensible without reference to their position within the world capitalist system.

## Neo-Marxism rediscovers politics

Despite its Marxist associations, dependency theory had many neo-Marxist critics. In an argument paralleling modernization revisionists' criticism of modernization theory, they rejected its assumption that capitalism wiped out pre-capitalist forms. This view,

they argued, was based on falsely equating capitalism with the market, rather than seeing it as a system of production. In fact capitalism as a dominant 'mode of production' could interact or 'articulate' with pre-capitalist modes. This further implied that different 'social formations' or countries on the periphery could have very different social systems (see Foster-Carter 1978).

At a more directly political level, neo-Marxist interest in developing societies was also stimulated by hopes that the socialist revolution that had failed to materialize in the West would begin there instead. Such hopes were raised by a 'third wave' of revolutionary developments (following a first wave centred on China, and a second wave from the late 1950s including Cuba and Algeria). The third wave from the late 1960s included communist victories in Vietnam, Cambodia, and Laos, revolution in Ethiopia, overthrow of Portuguese regimes in Africa, and revolution in Nicaragua (Cammack 1997). For these reasons neo-Marxists engaged in a much more detailed and rigorous analysis of social structure which was in some sense aimed at assessing the eligibility of different social categories—peasants, the lumpenproletariat (the urban poor who were not regular wage-earners), and so on—to inherit the role of revolutionary vanguard originally attributed to the industrial working class. As with 'modernization revisionism' this generated much valuable, careful research into what developing societies were actually like, although the appropriateness of the Marxist categories of social analysis imposed on them was often questionable.

As a corollary of this less determinist view of politics, there was a new interest in what Marxists typically referred to as the **'post-colonial state'**. Marx himself generally depicted the state as a simple instrument of class domination—in the famous words of the *Communist Manifesto* (1872) 'The executive of the modern state is but a committee for managing the common affairs of the whole bourgeoisie'. But his writings sometimes alluded to a second possibility, as in France during the second empire under Louis Napoleon, when the weakness or divisions of the bourgeoisie allowed an authoritarian state to emerge which was 'relatively autonomous' from any particular social class. This notion was taken further by neo-Marxists such as Gramsci (1891–1937) and more recently Poulantzas (1936–1979) analysing capitalist states in the West but was also subsequently seized on to explore the relationship between the state and social classes in post-colonial societies. Alavi (1979), for instance, argued with particular reference to Pakistan, that the post-colonial state enjoyed a high degree of autonomy. This was first because it had to mediate between no less than three ruling classes but second because it had inherited a colonial state apparatus that was 'over-developed' in relation to society because its original role was holding down a subject people (others later questioned whether the post-colonial state in Africa could be described as over-developed, however). With reference to some African countries, there were also debates about whether the state itself could give rise to a new ruling class.

## Globalization theory

By the early 1980s, and despite their diametrically opposed starting points, it is possible to argue that the lines of thought evolving out of early political development theory on the one hand and dependency theory on the other were converging around a reappreciation of the independent importance of 'the political' and an interest in strong government and/or the state. But both these lines of thought were also tending to run out of steam. Although strong government arguments gave the politics of modernization perspective a seeming new lease of life and, Higgott (1983) suggests, such arguments persisted into the 1980s in the guise of a spate of public policy studies, this whole approach remained vulnerable to the charge of insufficient attention to the economic and international context. The Marxist-inspired approach, never in any case enjoyed levels of funding comparable with the more mainstream modernization approach; and if dependency theory was increasingly challenged by the experience of oil-producing states in the Gulf, **newly industrializing countries (NICs)**, and so forth, by the mid-1980s the neo-Marxist focus on socialist revolution in turn appeared increasingly anachronistic.

Reflecting these changes in the global environment, by the 1990s a new 'macro' approach was emerging, globalization theory, that tended both to absorb and displace the previous two (for a valuable overview see McGrew 1992). Globalization theory should more properly be referred to as globalization theories, since it takes many different forms. As with the previous two approaches it can also often seem closer to an ideology or policy strategy than a theoretical framework. Globalization theory focuses on a process of accelerated communication and economic integration which transcends national boundaries and increasingly incorporates all parts of the world into a single social system. Although this process is often seen as originating in the distant past, there is general agreement that it accelerated in particular from the 1970s, spurred by developments in transport and communications and subsequently by the collapse of the Soviet bloc and end of the cold war.

Probably the most important dimension of this process is economic (see Chapter 2). Globalization theory cites trends in three spheres. First is the continuous growth in world trade. Secondly, it points to increasing global integration of the process of economic production of goods and also recently of services, with so-called TNCs (Transnational Corporations) playing a key role. Technological developments have enabled TNCs to shift different stages of production to sites about the world where they can achieve the most favourable deal in terms of economies of scale, labour costs, and so on. This has been partly facilitated, thirdly, by revolutionary changes in the sphere of finance. The information revolution, along with deregulation, has created a network of financial markets trading twenty-four hours a day, dramatically increasing the mobility of capital.

Associated with these economic trends has been a significant cultural dimension of globalization that is increasing cultural awareness and interaction across national boundaries. Central to this process has been the remarkable development and expansion of information technology and the new electronic mass media, enormously extending the scope and immediacy of communication. The consequences of this process are undoubtedly complex and contentious. Despite the emergence of powerful media industries in a number of developing countries such as India, Brazil, and Mexico, it is questionable just how truly 'global' in the sense of multi-directional, cultural communications have yet become. For writers like Sklair (1991: 41) the predominance of US-based media conglomerates has meant the diffusion of images and lifestyles that promote the 'culture-ideology of consumerism'. By the same token, however, the perceived threat of cultural globalization has prompted complex counter-trends, including reassertion of local and national cultural identities (on religious identity see Chapter 6).

Different forms of globalization theory emphasize different aspects—economic, cultural and so on. They differ in what they understand to be the prime moving mechanism of the globalization process: some see it as driven by the underlying logic of unfolding capitalism, others as primarily a consequence of developments in communications, others a combination of factors. Some accounts, echoing modernization theory, are essentially optimistic: they stress, for instance, the extent to which a globalizing economy, in which capital is increasingly mobile, hugely extends opportunities for investment and employment for those who are enterprising and adaptable. Others, echoing the mistrust and many of the arguments of dependency theory, are pessimistic; they depict an increasingly unfettered global capitalism, ruthlessly exploiting people and resources (such themes have of course been taken up by the so-called 'anti-globalization' movement).

Given the boldness of its claims, globalization theory has encountered opposition on a range of grounds. One of the most effective critiques of the thesis of economic globalization has come from Hirst and Thompson (1996). They suggest that most companies remain nationally based, rather than genuinely transnational and that the main flows of trade, finance, and investment rather than being global in scope remain concentrated between the 'triad' of Europe, Japan, and North America. However it is ultimately very difficult to 'prove' or disprove the globalization thesis since it describes a process, not an achieved state, and since it also envisages this process as 'dialectical', not proceeding straight in one direction but encountering resistance and progressing in fits and starts.

Although the voluminous literature on globalization has relatively little directly to say about politics in the developing world, its implications are far-reaching. First it suggests changes in the character of politics as a whole. While it would be premature to talk about a process of political globalization comparable with what is claimed in the economic and cultural spheres, one can point to a series of developments that incline that way, including the increasing perceived urgency of a number of issues—such as global warming, refugee flows, terrorism—whose origin and solution transcend national borders; the proliferation of international regulatory organizations, and non-governmental organizations; and the growth of transnational social movements.

At the same time, globalization theory emphazises ways in which the nation-state is losing autonomy. It is increasingly difficult for the individual state to control the flow of information across its borders or to protect its people from global security threats. Likewise, globalizing trends have greatly reduced its economic options, for instance, its ability to fend off the consequences of economic upheaval elsewhere, such as the 1997 East Asia financial crisis, or to successfully promote 'Keynesian' economic policies, to enhance welfare and protect employment, when these run counter to the logic of the global economy. With reduced autonomy comes reduction in the state's perceived competence and accordingly in its legitimacy. It comes under increasing pressure from within, as well as without, contributing to a process of 'hollowing out' the state. Critics of the globalization thesis have argued that this greatly overstates the threat posed to the nation-state, pointing out, for example, that many states, including the East Asian NICs, have actively promoted and benefited from the process of economic globalization, and suggesting that states may be able to invoke or harness nationalist reaction to globalizing pressures as an alternative source of legitimacy, as in India. However these objections seem less relevant for many of the poorer, smaller developing countries. Clapham (2002: 785) suggests that in such countries 'the logic of incorporation into the modern global system . . . has undermined the state's coercive capabilities, weakened its legitimacy and subverted its capacity to manage the inevitable engagement with the global economy'.

But globalization theory also creates difficulties for the notion of a distinct 'developing world'. Even if we talk about a 'developing world' rather than a 'Third World' and are careful about which countries we include or exclude, this still implies a distinct geographic entity. However, globalization theorists like Berger argue that if we want to retain the idea of a 'third' or developing world, this should be conceived of in sociological rather than geographic terms. The ongoing process of economic globalization means that economically based social classes are increasingly transnational or global in span. So, on this analysis, dominant classes in the developing world are more oriented, economically and culturally, to Western capitalist centres, where 'they have their bank accounts, maintain business links, own homes and send their children to school', than to their own countries (Berger 1994: 268). On the other hand countries in the 'developed world', not least the United States, each have their own underclass (or 'Third' or developing world), even if there are few signs that such underclasses are coming together at a global level.

Overall it is difficult to assess the globalization perspective as a framework for understanding politics in the developing world, because it takes such a variety of forms and reflects such a range of ideological positions, extending from a messianic optimism that echoes the crassest forms of modernization theory to doom-laden warnings that come close to the claustrophobic determinism of unmodified dependency theory. However, arguably even the left-wing version of globalization theory goes much further than dependency theory in recognizing the *inter*dependence of developed and developing economies. Globalization theory is much more open-ended than dependency theory; ultimately it envisages an integrated global economy but in the shorter term acknowledges developments are unpredictable and could include increasing differentiation between beneficiaries and losers. Perhaps its most valuable contribution to understanding politics in the developing world is that, like dependency theory, it emphasizes the impact of global processes. But in other ways it poses problems for this field of study. First, it calls into question the concept of the 'developing world' as a geographically distinct entity. Second, whilst it does not discount the political level, it tends to depict economic and/or technological change as driving cultural and political change and thereby to downplay the importance of the independent effects or autonomy of the 'political' and certainly of the state.

## Key points

- The politics of modernization approach emerged in the 1950s, initially taking the form of political development theory.

- Political development theory was criticized by 'revisionists' for simplifying and underestimating the role of tradition and by advocates of political order for excessive optimism.

- From the left, dependency theory criticized the modernization approach for ignoring former colonies' continuing economic and thus political dependence.

- Neo-Marxists criticized dependency theory's determinism and explored the relative autonomy of politics and the state.

- Globalization theory, drawing on both modernization and dependency theory, emphasizes increasing global economic integration.

- Globalization theory calls into question both the existence of a distinct developing world and the importance of the state.

# Current approaches

It is more difficult to characterize the study of politics in the developing world today. The main emerging trends will become clearer in retrospect but some preliminary comments are in order.

## A state of 'disarray'?

Both modernization-based approaches and Marxist-inspired approaches were found increasingly wanting by the 1980s. Although globalization theory incorporates significant elements of both, it too tends to undermine the rationale for studying politics in the developing world as a distinct field. Moreover globalization theory reflects changes in the real world, including increasing differentiation amongst countries of the 'developing world', which pose further problems for meaningful generalization.

These developments within the field have coincided with a wider disillusionment with attempts at grand theory building in the social sciences. (Globalization theory may well seem an obvious exception to this aversion but it has been attacked precisely for its sweeping generalizations and also it nonetheless contrives to be extraordinarily open-ended and flexible.) One general school of thinking, originating in linguistics and philosophy, that has contributed to and helped to articulate such misgivings has been **post-structuralism**. Post-structuralists question the epistemological basis and claims of the great theoretical approaches or 'meta-narratives' such as liberalism, Marxism, or indeed 'modernization'. Foucault (1926–84) in particular has preferred to see them as 'discourses' which are historically contingent and which reflect and construct relations of power. Despite political science's general resistance to discourse theory as an exclusive approach in its own right, many practitioners—including those studying politics in the developing world—draw selectively on its concepts and arguments in their own analysis (see some of the essays in Manor 1991).

There has also been a steady growth of information about politics in different developing countries since the first attempts at generalization in the 1950s. Western governments, above all the US government, have funded research and teaching, some of it under the rubric of 'area studies'. Professional associations of area specialists, conferences, and journals have proliferated. At the same time there has been growth in political science expertise within a number of developing countries such as India. All of this has heightened awareness of the complexity and diversity of politics across this great tranche of the world's countries. Surveying all these developments, one might well conclude that politics in the developing world no longer even has pretensions to being a coherent field of study; rather, to quote Manor (1991: 1), it is 'in disarray'.

## Themes and agendas

But a consideration of the general character of publication and research in the broad field of politics in the developing world over the last few years suggests that this is an exaggeration. Even though one of the logical implications of globalization theories may be to call the need for this distinct field into question, the frequent presence in such work of ideas about globalization does provide one significant element of theoretical common ground. Moreover, against this globalization background, three, partly overlapping, themes or research issues tend to predominate and shape lines of current comparative enquiry.

One is democratization (see Chapter 12). When the '**third wave**' of democracy broke in the mid-1970s, spreading through South America in the 1980s and much of tropical Africa in the 1990s, it served to confound the expectations of a generation of political scientists who had come to see political authoritarianism or decay as an intrinsic political feature of the developing world. Nonetheless the global reach of democratization was extended not only as a consequence of pressures within developing countries, or of the collapse of the Soviet bloc and end of the cold war but by more deliberate interventions of Western governments and intergovernmental organizations. As Chapter 12 describes, these included attaching political conditions to forms of economic assistance but also more direct 'international democracy promotion' through financial and other forms of support to democracy projects. Linked to this drive, Western government and research foundation funding has helped to generate a huge literature apparently covering every aspect of democratization—its stages, causes, the conditions that produce the most favourable democratic outcome, why democratization has proceeded further in some developing countries than others, and so forth.

This focus on democratization, as Cammack (1997: 217–18) observes, is not really underpinned by a specific systematic body of theory. He cites a number of key authorities in the democratization literature—who explicitly declare that they are not aiming to produce an integrated theory of democratization and doubt whether it would in any case be possible. Even so, the very preoccupation with the process and prerequisites of democratization echoes the original political development literature, in which some form of liberal-democracy was typically upheld as the end-state to which developing countries were progressing or should aspire. Furthermore, features of democratization in the developing world, including international democracy promotion and especially the transnational diffusion of democracy as an ideal, are highly compatible with notions of political globalization, an idea which may have achieved its high point with Fukuyama's hubristic claim (1992) that liberal democracy could represent the 'end point of mankind's ideological evolution' and 'final form of government'.

The second theme is the relationship between politics and economic development or growth. This overlaps with the theme of democratization since an influential strand of thinking now sees good governance and even democracy as a prerequisite of economic growth. As noted by Leftwich (1993) this represents an inversion of the early political development literature where economic growth was generally assumed to be a condition of democracy. The concern with the politics of growth has also led to a reassessment of the importance of the state by bodies like the World Bank, which opens its 1997 report, *The State in a Changing World*, by declaring that the state is central to economic and social development, not so much as a direct provider of growth but rather as a partner, catalyst, and facilitator. It has also led to an interest in the economic role played by **civil society** organizations and **'social capital'**. This theme, again, lacks a fully elaborated theoretical context but owes something to the strong government variant of the politics of modernization. But again, like the democratization theme, it is clearly partly driven by concerns of western governments and intergovernmental organizations.

A third increasingly prominent theme concerns peace and security versus conflict and risk. Again this overlaps with the two previous themes: domestic conflict inhibits the emergence of political conditions conducive to economic growth, for instance, whilst many champions of democratization believe that democratic values and institutions provide the best guarantee both of domestic and of international security and order. The growing focus on causes and consequences of conflict and instability within developing countries is also, however, due to the perception that such conflict has been on the increase since the end of the cold war. In this context there has been growing interest on the one hand in the pathology of 'failed' or **'collapsed' states** and on the other in the 'politics of identity', especially ethnic and religious identity, in developing countries (see Chapters 5, 6, and 11).

These three themes do not amount to, or derive from, one coherent analytic framework although they echo and incorporate elements of the earlier dominant paradigms as well as globalization ideas. But they do overlap in the sense that democratization, economic performance, and the presence or absence of internal conflict either do, or are seen to, significantly affect one another. These themes also clearly relate to observable trends in the developing world and resonate strongly with important constituencies there. At the same time, however, they reflect the concerns, interests, and research-funding priorities of international agencies, Western governments, and to a lesser extent non-governmental organizations (NGOs).

## Key points

- Decline of modernization- and Marxist-based approaches and ascendancy of globalization theory have coincided with questioning of the need for grand theory in political studies.

- Expanding scholarship has increased awareness of the empirical complexity of the field.

- However, some coherence is provided by key themes of democratization, politics and economic development, and conflict.

# Conclusion: do we need a distinct analytical approach?

We are left with the difficult final question of whether a distinct approach for analysing the politics of developing countries is necessary or desirable. The dominant paradigms in the past, associated with modernization theory and dependency theory, were valuable to the extent that by suggesting the importance of particular factors or relationships, they helped to generate debate; also, they encouraged political analysis and generalization beyond the particularities of individual country case studies. But at the same time, they were overgeneralized, excessively influenced by Western ideological assumptions and agendas, whether 'bourgeois' or 'radical', and Western historical experience and based on inadequate knowledge and understanding of the developing world itself. They created, as Cammack et al. (1993: 3) phrased it, 'a problem of premature and excessive theorization'.

Over time our knowledge of the developing world has grown and with it inevitably our awareness of its diversity and complexity. Moreover, that developing world itself has become increasingly differentiated. Especially in the context of globalization theory, this greater recognition of diversity has called into question the coherence of the 'developing world' as a geographic—and political—category. These developments have coincided with a tendency for political science to rein in its theoretical aspirations, focusing on 'middle-range' rather than grand theory.

Presently, then, whilst the question of whether we need a distinct approach or theoretical framework for studying politics in the developing world is rarely put directly, one can distinguish two implicit responses. The first is that we should approach politics in developing countries just the same way, asking the same sorts of questions, using the same theoretical tools and methods of analysis, as in the developed world. This view is particularly evident in much of the democratization literature. Thus we find a growing use of conventional electoral analysis, interest (reflecting trends in political science as a whole) in the role of political institutions and constitutions,

and the application of different forms of rational choice theory. There is a parallel extension to the developing world of interest in more 'radical' issues like gender relations, human rights, and the environment.

The alternative approach is even less of an explicit or coherent viewpoint. Rather, from different perspectives and in specific contexts, a number of writers (still) question how far assumptions and approaches derived from Western experience can really capture the nature of politics in developing countries. There are at least two rather different variants of this argument. There is first a long-standing tradition stressing the cultural 'otherness' of what we now call the developing world. Edward Said (1995, originally published 1978) wrote about the lens of **'Orientalism'** through which many Western scholars interpreted Asian and Middle Eastern societies, in imperial times. More recently, in the post-cold war environment, writers like Huntington (1996a) with his **'clash of civilizations'** thesis have seemed to echo this 'orientalist' view. Huntington identifies a series of long-lasting civilizations, in particular Western, Sinic, Japanese, Hindu, and Islamic. He argues that deep-rooted cultural differences associated with these civilizations, always present but temporarily obscured by ideological divisions of the cold war, have become increasingly visible and serve as important anchors of political identity. He also stresses the extent to which Western and other cultures, especially Islam, are mutually alien and uncomprehending.

More pragmatically, some political area specialists criticize the literature, especially that concerning democratization and governance, for its failure to understand what is really going on. For instance, in *Africa Works*, Chabal and Daloz themselves make use of 'universal' rational choice assumptions but criticize the literature for its emphasis on formal political institutions: 'political action operates rationally, but largely in the realm of the informal, uncodified and unpoliced—that is, in a world that is not ordered in the sense in which we usually take our own politics in the West to be' (1999: p.xix). Similarly O'Donnell (1996) argues that excessive emphasis on formal political institutions in the process of democratic consolidation in South America obscures the importance of the 'informal, pervasive and permanent' institution of **clientelism**.

Ultimately it seems a distinctive approach to, let alone a theory of, politics in the developing world is neither possible nor any longer desirable. But in their absence we need to be critically aware of what are the dominant themes in the literature and the interests and agendas these reflect. Moreover we need to employ general political science categories intelligently and flexibly, taking into account as far as possible how their 'translation' to different developing country contexts will be affected by notable variations in, among other things, culture, history, and institutions.

## QUESTIONS

**1**  What were the main shortcomings of political development theory as a way of understanding politics in the developing world?

**2**  In what ways does globalization theory draw on modernization theory and dependency theory?

**3**  What are the implications of globalization theory both for the character of politics in the developing world and the way in which it should be studied?

**4**  Which theoretical approaches to politics in the developing world shed most light on the relative autonomy of politics and the state?

**5**  Is the field study of politics in the developing world currently in 'disarray'?

**6**  Do we need a distinct theoretical framework for analysing politics in the developing world?

## GUIDE TO FURTHER READING

Berger, M. (ed.), 'After the Third World?', special issue of *Third World Quarterly*, 25/1 (2004). Collection of articles that reflect upon the historical significance and contemporary relevance of the notion of a 'third world'.

Cammack, P., *Capitalism and Democracy in the Third World: The Doctrine for Political Development* (Leicester: Leicester University Press, 1997). Well-argued, critical reflection, from a left-wing perspective, upon 'mainstream' accounts of the political development literature.

Hagopian, F., 'Political development revisited', *Comparative Political Studies*, 33/6 and 7(2000), 880–911. Recent retrospective overview of political development thinking.

Higgott, R. A., *Political Development Theory* (London and Canberra: Croom-Helm, 1983). Account of the development and persistence of political development thinking.

Manor, J. (ed.), *Rethinking Third World Politics* (London: Longman, 1991). Collection of essays, some using post-structuralist concepts or approaches, seeking to go beyond old theoretical perspectives.

Moore, M., 'Political Underdevelopment', paper presented to 10th Anniversary of the Institute of Development Studies Conference, September 7–8 2000. See also at **www.ids.ac.uk/ids/govern**. Recent attempt to rework the notion of political development, focusing on state legitimacy.

Randall, V., and Theobald, R., *Political Change and Underdevelopment: A Critical Introduction to Third World Politics*, 2nd edn (London: Macmillan, 1998). Provides an account of theories and debates concerning politics in the developing world, from political development to globalization.

Smith, B. C., *Understanding Third World Politics*, 2nd edn. (Basingstoke: Palgrave, 2003). Useful, recently updated, overview of themes in the study of the politics of the developing world.

 **COMPANION WEB SITE**

For additional material and resources, see the companion web site at:
**www.oup.com/uk/booksites/politics/**

# 2 The developing world in the global economy

*Stephen Hobden*

## OVERVIEW

This chapter and the following inter-linked one provide an overview of the international context in which politics in the developing world operates. In this chapter the focus is on the global economy. It examines especially the important contribution made by the significant increase in trade in the last fifty years to the general increase in global economic integration, or what has come to be styled '**globalization**'. However, with some notable exceptions, most developing countries have not benefited from this expansion. Is this because, as some argue, they have not embraced free trade with sufficient enthusiasm, or because, as others suggest, the global trading system is inherently unfair?

# Introduction: The emergence of a global economy

The term 'global economy' is understood as the total of all international economic transactions, the bulk of which are trade plus foreign direct investment (more commonly known by its initials as FDI). Many observers claim to see evidence of increasing global economic integration, and the term 'globalization' has been coined to refer to this phenomenon. The meaning of the concept of globalization has been much debated and is still in dispute, while there is considerable disagreement over the precise implications of whatever globalization means for economic well-being in the developing world. A prudent assessment would be that it contains both positive and negative potential, and that different developing countries have been affected differently; some countries and within individual countries particular social groups are much more marginal to the process than others.

A major component has been the growth in the value of trade. Between 1950 and the close of the twentieth century world merchandise trade increased almost twenty times while world merchandise production increased only sixfold (Dicken 2003: 35). And for many writers the economic growth of the West is largely explained by its involvement in an international trading system, leading to the view that 'free trade' is inherently beneficial. Yet, despite the developing world's increasing inclusion in the global economy, the benefits from trade do not appear to have reached the large proportion of the globe's population who live in absolute poverty. Indeed, although the developing world increased its share of world manufacturing output from a mere 5 per cent in the early 1950s to close to 25 per cent by the end of the century, much of this was accounted for by only a handful of countries that includes China in addition to, for instance, Brazil, South Korea, and Taiwan (Dicken 2003: 37). The same is true of the increase in merchandise exports, where again China and Hong Kong dwarf the other exporting countries such as Mexico, Singapore, and Taiwan. The arguments that lead many to suggest that there are enormous benefits to be gained from joining the world economy must be balanced against a consideration of the reasons why developing countries are not always able to exploit the potential gains from

trade. The precise location in the global economy could determine the ability to derive the benefits.

There is evidence of trade between different social groups for as long as written records have existed, and it has provided much of the motivation for people to explore the globe. By the end of the nineteenth century much of Asia and Africa had been included in the European empires, and trade between the colonial powers and their subject states provided the bulk of trade between what came to be called 'First' and 'Third' worlds. The colonies provided guaranteed sources of essential raw materials, and also markets for manufactured goods from the metropolitan centres. One historian of empire notes that 'Britain prospered . . . by manufacturing articles for sale abroad, which her customers paid for in raw materials and food' (Porter 1996: 4). An international division of labour developed in which European powers exported manufactured goods to the colonies and imported the materials needed to make these goods (McMichael 2000: 8–13). One way of imagining this process is to think of the international trading system as a number of segments, each segment comprising the colonial power and its colonies. A considerable amount of trade took place within the segment, and to have an empire was seen as essential for the economic well-being of the core.

Standing outside this segmented economic system was the United States, which in the early twentieth century was becoming a significant source of global production. Successive US administrations sought a larger role in the international economy, which would require the breaking up of the European imperial systems of trade. At the outbreak of the Second World War, planners in the United States started to think about what the post-war economic and political order might look like. The fruits of this planning emerged in a document known as the Atlantic Charter signed by the British Prime Minister Churchill and President Roosevelt in 1941. At the core of the charter was a commitment to the end of empire and the creation of an open world economy.

Despite the resistance of the European powers, decolonization gradually occurred following the end of the Second World War. However, as a result of the cold war, a world economy segmented by the European colonies was replaced by a world economy divided between, on the one hand, the USA, its allies and client states, and, on the other, the Soviet Union, its allies and client states. These systems resembled in many ways the imperial systems which had preceded them, in the sense that the cores provided manufactured goods whilst developing countries were major sources of raw materials. Despite an increasing level of contact between the capitalist and communist systems, it was not until the collapse of Communist Party rule in the Soviet Union that it is possible to start talking of a global economy—one, exclusively capitalist, system.

In terms of economic growth, how have the countries of the developing world fared in this economic system? The simple answer is that there has been a huge differential in terms of economic growth between different countries. As a consequence there has been growing inequality of average incomes across countries, in addition to increasing inequalities within many individual countries. Admittedly, differences between incomes of the rich and the poor, ignoring the country to which they belong, have actually reduced. The average global citizen has become better off. However, that owes mainly to strengthening economic performance in a few very populous countries, most notably China, and also India and

Vietnam. Thus over the last half-century or so while some countries like South Korea, for instance, have done well, others like Guatemala have done badly. Clearly there are many reasons for the disparities; they are not just a result of countries' involvement in the global economy. For many analysts there are very close links between trading and higher levels of economic growth, just as there are also many who claim the benefits of free trade are not being shared equally.

## Key points

- For most economists there is a direct link between international trade and economic growth, but continuing, and growing, economic disparities between developed and less developed countries suggests that the potential 'gains from trade' are not being shared equally.
- During the period of European colonialism the major pattern of trade was for the colonies to export raw materials, while the metropolitan cores exported manufactured goods. These structures of trade have persisted into the post-colonial period.
- Following the end of the cold war it is possible to talk about the emergence of a global economy—a single, capitalist system.

# The case for free trade

The view that free trade works in the interests of all participants now holds a predominant position in economic thinking. The idea that unimpeded trade will lead to a material benefit to developing countries is a core idea of the **neo-liberal agenda**, and is expressed in what became known as the '**Washington consensus**'. The neo-liberal agenda derives from classical liberal economics. The 'consensus' denotes the primacy of related ideas in the World Bank and the International Monetary Fund (IMF), both based in Washington (see next chapter), while the term itself dates from a paper on policy reform for Latin America written by John Williamson in 1989 (Williamson 2003). These ideas have proved to be very powerful. Policies based on the theory of

**comparative advantage**, implemented by international organizations, have dramatically affected the lives of millions of people around the globe. Gill (1995 and 2003) has described this process as 'disciplinary neoliberalism' because of the role of these policies in conditioning individuals and societies for a role in the global economy.

## Antecedents of the neo-liberal agenda

As the terms neo-liberal and neo-classical economics suggest, these are a restatement, or revisiting, of established sets of ideas. Two classical writers stand out in terms of advocating free trade—Adam Smith and David Ricardo.

Adam Smith's (1723–90) major work, *An Inquiry into the Nature and Causes of the Wealth of Nations* (1776), remains one of the key statements of economic theory. For Smith the maximum benefit to society would be gained from individuals pursuing their own economic interests. Competition between individual producers would lead to the manufacture of goods in the most efficient and effective ways, to the benefit of society as a whole. Left to their own devices markets would tend towards a position of equilibrium (or stability), where production of goods matched the desires of consumers to purchase. This was through the action of a 'hidden hand', which would reward efficient producers and drive inefficient enterprises out of business. The actions of governments frequently blocked the working of this 'hidden hand' by placing restrictions on entrepreneurs, making production less efficient and society poorer as a result.

Smith's book provides the classic statement of the argument that producers and consumers should enjoy freedom to make and purchase goods without hindrance from government. In essence he argued that the wealth of the nation would be maximized by allowing the market to follow its own course. This was primarily an argument about a domestic economy, though he did argue that specialization should be extended to trade between countries. Ricardo (1772–1823) extended these ideas. He argued that countries would gain the greatest economic benefit from specializing in the production of those goods in which they were relatively more efficient, or in which they had a '**comparative advantage**'. This has been taken to mean that developed countries should specialize in the production of manufactured goods and developing countries concentrate on raw materials and agricultural goods. In this way both would benefit because they were specializing in the area in which they held a comparative advantage.

The views of 'classical' economic thinkers such as Smith and Ricardo were dominant through much of the nineteenth century (when Britain was the leading advocate of free trade), and early twentieth century. However free market views suffered a severe challenge during the world depression of the 1930s when traditional policies seemed to be no longer working. A new orthodoxy emerged, based on the writings of John Maynard Keynes, and inspired by the 'New Deal' in the United States, that governments could intervene in their economies to promote growth and stability. Through much of the middle of the twentieth century, European and US governments, of various political backgrounds, pursued interventionist policies. However, by the severe economic downturn of the 1970s there was a view that there were limits to which governments should intervene in the economy. Political and theoretical room opened up for a revival of classical economic theory. Such a renewal came from various writers, but perhaps the most influential was the Chicago economist Milton Friedman. In essence his work was a restatement of some of the key elements of Smith. A government's role in the economy should be reduced to the absolute minimum, and all restrictions on international trade should be removed. In all areas of economic life the market should be left to work its 'magic' unsupervised, and, as far as possible, unregulated.

## Policies

This view of how the global economy works has led to a number of policy recommendations which free trade advocates have suggested would be of benefit to all. These policies can be summarized as aiming to remove constraints on the operation of markets. They have formed the basis of the packages of measures routinely recommended by the World Bank and IMF as a price for assistance, in the wake of the debt crisis (see next chapter).

The package of measures associated with the 'neoliberal agenda' comprises both national and international elements. At the national level free trade policies fall into two main areas: the promotion of a more efficient use of labour, and the reduction of the role of the state in the economy. The first requires the labour force to be flexible, which can often require the power of trade unions to be curbed. The second is premised on the assumption that the state acts as a drag on the free operation of the markets, and that its role should be reduced to providing a minimal set of public goods such as national defence and overseeing the legal system. At the international level policies are advocated which aim to remove hindrances to trade and to promote the inflow of FDI.

Tariffs on imports or exports are seen as a major impediment to trade. Tariffs are a form of taxation that are levied on the value of goods which are entering or leaving a country. They can be both a form of revenue and a way of protecting domestic industries. For free trade advocates tariffs are seen as acting to undermine the potential gains to be derived from comparative advantage. Therefore it is argued that removal or reduction of trade tariffs will promote trade and lead to a more efficient use of resources, as domestic industries are exposed to international competition. Free traders have also argued in favour of allowing currencies to float freely rather than being managed by governments. In the past currencies have frequently been overvalued, making imports cheaper and exports more expensive. As part of free trade regimes countries have been persuaded to allow their currencies to float freely. This often means devaluation of the currency, making domestic production more competitive internationally, while increasing the cost of imports. Many developing countries also placed considerable restrictions on the permitted levels and forms of international investment in their economy. Restrictions on the parts of the economy in which foreign investment is allowed, higher levels of taxation for international firms, and limits on the expropriation of capital have all been typical in the past, especially before the 1980s. However, free market policies argue that there should be no discrimination against foreign capital wishing to invest in the country, and that any barriers to investment should be removed. Boxes 2.1 and 2.2 highlight Chile and the **newly (or new) industrialized (or industrializing) countries (NICs)** of South-East Asia respectively, which have been argued to be successful examples of the implementation of free trade policies.

## Box 2.1 **Chile as an example of free market policies**

The developing country where free market policies have been followed most radically is probably Chile. Through the 1970s and 1980s, during the dictatorship of Augusto Pinochet, Chile effectively became a testing ground for the neo-liberal agenda. The economic policies implemented in the wake of the coup were devised by a group of economists trained by Milton Friedman. On the domestic front, the rights of labour were severely curtailed. Unions were banned and strikes were outlawed. All mechanisms for collective bargaining were abandoned. Taxes were reduced and public spending was cut dramatically. Much of the economy, previously controlled by the government, was privatized. Additionally, price controls, introduced to ensure that essential goods were affordable by the poorest parts of society, were abolished. The Peso was devalued, and import duties lowered. The so-called 'shock treatment' had enormous impact. Gross domestic product fell sharply, as did wages, while unemployment rose to over 20 per cent. However, in the longer term the picture is more mixed. Advocates of free market policies point to the country's success in capturing export markets, particularly in agricultural products. Additionally industrialization has increased, with Chile sometimes being described as a Latin American NIC. Furthermore the country feels sufficiently confident to apply for membership of the North American Free Trade Agreement (NAFTA).

Critics, while acknowledging the transformation of the Chilean economy, point to the huge social costs. Compared to much of Latin America, Chile can be regarded as an economic success story. Yet this does not give the entire picture. The human rights abuses of the Pinochet era are well documented, with arbitrary arrest, torture, and death for many who criticized the regime. Furthermore the effect of the economic policies was to severely widen the gap between the richest and poorest. The richest sections of society profited from the tax reductions, and made fortunes through their involvement in privatization programmes. Meanwhile for the poorest sections, the removal of price controls made essential goods more expensive and reductions in government spending reduced the levels of social services. Critics also point to the high level of foreign ownership of industry, attracted by the low level of workers rights, low wages, and low levels of taxation. This could make the Chilean economy less stable, if foreign capital withdraws in times of economic crisis, or moves on to more profitable parts of the global economy. For further discussion with special reference to the role of the Chilean state see Chapter 18 in this book.

## Box 2.2 The Newly Industrializing Countries of South-East Asia and export-led industrialization

The so-called NICs include Taiwan, South Korea, Hong Kong, and Singapore, with perhaps a second wave including Malaysia, Indonesia, and the whole of the People's Republic of China. The NICs have seen a remarkable turnaround in their economic fortunes, developing from being very poor, largely agricultural economies in the wake of the Second World War to industrialized countries, some with average incomes comparable to the developed world. On some measurements, for example, Singapore is now among the top ten countries in average income per capita. Free trade advocates have cited the NICs with varying justification as models for how to develop an economy.

The economic success of the NICs has many possible explanations, for example, their exceptionally favourable geopolitical location during the cold war period and even the cultural attributes of the people. But to most economists a major reason is their adoption of policies of export-led industrialization. This can be contrasted with the policies of import substitution industrialization. The policy of the NICs has been to direct industrialization to fulfil the demands of world markets, and gradually to expose their industries to world competition through lowering tariff barriers. They have been prepared to switch production in order to maintain their position of comparative advantage—starting with textiles, then moving into mass production items such as toys, and then into more high-tech goods. The NICs in particular have been successful in specializing in areas of production that have become unprofitable in the more developed world.

Those economists who wish to promote free trade have seen the NICs as a good model because of their willingness to trade in the global economy, and their readiness to reduce tariff barriers over time. Furthermore the NICs have succeeded in exploiting their comparative advantage. However, as with the example of Chile, the position is more complicated. It is true that the NICs have reduced tariffs over time so that their industries are now more exposed to international competition. But they have been prepared to use tariffs to protect their industries in the early stages while they were becoming established. This is known as infant industry protection, and was used as an argument for the protection of industry in Europe during the nineteenth and early twentieth centuries. A further point that is often overlooked is the important role the state played in developing industry in the NICs (see Chapter 21 on the example of South Korea). The state maintained subsidies and investment as a way of developing parts of the economy that were perceived to have the greatest potential or were strategic in some sense. As with the use of infant industry protection, this suggests that the history of the NICs is more complicated and perhaps more difficult to replicate than is suggested by free market proponents.

## Key points

- The theory of comparative advantage provides the theoretical foundation for free trade. It claims that all countries should specialize in the production for export of those commodities that they can produce relatively more efficiently.

- For many developing countries this means raw materials and labour-intensive manufactured goods and services (textiles for example), owing to their relatively large reserves of cheap labour.

- A wide range of economic and social policies advocated in the name of freer trade has included restrictions on the activities of unions, reducing the role of the state in the economy, reducing tariff barriers, and allowing currencies to float freely.

# Limits on comparative advantage for developing countries

The examples of the Asian NICs and Chile suggest that in certain circumstances free market policies can contribute to rapid economic growth. Why have other developing countries not been able to replicate this success? Why has the enormous growth in international trade not resulted in a wider distribution of the fruits of that trade, as Ricardo's theory of comparative advantage would suggest? And why have some parts of the developing world barely participated at all in the growth of world merchandise trade—Africa's share of such trade is now less than half its contribution of over 5 per cent in 1980 and the developing countries of the Americas remained static at just under 6 per cent (UNCTAD 2003: 3)? Critics of the neo-liberal agenda suggest that in some ways the developing world is in a disadvantaged position in the global economy compared to more developed countries.

## The 'colonial legacy'

The term colonial legacy has been used to cover a wide range of social, political, and economic problems that developing countries confront. Two issues of particular relevance to trade are, first, a reliance on primary commodities, and second, lack of inward investment.

Following de-colonization the same basic pattern whereby the developing areas under colonialism were primarily providers of raw materials and markets for manufactured goods has largely persisted, with some notable exceptions (see Weiss 2002). Although several developing countries have seen increasing levels of industrialization, for example Mexico and Brazil, while some developed countries like the United States, Canada, and Australia continue to be major producers and exporters of commodities including certain agricultural commodities such as wheat, the developing world as whole continues to rely heavily on trade in raw materials or primary commodities. For many Non-Asian developing countries over 70 per cent of exports still comprise primary products. For many sub-Saharan African countries the figure is over 80 per cent (World Bank 1999). Given that the theory of comparative advantage suggests that countries should specialize in the production of those goods in which they have a relative advantage, why should this be a problem?

Writers from the **dependency theory** or perspective have argued that when developing countries have relied on primary commodities for export they have confronted deteriorating terms of trade. This means that developing countries have to export more and more raw materials in order to buy the same level of manufactured goods. Raúl Prebisch, the first director of the United Nations Economic Commission for Latin America (UNECLA; now called Economic Commission for Latin America and the Caribbean), put forward this idea in the 1950s, on the basis of examining economic data for Britain's imports and exports between 1870 and 1939, where he found that the prices of Britain's manufactured exports rose by nearly a third compared to the prices of imported raw materials. Various writers have attempted to replicate his research using wider data, with some arguing they have confirmed his thesis and others taking the opposite view (Todaro and Smith 2003: 522–5), although over the long term world trade in most primary commodities has certainly grown less rapidly than manufactures.

Regardless of the true position—and there is general agreement that the terms of trade for certain commodities among developing world exports have deteriorated over recent decades (Nixson 2001: 86–92)—there is a consensus that the value of raw materials are subject to greater volatility than manufactures. Between 1997 and 2001 the UNCTAD combined price index of all commodiites in US$ fell by 53 per cent in real terms; that is, primary commodities lost more than half their purchasing power relative to manufactures (UNCTAD 2003: 19). Movements like this make it harder to predict what revenues will be derived from exports in any particular year. Agricultural products are particularly prone to large price fluctuations. Years when there is a glut in production can lead to price falls, while crop failures can lead to massive price increases. Agricultural production can also be hit by changes in fashion in the developed world. See Box 2.3 for a discussion of some of the problems that are confronted by coffee-exporting countries specifically.

Many developing countries have also been hampered in their attempts to participate more fully in the global economy by a continuing and chronic shortage of capital. Investment is significant for trade, particularly in the modern world economy, because it is only possible to compete in the most profitable areas with the most up-to-date equipment. Where

---

## Box 2.3 **Coffee**

Coffee is a commodity that illustrates clearly the problems that can confront the producer of raw materials, especially agricultural products. With the exception of oil it is the commodity that earns the most for developing countries. An estimated 125 million people in the developing world depend on coffee production for their livelihoods. Yet it is an item whose price fluctuates wildly, and in recent years has shown a dramatic fall in price.

*Coffee basics*: there are two main types of coffee beans—*Robusta*, grown in lowland areas in, for example Brazil and West Africa, and the main source of instant coffee, and *Arabica* grown in highland areas such as Kenya and Colombia, which is the main source of expressos and filter coffees. Most coffee is grown on small independent farms, in contrast to, for example, bananas, which are frequently grown on large plantations. It takes three years from planting a coffee bush until it produces the first beans.

*Coffee prices*: over the past twenty-five years, international coffee prices declined rapidly. After frost destroyed much of the coffee harvest in Brazil in March 1977, coffee reached a peak price of £3,000 a tonne from £500 per tonne in 1975). Since then it has declined rapidly to a price of around £350 per tonne.

*Coffee problems*: three main problems confront the producers

- *Price fluctuations*: the price hike of 1977 demonstrates what can happen when a harvest fails. The fall in output (or even a fear of a fall in output) from one region can send the price rocketing. For a short while the production of the commodity can be extremely profitable, and this of course can prompt new producers to switch to growing the product, in the (mistaken) belief that the price will remain high.

- *Oversupply*: the price of coffee on the international market has fallen dramatically because too much was being grown. Global over-production has been exacerbated by a World Bank programme to introduce coffee production into Vietnam, which has risen rapidly to account for 10 per cent of global production now.

- *Structure of the industry*: although the large fluctuations in price and the oversupply of raw commodities are not unique to coffee, the industry's structure adds special problems. The millions of small farmers, with very limited power, face a very small number of producers with enormous power to dominate the final retailing of the product. In between there are numerous levels of wholesalers and other intermediaries. Coffee beans can change hands more than 150 times between farmer and supermarket shelf, and each time it changes hands a smaller proportion of the final price reaches the grower. Thus while the coffee growers earned $10–$12 billion of the $30 billion global retail market for coffee in the early 1990s, by 2004 they were forecast to earn just $5.5 billion from a market now worth $70 billion.

**Can fair trade provide an answer?** Much has been made of the increasing share of the coffee market that sells under the label of Fair Trade. Fair trade coffee aims to benefit growers by dealing directly with farmers, eliminating layers in the supply chain. Farmers are guaranteed a floor price that at least covers the costs of production. Additionally a bonus is always paid above international prices should they rise above the floor. The premium is earmarked for development projects agreed with the producers. Clearly fair trade is advantageous for those producers fortunate to be included. However, although fairly traded coffee as a proportion of the total is increasing, the figure is still very low, benefiting only thousands of farmers out of the millions involved in coffee production.

(UNCTAD 2003: 24–5)

**Table 2.1** Foreign direct investment inflows by region, 2000 (US$ billion)

| Region | 1989–1994 annual average | Percentage of total | 2000 | Percentage of total |
|---|---|---|---|---|
| World | 200.2 | | 1,270.8 | |
| Developed world | 137.1 | 68 | 1,005.2 | 79 |
| Developing world | 59.6 | 30 | 240.2 | 19 |
| Central and Eastern Europe | 3.4 | 2 | 25.4 | 2 |
| Africa | 3.9 | 2 | 8.2 | 0.6 |
| Latin America and the Caribbean | 17.5 | 9 | 86.2 | 7 |
| Asia | 37.7 | 19 | 143.8 | 11 |

*Source*: United Nations Conference on Trade and Development (UNCTAD) 2001: Table B1, 291–5.

equipment is outmoded, or the technology outdated, it becomes harder to manufacture goods, or even to extract raw materials or grow crops that can compete on the global market.

Table 2.1 provides a global snapshot of global foreign direct investment in 2000, with a comparison to 1989–1994. Overall, FDI levels have increased dramatically over the decade of the 1990s, but the proportion being invested in the developing world has declined. Much less than 1 per cent of the world's foreign investment is made in sub-Saharan Africa. Taking the figures for Hong Kong and the rest of the People's Republic of China together, approaching half of all investment in the developing world is directed to just one country, and the top ten recipients account for over 80 per cent (see Table 2.2). Provisional estimates for 2003 from the United Nations Conference on Trade and Development indicate that China accounted for more than half of total inflows into Asia and the Pacific and received as much as all of Africa, Latin America, and the Caribbean together.

**Table 2.2** Top ten recipients of foreign direct investment in the developing world, 2000

| Country | US$ billions | Percentage of developing world total |
|---|---|---|
| Hong Kong, China | 64.5 | 27 |
| China | 40.8 | 17 |
| Brazil | 33.5 | 14 |
| Mexico | 13.2 | 6 |
| Argentina | 11.2 | 5 |
| South Korea | 10.2 | 4 |
| Bermuda | 6.6 | 3 |
| Singapore | 6.4 | 3 |
| Malaysia | 5.5 | 2 |
| Taiwan | 4.9 | 2 |

*Source*: United Nations Conference on Trade and Development (UNCTAD) (2001): Table B1, 291–5.

# Operation of the global economy

Despite a 'colonial legacy' some countries have made a transition to a more industrial economy. Free trade zones inside national borders have been effective in attracting investment in some instances. Therefore, in order to explain continued underdevelopment some writers have stressed structural factors to argue that even where certain historical legacies cease to apply there are other factors inherent in the global trading system preventing the developing countries from deriving the full benefits.

## Unequal exchange

The concept of **unequal exchange** has been widely used by writers from within the dependency and world systems perspectives (Frank 1969; Emmanuel 1972; Wallerstein 1974). In essence the argument is that trade between the North and the South does not occur on an equal playing field, and will always be more advantageous for the North than the South. Goods from the North are always sold above a 'fair' price, while those from the South will always be sold below a 'fair' price. Hence trade will always be more profitable for the developed world, and less so for the developing world.

Various explanations have been given for this alleged lack of fairness. Prebisch, for example, argued that the slow diffusion of technology meant that the North was always at an advantage in terms of production. Emmanuel claimed that unequal wage rates were a central cause of unequal exchange. He argued that, because the labour force was smaller in the developed world, wage rates could be bargained higher, particularly in boom times. Wage rates would always be lower in the developing world because of the larger labour supply. Even if wage rates can be negotiated higher in the short term, it would always be possible to find someone who would accept a lower wage. Hence goods from the North will always be comparatively more expensive because the amount paid for the labour proportion will always be higher.

## Protectionism

The concept of unequal exchange is a highly contested one, and along with the theory that primarily advocated it, dependency theory, it is now somewhat out of fashion. A more glaring and widely accepted inequity in the global economy is the high level of protection barriers that the developed world has erected against goods of various types from the developing world.

Protectionism comes in many forms. Perhaps the simplest is the implementation of a trade tariff, the application of a tax on imports, as discussed above. A large element of the Common Agricultural Policy of the European Union involves the use of tariffs to protect farmers from certain agricultural products from outside Europe. Another form of protectionism is the use of subsidies, so for example cotton farmers in the USA receive large subsidies on their production. Furthermore there are non-tariff barriers, such as quotas, whereby only specified quantities of a product can be imported, and other restrictions such as safety requirements, environmental, or labour standards that must be adhered to and which might be judged unreasonable. This whole area has been described as the **'new protectionism'** because governments have sought to defend domestic industries, while at the same time honouring commitments to lower trade tariffs as part of international agreements.

According to Oxfam (2001) developing countries are losing $US100 billion each year from protectionist measures in industrialized countries. Tariff barriers are far higher in developed countries than in the rest of the world. At the same time the richest countries in the world have increased subsidies to their agricultural industries, making it harder for developing countries to compete.

## Key points

- A combination of factors, both historical and related to the operation of the global economy, may explain why some countries have been unable to benefit so effectively from comparative advantage.

- Many developing countries rely on the export of primary commodities. Some economists argue that over the long term the value of commodity exports does not match those of manufactured goods, and in any case are more prone to large fluctuations in value.

- The flow of foreign direct investment to the developing world has increased enormously over the past decade, but as a proportion of total, investment flowing to the developing world, and in particular Africa has declined.

- 'New protectionist' barriers provide a hidden way of limiting access to the markets of the developed world, either by constraining the volume of goods that can be sold or by placing unachievable restrictions on the character of their production.

# Developing world's responses to the world trading system

This section examines some of the ways in which developing countries have attempted to overcome the constraints and biases of the global trading system.

## Import-substituting industrialization

The aim of **import-substituting industrialization** (ISI) was to foster manufacturing in developing countries. By promoting localized manufacturing it was seen to have a number of advantages. It would employ local labour and thereby reduce unemployment, and allow production of manufactured goods at prices lower than available on international markets. Producing locally would reduce imports, potentially allow some of the production to be exported, and promote the introduction of new technology.

However, it is not straightforward to create a new industry from scratch. Often it requires specialist machinery, a knowledge of how to use and repair that machinery, and high levels of investment that are typically not available. For ISI to work, investment had to come from the state, usually obtained from international borrowing. In the short term at least, it is unlikely that manufactured goods could be produced cheaper than those available internationally, because of a 'learning curve'. In order to promote a local market for production, tariff walls have to be set up to make imported goods more expensive. Two key elements therefore have typified ISI programmes— a high level of government investment, and tariff walls to protect the 'infant' industry.

ISI is generally regarded as having been a failure for the developing world. In general it did not promote the stated objectives, but resulted in rather inefficient government-owned industries that were unable to compete internationally. The reason for this is generally cited as being a reluctance to move towards reducing the tariff walls so that the industries are forced to compete internationally. Particularly in Latin America

pressure was put on governments to maintain subsidies and high levels of protection underpinning the industries. A further problem was that in many developing countries the market was not large enough to reap economies of large-scale production. Finally, ISI did not even break the reliance on imports: instead of relying on imported manufactured goods, the countries became reliant on the import of machine tools, spare parts, and specialized knowledge.

Although ISI is normally now depicted in negative terms, it should be remembered that much of European and US industrialization occurred behind tariff walls, and that the success of the NICs depended to varying degrees on this approach. The key issue is the point at which the tariff protection is withdrawn and industries move from being 'import-substituting' to being 'export-generating'. This was a transition that many countries, particularly in Latin America, were not able to make. However this was not the lesson that was learnt at the time; rather the failure of ISI was largely seen as being due to the small size of the domestic market, and regionalism was promoted as a way of increasing the number of potential customers.

## Regionalism

**Import-substituting industrialization** featured strongly in the attempts of developing countries to overcome their problems with the world economy in the 1940s and 1950s. Regionalism emerged as a separate strategy with a first wave in the 1960s, but which had run its course by the early 1970s, and a second wave or 'new' regionalism in the 1990s. The prime aim of the first wave of regionalism was to increase the size of the market for their manufactures. Regional blocks were also thought potentially to increase negotiating power in international organizations. One of the features of the first wave of regional organizations, such as the Caribbean Common Market, was the attempt to implement a high level of political control over production, so that decisions about the siting of industrial production were supposed to be made at a regional level. The idea was that by sharing out industrial production, the benefits from economies of scale could be maximized. This proved to be both politically and economically unviable. The first wave of regionalism soon ran into serious problems, because the required degree of political cooperation and coordination never materialized. The maintenance of high tariffs once again resulted in inefficient industries, unable to compete internationally, and weak transport and other infrastructural links also played a part.

By the mid-1970s many of the first wave of regional organizations were moribund in all but name. However in the 1990s, a 'new' regionalism emerged, inspired by the European Union. These organizations adopted a much larger free market agenda, without the political baggage associated with the first wave. Some formerly dormant organizations such as the Central American Common Market have been revitalized, and other new groups have emerged, such as MERCOSUR—the common market of the Southern cone, in South America. The aim of these organizations has been to promote inter-regional trade through the lowering of internal tariffs, without ambitious attempts at controlling the economic diversification of the countries involved (see Appendix 2: Regional Inter-governmental Organizations in the Developing World).

## Commodity agreements

When, by the mid-1970s, many of the attempts at promoting growth through regional organizations were faltering, creating a dissatisfaction comparable to the disillusionment with ISI in the 1960s, a new strategy gained support. The success of the Organization of Petroleum Exporting Countries (OPEC, see Box 2.4) indicated that the prices commodities fetch on world markets could be influenced through manipulating supply. OPEC achieved this through operating an export quota system; other commodity agreements resorted to employing buffer stocks. A problem for commodities is that the price falls when there is a high supply, and rises when supply is restricted. The aim of buffer stocks is to smooth out

these fluctuations, by buying up stocks when the price falls (thus restricting supply and maintaining the price), and releasing the product when the price starts to rise, so that an increase in supply ensures that the price doesn't rise too far. Commodity agreements pre-date the 1970s. For example, attempts had been made to stabilize sugar prices from the mid-1930s. OPEC's success in the 1970s prompted increased interest in ways of stabilizing and raising commodity prices. The establishment of commodity agreements became a central part of the call for a **New International Economic Order** (see Chapter 3, Box 3.1).

In practice the overall record of attempts to manipulate, or at least stabilize, commodity prices has not been successful. OPEC itself lost some of its power as new oil producers in the North Sea, Egypt, Mexico, and Russia captured a growing share of world markets without even joining OPEC, and the development of alternative forms of energy and energy conservation measures in the rich countries have also played a part. OPEC's success in the 1970s was not repeated with other commodities, and the majority of the other agreements have not survived. With the move towards **neo-liberalism** and a greater advocacy of free trade policies from the 1980s, the developed world has been less willing to cooperate with commodity agreements.

## Key points

- Developing countries have employed various strategies to overcome the perceived inequities of the global trading system, such as import-substituting industrialization, regionalism, and commodity agreements

- The strategies by and large have been unsuccessful. Advocates of free markets claim this is because they introduce economic inefficiencies; others argue that it reflects the character of power relations between the North and South and the enormous difficulties facing developing countries trying to catch up economically with the developed world.

- The first wave of regionalism was an attempt to increase the size of markets for local industrial production, while the second, less ambitious wave is an attempt to reduce tariffs to boost production.

## Box 2.4 Organization of Petroleum Exporting Countries

Oil represents a special case. Nevertheless it highlights further the difficulties that commodity exporters face. Other commodity agreements have not had the success of OPEC (Organization of Petroleum Exporting Countries).

*Oil basics*: amongst oil's many uses are: as a source of energy for domestic and industrial electricity; to power transportation systems; as a lubricant; as the raw material for plastics. It has become central to the way of life of the developed world, but ultimately is a limited resource.

OPEC was founded in 1960 by a number of oil-producing countries in the developing world in an attempt to increase export revenues. In the 1950s world oil consumption was growing rapidly. But oil prices fell throughout the decade. However, between 1970 and 1973 OPEC succeeded in doubling oil prices, through negotiation with Northern governments. Then, between October 1973 and January 1974, OPEC was able to further quadruple oil prices, by reaching an agreement between the members to restrict supply. In the 1970s OPEC's success in increasing oil prices seemed to be a signal to developing countries that others too could get a better price for their commodity exports. But was oil a special case?

*Accounting for OPEC's success*: OPEC is an example of an export quota commodity agreement. Its members have been able to manipulate the price by regulating the supply. But this is not easy.

- On the supply side, export quota commodity agreements tend to be fragile because there is always a temptation for producers to defect. When prices rise through joint action to limit supply, there is always a risk that some member(s) will exploit the situation by increasing their supply to take advantage of the higher price. At times this has been a problem for OPEC and would be a much bigger issue where the number of producers is larger, like millions of coffee growers. Moreover oil is not perishable, and to leave it unexploited for a few more years will not affect its quality, unlike agricultural goods, which cannot be stored indefinitely.

- On the demand side, there are ways of reducing its use (seeking other non-OPEC controlled sources, using increased insulation, using coal or synthetic substitutes, or reducing energy use generally), but these take time to introduce. Oil is still an essential item. And although oil as a proportion of total energy use has declined since the 1970s (in 1973 oil supplied 45.1 per cent of the world's energy requirements, compared to 35 percent in 2001) this decline has to be seen in the light of an overall increased consumption of energy, of 66 per cent, so the quantity of oil being used has actually increased.

Oil appears to be a special case, and perhaps the best demonstration of this is that OPEC is really the only commodity agreement to remain active, even though it is no longer as powerful as it appeared to be in the 1970s. In 2002 OPEC countries accounted for only 38.4 per cent of the world's production of oil, although perhaps more significantly they controlled 78 per cent of the world's proven oil resources. It is not in OPEC's interests to drive oil prices ever upwards, for this can provoke recession in the industrialized countries and accelerate the search for alternative sources of energy.

(BP 2003; International Energy Agency 2003)

# Conclusion

After 1945 the global economy has seen not only massive increases in the levels of world trade, but also an enormous growth in the prosperity of the developed world. For most analysts these two features are closely linked. But this prompts the question of why possible gains from trade do not seems to have been obtained by the majority of developing countries. Why, in an era of a global economy and neo-liberal policies, are some countries poorer than they were a decade or even much longer ago?

Various answers to this question exist. A free market analysis would suggest that there are still too many blockages to the free movement of investment and goods. Poorer countries have undermined their own prospects of development by working against the market. A second position maintains that trade is potentially beneficial but because developing countries are behind the developed world in terms of industrialization, reforms to the global economy are required. A more radical position, derived from dependency theory and world-systems theory, would argue that the global trading system entrenches inequality between the richest parts of the world and the poorest.

Each of these positions implies radically different policy options. For the past twenty years the free market philosophy has dominated policy. But although many developing countries have followed neo-liberal prescriptions, they still face protectionist measures imposed by governments in the developed world. This makes it more difficult to persuade the developing countries to proceed faster or in a more comprehensive fashion. Reformers who believe that the impacts of the global economy can be mitigated suggest varying mixes of policies, such as foreign debt forgiveness, concessionary aid inflows to promote industrialization, commodity agreements to protect prices, and preferential terms for trade. Two major problems confront this approach. First, many such policies have been tried, and as with commodity agreements, have been found wanting. In an increasingly global economy attempts to override the market become more heavily penalized as capital moves more freely from location to location. Secondly, the size of resource transfers needed to significantly lift living standards in the developing world and meet current United Nations' **Millenium Development Goals (MDGs)** (see Box.13.1 below) is generally reckoned to be about twice current levels (around $US68 billion in 2003) and is politically unacceptable for most governments in the rich world.

From a more radical perspective, trade is not the solution to the developing countries' problems but instead is a contributory factor in underdevelopment. Unequal trading relations reflect underlying power realities. In exceptional circumstances escape from the periphery may be possible through heavy state intervention, but there is no one set of measures that will lead to this. Such an analysis would suggest a policy of attempting to break out of the system, or at least to reduce trade with the developed world. A view that production should be local is a keystone of the anti-globalization movement (Mandel 2003: 49–51). The problem for this position is the shortage of viable models for countries seeking an alternate development approach. With the transformation of the Soviet Union, there is no alternate trading system. Models of development offered by Cuba and China hardly seem relevant. Both pay lip service to socialism, but have opened their doors to capitalist investment. North Korea as an example of autarchy is not attractive either, given its very serious development failings that make it routinely dependent on international humanitarian food relief aid.

The reasons for the disparity of wealth in the global economy will be disputed indefinitely. For the foreseeable future developing countries will have to make their way within a global capitalist environment. The operation of global markets has the potential to generate enormous wealth as well as the capability to exploit the most vulnerable. The governments of developing countries have the awesome task of trying to minimize the negative impacts of global capitalism, while attracting the potential benefits for their populations. The challenge for governments in the developed world is to resolve the contradiction of promoting free trade as a solution for the developing world while maintaining protectionism at home. While they fail to do this it would appear that the global economy operates largely in the interests of the rich and powerful and against some of the poorest and least influential parts of the world.

## QUESTIONS

**1** How useful is Ricardo's theory of comparative advantage in explaining trade relations between the developed and developing worlds?

**2** Account for the failure of import-substituting industrialization in many parts of the developing world.

3   What are the arguments for and against developing countries adopting free trade policies and how persuasive are they?

4   Does the reliance of many developing countries on the export of raw materials place them at a disadvantage in the global economy?

5   To what extent can the newly industrializing countries of South-East Asia provide a model of development for the developing world?

## GUIDE TO FURTHER READING

Dicken, P., *Global Shift: Reshaping the Global Economic Map in the 21st Century* (London: Sage, 2003). Clear overview of the emergence of a global economy, with good sections on the Newly Industrializing Countries.

McMichael, P., *Development and Social Change: A Global Perspective*, 2nd edn. (London: Sage, 2000). Comprehensive account of approaches to development, with many case studies.

Mandel, J. R., *Globalization and the Poor* (Cambridge: Cambridge University Press, 2003). A good overview of arguments for and against economic globalization.

Spero, J., and Hart, J., *The Politics of International Economic Relations*, 6th edn. (New York: Wadsworth, 2003) Superb discussion of key theories of international political economy.

Todaro, M., and Smith, S., *Economic Development*, 8th edn. (Boston, Mass.: Addison Wesley, 2003). Regularly revised and updated, contains excellent chapters on the role of developing countries in the global economy and on theories of trade.

van Marrewijk, C., *International Trade and the World Economy* (Oxford: Oxford University Press, 2002). Excellent introduction to theories of trade and investment in the global economy.

Weiss, J., *Industrialisation and Globalisation: Theory and Evidence from Developing Countries* (London: Routledge, 2002). A very detailed account of the processes of industrialization in the developing world.

## WEB LINKS

**www.freetrade.org**   The site of the Center for Trade Policy Studies, Washington, DC, whose 'mission' is to increase public understanding of the benefits of free trade and costs of protectionism.

**www.twnside.org.sg/trade.htm**   Third World Network page on trade issues, provides research critical of current global economic policies.

**www.oxfam.org**   The site of the non-governmental organisation Oxfam (UK), containing many of its reports on trade and protectionism:

**www.undp.org**   United Nations Development Programme—the United Nations body that focuses on development issues and produces annually a human development report.

 **COMPANION WEB SITE**

For additional material and resources, see the companion web site at:
**www.oup.com/uk/booksites/politics/**

# 3

# The developing world in international politics

*Stephen Hobden*

## OVERVIEW

This chapter focuses on the politics of North–South relations. It makes the argument that the discipline of International Relations has traditionally overlooked the significance of the developing world in global politics. It examines international relations between the North and South especially during the cold war and discusses the role of developing countries in international organizations. A section on the debt crisis links this chapter to the previous one by showing how economic and political forces interact in North–South relations.

# Introduction: international relations and the developing world

For much of the history of the discipline of International Relations, the developing world has been a minority issue.[1] The discipline has primarily been concerned with relations between the great (or super) powers. Although perhaps understandable, this concentration is deeply problematic. It meant that at least four-fifths of the global population was excluded as a subject of study. This has reflected a Western perspective on the world. Furthermore, it failed to acknowledge that while, during the cold war, there was a 'long peace' in Europe, many parts of the developing world were deeply mired in violent conflict, in which the superpowers were frequently involved. There the rivalry between the superpowers was played out in a way that was far from 'cold', fuelling **proxy wars** for instance in southern Africa and the horn of Africa. Finally, the opening years of the twenty-first century appear to be characterized by increasing conflict between parts of the developed and developing worlds, as most notably in Iraq.

The focus on the superpowers may reflect a deeper problem with the discipline. That is quite simply that traditional International Relations theory does not have the tools to understand the developing world. The traditional world-view of International Relations is one where the state is the key actor, and is the guarantor of the 'good life' for its citizens. States operate in a situation of 'anarchy', where they all have equal sovereignty, and must all in the final instance be liable for their own self-defence. Within the confines of the state there is order and hierarchy, outside lies a lack of order. From the developing world this world-view may make little sense. The state rather than being the guarantor of the 'good life' has frequently been a major threat to the well-being of the citizen. Many developing countries have been governed at some time or another by military regimes, which have targeted sections of the society for repression. The states of Latin America have, by and large, lived at peace with each other since the 1930s, but regimes in virtually every country in the region have practised major human rights abuses. The anarchy has been on the inside rather than the outside. Furthermore, the state, rather than being the key actor, has had to compete with numerous other powerful actors, such as **warlords**, guerrilla groups, and drug cartels, which in some places appear to threaten its very existence. More recently, when developing countries acquiesced in World Bank **structural adjustment** agreements, external actors have had more power over the running of the society than the state itself. At the same time that domestic politics in the developing world perspective can be viewed as disordered, the external world appears to be more hierarchical, with the most powerful states determining the fates of the less powerful. Sovereignty, the right of states to govern within their own territory without external interference, a fundamental tenet of the charter of the United Nations, has been breached many times since 1945.[2]

This chapter stresses the importance of the developing world in the cold war and post-cold war periods. It begins by considering the situation of developing countries during the cold war, followed by the implications of the collapse of the Soviet Union and the emergence of the United States as the dominant global power. It also examines the role of developing countries in international organizations, particularly the United Nations. A final section considers how the politics of North–South relations cannot be separated from the developing countries' economic position, by analysing the role of the international financial institutions in dealing with the so-called 'Third World debt' crisis.

## Key points

- The discipline of International Relations has tended to focus on the role of the great (or super) powers.

- This focus has ignored the vast proportion of the global population, and the key role that the developing world has played in the global politics of the cold war and post-cold war periods.

# North–South relations since 1945

## The cold war

The now obsolete notion of a 'Third World' is closely linked to the period of the cold war, and is derived from a perceived tripartite division of the world:

- a 'first world', the United States, and its allies,
- a 'second world', the Soviet Union, and Eastern Europe,
- a 'third world' comprising the rest—the newly decolonized countries of Asia and Africa, and the countries of Latin America, most of which had gained their independence at the start of the nineteenth century.

This was a ridiculous oversimplification, though the ideological and strategic conflict played out between the superpowers certainly had a major impact felt by most countries of the 'Third World'. This conflict took a variety of forms. There were cases of direct military intervention by the superpowers, such as the USA in Vietnam, and the Soviet Union in Afghanistan. There were many examples of indirect intervention using either the carrot of aid policy, or the stick of sanctions, or the threat of the withdrawal of aid. There was also the use of proxy fighting forces to avoid direct intervention. Examples here include the funding by the USA of the Mujahidin to challenge the Soviet Union in Afghanistan, and the use of the Cuban army in southern Africa.

Once both superpowers had access to nuclear weapons, any direct confrontation would have been, in the terminology of the time, MAD—Mutually Assured Destruction. A range of interests underpinned the superpowers' policies towards the developing world. For both there were security issues, both had trading concerns, and for both there were ideological issues that related to their views of themselves as nations. These different interests played out in different ways at different times.

In the beginning of the cold war the US government's main interest in the developing areas was in supporting the calls for decolonization, in line with its world-view that a decolonized world would be more in its own interests. This was coupled, however, with a concern that newly independent countries should not fall under Soviet influence. Therefore there was a tension between the USA's support for decolonization, and its wish to maintain international stability. Additionally, with the triumph of Mao's revolutionary army in China, and the invasion by North Korea of the south of the country (see Chapter 21*b* below) there was fear that communist influence was spreading in East Asia. The Soviet Union was barely engaged at this time. Stalin, now in physical decline, did not try to exploit Lenin's theory that the developing world was a weak link for the capitalist system, and had done little to support the Communist Party in China.

From the late 1950s and through the 1960s both superpowers increased their activities in the developing world. The USA was particularly active in its own 'back yard', supporting the overthrow of democratically elected President Arbenz in Guatemala (1954), and attempting to overthrow Castro in Cuba (1961 onwards). Through this period it also became increasingly involved in the war between North and South Vietnam. Following the death of Stalin the Soviet Union gave more attention to the newly independent countries, seeking to draw them under its influence. However it lacked the power projection to protect potential satellite states. For example, in 1960 Prime Minister Lumumba of the Congo sought military aid to counter secessionists in his newly independent country, but the Soviet Union was not able to respond and the country soon came under the rule of Joseph Mobutu, who looked to the West (see Chapter 18*b* below). The Soviet Union ultimately did not offer protection to Cuba when its missiles were found on the island in the autumn of 1962.

As the USA became increasingly drawn into the Vietnam 'quagmire', confidence about its role in the world declined, and anti-US sentiment grew. During the 1970s the Soviet Union appeared able to exploit this weakness. The West seemed to be in disarray, as the USA attempted to withdraw from Vietnam and President Nixon's administration was shaken by the 'Watergate scandal' (1973–4). Furthermore the economies of the West went through deep upheavals in the wake of the OPEC oil price rises. The Soviet Union was now getting closer to strategic parity with the USA and was able to project its power with greater confidence. It gave direct support to revolutionary movements in Vietnam, Ethiopia, and Angola, and as a result gained strategic bases in Africa and Asia. It also supported revolutionary movements in Central America, giving it influence very close to the United States. This growing confidence led it to launch a major military intervention in Afghanistan in late 1979 to support a friendly regime on its southern border.

The global situation changed dramatically in the following decade. It was now the Soviet Union that was mired in a foreign war, and the USA under President Reagan exploited the situation. The USA sought 'rollback'—reversing Soviet gains of the 1970s, and under the 'Reagan doctrine' support was given to anti-communist guerrillas. In Afghanistan the USA supported the Mujahidin, in Nicaragua the 'Contras', and in Angola UNITA (National Union for Total Independence). As the decade drew on the cold war moved to a close. Mikhail Gorbachev's 'new thinking' in the Soviet Union sought a new relationship with the West and a Soviet withdrawal from Afghanistan. The impact of the Afghan war on the Soviet Union was at least comparable to that of the Vietnam war on the USA, where considerable social ferment followed especially among the young. Although not the only cause of the collapse of the Soviet Union, within two years of the withdrawal from Afghanistan, Communist Party rule had ended. At the same time, material support for former satellite states, even Cuba, also ended.

The cold war was a time of great of upheaval for the developing world. In the period immediately after the Second World War, most of it was still was under colonial control. By the end of the cold war it was mostly independent. This wave of decolonization was accompanied by an international conflict between the two superpowers, fought over and in developing countries. For their governments it meant making a choice to align with one superpower or the other. This pressure provoked the creation of the Non-Aligned Movement in 1961—a collection of states that claimed to reject both superpowers, although in reality most states, Cuba for example, were aligned with one or other superpower.

However the existence of two competing superpowers did mean that a choice existed for developing countries. Many countries were courted by both sides, with rival offers of financial and economic aid. For some the possibility existed to switch allegiances (or at least to threaten to switch). Egypt in the early 1970s changed its alignment from the Soviet Union to the United States, becoming one of the largest recipients of aid. The cold war provided these countries with at least an option between two superpowers with two ideologies concerning the operation of social and economic systems and the goals and modalities of development.[3]

## The post-cold war period

The end of the cold war in the late 1980s was greeted with optimism. The prospect of imminent nuclear destruction, which had hung over the world since the late 1950s, receded. In a 1991 speech US President George Bush spoke of a 'New World Order' which would be 'an historic period of cooperation . . . an era in which the nations of the world, East and West, North and South, can prosper and live in harmony' (quoted in Acharya 1999: 84). In the early 1990s there was a sense that a new form of global cooperation could result in solving many of the world's problems. For many in the developed world this sense of peace and well-being was enhanced by a prolonged economic boom through much of the 1990s.

For developing countries too there were reasons to be optimistic. The cold war had been a cause of instability, and its end promised greater peace and stability. Accompanying the end of the forty-year superpower conflict a number of regional conflicts were also resolved—particularly in southern Africa (Mozambique, Namibia, and, temporarily, in Angola) and Central America (Nicaragua and El Salvador). A new spirit of cooperation in the United Nations Security Council enabled that organization to become more active in conflict resolution. The UN achieved notable successes in Namibia, El Salvador, and Cambodia. It authorized an international military response to Iraq's invasion of Kuwait in 1990. Furthermore a number of corrupt regimes which had been supported by one side or the other were replaced by democratic governments. There was much talk of a 'peace dividend' and considerable reductions in arms spending which could be funnelled towards development projects. Then, at the Millennial UN General Assembly ambitious commitments were made by the member states to reverse global poverty. Also, the prospect of a truly global economy appeared to promise more extensive trading links with the hope of generating greater wealth.

Following the terrorist attacks on the USA in 2001 ('9/11') the optimism of the post-cold war period has been replaced by a 'global melancholy' (Halliday 2002: 214). The opportunities that appeared to be emerging for developing countries now look less promising. While the end of the cold war did provide greater stability in some areas, there has been greater instability in other regions. Afghanistan, for example, has been in a constant state of upheaval, and the Democratic Republic of Congo descended into chaos, with its neighbouring countries intervening on opposing sides (see Chapter 18*b* below). There have also been concerns about how the USA will use its position as the only superpower. In the wake of 11 September 2001 the US government declared its willingness to act unilaterally and pre-emptively to further its national security interests, and the invasion of Iraq in 2003 occurred without the clear support of the United Nations Security Council. Furthermore the hoped for increases in development aid failed to materialize; levels of aid, particularly to Africa, fell throughout the 1990s.

The global picture for developing countries is therefore mixed. Some states have benefited from a greater stability, while for many citizens the end of the cold war has meant greater instability. The post-cold war boom of the 1990s also offered increased possibilities for more countries to participate in the global economy. However, the demise of the Soviet Union has removed an option of choice. There is now one global economy, and one system—capitalism—and the costs of defaulting from this system have become higher. The option of playing one superpower off against the other no longer exists, and hence the room for manoeuvre has been reduced.[4]

## Key points

- During the cold war the superpowers intervened in the developing world in a variety of different ways.

- The superpowers were motivated by a variety of different interests: military security, trade, and ideology. The significance of these interests varied over time and location.

- The cold war was a source of instability for many countries in the developing world. However, in a world where neutrality from the global struggle was difficult there was a choice of ideology and model of development.

- A post-cold war peace dividend has failed to appear for the developing world. Although some areas have experienced greater stability, many have not. There are also increasing fears regarding the deployment of US power.

# The developing world in international organizations

Having considered the broader environment of international relations, the role of developing country states in international organizations merits closer attention, particularly in view of the clear majority of seats they now command in the United Nations General Assembly.

## The United Nations

The United Nations is an enormous and complex institution, and it is normally described as the UN system. This system comprises the six principal organs (the General Assembly, the Security Council, the Trusteeship Council, the Economic and Social Council, the Secretariat, and the International Court of Justice), plus numerous subsidiary organs, agencies, and programmes. Many of these subsidiary organizations are of direct relevance here, especially the Development Programme (UNDP), the Children's Fund (UNICEF), and the International Monetary Fund and World Bank (which are discussed below).

In theory the core of the organization is the General Assembly. All nations that are members of the United Nations have a seat in the Assembly. Its decisions are taken on the basis of sovereign equality (namely one member one vote). The vote of the United States is the same as that of Haiti, and China (with approximately one quarter of the world's population) has the same vote as Tonga (which has a population of 104,000). The full Assembly meets once a year, between mid-September and December, though special sessions can be called by a majority of members, or by the Security Council. Most of the work of the Assembly is done by a series of sub-committees which discuss issues ranging from international security to the budget of the UN. Members of the Assembly can raise any issue for discussion that falls within the range of the Charter. The call for a '**New International Economic Order**' (NIEO) was launched in the General Assembly (see Chapter 2, and Box 3.1).

## Box 3.1 **The call for a New International Economic Order (NIEO)**

The demand for a New International Economic Order can be seen in the context of a series of meetings and conferences held during the 1950s and 1960s. It represents the highpoint of cooperation between developing countries. The call for a NIEO was first officially voiced at a meeting of the Non-Aligned Movement in Algiers in 1973, at a time when Western capitalism seemed to be weakened in the face of the OPEC oil rises.

The NIEO envisaged a radical reordering of the world economy, an end to dependency and a major spur to development. The demands were:

- *Trade*. The NIEO envisaged the linking between prices of commodities with those of manufactures, in an attempt to overcome the problems of declining terms of trade. Furthermore there were calls for the setting up of a Common Fund to support and stabilize the prices of commodities. Also there was a demand for increased access to the markets of the developed world for Third World manufactured goods.

- *Investment*. A call for control over the actions of TNCs, frequently regarded as exploitative by developing countries. In particular a code of conduct was sought to control the activities of multinational companies.

- *Technology*. A demand for increases in technology transfer, particularly cheaper access to more appropriate technology.

- *Aid*. More aid was sought, along with a reduction in preconditions.

- *Reform of International Organizations*. The NIEO called for the reform of international organizations to give developing countries greater influence over decision-making.

The UN General Assembly became the forum where the call for a NIEO was largely debated. In spring 1974 a special session approved 'The Declaration and Program of Action on the Establishment of a New International Economic Order', though the voting divided the developed and underdeveloped worlds. In the autumn a 'Charter of Economic Rights and Duties of States' was approved by 120 votes to 6, with 10 countries abstaining. Again, many of the countries of the North either voted against or abstained.

Few of these demands were met. The Lomé agreement between Europe and its former colonies in Africa, the Caribbean, and Pacific allowing preferential access to European markets was one result. A common fund for commodities was finally set up in 1989, though in restricted form. A voluntary code of practice for transnational corporations was finally agreed in 1976, though, being voluntary was largely seen as ineffective. Many of the key demands with regard to trade, aid, and the reform of international organizations remain unmet.

The reasons for this failure are complex. The call for a NIEO came at a time when perhaps the South was at its most united and powerful, and at a time when Western capitalism appeared vulnerable. However the North maintained its unity, while divisions emerged among developing countries. At a deeper level the call for a NIEO poses questions regarding the extent to which a capitalist global economy is possible of reform, or whether a more radical way of seeking a fairer distribution of the world's resources is required.

The Assembly can make recommendations to the Security Council, and it can initiate studies. It also approves the budget for the organization.

Although the General Assembly appears to be at the centre it is the Security Council which has the real power. It comprises five permanent members (Britain, China, France, Russia, and the United States), plus ten non-permanent members. The non-permanent members are elected by the General Assembly and have a seat for two years. The non-permanent seats are allocated on a regional basis— five for Africa and Asia, two for Latin America, one for Eastern Europe, and two for Western Europe. The charter imbues considerable power in the Security Council. Under Article 24(1) the Council is given 'primary responsibility for the maintenance of international peace and security'. Article 25 commits all UN members 'to accept and carry out the decisions of the Security Council'. Under Chapter 7 of the charter the Council can 'identify aggressors' in a conflict situation (article 39), it can 'decide on enforcement measures' (articles, 40, 41, and 42) and it can call upon other members to provide armed forces (articles 43, 44, and 45).

The key to understanding the decision-making process of the Security Council is the voting procedures. Two types of votes are held. First there are votes on procedural issues. These include votes on the agenda for meetings, for calling special sessions of the Assembly, or invitations to non-members to address the council. These votes are taken on a simple majority—nine affirmative votes. Secondly there are votes on substantive issues. These votes relate to the significant activities of the Council. For these votes there have to be at least nine affirmative votes, plus all of the permanent members have to concur, or abstain. If one of the permanent members votes against a proposal this is described as using its veto. If the veto is used the motion falls—even if all the other members of the council are in favour. For example, the United States has often used its veto to defeat motions critical of Israel. In the 2003 war against Iraq a vote was not taken on a resolution committing the UN to war as it was likely that France or Russia would have used the veto, even though it is possible that a majority might have voted in favour.

The Economic and Social Council (ECOSOC) is part of the UN that has particular relevance for developing countries because it has specific responsibility for overseeing development-related activities. ECOSOC comprises fifty-four members elected by the General Assembly, each serving for a period of three years. ECOSOC primarily has a coordinating role, overseeing the activities of the various UN institutions having economic and social responsibilities. For example, in theory the International Monetary Fund is a subsidiary institution of ECOSOC. In addition, ECOSOC is the key forum in the UN for the discussion of economic and social issues. It can initiate studies and organize conferences and make recommendations to the Security Council. It also has a key role in promoting Human Rights (see pp. 240–1 below in Chapter 15). Box 3.2 assesses some of the successes achieved by the UN with regard to development issues.

The Trusteeship Council has also played an important role in the developing world as the body charged with overseeing the road to independence of a number of countries. Immediately following the Second World War three types of territory were envisioned as coming under its jurisdiction. First, a number of territories had been mandated to the League of Nations. These were primarily German colonies, which were removed from its control after the First World War, for example Tanganyika. Secondly, there were the colonies confiscated from Italy and Japan following the Second World War. Finally, the provision existed for colonial powers to voluntarily hand over the administration of territories to the Trusteeship Council, though, perhaps unsurprisingly, this option was never utilized. In one sense the Trusteeship Council can be regarded as one of the most successful components of the UN. It has been so successful in overseeing its charges to independence that it no longer has an active role. The crucial role that the UN played in decolonization is summarized in Box 3.3.

# The International Monetary Fund, the World Bank, and the World Trade Organization

These three international organizations have their origins in the conference held at Bretton Woods, USA, in July 1944, although the World Trade Organization

---

## Box 3.2  United Nations achievements in development

The UN has been involved in development issues in a number of ways:

- As an information source, with experts in economics, agriculture, and industrial development.

- Direct assistance in emergency situations.

- The creation of regional organizations to address the particular problems of specific areas, for example, the Economic Commission for Asia and the Far East.

- Specific development responsibilities of UN agencies, for example, the UNDP (Development Programme) and the UNHCR (High Commissioner for Refugees).

- Numerous resolutions in the General Assembly related to development issues.

- A series of 'development decades', intended to keep issues such as global inequality on the agenda.

The UN can point to a number of areas of success:

- Life expectancy globally has increased.

- Child mortality rates for under-5s have decreased.

- Immunization levels have improved, as has access to primary health facilities, availability of clean water, and literacy levels.

- An achievement that can be directly attributed to a UN agency is the eradication of smallpox, coordinated by the World Health Organization.

That the organization retains such goals is demonstrated by the Millennium Declaration adopted in September 2000. This pledged the member states to work towards ambitious goals including halving the proportion of the world's population living on less than $US1 a day, and ensuring that all the world's children receive a primary education (see Chapter 13).

---

was not established until 1995. The International Monetary Fund (IMF) is primarily concerned with maintaining the operation of the global financial system. The World Bank concentrates on providing loans to developing countries. The World Trade Organization (WTO) focuses on improving trade relations between its members. All three have had profound implications for the developing world.

### The IMF

The aims of the IMF are laid out in its Articles of Agreement. They are:

- to increase monetary cooperation between member states,

- to facilitate increased trade,

- to promote foreign exchange stability,

- to help member states overcome balance of payments problems,

- and to reduce the duration of international financial disequilibria.

The running of the IMF is divided between a board of governors and an executive. The board of governors is made up of one representative from each member state. The governors meet once per year in September, and their main business is to consider applications from potential new members and to consider the levels of quotas that each member pays and the corresponding voting rights. The executive is concerned with the day-to-day running of the organization. It is made up of representatives from twenty-four countries. Of these the United States, Britain, France, Germany, Japan, Saudi Arabia, and Japan are permanent members, while the rest are elected. The function of the executive is to consider applications by members for loans and to consider the requirements that are attached to such loans. These requirements frequently take the form of structural adjustment packages.

Unlike the UN General Assembly, voting in the IMF is not based on one country one vote—instead the voting is based on the size of the quota that each country pays into the fund. This in turn is related to the size of the country's economy. Hence the USA with the largest economy has the largest proportion of the vote (approximately 17 per cent), while many of the poorest countries have a mere 0.001 per cent. As a result the developed world always has a majority.

The activities of the IMF have changed since its formation, reflecting both the changed character of

## Box 3.3 **The United Nations and decolonization**

The end of the European empires is one of the most significant developments of the last century. It was a global transformation in which the United Nations played a key role. The oversight of this process is perhaps one of the organization's greatest achievements. The notion of self-determination is at the core of the Charter, articulated in Article 1(2) and repeated in Article 55. Furthermore, a pledge to develop self-government in non-self-governing territories (a euphemism for colonies) is made in Article 73.

In the immediate aftermath of the Second World War a small number of countries became independent. For example, India gained independence from Britain in 1947, while Indonesia became independent from the Netherlands. The first move of newly independent countries was to take up a seat in the UN General Assembly as a mark of sovereignty and independence from the colonial power. The newly independent states were generally critical of the continuation of empire, and the general assembly became the main forum where calls for decolonization were voiced. By 1960 there were sufficient members to allow the passing of resolution 1514, which condemned the continuation of colonialism. In the 1960s several African states became independent and further resolutions were passed calling for colonialism to be eradicated.

The UN also acted in a very practical way to smooth the process of decolonization. The withdrawal of colonial powers from territories was seldom a straightforward affair, frequently leaving civil strife and disastrous levels of underdevelopment. The UN was frequently drawn into such situations, as peacekeeper and as provider of essential services. With the withdrawal of the British from India, massive unrest broke out between the Hindu and Muslim populations of India and the newly created state of Pakistan. There was massive loss of life and displacement of population. The UN Security Council voted to send an observer group to monitor the situation in the hope that an outside group might calm the situation. UNMOGIP

(United Nations Military Observer Group in India and Pakistan) was created in 1949 to patrol the border area in Kashmir. It remains in place today.

Decolonization also transformed the organization itself. There were fifty-one original members in 1945. Of these thirty-one came from the developing world. There were very few representatives from Africa and Asia, and over 750 million people lived in 'non-self-governing trusts'. Hence the USA and the West in general had a built-in majority in the General Assembly, and the majority of votes would swing in line with the wishes of the USA. By 1960 (when resolution 1514 was passed) the situation had changed dramatically—to 100 members, of whom sixty-six were from the developing world including forty-six from Africa and Asia. By this point the General Assembly was supporting the position taken by the United States in around half of all votes taken. By 1980 more than half of the UN consisted of non-founder members, which had not been sovereign states in 1945. Their loyalty to a US-dominated world order was low and the vast majority of the votes in the assembly were against the US position and in support of the Soviet Union.

The General Assembly became the forum for further issues that were a priority for the developing world. On the Middle East the assembly has consistently supported the position of the Palestinians and has passed resolutions critical of the Israeli government. The General Assembly took a large part in the struggle against apartheid, passing a first resolution calling for sanctions to be implemented against South Africa in 1962. When Central America became a flashpoint during the cold war the General Assembly consistently passed resolutions critical of US intervention in the region. With the numerical dominance of the developing countries, the USA, which had done so much to create the UN, became lukewarm in its support, as reflected in protracted delays in paying its annual dues.

---

the global economy, and changing economic orthodoxy. The prime activity of the IMF has always been to make short-term loans to countries undergoing balance of payments crises (when the value of imports exceeds those of exports for a prolonged period). Countries can borrow money in '*tranches*', but the more they borrow the greater the level of

'**conditionality**'. Conditionality means the level of influence that the IMF endeavours to exert over the financial and economic policy of the borrowing country.

In recent years the IMF has concentrated on four main functions. First, it has taken a surveillance role, both of member states and of the global economy.

It produces a bi-annual World Economic Outlook giving information on the main economic trends. Through its publications it also seeks to promote its own preferred neo-liberal policy preferences. Secondly, it has intervened to a large extent in the economic policies of a number of countries, particularly as a result of the debt crisis (see below). For many countries it has been essential to get an IMF 'seal of approval' in order to be able to attract finance from other sources. Thirdly the IMF provides training for government officials, and technical assistance missions to assist governments with economic planning. Finally the IMF has been involved in a number of global initiatives to help resolve particularly large financial crises, for example in Mexico (1994), several countries in South-East Asia (1997), and Brazil (1999).

## The World Bank

The World Bank is in a sense a more complex organization than the IMF. It makes more sense to talk of the World Bank Group, rather than a single organization. At the core of the group is the International Bank for Reconstruction and Development, usually known as 'The Bank'. This started off by making loans to aid the reconstruction of Europe following the destruction wreaked by the Second World War, but now specializes in making loans to finance major projects in the developing world. In terms of its organization the World Bank group operates in a way very similar to the IMF. It has a Board of Governors, one from each member, which meets twice per year, while an Executive of twenty-four meets twice a week to oversee the normal running of the group. The mix of elected and permanent members is similar to the IMF, as is the system of weighted voting.

A contradiction lies at the heart of the World Bank in the sense that it operates in many ways similarly to a commercial bank yet has development objectives of reducing poverty and promoting economic growth. As a result its policies have tended to change. From the 1950s to the 1970s it promoted state-led development, seeing government very much as the agent of development, and its loans reflected this view. From the 1970s it started to accept the neo-liberal agenda, and its loan policies reflected the view that states should now withdraw from direct intervention in many development activities. Most recently it has engaged with the notion of participatory development, which means seeking to gain wider agreement in society for development policies.

## The World Trade Organization

The idea of establishing an international trade organization was originally discussed at the Bretton Woods conference. However this ambitious project was replaced by the more limited General Agreement on Tariffs and Trade (GATT). The title of the GATT makes it sound like a one-off trade agreement, but in fact it turned into an ongoing process of negotiation. In line with the general assumption of the immediate post-war period that the great depression of the 1930s and the move into protectionism bore heavy responsibility for the Second World War, the GATT was an attempt to promote international trade through lowering barriers to trade. The members of the GATT first met in 1947 and then proceeded, through a series of 'rounds' or series of agreements, to extend the range of items that are covered by GATT agreements.

During the 'Uruguay Round' of the GATT 1986–94, the decision was made to create the WTO as a more formal organization to oversee the working of the global trading system. The WTO has three main roles. First, it provides an institutional and legal framework for the operation of world trade. Secondly, it provides the arena where international trade issues can be discussed and policies formulated. Finally, it provides a mechanism whereby trade disputes between members can be settled. The latest, so-called 'development' round of WTO talks was launched at Doha in 2001, but foundered at the follow-up summit in Cancun, Mexico, September 2003. In what may retrospectively come to be seen as a landmark event, a 'Group of 21' developing member states, led by Brazil, India, and China refused to proceed to discuss the 'Singapore' agenda of issues that had first been introduced at the Singapore summit in 1996. Those issues included investment and government procurement. First they wanted to see the question of EU and US subsidies to agriculture (see previous chapter) satisfactorily resolved.

Supporters of the organization argue that it is a technical rules-based organization and point out that all members have one vote. Compared to the World Bank and the IMF the voice of the developing world can be expressed much more forcefully, as happened at the Cancun summit. However, critics of the organization argue that the inequalities of the global system are woven into the organization. The poorest countries find participation in its proceedings costly whilst, according to critical non-governmental organizations, much of the real decision-making takes place 'behind the scenes'. More fundamentally, even though it gives the appearance of being based on rules and equality of power, it is still possible for the richer countries to manipulate the system in their own interests and maintain the liberalization agenda which works in their favour (see Stiglitz 2002; Thomas 2000).

## Key points

- International organizations have had a profound effect on developing countries, whilst providing them with a forum to raise development issues.
- The UN general assembly has frequently been used to pass resolutions critical of the developed world.
- The IMF, World Bank, and WTO have been significant actors in global finance and trade. Critics of these organizations argue that power over decision-making is held disproportionately by the richest countries.

# The debt crisis

The debt crisis links together several of the issues raised in this chapter and the previous one, and demonstrates the very close links between global political and economic relations. The term 'Third World debt crisis' is usually used to describe the very high levels of indebtedness experienced by many developing countries since the early 1980s. The term, however, obscures the fact that the crisis took many forms. There was a debt crisis for the banks in the rich countries, which had lent heavily to developing countries and now faced 'non-performing loans'. The character of the crisis for the countries of Latin America (which had primarily borrowed from commercial banks), was different from those of sub-Saharan Africa (which had primarily borrowed from multilateral agencies). Meanwhile for the citizens in countries who confronted and continue to confront austerity programmes instituted by the IMF, there is an ongoing crisis as social programmes have been cut and development possibilities postponed or reduced.

During the 1970s Western banks became very heavily involved in lending to developing countries for two main reasons. First, they were holding very large deposits as a result of the OPEC oil price rises. Second, because of the economic downturn in the West, primarily sparked by the oil price rises, there was less home demand for finance for investment. The banks were caught with large cash reserves at a time when there was little demand for borrowing. Hence they looked for

new markets. This was a time when interest rates were low, and borrowing looked attractive. However interest rates rose rapidly in the early 1980s following the elections of the Thatcher and Reagan governments in Britain and the United States. As part of their economic policies they instituted much higher rates of interest in order to reduce inflation levels. Because much of the borrowing in the developing world (though particularly Latin America) had been from private banks this had the result of increasing repayment levels dramatically. It became much harder to attract new lending so as to service existing debt. Accordingly countries experienced great difficulties maintaining the levels of debt they had previously contracted.

The debt situation became a 'crisis' for Western banks when in August 1982 Mexico announced that it was no longer able meet its interest payments. The size of Mexico's debts brought the stability of some international banks into question, and some commentators even speculated that the capitalist system itself was at risk. It became crucial that Mexico's crisis not spiral out of control and send shock waves further afield. The USA made short-term bridging loans to enable Mexico to maintain its interest payments, and by November Mexico had agreed a package of measures with the IMF that allowed the extension of further loans to the country.

A similar approach was applied to other countries throughout Latin America as they faced an inability to make interest payments. However the IMF on its own could not resolve the gathering crisis that deepened through the 1980s. In 1985 the US Treasury Secretary, James Baker, announced a plan that would encourage the World Bank and commercial banks to increase lending to fifteen of the most indebted countries, in exchange for thoroughgoing restructuring of their economies. The 'Baker plan' was superseded in 1989 by the 'Brady Initiative' (after Treasury Secretary Nicholas Brady). The Brady Initiative extended the Baker plan by attempting to introduce some mechanisms by which debt could be forgiven or at least reduced. IMF Structural Adjustment programmes became the standard by which a country's eligibility for relief under the Baker Plan and Brady Initiative could be assessed. The Baker plan and the Brady initiative were, together with a number of other piecemeal measures, sufficient to avert an international banking crisis.

For those countries whose debts were owed primarily to rich world governments or multilateral organizations, a number of attempts have been made to

**The ten most indebted 'developing countries' measured by comparing debt to national wealth**

| 'Developing country' | Total external debt as % of gross national income |
|---|---|
| São Tomé and Príncipe | 735 |
| Liberia | 487 |
| Guinea-Bissau | 336 |
| Nicaragua | 306 |
| Congo, Dem. Rep. | 257 |
| Congo, Rep. | 231 |
| Mauritania | 222 |
| Guyana | 218 |
| Sierra Leone | 178 |
| Zambia | 178 |

A further way of examining the level of indebtedness is the ratio of the total debt service (annual debt repayments) to the total a country earns each year in exports. This is a significant ratio, because it is through the export of goods and services that a country can earn the foreign currency needed to pay off the debt. Additionally this ratio reflects different types of debt (rates of interest tend to be higher on commercial debt than multilateral debt).

## Table 3.1 Measuring indebtedness

Measuring a country's level of indebtedness is not straightforward. The logical point to begin would be to examine the total level of external debt:

**The ten 'developing countries' with the largest overall debt (as at December 2001)**

| 'Developing country' | Total external debt $US millions |
|---|---|
| Brazil | 226,362 |
| China | 170,110 |
| Mexico | 158,290 |
| Russian Federation | 152,649 |
| Argentina | 136,709 |
| Indonesia | 135,704 |
| Turkey | 115,118 |
| India | 97,320 |
| Thailand | 67,384 |
| Poland | 62,393 |

However, measuring the total debt ignores the ability to pay. Another way of looking at debt is to compare the size of the debt with a country's gross national income:

**The ten most indebted countries measured by comparing debt servicing to exports**

| Country | Total debt service as % of exports |
|---|---|
| Sierra Leone | 89 |
| Brazil | 81 |
| Argentina | 67 |
| Lebanon | 50 |
| Hungary | 42 |
| Turkey | 40 |
| Burundi | 39 |
| Bolivia | 38 |
| Guinea-Bissau | 38 |
| Nicaragua | 37 |

*Source:* World Bank (2003a: Tables A.43 and A.51).

provide debt relief. Of these the most significant has been the **Heavily** (also sometimes called Highly) **Indebted Poor Countries Initiative** (HIPC), launched by the World Bank and IMF in 1996. This initiative has gone through several iterations since then, and in its current manifestation requires governments to initiate **poverty reduction strategies** (PRSPs) devised in consultation with **civil society**. Nevertheless, although HIPC aims to provide a framework to relieve countries confronted by the worst debt situations, the price of conforming to IMF programmes has been great, and the countries that are prioritized are still not necessarily those whose governments have the greatest difficulties in tackling poverty. Table 3.1 examines some issues regarding the measurement of indebtedness, and demonstrates that for many countries the debt crisis remains a crisis even today.

The reactions of the developed world and of the IMF and World Bank to the debt crisis have had two main effects. First, the crisis has been 'managed'. Although debt remains a problem, the crisis was dealt with in such a way that the entire banking system was ultimately not threatened. Secondly, it shifted the crisis onto the poorest peoples of the developing world. An extensive literature describes the effects of IMF austerity programmes (for example Chossudovsky 1996; Mihevc 1995; Bello 1999). Many governments found themselves in a situation where annual budget allocations for servicing foreign debt service exceeded health or education spending and often those two heads combined—a situation that the introduction

of PRSPs beginning in late 1999 is supposed to address. Yet in many cases it was unrepresentative and unaccountable governments, for example military regimes, that had contracted the debts. Furthermore the emphasis that structural adjustment programmes have placed on promoting exports to earn revenue so as to service debts has meant that many developing countries have increased their reliance on commodity exports, notwithstanding the economic drawbacks and negative environmental impact.

## Key points

- The debt crisis emerged in the wake of the OPEC oil price rises in the 1970s. Cash-rich Western banks made extensive loans to developing countries. When global interest rates rose in the 1980s and the banks became more cautious, repayments on these loans became unsustainable for many developing countries.

- The debt crisis has taken a variety of different forms. Latin American countries were primarily indebted to commercial banks, whilst sub-Saharan countries were and still are primarily indebted to governments and multilateral agencies.

- International organizations, in particular the IMF and World Bank, have taken a key role in managing the crisis. Their priority has been to protect the global capitalist system, above social provision and development in the South.

- For many in the developing world the crisis remains.

# Conclusion

The notion of a 'Third World' was primarily a construction of the cold war. As the conflict drew to an end increasing diversity between regions based on divergent rates of economic growth and competition between countries for the supposed fruits of **globalization** has eroded the perception of shared interests that underlay earlier groupings, such as the Non-Aligned Movement. It is too early to say whether this is a permanent feature, or whether durable new alliances will be forged in response to an emerging US-dominated world order.

Three main constraints now confront developing countries. First, many of them are small. Eighty-seven of the world's countries have a population of less than 5 million (Chapter 19b below provides illustration from the Pacific). They have little economic power, no military capability, and little access to technology. A second constraint lies in the working of the world trade system, which still leaves many countries reliant on certain forms of trade of low profitability and subject to wide fluctuations in prices, and possibly a long-term decline in their relative value. Thirdly, in international organizations (with the exception of the General Assembly of the UN) developing countries have little capability of exerting pressure on the developed world. The voting procedures in the Security Council, IMF, and World Bank confine power to a few wealthy countries. Although the WTO operates a system of one country, one vote, cooperation amongst the richer countries and splits amongst the developing world has usually reduced its effectiveness as a vehicle to promote developing country interests.

Despite these constraints, there are opportunities for developing countries in international relations. Organizations such as the Non-Aligned Movement provided a voice during the cold war. However, the diversity of patterns of development now means that organizations claiming to represent all less-developed countries are unlikely to be effective. The new drive to regionalism (see Chapter 2) provides an alternative forum and possibilities of exerting greater influence in negotiations with the developed world. The emergence of a global economy also offers immediate advantages to some. Where capital is more mobile, developing countries can exploit their advantage of lower wages. Countries where there are high educational standards are particularly likely to be able to gain

from this. For example, India has been particularly successful in attracting jobs in the information technology and call centre sectors. Not all developing countries are small. India, Brazil, and China are all regional superpowers, able to exert their influence internationally, and in due course the first two might gain more formal institutional recognition in the UN Security Council if that body is reshaped. A further area of possibility for developing countries is in the emergence of what has been described as a global civil society. Neo-liberalism is under attack from some quarters in the developed world, as the anti-globalization movement has demonstrated. There are increasing avenues for the development of transborder and supraterritorial alliances between the peoples of the North and South.

This chapter has demonstrated the key, though often neglected, role of the developing world in the international relations. Although the character of the global system remains unsettled following the end of the cold war, the situation of the majority of the world's population who reside in the developing world should become a more central area of study for those who seek to comprehend international processes.

## QUESTIONS

1  'If the United Nations didn't exist it would have to be created'. Discuss.

2  Evaluate the effectiveness of the World Bank in promoting development.

3  Account for the failure of a debtors' cartel to emerge as a result of the debt crisis.

4  Why do developing countries accept IMF structural adjustment policies?

5  Why was the demand for a New International Economic Order ineffective?

6  Was there a 'cold' war in the 'Third World'?

7  What reforms to the international system would prospectively offer most benefit to development in poorer countries?

## GUIDE TO FURTHER READING

Baylis, J., and Smith, S. (eds.), *The Globalization of World Politics: An Introduction to International Relations*, 2nd ed. (Oxford: Oxford University Press, 2001). An excellent primer in international relations, containing several chapters relevant to the study of the developing world.

Duffield, M., *Global Governance and the New Wars: The Merging of Development and Security* (London: Zed, 2001). Analyses the position of the developing world in the emerging world (dis?)order.

Halliday, F., *Cold War, Third World: An Essay on Soviet-US Relations* (London: Hutchinson Radius, 1989). Wide-ranging discussion of the developing world during the cold war.

Roddick, J., *The Dance of the Millions* (London: Latin America Bureau, 1988). Clearly written introduction to the origins of the debt crisis in Latin America.

Stiglitz, J., *Globalization and its Discontents* (London: Allen Lane, 2002). A critical account of the role of global institutions in the management of the global economy, written by a former World Bank chief economist, and vice-president.

Thomas, C., *Global Governance, Development and Human Security: The Challenge of Poverty and Inequality* (London: Pluto, 2000). Excellent study of the role of international organizations in dealing with development and security issues.

## WEB LINKS

**www.twnside.org.sg/econ_1.htm**   Third World Network reports on international organizations.

**www.un.org**   Official site provides overview of the organization and workings of the United Nations.

**www.imf.org**   Official site provides details of role of the International Monetary Fund.

**www.worldbank.org**   Official site provides complete overview of the operation of the World Bank Group.

**www.wto.org**   Overview of history, purpose, and working of the World Trade Organization.

**www.jubilee2000uk.org**   Successor organization to the Jubilee 2000 campaign against 'third world debt', it provides a wealth of information on debt-related issues.

**www.worldbank.org/hipc**   The World Bank Group's site for the heavily indebted poor countries initiative, containing much useful statistical and other information.

 ## COMPANION WEB SITE

For additional material and resources, see the companion web site at:
**www.oup.com/uk/booksites/politics/**

## NOTES

1. In this chapter, capitalized International Relations denotes the discipline; international relations refers to the subject of study.

2. On the failure of International Relations to consider the developing world, see discussion by Dickson (1997: ch. 1) and Neuman (1998: 2–12).

3. For discussions of North–South relations during the cold war see Allison and Williams (1990), Halliday (1989), Hough (1986), Merrill (1994), Shearman and Williams (1988).

4. For discussions of North–South relations following the cold war see Fawcett and Sayigh (1999), Halliday (2002), Mesbahi (1994), Swatuck and Shaw (1994).

# Part Two

# Society and state

In Part Two we introduce the social and cultural aspects of developing countries within which their politics are embedded, and which are so central to understanding political behaviour. The part has two main aims. The **first** is to indicate the great diversity of social structure found in the developing world and in countries individually; the variety in terms of religious, ethnic, and other identities; and the divisions that these features together with gender- and economically-based inequalities give rise to. In contemporary social science civil society also ranks very high as both a constituent feature and determining influence upon politics; that too can vary widely in practice. The second **aim** is to show the political significance of these complex social contexts and how problematic they can be for political management, by posing challenges as well as opportunities for the institutional arrangements centred on the state. The contents of this part thus set the scene for the investigation in Part Three of how developing world states have responded to the many internal and external demands on them and to their transformation in recent decades. So, for instance, societal features introduced in Part Two can help explain tendencies towards state collapse and the pressures to engage in political liberalization and democratization as well as the forces resisting those agendas. The illustrative material included in Part Two is drawn widely from around the developing world. By comparison, case studies of individual countries selected to illustrate specific themes can be found in Part Five. For example Chapter 8 on civil society is complemented by more detailed explorations of how active or passive civil society really is in two contrasting countries, namely India and Saudi Arabia, in Chapter 17. Readers are encouraged to consult the relevant case studies in Part Five when reading the chapters in Part Two.

# 4

# Inequality

*Jenny Pearce*

## OVERVIEW

The relationship between inequality and development is hotly debated within development studies and practice. Differences have emerged over the value attached to equality as a goal of human development. The first section of this chapter traces the history of the conceptual debate, beginning with the argument that growth can exacerbate inequality and leave the poorest excluded from its benefits. The second section explores the impact of inequality thinking on the developing world and the third section explores the questioning of equality as a goal of development in the 1980s. At the beginning of the twenty-first century, inequality has regained ground as a core development concern. It is accepted that entrenched social and economic inequalities can constrain the poverty reduction impact of growth. Contemporary views on the idea of inequality are raised in the fourth and final section. The idea of the 'equality of man' as an ontological assumption has been challenged by the acknowledgement that human beings are diverse. This has implications for the political arrangements within states and for policies too. Furthermore inequality affects the very character of the political process itself, in particular who participates in it and who shapes its goals. Will the challenge of the construction of complex political mechanisms for achieving greater equality ever be fully taken up without the energetic participation of those presently disadvantaged?

# Introduction

The issue of inequality was raised by development economists soon after 'development' emerged as a field of policy and study. Harvard economist Simon Kuznets (1955) put forward his 'inverted-U hypothesis', arguing that relative income inequality increases in the early stages of economic development and does not improve until countries reach middle-income levels. If economic growth leads to increased inequality in this way, it could take many years to eradicate poverty in the so-called 'developing' countries. In the post-war years, the inequality and development debate remained framed in terms of income and wealth disparities. But major conceptual ebbs and flows in social theorizing have also been influential.

The implicit post-war consensus in the industrialized world that government has a responsibility to address inequalities was disturbed in the 1980s when the rise of the paradigm of market liberalism posed a serious theoretical and practical challenge to redistributive theories of justice. Concern with income inequality as a goal of development policy declined. In its 1990 *World Development Report* (1990: 47) the World Bank charted the effect on poverty of economic growth in eleven countries, concluding 'in the low-income countries inequality consistently improves (contrary to the Kuznets' hypothesis), and there is no case in which the effect of growth is offset by changes in inequality . . . In short growth reduces poverty.' This signalled a major shift in mainstream thinking about the relationship between inequality, poverty, and development. Pro-poor growth rather than the impact of growth on distribution became the core goal of development.

Paradoxically, the conceptual debate on inequality remained lively. The collapse of universalizing social theory has resulted in an unprecedented uncovering of differential life experiences throughout societies all around the world, which has favoured new thinking on social stratification dynamics. The cultural dimensions of inequality were exposed, while recognition of human differences suggested that the 'equality of man' is not the best foundation for egalitarian theory. In its 2001 *World Development Report* the World Bank acknowledges that 'high initial inequality' reduces the poverty impact of a given rate of growth, and that there may even be circumstances in which addressing asset inequality can enhance economic efficiency and benefit growth. In addition it now recognizes that **gender** inequalities have a particularly negative impact on economic growth, and that interventions in the market can aid poverty eradication amongst such socially disadvantaged groups as indigenous peoples and certain castes and tribes.

The building of appropriate new social, political, and economic arrangements and institutions at the global and national levels remains, however, a distant goal. Improving individual advantages through aggregative growth approaches is still considered preferable on efficiency grounds to redistributive policies aimed at reducing the inequalities in the distribution of advantages. The main challenge to this assumption now comes from social movements seeking social justice. These extra-institutional challenges suggest that the inequality that has been confronted least is that of power and its impact on all the other forms. Who, on what grounds, and through what process, is to determine the developmental goals a society and indeed all of humankind sets for itself when initial inequalities become so embedded over time within power relationships that they are not recognized as such? Inequality not only impedes access to the fruits of development, it limits access to decision-making and the exercise of full citizenship.

## Key points

- Post-war development thinking was influenced by the argument that economic development may enhance income inequality.

- Post-war acceptance that governments have some responsibility to redress inequality was challenged by the rise of **neo-liberalism**.

- Recognition of human differences came to challenge the idea of 'equality of man'.

- Major development institutions now acknowledge that high existing inequality can retard poverty reduction.

- Inequality impacts on the exercise of citizenship and ultimately who determines the goals of development within and between nations.

# Charting the conceptual waters

The importance that we attach to the issue of inequality is rooted in some fundamental questions of political philosophy and shifting values and norms. Do societies think that equality is a legitimate aspiration? And if so, how is it to be achieved? Over the past two centuries or more these questions have been discussed repeatedly. During this period there was a 'steady erosion in the **legitimacy** accorded to social inequality ... for students of social stratification, this ... is perhaps the most important feature of the nineteenth and twentieth centuries' (Béteille 1969: 366). However, by the end of the twentieth century the pursuit of greater social and economic equality has become increasingly discredited; such concepts as 'social exclusion' and pro-poor growth have gained ground. The poor became 'targets' of anti-poverty programmes. Traditional leftist concerns about distribution and **'exploitation'** have been abandoned. At the same time, interest has grown in human diversity in terms of identity and culture and its relationship with equality—a development Fraser (1997) calls a shift from the 'politics of redistribution' to the 'politics of recognition'. The implications for the politics of development could be profound.

## Ontological equality and equality of outcome

The relative material prosperity achieved by American colonizers by the eighteenth century demonstrated that poverty was not inevitable. However it was the French Revolution of 1789 that brought equality and the 'social question' to world attention. It showed not only that traditional social stratifications were not divinely sanctioned but that they could be challenged by the people acting collectively as citizens with equal rights. The First Article of the 1789 Declaration of the Rights of Man and Citizen states famously 'Men are born and remain free and equal in rights. Social differences, therefore, can only be based on common utility.'

The idea that men are born equal had emerged as a philosophical challenge to the prevailing assumption that social stratification was a result of natural differences of rank between individuals. The Greeks had built the *polis* on that assumption, and equality only existed in that realm; it was an attribute gained through citizenship not birth. Rousseau (*Discourse on Inequality*, 1755) began his investigation into inequality by assuming instead the equality of men in a pre-social original state of nature—an assumption of **ontological equality**. In the course of the eighteenth century, the idea that men are equal rather than unequal by nature took hold with powerful political and intellectual consequences. But it inevitably led to the question, what are the origins therefore of inequality? Rousseau's answer is usually summed up as 'private property', starting a debate that has raged ever since. Those who came to see private property as a social evil emphasized the need for society to promote **equality of outcome** despite individual human differences. Karl Marx made equality of outcome the central tenet of his vision of the good society.

For Marx writing in 1845–6, inequality had its origins in the division of labour as well as private property. It is the former which 'implies the possibility, nay the fact that intellectual and material activity —enjoyment and labour, production and consumption—devolve on different individuals'. And with the division of labour comes the question of distribution and 'indeed the *unequal* distribution, both quantitative and qualitative, of labour and its products, hence property, the nucleus, the first form of which lies in the family, where wife and children are the slaves of the husband' (Marx 1970: 52). Capitalism is the most advanced system of labour division yet, in which the capitalist class owes its wealth to its exploitation of another class with only its labour to sell. Marx not only places this unequal relationship to the means of production at the heart of his class analysis of history, but the emphasis on exploitation indicates that such inequality between classes is unjust. Inequality between classes results in antagonism and struggle that under capitalism is carried forward by the class that will eventually act for humanity as a whole by overthrowing the capitalist order and restarting history on the basis of a new logic. Although class and the exploitation of surplus value did not appear in reality to constitute the only form of inequality that matters in human sociability, Marx's writings were extraordinarily influential. Nationalist as well as socialist movements mobilized around egalitarianism including in many places in the developing world.

Marxist thinking tapped into deeply felt injustices at the popular level. For some, largely pre-industrial, developing societies, Marxist ideas appealed to the desire to retain some of the primitive communal forms of equality that persisted in agrarian societies and to restrain the differentiating process that comes with socio-economic change. Much 'Third World' sociology in the post-war years was an effort to clarify its distinct forms of class composition and social inequality and the relationship between class formation and development. A particularly vibrant debate concerned the analytical categories for exploring relationships between the developed and under-developed worlds. Could one nation exploit another? Gunder Frank (1971) powerfully argued that it could and traced the history of **underdevelopment** from 'core' to 'periphery'. He was criticized by others who claimed that he saw feudalism and capitalism only in terms of market exchange, not in Marx's true sense of relations to production and class exploitation. The ideas of **unequal exchange** and **dependency** would nevertheless provide one of the most important frameworks for understanding inequalities between countries in the North and the South in the early post-war decades.

## Differentiating inequalities: class, status and power

Max Weber, writing in the twentieth century, provided a more differentiated categorization than Marx. He argued that social divisions and the distribution of power they convey encompass a range of non-economic as well as economic determinates. He said 'The emergence of economic power may be the consequence of power existing on other grounds', arguing:

Man does not strive for power only in order to enrich himself economically. Power, including economic power, may be valued 'for its own sake'. Very frequently the striving for power is also conditioned by the social 'honour' it entails. Not all power, however, entails social honour . . . Quite generally, 'mere economic' power and especially 'naked' money power, is by no means a recognized basis of social honour. Nor is power the only basis of social honour. Indeed, social honour, or prestige, may even be the basis of political or economic power, and very frequently has been. (Weber 1970: 180–1)

For Weber, in addition to class stratifications that emerge out of a person's relationship to the market, there is **status**—a quality of social honour or a lack of it, which is mainly conditioned as well as expressed through a specific style of life. Social honour can adhere directly to a class situation, and for most of the time will be determined by the average class situation of the status-group members. This, however, is not necessarily always the case. Status membership, in turn, influences the class situation in that the style of life required by status groups makes them prefer special kinds of property or gainful pursuits and reject others. A status group can be closed ('status by descent') or it can be open. Weber's understanding of the distinctiveness of status groups was particularly helpful for those wishing to understand social differentiations in situations where market transactions were fairly simple and class formation limited. He also observed, however, that technological advances and economic transformation threaten stratification by status and will push the class situation further into the foreground.

So, between Marx and Weber there is a 'hard' and a 'soft' view of inequality. The former only includes exploitation and injustice and the struggle between exploited and exploiting classes as a motor for historical development. Weber did see what he calls communal action flowing out of class interest in particular situations, but this will not necessarily be an outcome of the economic interest that creates 'class'. His 'softer' view of inequality has also had an enduring impact. In terms of the developing world, Weber was able to draw into the picture the forms of social stratification that Marxists have often found particularly difficult to explain, such as caste and tribe and the distinctions between them. Caste, Weber argued for instance, belonged to the 'closed status group', where status distinctions are guaranteed not just by conventions and laws but also by rituals, such as stigmatizing any contact between lower and higher castes through religious acts of purification.

He explored the complexity of the **Hindu caste system** in India in some detail, seeking to explain its relationship to economic change and its 'elasticity' and hence survival in the face of the logic of labour demands in the modern economy.

The nature of these traditional relationships and the impact of processes of economic change are particularly significant for an understanding of social divisions in the developing world. Systems of 'inherited inequality' such as those based on descent, lineage, and kinship have persisted in many parts of the developing world. Anthropologists have long studied the lineage and kinship stratifications of indigenous populations. For example Sahlins (in Béteille 1969: 239), who studied kinship in Polynesia in the 1950s, referred to 'a graduated series of different degrees of stratification'. He distinguished between stratified and egalitarian societies, and implied that ranking processes emerge in all human societies, but they vary a great deal in terms of ranking criteria and how far they formally sanction social inequality. This is why writers like Béteille (1969) have emphasized the values and norms that underpin social inequality or its qualitative dimensions. It has often been assumed that ranking on the basis of the hereditary principle will disappear with the process of economic development, and that industrialization will overcome the differentials associated with traditional and agrarian societies. The persistence of caste in India, where status is determined by birth and legitimized by religio-cultural belief, questions that assumption. In modern India caste and class intersect in particularly complex ways, creating a potent and enduring source of social, economic, and political inequality (see Chapter 17a).

But across the developing world even where 'closed status group' systems such as caste do not exist, kinship and ethnic group identity have been the basis of stratified as well as segmented forms of social differentiation. As segmented differentiation, it is possible to identify a large number of horizontally distinct cultural affiliations or ethnic communities in the developing world coexisting with each other. These often construct their **ethnic identity** in the language of blood and birth although ethnic identity does not coincide with objective racial differences. Such ethnic communities may be segregated communities that exclude intermarriage with other groups.

Ethnic coexistences have become the source of ethnically based stratifications at various points in history. Pre-colonial conquests, colonialism, and post-colonial political mobilization have all played a critical role in privileging some ethnic groups over others and usually for some political as well as economic gain. As market economies expanded, so some ethnic groups were in a more privileged position than others to take advantage of opportunities. In this context, the debate about whether emerging stratifications are derived from market positioning, or from the logic of capital and its search for exploitable labour, or from ethnic identity per se has been particularly protracted. Thus relationship to production is a source of inequality but not the only source of social differentiation. When class and status, economic and social power coincide, however, one of the most powerful sources of inequality is created with capacity to perpetuate itself through the generations.

## Box 4.1 **Béteille on inequality**

Béteille (1969: 365) points out that the sanctioning of social inequality has taken place on very distinct grounds often legitimized by religious systems that paradoxically and simultaneously contain messages of equality. In the United States, commitment to the equality of man was a strong feature of cultural values and political ideals, though black people were denied the vote and were evidently not treated as equals by the dominant white population. Most societies have denied and many still deny women formal as well as informal social, economic, and political equality.

## The political consequences of inequality

One means by which inequality perpetuates itself is through the political system that develops around it. Unequal societies, no matter what the source of inequality, generate differential means of influencing political processes, and this is true at all levels from micro to macro, and in traditional as well as more 'modern' development contexts. That means power and powerlessness grow out of inequality and create the source for recycling it. As societies undergo transitions from more traditional to 'modern' economies, traditional power structures and ways of exercising power have often adapted to changing social conditions so that they survived more or less intact or persisted in new but recognizable forms. As the idea of political contestation (if not modern democracy) began to take root in the developing world, it frequently did so in contexts where political and economic power was already tightly meshed. The 'delivery' of the political support of a dependent rural population to particular leaders and interests quickly became the norm. Such practices were then adapted to urban contexts, where the rapid growth of cities without adequate services or employment gave brokerage power to individuals with access to elites and decision-makers. **Clientelism** and **patronage** networks emerged throughout the developing world, creating vertical links to tie the poor to political power structures through favours granted in return for support. Such networks reflect differentials in power and income and act as obstacles to independent political action and democratization, further entrenching the pre-existing structures of inequality.

## Equality strategies and equality theories

The French Revolution placed equality on the political agenda, but some later argued that it succeeded only in abolishing the arbitrary privileges and restrictions imposed by the old regimes. Tawney (1952: 106) argued this powerfully, claiming that it resulted in the view that 'the inequalities of industrial society were to be esteemed, for they were the expression of individual achievement or failure to achieve'. However, he pointed out: 'Opportunities to "rise" are not a substitute for a large measure of practical equality . . . The existence of such opportunities in fact, and not merely in form, depends, not only upon an open road, but upon an equal start.'

Tawney's essay was an appeal for measures that would ensure that society actively aimed at 'eliminating such inequalities as have their source, not in individual differences, but in its own organization, and that individual differences, which are a source of social energy, are more likely to ripen and find expression if

social inequalities are, as far as practicable, diminished' (Tawney 1952: 57). He made the critical distinction between equality of capacity or attainment, and that of circumstance, institutions, and manner of life. He had in mind strategies such as progressive taxation, the strengthening of trade unionism and industrial legislation and economic policy for the communal good.

Over the next five decades, equality as a goal was hotly debated in the advanced industrial countries, and the view that governments had some responsibility to pursue strategies of greater equality was broadly accepted. But there was little agreement on which strategies, and conservatives worried that they would limit individual freedom and choice. Nevertheless by the 1960s social scientists on both sides of the Atlantic were challenging claims that their societies were moving towards greater equality despite the welfare state, estate duties, and higher taxation (in the UK), and the reforming impetus towards equal opportunity (USA). In doing so they raised important questions about the relationship between equality strategies and social justice theories. And they helped shape the conceptual frameworks that development practitioners and policy makers brought to their understanding of development imperatives in the developing world. For example Jenks (1975: 264) in the USA concluded that no progress would be made in addressing economic inequality unless it was possible to 'alter people's basic assumptions about the extent to which they are responsible for their neighbours and their neighbours for them'. This raises the question whether it is possible to have an agreed standard of social justice and equality in terms of which any social inequalities would have to be justified. The utilitarian view which prevailed in Anglo-American thinking argued that a just society should aggregate the basic principle that each individual should realize his own interests and pursue his own greatest good, rationally balancing present and future losses against present and future gains. Similarly, society should arrange its institutions in order to 'maximise the net balance of satisfaction' of all the individuals belonging to it.

Rawls's *Theory of Justice* (1971), constructed an alternative and influential challenge to the tendency towards meritocracy that can be fostered by equal opportunity approaches. He started with the premises of equal liberty, equal opportunity, and equal distribution of income and wealth. But, he asked, if there are inequalities in the basic structure that work to make everyone better off in comparison with the benchmark of initial equality, why not permit them? Thus Rawls put forward a conception of justice in which 'All social values—liberty and opportunity, income and wealth and the bases of self-respect—are to be distributed equally unless an unequal distribution of any, or all, of these values is to everyone's advantage. Injustice, then, is simply inequalities that are not to the benefit of all' (Rawls 1971: 62). What Rawls calls '**primary goods**', which are basic social values, have been much debated, but social democratic thinking in developed countries continues to be influenced by the idea that equality of income and wealth form the ideal and inequalities can only be justified if they are of benefit to those least favoured in terms of the 'undeserved inequalities' of birth.

## Key points

- Both Rousseau and the French Revolution challenged previous assumptions that inequality and social division were natural or divinely sanctioned.

- If private property (Rousseau) and the division of labour (Marx) created inequality, the good society was one dedicated to overcoming these ills and promoting equality of outcome for all citizens.

- Weber's notions of status and honour, derived from non-economic as well as economic determinants, assisted understanding of social stratification in the developing world.

- Rawls advanced a new approach to equality thinking when he sought in the early 1970s to find the basis for an agreed standard of social justice and equality.

# The politics of inequality in developing countries

Moral and political arguments for an equitable model of economic development found concrete expression in a number of experiments that spanned the post-war decades, such as the model of socialism which followed the 1959 revolution in Cuba; the 1967 Arusha declaration and *Ujamaa* (kiswahili for community-hood) Socialism of Nyerere's government in Tanzania; and the Chilean Road to Socialism of Salvador Allende between 1970 and 1973. These experiments went further than economic egalitarianism. They were also about new forms of political participation and how to address the impact of inequality on political decision-making.

The inequality question is partly about these morally and politically based arguments but it is also partly about the facts and how to measure them. Development economists in the Bretton Woods institutions (World Bank, International Monetary Fund) and universities were concerned with measurement and the potential trade-off between economic growth and inequality that Kuznets had highlighted. Their objective was to understand the contribution that factors of production such as land, labour, and capital make to output, and not who gets what and

why. Inequality mattered if it impacted negatively on growth and development. Quantitative surveys during these decades broadly tended to confirm Kuznets's findings but they did not show a fixed relationship in all cases. However, the argument that inequality was impeding development appeared to have been partially accepted when in the mid-1970s, the World Bank embarked on a new strategy of 'redistribution with growth'. At the same time, arguments that a New International Economic Order should address the inequalities between nations were also topical.

Income distribution measurement is by no means straightforward. Unreliable data, choices over the best unit of measurement (individuals or households), the timescale of measurement, and the definition of income itself, which given the high level of informal and unregistered earnings is particularly problematic in developing countries, all represent significant problems. Fields (1980: 66–7) identified four approaches to measurement in 1980: relative inequality (income changes of various groups relative to others), absolute income (changes in various groups' incomes), absolute poverty (focus on changes in economic

## Box 4.2 Tanzania's President Julius Nyerere on equality

Tanzania's President Julius Nyerere set out the country's broad policy on socialist development in a document called the Arusha Declaration, adopted by the ruling party in 1967. The opening proposition declared that all human beings are equal. The Arusha Resolution that accompanied the Declaration stated that every party and government leader must be either a peasant or a worker and should in no way be associated with the practices of capitalism or feudalism. Leaders were forbidden to hold shares in any company or directorships in privately owned enterprises. They should not receive two salaries or own houses that were rented out to others. Ten years later, in a review of the Arusha Declaration that he presented to the ruling party's Executive Committee, Nyerere defined three aspects to the goal of equality. First, in respect of differentials in personal incomes; second, in access to public services; and third, in the extent to which taxation-supported activities served the interests of the people as a whole rather than those of a small minority.

well-being of the poor ignoring the remainder of income distribution), and relative poverty (absolute income received by poorest 40 per cent or some other defined percentage).

The most frequently used approaches to measurement are the Lorenz curve and the **Gini coefficient** . The Lorenz curve, named after the American statistician Lorenz, who developed it in 1905, uses a vertical axis (percentage of income earned) and horizontal axis (percentage of the population earning that income); the greater the bow of the curve, the larger the degree of inequality. The Gini coefficient, named after the Italian statistician who created it in 1912, uses areas of the Lorenz curve and is the ratio of the area between the line of equality and the Lorenz curve, and the total area under the line of equality. It offers an aggregate measure of inequality and can vary between 0 (perfect equality) and 1 (perfect inequality). The Gini coefficient for countries with highly unequal income distribution tends to lie between 0.50 and 0.70, while for those with relatively equitable distributions it is between 0.20 and 0.35.

The World Bank in addition uses a numerical format, the distribution by quintiles (20 per cent of the population) measured by household or individuals (see Fig. 13.1, p. 209 below for inequality measured by Gini index in selected countries).

Following Kuznets's challenge, many studies in the 1960s and 1970s sought to explore and measure the impact of economic growth on income distribution and the influence of income distribution on growth. Large-scale cross-country surveys were undertaken using improving data sets. Some confirmed the trend towards rising inequality in the less developed countries, although they varied in terms of whether the trend was weak or strong, that is whether the trend reflected a prolonged absolute impoverishment of large sections of the population in the course of development. Evidence was clearly not uniform across countries. Chenery (1974) argued that ultimately the evidence and judgements cannot be separated from 'social and ethical postulates'. In other words, the patterns of growth and distribution reflected political priorities and values in particular countries. He discussed three models: growth-oriented patterns, illustrated by Brazil and Mexico, including an equity-oriented, low-growth variant, illustrated by Sri Lanka; rapid growth with equity, illustrated by Taiwan, Republic of Korea, and Singapore; and an average pattern illustrated by India, the Philippines, Turkey, and Colombia, where patterns of growth and distribution follow the average relations of the Kuznets curve.

A great many qualitative, but empirically based studies tried to identify the causes of income inequality, and some examined its consequences. These explorations began to bring in non-economic as well as economic factors. The distribution of ownership of assets between households (the question of asset distribution *within* households was not yet on the agenda) was clearly vital, but it could be influenced by historical, institutional, and political forces as well as economic and policy ones. Adelman and Morris (1973) analysed data for forty-three countries in the 1950s and early 1960s and found that on average the poorest 60 per cent received around a quarter of total income; the share was smallest where a sharply dualistic development process had been initiated by well-entrenched expatriate or military elites geared to taking the lion's share of the benefits. Although their methodology was widely criticized their basic conclusion found an echo amongst many observers, namely that economic structure, not level of income or rate of economic growth, is the primary determinant of patterns of income distribution.

So-called structuralist theorists of development emphasized the impact on income inequality of such factors as historically unequal landownership patterns and social structures that excluded people on such bases as caste, race, sex, or religion. The concentration of physical and financial capital as well as land in the hands of a small elite enabled them to buy access to educational opportunity and control an ever greater proportion of national product. The consequences of this unequal distribution included malnutrition, poor housing, and education for the majority, resulting in low levels of productivity. In contrast the argument was made that a redistribution of income would increase production by increasing the consumption and hence the health and productivity of the poor.

Non-structuralists countered that inequality was the logical (some would say inevitable) outcome of economic growth. The apparent increase in inequality during the early stages of development is because development does not start at the same time in all parts of the economy. Growth in a poor, underdeveloped country will always raise some people's income before others, notably those where the growth is first located, for instance in urban rather than rural areas. Shifts in a country's structure of production will inevitably create inequalities between those engaged in agriculture compared to those in new, more highly remunerated industries. The non-structuralists argued that these inequalities would not necessarily result in absolute impoverishment but only a relative decline in income of the poorest. The argument that the poor would see their living standards rise through economic growth even though their relative share of income might not, would gain ground in the 1980s.

However, structuralist arguments and the prevailing climate of normative opinion against economic inequalities were still ascendant in the late 1960s and early 1970s. The early conviction that economic **modernization** and growth would trickle down had been gradually eroded by the evidence of persistent poverty and inequality. Radical movements called for land reform, wealth redistribution, and state economic planning to guarantee egalitarian develop-

ment. Structuralists who remained committed to economic growth maintained that state intervention could ensure that such growth and economic diversification, particularly industrialization, would gradually incorporate labour into the higher wage and more productive sectors. But by the 1970s, they too were becoming sceptical. For example Dudley Seers, influential Director of Britain's Institute of Development Studies at Sussex University and a key figure in International Labour Organization missions to Sri Lanka, Colombia, and Kenya, expressed the disillusionment thus:

> The questions to ask about a country's development are therefore: what has been happening to poverty? What has been happening to unemployment? What has been happening to inequality? If all three of these have declined from high levels, then beyond doubt this has been a period of development for the country concerned. If one or two of these central problems have been growing worse, especially if all three have, it would be strange to call the result 'development', even if per capita income doubled. (cited Hunt 1989: 260)

Even the President of the World Bank, Robert MacNamara, was forced to admit that despite a decade of unprecedented increase in the gross national product of the developing countries, the poorest segments of their population had received relatively little benefit. Policies aimed primarily at accelerating economic growth in most developing countries had benefited at most the upper 40 per cent of the population.

Thus considerable attention was given to the question of whether an egalitarian development process was possible. Much depended on whether 'egalitarian' meant equality of outcome or opportunity or condition, distinctions that were rarely made. Reforming economists put forward a range of policy measures that could combine changes in the distribution of the ownership of productive assets while maximizing the development effort and even accelerating the growth rates. Radicals pointed to the political obstacles to such measures, which came not only from the governments and ruling elites in the developing world but also from Western governments opposed to what they judged non-capitalist paths to development. Cuba and Chile faced active hostility from the United States in their pursuit of more egalitarian development, while even Tanzania, one of the most heavily aided countries, found its strategy of self-reliance and equality extremely difficult to combine with growth and development.

## Key points

- Egalitarian thinking influenced several experiments in egalitarian development in developing countries from the 1960s but they ran into difficulties.
- A general trend towards rising inequalities in the less developed countries was not uniform, and patterns reflected local policy priorities and choices.

- Structuralists argued that economic structures and ownership patterns largely determined inequality.
- Non-structuralists argued that economic growth inevitably entailed some inequalities, but this did not mean absolute impoverishment, only relative impoverishment for the poorest.
- From the 1970s as agreement grew that economic modernization was not benefiting the poor, international development policies focused on raising their living standards but without radical redistribution.

# Equality questioned

By the 1980s support for the idea that the pursuit of inequality is a task of government eroded in the Anglo-American world especially and in the international institutions it influenced. The global economic recession which followed the 1973 oil shocks had resulted by the end of the decade in a shift from Keynesian policies of demand management and welfare-oriented state interventions, to monetarism, which cuts public expenditure on welfare and prioritizes investment and profitability. Toye (1987: 71) called this a counter-revolution in development thinking, referring specifically to the thinking of P. T. Bauer. Bauer had argued that some individuals are better off than others because of different aptitudes and personal advantages. Measures to counteract economic differences, 'the pursuit of the holy grail of economic equality', he argued, 'would exchange the promised reduction or removal of differences in income and wealth for much greater actual inequality of power between rulers and subjects. There is an underlying contradiction in egalitarianism in open societies' (Bauer 1981: 8).

Bauer attacked the political consequences of an increasingly coercive and bureaucratic state pursuing egalitarian goals. Many developing world egalitarian states had indeed shown that these dangers were real. Even where such states had consciously sought to avoid such tendencies, for example Nyerere's Tanzania (1962–85) and the Sandinistas' Nicaragua

(1979–90), they could not entirely avoid state-heavy political structures that concentrated power in new elites, such as the 'bureaucratic bourgeoisie' of the former and the party *caudillos* of the latter. Bauer also maintained that promotion of economic equality and the alleviation of poverty are distinct and often conflicting goals, and that to make the rich poorer does not make the poor richer. Others added that good government is something that promotes opulence through a policy of promoting liberty by establishing laws of justice which guarantee free exchange and peaceful competition, leaving the improvement of morality to non-governmental institutions.

These and related ideas informed the broad trend in thinking away from government regulation and intervention in markets for any purpose, including social justice. The argument against Kuznets that in any case inequality had no inevitable consequences for poverty gathered support in the 1980s, boosted by the publication of several time series studies showing that income inequality does not in any case change much over time, so economic growth must reduce poverty to some extent. The pattern of overall distribution of goods in society now seemed less important than individual well-being and freedom to pursue private interests in the marketplace. In the developing countries market liberalization echoed this shift. But while inequality and social justice tended to fall from the mainstream political agenda, equity meaning fairness did not. Gender equity and sometimes equality, in particular, won a place in the new development thinking, as an increasing body of evidence showed that gender discrimination and inequality adversely affect a wide range of development indicators. New concepts that tried to confront the problems of disadvantage and discrimination began to gain ground in the 1990s, most notably social exclusion. That concept has attracted much debate and little consensus on its core meaning or even its relationship to poverty. It is not inevitably linked to poverty; for disability, drug addiction, age, and so on can all be linked to exclusion. Some writers try to link it to inequality and to assess its relative importance alongside social integration as mechanisms of differentiation and stratification. The concept's resilience seems to lie in its ability to take in both distributional and relational approaches to inequality. Distributional approaches refer to the ways different factors such as income wealth, occupation, education, and power are distributed. Relational approaches emphasize the ways in which 'individuals differentiated by these criteria are related to each other within a system of groups and categories' (Béteille 1969: 13). Although it lacks the elements of exploitation and justice, 'social exclusion' has offered more scope for keeping inequality on the agenda than would an anti-poverty focus *tout court*. It does not, however, represent the end of the discussion about the relative weight of the distributional and relational aspects of inequality, which has taken on new directions as the complexity of human diversity and the stratifications we make within it become increasingly recognized.

## Key points

- In the 1980s priority was given to market-driven growth and new arguments were mounted to suggest why economic growth was bound to be positive for the poor.
- Inequality and social justice were no longer on the mainstream political agenda, although gender equity and the problem of social exclusion were.

# Equality and human diversity

Various egalitarian theories have identified at least three different kinds of socio-economic injustice: exploitation, **economic marginalization**, and **deprivation**. In Fraser's words (1997: 13) exploitation means 'having the fruits of one's labour appropriated for the benefit of others'; economic marginalization is 'being confined to undesirable or poorly paid work', and deprivation is 'being denied an adequate material standard of living'. She contrasts these approaches with those that emphasize cultural or symbolic injustice, rooted in social patterns of representation, interpretation, and communication, but allows that the different forms can intersect. Economic institutions are imbued with cultural meanings and norms, while cultural practices have a political-economic dimension. The dilemma that interests Fraser is that while the claim for redistribution calls for the abolition of economic arrangements that underpin group specificity, such as the gender division of labour, recognition claims call attention to the specificity of a group and the affirmation of its value as a group. How can a society's social and political arrangements embrace both imperatives together? In the developing world, such questions have considerable salience for ethnic as well as gender stratifications. A great deal of debate is now taking place around these issues amongst scholars of multiculturalism, indigenous and minority rights, and citizenship. Progress has been made in terms of the abandonment of the single axis of difference such as woman or class, and the acknowledgement of the differences between women, for example, and the interaction among race, gender, and class identities. But how are the multiple connections between identities and social position linked to the question of equality in terms of the practical design of human social arrangements? And without some rethinking of those arrangements, are not certain people doomed to political as well as social exclusion, unable to effectively influence decision-making processes because of entrenched social and cultural hierarchies and power imbalances?

Sen, in *Inequality Reexamined* (1992) offers one of the most sophisticated efforts to address the relationship between human diversity and equality. It has been particularly influential in development studies, refocusing attention away from income as a poverty and development measure, to human capabilities—a shift that can be followed in the evolution of the United Nations Development Programme's annual *Human Development Reports*. Sen is not concerned to justify equality as such, but is more interested in the question, 'equality of what?' which in itself clarifies the question 'why equality?'. His thinking is heavily influenced by Rawls here, but he has gone beyond Rawls in moving the emphasis from the *means* of freedom, that is primary goods in Rawls's account, to the **extents of freedom**. In Sen's terminology that means the capabilities or the *freedom* to achieve whatever functionings an individual happens to value.

The logic of Sen's argument is based on the assumption of human diversity. Equality claims must come to terms with this fundamental empirical fact, as there are times when equal consideration for all may demand unequal treatment in favour of the disadvantaged. Indeed because we are diverse in our personal qualities, such as age, gender, talents, proneness to illnesses, physical abilities, as well as in our external circumstances like material assets, social backgrounds, and environmental circumstances, insistence on egalitarianism in one field may imply rejecting it in another. Disadvantage is itself diverse. Moreover disadvantage is not just about consumption of resources; Sen recognizes the active agency in human beings that can be unleashed in other ways than the allocation or reallocation of goods. The 'focal variable' for the inequality that matters is itself internally diverse, so that for Sen the question 'equality of what?' has a plurality of potential answers. Income alone cannot be an adequate measure of inequality. Our capabilities to achieve whatever we value do not ultimately depend on income but on all the physical and social characteristics that make us what we are and which affect who we are. Substantial inequalities in well-being and freedom can, given our variable needs and disparate personal and social circumstances, result directly from an equal distribution of incomes.

Sen turns our attention to the fact that some countries with higher per capita incomes enjoy lower life expectancies. The Indian state of Kerala has one of the lower real per capita incomes in India but the highest life expectancy, lower infant mortality and higher general literacy, particularly female literacy. This is true even if the average Gross National Product is adjusted for distributional inequality; Kerala remains even with this statistical adjustment one of the poorer Indian states. The explanation lies in the history of public policy, most notably education (particularly female literacy) health services, and food distribution, which reaches the rural as well as urban population (Sen 1992: 128).

The UNDP's annual *Human Development Reports* have introduced a range of new indices that try to take into account non-income measures of development and enable us to view the performance of a country in terms of both growth and freedoms. The best known is the human development index, which incorporates data for human longevity and educational attainment as well as material living standards.

So it is now possible to appreciate the diversity of inequalities and to take a wider view of the social arrangements that should be aspired to. However, we are still left with what some would term the structural or embedded stratifications and subordinations that

---

### Box 4.3 **Human Development Index**

Comparing countries by their place in the Human Development Index produces a very different picture to a rank that is based on the Gini coefficient alone. For example Chile and Guatemala have a comparable level of inequality measured by the Gini coefficient, that is very high. But in human development terms Chile easily qualifies among the top fifty countries (high human development) whereas Guatemala is in the middle of the medium human development range, placed about seventy countries below Chile. The contrast between for instance South Korea and Rwanda is even greater. Similar in terms of the Gini coefficient (where both appear significantly more equal than say the United States or United Kingdom), in human development Rwanda features among the least developed countries anywhere while South Korea features in the top thirty countries of the world.

lie behind the persistent but diverse inequalities of the South. And the World Bank in its 2001 *World Development Report* acknowledged that social discrimination can have economic effects that will undermine efforts at pro-poor growth. Redistributive policies that do not impede the functioning of markets have been somewhat reluctantly conceded to be a possibility. But making 'public spending pro-poor' enters the terrain of political power and counter-power: 'Governments face important political issues in redistributing public spending to support asset accumulation by poor people. With finer targeting, public funds may in principle reach more poor people. But such targeting may lack political support from powerful groups that may lose out. Hence the importance of building pro-poor coalitions' (World Bank 2001: 82) (for more on the policy issues see Chapter 13). In the meantime, the poor and their allies build their own movements and engage in multiple forms of collective action. This includes challenges to the World Bank's own perceived contribution to global and local inequality through market-driven policies that failed to take into account the

initial inequalities. It is precisely those inequalities that have allowed some people to maximize their advantage in the market while others had not even begun to enter it. Thus the World Bank (2001: 32) appears to be correct when it writes 'Inequality is back on the agenda—in the realm of ideas and experience and in the political discourse of many developing (and developed) countries'.

## Key points

- New awareness of social and cultural diversity has increased the complexities of the inequality issue.
- Sen, taking human diversity as a starting point, argues that policies need to recognize that people are diverse in their disadvantages and advantages.
- The UNDP has introduced new measures to estimate non-income aspects of inequality.
- Recognition that structural factors continue to disadvantage large numbers of people has renewed the focus on inequality in debates about development.

# Conclusion

The conceptual waters of the inequality debate have ebbed and flowed since the eighteenth century, with ontological equality displaced by the end of the twentieth century with equality based on human diversity. Sen has advanced on Tawney's vision of the 'largest possible measure of equality of environment', to the multiple environments that must be tailored to the capability enhancements of a diverse humanity. However, humankind is a long way from constructing the new social, political, and economic arrangements that would enable inequalities to be addressed in the multiple 'spaces' in which they appear. Equality practice has foundered on the power at the global, national, community, and family levels that protects embedded inequalities and allows some people to exploit, marginalize, and deprive others of a full life. In turn, inequality impacts on the political system, limiting participation of poor and discriminated people and hence the possibilities of prioritizing the

search for new solutions that might truly enhance the life chances of all.

The prevailing development discourse has shifted since the 1980s but still has a long way to go before inequality is given full weight in the measurement of economic development. Social policy continues to prioritize efficiency over equity and to assume there is a tension between the two. The idea that the success of economic management should be assessed in terms of increasing social cohesion and lessening social disparities rather than growth and efficiency, is barely on the agenda even today. In the meantime, according to the *Human Development Report 2002* (UNDP 2002), the level of worldwide inequality is 'grotesque'—the world's richest one per cent of people being reckoned to receive as much income as the poorest 57 per cent, and the combined income of the world's richest 5 per cent being fourteen times that of the poorest 5 per cent.

Embedded, 'initial', or structural inequalities remain huge obstacles to the possibility of new egalitarian societal strategies that acknowledge human diversity, and respond appropriately to the diverse forms of inequality that arise from it. These are due to such long histories that people have often forgotten the social origins of the inequalities. Those who lose out come to assume they are less equal and that this may be so in several 'spaces of inequality' at once; those who gain have accumulated power to enforce and defend the visible and invisible boundaries between them and disadvantaged others.

Some analysts have argued that the moral interests of society must be promoted not by the state but by other actors, for example voluntary non-governmental agencies. Those that disagree have not yet come up with a vision of the kind of state that might counter their fear of the more adverse effects of ignoring inequality. Some have put their faith in democratization. Many believe that stronger civil societies will also help. However, neither of those purported solutions is immune from the exclusionary impact of embedded inequalities. Who participates and what impact they might have in the new public spaces that have opened up in some developing countries and certain global arenas remain key questions in assessing the prospects for renewed public and global debate on inequality thinking and practice.

## QUESTIONS

**1**  Why is it important to distinguish between equality of opportunity and equality of outcome?

**2**  Does it matter if the evidence shows that economic growth increases inequality but nevertheless raises absolute living standards amongst the poor?

**3**  To what extent should the state address the question of inequality as well as poverty in its development strategies?

**4**  Assess the evidence that there is a relationship between neo-liberal globalization and increasing inequality between and within nations?

**5**  Can embedded or structural inequality be addressed by political institutions that reflect those structures, and if not, how can it be challenged?

**6**  Can cultural and social inequality be tackled by addressing income inequality?

**7**  To what extent does Sen's approach to inequality, human diversity, and capabilities satisfy a feminist critique of social inequality?

## GUIDE TO FURTHER READING

Bauer, P. T., *Equality, the Third World and Economic Delusion* (London: Methuen, 1981).
A major source of the neo-liberal questioning of the goal of pursuing equality in development.

Béteille, A. (ed.), *Social Inequality* (Harmondsworth: Penguin, 1969). A good set of conceptual and anthropological essays on social inequalities which still merits reading.

Chenery, H. et al., *Redistribution with Growth* (New York: Oxford University Press, 1974).
Had a major impact on World Bank and other institutions involved in development policy in the 1970s.

Fraser, N., *Justice Interruptus, Critical Reflections on the 'postsocialist' condition* (London: Routledge, 1997) A very useful discussion on the relationship between the redistributionist and recognitionist emphases within inequality thinking.

Kuznets, S., 'Economic growth and income inequality', *American Economic Review*, 45 (1955), 1–28. An important benchmark study on the relationship between inequality and development.

Rawls, J., *A Theory of Justice* (Oxford: Oxford University Press, 1971). A very influential contribution to the political philosophy of inequality.

Sen, A., *Inequality Reexamined* (Oxford: Oxford University Press, 1992). Includes good discussions of both the state of welfare economics measurement and the relations between aggregative and distributional considerations and economic efficiency.

Tawney, R. H., *Inequality* (London: Allen and Unwin, 1952). A classic essay on inequality which challenges the notion that equality of opportunity is a sufficient approach to the question.

## WEB LINKS

**www.worldbank.org/poverty/inequal**   The World Bank Group site on the concept inequality and its links to poverty and to socio-economic performance, and pro-poor growth specifically.

**www.wider.unu.edu/wiid/wiid.htm**   Contains United Nations-World Institute for Development Economics Research Database on world income inequality.

**http:/ucatlas.ucsc.edu**   The University of California, Santa Cruz Atlas of Global Inequality, includes downloadable maps and graphics.

**www.undp.org**   Site of the United Nations Human Development Programme contains links to its annual *Human Development Report*.

 ## COMPANION WEB SITE

For additional material and resources, see the companion web site at:
**www.oup.com/uk/booksites/politics/**

# 5

# Ethnopolitics and nationalism

*James R. Scarritt*

## OVERVIEW

This chapter stresses the significance of both: (1) differences among ethnic, ethnopolitical, and **national identities**; and (2) different types of relations among groups having these identities in countries of the developing world. **Ethnic identities** are constructed and reconstructed over time, and some but not all are politicized. Specific processes for construction and politicization and their variations across countries are discussed. National identities in the developing world, which are inherently political, vary in strength as well as the degree to which they are civic, multi-ethnic, or ethnic, and the chapter explains these variations. Both types of identities have been strongly influenced by European colonialism. Both types interact variously with group morphology, group advantages and disadvantages, organizations, institutions, mobilization and state response histories, and international influence. Based on such interactions ethnopolitical groups engage in conflict, competition, and cooperation with one another and the state in different countries and at different points in time. Different interaction patterns are explored. Since national identities are relatively weak in many developing countries while sub-national ethnopolitical identities and groups are often stronger, developing states more or less successfully engage in a variety of **nation-building** activities; the chapter describes these activities and explains their degree of success in the current era of electoral democracy and globalization.

# Introduction

Defining ethnicity and nationalism in ways that are uncontroversial is probably an impossible task. Yet these are vitally important topics in the politics of the developing world, affecting and affected by the other social and economic cleavages and characteristics discussed in this book, the nature of the state and its degree of democratization, and policies for economic development and human rights protection. Boldly stated, a reasonably strong sense of civic or multi-ethnic nationalism and interactions among politicized ethnic groups based primarily on cooperation and institutionalized competition rather than on conflict tend to moderate economic and religious cleavages, strengthen civil society, and enhance state-building, democratization, economic development, and the provision of human rights. Although these generalizations are only tendencies rather than universal relationships, and reverse causal effects of other cleavages, civil society, state-building, democratization, economic development, and human rights on ethnopolitics and nationalism are also important, these relationships leave no doubt about the vital importance of ethnicity and nationalism.

Rather than dwell on controversies about the definition of ethnicity and nationalism, this chapter assumes that: (1) they are different and only sometimes closely related; (2) both are socially constructed identities that are subject to change in interaction with group morphology, group advantage or disadvantage, political organizations and institutional rules, mobilization histories, and international influences; and (3) ethnicity is only politicized in some cases, but nationalism has an inherent political component. The discussion thus begins with the construction and politicization of ethnic identities, or—in other words—the construction of ethnic and ethnopolitical identities, and then turns to the construction of a variety of nationalist identities. The next section deals with the conflictual, competitive, and cooperative interactions of groups based on these identities with one another and with states, while the final section deals with states' efforts to mould these interactions in ways that enhance the legitimacy of state-based nations and their support from various groups.

# The construction and politicization of ethnic identities

Ethnic identities are constructed when some people self-consciously distinguish themselves from others on the basis of perceived common descent (perhaps mythical), shared culture (including values, norms, goals, beliefs, and language), or—most commonly—both. There is thus a wide variety in the specific contents of these identities even within a single country, to say nothing of across the countries of the developing world. Actual commonalities of language, a broader culture, or a common line of descent are often but not always central to ethnic identities. In spite of this wide variety in specific content, the common characteristics of these identities are sufficient to

separate them clearly from other identities and to justify generalizing broadly about them (Eriksen 1993: 10–12; Gurr 2000: 3–5; Horowitz 1985: 51–64). Religious identities are the closest ones to ethnicity but, as discussed in Chapter 6, it is useful to separate them.

Many but not all ethnic identities are politicized (made politically relevant). This distinction is obviously very important for the analysis of the role of ethnicity in politics in the developing world and elsewhere. **Ethnopolitical identities** are those ethnic identities that have been politicized. This term deliberately emphasizes the interactive causal significance of the ethnic and political components of these identities in their formation, continuing mobilization, and interaction with concrete organizations, institutional rules, and international influences (Gurr 2000: 5–8; Mozaffar, Scarritt, and Galaich 2003: 382–3). There is much debate about the relative strength of each component of ethnopolitical identities, with a majority of recent analysts giving predominance to the political. But their relative strength, as well as the specific form of their interaction, may vary across ethnicities or countries and over time, so what is crucial is to emphasize their interaction and examine it empirically in different cases. Young (2001: 176) suggests that the political component is more important in Africa than in Eurasia. This point is examined in greater detail in the following paragraphs and in the section on ethnopolitical cooperation, competition, and conflict.

The fact that ethnopolitical identities are constructed through the processes just discussed, and thus change over time, does not mean that they are not often held with deep emotional intensity. They are constructed through a variety of interactions between leaders and masses in which everyone's rational calculations are structured by their existing values, norms, and identities. A theory of constructed identities involves much more than narrowly rational elite instrumentalism, although this is not recognized by all analysts (cf. Smith 1995: 30–41).

With very few exceptions, the countries of the developing world experienced European colonialism, which played a crucial role in the construction of ethnic identities and an even more crucial role in their politicization and organization into ethnopolitical groups. But the timing of colonial rule, the European powers involved, and the specific policies that affected ethnic identities varied sharply between Latin America and the Caribbean on the one hand and Asia, the Middle East and North Africa, sub-Saharan Africa on the other, and to a lesser extent among and within the latter areas. The Spanish and Portuguese colonized virtually all of Latin America and much of the Caribbean from the sixteenth century until the first quarter of the nineteenth century. They brought in large numbers of settlers from their own countries and other European countries, and it was the Creoles—the American-born descendents of these settlers (Anderson 1991: 47; Young 1976: 84)—who seized power from the decaying colonial empires at the time of independence. In many of these countries they were outnumbered by indigenous Indians alone, or (as in Brazil) in combination with imported African slaves, although extensive intermarriage created intermediate groups of people, many of whom adopted Creole identities. European or Creole, mixed-race or Mestizo, Indian and African ethnopolitical identities developed over the following decades, roughly in that order. The increasing strength of Indian identities as disadvantaged minorities—more focused on individual 'tribes' than on multi-tribal Indian populations in specific countries—has been the primary change in the landscape of ethnopolitical identities in recent decades. Ethnopolitical mobilization and the globalization of information have played crucial roles in strengthening these identities, as discussed below. British and French colonialism in the Caribbean began slightly later, and the British held on to their colonies until the end of the Second World War. Descendents of former slaves from Africa are the overwhelming majority of the population in most of these countries. However, those countries with substantial East Indian populations are deeply divided in terms of ethnopolitical identities.

English, French, Dutch, and Spanish/American colonialism in South and South-East Asia occurred somewhat later, beginning as early as the sixteenth century in the Philippines and as late as the late nineteenth century in Indochina, and lasting until after the Second World War. Very few permanent European settlers were brought in, although Chinese and Indian settlers were brought into some South-East Asian countries. A core pre-colonial ethnic identity existed in many but not all Asian colonies, and was usually reinforced and given increased political significance by colonial rule. Burma is a clear example of this pattern. But minority ethnic identities within or outside the core were recognized and also politicized, especially by the British. Minority identities were strengthened in the process of resistance to the colonial reinforcement of the core identity. The two largest Asian colonies—British India and Dutch Indonesia—and a few others were amalgamations of a vast array of ethnic identities without a single dominant core. The British politicized these multiple identities more intensively and intentionally (through granting limited political autonomy to indigenous princely states) than the Dutch did, but the latter's classification of customary law zones constructed and politicized the ethnicity of their residents (Young 1994: 270), and amalgamation of groups into a common state inevitably had a politicizing effect. Post-independence politics have intensified group politicization in both countries, reinforced by international support for some disadvantaged minorities.

English, French, Belgian, and Portuguese colonialism in sub-Saharan Africa occurred much later, not really penetrating the subcontinent beyond a few coastal areas, the Portuguese-influenced Kongo Kingdom (most of which is now in Angola) and areas of European settlement in South Africa until the 1880s. Colonial rulers' reliance on local agents to cope with the dilemma of maintaining control at low cost encouraged these agents to differentiate their groups from those not so privileged by colonial authority, either by recombining and redefining existing objective markers of ethnicity or by accentuating previously minor group differences. Colonial rulers' creation of administrative units to secure additional economies in the cost of governance incorporated culturally disparate groups within single administrative units or separated culturally similar groups into separate units.

At independence, therefore, sub-Saharan African countries inherited a distinctive ethnic morphology (the form and structure of groups) with three defining features: (1) marked differences in group size, such that virtually no major ethnopolitical group comprises an outright majority in a country, although some comprise a large plurality, (2) considerable variety and complexity in ethnic markers, such that, even as they produce politically salient inter-ethnic differences, they also produce politically salient intra-group heterogeneity even with limited cultural differences among large agglomerations of such groups, and (3) the territorial concentration of some ethnic groups that facilitates their construction as cohesive units for collective political action. These three features have combined with the accommodation by post-colonial regimes of instrumental ('pork-barrel') ethnopolitical demands to foster *communal contention* as the typical pattern of political interactions in which ethnopolitical groups serve as cost-effective strategic resources for organizing political competition for power and resources. Communal contention discourages political entrepreneurs from exaggerating cultural differences among groups and encourages them instead to maintain strong group and coexisting sub-group identities that are strategically sustained by their ability to access the state and secure valued goods and services for their followers (Mozaffar and Scarritt 1999: 239–42; Mozaffar, Scarritt and Galaich 2003: 382–3).

In sub-Saharan Africa, construction of *ethnopolitical* groups occurred through organized group mobilization (primarily in ethnic associations or cliques of leaders within the same party, the bureaucracy, or the military), articulation of grievances by leaders claiming to speak for a group rather than a party, participation in collective action or (violent or non-violent) conflict with other groups or the state and being subjected to state violence, encapsulation within or domination of an officially designated administrative unit, occupying a disproportionate number of high positions in the bureaucracy or the military, controlling disproportionate socio-economic resources, or forming or joining an ethnic or multi-ethnic political party (Mozaffar, Scarritt, and Galaich 2003: 383).

French and British colonialism came to North Africa with the French occupation of Algeria in 1830, fifty years before neighbouring Morocco and Tunisia, and the British occupation of Aden in 1839. The presence of numerous French settlers in Algeria who campaigned to incorporate the colony permanently into France was eventually a major force in politicizing Algerian and regional (Maghreb) Arab identity. Colonial rule by the same European powers came to the Asian Middle East the latest of all regions (the end of the First World War in which the Ottoman Empire—the former colonial power in most of this region—was defeated), and lasted less than thirty years. Ottoman rule was assimilative rather than alien, but it was more interventionist and integrative than previous localized rulers, and thus stimulated Arab nationalism within its territories, especially in its waning years. Post-independence interventionist states continued this process, as did the conflict surrounding the arrival of large numbers of European Jews in Palestine before and after the founding of Israel in 1948. Other Arab countries have had few European settlers. Thus the construction and politicization of Arab as the dominant ethnopolitical identity in the entire bi-continental region was a long process in which European colonialism played a more limited role than in other regions (Young 1976: 373–427).

Apart from the Kurds of Iran, Iraq, and Turkey, whose identity was politicized primarily in the twentieth century, and Berber speakers in western North Africa, the main lines of division are religious, as discussed in Chapter 6. The Western powers have been seen as opposed to the emergence of a transnational Arab identity, and not only with respect to Palestine. This opposition has been a powerful politicizing force.

## Key points

- Ethnic identities are constructed and then are often politicized to become ethnopolitical.

- The ethnic and political components of ethnopolitical identities are both important, but their relative importance varies among groups, countries, and regions.

- Most ethnopolitical (politically relevant ethnic) identities in the developing world were constructed during the colonial period, but some have been modified by post-independence politics.

- Differences among regions of the developing world in the timing of colonialism, the policies of the major colonial powers, and the presence of European settlers significantly affected the construction of ethnopolitical identities.

# Varieties of nationalism in the developing world

National identities are inherently political, emphasizing the autonomy and unity of the nation as an actual or potential political unit (Hutchinson and Smith 1994: 4–5; Smith 1995: 149). They can be broadly characterized as civic, multi-ethnic, ethnonational, or a combination of these types (Croucher 2003: 3–5; Eriksen 1993: 118–20; Scarritt and Mozaffar 2003). Civic national identities involve unity among citizens of an autonomous state. Whatever social cleavages may divide these citizens are irrelevant; their common citizenship unites them. The only cultural uniformity that is demanded is commitment to the existence of the nation and its political institutional norms and values. Ethnonational identities define the nation in ethnic terms, attaining unity through the merger of ethnic and national identities, and demand autonomy for ethnic nations. Multi-ethnic national identities define the nation in terms of several ethnic identities that are united by or nested within citizenship and political interaction in an autonomous state, while often excluding other ethnic identities. They differ from **civic nationalism** in accepting the legitimacy and political utility of ethnopolitical identities, as long as they do not undermine national unity. This difference is not sufficiently recognized in the literature on nationalism. Very few national identities in the developing world are purely civic, but a substantial majority of them contain civic or multi-ethnic aspects, so that they do not identify the nation with a single ethnic group.

Consequently there is an ongoing tension between the ethnic, multi-ethnic, and civic aspects of these identities in their interaction with group advantages and disadvantages, concrete organizations, institutional rules, and international influences. There is a similar tension between what Varshney (2003) calls the nationalism of exclusion and the nationalism of resistance against external control. Both aspects are present in all nationalism, but resistance was the dominant aspect during the struggle against colonialism while exclusion has gained in importance since independence.

Since nationalism is a constructed identity, the significant variations in the specific nature of nations in the developing world are not surprising. Colonialism played an even greater role in the construction of national identities than it did in the construction of ethnopolitical identities. The boundaries of the vast majority of developing states were determined by colonial rulers, and the varieties of nationalism are products of the interaction between the states that rule within these boundaries and the morphology of ethnopolitical identities, the tactics of ethnopolitical groups, and the presence of alternative identities within the same boundaries, which is discussed in the next section of this chapter. 'The normative model of the contemporary polity calls for the coincidence of nation and state' (Young 1976: 70). States attempt to create national identities that are coextensive with their boundaries, and the constituent ethnopolitical groups support or oppose these identities. Disadvantaged minority groups are especially likely to oppose ethnonational identities, and groups that are politically dominant demographic majorities are likely to oppose civic or multi-ethnic national identities, but other patterns of support and opposition also occur. National identities are still being constructed, and this process is more advanced in some regions of the developing world than in others. But only in a very few developing countries have national identities become banal—accepted as a matter of course and constantly reinforced by popular culture—as these identities are in most developed countries (Billig 1995). Thus nationalism in every country—one nation in a world of nations—develops in relation to nationalism in all other countries, but especially in relation to nationalism in neighbouring countries and to the strong nationalism of the former colonial powers including the United States, which is all the more galling to the developing world because it is banal. It is impossible to specify exactly the number of nations or potential nations in the developing world, but if one includes every state and every ethnopolitical identity that engenders an ethnonationalist movement, there are probably several hundred.

Latin American states are former colonial administrative units. 'The first century of independent life saw the gradual transformation of what began primarily as the territorial heirs to colonial administrative divisions into nation-states' (Young 1976: 85). These countries officially pursue civic nationalism but until the late twentieth century this was actually a cover for Creole assimilationist ethnonationalism. Since the awakening of indigenous and/or African ethnopolitical identities in most countries, there has been a struggle by these groups to redefine national identity in more multi-ethnic terms. Because of Creole elite resistance, the outcome of this struggle is very much in doubt. Civic and ethnic nationalism tend to merge in racially homogeneous Caribbean countries, but civic national identities are much weaker and ethnonational ones much stronger in countries such as Trinidad and Guyana with significant East Indian populations.

Nationalism in Asian countries having politicized ethnic cores has tended to be ethnonationalism focused on these cores, and thus is often rejected by members of non-core cultural groups who advocate civic or multi-ethnic nationalism or desire secession. As discussed in the next section, this can lead to violent conflict over the definition of the nation. In substantially different ways, multi-ethnic India and Indonesia constructed relatively strong multi-ethnic national identities during the struggle for independence and the first decades of post-colonial rule. In India, the multiplicity of types of ethnic identities and the integrating force of the multi-ethnic and nationalist Congress Party facilitated the emergence of a multi-ethnic national identity, while the adoption of a *lingua franca* developed through trade as the national language did the same for Indonesia. These multi-ethnic national identities have weakened substantially in recent decades, as discussed in the following section and in Chapters 16 and 17. The role of religion in weakening these identities is discussed in Chapter 6.

Sub-Saharan Africa is the region in which multi-ethnic nationalism is most commonly found, although ethnonationalism is by no means absent there. The predominance of ethnopolitical cleavages, their complex multi-level morphology described above, the absence of large cultural differences in most African countries (in contrast to the multi-ethnic societies of Asia, Latin America, and the Caribbean), and the politics of communal contention (mentioned above) combine to produce multi-ethnic national identities that most effectively integrate national and ethnopolitical identities in this context. The presence of substantial numbers of foreign Africans in the presently or formerly wealthier African countries helps to solidify the multi-ethnic national identities that exclude them but include all ethnic groups comprised primarily of citizens. It should be noted that these identities are emerging rather than fully formed, and that they mitigate rather than eliminate ethnopolitical conflict. A minority of African societies are deeply divided, and thus torn by conflicts about national identity. That small cultural differences do not always eliminate such conflict is amply illustrated by Rwanda and Burundi, which can be called culturally homogeneous because the pre-colonial Tutsi conquerors adopted the culture of the conquered Hutu, but in which colonial policies and post-independence political competition have created violent deeply divided societies.

In the Middle East and North Africa the national identities of states with colonially (Ottoman or European) created boundaries compete with the transnational Arab nationalism—the primary competitor in the middle decades of the twentieth century, transnational Islamist identities (see Chapter 6)—the primary competitor today, transnational non-Arab identities—Berber in Algeria and Morocco and Kurdish in Iran, Iraq, and Turkey, and small sub-national identities. Consequently, these national state identities are probably the weakest in the developing world.

## Key points

- National identities are inherently political.
- National identities can be ethnonational, multi-ethnic, and civic in varying degrees.

- Most national identities in the developing world were constructed during the colonial period, but some have been modified by post-independence politics.
- Differences among regions and countries of the developing world in the morphology of ethno-political identities, the tactics of ethnopolitical groups, the policies of the major colonial powers and post-independence states, and the presence of alternative identities significantly affected the construction of national identities.

# Ethnopolitics in multi-ethnic and deeply divided societies

## Ethnopolitical morphology

The discussion of the construction of ethnopolitical and national identities in various regions of the developing world has revealed that the morphology of ethnopolitical groups varies greatly among the developing countries. Borrowing from Young (1976: 95–7), it is possible to specify five patterns of ethnopolitical morphology: (1) homogeneous societies such as Korea, Lesotho, and Haiti; (2) societies with a single clearly dominant group, numerically and socially, and minorities such as Algeria, Burma, and Nicaragua; (3) bipolar or deeply divided societies such as Burundi, Guyana, Rwanda, and Sri Lanka; (4) multi-polar societies, divided primarily on a single dimension, with no dominant groups, such as many sub-Saharan African countries; and (5) societies with a multiplicity of cultures, with more than one dimension of differentiation, such as India and Indonesia. Countries having the last two patterns and those having the second pattern in which the minorities do not cohere (a substantial majority of societies in that pattern at most points in time) can be called multi-ethnic societies.

Another approach to comparing ethnopolitical morphologies is to develop an index of fractionalization

or fragmentation for each country. To do this, one must first specify all of the ethnic or ethnopolitical groups that exist in each country of the developing world because of past construction processes. Fearon (2003) has recently attempted to do this; Scarritt and Mozaffar (1999) have attempted to do it for Africa; and Gurr and his associates in the Minorities at Risk (MAR) project (1993, 2000) have attempted to specify a narrower list of groups 'at risk'. These authors have different definitions of politically relevant ethnic groups; it may be the case that different groups have been politicized for different purposes, including economic policy-making (Fearon), electoral politics (Scarritt and Mozaffar), and political protest and rebellion (Gurr); and construction and politicization are ongoing processes. But it is nevertheless useful to examine these efforts to specify groups, as is done in Table 5.1, in order to get an idea of the very large number of them and to show that the regions are ranked in the same order in the three data sets in terms of the number of groups specified: sub-Saharan Africa first, Asia second, Latin America and the Caribbean third, and the Middle East and North Africa last.

Only Fearon's data allow comparison of countries and regions in terms of fractionalization, which varies

**Table 5.1** Numbers of ethnopolitical groups in the developing world

| Region | Fearon | Scarritt/Mozaffar | Gurr |
|---|---|---|---|
| Latin America–Caribbean | 84 | | 32 |
| Asia | 108 | | 59 |
| Sub-Saharan Africa | 351 | 382 | 67 |
| Middle East–N. Africa | 70 | | 28 |
| Total | 613 | | 186 |

**Table 5.2** Ethnic fractionalization in the developing world

| Region | Average | Range | % of countries with majority group |
|---|---|---|---|
| Latin America–Caribbean | 0.41 | 0.743–0.095 | 0.78 |
| Asia | 0.44 | 1.00–0.002 | 0.78 |
| Sub-Saharan Africa | 0.71 | 0.953–0.180 | 0.28 |
| Middle East–N. Africa | 0.45 | 0.780–0.039 | 0.84 |

in his scale between 0 (homogeneous) and 1 (totally fragmented). These data (Fearon 2003: 204, 209, 215–19), summarized in Table 5.2, show that, within the developing world, the average level of ethnic fractionalization is lowest in Latin America–Caribbean, slightly higher in Asia and the Middle East–North Africa, and much higher in sub-Saharan Africa. The range of countries in terms of fragmentation is greatest in Asia, almost as great in sub-Saharan Africa, and less in the other two regions. Finally, the percentage of countries in which the largest group comprises the majority of the population is only 28 per cent in sub-Saharan Africa and between 78 per cent and 84 per cent in the other three regions. Thirty African countries (70 per cent of the total) have fragmentation scores above 0.7, while only four Asian countries (including the two largest ones, India and Indonesia), three Middle Eastern countries, and one Latin American country have scores this high. Fearon's data thus support the conclusion that most African countries are far more fragmented than most countries in other regions.

Other relevant aspects of ethnopolitical morphology are geographic concentration, the extent of

cultural differences among groups, and the presence of ethnic groups that have not been explicitly politicized as described above. Available data indicate that ethnopolitical groups in sub-Saharan Africa tend to be the most geographically concentrated and to have the smallest cultural differences, and that there are more ethnic groups that have not been politicized there than in other regions of the developing world (Fearon 2003: 211–14; Gurr 1993: 344–51; Scarritt and Mozaffar 2003: 9–10).

## Collective action and interaction

These different ethnopolitical morphologies interact with group advantage or disadvantage, political organizations and institutional rules, mobilization and state response histories, and international influences in causing different types of collective action by ethnopolitical groups and different types of interaction among them or with the state. Human agents who are rational within their belief and normative frameworks carry out these processes within the constraints imposed by social structures (Gurr 2000: 65–95; Mozaffar 1995; Mozaffar, Scarritt, and Galaich 2003: 380–2, 385–7; Scarritt and Mozaffar 2003: 12–16). Ethnopolitical interactions cannot be fully explained without taking all of these factors and their interactions into account; the following presentation is organized factor by factor but incorporates interactions among factors into the discussion of each one. Group advantage or disadvantage can be economic, political, or cultural, or any combination of these forms. Crucial political organizations include various civilian state agencies, the military and police, political parties, and interest associations that are not ethnically based. Some are more institutionalized than others. Institutional rules can be broadly categorized as democratic, transitional, or autocratic (Gurr 2000: 154). Rules about the formation and control of ethnopolitical associations and the conduct of elections are of special importance. Group collective action and state responses have historical patterns that have varied in violence and intensity in different countries of the developing world, although these patterns are more firmly established in some countries than in others. These patterns are of course subject to change, but they have self-perpetuating qualities that resist change unless the forces supporting it are sufficient to overcome them. Finally, although ethnopolitics is primarily internal to states, it is significantly influenced by several aspects of globalization, diffusion, and contagion among identical or similar groups across state boundaries, and external political and material support.

Interaction among groups and between them and the state can be categorized as cooperative, competitive, or conflictual. The boundaries among these three types of collective interaction are by no means perfectly clear, and a given action by a group or the state may involve any two or all three types vis-à-vis various targets. The relative importance of these interaction patterns nevertheless provides a very useful way of comparing ethnopolitics in the countries of the developing world. As illustrated in Box 5.1, the literature on ethnopolitics there (Gurr 1993, 2000; Horowitz 1985; Young 1976) emphasizes the complex causation of conflict involving some degree of violence, and to a lesser extent competition, but a

greater emphasis on the latter and the inclusion of cooperation are necessary for a more balanced treatment. To highlight this point, it is useful to separate—within the discussion of each factor and its interactions with others—the explanation of cooperation, institutionalized competition, and peaceful protest from the explanation of conflict and non-institutionalized competition.

Cooperation and institutionalized competition among ethnopolitical groups and states in the developing world do not get much attention in the global media, yet they occur with great frequency and have significant consequences. They are substantially greater in frequency and consequences than conflict is in many countries, although they often coexist with conflict (involving the same or other groups). Peaceful protest attracts more media attention. It is not institutionalized but is more properly seen as competition rather than conflict, although it is easy for such protest to turn violent and thus become conflictual through the actions of the protesters or the authorities (usually the police). This is one reason why the boundaries between cooperation and competition and between competition and conflict are often difficult to draw. On the other hand, conflict in the forms of violent protest, rebellion, and repression, as well as its almost indistinguishable cousin non-institutionalized violent competition, get a great deal of attention from global media (and scholars); they are 'newsworthy'. The consequences of such conflict can indeed be horrific, but this is not always the case, and the media's view of ethnopolitical conflict as prevalent in most developing countries is distorted.

## Ethnopolitical morphology and types of ethnopolitical interaction

Cooperation, institutionalized competition, and peaceful protest, aspects of the politics of communal contention, are much more frequent and consequential in multi-ethnic than in deeply divided societies, although they are not limited to the former type. The impossibility of majority support for the regime (which is important even for autocratic regimes) in the absence of such cooperation in the former type of society and the tendency towards the mutual fears and hopes of ethnonationalist winner-takes-all

---

### Box 5.1 Two conceptions of the causes of ethnopolitical conflict

**Horowitz**: An adequate theory of ethnic conflict should be able to explain both elite and mass behavior. Such a theory should also provide an explanation for the passionate, symbolic, and apprehensive aspects of ethnic conflict. Group entitlement, conceived as a joint function of comparative worth and legitimacy, does this—it explains why the followers follow, accounts for the intensity of group reactions, even to modest stimuli, and clarifies the otherwise mysterious quest for public signs of group status

(Horowitz 1985: 226).

**Gurr**: The motivations at the heart of ethnopolitics are assumed to be a mix of grievance, sentiment, solidarity, ambition, and calculation. It is simplistic to argue that one kind of motivation is primary and others subsidiary. Ethnopolitical protest and rebellion are consequences of complex interactions among collective experience, normative commitments, contention for power, and strategic assessments about how best to promote individual and collective interests

(Gurr 2000: 66).

politics among both groups in the latter type of society account for this difference. Small cultural differences and the presence of non-politicized groups (impossible in deeply divided societies) facilitate cooperation, while geographic concentration (less likely in deeply divided societies) has more ambivalent effects. Conflict and non-institutionalized violent competition are more likely to occur in deeply divided than in multi-ethnic societies, although they are not limited to the former type. The reasons for this are the inverse of those for the greater significance of cooperation in the latter type of society. Organizations such as political parties and the military tend strongly to be arenas of conflict in deeply divided societies (Horowitz 1985: 291–525). But within each type of society, other factors account for substantial differences in cooperation, competition, and conflict.

## Group advantages and disadvantages and types of ethnopolitical interaction

Cooperation is easier the smaller the advantages or disadvantages of different groups. Advantages or disadvantages can be economic, political, or cultural, and can be due to discrimination in either state policies or well-established social structures, or to more accidental factors such as regional differences in resource endowments. Disadvantages that are seen as caused by discrimination in state policies make cooperation especially difficult (Gurr 1993: 34–60; 2000: 105–32), but disadvantages caused by social structural discrimination and not counteracted by state policies also hinder it. Since many groups in most countries of the developing world have advantages or disadvantages caused by discrimination (as described below), ethnopolitical cooperation and the reduction of discrimination through state policies tend to go together.

Conflict is more likely to occur the greater the advantages or disadvantages of different groups, especially if these advantages or disadvantages are seen as due to discrimination in state policies. Horowitz (1985: 32) indicates that 'virtually all ranked systems of ethnic relations [in which class and ethnicity coincide] are in a state of rapid transition or of increasing coercion

by the superordinate group to avert change'. Almost 90 per cent of the 186 groups in the developing world that were included in the MAR survey in the mid-1990s because they were judged to be at risk of being involved in violent conflict experienced one or more forms of discrimination, and most of the rest were at risk because of advantages gained from such discrimination. Over two-thirds of these groups experienced economic discrimination, and 40 per cent experienced high levels of such discrimination. Within the developing world economic discrimination is greatest in Latin America and the Caribbean (where indigenous peoples are subject to severe discrimination of all types), followed by the Middle East and North Africa, Asia, and sub-Saharan Africa in that order. Political discrimination is even more prevalent in the developing world. Over 80 per cent of the 186 groups experienced political discrimination in the 1990s and over half experienced high levels of such discrimination. This form of discrimination is also greatest in Latin America and the Caribbean and least in sub-Saharan Africa, but Asia ranks a close second in this case. Finally, cultural discrimination is less frequent, with small majorities of groups experiencing it in Latin America and the Middle East, a large minority of groups in Asia (mainly 'hill tribes'), and only a few groups in sub-Saharan Africa. Unlike the other forms of discrimination, a majority of groups that experience cultural discrimination experience it at low or medium levels. These forms of discrimination were highly correlated with group disadvantages (Gurr 2000: 105–27).

## Organizations, institutional rules, and types of ethnopolitical interaction

Cooperation among ethnopolitical groups occurs primarily within the political organizations listed on p. 81, operating with more or less firmly institutionalized rules. Institutional differences are probably the most important factor in explaining cooperation in such organizations. Cooperation requires a relatively high degree of institutionalization of the organizations within which it occurs, although it is impossible to specify the required level exactly. Democratic institutions, particularly if they are strong (highly institutionalized), promote cooperation, are the primary basis of institutionalized competition, and allow—and in some ways encourage—relatively peaceful protest. Institutional rules providing relatively unrestricted freedom for group activities are crucial for both institutionalized competition and peaceful protest. Not surprisingly, the MAR data demonstrate the greater use of peaceful protest and less ethnopolitical conflict in democratic countries and, perhaps more surprisingly, in transitional countries in the developing world as well.

In multi-ethnic societies, political parties contesting democratic elections need multi-ethnic support to win unless one group constitutes a majority of the population or is close enough that a non-proportional electoral system can give them control of a majority of seats in the legislature (Scarritt and Mozaffar 2003: 1). But even in the latter cases, democratic institutions value inter-ethnic cooperation and thus multi-ethnic parties more than autocratic institutions do. Multi-ethnic parties predominate in sub-Saharan Africa, and are found in a number of countries in other regions of the developing world. There is considerable debate about whether proportional representation or first-past-the-post electoral institutions are more likely to promote cooperation in multi-ethnic parties. The influence of such electoral institutions is probably outweighed by other factors. Horowitz (1985: 291–440) has analysed the ways in which ethnic parties, whose support comes overwhelmingly from a single ethnopolitical group, enhance conflict in deeply divided societies by unreservedly pursuing the interests of that group and failing to form stable majority coalitions.

Conflict and non-institutionalized violent competition occur within and among the organizations in which cooperation occurs (Horowitz 1985: 291–525), but more frequently occur outside formal organizations in the forms of violent protest, armed rebellion, and state repression varying from restrictions on civil and political liberties through conventional policing to genocide. Conflict has been most violent in deeply divided societies, when groups are severely disadvantaged by multiple forms of discrimination, and under weak autocratic institutions. In the MAR data violent rebellion between 1985 and 1998 had a mean annual magnitude in autocracies that was two and a half times that in new democracies. Rebellion in transitional regimes was much closer to the level in new democra-

cies. Partial or failed transitions in the developing world tend to increase protest but decrease rebellion (Gurr 2000: 151–63). The data show that, in part, democratization decreases conflict by decreasing discrimination (Gurr 2000: 163–77). Thus, while the institutional instability engendered by democratization can increase ethnopolitical conflict, as Snyder (2000) suggests, this is not its most common effect, at least beyond the transition period, and his idea of postponing democratization until strong institutions emerge (2000: 41, 265–9, 316–20) is not justified in the developing world other than in the deeply divided societies that he discusses.

## Mobilization, state response, and types of ethnopolitical interaction

Ethnopolitical identity construction and ethnopolitical group mobilization are closely related processes that tend to occur together over time. As discussed above, mobilization of ethnic associations is part of the politicization of ethnic identities, which then leads to ethnopolitical mobilization through political parties. Thus ethnopolitical mobilization has a history going back to the colonial period in most countries of the developing world. Since independence, such mobilization has been most intense and the most violent in deeply divided societies, when groups are severely disadvantaged by multiple forms of discrimination, under weak autocratic institutions, and in the presence of international political and material support for or against mobilization. It has been least intense and most peaceful in highly multi-ethnic societies, when few or no groups are severely disadvantaged by any form of discrimination, under strong democratic institutions, and in the absence of international political and material support. The longer a specific pattern of mobilization occurs, the more likely it is to be self-perpetuating unless changed deliberately by powerful actors. It is very difficult to change a primarily conflictual pattern of collective interaction into a primarily cooperative pattern or vice versa, and somewhat difficult to institutionalize un-institutionalized competition or change violent protest into peaceful protest.

The tendency for patterns of mobilization to be self-perpetuating is reinforced by state repression of a pattern of mobilization or the absence of such repression. Not surprisingly, the more intense and violent the mobilization the more severe the repression. In the MAR data repression varies from conventional policing to genocide (extermination of an ethnic group) and politicide (extermination of political enemies). Between 1955 and 1995 extensive ethnopolitical repression occurred in all areas of the developing world. It involved the largest number of groups in Asia and sub-Saharan Africa, but was least intense in Latin America and the Caribbean during the last decade of that period. Repression was far more likely to intensify violent mobilization than to stop it. Harff (2003: 66) found that genocide or politicide is most likely to occur or to be repeated after political upheaval in autocracies based on the support of advantaged minorities with exclusionary ideologies. State response to peaceful protest, most common in democratic states, has often been to grant only a small proportion of the protesters' demands but not to engage in repression. This response has typically led to the continuation of peaceful protest.

## International influences and types of ethnopolitical interaction

International influences have fostered both ethnopolitical cooperation and ethnopolitical conflict. Scholars have given some attention to the direct diffusion or indirect contagion of ethnopolitical conflicts across national borders through the presence of the same or closely related groups on both sides of the border. Much less attention has been paid to the diffusion of ethnopolitical cooperation, which is more difficult to study. But as democracy has been diffused to much of the developing world since the end of the cold war it is possible to argue that ethnopolitical cooperation and institutionalized electoral competition have often been diffused with it.

During the cold war, the superpowers and former colonial powers frequently gave material, political, and/or military support to parties to ethnopolitical conflict in the developing world. This was done to further the objectives of the powers giving aid, but it undoubtedly substantially exacerbated such conflict in a number of countries, including Afghanistan, Angola, Ethiopia, Guatemala, and Nicaragua. It is argued below that international intervention in ethnopolitical conflicts has been less self-interested since the end of the cold war, but the combination of the persistence of some degree of self-interest and lack of adequate information about the consequences of specific forms of intervention mean that political and/or material support can still have conflict-enhancing effects. French intervention in Rwanda in favour of the existing government (and thus of its followers who were bent on genocide) before and during the genocide of 1994 is a case in point. Regional powers within the developing world have also supported parties to ethnopolitical conflict in their regions out of self-interest, which formerly included rewards from their cold war patrons. Finally, regional and international organizations—governmental and especially non-governmental—have struggled to resolve a number of ethnopolitical conflicts with consequences that have varied from success to exacerbating the conflict, but it appears that some of them are becoming more successful.

Globalization has stimulated ethnopolitical mobilization and probably terrorism as tools in ethnopolitical conflict, but it has also strengthened international norms of democratization, human rights, and non-discrimination. International norms now favour ethnopolitical cooperation, institutionalized competition, and the peaceful resolution of ethnopolitical conflicts to a greater extent than ever before. Economic globalization has strengthened national identities in the developing world, while also weakening the capacity of most developing states to carry out nationalist policies that challenge multinational corporations or international financial institutions. Globalization of communications has provided new tools for constructing ethnopolitical groups as well as nations. But, as Billig (1995: 128–43) argues, global culture cannot serve as the primary basis of resistance to economic globalization because it is less banal than those of the developed nations, which support such globalization.

## Key points

- Ethnopolitical morphology takes a variety of forms in the countries of the developing world ranging from highly multi-ethnic to deeply divided and homogeneous.

- Interaction among ethnopolitical groups and between them and states involves a mixture of cooperation, competition, and conflict.

- Cooperative interactions are most easily achieved in multi-ethnic societies that have small group advantages and disadvantages, democracy based on relatively institutionalized multi-ethnic parties, a historical pattern of non-violent ethnopolitical mobilization and minimal repression of it, and international influences that support 'managed heterogeneity' rather than one side of ethnopolitical conflicts.

- Cooperation is possible when some of these conditions are absent.

# The state and nation-building in the developing world

Nationalism was relatively weak in most developing states at independence, and was essentially absent in those that lacked meaningful nationalist movements and won their independence through a combination of the spillover effect of nationalist movements in neighbouring countries and the colonial powers' desire to extricate themselves from their colonies. 'The initial "nation-building" ethos [in Africa] proposed to resolve the ethnic question by confining it to the private realm. Across the continent, ethnic categories were removed from census exercises and "tribal associations" were proscribed' (Young 2001: 174). Civic nationalism was asserted ideologically in spite of its empirical weakness. But authoritarian 'banishment of ethnicity from political assertion merely drove it underground' (Young 2001: 176), while rulers continued to make ethnopolitical calculations in appointments to high political positions and the placement of development projects. Many essentially similar histories of failed efforts to extinguish ethnopolitical identities and movements and either create civic nationalism by fiat or assimilate minorities into the core ethnonational identity by force are found in other regions of the developing world. Forced assimilation to ethnonationalism has had the more severe consequences; in deeply divided societies with long histories of ethnopolitical mobilization, especially those characterized by great group differences and external material and political support for one side or the other, it has usually led to extremely violent conflict.

Due in part to the desire to reduce the negative effects of economic globalization and the support received from international norms and the globalization of communications, there has been a shift in some developing states from these unsuccessful policies of trying to impose civic nationalism by fiat or majority ethnonational identities by force to accepting multi-ethnic national identities as a viable compromise. This shift has been easier in multi-ethnic societies than in societies with a single dominant group or deeply divided societies, but multi-ethnic national identities are potentially viable in all of these societies (Snyder 2000: 33). They tend to make state and nation mutually reinforcing; 'the persistence of states, however challenged or changed by globalization they may be, offers a partial explanation for the continuation of nationhood as a salient form of belonging' (Croucher 2003: 14). Immigration compels states to clarify and reinforce national boundaries; responses to terrorism have the same effect. 'Nationhood, then, continues to be a functional, familiar, and legitimate mechanism for belonging' (Croucher 2003: 16). The aspirations of stateless peoples to national states prove its value.

Similarly, Smith (1995: 154) argues that 'Only nationalism can secure the consent of the governed to the territorial units to which they have been assigned, through a sense of collective identification with historic culture-communities in their "homelands". As long as any global order is based on a balance of competing states, so long will the principle of nationality provide the only widely acceptable legitimation and focus of popular mobilization.' He cites the rarity of defections from, and the frequency of self-sacrifice for, nationalism as evidence in support of this claim. Although Smith exaggerates the significance of long-established traditions for national identities, as well as the differences between national and other identities, he is right about the functionality of nationalism in the contemporary world. He does not recognize, however, that this is a multi-ethnic nationalism with civic overtones in the vast majority of countries of the developing world that are not homogeneous.

Gurr (2000: 195–211, 275–7) presents data, summarized in Box 5.2, to show that the number and severity of ethnopolitical conflicts have declined since the end of the cold war, reversing the upward trend of the preceding three decades. He attributes this change to the emergence of a 'regime of managed ethnic heterogeneity, shorthand for a bundle of conflict-mitigating doctrines and practices' (2000: 277–8). This regime has both domestic components—essentially those described above as promoting ethnopolitical cooperation—and international components—international norms and changes in the behaviour of outside states and transnational organizations reflecting decreased self-interest and increased competence. It fosters multi-ethnic nationalism. But Gurr (2000: 223–60) also acknowledges that some ethnopolitical groups are still at risk of being involved in future violent conflicts because they maintain the interaction patterns with other groups and states that have led to violent conflict in the past. The United States, an important player in this international regime, has moved back to self-interest since Gurr wrote. It is far too soon to declare the demise of ethnopolitical conflict, exclusionary ethnonationalism, or their exacerbation through foreign intervention.

> ## Box 5.2 Gurr on the post-cold war decline in ethnopolitical conflict
>
> A global shift from ethnic warfare to the politics of accommodation is amply documented in previous chapters. In the late 1990s the most common political strategy among the 275 ethnopolitical groups surveyed in the Minorities at Risk study was not rebellion; it was symbolic and organizational politics. Equally important, the number of groups using armed violence has been declining after decades of increase. The eruption of ethnic warfare that seized observers' attention in the early 1990s was actually the culmination of a long-term general trend of increasing communal-based protest and rebellion that began in the 1950s and peaked immediately after the end of the cold war.
>
> (Gurr 2000: 275–6).

## Key points

- Many states of the developing world have attempted to suppress ethnopolitical identities and conflicts by declaring civic nationalism by fiat or assimilating minorities into their core ethnonational identity by force, but more are now accepting multi-ethnic national identities as a viable compromise.

- National identities in the developing world, usually based on existing states, continue to be viable in the era of globalization, and offer a basis for resisting the negative effects of economic globalization.

- The number and severity of ethnopolitical conflicts have declined since the end of the cold war because of the emergence of a 'regime of managed ethnic heterogeneity', but some violent conflicts persist.

# Conclusion

In conclusion, we can briefly summarize the major themes of this chapter. Ethnopolitical and national identities are different, although both are socially constructed and thus change over time. The pattern of ethnopolitical identities (the ethnopolitical morphology) within countries involves the number and relative size of groups, their geographic concentration and degree of cultural differences, and varies from deeply divided to highly multi-ethnic. National identities are civic, multi-ethnic, or ethnonational. Collective action by ethnopolitical groups and cooperative, competitive, and conflictual interactions among them and with states are influenced by the interaction of ethnopolitical morphology, group advantages and disadvantages, political organizations and institutional rules, mobilization and state response histories, and international influences. Cooperative interactions are most easily achieved in multi-ethnic societies that have small group advantages and disadvantages, democracy based on relatively institutionalized multi-ethnic parties, a historical pattern of non-violent ethnopolitical mobilization and minimal repression of it, and international influences that support 'managed heterogeneity' rather than one side of ethnopolitical conflicts. These interactions, in turn, tend to promote nation-building through multi-ethnic nationalism. There is evidence of a shift in this direction in some countries of the developing world, but conflictual interactions and failures of nation-building still occur all too frequently.

## QUESTIONS

**1** If one accepts that ethnopolitical and national identities are constructed and thus change, how rapidly do they change?

**2** Are multi-ethnic and civic national identities really different?

**3** Why is it so difficult to specify the number of ethnopolitical groups and nations in the developing world?

**4** Can democracy be effective in deeply divided societies in the developing world?

**5** Is it possible for groups to cooperate when some have great advantages and others have great disadvantages if other factors that favour cooperation are present?

**6** If the amount of violent ethnopolitical conflict has declined in the developing world as a whole, why is such conflict still so strong in some countries?

## GUIDE TO FURTHER READING

Eriksen, T. H., *Ethnicity and Nationalism: Anthropological Perspectives* (London: Pluto Press, 1993). Presents an anthropological perspective on ethnicity, identity, ethnic relations, nationalism, and relations between states and ethnic minorities.

Fearon, J. D., 'Ethnic Structure and Cultural Diversity around the World: A Cross-National Data Set on Ethnic Groups', *Journal of Economic Growth*, 8 (2003): 191–218. Describes a global data set under construction on ethnic and linguistic/cultural groups and compares it to other data sets; highlights the difficulties encountered in specifying ethnic groups cross-nationally.

Gurr, T. R., *Minorities at Risk: A Global View of Ethnopolitical Conflicts* (Washington: United States Institute of Peace Press, 1993). The first book based on the Minorities at Risk project. It identifies communal groups at risk and analyses forms of risk, group grievances, group mobilization, group protest and rebellion, and the resolution of group conflicts; it includes chapters on the Middle East and Africa.

Gurr, T. R., *Peoples Versus States: Minorities at Risk in the New Century* (Washington: United States Institute of Peace Press, 2000), is the second book from the same project. It analyses the same topics as its predecessor plus the role of democracy and the risk of future ethnic violence; it includes a number of illustrative sketches from the developing world.

Horowitz, D. L., *Ethnic Groups in Conflict* (Berkeley: University of California Press, 1985): presents a definition of ethnicity and a theory of ethnic conflict among unranked groups derived primarily from social psychology; discusses the roles of political parties and the military in ethnic conflict and strategies for its resolution; emphasizes deeply divided societies in South-East and South Asia, Africa, and the Caribbean.

Hutchinson, J., and Smith, A. D. (eds.), *Nationalism* (Oxford: Oxford University Press, 1994), a very comprehensive reader that includes selections from classic works on the definition of nationalism, theories of nationalism, nationalism in the developing world, and the effects of trends in the international system on nationalism.

Scarritt, J. R., and Mozaffar, S., 'The Specification of Ethnic Cleavages and Ethnopolitical Groups for the Analysis of Democratic Competition in Contemporary Africa', *Nationalism and Ethnic Politics*, 8/1 (Spring 1999): 82–117. Lists African ethnopolitical groups that are relevant for electoral politics and describes the methodology developed to specify them.

Young, C., *The Politics of Cultural Pluralism* (Madison: University of Wisconsin Press, 1976). Discusses cultural pluralism, identities, the state, nationalism, and cultural mobilization in Africa, the Arab world, Asia, and Latin America; includes comparative case studies from these regions.

## WEB LINKS

**webhost.bridgew.edu/smozaffar**   The website for the Scarritt/Mozaffar data set on African ethnopolitical group fragmentation and concentration.

**www.minoritiesatrisk.com**   The website of Minorities at Risk project, covering 285 politically active ethnic groups coded on approximately 1,000 variables. Qualitative assessments of every group's risk are included.

 **COMPANION WEB SITE**

For additional material and resources, see the companion web site at:
**www.oup.com/uk/booksites/politics/**

# Religion

*Jeff Haynes*

## OVERVIEW

Recent decades have seen widespread involvement of religion in politics, especially in parts of the developing world. This chapter, examining the relationship between religion and politics, is structured as follows. First, the concept of religion is defined and its contemporary political and social salience in many developing countries is emphasized. Second, the chapter examines the notion of religious fundamentalism, not least because it is often associated with religious competition and conflict. Third, a survey of extant religious competition and conflict in the developing world is presented, with brief examples drawn from Christianity, Islam, Hinduism, and Buddhism. Fourth, the chapter considers the extent to which, after 'September 11', the world has changed in terms of the political salience of religion, by examining the importance of both domestic and external factors in conflicts characterized by religious concerns in the developing world.

# Introduction

Open a 'quality'—that is, a 'broadsheet'—newspaper on almost any day of the week and turn to the foreign news pages. You might be struck by the number of news items with religious and political dimensions (**religio-politics**). For example, a recurring theme is widespread Islamic militancy or 'fundamentalism', particularly in the Arab Middle East. It sometimes seems that the entire region is polarized between Jews and Muslims—both over the status of holy sites claimed by the two sides and the political and economic position of the mostly Muslim Palestinians.

However, it is not only international relations that are informed by Islamic militancy. For example, Algeria has endured a decade of civil war between Islamic 'fundamentalist' (or, as I prefer, for reasons to be noted later, Islamist) rebels and the state. The roots of this conflict go back to a contested election in the early 1990s and, more generally, highlight the often problematic political relationship between religious and secular actors in the Middle East. In December 1991 Algeria held legislative elections which most independent observers characterized as amongst the freest ever held in the Middle East. The following January, however, Algeria's armed forces seized power to prevent what was likely to be a decisive victory in the elections by an Islamist party, the Front Islamique du Salut (FIS). The assumption was that if the FIS achieved power it would then erode Algeria's newly refreshed democratic institutions. In London *The Economist* posed the question, 'What is the point of an experiment in democracy if the first people it delivers to power are intent on dismantling it?' (2 January 1992). The answer might well be: 'This is the popular will, it must be respected—whatever the outcome.' Instead, Algeria's military leaders imposed their preference. The FIS was summarily banned, thousands of its supporters were incarcerated, and, so far, around 120,000 Algerians have died in the subsequent civil war.

Islamists are also active in other countries. For example, in Africa, Nigeria is increasingly polarized politically between Muslim and Christian forces, fragmented Somalia may eventually have an Islamist government, while Sudan has also experienced a long-running civil war between Muslims and non-Muslims.

But it is not only Islamists who pursue political goals related to religion. In officially secular India, there has been growing militant Hinduism highlighted by, but not confined to, the Babri Masjid mosque incident at Ayodhya in 1992 that was instrumental in transforming the country's political landscape. This mosque, according to militant Hindus, was built on the birthplace of the Hindu god of war, Rama. As long ago as 1950, the mosque was closed down by the Indian government, for militant Hindus wanted to build a Hindu temple there. Since then, Hindu militants or 'fundamentalists', whose primary political organization is the Bharatiya Janata Party (BJP), have grown to political prominence. Between 1996 and 2004 the BJP has been the dominant party in three ruling coalitions.

On the other hand, religion can significantly contribute to political and social stability, for example, in the way that the Roman Catholic Church was a leading player in the turn to democracy in Latin America in the 1980s and 1990s.

## Key points

- The last three decades have seen widespread involvement of religion in politics, especially in many countries in the developing world.

- Several religious traditions have experienced increased political involvement.

- Religion and democracy do not always seem compatible, although religious actors have contributed to democratization.

# Religion and politics

Before proceeding, it is necessary to define 'religion'. In this chapter, religion has two analytically distinct, yet related meanings. In a *spiritual* sense, religion pertains in three ways to models of social and individual behaviour that help believers organize their everyday lives. First, it is to do with the idea of *transcendence*, that is, it relates to supernatural realities. Second, it is concerned with *sacredness*, that is, a system of language and practice that organizes the world in terms of what is deemed holy. Third, it refers to *ultimacy*: it relates people to the ultimate conditions of existence.

In another, *material*, sense, religious beliefs can motivate individuals and groups to act in pursuit of social or political goals. Very few—if any—religious groups have an *absolute* lack of concern for at least *some* social and political issues. Consequently, religion can be 'a mobiliser of masses, a controller of mass action . . . an excuse for repression [or] an ideological basis for dissent' (Calvert and Calvert 2001: 140). In many countries, religion remains an important source of basic value orientations; and this may have social and/or political connotations.

One final point concerns the relationship between religion and ethnicity. As Chapter 5 demonstrates, religion is a very common basis for ethnic identity. For instance in India, Sikh ethnic identity has been defined largely in terms of adherence to a common religion. It could seem then that ethnicity is the overarching concept and religious identification is one sub-type. However, there are situations where people sharing a single religion are divided by ethnicity, as for example in Pakistan where people share a common Islamic faith but are ethnically divided on the basis of region and language. Moreover appeals to religion often seek to transcend particular local or ethnic identities in the name of a supposedly universal ideal. It is wisest, therefore, to see ethnicity and religion as terms whose potential meaning and content overlap but remain distinct.

An American commentator, George Weigel, claims there is an **'unsecularization** of the world', that is, a global religious revitalization (quoted in Huntington 1993: 26). This is manifested in a global resurgence of religious ideas and social movements, not confined to one faith or only to poor, developing countries. This

unexpected development can be explained in various ways. No simple, clear-cut reason or single theoretical explanation covers all the cases. Yet the widespread emergence of religious actors with overtly social or political goals is often linked to **'modernization'**—that is, the prolonged period of historically unprecedented, diverse, massive change, characterized by urbanization, industrialization, and abrupt technological developments that people around the world have experienced in recent times. Modernization is said not only to have undermined traditional value systems but also to have allocated opportunities—both within and between countries—in highly unequal ways. This has led many people to feel both disorientated and troubled and, as a result, some at least (re)turn to religion for solace and comfort. In doing so, they seek a new or renewed sense of identity, something to give their lives greater meaning and purpose.

A second, although linked, explanation for apparent religious resurgence moves away from the specific impact of modernization to point to a more generalized 'atmosphere of crisis'. A key factor is said to be widespread popular disillusion with the abilities of secular state leaders to direct their socio-economic polities so that people generally benefit. Such disappointment can then feed into perceptions that these leaders hold power illegitimately—a sense bolstered when leaders resort to political oppression. Adding to the sense of crisis is widespread popular belief that society's traditional morals and values are being seriously undermined, not least by the corrosive effects of globalization, Westernization, and **secularization**—the reduction in influence or even withdrawal of religion from the public realm. These circumstances are said to provide a fertile milieu for many people's 'return' to religion.

This suggests that the influence of religion will not be seen 'only' in relation to personal and social issues. Commentators have additionally pointed to *political* effects of the 'return of religion' where, in many developing countries, highly politicized religious groups, institutions, and movements have emerged—or adopted a higher profile—in recent years. Such actors are found in many different faiths and sects and what they have in common is a desire to change domestic, and in some cases international, arrangements, so as to (re)place religion as a central societal and political influence. They adopt a variety of tactics to achieve their goals. Some confine themselves to the realm of legitimate political protest, seeking reform or change via the ballot box; others resort to violence and terror to pursue their objectives.

Other explanations are offered for what is widely seen as a global religious revival and revitalization, but some commentators suggest that, in the developing world, there is not a religious resurgence per se; rather, political religion is simply more visible—largely as a consequence of the global communications revolution. In other words, religion is not a novel political actor, so much as a stubbornly persistent one. For Smith (1990: 34), 'what has changed in the present situation . . . is mainly the growing awareness of [global manifestations of political religion] by the Western world, and the perception that they might be related to our interests'. This makes the recent trends just the latest manifestation of *cyclical* religious activity, made more highly visible (and to many alarming) by advances in communications technology and availability.

Such claims are bolstered by the fact that, in the developing world, various religious traditions—for example, Hinduism, Buddhism, and Islam—all experienced periods of pronounced political activity in the first half of the twentieth century in what were then mostly colonized countries. In the 1920s and the 1930s, religion was frequently used in the service of anti-colonial nationalism, and was a major facet of emerging national identity in opposition to alien rule (see Haynes 1996: 55–6). For example, in various Muslim countries, such as Algeria, Egypt, and Indonesia, Islamic consciousness was the defining ideology of nationalist movements. In 1947, immediately after the Second World War, Pakistan was founded as a Muslim state, religiously and culturally distinct from India, which was 80 per cent Hindu. A decade later, Buddhism was politically important, *inter alia*, in Burma, Sri Lanka, and Vietnam. Later, in the 1960s in Latin America, both **Christian democracy**—the application of Christian precepts to politics—and **liberation theology**—a radical ideology using Christianity as the basis of a demand for greater socio-economic justice for the poor—were politically consequential. More recently and in diverse countries including Iran, the United States, and Nicaragua, religion (re)appeared as an important political actor. Religious actors became skilled at using the media to spread their political messages (Tarrow 1998: 115). In sum, political religion is nearly always in opposition to the status quo; and in the developing world this has been the case since at least the early years of the twentieth century, a time of widespread external colonial control. Current manifestations of political religion can be located in this historical continuum and context, to stress *continuity* rather than *change*.

## Key points

- Religion has spiritual, material, and in some cases political, aspects.

- Religion played an important political role in many developing countries during the last years of colonialism.

- Patchy modernization and/or a more generalized 'atmosphere of crisis' are said to underpin religious resurgence.

- It is often claimed that there is a near-global religious revival but globalization may simply be rendering religion in politics more visible.

# Religious fundamentalism

Many religious actors with political goals are routinely labelled 'fundamentalists'. **Religious fundamentalism** has been described as a 'distinctively modern twentieth-century movement' albeit with 'historical antecedents' (Woodhead and Heelas 2000: 32). The label, 'religious fundamentalism' has been widely employed since the 1970s, especially by the mass media, to describe and account for numerous, apparently diverse, religious and political developments around the globe. The term's genesis is in a group of socially conservative evangelicals inside the mainstream Protestant denominations in the United States. There, in the early twentieth century, such people first applied the designation 'religious fundamentalist' to themselves. Now, however, as a generic term, it is widely applied to groups outside the corpus of Christianity, notably Hindu and Islamic entities.

What fundamentalist doctrines generally have in common is that their character and impact are located within a nexus of moral and social issues revolving in many cases around state–society interactions. In some cases, the initial defensiveness of beleaguered religious groups later developed into a political offensive that sought to alter the prevailing social and political realities of state–society relations. Religious fundamentalists often accused their rulers of performing inadequately and/or corruptly; with the exception of Buddhist and Hindu fundamentalists, they criticized contemporary developments in the light of religious texts, such as the Bible or the Koran.

The significance of this from a political perspective is that religious fundamentalism can, and often does, supply an already restive group with a ready-made manifesto for social change: fundamentalist activists use suitable religious texts both to challenge secular rulers and to propose a programme for radical political and social reform. Under these circumstances, it can be relatively easy for fundamentalist leaders to gain the support of people who feel particularly aggrieved that, in various important ways, society's development is not proceeding according to God's will and/or the community's interests.

Contemporary examples of religious fundamentalism are often said to be rooted in the failed promise and impact of modernization, such as apparently declining morals. To many fundamentalists the current era is one where God is in danger of being superseded by a gospel of technical progress accompanying sweeping socio-economic changes. The pace of change strongly challenges traditional habits, beliefs, and cultures. In an increasingly materialist world, individual worth often seems to be measured according to standards of wealth and status, while religion is ignored or belittled. This development is thought to lie behind the growth of religious militancy and to account in general terms for the recent rise of religious 'fundamentalism'.

But some argue that, in fact, religious 'fundamentalism' is an empty and therefore meaningless term, erroneously and casually employed 'by western liberals to refer to a broad spectrum of religious phenomena which have little in common except for the fact that they are alarming to liberals!' (Woodhead and Heelas 2000: 32). Critics contend that the range of so-called fundamentalist groups is so wide—for example, resurgent Islam in Iran and Latin American Pentecostalism—that the term has no meaning and, moreover, is insulting to many people described as 'fundamentalists'. Such groups actually differ markedly among themselves: some aspire to influence or even control the public and political arena; others actively work to disengage from social and political issues. As a consequence, Hallencreutz and Westerlund (1996: 4) argue the

broad use of the term has become increasingly irrelevant. In sum, viewed as a derogatory concept, tied to Western stereotypes and Christian presuppositions, the casual use of the term easily causes misunderstandings and prevents the understanding of the dynamics and characteristics of different religious groups with explicit *political* objectives (my emphasis).

In contrast, those accepting the analytical relevance of the term do so because they perceive contemporary movements of religious resurgence—albeit encompassing different religious traditions—as having features in common which denote a shared concern with 'fundamentalism'. In general, fundamentalist doctrines share the following: (*a*) a strong desire to return to what are believed to be a faith's fundamentals; (*b*) forceful rejection of Western-style secular modernity; (*c*) 'an oppositional minority group-identity maintained in an exclusivist and militant manner' (Woodhead and Heelas 2000: 32); (*d*) rejection of secularization, and a demand to retrieve the public realm as a place of moral and religious purity; and (*e*) perception that patriarchal and hierarchical ordering of relations between the sexes is both morally and religiously appropriate.

Drawing on data from a large variety of fundamentalist movements, Marty and Scott Appleby (1993: 3) define religious fundamentalism as a 'set of strategies, by which beleaguered believers attempt to preserve their distinctive identity as a people or group' in response to a real or imagined attack from those who, it appears, want to draw the religious believers into 'syncretistic, areligious, or irreligious cultural milieu[s]'. Such defensiveness may develop into a political offensive aiming to alter prevailing socio-political realities.

So far, then, it seems that what religious fundamentalists share is the fear that their religiously orientated way of life is under threat from unwelcome alien influences, especially secular-orientated governments. As a result, they often seek to reform society in accordance with what they believe are suitable religious tenets, to change laws, morality, social norms, and, if necessary, the polity. They may seek to create a traditionally orientated, less modern(ized) society, and are willing in some cases to fight governments if the latter's jurisdiction appears to be encompassing areas which the fundamentalists believe are integral to its realization—education, gender relations and employment, and social morality. Fundamentalists may also attack those they see as 'nominal' or 'backsliding' co-religionists and members of opposing religions.

Drawing on the example of contemporary Christian fundamentalists in the United States, many analysts who employ the term fundamentalism also suggest that it is only properly applicable to Christianity and other Abrahamic religions of the 'book': Islam and Judaism. This is because, like fundamentalist Christians, Muslim and Jewish fundamentalists take as their defining dogma what is believed to be the inerrancy of God's own words set out in holy books like the Bible. In other words, in these three religions, singular scriptural revelations are central to each set of fundamentalist dogma. The inference is that, because neither Hinduism nor Buddhism have central tenets of political, social, and moral import conveniently accessible in holy books, it is not logically possible for there to be Hindu or Buddhist fundamentalism. However, in recent years a popular 'fundamentalist' movement within Hinduism has emerged in pursuit of demonstrably political goals. Such a group is not defined by its absolutist insistence upon the veracity of God's revealed will, but instead by a desire to recapture elements of national identity that are perceived as being lost, either by dint of cultural dilution or mixing, or by perceived deviations from the religious philosophy and/or teaching (Ram-Prasad 1993: 288).

## Key points

- All major religious traditions have fundamentalist variants.
- Fundamentalist doctrines are concerned with moral, social, and sometimes political, issues.
- Fundamentalist concerns may supply an already restive group with a manifesto for social and political change.
- Fundamentalists fear their way of life is under threat from secular forces.

# Religious fundamentalism and politics in the developing world

This section considers four kinds of religious fundamentalism, most prominent in the developing world—Islamic, Christian, Buddhist, and Hindu—focusing on their main socio-political characteristics.

## Islamic fundamentalism

Like Christianity, Islam is by no means monolithic but has taken many different forms, one important distinction being between the 'Sunni' and Shia traditions. In 2004 clashes between these two communities in Iraq and Pakistan were only the latest tragic reminder of the endurance of these divisions. Both these main branches however have given rise to 'fundamentalist' movements.

A defining character of religious fundamentalism is that it is always socially but not necessarily politically conservative. Thus some Islamic fundamentalist ('Islamist') groups seek to overthrow the existing socio-economic and political order by various means, including violence or terrorism, incremental reform of existing political regimes, or winning elections through the mobilization of a political party. Islamists take as their defining dogma what are believed to be God's words written in their holy book, the Koran. In other words, singular scriptural revelations are central to Islamic fundamentalist beliefs.

Modern Islamic resurgence dates from the 1920–40 period, when growing numbers of countries in the Middle East were demanding—and in some cases receiving—national self-determination. The main point of contention was how far these predominantly Muslim states should employ the tenets of *sharia*—that is, Muslim religious—law in their legal systems. This example of a desire to Islamicize polities had its precedents in the Muslim world in anti-imperialist and anti-pagan movements (*jihads*), periodically erupting from the late nineteenth century, especially in parts of West Africa and East Asia (see Haynes 1993). In these regions, conflict between tradition and modernization and between Islam and Christianity was often acute.

In the early stages of Islam, over 1,300 years ago, religious critics of the status quo periodically emerged in opposition to what they perceived as unjust rule. Contemporary Islamists are only the most recent example of such a phenomenon, often characterizing themselves as the 'just' involved in a 'holy war' against the 'unjust'. This dichotomy between 'just' and 'unjust' in the promotion of social change parallels the tension in the West between 'state' and 'civil society': both juxtapose mutually exclusive concepts where a strengthening of one necessarily implies a weakening of the other. The implication is that the 'unjust' inhabit the state while the 'just' look in from the outside, aching to reform the corrupt political system. The Islamic 'just' strive to achieve their goal which is a form of direct democracy under the auspices of *sharia* law, in which the ruler uses his wisdom to settle disputes brought before him by his loyal subjects. The Islamic concept of *shura* (consultation) by no means necessarily implies popular sovereignty, which is with God alone; 'rather it is a means of obtaining unanimity from the community of believers, which allows for no legitimate minority position' (Dorr 1993: 151–2).

The goal of the 'just' is an Islam-based society. Currently, in many Muslim countries, Islamist groups believe themselves to be the appropriate vehicle to achieve this goal. For them, Western-style liberal democracy is fatally flawed and compromised, a concept relevant only to secular, Western(ized) societies which appear unacceptably decadent. As a young Algerian graduate of the Islamic Science Institute of Algiers averred in the early 1990s, 'The modern world is going through a major moral crisis which can be very confusing to young people. Just look at what is happening in Russia. Personally I have found many of the answers and solutions in Islam'(cited in Ibrahim 1992).

The global Muslim community, the *umma*, is a good example of a transnational civil society (the Roman Catholic Church, with its institutional support for democratization in the 1990s, is another), containing the seeds of both domination and dissent. Shared beliefs, relating especially to culture and identity link Muslims. For this reason it is unsurprising that international manifestations of Islamic resurgence appeared after the humbling defeat of Arab Muslims by Israeli Jews in the six-day war of June 1967. Since then a combination of poor government, growing unemployment, and generalized social crisis in the Muslim world has produced Islamist movements. When possible, as in the Persian Gulf, rulers have been content to live on the 'rents' accrued from their control of oil exports with little done to reduce unemployment and underemployment, develop more representative polities, or plan successfully for the future. In short, there has been a skewed modernization; urbanization and the creation of a centralized state proceeded at the same time as many people became increasingly dissatisfied with the way that their rulers rule.

## Christian fundamentalism

This section focuses on Christian fundamentalism in Nigeria because of its significance to the country's political and economic developments. Since the 1970s there have been growing signs of tension between Islamists and the state in Nigeria. This has paralleled increasing hostility between Muslim and Christian communities leading to the emergence of an organization representing fundamentalist Christians whose main purpose is to comment on both religious and political issues. The Pentecostal Fellowship of Nigeria (PFN) is an influential voice in the inter-denominational Christian Association of Nigeria that claims to represent the interests of the country's Christians at both federal and national levels. The PFN was formerly an avowedly apolitical organization. It re-evaluated its traditional stance of indifference to political issues in the mid-1980s because of its fear of creeping Islamicization. Some influential figures in the PFN, including Benson Idahosa, founder of the international Church of God Mission, have warned of religious war in Nigeria—if tensions between Muslims and Christians are not diminished.

Somewhat ironically, religious tensions were exacerbated in Northern Nigeria in the 1990s in part because of the aggressive proselytizing of missionaries of several of the fundamentalist churches, including Idahosa's, which led to some conversions in the predominantly Muslim north. In that region, where sociocultural norms make Islam an integral facet of many people's lives, conversion to Christianity was facilitated by a modern variant of the colonial missionaries' 'gospel of prosperity' argument. During colonial times, Christianity was seen to bring medicine, education, and wealth to the country, so it was quite sensible for those who wished to share these benefits to follow the Christian faith. 'Muslims in power know that they have nothing to offer the country,' claimed Idahosa (Elliot 1993), alluding to the three decades of 'Muslim rule' that saw living standards of most Nigerians plummet.

In Nigeria, the Christian fundamentalist churches consider themselves involved in a three-way conflict, not only with Muslims, but also with mainstream Christians. They accuse the latter of being apostates who have abandoned the fundamentals of the Christian faith, while their leaders have set themselves up as individuals whose power challenges that of God. In short, all people of whatever religious faith outside the community of Christian fundamentalists are beyond the pale of true believers and can only be saved from Hell if they convert.

The growth of fundamentalist churches in Nigeria has probably been encouraged by the country's deteriorating socio-economic conditions over the last twenty years (see Chapter 19a). The volatility of the religious environment mirrors the unpredictability of the political arena: the battle for power between various ethnic groups, and between civilian politicians and military figures, corresponds to the fight for 'theological space' between traditional and *arriviste* religions. Interlinked economic, social, and spiritual crises help to spread fears of the end of the world and an accompanying, increasingly desperate, striving for salvation. This combination of predicaments is good business for the plethora of emergent preachers who capitalize on fear and a common desire for order, stability, and community. Traditionally, politics, business, and religion have been the three areas of endeavour from which individuals may expect financial reward; politics in Nigeria has long been the domain of a homogeneous (northern-military) elite. Business success requires capital, contacts, and luck, all generally in short supply, while religious success may only require a charismatic personality with the ability to attract disciples and followers. The supporters, as a sign of their faith, are often willing to pay for the costs of running a church and the considerable expenses incurred by its leader.

With economic decline in the 1980s and 1990s and increasing social disorder, the hierarchies of the mainstream Christian churches conspicuously failed to speak up for ordinary people, or even to criticize the inept political system and the accompanying corruption in public life. The fundamentalist churches offered, in contrast, a sense of solidarity between co-religionists, a code of behaviour, moral values, and, above all, a sense of stability in a world profoundly disrupted. The Christian revival involved a movement away from the crassly materialist ways of the established churches and an attempt to reconstruct a new type of socially responsive organization. It stressed a fundamentalist return to the tenets of the Bible, calling on Christians to experience spiritual rebirth.

In sum, the growth of fundamentalist Christian communities in Nigeria is linked to the country's socio-economic deterioration that, in turn, follows the fortunes of the oil industry. Like fundamentalist churches elsewhere in Africa, those in Nigeria have offered their followers the possibility of joining a new Christian community—where solidarity between individuals is a function of religious belief. At the same time Nigeria's Christian fundamentalists' political concerns have been forged by the fear of a growth in Islamist groups in the country.

## Hindu fundamentalism

The roots of Hindu fundamentalism are said to lie both in the desire of some Hindu nationalists in India to privilege their culture over others and in the perception that 'Hindu' India is surrounded and threatened by Islamic resurgence—notably in

Pakistan (where the Kashmir issue focuses such concerns), Iran, and Afghanistan. We should note, however, that Hindu nationalism is not a new development. Mahatma Gandhi, the leading Indian nationalist and a committed Hindu, was assassinated by a Hindu extremist in 1948 for the 'crime' of appearing to condone the creation of a new homeland—Pakistan—for India's Muslims. More recently, Prime Minister Indira Gandhi played to such sentiments in the early 1980s, in her confrontation with Sikh militants. From that time also simmering Hindu fundamentalist suspicion of India's largest religious minority—the Muslims, comprising about 11 per cent of the population, more than 100 million people—has been reflected and fostered by a growing 'family' (parivar) of organizations embodying the Hindu chauvinist doctrine of *Hindutva*, and reached a kind of apotheosis in the violent destruction in 1992 of a historic mosque at Ayodhya in Uttar Pradesh. Since then we have seen that the BJP, the political party that has grown out of this movement, has become an increasingly important political player; by 2004 it had been leading the ruling NDA (National Democratic Alliance) coalition government for six years, though it was ousted from power in that year's General Election.

## Buddhist fundamentalism

In Thailand, a neo-Buddhist movement, Santi Asoke, made a unilateral declaration of independence from the orthodox Thai *sangha* (body of monks) in 1975. One of its most prominent followers, a former governor of Bangkok, Major-General Chamlong Srimaung, formed a political party in the late 1980s, called Palang Tham (*tham* means both 'moral' and 'dhamma' in the teachings of Buddhism). Some have argued that Palang Tham's ultimate goal is the creation of a radical Buddhist state in Thailand. The ambition would be to create a corruption-free political environment with the role of the military downplayed and with state ideology rooted in Buddhist ideals and teaching. However, despite some initial political success, for example, winning fourteen parliamentary seats in the 1988 elections, Palang Tham's Buddhist fundamentalist message generally failed to influence Thais.

## Key points

- Many Islamic fundamentalists in the developing world seek to change political arrangements by a variety of methods.
- Christian fundamentalists in Nigeria fear Islamicization.
- Hindu fundamentalists feel under threat from Muslims, both within India and without.
- Buddhist fundamentalist groups have failed to make much political headway.

# Religion and the state

These examples of religious fundamentalisms in the developing world point more generally to the importance of **state–church relations**, that is, the interactions in a country between the state and the leading religious organization(s). A major difficulty in trying to survey existing church–state relations in the developing world is that the very concept of *church* reflects a somewhat parochial Anglo-American standpoint with most relevance to Western Christian traditions. The concept derives primarily from the context of British **establishmentarianism**—where one church alone is legally recognized as the established church. Thus when we think of church–state relations we tend to assume a single relationship between two clearly distinct, unitary and solidly but separately institutionalized entities. In this implicit model, there is but *one* state and *one* church; and the entities' jurisdictional boundaries need to be carefully delineated. Both separation and pluralism must be safeguarded, because, it is assumed, the leading church—like the state—will seek institutionalized dominance over rival organizations. For its part, the state is expected to respect individual rights, even though it is assumed to be inherently disposed towards aggrandisement at the expense of citizens' personal liberty.

The traditional European-centred perspective is that both church and state have a fair degree of power in relation to each other. Yet, for instance, in Eastern Europe (late 1940s–late 1980s) communist states presided over—and rigorously enforced—an institutional interpenetration of political-administrative and religio-ideological orders. Even in Western Europe the church's position has declined in most countries, while the political saliency of church–state issues has declined in importance as secularization— that is, the gradual diminution of the influence of religion on public affairs—has penetrated the social fabric.

Extending the question of church–state relations to non-Christian contexts necessitates some preliminary conceptual clarifications—not least because the very idea of a prevailing state–church dichotomy is culture-bound. *Church* is a Christian institution, while the modern understanding of *state* is deeply rooted in the post-Reformation European political experience. Overloaded with Western cultural history, these two concepts cannot easily be translated into non-Christian terminologies. Some religions— for example, Hinduism—have no ecclesiastical structure at all. Consequently, there *cannot* be a clerical challenge to India's secular state comparable to that of Buddhist monks in parts of South-East Asia or of *mullahs* in Iran. However, political parties and movements energized by religious notions—such as Hinduism and Sikhism—have great political importance in contemporary India. Within the developing world, only in Latin America is it pertinent to speak of church–state relations along the lines of the European model. This is because of the historical dominance in the region of the Roman Catholic Church and the creation of European-style states in the early nineteenth century.

The differences between Christian conceptions of state and church and those of other world religions are well illustrated by reference to Islam. In the Muslim tradition, mosque is not church. The closest Islamic approximation to 'state'—*dawla*—means, conceptually, either a ruler's dynasty or his administration (only with the specific proviso of *church* as generic concept for *moral community, priest* for *custodians of the sacred law*, and *state* for *political community*, is it appropriate to use these concepts in Islamic and other non-Christian contexts). On the theological level, the command–obedience nexus that constitutes the Islamic definition of authority is not demarcated by conceptual categories of religion and politics. Life as a physical reality is an expression of divine will and authority (*qudrah'*). There is no validity in separating the matters of piety from those of the polity; both are divinely ordained. Yet, although both religious and political authorities are legitimated Islamically, they invariably constitute two independent social institutions. They do, however, regularly interact with each other. In sum, there is a variety of church–state relations in the contemporary world (see Box 6.1). Note, however, that the typology is not exhaustive but instead identifies common arrangements.

In the *confessional* church–state relationship, ecclesiastical authority is pre-eminent over secular power. A dominant religion—Islam in the countries in the

---

### Box 6.1 **A typology of church–state relations**

| Confessional | 'Generally religious' | Established faith | Liberal secular | Marxist secular |
|---|---|---|---|---|
| Iran, Saudi Arabia, Sudan, Afghanistan (under the Taliban) | Indonesia, USA | England, Denmark, Norway | Netherlands, Turkey, India, Ghana | China, Albania (until 1991), Russia (until 1991), North Korea |

box—seeks to shape the world according to its leadership's interpretations of God's plan for humankind. However, confessional states are rare in the early twenty-first century. One of the most consistent effects of secularization is to separate religious and secular power almost—but not quite—regardless of the religion or type of political system. However, as events in Saudi Arabia after the country's creation in 1932, in Iran since the 1978–9 Islamic revolution, and in Sudan and Afghanistan from the 1980s indicate, several Muslim countries have sought to build confessional polities.

Because of Islam's pivotal role, the overthrow of the Shah of Iran in 1979 was one of the most spectacular political upheavals of recent times. The outcome of the revolutionary process was a clerical, authoritarian regime. The Shah's regime was not a shaky monarchy but a powerful centralized autocratic state possessing a strong and feared security service (SAVAK) and an apparently loyal and cohesive officer corps. Unlike earlier revolutions in other Muslim countries, such as Egypt, Iraq, Syria, and Libya, Iran's was not a secular, leftist revolution from above, but one with massive popular support and participation. The forces that overthrew the Shah came from all urban social classes, Iran's different nationalities and ideologically varying political parties and movements. Nevertheless an Islamic Republic was eventually declared. In these events the *ulama* or Muslim clerics, who adhere like the bulk of Iran's Muslims to the Shia tradition, played a central role. Organized in and by the Islamic Republican Party, they came to power, established an Islamic constitution and dominated the post-revolutionary institutions.

The Iranian revolution was internationally significant in a number of ways. It was the first since the anti-monarchist, anti-confessional French Revolution of 1789 in which the dominant ideology, forms of organization, leading personnel, and proclaimed goals were all religious in appearance and inspiration. The guide for the post-revolution Iranian state was the tenets of the Muslim holy book, the Koran, and the Sunnah (the traditions of the Prophet Muhammad, comprising what he said, did, and approved of). While economic and political factors played a major part in the growth of the anti-Shah movement, the leadership of that movement (the clerics) saw the revolution's goals primarily in terms

of building an Islamic state that rejected Western materialism and political ideas. This in turn came to determine poor relations with the West.

The radicals within Iran's ruling post-revolution elite began to lose ground following the death of Ayatollah Khomeini, the revolution's charismatic leader, in June 1989, just months after the end of the bloody Iran–Iraq war (1980–8). As it became clear that Iran was in dire need of foreign investment and technology, the then state president, Hashemi Rafsanjani, and his political allies seemed to gain ascendancy. The lesson was that even a successful Islamic revolution could not succeed in splendid isolation. Iranians, like people everywhere, hoped for improving living standards. They were not content with increased Islamicization of state and society, which many perceived as little more than political and social repression behind a religious façade. More recently, however, the reformist President Khatami, in office since 1997, has found himself caught between the demands of those wanting social and political liberalization—headed by radical students—and the conservatives, led by the *mullahs*.

Alongside the confessional states such as Iran there are the 'generally religious' states, like the USA and Indonesia. They are guided by religious beliefs in general, but are not tied to any specific religious tradition. Both have a belief in God as one of the bases on which the nation should be built. In Indonesia, under General Suharto (1965–98), such a belief formed one of the five pillars of the state ideology, *Pancasila*. This position is very similar to the notion of 'civil religion' in the USA. However, whereas the 'generally religious' policy of religion in Indonesia is an official policy, civil religion in the USA is not formally recognized.

Then there are countries that have an officially established faith but are also socially highly secular, of which the Scandinavian countries and England are examples. Over time the voices of the established churches in public policy issues have become increasing marginal. However, in England at least, the Anglican Church has recently begun once again to try to add its voice to demands on social policy issues.

Next, and frequently encountered in the modern era, is the *liberal secular* model that encapsulates the notion of secular power holding sway over religion, with distance, detachment, and separation between church and state. Here, the state strives to use religion for its own ends, to 'legitimate political rule and to sanctify economic oppression and the given system' of social stratification (Casanova 1994: 49). Secularization policies are widely pursued as a means of national integration in post-colonial multi-religious states, like India. It is worth noting, however, that the concept of secularism is not necessarily straightforward. For example, Hindu critics of India's religiously 'neutral' Constitution contend that it is not neutral but rather privileges India's religious minorities, including Muslims, Sikhs, and Christians. In the liberal-secular model, no religion is given official predominance. In fact, in vigorously modernizing countries such as India and post-Ottoman Turkey, state policies of modernization were expected to lead—inevitably—to a high degree of secularization; hence, their constitutions are neutral towards religion. But things turned out differently: in recent years, democratization and secularization have worked at cross purposes. Increasing participation in the political arena has drawn in new social forces in India, religious Hindus, Sikhs, and Muslims—who, in demanding greater formal recognition of their religions by the state, have been responsible for making religion a central issue in contemporary politics. In Turkey, the accession to power of the Islamist Welfare Party (*Refah Partisi*) in 1996—claiming to be the party of the poor and the alienated—suggests that even when secularization is pursued with great determination over a long period—in Turkey's case for eighty years—there is still no certainty that, for important constituencies, the socio-political appeal of religion will wither.

Finally, there is the category of *Marxist secular* states. Before the overthrow of communism in 1989–90, Eastern Europe contained anti-religious polities where religion was stifled by the state. Most Marxist regimes were less hardline than Enver Hoxha's Albania—where religion was 'abolished'—but religion was typically permitted to exist only as the private concern of the individual. This constituted a kind of promise that the authorities would respect the people's religious faith and practice—as long as it remained behind closed doors. Skeletal religious organizations were, however, allowed to exist—but only so the state could use them for purposes of social control. They were reduced to liturgical institutions, with no other task than the holding of divine services. Numbers of permitted places of worship were greatly reduced.

Paradoxically, however, even the most strident and prolonged Marxist anti-religion campaigns failed to secularize societies. The pivotal role of the Christian churches in the democratic openings in Eastern Europe and non-Marxist Latin America in the 1980s and 1990s, and the contemporary revival of Islam in some of the formerly communist Central Asian countries, indicate that popular religiosity has retained immense social importance. But we should not take it for granted that Marxist, 'anti-religion' states are only of historical interest. For example, the government of China—home to more than a billion people—launched a fierce campaign in the mid-1990s to 'teach atheism to Tibetan Buddhists'. This was necessary, the Chinese government argued, to enable Tibetans to 'break free of the bewitchment' of religion.

In sum, none of the various models of church–state relations has been permanently able to resolve the tension between religion and the secular world. The chief manifestation of this tension in recent times is the desire of many religious organizations not to allow the state to sideline them as—almost everywhere—increasingly secularized states seek to intervene ever deeper into social life.

## Key points

- 'Church' is a concept that derives from Christianity and may have little relevance in other religious settings.

- There are various relationships between 'church' and state in the developing world.

- States often seek to secularize their societies, to the dismay of religious actors.

- No model of 'church'–state relations has been permanently able to resolve tensions between the religious and the secular world.

# Religion in international politics after 'September 11'

So far, we have been concerned primarily with the domestic interaction of religion and politics within developing countries. However, no survey of the issue can legitimately ignore the impact of the terrorist events of 11 September 2001 ('9/11') on issues of religion and politics in general and those of the Muslim world and the West, in particular.

Prior to the eighteenth century and the formation and development of the international state system, religion was the key ideology that stimulated conflict between social groups. However, following the Peace of Westphalia in 1648 and the consequent development of centralized states, religion took a back seat as an organizing ideology at the international level. As already noted, it was not until the Iranian revolution of 1978–9 that religion resumed a significant political role. Ten years later in 1989, the cold war came to an end. Since then, international politics has been characterized by four significant changes:

- Change from a bipolar (USA, Soviet Union) to an arguably unipolar (USA) structure of power.
- Culture replacing ideology as a chief source of identity, leading to changes in extant affiliations and antagonisms in world affairs.
- Some commentators argue that there is a religious resurgence in countries around the world, excepting Western Europe.
- The nature of international conflict has changed, with fewer inter-state wars. Of the 110 major conflicts during the 1990s—that is, those involving more than 1,000 fatalities each—only seven were interstate wars, while 103 were civil wars. Of the latter, over 70 per cent are classified as communal wars: that is, wars among ethnic and other national groups, with religion very often playing an important part.

Western Europe, including Britain, is characterized by both religious privatization and secularization. In contrast, over half of all US citizens claim to attend regular religious, mostly Christian, services. Moreover, eight words are juxtaposed—'In God We Trust' and the 'United States of America'—on all US currency, both coins and notes.

The issue of what role religion should play there was sharpened by the arguments of the US academic, Samuel Huntington (1993; revised and expanded version, 1996a), in his now (in)famous 'clash of civilizations' thesis. Huntington's key argument is that following the end of the cold war, future international conflicts are increasingly likely to be along cultural fault lines. In his view, this would replace the forty years of competition between two secular ideologies: liberal democracy/capitalism and communism. Now, he suggests, new rivalries are most important, notably between the (Christian) 'West' and the (mostly Muslim, mostly Arab) 'East'. In short, the core of Huntington's argument is that in the post-cold war era the 'Christian', democratic West is likely to find itself in conflict with radical Islam ('Islamic fundamentalism'), a global anti-Western political movement said to be aiming for fundamental changes to the political order. Another influential US commentator, Francis Fukuyama (1992: 236), argued that 'Islamic fundamentalism' is the antithesis of Western liberalism, with 'more than superficial resemblance to European fascism'.

Critics of such arguments argue that although many radical Islamist movements and political parties would not classify themselves as liberal democratic, we cannot assume this necessarily implies that such actors are willing to engage in violent conduct, including terrorism, to pursue their aims. The 'September 11' atrocities in the USA—as well as the Bali and Kenya terrorist incidents that followed—appear to have been carried out by a shadowy transnational terrorist group—al-Qaeda. However, it is by no means clear that most 'ordinary' Muslim men and women support either its goals or the violent means it employs.

It is also important to see the struggle in the Islamic world of groups like al-Qaeda as directed against their own rulers as well as the West, especially the USA. Since the beginning of Islam in the seventh century,

Muslim critics of the status quo have periodically emerged to oppose what they perceive as unjust rule. Current Islamists, including, arguably, bin Laden and al-Qaeda, are contemporary examples, who portray themselves as the 'just' involved in struggle against 'unjust', 'anti-religious' rulers and their allies. Bin Laden's key goal is said to be the creation of a pan-Islamic state to revive the glories of the Ottoman califate that collapsed after the First World War. Bin Laden and his followers certainly oppose Western interpretations of democracy, where sovereignty resides with the people, because it is seen as a system that negates God's own sovereignty. Finally, it is suggested that Western support for so-called 'un-Islamic' rulers in, for example, Algeria and Saudi Arabia, led some radical Islamist groups to target the West. For example, French support for the military junta in Algeria is said to be why Islamist terrorists detonated bombs on the streets of Paris in the mid-1990s. Similarly, US support for Saudi Arabia's allegedly unpopular rulers is said to be part of the reason why America was targeted on 'September 11'.

But it would be wrong to see the rise of Islamist groups—now found throughout the Arab countries of North Africa and the Middle East—as the result of bin Laden's influence. Instead, we might look to the failure of state-sponsored modernization as a key explanation. The contemporary Islamist resurgence is argued to be a vehicle for popular disillusion in the Muslim world, as many governments have failed to achieve what they promised—both developmentally and politically—since independence from colonial rule. In addition, existing communitarian structures have been confronted by state power that apparently seeks to destroy and replace them with the idea of a national (increasingly secularized) citizenry. A common response has been the rise of popular (as opposed to state-controlled) Islamist groups to become in many places a major vehicle of popular political aspirations. Thus the widespread Islamic awakening can be seen in relation to its *domestic* capacity to oppose what are perceived as oppressive states: 'It is primarily in civil society that one sees Islam at work' (Coulon 1983: 49). The point is that this domestic response does not necessarily translate into a wider Muslim threat to *global* order.

## Key points

- Religion now plays a central role in international politics.
- Most Islamic critics of the status quo see their own governments as the main cause of political and developmental failures.
- 'September 11' is sometimes said to provide evidence of an emerging 'civilizational' clash between Christianity and Islam, but most Muslims were probably appalled by these and related terrorist acts.

# Conclusion

The last thirty years have seen much involvement of religion in politics. A serious new threat to world order, some claim, now emanates from Islamic 'fundamentalism', with 'September 11' as the key example. However, such fears do not appear to have very strong foundations. In the case of Islamic 'fundamentalism' (Islamism), various domestically orientated groups threaten the incumbency of their own rulers rather than the security of the global order. In short, there is very little—if anything—in the spectre of an 'Islamic' threat per se to global order.

Globally, the recent political impact of religion falls into two—not necessarily mutually exclusive—categories. First, if the mass of the people are not especially religious—as in many Western countries—then religious actors tend to be politically marginal. However, in many developing countries, most people are already religious believers. Unsuccessful attempts by many political leaders to modernize their countries have often led to responses from various religious actors. Often, religion serves to focus and coordinate opposition, especially—but not exclusively—that of the poor and ethnic minorities. Religion is often well placed to benefit from a societal backlash against the perceived malign effects of modernization. In particular, various religious fundamentalist leaders have sought support from ordinary people by addressing certain crucial issues. These include: the perceived decline in public and private morality and the insecurities of life, the result of an undependable market where, it is argued, greed and luck appear as effective as work and rational choice.

And what of the future? If the issues and concerns that have helped stimulate what some see as 'a return to religion'—including, socio-political and economic upheavals, patchy modernization, increasing encroachment of the state upon religion's terrain—continue (and there is no reason to suppose they will not), then it seems highly likely that religion's political role will continue to be significant in many parts of the developing world. This will partly reflect the onward march of secularization in many countries and regions, linked to the spread of globalization—which no doubt will be resisted by religious leaders and their followers, with varying degrees of success. This suggests that a period of religious reinterpretation will follow—spurred by changes both within individual countries and at the global level. For this reason it would be very unwise to neglect religion in analyses of contemporary politics in the developing world.

## QUESTIONS

**1**  Why is there said to be a global religious resurgence?

**2**  Why do religious fundamentalists want fundamental social, moral, and often political changes?

**3**  Why are religio-political actors found in so many parts of the developing world?

**4**  In what ways, if at all, did 'September 11' change the world?

**5**  To what extent is secularization undermining the power of religion?

**6**  In what ways is globalization contributing to the spread of religio-political doctrines and actors?

## GUIDE TO FURTHER READING

Beyer, P., *Religion and Globalization* (London: Sage, 1994). Surveys transborder religious interactions in the context of globalization.

Haynes, J., *Religion in Global Politics* (Harlow: Longman, 1998). A survey of religio-political developments around the world.

Huntington, S. P., *The Clash of Civilizations* (New York: Simon and Schuster, 1996). Articulates the thesis that the world is poised to enter an era of 'civilizational clashes'.

Mainuddin, R. (ed.), *Religion and Politics in the Developing World: Explosive Interactions* (Aldershot: Ashgate, 2002). Examines a number of key religio-political interactions in the developing world.

Volpi, F., *Islam and Democracy. The Failure of Dialogue in Algeria* (London: Pluto, 2003). A well-researched account of the failure of religious and political actors to arrive at a *modus vivendi*.

Westerlund, D. (ed.), *Questioning the Secular State. The Worldwide Resurgence of Religion in Politics* (London: Hurst, 1996). Series of predominantly developing country, national case studies examining the attitudes of 'fundamentalist' groups to the state and state policies.

Woodhead, L., and Heelas, P. (eds.), *Religion in Modern Times* (Oxford: Blackwell, 2000). A very useful survey of the contemporary position of religion.

## WEB LINKS

**www.eppc.org/publications/xq/ASP/pubsID.1209/ qx/pubs_viewdetail.html**
'Religion, Culture, and International Conflict After September 11. A Conversation with Samuel P. Huntington'—the transcript of an extended conversation between Samuel Huntington and a group of American journalists.

 **COMPANION WEB SITE**

For additional material and resources, see the companion web site at:
**www.oup.com/uk/booksites/politics/**

# 7 Women and gender

*Kathleen Staudt*

## OVERVIEW

Nearly all nations in the world could be considered still 'developing' or not yet developed if judged against full democratic standards both of women's representation in decision-making positions and of responsiveness to women's policy interests. Only a few exceptions exist, most notably Scandinavian, but even there countries became more inclusive and responsive to women only in recent decades, a result of women's organized strength (including in unions), progressive public policies since the 1930s, and especially open and democratic political structures. This chapter draws attention to the widespread reality that women have little voice in established politics, and their 'interests' are muted, given the existence of overwhelming male privilege and preference in the policy-making and policy implementation processes. Here and there women's activism has produced some change in policies, altering power relations between men and women.

The chapter first examines key ways in which men's privileges became institutionalized in the state, political institutions, and governments during history. In so doing, it will incorporate the language of **gender** which leads to an examination of social structures that 'construct' male and female differently in different nations, regions, and historical eras. While the term gender is contested and does not translate well into all languages, it facilitates emphasis on the larger social structure, including relations between men and women, and away from biology as the essential determinant of behaviour. The chapter then considers women's work, paid and unpaid, and women's reproductive capabilities in order to outline typical obstacles that women face in different places and why gendered 'stakes' have been maintained or changed in the policy status quo. It moves on to examine women as voters, activists, and decision-makers in different nations and the effects of their actions on policy responsiveness. Finally, more global and local perspectives are introduced as being essential to moving towards gender-fair politics and policies.

# Introduction: historical perspectives

In geographic spaces around which national boundaries are drawn, relatively stable institutional structures and decision-making patterns have emerged that reflect values and ideologies, including beliefs about men and women. This structure is known as the state, and it is different from the regional units of government also known as states, provinces, or districts, such as the State of Coahuila in Mexico, Western Province of Kenya, or the State of Texas in the United States. From the outset of the modern state in Europe, men, not people generally, crafted the skeletal structure of the state during an era when men spoke for most women and children in both societies and families, as fathers, husbands, and brothers. While wealth, position, and authority concentrated power among the few, virtually all men exercised formal power and authority in 'their' households. Power is relational: the relatively more and less powerful can shift the balance through force, knowledge, and resistance, among other things, opening opportunities for women to exercise power. Rights to hold office and to vote first benefited men, and only much later, women. These rights and opportunities themselves augmented the social construction of gender in ways that associated men with the public sphere of politics and paid labour, and women with the private sphere of family and household.

**Patriarchy**—the ideology and institutions of male rule, male privilege, and female subordination—exists in most societies to different degrees. It is embedded in all states, made 'normal' and routine in laws and public policies that often change only incrementally over time. By the twentieth century, state policies and laws institutionalized male privilege and transplanted the tools, ideology, and machinery of privilege from one nation to another, and throughout colonial empires in nearly global breadth. This gender baggage constructed men as family breadwinners, legally and financially responsible for land and households, and attendant policies benefited men through education, training, and employment. For Latin America and the Caribbean, colonial masters included Spain, Portugal, the Netherlands, Britain, and France. For Africa, the masters included Britain,

Belgium, France, Germany, Italy, and Spain. For Asia from west to east and south, the masters included France, the United States, Britain, and the Netherlands. Nations like China and Japan, despite alternative and historically deeper indigenous patriarchal sources in those states, also exhibited male dominance in and benefit from the public sphere.

Male privilege and gender social constructions have enduring legacies for women's quality of life and opportunity. Life itself may be in question. Using demographic data for Asia, some regions of which showed highly imbalanced gender ratios for regions with strong patriarchal traditions, Sen (1990) found that 100 million women were 'missing' in existing demographic ratios. What he meant was that gender ratios, usually displaying relative balance (slightly over or under) 100:100, exhibited skews as disparate as 88 females to 100 males. In northern India and elsewhere, girl infants and children are ignored so badly that some die needlessly for lack of food, amounting to the waste of enormous numbers of female lives. Patriarchal traditions like these developed long before colonialism. Many indigenous societies vested control over economic resources and political voice in men rather than women or both. Deep patriarchal traditions, both indigenous and 'modern', are legacies that people will have difficulty shedding.

## Key points

- Laws, public policies, and decisions about how to implement public policies are deeply and historically embedded in states, with their concentrated political authority in government that affects the whole of society.

- Men captured and controlled these political institutions in ways that disempowered women and muted their policy interests.

- In the developing world, this patriarchal state model both emerged from indigenous practices and/or was spread through colonialism.

# Women's policy interests

Women and men have stakes in any and all public policies, from education to health, safety, and employment. Policies articulate official decisions on issues that have been perceived as public, rather than private matters; and governments raise money—through taxes, tariffs, and fees—and spend that money (documented in budgets) in ways that resemble official policies. However, policy implementation is crucial, for much policy is merely rhetoric, lacking budgetary resources, staff, and commitments to put policy decisions into practice.

## From private problems to public policies

The social construction of gender has given men and women different stakes in policies, for the ways that policies are formulated, finalized, implemented, and evaluated have usually meant that women's and men's 'interests' were benefited and burdened in distinctive ways. **Women's policy interests**, then, refer to their shared stakes in issues over which governments exercise decision-making, spending, or withholding money for implementation. The identification of shared stakes is complex, given the differences that exist among women based on ethnicity, class, age, geography, and other factors. People contest whether policies should be neutral to gender or take into account gender specifics, such as realities over who—men or women—care for infants after birth. In other words, questions can be raised about whether public policies should be neutral to gender (for example parental leave from paid employment obligations after birth, rather than just maternal leave) or should recognize gender difference, whether constructed through social norms or reduced to biological factors, such as reproductive organs. And if difference is recognized, will that reinforce and sustain gender difference?

Often extraordinary efforts are required to bring issues and problems deemed part of a 'private' sphere onto the public policy agenda. A key example is found in sexual assault and domestic violence, which primarily burdens women. Only in the last three decades have most governments treated violence against women as a public, rather than a private, problem. And the few changes that have taken place in public attitudes have come about only as a response to women organizing for change. Weldon (2002) compared thirty-six countries in various regions and different levels of development with respect to factors that led to seven progressive policy responses. She examined cultures—notoriously difficult to generalize about—women politicians, women's offices in the bureaucracy, and social movements and non-governmental organizations (NGOs) to find that the last two are the most significant factors. Public policies to diminish violence against women are a recent innovation for most countries. Governments with better records than most on the issues include Costa Rica in the developing world and Canada.

## Women and wage inequalities

Until the latter part of the twentieth century, it was considered to be no violation of cultural norms or laws to pay women lower wages and salaries than men. While the United Nations-affiliated International Labour Organization produced conventions that established principles (such as 'Equal Pay for Equal Work'), agreed to in tripartite negotiations among government, business, and labour, national governments enforced these principles only to the extent that internal political forces and laws supported such measures. For women who laboured for income in the **informal economy**, laws and regulations had no impact on earnings.

Women work in many kinds of occupations, from paid to unpaid. But virtually everywhere, women earn less than men in paid employment. The United Nations Development Programme (UNDP) annual *Human Development Report* shows no countries without gender wage gaps, even the Scandinavian countries. But wage gaps range in degree, with some countries that govern by rule of law instituting

## Box 7.1 Latin American wage struggles

Labour unions have been slow to organize women workers. Historically, men organized men, viewed as the family breadwinners, to obtain 'family wages' that could support women and children. In many countries, the percentage of economically active people organized into unions diminished by the close of the twentieth century. Informal workers are rarely organized despite their labour burdens: they work outside regulations on minimum wage, social security benefits, and maximum hours.

In most Latin American countries, the most common paid job for women has been domestic labour: working as servants in other people's households. Live-in maids are notoriously exploited, with employers calling upon them for far more than a forty- or fifty-hour working week. And their pay supplements may consist of discarded clothing and left-over food. Employer–employee relationships take on feudal overtones, and women may be labelled *muchachas* (girls) well beyond the age of adulthood. Chaney and Castro (1989) document the struggles of domestic workers to organize themselves in cities like Bogotá, Colombia, and Mexico City. They show that although organized *trabajadoras domesticas* agree on wage rates and hourly commitments, organizing domestic workers is very challenging, given the competition for work and desperation that characterizes many who seek earnings.

laws that require equal pay for equal work or equal employment opportunity. Yet many women do not take advantage of these laws, or enforcement of the laws requires access to expensive and time-consuming legal services.

Because women generally form at least a third to a half of the labour force, the unequal pay adds up to considerable value or profit that is extracted from, but does not benefit women. Worldwide, labour unions are the collective means by which workers use the power of numbers to threaten work stoppage, strike, and/or negotiate with generally more powerful employers, whether nationals or foreigners. Only a minority of paid workers belong to such organizations; and genuinely independent unions, able to negotiate on national and transnational bases, are rare. Moreover, lower wages, discriminatory job entry, and/or high unemployment levels leave many women dependent upon men.

With the rise of the global economy, much attention has focused on the recruitment of young women into export-processing factories such as garment and electronics manufacturing. Compared with work as maids or street vendors, the factory jobs have fixed hours and pay the legally minimum (although artificially low) wages. However, the jobs are often unsafe and insecure, involving minuscule wages compared with profits earned or executives' salaries. In Mexico, workers' minimum wages are less than $US5 daily,

compared with $US1 daily or less in parts of Asia (or ten to thirty times those values in many developed countries, or fifty to a hundred times those values for management executives) (Staudt and Coronado 2002; UNDP *Human Development Reports*).

## Unpaid labour in households

Women also invest considerable unpaid labour in households, from food cultivation to preparation to care for family members, especially children. In subsistence economies, which characterize many parts of the developing world in Asia and Africa, female labour time in unpaid labour to grow food, process it, cook and feed, and provide water for families usually exceeds male labour time in unpaid labour.

Managing households is a time-consuming activity in most societies, considering the child-rearing and emotional care that is generally thought necessary to hold families together. Women are primarily caregivers in families. In societies lacking running water and basic technology, tasks that seem manageable in the developed world take on onerous physical and time constraints. For example, carrying water from rivers or collecting firewood from forests surrounding villages can consume an inordinate number of hours each day. Or pounding dried grains to make flour for cooking can take hours of arduous labour.

## Box 7.2 **Kenyan women farmers**

In many cultural groups, women grow food for home consumption. Occasionally they sell surplus food, or brew grains into beer to earn cash incomes. When colonial authorities attempted to 'modernize' agricultural economies, they introduced cash crops like coffee and tea to men, bypassing women, as Ester Boserup analysed in *Woman's Role in Economic Development* (1989, originally published in 1970). Colonial agricultural ministries established agricultural extension systems in colonial headquarters, focused on men delivering advice, training, and credit to men farmers. But many men disdained agricultural work, seeking wage labour in distant locales to which they migrated. After gaining independence, countries maintained the bureaucratic status quo in many instances. Kenya is an example, where large numbers of men migrate away from agricultural households, where women remain to grow food and feed their families. Studies of agricultural policy implementation showed that few extension officers visited women even when sizeable numbers, up to 40 per cent, managed farms on their own. And women rarely receive credit, in many societies because they have limited opportunity to own the land and so have no collateral to offer. In Kenya women's voices have been virtually silenced in the man-made political machinery (Nzomo and Staudt 1994). Yet women continue to operate self-help groups, rotating savings among themselves, even as small numbers of women are elected and appointed to political office.

## Reproductive choices

Many women lack the abilities to make decisions about their bodies and voluntary motherhood, given customs and state policies. Although, historically, women relied on indigenous knowledge and practices related to birth, most states until the last few decades have been **pronatalist**, that is, encouraging multiple births and restricting contraception and abortion. As primary care-givers, multiple births consumed much female time and energy. As **overpopulation** became a global issue with United Nations conferences beginning in 1972 (Stockholm) and cheap contraception technology widespread, more governments began to legitimate and to disseminate advice and the means of contraceptive use. Countries like Yemen, Angola, Mali, and Niger have Total Fertility Rates (average numbers of births per woman) as high as 7 or more, in contrast to developed country figures like 1.2–3 per woman (UNDP 2002: 163–5). However, the population policy agenda has often appeared to prioritize government planners' desires to slow population growth, rather than enhance women's choices over healthy and voluntary motherhood. Exploration of the connections between user-friendly women's health and development emerged in the United Nations International Conference on Population and Development in Cairo in 1994.

## Key points

- Women may have different policy interests than men, requiring policies that recognize gender rather than being gender neutral.

- Many issues affecting women are defined as 'private' and it is a struggle to get them onto the public agenda.

- Women workers are regularly paid less than men and the value of women's unpaid domestic and agricultural labour is insufficiently recognized.

- Women generally lack autonomy over reproductive choices.

# Policy injustices

How and why could these unequal gender patterns prevail for so long? The answers involve a confluence of education, discrimination, state inaction, economic inequalities, and women's muted political voices. The most privileged people rarely organize to dismantle privilege, so organized constituencies and political parties rarely advocated gender equality until women acquired voices, rights, economic strength, networks, and organizations to promote change. This section looks first at educational inequalities, then voting rights, and finally the expanding field of women's movements.

Mass education arrived only in the twentieth century in most countries, but usually boys had preferential access and wider opportunities for education that prepared the privileged among them for technical, management, legal, business, health, and other professional occupations. Even in the twenty-first century, girls are the majority of illiterates in South Asian and some African countries, although equal access to primary and secondary education now exists in many Latin American countries.

The UNDP *Human Development Report* collects data on gender-disaggregated adult literacy rates. In thirty-nine developing countries, there is a gender gap of fifteen points or more (UNDP 2002: 223–5). Table 7.1 gives illustrative examples in different world regions, placed in descending order from countries with a relatively high score in their Human Development Index to countries with lower scores. They are concentrated in the band of deep patriarchy (West Asia and North Africa) and impoverished countries of Africa and South-East Asia. The figures show stark gender disparities, but they also reflect the desperate poverty within many of the countries. However, poverty and opportunity are structured to produce different outcomes for men and women, the essence of a gendered approach.

Who is responsible for the massive historical disinvestment in girls' education, parents or governments? In nations without social security and state-provided welfare or poverty alleviation programmes, parents have typically relied on grown children to support them in old age. Marital and settlement customary

**Table 7.1** Female and male literacy rates (%)

| Country | Female literacy | Male literacy |
| --- | --- | --- |
| Saudi Arabia | 67 | 83 |
| Turkey | 77 | 94 |
| China | 76 | 92 |
| Tunisia | 61 | 81 |
| Syria | 61 | 88 |
| Egypt | 44 | 67 |
| Morocco | 35 | 62 |
| India | 45 | 68 |
| Pakistan | 30 | 56 |
| Bangladesh | 30 | 52 |
| Nigeria | 56 | 72 |
| Tanzania | 67 | 84 |
| Senegal | 28 | 47 |
| Mozambique | 29 | 60 |
| Niger | 8 | 24 |

patterns tended to result in girl children joining their future husbands' families upon marital age, but with boy children remaining near home, therefore expected to support parents. Yet, historically, governments did little to alter inequalities.

In the late twentieth century, states like Bangladesh, Pakistan, and Nepal offered incentives such as free uniforms, subsidized fees, and books to parents with girl children in school attendance. These incentives, sometimes funded through international assistance, reduce the costs of female education to parents. However, even under such conditions of equal access, girls' and boys' experiences may be quite different, for subtle but accumulating cues are communicated to both boys and girls that men are and should be the household breadwinners, leaders, and household decision-makers. Women often resort to self-employment, usually part of the informal economy, in income-generating strategies outside the state regulatory apparatus. A prominent example from Bangladesh is the NGO the Grameen Bank, which has been emulated in many other countries, and which channels credit to micro-entrepreneurs, either as individuals or in groups, where peer pressure and responsibility provides the guarantee for loans.

Even when girls and boys complete primary and secondary school in relatively equal proportions, gender patterns diverge in higher education, especially in coursework that results in marketable employment and political careers. In most societies, professional, business, and economic careers are the occupational groups from which leaders emerge, as well as providing the material resources to fund political careers and organizations. Men are channelled into these occupations, thereby accumulating wealth and contacts that translate into political recruitment opportunities. 'Money talks' in many countries, despite attempts to create democratic machinery and voting rights that seemingly foster equality.

On voting rights, when foreign powers controlled large parts of the developing world during the eras of imperialism and colonialism, few (male) inhabitants exercised political voices except those appointed to or co-opted in the colonial state. After the Second World War and the general movement towards independence, women participated in nationalist movements, but often did so primarily as budding nationalists, not advocates of women's interests. But, as such, the voting franchise was often granted to all adults—women and men—once independence came, in countries that instituted elections. The countries in which women currently still lack the right to vote include Brunei, Kuwait, Oman, Saudi Arabia, and the United Arab Emirates.

Finally there is the expansion of women's movements. The structure of the male-dominated state that preserved male privilege has consolidated after independence. Women's movements began to challenge policies only in the latter quarter of the twentieth century, legitimized with the global organizing around the United Nations-sponsored International Women's Year of 1975, which turned into an International Women's Decade, followed up with global conferences in 1980 (Copenhagen), 1985 (Nairobi), and 1995 (Beijing). These conferences fostered the development of more networking, from global to regional, and local, and gender visibility at other UN meetings. Naturally, women's movements experienced resistance to change from those with stakes in perpetuating the status quo and the privileges they enjoyed.

Women's movements rose hand in hand with the emergence of diverse **feminist** philosophies, which at a generic level focus on inequalities and injustices between men and women, especially in the areas of income, political voice, and violence (Staudt 1998: chapter 2). Ironically, many women's movements do not use feminist labels, so as to avoid the appearance of replicating or accepting philosophies developed elsewhere rather than customizing issues within their own communities and nations. Feminist approaches are wide-ranging, preceded with adjectives that provide distinctive ways in which to problematize and address injustices: liberal, socialist, radical, black, maternal, conservative, and others. But by the late twentieth century, some feminists were converging in their efforts to deal with typical widespread injustices like, for instance, domestic abuse and sexual violence. For example, liberal feminists who had worked within given political-economic systems to change the laws found common ground with radical feminists, who are suspicious of the state. They combine forces to demand stronger laws regarding rape, policy implementation over police training to enforce domestic violence laws, and resources for battered women's shelters and counselling for abusers.

Not everyone agrees that political power is the key to generating greater equality. Some focus on strengthening women's ability to earn and control income and other assets. If women had greater economic resources, or resources comparable to men, then they could either make individual choices to benefit themselves or organize collectively to press governments to change. After all, public policy often changes in response to constituencies with money. But it is only public policies that have the capacity to make systemic change, involving large numbers of people.

## Key points

- In women's everyday lives, from unpaid and paid work to reproductive activities, the political framework has devalued women's experiences and increased their dependency on men.

- Gradually, once private issues within the household have entered the public policy agenda, women have made gains that increase their value and autonomy.

- The explanations for past policy disadvantage are numerous, herein focused on (still lingering) educational inequalities, economic inequalities, and delays in women's exercise of their political voices. Those causes for policy disadvantage invite specific solutions: women's increasing economic and political power will enhance their ability to gain responsive and accountable government that serves their interests and needs.

# Women's political activism: movements, non-governmental organizations, and decision-makers

Women's political activism has gradually increased at the local, regional, national, and international levels, both in government and non-government organizations. Still, however, the power that women exercise collectively is far less than men, and few countries exhibit gender-balanced decision-making. Men continue to monopolize politics, and much of that monopolization contributes to sustaining male privileges in the status quo.

In preparation for the United Nations-sponsored women's conference in Beijing in 1995, the United Nations Development Programme (UNDP) *Human Development Report* produced a special publication on gender (1995). One of its chapters focused specifically on women in political decision-making positions and politics. That represents a baseline from which to examine change in women's participation, around ten years later.

## Political structure matters

In the 1995 UNDP report the concept of a 'participation pyramid' was introduced and graphed. It illustrated how men's monopolization was stronger at the pinnacle of the pyramid, for chief executives, and how this steep pyramid broadened only slightly in descent from the top, to cabinet members, elected representatives of the legislature, and finally to eligible voters, the bottom of the pyramid that exhibited greater gender balance. In some parts of the world, namely western Asia, no women serve in cabinets. Often there is only a token female presence in cabinet,

serving in posts with limited resources, staff, and authority. Yet there are differences among countries, based on their political structures. Even democracies come in different forms, and questions have often been raised about which form is the more gender-friendly.

Chief executives in government consist primarily of presidents and prime ministers, illustrating two variations in democracy: presidential and parliamentary (though hybrid systems also exist). Presidential forms of government, most common in the western hemisphere, have three separate branches (executive, legislative, judicial) that, ideally, are equal and check one another's power. The president is elected separately from legislators, members of congress in what is often a bicameral system of a lower and upper house. The president appoints cabinet members from various walks of life: interest groups, campaign supporters, loyal friends, experts, and/or academics. These cabinet members are not elected, but are accountable to the people indirectly through the appointment process. Presidential systems, as is evident, are fragmented, consuming a great deal of time for decision-making. Their officials are elected for fixed terms, lending stability to the system but also less responsiveness. Yet presidential systems also offer many decision points at which to advocate or resist policy change, including policy that concerns women especially.

Parliamentary forms of government, most common in European and former European colonies in Asia and Africa, fuse the executive and legislature in the form of a chief executive called prime minister.

The prime minister is elected to parliament, and rises to executive leadership as a result of leadership in the majority political party or party coalition. Cabinet ministers come from the majority party or a coalition of parties, and are thus elected officials. As is evident, parliamentary systems concentrate power, thus making the decision-making process potentially more efficient. They can be more responsive to the people because new elections can be called if, on important measures before parliament, a majority vote does not prevail (that is, a 'vote of no confidence').

## Women in decision-making positions

Few women have risen to become a chief executive in democratic governments. In the 1995 *Human Development Report* only twenty had ever achieved the position, about equal numbers of presidents and prime ministers. In the early twenty-first century, only a handful more women have been added; the Philippines, Sri Lanka, and Bangladesh are the only countries to have elected two different women as chief executives.

Women are beginning to be selected or appointed for cabinet positions in larger numbers than two decades past. For the 1995 report, women held 7 per cent of cabinet posts, and in two out of every five governments, men monopolized all the cabinet posts. Often, however, women's portfolios involved 'women's affairs', 'family affairs', or peripheral bureaucracies not central to core government missions and budgets. Mexico has appointed women to the Fisheries Secretariat in several administrations. Only twenty years ago, many governments had no woman in the cabinet, or a single token woman. Now, pairs or handfuls of women lead government bureaucracies, their programmes, and employees.

Moving down to legislatures, the 1995 *Report* calculated an average of 10 per cent women's participation for democratic and non-democratic countries. These figures illustrate men's near-monopolization of legislative politics. The average figures had actually decreased, from 13 per cent in the late 1980s when women's participation was slightly inflated until the demise of the former Soviet Union and authoritarian Eastern European countries, many of which installed quotas that guaranteed seats for women. In the 1990s, democratic countries have installed quotas that resulted in substantial increases in women's share of seats, at a quarter or more, such as South Africa and Argentina.

Women's representation varied by world region a decade ago. Asian, European, and Latin American figures surpassed world averages, while African, Pacific, and Arab countries were well below world averages. But the differences were not dramatic. Since 1995, women's participation in legislatures has risen slightly, back to its 1980s level of around 13 per cent. When there is a bicameral system, women's representation is usually greater in the lower rather than higher house (the latter, often called the Senate). The Inter-Parliamentary Union compiles data on parliaments for 181 countries. Scandinavian countries and the Netherlands are always at the top, exhibiting critical masses of women, at a third or more of the representatives. Of course, one-third never constitutes a majority—the proportion usually required for voting bills into laws! Updated lists are easily available for readers who wish to consult each and every country (**www.ipu.org**).

The regional patterns outlined for a decade ago still persist. That is, the Latin American region retains the highest level of female participation in the legislature, among developing countries, with African, Pacific, and Middle Eastern countries following in that order (IPU 2003). The highest levels in Latin American are found in Cuba (36 per cent) and Costa Rica (35 per cent), while the lowest are in Colombia (12 per cent) and several Caribbean countries. In Africa, the highest levels are found in Mozambique (30 per cent) and South Africa (29.8 per cent), while the lowest are in Niger (1.2 per cent) and Egypt (2.4 per cent). In Asia, the highest levels are in South-East Asia (Vietnam, 27.3 per cent) and Laos (22.9 per cent), and the lowest in Nepal and South Korea, at 5.9 per cent each. In several Pacific, Arab, and/or Middle Eastern countries, there are no women elected to the legislature: Bahrain, Kuwait, Micronesia, Nauru, Palau, Solomon Islands, Tuvalu, United Arab Emirates.

Why the variation? The answers lie in political party actions and in the structure of electoral systems. Proportional Representation electoral systems produce higher percentages of women in politics than do single-member constituencies.

Political parties are also crucial, and in some countries parties commit themselves to greater gender balance. Both national governments and political parties have adopted special measures like quotas to assure that critical masses of women are elected. For example, Argentina has a national quota law of 30 per cent for the legislature. In 1992, India passed a law that required women to hold one-third of all local council (*panchayats)* seats, although a similar law was not passed at the national level. This introduced nearly a million women into public decision-making positions, theoretically a stepping-stone into other political offices (Rai 2003). Yet India falls well below the international median in national representation rates for women—in the 1999–2004 parliament 8 per cent in the lower house, 10 per cent in the upper.

Do women in the legislature expand the policy agenda and address gender inequalities? This is a perennial question in research on women in politics. Women often follow different pathways into the political process, such as through non-government organizations with possible commitments to women's policy interests. As a result, they may even bring a new way of interacting with colleagues and constituents. Once in office, women's party loyalties, ideologies, and constituencies influence their legislative behaviour. Women in office may come from markedly different and privileged income backgrounds than the majority of (poor) people. And women may belong to political parties that operate under ideologies that ignore 'private' injustices. Conservative politicians cut public spending programmes from which poor women may benefit. Yet women have sometimes coalesced across party lines to vote for women's policy interests. This happens periodically in Mexico around anti-violence laws.

## Non-governmental organizations

The crucial ingredient for bringing about more gender-just policies and better accountability lies with the political engagement of NGOs and social movements with women (and men) representatives. NGOs come in many different forms, active at the local, regional, national, transnational, and international levels. Some NGOs are registered with the United Nations or with government (the latter seeking to qualify for tax-exempt status), known as non-profit organizations or *asociaciones civiles* in parts of the Spanish-speaking world. Others are looser informal networks or coalitions, including movements that may avoid registration (particularly with undemocratic governments). In these circles consultants create organizations, but tend to operate more like a business. Just as governments need to be accountable to their citizens and residents, so must NGOs become more accountable than many of them actually are.

In many countries, NGOs work with political parties, legislatures, political executives, and bureaucracies to press for more responsive policies and resources. They push for goals like equal employment opportunities, non-sexist education, better health care, loans for micro-businesses, and laws to prevent violence against women, among many other areas. It is NGOs that give life and energy to democracies and the women (and men) who are elected and appointed to office.

## Tools for policy change

Women are gradually increasing their share of power in public affairs, in NGOs and governments. Women's participation expands public policy agendas to include women's policy interests. What tools exist to ensure that policies are implemented?

Once public officials adopt new policies, some resistance can be expected in the policy implementation process of government bureaucracies. The last quarter-century has pioneered the use of several tools to overcome that resistance, including more academic research and the innovative policy tools associated with gender **mainstreaming**, such as establishing women's 'machinery' in government and introducing gendered budget-making (BRIDGE 2003).

Although policy-making is an inherently political process, in which power is brought to bear on policy adoption, the idealized policy-making process involves the application of research findings to policy deliberation and adoption. There is now a considerable body of findings concerning various developmental, educational, and health policies relevant to women and gender. This research has been spurred on by the rise of policy, programme, and project evaluation. **Evaluation research** typically asks: What outcomes occurred as a result of the programme intervention or policy changes? Who benefited and who was burdened? How well were programme and policy goals accomplished? What lessons can be learned for future change? Evaluation research of this type has lent itself well to addressing inequalities, whether by gender, ethnicity, class, and/or geographic regions.

Other innovations have moved beyond just policy rhetoric that promises greater equality and more responsive governance towards initiating real action in government bureaucracies as they interact with people. The first such innovation involved the creation of what the United Nations initially referred to as **women's machinery**, or units within government such as women's bureaux, commissions of women, ministries of women, and women's desks. Within ten years, virtually all governments hosted some women's machinery, but many had minimal staff and low budgets. They tended to operate in isolation, without really influencing the core of government policies and programmes. This separate sidelining gave rise to strategies to 'mainstream' all government efforts, even those without obvious women's policy interests or those based on women's special needs (Staudt 1997; Rai 2003). However, the effectiveness of mainstreaming strategies depends on good leadership, wide receptivity, adequate resources, strong incentives for change, and strategic locations within government agencies. Moreover, the machinery was not always connected well enough to NGOs, highlighting concerns raised generally about the need for transparency and accountability in democratic governance.

Gender mainstreaming machinery has not operated with sufficient power and resources to transform government, giving rise to a more recent innovation, one that would analyse budgets in gendered ways. Budgetary decision-making is at the very heart of the political process, and some countries have pioneered methods to dissect budgets by gender and make the process more transparent in this way, and to involve more women and their organizations. The phrase 'gender audits' has also been used to analyse spending, and it resonates well with the technical accountability tools deemed necessary to exercise oversight on government.

## Key points

- Women are gaining power both in official positions and in relation to government through social movements and NGOs.

- Political structure matters: democratic systems that are parliamentary, with political parties that gain seats through proportional representation that implement goals for more critical masses of women, have higher rates of women representatives than presidential systems, although fewer decisional access points.

- However, once in office, bureaucratic or elected, women decision-makers will respond to women's interests and needs only if committed to justice in a political party that does the same and where accountable to relevant NGOs.

- Tools available to nudge the more resistant bureaucracies include mainstreaming strategies, budgets, and audits.

# More global dimensions

This chapter has focused primarily on nations, but it cannot close without noting the growing global inequalities in which nations are fixed. Even as developed countries exhibit average annual per capita incomes of many thousands of dollars, there are numerous countries in which per capita income is equivalent to only a few hundred dollars. The *Human Development Report* (UNDP 2002: 19) reckons the world's richest 1 per cent of people receive as much income as the poorest 57 per cent and the income of the world's richest 5 per cent is 114 times that of the poorest 5 per cent. Women in developing countries are burdened by this grave poverty.

International conferences, many of them held under the auspices of the United Nations, have provided space for women to articulate their interests.

These meetings range from those that focus specifically on women, such as the women's conferences of 1975, 1985, and 1995 (mentioned earlier), and those that focus on public policies in which women have stakes, such as the environment, population, and others. Typically, official delegations meet and at the same time parallel meetings of international or national NGOs also take place. Transnational networks and bonds are formed, and resolutions are passed. While the United Nations exerts little authority over sovereign countries (save peacekeeping missions), the passage of resolutions provides leverage for local and national organizations to press their governments for accountability and change. Legal instruments such as the UN Convention on the Elimination of All Forms of Discrimination against Women, also provide leverage for change.

International women's NGOs work on transnational bases on a variety of issues, from human rights and business to research and labour solidarity. They include the Association for Women's Rights in Development, the Solidarity Center in Mexico City (affiliated with American Federation of Labor-Congress of Industrial Organizations, the largest labour union in the United States), Women Working Worldwide (with a UK base), Women's International League for Peace and Freedom, and the International Federation of Business and Professional Women. Other national organizations have acquired international fame, such as the Self-Employed Women's Association (India) and GABRIELA (Philippines). While many of these organizations are registered with the United Nations, most operate with focused agendas and have useful websites. Yet it is important for them to be grounded in concrete personal relationships that are linked regionally, nationally, and internationally, as occurs in international border communities (see Staudt and Coronado 2002).

One example of grounded cross-border, transnational work is the Coalition Against Violence towards Women and Families at the US–Mexico Border. The Coalition is a binational network of organizations and activists who focus on the unsolved murders of more than 300 girls and women in Cd. Juarez, Mexico's fifth largest city, over the last decade. A third of the victims are mutilated before death, and victims' families are treated with disdain by judicial authorities, who routinely operate with impunity. The Coalition and other NGOs have networked with western hemispheric and UN-affiliated human rights officials and international NGOs to bring attention to the problems, and to demand solutions that will be effective on both sides of the border. The Coalition has fostered some cooperation among police departments on both sides. Yet violence against women continues to be a deep, complex, and substantial problem, and the police in Mexico are as recalcitrant on these as on other crimes. The police may be part of the problem.

## Key points

- Analysts must think outside the box of nation-states to understand the global politics of over-prosperous women (and men) versus desperate women (and men) struggling for basic amenities. Gender balance within the nation-state obscures those politics.

- Global and local forces structure women's everyday lives and gender relations.

- It is a challenge to organize across borders, even in crisis-laden policy areas such as violence against women.

# Conclusions

Women and their policy interests have been marginalized as a result of historic state structures and political institutions that privilege men and their voices in the decision-making process. Over the last century, women have gradually increased their participation in politics as voters, decision-makers, and members of non-government organizations. Public policy agendas have widened, taking into account discrimination and gendered inequalities. Progressive policies have yet to be fully implemented, but various bureaucratic tools and NGO oversight increase the prospects for implementation and accountability. Women are gaining ground in most nation-states, thus altering power relations between men and women. The meagre pace of change in most countries, however, may mean that our great grandchildren will be among the first to experience a gender-balanced polity in most of the developing (and developed) nation-states.

## QUESTIONS

1   Discuss the role of the state in the subordination of women and in facilitating gender equality for both historical and contemporary times.

2   Do women share identical policy interests?

3   Compare the contribution of economic and political power in facilitating gender equality.

4   What role does reproductive choice have in facilitating gender equality?

5   Will poverty-alleviation policies automatically address gender inequalities? Make reference to education and literacy in the response.

6   Discuss three features of the political structure that open or close spaces for women's voices, individually and collectively.

7   Do women in the legislature expand the policy agenda and address gender inequalities?

## GUIDE TO FURTHER READING

Basu, A. (ed.), *The Challenge of Local Feminisms: Women's Movements in Global Perspective* (Boulder, Colo.: Westview Press, 1995). A collection of chapters on grass-roots women's movements in Asia, Africa, and Latin America, most of them authored by women from those areas.

BRIDGE Development—Gender. *Gender and Budgets* (Brighton: Institute of Development Studies, University of Sussex, 2003). Offers valuable concepts for application to real problems in government and organizations.

Goetz, A. M. (ed.), *Getting Institutions Right for Women in Development* (London: Zed, 1997). About transforming and tinkering with institutional machinery to make it more accountable to women and gender equality.

Jahan, R., *The Elusive Agenda: Mainstreaming Women in Development* (London: Zed, 1995). A comparison of two multi-lateral organizations (World Bank and UNDP) and two relatively progressive bi-lateral technical assistance institutions (NORAD-Norway and CIDA-Canada).

Jaquette, J. S., and Wolchik, S. L. (eds.), *Women and Democracy: Latin America and Central and Eastern Europe* (Baltimore: Johns Hopkins University Press, 1998). About women activists and politicians in regions undergoing 'transitions to democracy', with transitions either opening or closing space to women and gender policy issues.

Pettman, J. J., *Worlding Women: A Feminist International Politics* (London: Routledge, 1996). An overview of international/global and comparative gender issues.

Stromquist, N. P. (ed.), *Women in the Third World: An Encyclopedia of Contemporary Issues* (New York and London: Garland Publishing, 1998). A 683-page reference work with geographic, functional, and international sections, divided into seventy plus chapters and selections.

## WEB LINKS

**www.ids/ac.uk/bridge**    From *Gender Websites*, by Sonja Boezak, Ra'ida Al-Zubi, Palo Brambilla, Elena Krylova and Emma Bell, BRIDGE Development—Gender, Institute of Development Studies, University of Sussex [itself a source of useful reports and newsletters], 2002.

**www.icrw.org**    International Center for Research on Women—policy research.

**www.aviva.org**    Aviva—women's groups, resources, news, events.

**www.wedo.org**    Women's Environment and Development Organization.

**www.wluml.org**    Women Living Under Muslim Law.

**www.awid.org**    Association for Women's Rights in Development (English, Spanish, French).

**www.whrnet.org**    Women's Human Rights Net Global Fund for Women.

**www.globalfundforwomen.org**    (English, Spanish, French, Portuguese, Arabic).

**www.ipu.org**    Inter-Parliamentary Union.

**www.undp.org/unifem**    United Nations Development Fund for Women (UNIFEM).

**www.worldbank.org/gender**    World Bank Gender Home Page.

**www.undp.org/gender**    United Nations Development Programme (UNDP).

**www.un.org/womenwatch**    United Nations gateway on women's advancement and empowerment, including the UN Division for the Advancement of Women (DAW) **www.un.org/womenwatch/daw**.

**www.sewa.org**    Self-Employed Women's Association (SEWA), India.

 **COMPANION WEB SITE**

For additional material and resources, see the companion web site at:
**www.oup.com/uk/booksites/politics/**

# Civil society

*Marina Ottaway*

## OVERVIEW

The expression 'civil society' has metamorphosed during the 1990s from a relatively obscure concept familiar mostly to scholars of Marxism into a mainstream term freely used by social science analysts in general and by practitioners in the international assistance field specifically. Several factors contributed to these developments. First, there was growing interest by the United States and many European countries in promoting democracy abroad during the 1990s. The demise of the Soviet Union and the Eastern European communist regimes triggered a wave of more or less successful democratic transitions further afield, where regimes formerly influenced by the Soviet model and often by the Soviet government struggled to transform themselves into something both more acceptable to their populations and less anachronistic internationally. This wave of political transformations provided an opportunity for the industrialized democracies to actively promote the spread of political systems similar to their own. As international actors devised democracy promotion strategies, they focused much effort on promoting citizen participation and activism— what quickly came to be known as a vibrant civil society.

Another factor was the changes taking place in the established democracies themselves. Many organizations of what used to be called broadly 'the left', inspired by socialist or social democratic ideals of socio-economic equity and justice, were replaced by newer groups whose concept of justice extended beyond the traditional concerns of socialist parties and labour movements. They embraced a broad array of causes such as environmental protection and sustainability, opposition to globalization, and protection of gay rights. The old left was rooted above all in political parties and labour unions. The new activists were organized in smaller **non-governmental organizations**, often loosely tied in broad networks, that saw themselves as the embodiment of a mobilized civil society.

Disenchantment with the performance of state institutions was an additional factor, as political leaders made concerted efforts to narrow the functions of government and enlarge the spheres of the private and non-profit sectors. At the same time, the corruption and inefficiency of many developing countries' governments prompted international development agencies to rethink the assumption that development required state intervention. As a result, they sought ways to bypass governments and implement some development projects and programmes through non-governmental organizations.

Needless to say, the popularization of the concept of civil society has led to a blurring of its meaning. It has also led to a blurring of its political connotations: a greater role for civil society is now extolled by conservatives, liberals, and radicals alike as a crucial component of political and even economic reform. Analysts of different persuasions do not agree about which organizations should be considered part of civil society and which should not, but they all agree that civil society is a good thing.

# Introduction: defining civil society

Defining the meaning of civil society is difficult because the term is laden with theoretical assumptions, unsolved problems, and value judgements. According to Hegel's oft-cited but ultimately unsatisfactory definition (in his *Philosophy of Right*, 1821), civil society comprises the realm of organizations that lie between the family at one extreme and the state at the other. While superficially clear and logical the definition generates a lot of conceptual confusion and some political booby traps. The result is that very few scholars, and virtually no practitioners of democracy promotion, now accept such a broad definition in practice, even if they cite it.

## Intellectual conundrums

The definition is clear on one point: civil society is not the whole society, the entire web of social institutions and relations, but only one part of it. The problem is how to define that part with any degree of precision. Citing the realm of voluntary associations between the family and the state does not provide sufficient clarification. Three problems deserve special attention: (1) distinguishing organizations that are truly voluntary from those that are not; (2) determining whether all voluntary organizations between the family and the state deserve to be considered civil; and (3) determining whether there is a conceptual difference between civil society and political society, as some argue, or whether this is a distinction with little analytical value, which has gained currency for reasons of political expediency.

The concept of voluntary association contains ambiguities, particularly when applied to the less formal organizations that constituted civil society in the past and are still important in the developing world. According to definitions that stress civil societies' voluntary character, a civil society group is a formally constituted association of which individuals become members as part of a completely free choice—a club, for example, is undoubtedly a voluntary association. The family is not, because membership in it is not chosen. But there is a grey area of groups in which membership is not formally compulsory, but is not completely a matter of free choice, either. Religious associations offer one example. Very often people are born into a church or another type of religious association by virtue of having been born in a family, and inertia explains continued membership; in other cases, membership in a religious group is a truly voluntary choice. Similarly, people are born members of a clan, tribe, or ethnic group, but membership in an organization that claims to represent that group is a political choice made voluntarily and deliberately by some but by no means all members of that particular group. South Africa provides a telling example of how membership in an ethnic group can be an accident of birth or a voluntary decision to join a group. In the early 1990s, at a time of intense fighting between the supporters of Inkatha, a political party with a Zulu nationalist agenda, and other black South Africans, ethnic Zulus who did not support the party and its agenda referred to Inkatha supporters, but not to themselves, as Zulus.

The ambiguities even extend to organizations that appear at first sight to be clearly voluntary, such as political parties. In the early twentieth century many Europeans were born as members of social democratic parties, figuratively, because of their families' allegiances, or even literally, being delivered by 'mid wives' paid by the party as a service to their members. Membership was voluntary in that anybody could stop paying dues and quit the party, but, for many, membership became part of an identity acquired at birth. A contemporary example of this phenomenon is offered by the Sudan, where major religious brotherhoods, into which people are born when families belong, have formed political parties to which adherence is equally automatic.

Another common problem in determining whether an association is voluntary or not arises in relation to ruling political parties and the mass organizations they control. Membership in the party or mass organization is rarely compulsory, but the absence of membership has negative consequences and many are forced to join. One of the difficult tasks faced by the United States as the occupying power in

Iraq in 2003 was to distinguish between committed members of the Baath Party, who were part of the defunct regime of Saddam Hussein, and those who had joined in order to keep their jobs so as not to attract undue attention to themselves.

A second thorny problem in determining the boundaries of civil society is ideological in nature, hinging on the interpretation of the word 'civil', which can mean both 'relating to citizens or the general public' and 'civilized'. The expansive definition of civil society as comprising all voluntary associations between family and state is based on the first meaning. For many, this is an unacceptable approach because it combines in one category, for example, human rights groups and terrorist organizations. In practice, the word civil society is almost invariably used to denote organizations that share certain positive, 'civil' values. But there is no consensus on that point. During the 1980s, Scandinavian countries considered the organizations fighting apartheid in South Africa as 'civil' and provided support. The United States defined them as terrorist organizations and refused to help; Nelson Mandela, the much acclaimed first president of post-apartheid South Africa, was once considered a terrorist by the United States. Many liberals or radicals have no problem accepting labour unions as organizations of civil society, but are often reluctant to see a federation of employers in the same light.

Another controversial issue influenced by political and policy consideration is whether it is valid to draw a distinction between civil and political society. Those who defend the distinction, first made by Gramsci (in 1929–35 in *Prison Notebooks*), admit that both civil society and political society play a political role and seek to influence policy decisions. But the political role of civil society is indirect: civil society groups do not aspire to control the government and exercise power, but see their role as that of influencing policies in the public interest. Political society organizations—essentially, political parties—want to control the government. A corollary of this view is that the civil society is virtuously dedicated to giving citizens a voice, while political society is power-hungry, self-interested, and considerably less virtuous. A second corollary is that international agencies seeking to promote democracy can and should provide assistance to civil society organizations; supporting political society, which aspires to power and thus is partisan

by definition, would be morally questionable and would also represent unjustifiable interference in the domestic politics of another country.

The distinction between civil and political society has theoretical justification. Its usefulness, however, is scant, because most civil society organizations are, overtly or covertly, more partisan and political than they claim to be. True, there are organizations of civil society that act purely as pressure or advocacy groups and have no intention of contesting public office. But civil society activists are often close to specific political parties, and many move freely between civil society organizations and parties. Furthermore, many political parties, including some in power, set up organizations of civil society in an attempt to capture some of the assistance that is available only to civil society organizations.

Examples of the blurring of the lines between political and civil organizations exist in most countries, though more pronounced in some than in others. Civil society organizations may be pushed into close alliance with political parties by government repression. Many non-governmental organizations (NGOs) in Zimbabwe, for example, developed during the 1990s as bona fide, non-partisan civil society organizations lobbying for improved human rights, constitutional reform, better legal services for the poor, and a variety of similar causes. As the government, when challenged by the opposition party, the Movement for Democratic Change, turned increasingly repressive, violating laws and human rights principles in order to stay in power, civil society organizations increasingly became part of the political opposition. Formally organized NGOs operating at the national level are particularly likely to become politicized when confronted by a repressive regime. But less formal, local groups, sometimes referred to as community-based organizations (CBOs), rarely become openly political. CBOs are usually concerned about local level development and welfare issues, focusing on service delivery or simply self-help.

## Politics and expediency

The abstract problems of how to define civil society remain a source of debate among academics, but in the meantime, civil society is being defined in practice by the policies of bilateral and multilateral aid agencies, by the governments of countries receiving democracy assistance, and by civil society organizations themselves.

Bilateral and multilateral international aid organizations define the boundaries of civil society when they decide which organizations are eligible for assistance under democracy promotion programmes or should be consulted in the preparation of an assistance strategy. This definition is based on a mixture of political considerations and administrative requirements. The major political requirement is that such organizations focus their activities either on civic education or advocacy for democratic reform. Civic education programmes, particularly common in countries in the early stages of political transition, seek to convey the basic meaning of democracy as well as teach about the political and institutional mechanisms of democratic systems. In its more sophisticated, advanced form, civil education is also training for political activism: citizens are encouraged to scrutinize the action of politicians, to lobby them to enact reforms, and to hold them accountable by voting them out of office. Advocacy organizations that attract international support focus on human rights, women's rights, legal reform, judicial reform, and, occasionally, environmental sustainability. To be part of civil society thus means to belong to one of these types of organizations.

The aid agencies' definition of civil society is further narrowed by their administrative requirements. The groups must be organized in a formal way because donors cannot provide support for an organization that is not registered in some way, that does not have a name and address, or that cannot be audited. Informal networks or vaguely organized civic movements may play an important part in a society or a democratic transition, but they do not meet donors' needs and only some foreign funders will provide support for them on an exceptional basis. For practical reasons, donors also prefer to deal with organizations that speak, literally and figuratively, the same language.

As a result, the donors' civil society is an entity very different either from the society at large or from civil society as the realm of voluntary organizations between the family and the state. The term civil society as used, and financed, by the international aid agencies refers to 'a very narrow set of organizations: professionalized NGOs dedicated to advocacy or civic education work on public interest issues directly relating to democratization, such as election monitoring, voter education, governmental transparency and political and civil rights in general' (Ottaway and Carothers 2000: 11).

Direct funding of civil society is not the only way in which international assistance agencies define that society. Their influence is strengthened by the requirement under which many now operate that they consult with local civil society in implementing a wide variety of development and democracy aid programmes. The World Bank has such civil society requirements and many bilateral agencies also hold wide consultations. In practice, many of the groups so contacted are the same organizations the assistance agencies helped set up or fund in the first place—the ones they know and are capable of sending representatives to meetings.

The governments of countries that are recipients of democracy assistance also try to shape the definition of civil society by imposing registration requirements, which are sometimes very strict and used to prevent the formation of antagonistic organizations. Many also try to limit the access to donor funding to only some categories of organizations or to prevent it outright. Some international agencies are willing to circumvent such regulations and provide funding covertly, others are more anxious not to antagonize the government.

Civil society activists have also played a very important part in determining which organizations are recognized as part of civil society. Transnational networks of NGOs, usually led by the better-funded groups of the industrialized countries, have been particularly influential here. For example, they successfully pressed the United Nations to accept their presence at international meetings; and the World Bank agreed to undertake re-evaluations of some of its practices, particularly lending for the construction of dams, and to consult with the NGO sector before reaching decisions on certain issues. For example oil companies in Chad are now required to pay royalties into specially controlled funds where they are administered under strict controls with the participation of civil society organizations. These examples of success are counterbalanced by more numerous examples where the militancy of transnational civil society networks has failed to earn them recognition as rightful participants.

## Key points

- The widespread agreement about the importance of civil society is accompanied by a great deal of controversy about what civil society is, not only among theorists but also among practitioners.

- The term has been given a concrete meaning by the policies of international assistance agencies and to a lesser extent by the efforts of civil society organizations.

# Traditional and modern civil society

It is common for donors to bemoan the weakness, or even the absence, of civil society in countries where they try to promote democracy. This concern has spurred governments of industrialized countries, as well as international NGOs and private foundations, to launch an array of civil society assistance programmes to strengthen what is invariably referred to as a 'fledgling' civil society. In many instances, even after years of effort, donors express concern about the slow progress of civil society development and its continuing need for support. Paradoxically, in the countries where civil society is deemed at its weakest, for example in war-torn African countries, the population relies for survival on civil society networks that go well beyond the family and reveal a high degree of sophistication and organization. One of the problems faced by countries undergoing political upheaval is that some civil society networks quickly establish themselves in major fields of economic activity and even within parts of the government. The criminalization of the state that has been witnessed in failing states in West and Central Africa is the result of the disparity between the power of civil society organizations and that of a duly constituted government and administrative structure.

These considerations point to the need to put the discussion of civil society in a broader perspective. Following the current use of the term, the discussion so far has dwelt on 'modern' civil society, that is, the part of civil society organized into formal, professionalized NGOs typical of the late twentieth century. But in all countries, including the industrialized ones, there is another civil society—'traditional society'. This society is organized more informally, often

through networks rather than formally structured organizations, and often following patterns that existed in earlier times.

Traditional forms of civil society exist in most countries today, but particularly so in countries where the state is weak. Organizations that are traditional in form do not necessarily perform only traditional roles. On the contrary, they grow in new directions in response to contemporary needs and requirements. West African Sufi organizations such as the Mourides are ancient, but they establish control over the wholesale rice trade in Senegal, or set up mechanisms to help members of the brotherhood emigrate to the United States and find jobs there: they are performing definitely non-traditional functions in response to new challenges.

Modern and traditional civil society stand in inverse relation to each other. In countries where the state is strong, traditional civil society is weak and modern civil society is strong. If the state is weak, so is modern civil society but traditional civil society strengthens (Migdal 1988b). This explains the paradox outlined above: in countries in the throes of a difficult, state-weakening transition, citizens rely on civil society networks in many aspects of their lives even as donors bemoan the weakness of civil society.

## Traditional civil society

Organizations of civil society have taken a great variety of forms traditionally, from the very informal to the highly structured. Loosely structured but culturally sanctioned mechanisms for swapping labour and joining efforts in the performance of large collective tasks exist in all societies, as do more structured mechanisms—for example, the rotating credit associations that exist, under different names, almost everywhere. Compared to modern ones, traditional civil society organizations were less specialized and formal. They were extremely unlikely to have full-time organizers and certainly not offices. Even in industrial countries, the professionalization of civil society, hence its separation from the society at large, is a recent phenomenon. When Alexis de Tocqueville visited the United States in the first half of the nineteenth century and wrote *Democracy in America* (published in two volumes, in 1835 and 1840) he was struck by the American propensity to form intermediate associations in the pursuit of a wide range of interests and projects; he was looking at loosely structured, ad hoc groups, not at formal organizations with professional staffs.

Modern civil society defined as a set of NGOs has clear boundaries that separate it from the family and indeed from the rest of society as well as from the state. The expression 'members of civil society' refers to a rather small number of people who belong, and very often work for, such NGOs, not to all citizens. **Traditional civil society** has no such clear boundaries, but fades into the larger society at one extreme and non-state forms of political authority on the other. In non-state societies, governance was an extension of the overall social organization, not the activity of specialized institutions.

The blurring of the lines between the society at large, more organized associations within it, and political authority is not completely a thing of the past, but can reappear in extreme situations of **state collapse**, as in Somalia.

Traditional civil society performed important economic activities that today are considered to be the responsibility of state authority. For example, long-distance trade was once organized and carried out through private, civil society networks that extended over long distances. States took over much of the responsibility for protecting trade routes and otherwise making large-scale economic activity more feasible. In places where the state has collapsed or is severely weakened, civil society is taking on again some of those functions. This has been the case in the Democratic Republic of the Congo (formerly Zaire) since at least the 1980s, for example.

## Traditional civil society and the state in the contemporary world

Some traditional forms of civil society exist even in the industrialized countries and they pose no problem. On the contrary, they contribute to the reservoir of what Putnam (1993) calls **social capital**. When traditional forms of civil society grow very strong as a result of the weakness or total collapse of the state, however, they can become highly problematic. Traditional civil society in the contemporary world is both indispensable and dangerous. Where the state is incapable, it can help people survive and maintain a semblance of normal life under very difficult conditions. But in the absence of a strong state, civil society networks can also turn into a source of power and domination for an oligarchy, become estranged from the broader society, and thus prevent the rebuilding of the state and the introduction of democratic forms of governance (Migdal 1988b: 24–41).

The benign side of the reappearance of traditional civil society is apparent every day in countries where government is unable to perform functions expected of a modern state. The government cannot fund schools for all children, and civil society responds by setting up alternative schools. State collapse forces banks to close, and civil society responds by setting up informal systems that may not be officially recognized or formally registered. Noteworthy particularly in the Arab world (the *hawala* system), they move money rapidly and efficiently across continents and into remote villages. The formal economy cannot provide jobs for everybody, and civil society develops an informal sector that provides the livelihood of the majority of the population.

But there is unfortunately also a malignant side to the reappearance of traditional civil society, because it can further undermine the failed state institutions for which it is trying to compensate. During the transition from apartheid in South Africa, a weakened government lost its capacity to enforce the laws that kept peddlers away from the business district of Johannesburg. Informal sector businesses took over the sidewalks, to the benefit of the people who were trying to make a living by selling vegetables and braiding hair on the street. But the informal marketplace also became the territory of criminal gangs, legitimate businesses were driven out, and the once thriving business district became a 'no-go' area.

And parts of the civil society that flourish because of the absence of the state may be hostile to efforts to revive it. The trading networks that form in war-ravaged countries respond to a need, but they can also become profitable organizations that resist the efforts of the new, stronger government to revive institutions. Vigilante groups, such as those that operate in many parts of Nigeria, are a civil society response to insecurity. But they tend to turn into criminal organizations that end up by preying on those they were supposed to defend. In extreme cases, the re-emergence of traditional civil society is a threat to the continued existence of the state or can challenge its reconstruction, as in Somalia today where the clans, who constitute the traditional organizations of civil society, resist any transfer of power to the state.

The tension between traditional civil society and the state is also evident in the cultural domain. Traditionally, civil society has always been a major vehicle through which culture has been transmitted. In many countries public education has deliberately sought to create a new culture, different from that transmitted by civil society and in many ways alien to it. A central part of the new public education was the effort to create a new national identity, different and often hostile to the local identities transmitted by traditional civil society. Public education historically was part of a struggle between state and traditional civil society. Thus in Turkey under Kamal Ataturk the state tried to impose secular values on a traditional society that upheld Islamic ones. This cultural conflict between states and traditional civil society continues today even in the most industrialized, democratic societies—it is evident for instance in the disputes in France over the right of Muslim girls to wear a headscarf in school. In societies where the state is weaker, or less determined to influence the culture, the battle is often won by civil society—the re-Islamization of culture in Egypt after decades of secular public education is a striking example (Wickham 2002).

## Key points

- Traditional forms of civil society exist in all countries, but they do not necessarily perform traditional functions.

- When the state is weak, traditional civil society tends to be strong.

- Traditional forms of civil society help alleviate certain problems created by the weakness of the state, but they can also prevent the strengthening of the state.

# The modern state and civil society as a specialized entity

The rise of civil society as an entity separate from the broader society and from the state is part of an overall process of specialization that has affected all social and political institutions, particularly in the later part of the twentieth century. This specialization of functions has been accompanied by a formalization of the organizations that discharge those functions.

The phenomenon of specialization and formalization is visible everywhere. Governments are spawning increasing number of agencies and bureaux in order to perform a growing number of intricate functions. Although more evident in industrialized than in developing countries a trend towards specialization exists in the developing countries too, driven in part by similar factors: economic change and urbanization. The multiplication of government functions is made necessary by the increasing complexity of the economy and the requirements of more urban societies. The change in lifestyles resulting from industrialization creates the need for new social institutions while reducing the importance of others. In developing countries these trends are also driven by the example of the industrialized countries and by the direct pressure exercised by international development agencies that seek to reproduce familiar forms of organization.

Such pressure is entirely understandable and probably useful in some cases, but it can also create distortions. For example, the insistence by international financial institutions such as the International Monetary Fund and the World Bank that aid recipient countries set up special anti-corruption agencies could prove beneficial, at least if the agencies were to work efficiently. However, the creation of specialized organizations in this way can lead to development of a civil society sector that is poorly suited to the prevailing conditions and financially unsustainable. It may undermine forms of civil society organizations that are more in line with the resources and needs of the developing countries (Ottaway and Chung 1999).

## Contemporary civil society: myths and realities

In order to address the problem of whether the emergence of a specialized civil society in developing countries is a positive phenomenon or a distortion created by international development agencies, it is necessary to consider the main functions that civil society organizations perform in the contemporary world. This section focuses on three major functions of civil society and asks whether the new, specialized, and professionalized civil society can perform them in developing countries. The first and vaguest of these functions is the generation of social capital; the second, somewhat more specific, function is the representation of the interests and demands of the population; and the third, quite concrete, function is the provision of goods and, above all, services for the population. The specialization of civil society alters the way in which civil society performs these functions in all countries, but raises particularly serious problems in developing countries.

Take first the widely held view that civil society organizations generate social capital, a concept first set forth by Putnam (1993) in a study of regional government in Italy, as an explanation of why the same institutions functioned differently in the north

and south of the country. He observed that the inhabitants of the northern region shared a civic culture rooted in earlier experiences with self-government and sustained over the centuries by a rich associational life. These attitudes constituted the social capital that determined the way people viewed government and related to its institutions. This social capital was scarce in the southern regions, which had both a different historical experience and a dearth of associational life.

It is open to question to what extent the more specialized civil society organizations of today, with their professional staffs and narrow focuses, generate social capital. Professional, specialized organizations tend to have small or even non-existent membership and thus they do not reach many people. Even if they do, they engage them only on very specific issues. They probably do not inculcate in their members the attitudes of trust and cooperation that constitute social capital. Putnam argues that professional NGOs, even if devoted to democratic causes, contribute less to the social capital that supports democracy than seemingly irrelevant associations such as bowling leagues or the charitable and social clubs once widespread in American towns. He even sees in the decreasing popularity of these organizations a harbinger of the decline of American democracy.

Putnam's concern about the capacity of specialized and professionalized NGOs to generate social capital may be exaggerated in the case of the United States. There, many types of voluntary associations thrive and NGOs are numerous, extremely varied in their ideological and policy positions, and draw support widely, thereby contributing to pluralism. But in developing countries, many NGOs have small memberships, focus on a narrow range of issues and are highly dependent on foreign governments or international NGOs. Their contribution to social capital is highly questionable, particularly when compared to the social capital generated by more traditional social institutions. Such traditional institutions also teach values and attitudes, but not necessarily those extolled by Putnam as necessary for democracy. They may include, for example, extremely negative views of other ethnic or religious groups, deep distrust of all strangers, or demeaning attitudes towards women. The fact that the content of this social capital is different and may be contrary to democratic values does not alter the fact that it is deeply embedded in social relations and not easily erased, particularly by professional NGOs with weak social roots.

The second of the three functions attributed to civil society—the representational function—raises the question whether or how far such groups can actually represent the society vis-à-vis the government. The simple answer is that specialized civil society organizations do not represent society as a whole in any country. But in developing countries and within non-democratic international institutions, however, civil society organizations do broaden the range of interests that are expressed. Yet they do so in a lopsided way that favours groups with the capacity to organize and to access resources, even if their ideas are not widely held.

In well-established democracies, the problem of representation is solved by the existence of elected officials, freely chosen by the voters to represent their interests. Organizations of civil society are simply one among many types of organized interest group that put pressure on the elected officials to adopt the policies they favour. Professional NGOs are numerous and hold a variety of conflicting positions, as already stated, and compete for influence with a lot of other groups including paid lobbies; thus, they cannot advance a credible claim to represent the interests and the will of the entire population.

But in many developing countries representative institutions are often weak and elections fall short of being free and fair; as a result, civil society organizations may more credibly claim to represent voiceless citizens. Civil society organizations also have a degree of credibility when they claim to speak for unrepresented constituencies in international institutions, which are designed to represent states, but provide no formal channels through which popular demands can be expressed. Because lack of popular representation is a real problem in many developing countries and in international organizations, NGOs' claims that they voice the voiceless have won a degree of acceptance in recent years, and even gained them a place at the table in many policy discussions.

The issue whether NGOs should be consulted despite their lack of representativity remains highly controversial, and unlikely to be resolved soon. As long as countries do not have truly democratic institutions, the voice of NGOs adds an element of pluralism to the political system, and the distortions created by this imperfect form of representation may be an acceptable price for such a broadening of the political process. On the other hand, there is an element of risk in mandatory consultations with organizations that are not representative and above all not accountable to the people in whose name they claim to speak.

The third function performed by modern, professional civil society organizations is the provision of goods and services to the population. Many voluntary organizations provide a wide range of assistance—from the very basic, survival-oriented food distribution or provision of emergency shelter to the funding of research on rare diseases or the formation of support groups for people facing an almost infinite variety of problems. In this field too, there are considerable differences between the importance of this civil society in industrial and less developed countries, as well as in the issues raised by the existence of these organizations. On the one hand, these civil society organizations are much more numerous, better organized, and more capable in the industrialized countries. In developing countries they are usually highly dependent on external funding and very often find themselves in a subordinate position to the more affluent international NGOs that can access with greater ease money from rich countries and international organizations.

On the other hand, professional NGOs delivering goods and services often have a more important role in developing countries compared to richer counterparts in the industrialized West. In the poorest countries, for example, the assistance provided by NGOs is the main form of assistance available to the population, while in the richer countries NGOs supplement rather than replace the safety net provided by the government. This gives the foreign organizations that provide the funding for activities in developing countries a role that is often more important than that of the government. In extreme cases, the imbalance between the capacity of a developing country's government and that of the foreign and domestic NGOs operating there becomes dramatic and can hollow out the role of the government. To illustrate, in Afghanistan between January 2002 and March 2003, foreign donors channelled $296 million in assistance through the Afghan government and $446 million through international NGOs.

## Key points

- Professionalized and specialized civil society organizations generate little social capital.

- Specialized civil society organizations are not truly representative, but they broaden the range of interests expressed in the political process.

- Professional organizations can play a crucial role in the provision of services.

# Civil society and the state in the developing world

Relations between state and civil society, both in its traditional and modern forms, are quite complex in the developing world, more so than in industrial countries. Political systems are undergoing change in many countries, some states are still consolidating or conversely are on the verge of failure, modern civil society is a recent construct, and traditional forms of civil society are still making adaptations to a changed social and political environment. As a result, relations between state and civil society are in flux. In consolidated democracies, the relationship is more stable and thus more predictable.

Civil society organizations relate to state institutions and officials in one of three different ways: they ignore them and try to avoid their control; they oppose them and work for their replacement; or they seek to influence their policies. The pattern of avoidance is most often found in countries where the state is incapable of delivering services or other public goods. Civil society organizations give up on the state and seek to provide essential public goods on their own. Some of these activities are benign, for example the organization of alternative self-help schools for children neglected by the public system. Others are quite problematic; for example, in countries where the police force is incapable of ensuring a minimum of security for citizens, vigilante groups sometimes degenerate into protection rackets or become predatory. The organizations of civil society that flourish in the space left by a failing state are unregistered and unlicensed, often illegal. In terms of structures, they thus fall into the category of traditional civil society, although the functions they perform are a response to

contemporary problems created by state collapse and/or political repression.

When the state is capable of performing its functions, but the government is repressive and unresponsive, civil society organizations are more likely to take an antagonistic position. Some civil society organizations that take on an opposition role are simply fronts for political parties, deliberately set up to circumvent donors' rules against funding political organizations. As mentioned earlier, in some countries civil society organizations have strong party links. In others, civil society organizations turn into opposition groups after trying to influence the government and discovering they cannot do so. Many NGOs in Zimbabwe developed in the early 1990s as bona fide civil society organizations lobbying for improved human rights, constitutional reform, better legal services for the poor, and a variety of non-partisan causes. By the end of the decade, many had turned into anti-government forces as President Mugabe's government became increasingly repressive. Organizations that see themselves as guardians of universal principles—human rights organizations for example—are particularly likely to turn antagonistic when the government continues to violate those principles. Civil society groups that oppose the government can be organized as professional NGOs or along less formal lines as broad social movements or loosely structured networks. Such a broad, loosely structured alliance of hundreds of small local organizations or 'civics' formed in South Africa during the 1980s. The existence of this many-headed and elusive hydra was crucial in convincing the apartheid regime that peace could not be restored by repressive measures and that a political solution was necessary.

Finally, the relationship of civil society to state and government can be a cooperative one. This is the ideal promoted by democratization programmes. There are various forms of cooperation. Civil society organizations, which possess a degree of expertise in their specialized area, lobby the government to promote specific policy reforms and even provide the government with the expertise to implement the reforms, like helping to write legislation. Women's organizations, which are not usually seen as particularly threatening by governments although they may antagonize conservative social forces, are adept at this advocacy role. For example, they helped craft legislation in Uganda that expanded landownership rights for women, as well as a new divorce law more favourable to women in Egypt.

Another form of cooperation between government and civil society is found when the government contracts out the delivery of services to non-profit non-governmental organizations. This is rarer in developing countries than in Europe because it requires strong governments, capable of establishing a regulatory framework and providing supervision, and strong civil society organizations capable of delivering complex services. The existence of a weak government on one side and strong international NGOs, often backed by large amounts of foreign money, gives rise to the common complaint that in such conditions international NGOs de facto make policy, further weakening the government and undermining its capacity.

The relationship between state and civil society in developing countries is rarely an easy one. This explains why many governments see civil society organizations as dangerous enemies to be tightly controlled. In democratic countries, setting up and registering an NGO is an easy process and regulations aim above all at preventing abuse of tax-exempt status or the misuse of donations. By contrast, in many developing countries NGOs are subject to complicated regulations aimed at suppressing groups that aspire to an advocacy role, instead of merely dispensing charity. An important issue that emerged in the 1990s in some countries is whether organizations of civil society should be allowed to receive foreign funding. Most governments welcome foreign funding of charitable organizations—for example, groups that provide assistance to AIDS orphans in Africa. Foreign funding of advocacy organizations, on the other hand, is very controversial.

## Key points

- When the state is repressive, civil society organizations are usually antagonistic to it.

- When the state is weak and incapable of delivering services, civil society organizations seek to ignore the state and avoid its control, rather than press for reforms.

- When the state is strong and civil society organizations are well developed, relations tend to be cooperative and constructive.

# Civil society and democratization

The rapid transformation of the term civil society from an obscure concept known to a few scholars to one that finds its place in all discussions of political transformation is due to the rapid spread of democracy assistance initiatives that followed the end of the cold war. However, by the end of the 1990s it was clear that many so-called democratic transitions had led at best to the formation of semi-authoritarian regimes

rather than democratic ones (Ottaway 2003). Furthermore, the reform process was losing momentum almost everywhere (Diamond 1996). Nevertheless, democracy promotion abroad remains on the political agenda of most industrial democracies. And leaders in the developing world, including many with no democratic credentials and no visible intention of acquiring them, embraced the rhetoric of democracy.

The concept of civil society became an important part of all discussions of democratization for reasons grounded to some extent in theory—as discussed earlier—and to a larger extent in pragmatism. In order to provide democracy assistance, aid agencies had to break down the abstract idea of democracy into concrete component parts that could be supported with limited amounts of aid. Civil society was such a component, and a particularly attractive one. Developing civil society meant promoting government by the people and for the people. And when civil society was defined as a narrow set of professional NGOs, it was also an entity to which assistance could be easily provided.

NGOs are easy to organize and cheap to fund; small grants go a long way. Professional NGOs were also a new type of association in many countries. Without roots in the traditional civil society and the culture of their countries and highly dependent on outside funding, professional NGOs were easy to train and influence to conform to the funders' concept of what civil society should do. With donor support, NGOs multiplied rapidly in all regions of the world, displaying remarkably similar characteristics. This made the aid agencies' job of supporting civil society easier. It also raised the question whether these organizations were truly addressing the specific challenges of democratization in their countries.

Many studies of the donor-assisted civil society have reached the conclusion that pro-democracy NGOs tend to be quite isolated from the society at large. For instance this was a nearly unanimous conclusion of the contributors to *Funding Virtue* (Ottaway and Carothers 2000), with the only exception being two experts on the Philippines, where the growth of civil society was an indigenous process that owed much less to foreign assistance. This suggests that donor support is an important contributor to the isolation of civil society organizations. Many professional NGOs have small or no membership. They are often exclusively urban organizations with little reach in the countryside—only the best organized are able to extend their reach through networks of less formal community-based organizations (CBOs). Exchanges (often called 'networking') among the NGOs from different countries provide an opportunity for organizations to discuss their problems and learn from each other, but they also contribute to

> ## Box 8.1  Civil society in the Philippines
>
> In the Philippines, the NGO community has long played a significant political role—helping bring down the Marcos regime, challenging and helping define the national political agendas under presidents Aquino, Ramos and Estrada, and taking sides in the 1998 presidential elections to support Estrada over Ramos . . . a reason for the unusual strength of civil society is that the focus of most NGOs in the Philippines is not the promotion of a formal democratic system but the participation of citizens in promoting economic development and tackling the social problems that affect them directly. Democratic participation is thus not an abstraction but a means to an end that is directly important to the lives of people. Democratic participation becomes an extension of such efforts to improve one's life chances.
>
> (Ottaway and Carothers 2000: 297; 302)

creating a special international NGO world whose inhabitants talk to each other more easily than they do to their compatriots. These observations do not call into question the genuine commitment of many NGO leaders to democracy, human rights, or other causes. They do call into question, however, the capacity of these so-called organizations of civil society to influence their societies.

Democracy NGOs have other problems worth mentioning briefly. One is the opportunism that exists in the NGO world alongside genuine commitment—when assistance is available, setting up an NGO can simply be a way of making a living. **Corruption** also exists in the NGO world, which is unsurprising in view of its very rapid growth. And many, as mentioned earlier, become partisan organizations affiliated with political parties. These problems are tangible, but also inevitable to some extent and not particularly worrisome unless they are extremely widespread. They are simply part of the inevitable imperfection of the real world.

What is more worrisome is whether the growth of a small professional civil society actually contributes to democratization and whether the attention lavished on these organizations has led to the neglect of organizational forms that might have greater popular appeal and greater outreach within the population. Democracy promoters recognize the weakness of the NGOs they support and they equate it with the weakness of civil society. And yet, in many of the countries where the organizations officially designated as civil society are weakest, for example in many war-torn African countries, informal civil society organizations have proven very resilient in trying to address the most severe difficulties created by state collapse. In their search for a society that is civil by their definition and assistable in terms of its formal characteristics, aid providers may have marginalized groups with a proven record of effectiveness.

Arab countries, with their contrast between a vast Islamic civil society and their struggling official civil society, illustrate the problem particularly well. In Egypt the world of Islamic civil society is large and multifaceted. It includes charitable groups, organizations that provide free of charge medical services the state has stopped delivering, organizations that offer some educational opportunities for students under-served by failing public schools, groups that provide textbooks for university students who cannot afford them. It also includes organizations with political goals that do not satisfy the principles of liberal democracy, and terrorist groups that can only be defined as uncivil.

This Islamic civil society is well rooted in the society at large. Even organizations that are by no means traditional, but represent a contemporary and, from a religious point of view, aberrant response to contemporary problems, can cast themselves as part of a well-established tradition. They are certainly better rooted in the society than the modern, professional, pro-democracy NGOs favoured by donors. But the new, donors' civil society espouses the values of liberal democracy, while the more traditional Islamic civil society is at best ambiguous on this point. In the end, neither an isolated modern civil society nor a well-rooted Islamic one are good vehicles for democratic transformation.

---

### Box 8.2 Policy and advocacy NGOs only a part of civil society

The case studies make clear the assumption of NGOs' centrality is questionable. Other kinds of civil society groups frequently drive political change, eclipsing what is often the circumscribed role of policy or advocacy NGOs. In South Africa a social movement brought down apartheid. In Egypt, traditional professional associations are major players in the struggles over political liberalization. In Latin America, the profound struggles of the 1980s against dictatorship and repression were conducted by many social and political forces very different from the technocratic advocacy NGO donors would favour in the 1990s. And in the Philippines, Bangladesh, and elsewhere in Asia, citizens' groups focused on socio-economic issues are having major effects on long-term processes of societal change.

(Adapted from Ottaway and Carothers 2000: 295)

## Key points

- The difference between traditional organizations well rooted in the society, relatively close to the population, but not necessarily democratic or official and the civil society recognized by international democracy promoters may be starker in the Muslim world than elsewhere at this time, but is found in all parts of the developing world.

- Democracy requires a large, active, democratically oriented civil society, but what is found in most countries is a bifurcated situation: an official civil society—small, democratic, but essentially elitist; and a less formal, traditional civil society—large, popular, well rooted but of dubious democratic credentials.

- How to combine the democratic commitment of the former to the popular roots and outreach of the other is a major conundrum for democratization.

# Conclusions

The chapter started with an acknowledgement of the ambiguity of the concept of civil society and of its lack of definitional clarity. It ends on the same note, but with a normative addendum. Not only the concept of civil society is an imprecise, ambiguous one, but it must be accepted as such. The more strictly the concept is defined, the less it helps understand how people come together voluntarily to address problems that they cannot solve as individuals and that the state cannot or does not want to help solve for them.

It is of course possible to narrow down the definition closely. This is what the international development agencies do all the time when they pick the organizations to support on the basis of the civility of their goals and the adequacy of their organizational structures. But what is gained in terms of clarity is lost in terms of the understanding of the society. First, the narrow definition loses sight of the many ways in which people in any society organize themselves to pursue their interests and satisfy their needs. It may reduce the effectiveness of any outside intervention, by focusing attention on groups that may be quite marginal to the society but happen to appear all-important to aid agencies. Second, a definition that separates a democratic, virtuous civil society acting in the public interest from a non-democratic, uncivil one, selfishly promoting narrow interests is more normative than analytical. The idea of the common good and the public interest obfuscate the reality that all societies are made up of groups with different and often conflicting interests, and that all groups are equally part of the society, whether their goals conform to a specific idea of civility or not.

In conclusion, despite the caveat expressed at the outset, from an analytical point of view we need to accept that we cannot do better than accept that civil society comprises the entire realm of voluntary associations between the family and the state. It is a vast and complex realm. Voluntary associations take many different forms, ranging from small, informal self-help groups and ad hoc committees with narrow goals to large, professional and bureaucratic organizations with large budgets. In developing countries, civil society organizations perform a wide range of functions. At one extreme, there are narrowly focused groups that seek, for example, to provide support for AIDS orphans in a community or raise money to improve the track that connects a village to the nearest highway. At the other, there are organizations tied into transnational networks with goals such as changing the World Bank's outlook on the construction of dams or delivering humanitarian assistance to populations in need. Many voluntary associations in developing countries try to provide services the state is unable to deliver. Others form to help citizens resist pressure from predatory governments. Organizations citizens develop voluntarily are not always 'civil' in the normative sense of the word. The realm of civil society comprises organizations that promote human rights and vigilante groups that prey on the people they are supposed to protect. While it is tempting to narrow the definition of civil society to organizations with commendable goals, this is not helpful. If we want to understand how people come together to defend their interests or pursue their goals, we need to accept the diversity, the complexity, and in many cases the flaws of the associational realm that has become known as civil society.

## QUESTIONS

1   What is civil society, and why is it considered crucial to democratization?

2   What are the competing definitions of civil society?

3   Why are traditional forms of civil society reappearing in developing countries today, and what functions do they perform?

4   To what extent do civil society organizations represent the population?

5   Discuss the different ways in which civil society organizations relate to the state.

6   Compare the contribution professional organizations of civil society and traditional civil society organizations make to democratization.

7   What problems can strong organizations of civil society create in weak states?

## GUIDE TO FURTHER READING

Florini, Ann M. (ed.), *The Third Force: The Rise of Transnational Civil Society* (Washington: Carnegie Endowment for International Peace, 2000). Case studies of the role of transnational networks of civil society including the global anti-corruption movement, human rights movement, organizations for democracy, and against dam-building and for environmental sustainability.

Hann, Chris, and Dunn, Elisabeth (eds.), *Civil Society: Challenging Western Models* (New York: Routledge, 1996). A critical account.

Kasfir, Nelson (ed.), *Civil Society and Democracy in Africa* (London: Frank Cass, 1998). A critical view of conventional Western attitudes towards civil society in Africa.

Ottaway, Marina, and Carothers, Thomas (eds.), *Funding Virtue: Civil Society Aid and Democracy Promotion* (Washington: Carnegie Endowment for International Peace, 2000). A critical examination of civil society aid drawing on cases in Africa, Asia, the Middle East, and Latin America.

—— and Chung, Theresa, 'Debating Democracy Assistance: Toward a New Paradigm', *Journal of Democracy*, 10/ 4 (1999): 99–113. A cautious view of international 'democracy assistance' to civil society and to elections and parties too.

Putnam, Robert, *Making Democracy Work: Civic Traditions in Modern Italy* (Princeton: Princeton University Press, 1993). A seminal work on social capital.

Wickham, Carrie Rosefsky, *Mobilizing Islam: Religion, Activism, and Political Change in Egypt* (New York: Columbia University Press, 2002). A highly acclaimed analysis of the role of cultural identity, political economy, mobilization and organization in political Islam in Egypt.

## WEB LINKS

**www.ids.ac.uk/ids/civsoc**   The site of the civil society and governance research project at the Institute of Development Studies, University of Sussex, which examines the interplay of civil society and governments in 22 countries. Funded by the Ford Foundation.

**www.ceip.org/files/pdf/CarnegiePaper44.pdf.a**   *Middle Eastern Democracy. Is Civil Society the Answer?*, by Amy Hawthorne. A critical examination of the question.

**www.civilsoc.org**   Civil Society International aims to help civil society organizations worldwide through publicity, networking, and educational initiatives.

**www.un.org/partners/civil_society/home.htm**   Links to the ways the United Nations system works 'in partnership' with civil society on issues of global concern.

 **COMPANION WEB SITE**

For additional material and resources, see the companion web site at:
**www.oup.com/uk/booksites/politics/**

# Part Three

# State and society

The heading of Part Three reverses the order of the two terms contained in the previous part to signify that Part Three focuses chiefly on the institutions of state and their importance to society. In politics, institutions matter. The state is not merely one among many political institutions but historically has been the pre-eminent focus of attention. In the modern world, under the impact of rapid social, economic, technological, and other changes taking place at both the global and sub-state level the exact nature, role, and significance of the state are continually evolving. But it would be no less foolish to suggest the end of the state is nigh and to dissolve its analysis into a soup of exogenous actors and currents—domestic or international—than it is to ignore how those actors and currents set limits on what government can do. This part has two main aims. The **first** is to explore what the state means in a developing world context and how it differs from the state in more developed countries. Can one framework accommodate all the varieties of state formation including the special manifestations such as state failure? The **second** aim is to show how the governance capabilities of states and even more so the kind of political regime—the relationship between the institutions of government and society—have undergone significant change especially in the last two decades or so. This part is essential for enabling us to address important questions about how far the state in the developing world should be held responsible for dealing with fundamental developmental issues, and whether it is equipped to resolve pressing issues such as those affecting the economy, welfare, the environment, and human rights. For instance what is the relationship between democracy or democratization and socio-economic progress or human development? Is there a specific sequence in which these must arise, or is the situation more like that of chicken and egg? Do the connections between regimes and development in the developing world suggest the presence of virtuous circles or vicious circles? The relevant policy issues comprise the substance of Part Four and are best examined only when Part Three is read first. The illustrative material in Part Three is widely drawn from around the developing world. By comparison case studies of countries selected to illustrate specific issues and themes can be found in Part Five. For example, the discussion of state collapse in Chapter 11 is illustrated by the case of Zaire/the Democratic Republic of the Congo in Chapter 18b. The more positive experience of democratization, examined at a general level in Chapter 12, is illustrated by Mexico's experience, in Chapter 20b. Readers are encouraged to consult the case studies alongside the Chapters in Part Three.

# Theorizing the state

*Adrian Leftwich*

## OVERVIEW

Explanation of successful and failed states in the contemporary developing world requires an understanding of the provenance, characteristics, and functions of the modern state as it evolved in what is now the developed world. This chapter first explores the nature of institutions in general and, in particular, the modern state as a set of political institutions of rule, geared to the organization, promotion, and continuous management of economic development. Second, it analyses the emergence and distinguishing features of the state in what is now the developed world; and, third, it investigates the transportation of the modern state to the now developing world and the consequences of that. The central argument is that the characteristics of any state, anywhere, are largely defined by its relations with the economy and society which it reflects and both represents and dominates, in its historical, regional, and international context. The chapter concludes by arguing that, despite many problems, political processes in some developing countries could be moving towards the establishment of the state institutions of rule that could at last provide more stability and effectiveness for economic development and greater participation for citizens in decision-making processes. But the process is both very slow and very uneven.

# Introduction: institutions, politics, and the state

## Institutions

Human societies cannot endure, prosper, or—especially—develop without broadly agreed and appropriate rules and conventions governing the conduct of social, economic, and political affairs, and about how human and other resources are to be used and distributed. Such sets of rules are what political scientists mean by **institutions**. In essence, institutions are collections of (broadly) agreed norms, rules, procedures, and routines—whether they are formally established and written down (in law or by decree), as with constitutions, or whether they are informal understandings embedded in the culture (March and Olsen 1989: 21–6). Essentially, institutions direct and constrain human interaction. All societies have them; they must. The different institutional spheres often overlap (and sometimes conflict to produce undesired outcomes), and include social institutions (governing social interaction and behaviour), economic institutions (the customs, rules, and procedures governing economic behaviour, ranging from silent barter to rules governing stock-market behaviour)—and political institutions (governing relations of power).

## Political institutions and the modern state

Political scientists take a special interest in the evolution and forms of the last of these institutional spheres: that of politics and power, the sphere in which the *processes and practices of rule*, of *governing*, or of a particular form of *institutionalized domination*, emerged. The *forms of rule* expressed in different political systems, or *polities*, have varied widely across space and time. For instance, some polities initially involved only very basic forms of localized village headship or leadership; others, perhaps starting with such local and limited forms of rule and power, subsequently evolved at different speeds and with different intensities into steeper and more extensive hierarchies of centralized control and power over an increasing territorial space. The emergence of centralized polities (which some theorists refer to as early states) sometimes expanded over wide areas to encompass other societies so that they came to constitute what have been called 'centralized bureaucratic empires'.

However, the immense range of historical political systems which gave expression to the different forms and distributions of power has shrunk dramatically since the sixteenth century when one type of polity began to emerge in Europe and came to be the dominant political form of the recent and contemporary world: *the state* or, more accurately, the *modern state*. Some scholars see earlier polities as 'non-modern' states, classifying them for example as ancient city-states, feudal states, pre-modern, early modern, or absolutist states or even 'princely states'. But the *modern* state, as we understand it, is distinctive in its central characteristics, though found in a variety of forms.

In the main, the emergence of the modern state in Europe was an endogenous process, occurring primarily within the geography and history of particular regions and in the course of conflict, competition, and, especially, consolidation among them. To illustrate, in late fifteenth-century Europe there were some 500 independent political units, but by 1900 this had shrunk to about twenty-five. Such states, in turn, came to shape the histories and geographies of the emerging countries which they both represented and dominated. And from within this history of European state formation, there developed, from the fifteenth century, outward thrusts of discovery, conquest, and control, loosely called imperialism and colonialism. These imperial processes carved out new 'countries' (in most cases which had not existed beforehand), they established new institutions of rule in the form of the colonial state (which either suppressed or used and sometimes transformed existing institutions of rulership), and drew such countries (or parts of them) into different kinds of largely subordinate economic relations with the metropolitan countries of the increasingly dominant 'West'. The effects of all this were to be profound in the external 'shaping' of the states that emerged in the developing world, and persist today in the post-colonial era.

# Key points

- All human societies require institutions, informal or formal, to govern and promote their collective affairs.

- Institutions are best understood as collections of rules, procedures, practices, and routines.

- The emergence of specialist political institutions marks the differentiation of political systems or polities.

- The most recent and dominant form has been the modern state whose origins (and forms) were primarily European.

- This form was carried outwards by European imperialism and colonialism, and imposed on diverse societies, or adopted and adapted by them. The external provenance of the state in many developing countries has been a critical factor in shaping and influencing their particular forms and the politics associated with them.

# The modern state

## Traditional polities

The modern state was the product of slow evolution from prior political systems, prior polities, but by the nineteenth century its central features were clear. The German sociologist Max Weber (1964) theorized those features of the 'modern' state which distinguished it from prior 'traditional' institutions of rule, or systems of authority. These earlier forms, he suggested, like the 'patrimonial' form of authority as he called it, were characterized by two overriding features.

First, the absence of any sharp institutional distinction between the *rulers* and the *institutions of rule*. This was typical of the absolutist rule of some European monarchs well into the eighteenth century, and beyond in some cases (as well as earlier and elsewhere in East Asia and Middle America). For instance, Louis XIV, the king of France in the mid-seventeenth century, made the point with great effect when he is alleged to have said to the *parlement* of Paris in April 1655 *'L'État c'est moi'* (I am the state).

The second defining feature of traditional forms of rule (not only patrimonial or absolutist versions) was the relative absence of open, meritocratic entry, autonomy, independence, and security of tenure for the officials who surrounded the rulers. In a manner that distinguished those officials from the ideal-typical bureaucracy of the modern state, they were essentially the personal staff of the ruler, often paid by him or her, and with the more or less explicit requirement of personal loyalty to him or her.

## Defining the modern state

Many characteristics and functions distinguish the modern state. But it was the development of *institutions* of rule and governing which were formally separated from not just the rulers but the officials who ran them, on the one hand, and the citizenry, on the other hand, that was central in the shift from what Weber called 'traditional' forms of rule and authority, including patrimonial polities, to the modern state. Held, McGrew, Goldblatt, and Perraton (1999: 45) claim the modern state is a set of 'political apparatuses, distinct from both ruler and ruled, with supreme jurisdiction over a demarcated area, backed by a claim to a monopoly of coercive power, and enjoying **legitimacy** as a result of a minimum level of support or loyalty from their citizens'. Within this compact definition can be found all the essential elements of the complex set of institutions that make up the modern state:

*Public institutions*: the institutions of the modern state are all 'public' institutions, not private or privately owned institutions, and include not only 'the government' and legislature (of the day) but also the courts, civil service, army, and police, plus any state-owned agencies. All of these, though more or less coherently linked, are differentiated from other institutions (especially private and non-state institutions) and individuals, and from the incumbents of the offices and the citizens or subjects over whom they exercise authority.

*Sovereignty and hegemony*: the institutions of the state and the rules and laws made by it have authority over a particular demarcated geographical area (though there may be disputes about that, as in secessionist and irredentist conflicts). Moreover, the rules and laws of the modern state apply in theory to everyone within its territory.

*Formal monopoly of violence*: the modern state has a monopoly of the legitimate use of violence and it is, or should be, the dominant agency of rule and law, whether democratic or not, in principle superordinate over all others. In practice most modern states have struggled at times and still do struggle to achieve that dominance—as illustrated by the Peruvian state's battle to subdue the *Sendero Luminoso* guerrilla movement which exercised considerable power over parts of Peru in the 1970s and 1980s.

*Impartial bureaucracy*: the bureaucracy is (theoretically) impersonal, impartial, and neutral. Theoretically, too, it does not make law, but receives it from whoever makes it (whether legislature or dictator) and applies it. In practice, policy-making is much more complex, and, increasingly, specialist bureaucratic input into policy-making is the norm. Furthermore, different parts of the public bureaucracy have often very different interests and compete for resources to assert their policy preferences, expand their functions or increase their staff. Nonetheless, the central characteristic that distinguishes the modern state from prior forms of rule is the principle, at least, of *relative* independence and autonomy of the public service from both the elected political elites and parties and also from the public. Moreover, the offices (and the powers of the offices) of state officials, whether constitutional monarchs, presidents, ministers, legislators, judges, police, or civil servants belong to the state, not to them personally. It is a fundamental assumption of the modern state that these public offices (and associated powers) should not be used for *private* gain by the incumbents of such offices (what would normally be called **corruption**). Occupancy of such offices should entail no powers of private **patronage** nor be used for the support of any particular private client base (**clientelism**), whether personal, regional, ethnic, or economic.

These characteristics are of course ideal-typical; that is, they define the modern state in abstract and ideal terms. No state in the modern world has been, or can be, found which fulfils them to perfection. And while many (though not all) theorists may agree on this limited set of characteristics of the modern state, the most contentious issues of debate and interpretation in political science revolve around other central issues such as: is the modern state 'neutral'? Can it be? Do classes and their interests dominate its policy output and, if so, in each case, which ones? Does or can the state have its own interests? What should its role in economy and society be? How far should the state intervene in, or make rules for, the 'private' life of its subjects and be limited or constrained in what it does by constitutionally defined bills of rights?

Modern states differ with respect to many other variables, for example their *historical traditions* (some have longer continuous traditions of centralized rule than others, as in England, Russia, or Japan); their *structural properties* (for example whether unitary or, as in India and Nigeria, federal, and hence how state power is distributed regionally); whether they are formally *democratic or not* and for how long; their *electoral systems* and/or *consultative patterns* (and how these influence state power and policy-making); and the nature and extent of their *legitimacy* in the perception of their subjects.

## The modern state: imperatives, functions, and challenges

As the modern state consolidated, replicated, and proliferated through the nineteenth and twentieth centuries, more countries began to adopt its broad template as their system of rule, their polity. For example, many Latin American countries adopted and adapted from France and (to a lesser extent) the United States in shaping their constitutions (rules of the political game) as they gained independence from Spain and Portugal between 1811 and 1900.

But the really central point is that the modern state emerged in the course of the great transformation from agrarian to industrial societies (mainly in Europe) and in the consequential requirements for appropriate institutional and regulatory frameworks and functions to facilitate and extend this. It was both product and agent of that transformation. Indeed it is essential to understand that the fundamental defining role and function of the modern state has been to promote, organize, protect, and sustain this economic and social transformation to industrialism—and beyond into the 'post-industrial' era. In the nineteenth and twentieth centuries the history of the now industrial powers and more recent modern history of the contemporary developing world shows that successful and effective modern states and successful economies go hand in hand. This process of state formation was of course intensified through the competitive economic, military, and other forms of nationalism that it promoted, and by the turbulent socio-political changes associated with the economic transformation. And by the early twentieth century four critical issues had come to confront the modern state. The manner in which each state dealt with them in turn helped to define its specific shape and its character in its relations with the society it claimed both to represent and to manage. These four issues were: defence against external attack and internal security, the promotion and protection of the economy, democratization, and the associated demand for state provision of welfare.

First, with regard to defence, the period 1850–1939 saw an intensification of what has been called **despotic power**, that is the power to control and suppress, as opposed to **infrastructural power**, the power to penetrate and transform society (Mann 1986: 169–70; Weiss and Hobson 1995). But, second, as indicated above, national economic growth and development also was central to the emergence of the modern state and its defence and was closely associated with the competitive nationalisms of the nineteenth century. Thus successful modern economic growth and successful modern states with influence that extends beyond their borders have been inextricably linked. And there is nothing that sums this up better than the slogan 'National Wealth, Military Strength' (often translated as 'rich country, strong army') adopted by the new post-Meiji elites in Japan after 1870.

In pursuit of these goals, most of today's leading industrial economies used state-directed industrial, trade, and technological policies (Chang 2002: 58 and *passim*) to get ahead, and try to stay ahead (as in the case of Britain), or to catch up as Germany, Japan, and the United States began to do in the nineteenth century. The theory and practice of state involvement in promoting growth and protecting the national economy has varied from country to country and time to time, but three broad strategies, or models, may be identified (though each has contained a variety of sometimes quite distinctive forms). The first was the Anglo-American and Western European model which involved the state ensuring four prime conditions for the promotion of private, market-driven growth, as argued by Douglas North (1990): securing property rights, establishing a fair and efficient judicial system, setting out open and understood system of rules and regulations, and facilitating market entry and functioning. At certain times state action has gone much further than this as in the depression years in the USA and in the post-war years in Europe. The second model has been the Soviet model, of forced-march top-down industrialization, pioneered from the 1920s and involving pervasive state ownership, control and management of the economy, and the mobilization by the state, not the market, of resources (including human ones) in pursuit of transformative objectives. The third model is essentially the East Asian model of the **developmental state**, pioneered in Japan after 1870, and especially after the 1920s, which has been replicated in some other countries like Korea and Taiwan (Leftwich 1995). This involved a much closer symbiosis between state and private sector, (see Chapter 21*b* below) and has sometimes been called 'managed capitalism' or 'governing the market'.

All modern states, then, have had to engage with the central issue: to what extent, when, and how to promote and protect their economies in a sharply (and increasingly) competitive world economy, especially when motivated by the urgent need to reconstruct (after war) or catch up—or go under (as they saw it).

Modern states in the developing world have sought to adopt (with often quite substantial local modifications) versions of the three different strategies outlined above in the more or less serious pursuit of the goals of economic growth through industrialization. Crucially, however, successful intervention along any of the strategic paths has only occurred, and has indeed only been possible, where the appropriate political coalitions and distributions of power underpinning the state have allowed rather than hindered growth-promoting institutions and strategies. This has been one of the key differences between the older 'modern states' and the new 'modern states' of the developing world.

Finally, with regard to the third and fourth challenges besetting the modern state (those of democratization and redistribution), Huntington (1991) identified three great 'waves' of democratization occuring between 1828 and 1926, between 1943 and 1962, and from 1974 to the present. In each of these phases, and varying from country to country, dominant state elites responded to democratic pressures in different ways, hence shaping the character of the polity, depending on whether and to what extent they saw their interests being threatened by such demands. Where democratic progress occurred, the associated deepening and extension of civil society has had the effect of redistributing some political power through the institutional forms of electoral, bargaining, and consultative processes. Moreover, the growth of powerful and increasingly well-organized labour movements in particular has meant that few states in the developed world could afford to ignore the demand for redistributionist programmes, for example through taxation policy, welfare provision (health, old age, and education for instance), and wage-level agreements. In consequence, those societies managed effectively by modern states are (with a few notable exceptions) characterized by levels of income inequality far less extreme than in many parts of the developing world (see Chapter 4).

## Key points

- Modern states are the political institutions of rule which are in principle differentiated and distinct from both the rulers and the ruled.

- The modern state emerged, evolved, consolidated, and was borrowed as the centralized and organizing institutions of rule whose central function was to manage, promote, and protect national transitions from agrarian to industrial society, and to sustain economic growth.

- Historically, the modern state has been characterized, in ideal typical terms, by its public institutions, its sovereignty and hegemony, its formal monopoly of legitimate coercion (violence), and its theoretically impartial bureaucracy

- Though different states adopted different strategies, successful economic growth and successful states have without exception been inextricably linked.

- In promoting economic growth and development, modern states have had to provide defence and ensure law and order, respond to demands for a wider set of civic rights—notably greater democratic participation in policy-making—and manage some redistribution of resources through tax and welfare arrangements.

- The broad strategy adopted in the pursuit of economic growth has depended crucially on the character of the political forces and coalitions underpinning state power, which in turn has influenced the achievement of developmental goals.

# The state in the developing world: provenance and forms

## Introduction

Most of the conditions and capabilities associated with the state's emergence in the now developed world have been largely absent in the developing world. In short, the formation of modern states in colonial and post-colonial contexts was not geared to

the development of institutions of rule directed at promoting economic growth or transformative development, as occurred in Europe, and elsewhere, whether on a capitalist, socialist, or mixed economy basis. Moreover, most of the challenges that those earlier states had to meet—especially those of democratic pressures and redistributive demands—have thus far exceeded the capability of many of the newer states. And crucially, apart from some very important exceptions, this is explained by the quite diverse political forces and coalitions formed during or after the colonial era and which set up, inherited, adapted, or battled for control of the institutions of the modern state. Simply stated, these political forces, representing varying kinds of socio-economic elites and interests, seldom had the interest, the will, or the power to establish or encourage growth-promoting institutions in accordance with any of the three models sketched above. This is why so many states in the contemporary developing world have been associated with weak or uneven developmental performances. But before proceeding further, two important introductory points should be made.

First, we do not need a special political science for the analysis of the state in the developing world today. The problems facing these states have been no different to those which faced (or still face) states and societies in the now developed world, so-called; they may be different in complexity, intensity, and context, but not in principle. These problems have been (and remain) essentially those of how to establish and sustain the institutions of rule which promote the momentum of economic development, within or outside democratic polities, whether state-led or market-led, in the face of both more or less explicit pressures for democratization and redistribution, in an increasingly globalized political economy.

Second, it is always difficult to generalize about states and politics across continents. Historically, the kinds of modern state institution which developing countries inherited at independence varied widely and were everywhere shaped by the interaction of four main factors: the nature of the pre-colonial polities; the economic purposes of colonial rule; the characteristics of the colonial state institutions and the socio-political groups which dominated them; and the manner of incorporation of pre-colonial political processes and institutions in the systems of colonial and post-colonial rule. Accordingly, the contemporary developing world is at least as diverse as were those societies in which the modern state emerged; and the differentiation in economic circumstances and political structure has been considerable. Nevertheless there are some major, common underlying themes too.

# The modern state in the developing world: provenance

If the modern state in what we now call the developed world grew largely through complex *internal* political processes of conflict, consolidation, and regional contestation (nationalisms) in the course of the great transformations from agrarian to industrial societies, most states in the developing world owe their existence (and indeed the very borders over which they seek or claim to rule) to the geographical definitions and institutional impositions of the colonial era or to later adjustments. With few exceptions, the provenance of states in the developing world has largely been *external*, and few modern states there can trace their lineages back through indigenous systems and institutions of rule. In short, few developed endogenously from prior local polities. In Asia, the exceptions include Korea, Indonesia, and Thailand where some continuity can be traced back to prior local (absolutist, monarchical, and imperial) systems and institutions of centralized rule, as in Egypt and Ethiopia in the case of Africa. In Latin America the main pre-colonial political institutions, especially the great centralized tribute-extracting empires of the Aztecs (Mexico) and the Incas (Peru), were extinguished by the Spanish conquest from the early sixteenth century, though cultural legacies remain even today.

Although the patterns of colonial state institutions varied widely across time and space (Young 1994: 244–81), they everywhere left very important influences on the politics and state structures after independence. Everywhere, and almost without exception, the purpose of colonial rule and control was undertaken initially for the benefit of the metropolitan countries or their particular interests.

# Colonial states: imposed borders and the institutional patterns of rule

### External design and imposition of 'national' boundaries

Perhaps the most far-reaching influence and impact has been the external shaping of geographical boundaries and institutional structures, the most dramatic illustration being the '**scramble for Africa**', which produced the national boundaries of Africa today. Of course there were no 'countries' with formally defined 'national' boundaries before this—indeed the notion of 'nation' or 'nation-state' would have been alien in pre-colonial Africa: political boundaries were vague and porous. What there were, however, was a wide range of 'multiple, overlapping and alternative collective identities' (Berman 1998: 310) expressed in, through, and under an equally wide range of institutional political arrangements. Such was the artificiality of the new, imposed boundaries that some 44 per cent of those still existing today are straight lines (Herbst 2000: 75), representing lines drawn cartographically on open maps. There was almost no indigenous definition of geographical boundaries, nor were any major 'national' movements, or 'nationalist' sentiments, involved in establishing the boundaries of modern African nation-states. The Latin American experience was not much different, where the new states were carved from the huge Vice Royalties of the colonial system of rule in the course of the struggles for independence in the nineteenth century. Led largely by the conservative

*criollos* (colonial born Spaniards) the new states in consequence expressed political and socio-economic relations which even today reflect deep and profound inequalities between a small (and very rich) elite and a large (and very poor) mass.

In Asia, a similar pattern occurred and the Indian subcontinent provides the best example, where British rule brought diverse ethnic and religious communities, often tense with communal rivalries, not to mention over 500 Princely States, together in colonial India. But at independence, the country was divided between India and Pakistan, with East Pakistan (later to become independent as Bangladesh) being separated by a great chunk of India from West Pakistan. Indonesia emerged from Dutch rule as an improbable 'nation-state' of about 13,000 islands stretching for about 3,500 miles from west to east, containing diverse linguistic, cultural, and religious communities (see map on page 256 in Chapter 16). Cambodia, Korea, Thailand, Myanmar, and, to some extent, Malaysia have been notable exceptions to this pattern, each reflecting closer lineages with some historical polity.

### Extractive rather than developmental purposes of rule

The purpose of imperial control or rule—and hence the character of the institutions of the colonial states—was not developmental in the manner of the emerging modern states of Europe. On the contrary, all the major colonial powers (and often the early private companies that acted for them) saw the extraction of riches, raw materials and taxes as their primary objective.

### External design and imposition of the institutions of rule

In trying to understand the problems and failures of many states in the developing world it is fundamental to recognize that these extractive purposes shaped the kind of institutions of rule, which in turn formed the foundations for the states after independence. In so far as the institutions of colonial rule can be termed 'colonial states' (Young 1994), they were essentially states of extraction, and not aimed at promoting, and organizing national economic development. With the exception of Japanese rule in Korea, no colonial institutions of rule bore any resemblance to any of the three models sketched above. In short, throughout

---

### Box 9.1 **The colonial impact in Africa**

In Africa, large tracts of land were claimed by European powers as their possessions, either as colonies or protectorates or as in the case of King Leopold of Belgium, as private property in the form of the Congo Free State. The distribution among the powers' 'scramble for Africa' was formally recognized by their representatives at the Congress of Berlin, 1884–5. In all of this Britain, France, Germany, and Portugal paid no regard to the enormous differences among the different African societies that ranged from small-scale self-governing hunting and gathering bands to large, hierarchical political systems as in the empires of Mali, Ghana, and Songhay in West Africa. Peoples with diverse cultures, religions, languages, and political systems that had previously lived alongside one another, sometimes peacefully and sometimes in violent conflict or subordination, but without formal boundaries, were now pulled together into entirely artificially created 'nation' states.

## Box 9.2 **The extractive nature of imperial rule**

The Spanish conquistador and conqueror of Mexico, Hernando Cortés, in the sixteenth century, is reputed to have said 'I came to get gold, not to till the soil, like a peasant'. In the Caribbean, plantations exploiting unfree labour (first, indentured servants and then almost entirely slaves) were established for the production and export of cotton, tobacco, and especially sugar. In Indonesia, the 'culture system' of the Dutch, first under the Dutch East India Company and then through formal colonial rule, required Indonesians to deliver set amounts of spices to the authorities. Likewise, the ruthless requirements of King Leopold's Free State in the Congo demanded that rubber and ivory be collected, on pain of often cruel punishment (amputation of hands was not unknown) by villagers. Elsewhere, throughout colonial Africa raw materials such as palm oil, beeswax, wild rubber, cocoa, and, later, tea, plus diamonds, gold, and copper in the south flowed back to Europe.

## Box 9.3 **The authoritarianism of colonial rule**

Throughout the colonial world until well into the twentieth century the institutions of rule were authoritarian, in some places harsher than others. In Latin America, for example, Viceroys and their officials answerable to the King of Spain and his Council of the Indies ruled over vast areas. But it was the institutions of control in the silver mines and, especially, the *latifundio* or *hacienda*—the great estates of largely coerced labour—that ruled by force at the local level. In the British Caribbean, governors, appointed from London, ruled over systems of slave labour. Well after the abolition of slavery and the slave trade, the descendants of slaves had little effective say in the institutions of rule, until well into the twentieth century. Similar patterns could be found in all of colonial sub-Saharan Africa, where governors, responsible to London, Paris, or Brussels, with executive councils made up mainly of officials, ran vast territories. British rule in India, French rule in Indochina, and Dutch rule in Indonesia was little different in this concentration of power in the hands of colonial officials, until the early twentieth century when consultative and elementary electoral processes began to be introduced at local or provincial levels.

the colonial world, and until well into the twentieth century, the institutions of colonial rule and control were authoritarian, elitist, and geared to maintaining high levels of extraction for the benefit of interests in the metropolitan powers.

### Intensities and paradoxes of colonial institutions

The institutions of colonial rule displayed something of a paradox. At the centre, power was generally held very firmly, 'despotic' power that is: the capacity to deploy force and coercion (Mann 1986: 169–70) in order to suppress and control. Challenges to colonial rule were usually put down with sometimes spectacular brutality, commonly with the assistance of locally recruited indigenous police and soldiers. The real *locus* of despotic power was largely confined to areas of economic or strategic importance—such as the cities, mines, plantations, or ports.

Yet there was seldom much infrastructural power (Mann 1986: 169–70)—the capacity of the colonial institutions of rule to penetrate, administratively, the length and breadth of the country and to use that

capacity to facilitate, organize, or promote transformative programmes and policies of economic change and development (Migdal 1988*b*: 4). For example, large areas of non-urban Latin America, in the Amazon and the Andes and especially in the huge rural hinterlands of countries like Mexico, Brazil, and Argentina, though formally under Spanish or Portuguese colonial rule, remained far beyond effective control of the centre and were run in effect by the *patrons* and *hacendados* of the great estates and the emerging *caudillos*, the local strongmen. The same was true for much of sub-Saharan Africa and large parts of South-East Asia. This lack of infrastructural power should not be at all surprising, given that the central purpose of European colonial rule was extractive, not developmental or transformative, and much of colonial rule was done on a very limited budget and a minimal administrative presence. But this dearth of infrastructural power of the colonial state created a legacy that characterizes many new modern states in the post-colonial world, while despotic power—protecting the new elites which took over after independence—remained pronounced in urban centres.

Because of the weakness of infrastructural power, all colonial regimes came to depend on local-level 'bosses', 'big men', brokers, or oligarchs, some of whom derived their power originally from their traditional positions (such as the *caciques* of Latin America and—the sometimes artificially created—'headmen' or 'chiefs' in colonial Africa). The net overall effect of this was generally to constrain the emergence of effective and centralized modern states capable of establishing national institutions of rule for the promotion, management, and maintenance of national economic development. Indeed, the weakness of its infrastructural penetration required the central institutions of the state always to bargain and deal with the local brokers—often later institutionalized in federal political systems after independence, as in India and Nigeria and Brazil—thereby establishing complex reciprocal networks of political influence and patronage in and around the institutions of the state, and hence imposing serious constraints on their capacity and autonomy (Barton 1997: 49). The pattern could not be better expressed than in Parry's description of this political process in Latin America, in his account of the legacy of colonial rule there:

This is *caudillismo* or *caciquismo*: the organisation of political life by local 'bosses' whose power and influence derives from personal ascendancy, family or regional association. In most countries the concentration of formal authority at the centre, the weakness of lawfully constituted provincial and local authority, leave wide scope for the activities of such people. The real effectiveness of central government may depend upon the nature of the bargain which it can strike with those who wield local influence and power; while the prestige of the *cacique* (local boss) may be enhanced by the 'pull' which he can exert in the capital. (Parry 1966: 371–2)

## Patron–client relations and the politics of the new states

This particular 'organisation of political life', as Parry described it, was the context within which patterns of patronage and **patron–client relations** became so pervasive in the post-colonial world, frustrating the emergence and consolidation of the institutions of rule of the modern state. Patron–client relations have

typified human polities, before the modern state, almost everywhere. The basic characteristic of the institution of patron–client relations is of an unequal power relation between patrons ('big men' in African terminology) who are powerful, rich, and high in status, on the one hand, and clients ('small boys' in African terminology) who lack power, wealth, or status, on the other hand. The patron–client relationship is reciprocal but uneven in that the patron has control of, or access to resources and opportunities which he (it is usually a male) can provide for the client in return for deference, support, loyalty, and (in the context of post-independence electoral politics) votes. Patrons have an interest in maintaining their client base by being good 'big men', that is by delivering the goods, while clients (depending on the particular pattern of the relationship) may have some freedom to move from one patron to another from whom they might expect a better deal.

Clearly the rules defining the institution of patronage are entirely at odds with the rules underpinning the modern state, and bear a striking resemblance to the pre-state institutions of patrimonial rule, discussed by Weber. But as societies in the colonial world achieved their independence from metropolitan powers, and as attempts were made to build modern states, the principles and practices of patronage quickly established themselves in the interstices of the new institutions of rule, from top to bottom, thereby weakening state capacity and undermining its autonomy. Thus in Latin America, the patterns described by Parry continued. National leaders, whether on the left or the right politically, were constrained by the immense regional and local power of the old bosses, oligarchies, and political elites, in country and town, who could contain if not derail reform even under the toughest of military regimes, as in Brazil after 1965. And in Africa, where patrimonialism pre-dated the colonial impact and where, at independence, the commercial, capitalist, or landed classes were small and weak, it was almost inevitable that the resources of the state would be the target that competing groups would seek to capture after independence, to feed and fuel their patronage links to 'friends and followers', whether of a regional, kin, or ethnic character.

It was little different in much of south and South-East Asia during and after the colonial period. Only in those few cases where revolutionary political movements seized state power and largely crushed prior elites and dominant classes, as in Cuba and (North) Vietnam, has the power of patronage been contained, though it has sometimes reappeared. Other exceptional cases, where electorally or militarily dominant elites have taken over and pursued national economic growth for purposes of national defence—the classic recipe for state formation and consolidation—include South Korea, Taiwan, and Singapore.

## Key points

- Unlike the development of the modern state in Europe, most contemporary states in the developing world had their borders and main institutions imposed from without.

- With few exceptions, the original purpose and point of colonial rule and hence colonial institutions of state were extractive rather than developmental.

- The institutions of rule of the colonial state reflected these purposes, being characterized by generally authoritarian patterns, designed to promote extraction and the control of labour.

- Yet most colonial states were marked by the paradox of having strong 'despotic' (coercive) power and weak 'infrastructural' or transformative capacities.

- So, many countries in the developing world achieved independence in circumstances where powerful economic and political forces in society exerted considerable regional and local influence and hence constrained dramatically the emergence of centralized, autonomous, and effective modern states.

- Colonial rule commonly built on, extended, and institutionalized patron–client relations, from top to bottom.

- In the post-colonial era, these institutions of patronage merged with the formal institutions of the modern state, commonly transforming it so that it has been unable to perform the central function of the modern state, namely the encouragement, promotion, and maintenance of economic growth.

- Many of the characteristics of pre-modern politics and 'patrimonial' polities were entrenched within the institutions of the modern state, leading to their characterization as neo-patrimonial states.

# The state in the developing world: characteristics and features

## Introduction

Having explained the provenance of the modern state in the developing world and then explored the typical legacies that the colonial period bequeathed, it is now possible to assess the distinguishing structural characteristics of the post-colonial modern state in the developing world. As before, there are two important qualifications: all states are different and generalization is difficult; and second, notwithstanding that observation, there are enough common patterns—some more pronounced in some states than in others—to warrant the following general points.

## State characteristics in the developing world

### Public institutions

One of the central characteristics of the modern state is that its institutions are, or should be, essentially 'public', not owned or treated as their private domain by their incumbents, as was typical of many pre-nineteenth-century European public institutions. One of the greatest problems in establishing modern states in the developing world has been to liberate public institutions from private control or influence of political leaders, or from their 'capture' by special interests (Hellman, Jones, and Kaufmann 2000). The combined effects of patrimonial rule and patronage have been to erode the independence of public institutions—whether they be policy-making bodies, courts, bureaucracies, armies, or other state-owned agencies—and the net effect has often been the informal privatization of public institutions in so far as they have been used to advance the private interests and clients of (usually) long-standing civilian or military leaders who have become heads of state. At its core, this private use of public office and resources is the core definition of corruption. Certain heads of state, for instance Presidents Marcos and Suharto in the Philippines and Indonesia, Presidents Mobuto and Kenyatta of Zaire and Kenya; and Presidents Batista, Duvalier, and Somoza of Cuba, Haiti, and Nicaragua might quite easily have repeated the view of Louis XIV that 'L'État c'est moi' (I am the state). One of the key institutional instruments of the modern state in the developed world for protecting the public institutions (such as the civil service) has been the establishment of bodies such as civil service commissions, responsible for appointing, managing, and disciplining civil servants, thereby establishing clear differentiation from the political leadership and protecting bureaucrats from political interference. It has been profoundly difficult to establish and sustain the independence of such bodies in many developing countries.

## Sovereignty, hegemony, and the monopoly of violence

Many states in the developing world have had great difficulty in establishing their hegemony and maintaining sovereignty within their borders and in relation to regional and international political forces. This is not only because of the power of local, private, or regional 'bosses' or 'influentials', but because the legitimacy of the state has been commonly challenged by various groups (ethnic, religious, cultural, or regional) which do not wish to be part of it, or by political opponents who refuse (for good or bad reasons) to accept the incumbent regime. Also, secessionist, irredentist, and civil wars have plagued the modern states of the developing world from Peru to the Philippines and from Angola to Afghanistan.

The earlier generation of modern states also faced these 'nation-building' challenges; for instance state education policy in nineteenth-century France had as one of its prime concerns the building of a sense of national identity and unity. Indeed such issues persist to this day, as demonstrated in Basque separatism in Spain and Quebecois nationalism in Canada. However such challenges have arguably been much more severe in the developing world. There they have been compounded by the legacy of colonialism including the imposition of artificial borders and such practices as the importation of slave or indentured labour from afar and biased patterns of recruitment to (colonial) state institutions like the military. While the present chapter has not identified nation-building as itself one of the core tasks or imperatives of the modern state, it must nonetheless be recognized that failure to achieve some degree of national, or multinational, integration and cohesion will jeopardize the state-building project. In effect it is in Africa that the greatest incidence of conflicts of this kind and the adverse consequences are to be found. But there are many examples from elsewhere, such as Sri Lanka's long-running conflict between the Ceylonese majority in the south and Tamil minority in the north. Moreover, Indonesia struggled for many years to hold on to East Timor (see p. 261 below). Guerrilla movements, both urban and rural, have challenged the hegemony and legitimacy of a number of Latin American states since the 1960s, most notably the Shining Path (Sendero Luminoso) movement in Peru in the 1970s and 1980s. Many states in the developing world cannot claim a formal monopoly of violence, a characteristic which marks them off sharply from most states in the developed world although not all of those have in recent years been free from all violent internal conflict, as in Northern Ireland and Spain.

One consequence has been the often astonishingly high levels of military expenditure by the governments of developing countries, much of it deployed for purposes of internal control and the suppression of dissent or secession. Whereas in many developed countries military expenditure as a percentage of government expenditure averages under 7 per cent, the comparative figures for some developing countries (mostly outside Latin America) are remarkable—over 40 per cent in Angola and Sudan, and between a quarter and a third in Ethiopia, Pakistan, Sudan, and Cambodia.

Thus, weakened from within by internal conflict and held down by low rates of economic growth, many states in the developing world have found it difficult to maintain sovereignty. Sovereignty is a difficult concept at the best of times, rarely found in practice in an absolute sense anywhere. But poor countries find it harder to maintain their sovereign independence in the international arena than rich countries. Economic strength not only provides for defensive (or offensive) military capacity but also reduces dependency and increases bargaining capacity in international negotiations and discussions with public institutions like the World Bank, the International Monetary Fund as well as foreign governments, and also with sources of private investment and finance. In particular, where foreign aid inflows form a significant part of government expenditure, de facto sovereignty is seriously reduced as aid donors come to apply increasingly stringent and wide-ranging conditions. As a percentage of central government expenditures (World Bank 2002: 360–2), aid contributions have been very high in such countries as Kenya (16 per cent), Bangladesh (21 per cent), Burundi (40 per cent), Cameroon (31 per cent), Haiti (54 per cent), Madagascar (48 per cent), Nepal (46 per cent), Nicaragua (56 per cent), and Uganda (77 per cent). In other countries, with lower aid-dependency ratios, the figure has not been so high, such as Brazil (0.2 per cent), India (1.9 per cent), Morocco (6 per cent), Pakistan (5 per cent), and the Philippines (4 per cent). The second group have been better able to maintain a grip on their own policy-making, though this has not meant that they have escaped high levels of debt (see Chapter 3), another element that impacts on sovereignty. Debt payment obligations as a percentage of the value of exports or goods and services even in these less aid-dependent countries can be very high—for example in Brazil—though much lower elsewhere, as in India for instance.

### Impartial bureaucracies

The pervasive legacy of patron–client relations, the culture of patrimonialism within the state, the absence of democratic accountability (even in its limited electoral form), low levels of economic growth, the power—and wealth—of special private interests through 'state capture', limited and often aid-dependent state budgets, low pay, high levels of state involvement in the economy, and hence much opportunity for discretionary bureaucratic decisions have all contributed to the undermining of bureaucratic impartiality in many developing countries. Moreover, bureaucratic continuity in much of Latin America has been constrained by the politics of the appointive bureaucracy, a system whereby incoming governments are able to dismiss (often many thousands of) bureaucrats (especially senior ones) and appoint their 'own' men and women (Schneider 1999: 292–4). Corruption too erodes state capacity to pursue coherent and consistent policies of economic growth, undermines development, and institutionalizes unfairness. By discouraging political elites from taking the tough decisions that development requires and by disabling the bureaucratic institutions of the state from carrying out effective implementation, the consequences for development can be severe. The difficulties in achieving appropriate forms of land reform in many developing countries offer a prime example, of which President Bhuto's failed attempts at land reform in Pakistan in the 1970s provides an excellent case study (Herring 1979).

## Key points

- States in developing countries vary greatly but, in many, institutional and political legacies blur the boundaries between public institutions and private interests.

- Establishing institutions to monitor and control these boundaries have been difficult where there is no political will to do so.

- Many states in the developing world have found it difficult to maintain hegemony within their own territory, to protect their sovereignty and achieve a monopoly of violence.

- Impartial bureaucracies, protected from political or sectional interests, are less common in the developing than in the developed world.

- Patrimonialism and patronage, low levels of pay, and pervasive opportunities for discretionary behaviour all contribute to varying but sometimes intense patterns of corruption, thereby subverting the central purpose of the modern state: the promotion of economic growth and welfare.

# The state in the developing world: facing the challenges

## Introduction

The central function of the modern state has been the promotion, management, and maintenance of economic transformation and growth, and especially the shift from agrarian to industrial society, and all the complex social and political complexities which that entailed. The effective elimination of patronage, the de-institutionalization of corruption, the clear differentiation of private and public interests and institutions, and the establishment of relatively impartial bureaucracies have always and everywhere been both condition and consequence of national economic growth, managed directly or supervised indirectly by the institutions of the state. In the course of its evolution, the modern state has also had to respond to the challenges of democratization and the associated demands for redistribution of welfare, and has done so more or less successfully in the more developed economies in the course of the twentieth century.

The same cannot be said of many parts of the developing world where many states have not yet been able to organize or manage economic transitions on any of the three main models outlined earlier. Instead, where attempted, industrial capitalisms—and the institutions that might facilitate it—have been distorted by excessive state regulation, corruption, and the relative general weakness of the kinds of social and economic classes that would normally be forces for change. Elsewhere, revolutionary socialist 'forced march' state-led economic transformations and the state institutions of rule and management they have required of the kind that occurred first in the Soviet Union after 1917 and then in China after 1949, where the political forces that backed it were strong, have generally failed too. And the extraordinary symbiotic marriage of state and market typified by various forms of the 'developmental state' that have promoted economic progress in countries as different as South Korea, Taiwan, Singapore, Malaysia, Thailand, Mauritius, and Botswana (Leftwich 1995)

has simply been impossible to replicate elsewhere. It is the particular constellation of social, economic, and political forces that explains these states' success, and not whether they happen to be democracies or not. In all cases they illustrate the axiom that successful and effective modern states and successful economies go hand in hand.

Until the 1980s, few states in the developing world qualified as consolidated democracies, at least electoral democracies. There were important exceptions—India, Jamaica, Venezuela, Costa Rica, Mauritius, and Botswana are but some, though many would question whether they all counted as *liberal* democracies (Burnell and Calvert 1999). This is because in much of the developing world, conflicts—of class, regional, religious, or ethnic groups—have been so sharp that consensus about rules of the political game has proved to be impossible. Different groups tend to prefer rules that would protect or advance their own particular interests and limit or reduce the interests of others. Secondly, many though not all the conflicts—most dramatically in Latin America—have been about distributional issues: land, jobs, income, welfare support. Where economic growth has been slow or negative, it has simply proved impossible (even if desired) to meet such demands. Elsewhere, especially in Africa, cycles of military coup and counter-coup have been symptomatic of rival factions—ethnic, political, or regional—seeking to gain control of the state and hence its resources and opportunities, in order to feed their clientelistic chains. This again illustrates a central theme of the chapter. The modern state in the developed world has been compatible with democratic (at least electoral) politics only where it has ensured that economic growth could subsidize a steady (if slow and sometimes intermittent) increase in the broad welfare of the majority. The more the state has been able to do that, the more robust has been its legitimacy and the more consolidated has its democracy become.

## Key points

- Most states in the developing world have experienced great diffculty in overcoming the challenges of economic growth, democratic claims, and redistributional demands.

- With important exceptions, states in the developing world have been unable to establish the institutions of rule that would permit economic growth according to capitalist, socialist, or developmental state models.

- In the absence of economic growth and in the presence of profound inequalities, states in the developing world have found it impossible to absorb and institutionalize democratic demands.

- For the same reasons many states in the developing world have found it impossible to deliver improved human welfare through redistributional means.

# Conclusion

Strong and effective states are inconceivable without strong economies. And strong economies are inconceivable without the institutions of state that make them possible. All examples of sustained economic growth and development, not simply statist or developmental statist models, have required effective states to make (and adjust and adapt) appropriate institutions of rule and to facilitate the coordination of the public with the private institutions. Market-oriented models would have not been successful in the West without pervasive state support in the form of investment in human and infrastructural capital, the raising of taxes, the regulation of commerce, the establishment of judicial and legal systems and welfare provision—and much more. Top-down state-led Soviet-style post-revolutionary industrialization, likewise, has also required appropriate institutions for success, as have the complex developmental states of East Asia. But in each and every case, behind the state and the institutions of development it has created or facilitated, has been a coalition of political and social forces willing and able to establish, maintain, and adapt those institutions.

The problem in many developing countries has been that few such social and political forces existed or, where they did, were seldom strong enough to make the running. In short, the politics underpinning states in many countries of the developing world have made them inept, disjointed, and divided agencies of economic growth—whatever model they have adopted.

With the collapse of the bipolar world, the largely economic processes of globalization have accelerated.

If, as has often been argued, such processes do indeed stimulate capitalist growth, then—wherever that does happen in the developing world—it is unavoidable that social and political forces will also gather momentum there and help to build modern states on the template of their European precursors. Instead of being the agents and beneficiaries of patronage and corruption, such forces will become the agents of their destruction and of the creation of both the public and private institutions of rule that promote economic growth. In short, they will become much more like the states of the developed world. For sure, this will not happen everywhere, nor will it happen simultaneously. At the same time, such developments, where they occur, will bring into politics other popular social forces, already on the march in some of the now-industrializing countries of the developing world. They will use the space created by democratization to demand social and welfare reforms that will constitute new challenges for the state. How each responds and adapts is uncertain. But what is certain is that the political science and political economy of the modern state in the developing world, and elsewhere, has not by any stretch of the imagination reached its terminus.

## QUESTIONS

1  What are institutions?

2  In what ways do institutions of the state differ from private or informal institutions?

3   Why are state and other institutions so important for development?

4   In what ways did the provenance of many modern states in the developing world differ from the provenance of European states?

5   Explore how different economic systems in the colonial era influenced the character and capacity of the colonial and post-colonial states.

6   How do institutions of patronage differ from institutions of bureaucracy?

7   In what respects are political forces important in crafting the character and capacity of modern states in the developing world?

8   Will globalization erode or help to strengthen states in the developing world?

9   What makes developmental states so difficult to replicate in the post-cold war era?

## GUIDE TO FURTHER READING

Bates, Robert H., *Prosperity and Violence. The Political Economy of Development* (New York: W. W. Norton and Company, 2001). This short book is a brilliant and wide-ranging analysis of the kinds of political arrangements that have enhanced or hindered economic development.

Chang, Ha-Joon, *Kicking Away the Ladder* (London: Anthem Press 2002). A masterly account of how, from the eighteenth century on, the state in many now developed countries played an active role in the promotion of development.

Leftwich, A., 'Bringing Politics Back In: Towards a Model of the Developmental State', *Journal of Development Studies*, 31/3 (1995): 400–27.

—— (ed.), *Democracy and Development* (Cambridge: Polity Press, 1996).

Migdal, J. S., Kohli, A., and Shue, V. (eds.), *State Power and Social Forces* (Cambridge: Cambridge University Press, 1994) explores the relations between social and political forces and state power and capacity in a number of developing countries.

Woo-Cumings, M. (ed.), *The Developmental State* (Ithaca, NY: Cornell University Press, 1999). Explores the conditions and characteristics of developmental states.

Young, Crawford, *The African Colonial State in Comparative Perspective* (New Haven: Yale University Press, 1994). One of the finest accounts of the colonial state and its legacy, with insightful comparative observations.

## WEB LINKS

**http://globalcorruptionreport.org**   for the annual survey of corruption in the world, according to the non-profit non-governmental organization dedicated to its study.

**www2.pfeiffer.edu/~lridenes/DSS/Weber/BUREAU.HTML**   Max Weber on bureaucracy in the modern state.

**En.wikipedia.org/wiki/scramble_for_Africa**   Site on the 'scramble for Africa' contains material on Africa and global markets, strategic rivalry, the colonial encounter—with special attention to the Congo—and partition.

 ## COMPANION WEB SITE

For additional material and resources, see the companion web site at:
**www.oup.com/uk/booksites/politics/**

# State-building

*Brian Smith*

## OVERVIEW

This chapter explores the concept of state-building by means of categories which reflect concerns about state failure in the developing world and the consequences of **'weak' states** and a lack of developmental, institutional, and policy-making capacity. First, different forms of state building are identified and explained. Then the economic and social consequences of state incapacity are set out. Following this, attempts to understand state incapacity and the need for state-building are examined systematically, typifying the aims of state-building as political order, developmental capacity, institution-building, and policy capacity. The chapter ends with a brief consideration of the role of foreign assistance in state-building.

# Introduction: varieties of state-building

State-building has been a recurring theme in comparative politics. In the literature on state-building four themes or dimensions can be distinguished.

## Political order

The concept of state-building as political order reflects a concern over the inability of many post-colonial states to provide political stability, maintain social and political order, mobilize resources, and successfully enforce decisions, policies, and interventions. Problems of 'integration' have included territorial integration, or the ability of governmental authorities to control the whole area under their jurisdiction. Huntington (1968: 2) drew attention to the lack of authority, effective organization, and political competence in many developing countries regardless of type of regime, claiming 'governments simply do not govern'. Examples included Chad, Uganda, and the Central African Republic in Africa (Bayart 1993: 256), or the **'soft state'**, whether authoritarian Thailand and Indonesia or democratic India and Sri Lanka, that Myrdal found in Asia (1971: 212).

By the 1980s concepts such as 'negative sovereignty', 'juridical artefacts', and 'nominal', 'collapsed', or 'quasi' states had been devised to characterize states without a capacity for effective civil government (Jackson and Rosberg 1982; Jackson 1987; Zartman 1995). Migdal referred to a lack of 'capabilities' to regulate social relations and deploy resources in a controlled way, and the inability of leaders to get people in the society to do what they want them to do (1988a; 1988b). Despite governments being endowed with extensive constitutional powers, elaborate national plans, large bureaucracies, and an ability to 'penetrate' society they proved unable to enforce their own legislation, achieve their objectives and bring about social change. Even where the state appeared strong, as under Latin American authoritarianism, for example, and able to exercise effective power against subordinate classes and organized opposition, it could still demonstrate ineptness, impotence, and incapability, as in Mexico in the 1980s.

## Developmental capacity

Simultaneously it became clear that some East Asian societies had successfully built developmental capacity and achieved impressive records of industrialization, economic growth, and human development (though not by democratic means). Starting from the same level in the 1960s by the mid-1990s incomes in East Asia were more than five times those in Africa, creating an ever-growing gap in the quality of life. Throughout the 1970s Singapore's annual growth rate in GNP per capita averaged over 7 per cent, higher than many southern European countries. By 1990 life expectancy in Taiwan was within one year of America's and Germany's.

Such divergent developments within the developing world prompted attempts to explain a capacity for development on the part of some states. In the 1960s and 1970s the debate was mainly between those who believed that new states needed direct state intervention and ownership in order to achieve 'late' development and those who, faced with the ineffectiveness of national planning, widespread **corruption**, and disappointing economic and social achievements, advocated a more minimal state. Rapid economic growth in some new countries prompted another conclusion: that a certain kind of state could bring about successful industrialization (White 1984: 97–8; Clark and Chan 1994).

The concept of a **'developmental state'** (see also Chapter 9) as an objective of state-building first appeared in the late 1960s. It was used in the analysis of Latin American development from 1971 but made its greatest impact on the study of economic development in 1982 with the publication of Chalmers Johnson's studies of Japan (Johnson 1982). By 1990 the World Bank and International Monetary Fund were ready to acknowledge, contrary to their earlier hostility to state planning and public enterprise, that the state was crucial to the achievement of economic growth and industrialization.

## Institutional viability

A parallel interest in post-colonial state-building reflected the importance attached by economic historians to institutional viability. The need for political leaders to strengthen institutional capacity as a foundation for economic and social development was also recognized within functionalist comparative politics. In the 1970s and 1980s a set of ideas known as **new institutional economics** (NIE) challenged the emphasis in mainstream neo-classical economics on individual preferences, technological opportunities, physical and human capital, and market opportunities as the main constraints on economic development to the exclusion of institutions (Nabli and Nugent 1989: 1335). Such theorizing had a major impact on World Bank policy, shifting its focus towards the quality of a country's social, political, and economic institutions. In the 1990s interest in the role of institutions in development was encouraged by the perceived need to strengthen the operation of economic markets and democratic politics. The institutions most relevant to the social order which is necessary for economic and human development are property rights, bureaucracy, and the rule of law.

## Policy capacity

State-building as an interest within comparative politics in the 1960s also included the need to build policy capacity. It was predicted that the modernization of society would enable new states to develop a problem-solving capacity for policy-making and an administrative capacity for effective and efficient implementation. The 1970s saw the emergence of **'development administration'** to provide an understanding of administrative performance in the specific economic and cultural contexts of poor, non-Western societies. In 1983 the World Bank put public management at the centre of development efforts (Turner and Hulme 1997: 105). The focus now is on the need for a strong central capacity for formulating and coordinating policy, efficient and effective delivery systems, and motivated and capable staff.

## Key points

- Many developing countries have had states too weak to maintain political order and enforce their authority.
- Some states have impressive records of development, prompting debate about the economic polices and political conditions required for such achievements.
- Institutions are important for both economic development and human welfare, especially property rights, bureaucracy, and the rule of law.
- Efforts to promote policy capacity have proceeded against a background of debates about the role of the state in development.

# Failures in state-building

Much scholarly interest in state-building has been prompted by the social, political, and economic costs of failure to build state capacity in its different forms. Failure of the state to organize its apparatus of power effectively and so create *political order* has produced uncertain political authority, ineffective agencies, and corruption. Laws are not made, order is not preserved, social cohesion decays, security (especially for the poor) is lost, and legitimacy evaporates. The officials of the 'soft' state also practise widespread disobedience of the law and collude with groups whose activities they are meant to regulate. Policy becomes distorted by the time it is implemented so that behaviour is not changed and benefits fail to reach the intended beneficiaries. Weak law enforcement and the distortion of public policies has weighted political, legal, and administrative systems 'systematically and heavily' against the poor (Myrdal 1971: 223).

Weak state power has undermined economic development in other ways—through smuggling, tax evasion, the shrinking of the state's fiscal base, and the growth of black markets, which by 1983 in Ghana had virtually replaced official markets (Grindle 1996: 33). In sub-Saharan Africa multinationals have been able to exploit local resources for the benefit of foreign shareholders and the local political elite rather than the national economy (Sandbrook 1986: 327).

Too often, especially in Africa, the alternative to a *developmental state* has been a **predatory state** led by 'rapacious officialdom'. At the extreme, the form of state becomes a kleptocracy: less an agency for providing law, order, security, justice, and welfare, and more a device for endowing a small elite with power, wealth, and privilege. The state becomes **neo-patrimonial**, combining traditional obligations with arbitrary rule. Political legitimacy is weak, so power has to be secured by the exploitation of ethnic loyalties, patronage, coercion, and repression of political opposition (Evans 1995: 46–7; Jackson 1987: 526–7). The predatory state preys on the majority of its citizens, providing little or no collective goods in return. Bureaucracy, in the sense of an institution providing predictable, honest, efficient, and rule-governed administrative behaviour, is absent. Investment is discouraged, economic growth is severely restricted, and the country's public utilities and infrastructure—physical and social—disintegrate.

Lack of *institutional viability* is also detrimental for political, economic, and social development. Without effective property rights markets cannot develop, investor uncertainty increases, and productivity declines, for example from land that is not secured by registered titles. Poor returns are achieved from development projects. Without the rule of law, arbitrary government action disrupts business activity and threatens human rights. Economic policies can change without change in the law. Property can be expropriated and entrepreneurial minorities harassed (as in Idi Amin's Uganda). Political interference in the judicial process forces firms and individual citizens to find other ways to monitor contracts and enforce dispute resolution, for example by calling on social obligations based on personal connections, family networks or ethnic loyalties. The security and rights of the poor become particularly vulnerable.

Absence of honest, impartial, efficient, and rule-bound bureaucracy enables corruption to flourish. Politically, corruption erodes the state's legitimacy. Trust and confidence in the state evaporate as corruption provides political and judicial protection to organized crime. Administrative efficiency declines as officials respond to incentives to create scarcity, delay, and red tape, as scarce public resources are misallocated, as revenue is lost, and as public service morale in undermined by unequal access to one of the spoils of office (Heywood 1997; Rose-Ackerman 1999). Economically, corruption inflates business costs, distorts demand for the allocation of resources, and raises the cost of public provision when less efficient firms secure contracts with bribes. **Transaction costs** increase as access to officials and information has to be bought. Corruption also distorts incentives, diverts funds from productive activities (for example, in development projects), reduces tax revenues, and lowers the quality of government services. Socially, corruption strengthens inequality and has a disproportionate impact on the poor.

Weak *policy capacity* has undermined the ability of developing world governments with good policy objectives to bring about social and economic development. Failures in policy-making have meant that policies often contain incoherent proposals and unclear objectives with no proper plans for implementation. Coordination between departments and with finance ministries has often been poor. Important information has been unavailable, for example on public sector debt. Consequently plans are not realized. For example, in Zambia 75 per cent of Cabinet decisions taken between 1991 and 1993 (the first two years of a new government) were not implemented (Garnett et al. 1997: 79–81).

Budgets have been set without much idea of what a policy and its outcomes will cost. Budget forecasts have often rested on unrealistic assumptions. For example, in the mid-1990s in Tanzania there was on average a 50 per cent difference between planned and actual recurrent expenditure. Plans often lack a reliable budgetary base since revenues, limited by a narrow tax base, fall short of expenditure targets. Little emphasis is placed on getting value for money.

Delivery of public services has been marred by poor quality, high cost, waste, fraud, and corruption. Public assets are neglected as central decision-makers concentrate on planning new projects rather than budgeting for the completion and maintenance of existing ones. Frequently other institutions have to compensate for inadequate state provision of essential public services; for example, in East Africa **non-governmental organizations** (NGOs), community associations, and the private sector provide half the education, water, and health services (Brautigam 1996: 81).

## Key points

- Failure of the state to create political order produces uncertain political authority and legitimacy, ineffective public policies, and insecurity, especially for the poor.

- The alternative to a developmental state has too often been a predatory state.

- A lack of institutional viability stifles economic growth, encourages corruption and increases inequality.

- Weak policy capacity has produced ill-conceived public policies, poor quality public services, and deviation from the government's policy objectives.

# Building political order

The most systematic attempt to explain why some states have been unable to establish political order was made by Migdal, who focused on social limits to effective state power. (Note that 'society' is the entity referred to here rather than 'civil society' which—see Chapter 8—may only form one part of it.) He argued that the 'transformative' capacity of the state, or its ability to bring about far-reaching changes, should not be exaggerated. Nor should state sovereignty, or 'the actual imposition of supreme state authority over its claimed territory' be taken for granted (Migdal 1988a: 398).

Weak states lack the capability of penetrating society fully, regulating social relations, extracting and distributing resources, and implementing legislation, plans, and policies. They are not fully in 'social control', neither securing the compliance of the population to the state's rules, nor the participation of society in the state's policies and institutions. They lack legitimacy. In the international context states are constrained by their relations with other international actors—states, multinational corporations, and international organizations. The state's capacity to maintain order and intervene effectively in social and economic behaviour can also be weakened by the loss of diplomatic and economic alignments, foreign aid, and military support, as in the case of Cuba following the demise of the Soviet Union (Migdal 1988a: 395; 1996: 103). But it is the domestic arena of state–society relations that has the greatest impact on state-building.

In contrast there are many social organizations exercising social control, apart from the state: families, tribes, traditional political authorities, churches, castes, clans, and enterprises. These come into conflict with the state over who has the right to make rules in particular areas of social and economic life. Whether the state can strengthen its capabilities and ensure that social and economic behaviour changes in the direction indicated by law and public policy depends on interactions between the state and a 'mélange' of social organizations—see Box 10.1 (Migdal 1988a: 397; 1988b: 32).

Political conflict arises from attempts by the state to displace alternative sources of social control. Politics becomes a struggle for 'accommodations' between state and society, often taking place in localities far from the centres of national government. Resistance to government policy occurs because it seeks to change established rules and organizations, and the power of those who benefited from them, as in land reform, for instance. To overcome resistance the state

## Box 10.1  Migdal's concept of post-colonial society

Post-colonial society is not typically integrated or homo-genous. It is more a 'mélange of contending organiza-tions'. Different social groups and organizations come into conflict over economic interests and moral stances, many of which become policy issues, drawing social forces into conflict or collaboration with the state. Social conflict is not between integrated and national social forces, such as classes, but dispersed and localized. The 'mélange' changes under the impact of external and internal pressures, such as the penetration of global capital and demographic change. Relations with the state may be mutually empowering, as when farmers are rewarded for cooperating with a state's programme of agricultural reorganization. Or the goals of the state and social

groups may be mutually exclusive, as when the state attempts to redistribute resources at the expense of the wealthy.

The leadership of social organizations confronts the state as 'strongmen' who offer stability to society through their powers of social control in key sectors of society and economy. Such 'strongmen' (local political bosses, clan leaders, landlords, moneylenders, traditional leaders and businessmen) eventually become incorporated into gov-ernance, receiving state funding in return for delivering social control.

(Migdal 1994; 1996)

has to deploy economic and financial resources such as tax breaks, grants, and contracts to create rewards, sanctions, symbols, incentives, and lines of commun-ication to convince people that change is in their interest.

Unfortunately for the state leadership, these resources are not always used as intended by 'strong-men', who also gain control of organizations set up by the state, such as cooperatives, local government institutions, and local branches of political parties. Local state officials are particularly vulnerable to pressure from local elites, especially when allied to other local agencies and political organizations or when able to offer the electoral support of their dependents and clients (Migdal 1988b: 193–7 and 245–6).

To counter these trends, strong state agencies, including political parties and a bureaucracy whose members equate their interests with state power, have to be built to mobilize resources, provide viable alter-natives to the security offered by social organizations, and generate public support for state policies and agencies. But because parts of the state apparatus, most notably the army, may identify with interests opposing the enforcement of government policy, state leaders have to balance the need for strong agencies against the danger posed by internal concen-trations of state power. State leaders confront the

consequences by practising the 'politics of survival', using patronage, nepotism, co-option, bureaucratic expansion, and repression with deleterious implica-tions for policy formation and implementation

Illuminating as it is, Migdal's analysis of state-society relations may not enable states to be categor-ized as either 'weak' or 'strong', for three reasons. First, the interdependence of state and society blurs the distinction and exaggerates the social constraints on the state. Second, a clear distinction needs to be drawn between an interdependence of state and soci-ety that empowers the state, and conflict which obstructs it in its mission. State and society every-where consist of actors in complementary as well as conflicting relationships. States are capable of shap-ing societies—for instance by restructuring the polit-ical culture and activating some group identities, not others—as well as being shaped by them. The power game between state and society is not zero-sum. Third, states may be weak in some policy areas—trans-forming the economy or improving human welfare—but strong in others—repression or the exploitation of natural resources (Evans 1995: 45). A capacity to implement policies is affected by the availability of human and financial resources, the ability to control the state's territory, and the quality of state organiza-tions. Such variables are not necessarily spread evenly across policy areas.

## Key points

- Weak states are confronted by strong societies in which social organizations compete for social control.

- Political conflict arises from attempts by the state to displace alternative sources of social control.

- The leadership of social organizations is conceptualized as 'strongmen' who confront the state, yet may become incorporated into the state apparatus.

- Migdal argues that 'accommodations' between the state and 'strongmen' weaken state capacity for sustaining social order.

- Migdal's theory does not enable us to distinguish sufficiently between 'weak' and 'strong' states, since interdependence between state and society is as much a feature of strong as of weak states.

# Building a developmental state

The exceptional economic achievements of some East Asian countries initially prompted two theoretical claims. One argued that success had been due to restrictions on state interventions, leaving as much economic activity as possible to be determined by market forces. The other related economic success to a highly interventionist state controlling markets in favour of internationally competitive sectors selected by state technocrats. Here the state determined the scale and direction of economic growth to a greater extent than free markets, engaging in rational planning through incentives (e.g. credit and price controls), legislation (e.g. on investment, imports, and taxation) and expenditure (e.g. on research and development) to ensure the development of manufacturing, high-technology production and selected industrial sectors. It is now generally accepted that the latter view comes closer to explaining the policies of the developmental state, and that development requires not less, but better, state intervention and structures (Leftwich 2000: 169). Attempts to identify the key features of the developmental state have focused on two main factors: the relationship between state and society; and the nature of the regime, authoritarian or democratic.

## The political qualities of developmental states

A crucial requirement for a developmental state is a unified and competent bureaucracy, based on merit recruitment and offering stable and rewarding careers relatively free from political interference by sectional interests, such as traditional agrarian oligarchies, that might compromise the pursuit of economic growth. An example is South Korea, where merit recruitment into the service of the state has existed since AD 788, where recruits are drawn from the best graduates of the best universities, and where the civil service enjoys a strong *esprit de corps* and social solidarity. Meritocratic recruitment provides the state with professional, technical, and managerial talent, enabling economic planning to be placed in the hands of capable personnel with a sense of common purpose oriented towards national policy objectives and attracting the cooperation of business elites. Relatively small-scale bureaucracies have allowed control and accountability, and restricted interventions to strategic sectors of the economy (see Chapter 21*b*).

Developmental states have also been characterized by a 'determined' set of nationalistic political and bureaucratic elites, relating to each other in shifting coalitions but all committed to developmental objectives. They have been motivated by various factors including external threats to national security (e.g. Taiwan), shortages of raw materials (e.g. Singapore), relative material equality in the post-1945 period resulting from land reforms, and financial and technical assistance from the USA. State elites have imposed nationalistic aims on civil society, partly through repression, but also by improving living standards, reducing inequality and raising levels of educational achievement and health. Political elites have also enjoyed credibility in their commitments to development, convincing the private sector, foreign and domestic, that it could risk investment.

## State–society relations

Relations between the developmental state and society have entailed what Evans calls **'embedded autonomy'**. This refers to the way in which the developmental state orchestrates the activities of economic bodies, offering sources of capital and other inducements in return for cooperation in the implementation of industrial policy. The concept of 'autonomy' here refers to the ability of the developmental state to transcend the interests of classes and other social forces when necessary (Chapter 21b describes how this worked in South Korea). The state has consciously promoted the development of a capitalist class by providing the infrastructure needed by private enterprise, constraining working-class power, mediating between different capitalist interests (industrial, financial, and ethnic), and legislating in support of capital accumulation (Onis 1991: 116–20; Hawes and Liu 1993: 638–9; Evans 1995; Leftwich 2000: 164–5).

There has been a 'governed interdependence' between state and industry, though the state has had the power to choose which socio-economic interests to cooperate with. Linkages and collaboration between state agencies and leading private manufacturing firms, conglomerates, banks, and trading companies have been established, and members of the political elite have 'circulated' between the bureaucracy, political executive, and business. The integration of state and private sector (including foreign investors and multinational corporations (MNCs) has been facilitated by joint ventures, state-owned enterprises, and networks of government personnel and business interests, sometimes bound by a common ethnicity, as in Malaysia.

## A democratic developmental state?

Since most developmental states have been authoritarian rather than democratic during the decades of rapid economic growth and social development, it has sometimes been assumed that authoritarianism is a necessary condition of development. This is not necessarily the case; indeed, it has been argued that development can equally well be achieved under a democratic regime, with the added bonus of political freedoms and civil liberties.

Such a democratic developmental state would require a number of contradictions to be resolved: between autonomous and accountable political leadership; growth and redistribution; political consensus and social inclusion; the concentration of power in state and business elites and public participation. These are 'fundamental contradictions which are difficult to resolve in the real world of politics' (White 1998: 44). The institutional context would also have to be receptive: accountable bureaucracy, legal stability, a strong knowledge base, and public–private cooperation, most of which are long-term projects and underline the importance of institution-building and the development of administrative capacity (Onis 1991: 121–3).

## Building a developmental state

The question of how far the characteristics of a developmental state might be replicated elsewhere is central to any state-building project. The answer can only be conjecture, partly because of the variability of developmental states. Though common traits can be identified, there is no single model. For example, South Korea and Taiwan had stronger states than Malaysia, Indonesia, or Thailand during their respective periods of economic growth. 'Modes of involvement' in social and economic processes have ranged from the 'parametric'—providing the parameters for private economic activity—to the 'pervasive', with more direct state involvement in investment and production through state-owned enterprises, the control of labour, the political repression of classes opposed to industrialization, and the development and control of industrial associations and cartels (White 1984: 100–1). Developmental states have varied in political structures and policy strategies, as well as undergoing great changes since the 1950s, recently in the direction of democratization. There have been variations in the style of executive leadership, relations between political and bureaucratic elites, and linkages between government agencies and social interests. Levels of state autonomy have varied over time and across economic sectors. This makes it difficult to identify a clear link between economic success and a single type of developmental state (Moon and Prasad 1994: 370; Pempel 1999: 149–52).

## Key points

- Development needs better, not less, state intervention.
- All developmental states have competent bureaucracies and determined nationalistic elites.

- Relations between the developmental state and society have been conceptualized as 'embedded autonomy'.
- Developmental states have been characterized by authoritarianism.
- A democratic developmental state would need to be 'inclusive', raising fundamental political contradictions.
- The variability of developmental states makes it difficult to replicate their characteristics elsewhere.

# Building institutions

It is now widely accepted among theorists that economic, social, and political development is dependent on the quality of **institutions**. Institutions are more than organizations, though they may depend on organizations for their effectiveness. For example, the rule of law depends on an impartial judiciary. The regulation of markets needs regulatory agencies. Institutions may be likened to the rules of a game. They are humanly devised constraints on social interactions (North 1990: 33). For example, property rights over possessions are acquired within an institutional framework of legal rules, organizational forms, sanctions, and norms of behaviour. The institutions regarded as essential for development are property rights, the rule of law, and the principles of rational bureaucracy. The state is responsible for ensuring such institutions are strong.

For the economy, institutions that protect property rights—rules establishing ownership, enforcing contracts and governing markets, administrative probity and efficiency, and the rule of law—are crucial to the scale and efficiency of investments and thus to economic growth. In order to create market mechanisms institutions have to protect private property against corruption and unpredictable judiciaries. Institutions create incentives for innovation and accumulation. They reduce transaction costs and uncertainty for economic decision-makers. They encourage investment in machinery, equipment, education, and

the development of the financial sector. Institutions determine whether fiscal deficits cause high inflation (greater in Latin America than South Asia), whether credit programmes will be successful (as they have been in Sri Lanka but not Bangladesh), whether state-owned enterprises will be efficient (as they are in Singapore and Taiwan but not in Argentina, Bolivia, or Nigeria), and whether rural development programmes enhance productivity (as they have done in parts of South Asia to a greater extent than in Africa and Latin America) (Nabli and Nugent 1989; World Bank 1991: 134–5; Knack and Keefer 1995).

Socially, growth in incomes is dependent on a combination of good policies and strong institutional capacity (see Chapter 13). Social development, especially poverty alleviation, generally requires strong institutions, particularly efficient bureaucracy and the rule of law. Powerful classes are willing and able to obstruct reforms, and it is always difficult for the urban and rural poor to assert their rights. They need the protection of an independent and accessible judiciary and honest administration (Clague et al. 1997; World Bank 1997: 32–3; Edison 2003: 35).

Politically, institutional development forms a mutually supportive relationship with democratization. Historically there is a strong correlation between the institutions of representative government and the rights of property and contract. The securing of property rights and contracts creates vested interests supportive of democracy. Democratic political institutions such as the rule of law and professional bureaucracy are more favourable to property rights than authoritarian regimes. Other characteristics supportive of democracy are also supportive of property rights and therefore economic growth: responsiveness to economic interests, impartial adjudication of disputes, and equality before the law. Bureaucracy and the rule of law also support the democratic principles of equality and justice (for example, treating like cases alike in decision-making about entitlements created by government policies; and subjecting the actions of state officials to tests of legality). Democracy enables trust in rules and institutions to grow, encouraging behaviour according to them rather than avoidance of them (North 1989; Clague et al. 1997).

Claims for a positive relationship between development and institutions, though backed by quantitative comparisons, are controversial for at least three reasons. First, there are potentially contradictory outcomes of institution-building. The accumulation of wealth that is a consequence of private property rights may lead to a concentration of political power in classes tempted to subvert institutions that protect the rights of others, such as the rule of law and a politically neutral bureaucracy. There may even be groups seeking to use political power to weaken property rights, so that they can benefit from the problems this causes others and from the lower costs (to them as taxpayers) of enforcement. Institutional development is

a political process, differentially affecting entrenched sectional interests (North 1989: 1321; Hirschman 1993: 115).

Secondly, it is unlikely that institution-building can respond to urgent needs for economic and political reform, since it takes time for new rules, practices, and values to become established. Institutional change requires cultural change and is inevitably slow and incremental. Thirdly, there is a danger that all economic achievements or problems will be ascribed to institutions, to the neglect of natural resources, geography, and so forth.

## Key points

- There is a strong correlation between states with guaranteed property rights and economic growth.
- Social development is also dependent on institutional capacity, whether measured by incomes or the protection of rights.
- Institutional development and democratization are mutually supportive.
- Institution-building can have conflicting outcomes if it ignores inequalities of power.
- Institutional change requires cultural change, and is likely to be a slow and incremental process.
- Not all economic achievements can be ascribed to institutions.

# Building policy capacity

As the discussion of weak states shows, policy capacity includes both policy-making and implementation, since the latter exerts a strong influence on policy outcomes, sometimes leading to unintended consequences. Currently, reform efforts focus on both dimensions. The quality of the organizations supporting the institutional prerequisites of economic growth and human welfare is seen as critical for all types of development. Building a capable public sector focuses on three essentials: a strong central capacity for formulating and coordinating public

policy; effective and efficient service delivery mechanisms; and staff that are motivated and competent.

## Causes of policy incapacity

Political and managerial factors have combined to undermine the state's policy-making capacity. Political conflicts undermine support for policy objectives, leading to 'a vicious circle of collapsing political support and further policy paralysis' (Nelson

1990: 328). Political clientelism has meant lost revenues through the exemption of friends and relations. Electoral cycles have delayed needed policy reforms (as in Brazil in 1986 and the Philippines in 1984).

Policy formulation has also suffered because of the state's difficulties in retaining well-qualified professionals in key planning agencies. Poor management information has undermined policy responses to pressing problems. For example, lack of comprehensive data on private debt compounded the external debt crisis in Indonesia and Mexico in the 1970s. Poor coordination and communication between agencies such as ministries of finance and spending departments or different service providers in the same policy area (central departments, local authorities, NGOs, and donor agencies in primary health care, for instance) have adversely affected policy capacity. External factors such as global economic recession, causing shortages of foreign exchange, have contributed to policy weakness, as have environmental disasters, political turmoil, and internal economic crisis.

Service delivery has frequently been undermined by political manoeuvrings as when elites capture policy implementation and divert resources away from intended beneficiaries. Administrative inefficiency suits the political interests of some leaders who need to maintain control of key sectors for political reasons such as patronage or the general creation of public sector jobs. Conflicts within the political elite may be reflected in divisions between state agencies leading to failures in implementation. Organizational complexity brought about by a growing number of development projects and interventions with multiple objectives, such as integrated rural development programmes involving the supply of water, seeds, fertilizer, credit, extension services, marketing, and roads, has undermined service delivery in some countries. Recruitment to public services by patronage rather than on merit has lowered administrative capacity. Poor financial management systems mean theft and fraud are easy. Personnel problems have been exacerbated by overstaffing, especially at lower levels, when states have acted as 'employer of last resort'. Less essential areas have often been overstaffed, with critical shortages in key areas. Political interference in the management of staff is widespread, adversely affecting morale already depressed by budget cuts and job losses occasioned by externally imposed economic reforms.

## Prescriptions for administrative reform

To build *policy-making* capacity requires mechanisms which provide political executives with the costs and benefits of competing proposals, adequate technical and political information, a coordinated policy debate between the political heads of agencies, feedback from external 'stakeholders', and professional monitoring and evaluation of implementation. The types of mechanisms vary: secretariats for presidents, prime ministers, or cabinets; inter-ministerial coordinating councils; economic planning boards; consultations with front-line civil servants and user groups; and special policy units serving the cabinet (see Box 10.2).

---

### Box 10.2  Policy analysis at cabinet level

The Policy Analysis and Coordinating Division of the Zambian Cabinet Office was established in 1993. It was designed to produce more open government and a more democratic policy formulation process involving ministerial initiatives following consultation with civil society. Thus it reflects the transition from an authoritarian form of government under a single party regime, as well as the need for sound policy analysis. The twelve professional staff under a Permanent Secretary were divided into three groups: Financial and Economic Policy; Social and Human Resources Development Policy; and Domestic, Regional and International Affairs.

The Division's remit was

- to ensure high-quality proposals are submitted to the Cabinet;

- to serve as a secretariat to the Cabinet;

- to coordinate preparation and implementation of Cabinet decisions;

- to monitor and report on implementation of Cabinet decisions.

(Garnett et al. 1997)

Whatever the arrangement the common need is for agencies and deliberative councils with professional and technical capacity (Kaul 1997).

To provide more *effective and efficient implementation*, states have been advised to contract out service delivery to private firms or NGOs and introduce competition, for example in the management of schools and water supplies, or by the provision of funds supporting NGOs, community groups, and private firms administering social services or public works projects such as Bolivia's Emergency Social Fund (Turner and Hulme 1997: 126–9). The theory is that competitive tendering between providers will give greater value for public money. Other measures include setting up performance-based agencies with managerial autonomy but accountability for outputs and outcomes. Examples include tax-collection agencies in Ghana, Uganda, and Zambia. Performance indicators provide yardsticks for measuring the efficiency and effectiveness of such agencies.

Numerous reforms have been advocated and tried to strengthen levels of competence among public sector personnel including meritocratic recruitment and promotion and better pay. Singapore pays public servants the market rate for comparable private sector jobs—salaries that are very high by international standards. Salaries attractive to capable and qualified people might be funded by the elimination of surplus posts and 'ghost' workers, the enforcement of retirement age limits, the freezing of recruitment in some departments, and the introduction of voluntary redundancy schemes. It is also necessary for many governments to increase revenues and strengthen budgetary controls, as the case of Kenya shows.

Morale and *esprit de corps* can be improved by training, team-work, self-management, and the recognition of achievements as in Malaysia's Public Services Innovation Awards. Other incentives such as professionalization, job satisfaction, corporate mission, status, and working conditions can help retain good staff and induce improved performance A comparative study of budgeting, agricultural extension, and health care in Bolivia, the Central African Republic, Morocco, Ghana, Sri Lanka, and Tanzania strongly suggested that effective public sector performance is more dependent on organizational culture than on rules, regulations, and pay scales (Hilderbrand and Grindle 1997: 45–56).

## Lessons from administrative reforms

Past experience of administrative reform indicates that it is highly problematic. Stronger planning procedures have been undermined by unwillingness on the part of departments to share information and act as a team. In Africa, members of the political executive often have poor skills, or concede power to international aid agencies. Aid donors have fragmented central policy-making capacity through bilateral deals with agencies. Experience also suggests it may be better to strengthen existing organizations and human resources rather than introduce new roles, organizations, and strategies, concentrating on key agencies such as ministries of finance or central banks from which good practice can be diffused throughout the public sector (Bräutigam 1996: 102; Olowu 1999: 14).

Capacity building for policy formulation has tended to concentrate on the supply side (government agencies and personnel) when greater benefits might be had by strengthening the demand side. One aim here would be to improve the policy advice and advocacy coming from NGOs, trade unions, political parties, research institutes, and pressure groups. Another would be to strengthen the capacity of user and client groups as well as other sectional interests to demand better public policies. However, inclusion of clients in policy-making is relatively rare and runs up against professional hostility in public bureaucracies (Turner and Hulme 1997: 120).

Attempts to improve service delivery by contracts and competition may weaken accountability and provide new opportunities for corruption. The private sector may be too weak to take on contracts, government agencies may lack the specialist skills to write them properly, and the rule of law may be too weak to enforce them. Competition may not work in certain cultures which socialize people into avoiding conflict. A 'one size fits all' approach to public sector management risks failure in highly variable cultural contexts. Civil service reform programmes have often been too far-reaching, raising unattainable expectations. At the same time they have lost sight of ultimate objectives, such as service quality or accountability, concentrating on inputs such as training or downsizing. They have generally met with little lasting success. Retrenchment has been obstructed by senior officials or incurred huge costs—Ghana's 'downsizing' exercises between 1987 and 1990 caused cumulative financial losses (Olowu 1999: 15).

Furthermore, the concept of attractive salaries does not fit easily into administrative systems where wage bills already crowd out other recurrent spending as well as essential capital expenditure, or where the IMF has imposed a wage freeze as part of a loan agreement (Turner and Hulme 1997: 121). Other incentives also encounter obstacles. Such cultural obstacles as kinship obligations, tribal networks, consensus-seeking, and the importance attached to secure employment, leisure, and celebrations, can militate against bureaucratic norms. State employees may be risk-averse. Superiors may 'ratchet up' performance requirements, and subordinates may concentrate on measurable outputs to the exclusion of the non-measurable benefits of public service (Klitgaard 1997).

## The politics of building policy capacity

Capacity building efforts encounter powerful political obstacles. Domestic political support and commitment may be lacking because they are driven by foreign aid conditionalities. A sense of local 'ownership' is then missing. There are also vested interests in the public sector that are threatened by 'downsizing' and meritocratic recruitment or promotion. Political leaders stand to lose powers of patronage. A politicized civil service suits ruling elites for whom public service employment is a form of patron–client

linkage strengthening electoral support, serving the business interests of politicians, and enabling the punishment of opponents by, for example, withholding import licences, foreign exchange permits, bank loans, tax exemptions, public utilities (water, power, and telephone), and even cargo space in ports and on aircraft. Local political and economic elites also have little interest in administrative reforms, particularly those aiming to strengthen policy implementation, because these are likely to threaten their domination and exploitation of subordinate social groups and classes.

## Key points

- Policy capacity includes both policy-making and implementation.
- The state's policy capacity has been undermined by both political and administrative problems.
- Prescriptions for reform have focused on policy analysis and coordination, service delivery, and the quality of the public service.
- Competition, performance-based agencies, and performance indicators have been advocated to improve the performance of public services.
- Pay and morale have been identified as crucial for personnel reforms.
- Change to the policy process needs to recognize the role and defects of politicians, aid donors, civil society, the private sector, senior bureaucrats, and local cultures.
- Building policy capacity poses threats to ruling elites and local power-holders.

# Foreign assistance

Aid donors are heavily involved providing grants, loans, and expertise in support of projects (e.g. infrastructure investment), economic sectors (e.g. agriculture), institutions (e.g. property rights), and policy capacity (e.g. civil service reform). However, this has sometimes been part of the problem rather than a

solution. The international community has recognized the sovereignty of weak states, regardless of corruption, repression, misappropriation, or a general inability to govern. By sustaining weak or quasi-states the international order has made it difficult to ensure that the goods, services, technology, and skills provided for development purposes are properly used (Jackson 1987: 18–22).

Institutional development and policy capacity have often been poorly served by much development assistance. First, the availability of aid money has reduced the incentives for national governments to improve their own institutions and organizations. When aid is substituted for domestic savings, government revenues, and foreign exchange, and constitutes a very significant proportion of national income, the institutions associated with savings, taxation, and the control of public expenditure are undermined rather than strengthened (Bräutigam 1996: 98).

Moreover, donors have tended to provide expatriate staff as part of technical assistance and bypass state agencies in delivering project funding, so that nationals do not obtain relevant experience or sense of ownership. Skills are attracted away from state organizations. The use of experts by aid donors blocks the career paths of indigenous counterparts, causing deterioration in policy capacity. Lines of managerial responsibility become blurred as staff answer to donors rather than recipient governments.

Finally, institution-building takes aid agencies into sensitive areas of power politics of which they have little understanding. They may support organizations reluctant to accept political and economic reform, perhaps because they represent vestiges of an authoritarian regime in transition to democracy.

## Key points

- The international community has often shored up the sovereignty of repressive, corrupt, and venal states.
- Aid has often reduced incentives for the state to develop institutional and policy capacity.
- Indigenous public services have often been side-lined by aid interventions.
- Aid donors may be insufficiently sensitive to current political circumstances when intervening to strengthen state capacity.

# Conclusion: state-building and democracy

Throughout the post-colonial era political science has been concerned with state-building in one sense or another. A key distinction is between building political order, developmental capacity, institutions, and policy capacity. Political order has been resisted by strong societies with which states have had to make 'accommodations'. The idea that strong societies are able to weaken the state's effectiveness has implications for theories of democratization which maintain that a vibrant **civil society** is a necessary condition for the consolidation of democracy. Democracy presupposes that strong states and strong societies are mutually supportive.

Debates about the unique characteristics of developmental states, and especially their early authoritarian tendencies, are equally relevant to contemporary interest in transitions from authoritarian to democratic regimes. Whether the developmental state can be democratic depends upon which understanding of democracy is being used. A more inclusive, participative, and egalitarian conception of democracy could possibly experience greater difficulties in adopting strategies, institutions, and policies favouring growth in investment, output, and incomes than a purely procedural one with its emphasis on political rights and the constitutional rules of representative government.

Institutional capacity has implications not only for economic development but also for human rights, justice, and poverty alleviation. Institutions are important for democracy, especially the rule of law and impartial bureaucracy, which offer those who lack the political power associated with wealth and social status some guarantee that their rights will be respected whether as litigants before the courts, claimants before state officialdom, or participants in electoral competitions or policy-making. Institutions have the potential to empower people and make their citizenship effective.

Policy capacity is by no means a purely technical or managerial matter. It too has implications for democracy. Democratic governments need the capacity to formulate good policies and have them implemented so that targets are hit. If social hardship is to be alleviated, it is necessary that sound policies are legally enforceable, and that resources reach the intended beneficiaries. The more public servants administer regulations according to statute rather than unfairly discriminating under the influence of bribes, kinship obligations, prejudices, or fear of local elites, the greater the fairness in bureaucratic allocations and the more meaningful the equality of citizens. This in effect brings the discussion back to the topic of state strength and the relationships with society which enable states effectively to achieve their policy aims.

## QUESTIONS

1   How useful is Migdal's concept of the 'weak state'?

2   Does the interdependence of state and society necessarily weaken the state?

3   What are the key requirements of a developmental state?

4   What have been the main causes of failures in policy-making and implementation in developing countries?

5   What obstacles are reform efforts to strengthen or build policy capacity likely to encounter?

6   How can foreign aid and technical assistance harm capacity-building?

## GUIDE TO FURTHER READING

Appelbaum, R., and Henderson, J. (eds.), *States and Development in the Asian Pacific Rim* (Newbury Park, Calif.: Sage, 1992). Case studies of South Korea, Malaysia, Japan, Hong Kong, Singapore, and Taiwan show the importance of state interventions through both economic and social policy to the Asian 'miracle'.

Clague, C. (ed.), *Institutions and Economic Development. Growth and Governance in Less-Developed and Post-Socialist Countries* (Baltimore: Johns Hopkins University Press, 1997). Shows how economic performance is affected by property rights, democracy, and patterns of participation, while the rule of law and bureaucracy emerge as the most significant institutions supporting property rights and contract enforcement.

Evans, P., *Embedded Autonomy. States and Industrial Transformation* (Princeton: Princeton University Press, 1995). Using case studies of Brazil, India, and Korea during the 1970s and 1980s, this book advances our understanding of the developmental state.

Grindle, M. S., *Challenging the State. Crisis and Innovation in Latin America and Africa* (Cambridge: Cambridge University Press, 1996). Shows how states try to respond to crises by strengthening their institutional, technical, administrative, and political capacities, with particular reference to Mexico and Kenya.

Leftwich, A., *States of Development. On the Primacy of Politics in Development* (Cambridge: Polity Press, 2000). A comparative study showing that type of politics rather than regime (democratic or authoritarian) is important if a state is to become 'developmental'.

Migdal, J. S., *Strong Societies and Weak States. State–Society Relations and State Capabilities in the Third World* (Princeton: Princeton University Press, 1988). Argues that states can be arranged along a continuum between 'strong' and 'weak' depending on the degree of fragmentation of social control, with particular reference to Sierra Leone, Egypt, and Palestine.

Migdal, J. S., Kohli, A., and Shue, V. (eds.), *State Power and Social Forces. Domination and Transformation in the Third World* (Cambridge: Cambridge University Press, 1994). Case studies of relations between state power and social organizations including Brazil, India, Egypt.

Turner, M., and Hulme, D., *Governance, Administration and Development. Making the State Work* (London: Macmillan, 1997). A critical analysis of different approaches to public policy and its management, and their applicability to developing countries, which challenges the orthodoxies of 'new public management' and the 'minimalist' state.

## WEB LINKS

**www.worldbank.org/public sector/legal/ruleoflawanddevelopment**   A number of international organizations are working on various dimensions of state-building. The World Bank places institutional development, especially in the legal system, at the centre of development efforts.

**www.worldbank.org/publicsector/civilservice**   The World Bank also identifies policy capacity as an important area of reform.

**www.undp.org/governance**   The United Nations Development Programme supports capacity development, including institutional and social capital, and associates the democratic state with development, especially for the poor.

**www.oecd.org/department**   The Development Assistance Committee of the Organization for Economic Cooperation and Development (OECD) supports public sector reform and 'capacity development' through its Network on Governance, an international forum that brings together practitioners in bilateral and multilateral development agencies and experts from partner states.

**www/oecd.org/dac**   The site of the Development Assistance Committee of the Organization for Economic Cooperation and Development includes the most up-to-date information on flows of foreign aid to developing countries and analysis.

 ## COMPANION WEB SITE

For additional material and resources, see the companion web site at:
**www.oup.com/uk/booksites/politics/**

# State collapse and civil conflict

*Martin Doornbos*

## OVERVIEW

In examining the incidence of **state collapse**, two central themes predominate, one concerned with the search for causalities and the other concerned with appropriate responses. There is often a misplaced tendency to look for single causes and explanations of state collapse, and similarly to propose single, ready-made solutions. Instead, a more nuanced scrutiny that differentiates the distinctive factors leading to collapse in specific instances offers most insights, and calls for a reconsideration of possible responses and approaches by external actors. Such analyses must be related to the broader discussion of dynamics of civil conflict, which at times has given rise to the collapse of state systems. This chapter introduces these themes. First, it considers the complex web of conditioning and facilitating factors that can instigate a chain reaction eventually leading to state collapse, examining the extent to which any emerging patterns can be identified. This requires proper conceptualization and identifying different patterns or trajectories of state–society relationships. Secondly, it looks more closely at the response side to incidences of state collapse, specifically by the intenational community. Whilst external actors, notably the 'donor community', are trying to better prepare themselves for the eventualities of crises of governance and state collapse in various countries, designing more effective strategies and instruments, it is not obvious they have yet discovered a perfect 'fit' between the determinants and dynamics of state collapse and the responses and solutions for restoration.

An earlier version of this chapter appeared as 'State Collapse and Fresh Starts: Some Critical Reflections', in *Development and Change*, 33/5 (2002): 797–815. The author thanks the journal's publisher and editors for permission to use a new version here.

# Introduction

Until little more than a decade ago, it would have seemed almost inconceivable, even to professional political analysts, that incidences of state collapse would be on the increase, that the prospect of short-lived or more enduring statelessness would become more common, and that discussion about these phenomena would grow rapidly. For a long time, states were accepted as 'normal' in a very basic sense and scholarly perspectives commonly took such 'normalcy' as their point of departure. An extensive literature in history, archaeology, anthropology, and political science developed on the dynamics of state formation—discussing and weighing variables that may give rise to it, such as conquest, trade routes, population pressure, and many other factors—but generally there was little writing on state collapse. Normatively, once states had come into existence they were expected to last—and, in recent decades, to help sustain the international system that had in turn come to be based on them.

Yet understanding the dynamics of state collapse may be no less important than appreciating those at work in state formation. Moreover, a better grasp of processes leading to collapse should offer additional insights into what makes states work, as well as what fails to work. Indeed, although they seem to be situated at opposite ends of a continuum, there are several key connections between the dynamics of state 'formation' and state 'collapse', which, on closer inspection, are not as far apart as they first appear. Ali Mazrui, referring to the contemporary drama, asked the cardinal question: 'Have Somalia, Rwanda, Liberia, Angola, Burundi been experiencing the death pangs of an old order dying and groaning for refuge? Or are we witnessing the birth pangs of a real but devastating birth of a genuinely post-colonial order?' (Mazrui 1995: 22). Depending on one's understanding of 'collapse' and the political dynamics that give rise to it, it is conceivable to regard collapse as part of processes of state reconfiguration and formation. Certainly, a better understanding of processes of collapse is crucial to determine how political reconstruction might best be approached.

If incidences of state collapse seem on the increase, then obviously answers are needed to a number of 'why and how' questions. However, it is equally important to ask what we mean by state collapse and whether different understandings and definitions influence our assumptions about its incidence. What are the significant features of state collapse? How do we (how should we) define it? What triggers it? Are some state systems, or contexts, more prone to it than others, and if so, under what kind of conditions? What are the implications of collapse—both internally within the state system concerned, and externally with respect to the relations with the world outside? At another level, what does state collapse and the disappearance of the state mean for the idea of 'normalcy' and sovereignty of states, as now enshrined in the United Nations system? What is the international system's response to state collapse? What lies beyond collapse and how should we propose to handle the connections between state collapse and state formation or political reconstruction, in the contemporary era? These are the questions that this chapter seeks to address.

Two main themes are central to the debate concerned with the search for causalities and with appropriate responses respectively. Discussion of them requires examination of the connections between the two. There is often a tendency to look for single causes and explanations of state collapse, and to propose single, preferably 'quick-fix' solutions. However, a more differentiating scrutiny of the factors leading to collapse in specific instances and, in this light, a (re-)consideration of responses and possible external actor involvement, offer greater insight.

This chapter therefore disentangles 'collapse'—a term that, unwittingly perhaps, has come to be used to describe quite a range of different things, which is not helpful for clarity of analysis. Following this, the chapter addresses two related concerns.

First, even if we adhere to a strict definition of collapse as referring only to when 'the basic functions of the state are no longer performed', we are likely to find some quite distinct patterns of and different and contrasted trajectories, or paths leading to, collapse. It is thus important to investigate the complex web of conditioning and facilitating factors that may be responsible for a chain reaction eventually leading to state collapse. This will enable us to understand not only why certain dynamics, usually emanating from key social cleavages and civil conflict, might end in state collapse but also the extent to which we can identify any different patterns emerging. The latter would certainly have significant implications for further analysis, and, incidentally, for policy.

The second concern to address is the response side—how the international community addresses these peculiar situations. In some degree external actors, notably the 'donor community', now see fit to intervene and are looking for more effective strategies and instruments of response. Their actions are generally guided by assumptions as to how state systems in the contemporary world should be structured and how they ought to function, and by what appears to be called for—in that light—in order to restore or establish effective government. The big question here is whether there will be a 'fit' between the determinants and dynamics of state collapse in various situations and the responses and solutions for restoration offered. A key precondition for meaningful action here must be a careful scrutiny of the background and

dynamics leading up to the collapse. However, the achievement of such an optimal 'fit' can be hampered in situations where the crises are viewed from an inappropriate perspective or choice of fundamental premises.

## Key points

- Until relatively recently the social science literature was strongly focused on state formation but paid little attention to the analysis of state collapse.

- Processes of state collapse and state formation are closely related in different ways.

- The increasing incidence of state collapse qualifies the normalcy of state systems in the international arena.

- Closer analysis shows different and contrasted trajectories leading to state collapse.

- External responses often take insufficient account of the specific conditions that have led to state collapse.

# Understanding state collapse

To understand better some of the key questions thrown up by the incidence of state collapse, we need to unpack the notion of state collapse and investigate the different understandings of the failure of state functions. Some important definitional questions do indeed complicate our understanding of state collapse. To illustrate, one of the earlier authors on the subject, Zartman (1995: 5), submitted that 'collapse means that the basic functions of the state are no longer performed, as analysed in various theories of the state'. This seems straightforward.

However, when further delineating the concept, Zartman (1995: 6) writes that '[s]tate collapse . . . is the breakdown of good governance, law and order'. This is more problematic, as it links the signalling of instances of state collapse to our understanding of 'good governance', which is essentially judgemental and potentially controversial. Moreover, 'collapse' in

principle should not only be used to refer to the breakdown of 'good governance', but to that of any pattern of governance, good or bad. Otherwise we might find many more instances of 'collapse' than is analytically meaningful—as indeed seems underscored by Zartman who refers to 'many' current instances of collapse. Moreover, employing such a normative notion could lead to endless quibbles and disputes as to whether particular instances of deterioration in 'good governance' illustrate 'state collapse'. Historically, there have been many examples of 'bad' governance in which the functioning of the state system as such was in no way impaired, but where in true Machiavellian (or neutral Weberian) spirit it remained geared towards the implementation of the rulers' chosen objectives. In contrast, instances of complete collapse, in the sense of the decline and virtual disappearance of a once functioning state system, still seem rather exceptional. Somalia and Sierra Leone in recent years have provided the most clear-cut examples, closely followed by others like Liberia, the Democratic Republic of the Congo (DRC), Cambodia, and Afghanistan. Nonetheless, even if these remain exceptional cases, the incidence appears to be on the increase.

However, there are other important reasons to re-appraise notions of breakdown of '(good) governance, law and order', in Zartman's term, as defining the essence of state collapse. For can we assume that when a state no longer functions this must imply a breakdown of 'order', or even of 'law and order'? That would seem to imply viewing 'order' as 'state-given', essentially a Hobbesian view: take away the state, and 'order' too will disappear. While possibly true for various situations as in Liberia, Sierra Leone, and DRC at different recent intervals, it might nonetheless be wrong to assume too readily such a one-to-one relationship. Even the United States once essentially emerged out of a setting in which 'free and equal' individuals—future citizens—searched for meaningful ways of governing themselves before a state evolved. Historically, other examples could be cited. Also, early anthropologists contributed greatly to our understanding of these questions by pointing to the existence of **'stateless societies'** which had meaningful forms of government without state structures. The distinction then developed between 'states' and 'stateless societies' is worth revisiting in the light of the spread of uncertain political futures following cases of state collapse. From this perspective also, more thought should be given to the kind of factors that may either facilitate or block new departures in state formation in contemporary situations.

Now is an appropriate time to study political processes within stateless societies and the associated dilemmas. For ever since 1991 Somalia has done without the benefit of a state system, a situation which still largely obtains notwithstanding the fact that several attempts have been made to reintroduce a central government. Whatever this might eventually lead to, in several Somali regions people for more than a decade have managed to cope, and to cope relatively well and in relatively orderly ways, without a functioning state system—some might even say 'better' than when the state system was still intact. In various regions there has in fact been a fairly normal set of activities, socially and economically, except that

there is no state. This tells us that whatever useful functions states may have to offer, the presence of a 'state' and of 'order' cannot always be equated. By comparison it is worth recalling the opposite possibility, that of 'state terror' coinciding with severe 'disorder'—something that Somalia experienced at an earlier stage and which similarly had been the fate of Uganda under Idi Amin (1971-9), Ethiopia under Mengistu (1974-91), Cambodia under Pol Pot (1975-9) and in numerous other situations. For definitional clarity, therefore, it is helpful to limit the notion of 'state collapse' to the kind of situation in which a functioning state system ceases to exist— whatever that situation may imply in terms of 'order'. The term **'state failure'** is more appropriate for situations of less than complete collapse. This is another recent addition to our vocabulary, which may well require further specification as to which particular state functions have been 'failing'. For example we can distinguish between the failure to deliver essential public welfare services, the failure to provide basic security (vis-à-vis internal as well as external threats), and the failure to act as a moderator of opposed interests. Finally, though, while taking note of any such seemingly 'deviant' patterns, this is not to deny the possibility of state collapse turning into (or already resulting from) a situation of frightening anarchy.

Closely connected are some other important distinctions. Aside from instances of 'total' collapse of state frameworks, there have been some recent cases of partial collapse, where some state functions persist as in the DRC—and of territorially restricted collapse due to ethnic or other conflict, like in Sudan (1973–present) and Sri Lanka (1983–2001). Then there is merely temporary versus enduring state collapse, as illustrated by the cases of Albania and Somalia, and the occurrence of twilight states—a presence of state authority during the day, and rebel authority during the night—although these probably also qualify as as instances of state failure.

## Key points

- Conceptual clarity requires distinguishing between the debate on what constitutes 'good governance' and that concerned with the determinants of state collapse.

- 'Order' is not necessarily 'state given': conceivably 'order' may coincide with 'statelessness' while 'disorder' may follow from 'state terror'.
- The distinction made in anthropological analyses between 'states' and 'stateless societies' carries

- renewed relevance in the contemporary international arena.
- Aside from 'total' state collapse, 'state failure' in various forms and degrees may be distinguished.

# Dynamics of civil conflict and state collapse

The collapse of a state can hardly occur spontaneously, or all at once. If and where it happens, it is likely to have been preceded and initiated by complex and conflict-ridden processes of deterioration, decline, and erosion of state functions. Actual collapse is likely to constitute the final moment of such processes, and to occur when a certain point of no return has been passed. These processes have their own dynamics, which is not to say that they are strictly internal processes. Indeed, the precise ways in which external and internal determinants interact and coalesce in prompting processes leading to state collapse are extremely important for a better understanding of the phenomenon.

As processes, dynamics of decline are theoretically reversible. We can only speculate about the number of instances where timely intervention—from below or from above, from inside or outside—may have stopped a chain of events that could have culminated in state collapse. A trite yet relevant truism would be to say that proper performance and maintenance of state functions and institutions provides the best protection against state collapse. But the dynamic quality of the processes concerned also makes it difficult to identify with any certainty at what point in a spiral of potential collapse a state system may find itself. As with historical state formation processes, where one may recognize in retrospect that a state has emerged out of various formative processes, the root causes of state collapse will similarly have been at work well before any actual collapse manifests itself.

Just as generalizing about the meaning of 'state collapse' can be hazardous, the same is true when it comes to identifying the causes and consequences. Although in a sense the end result may appear to be uniform, namely the absence of a once functioning

state system, the trajectory—that is the pattern and dynamics leading to that condition—may differ greatly. Nor should this be surprising. The still fragile Sierra Leonean situation, for example, with its massive insecurity and violence at the hands of armed rebel groups enjoying significant external support (Reno 2000), appears qualitatively different from the fragmentation of the erstwhile Somali state system into different regional entities vying with each other for power (Doornbos 2002). Superficially, the common element in both cases seems to be the presence of '**warlords**'. But closer investigation shows there is much more to it than that and many differences between the two situations.

In the Somali case, it was the inability to accommodate conflicting interests, often articulated on a clan basis, and the instrumental use to which the state apparatus was put in the pursuit of this inter-clan violence, that brought about disintegration. For all its repressive qualities, the Somali state had a relatively 'thin' presence within the society, which meant that it could all the more easily collapse and be jettisoned when inter-clan conflict and repression came to a head. In Sierra Leone, it was the greed for profit from control over the lucrative illegal diamond trade that became a key factor fuelling the rebellion and by implication the progressive undermining of the state system. However, this still leaves open the question of why the rebellion started. Different explanations have been offered, most notably ethnic grievances spurred by unequal access to power and resources (Richards 1996). The Somali context in recent times has comprised several regions with ambitions for either far-reaching political autonomy (like Puntland) or full-fledged independence (namely Somaliland)—thus for statehood in one form or another. This again differs sharply from the Sierra Leonean situation, which is argued to comprise various powerful groups known to be negatively disposed to any resurrection of the state framework (Reno 2000).

Other examples also illustrate this differentiation of patterns. For instance, the complex dynamics that led to the crisis and collapse of the Cambodian state framework succeeded years of protracted and destructive struggle between the Pol Pot government and liberation forces. Eventually the UN led a complex effort to restructure a state system expected to be reasonably open to and representative of the various political strands. Other recent configurations of collapsing states have included the compound crises that occurred—and in several instances still continue—in Haiti, Liberia, DRC, and indeed Afghanistan. Each of these evidently requires its own explanation of what went wrong in terms of **failing state** systems no longer able to provide basic security, ending up in final collapse. In several cases, like Haiti or DRC, state power had for so long been personalized—resembling non-formal militias loyal only to the president—that the degeneration of the system caused the fragile state structure to become largely irrelevant and eventually to collapse. In Afghanistan, prolonged violent conflict started as a late cold war **proxy war** between the superpowers, in 1979, resulting in ongoing stalemate among the conflicting groups and pervasive social disorientation in the population at large. In the wake of this, and in the face of non-state forces with an entirely different cultural and ideological agenda—the Taliban—the former state largely became irrelevant. That saga was subsequently brought to completion with the externally induced collapse of the Taliban regime, which exposed the state system it had controlled to be in ruins.

Trying to better understand state collapse, therefore, must mean getting a better grip on the conditioning factors. That is what makes some political and economic contexts more vulnerable than others to dynamics leading to state collapse; what key variables lead to different tracks? Internally, as noted, there are various distinct factors to explore, such as a lack of meaningful linkages between state and society, greed for resources, excessive concentration of power, and gross institutional mismanagement. More generally still there is the nature and dynamics of social cleavages and civil conflict along class, ethnic, religious, or regional lines, or some combination of these.

Externally, again, several recurrent patterns seem to present themselves, working alone or in concert with others. One is the strategy of deliberate destabilization on the part of neighbouring powers, either for geopolitical reasons as in Lebanon or Cambodia (after 1979), or for economic gain as in DRC and Sierra Leone. Another is the general vulnerability of poor countries, especially African countries, vis-à-vis forces emanating from the world economy. With regard to Rwanda, for example, though strictly speaking not a case of complete 'collapse', there has been some debate about the role played by the slump in international coffee prices together with IMF/World Bank-imposed austerity measures, shortly before the 1994 genocide. Consumer prices and fees for health and education had indeed been rising in the context of austerity policies, adding to economic hardships. The recent Afghan case was special in its own way, with a state system that had by and large ceased functioning as a 'normal' state, though in the end receiving its *coup de grâce* with the American intervention.

## Key points

- State collapse occurs at the final end of complex and conflict-ridden processes of deterioration, decline, and erosion of state functions.

- Understanding state collapse requires sound analysis of the contextual and conditioning factors, including the interaction of internal and external variables.

- State collapse may result from significantly different tracks of civil conflict and the erosion of state functions.

# State–society linkages under threat

Clearly, therefore, discussions about state collapse are closely related to discussion of the causes and consequences of civil conflict. However, the latter evidently represents a much broader field than that concerned with state collapse as such. If we keep strictly to a bottom-line definition of state collapse as referring to situations where all normal state functions have ceased to exist, then *most or all recent patterns of state collapse will have been preceded by sub-state conflict and violence of one kind or another*. An all-out civil war, for example, can seriously weaken the central state and eventually cause its collapse. Ethnic or religious strife and other forms of sub-national conflict, as discussed in Chapters 5 and 6 of this volume, can severely affect the chances of survival of the state system as a whole. Again, as discussed in Chapter 4, widening socio-economic gaps within the population, induced or aggravated by factors emanating from the global economy, can fuel conflicts and eventually incapacitate the state system to handle them.

State collapse may itself constitute a moment in ongoing civil conflict, inaugurating new episodes in the strife, such as in Liberia. Again, as suggested earlier, state collapse in due course could open up processes of renewed state formation. But the relation between state collapse and civil conflict is not a chicken and egg one. If we reverse the equation, *it is by no means the case that all instances of civil conflict, no matter how severe, will lead to state collapse*. Historically, there have been numerous cases of prolonged or profound civil conflict which have not led to ultimate state collapse. If it appears to have done so more frequently in recent times, this may be due to particular conditions resulting from the fragility of state systems within the current global context having come to play a larger role—a point returned to later.

In discussing dynamics that may lead to state collapse, Zartman (1995) points to a 'necessary' factor which is contained in the paradox of 'the effectiveness of the state before collapse, through repression and neglect, in destroying the regulative and regenerative capacities of society: [T]he collapsing state contracts, isolates itself, retreats. As it implodes, it saps the vital functions of society' (Zartman 1995: 7).

Thus state collapse is seen here as one side of a coin of which **societal collapse** is the other. Linking the (mal-)functioning of the state to that of societal processes and capacities touches on an important dimension.

Nonetheless, that kind of crisis can arguably occur more easily in some situations than in others, notably in those where the fabric of linkages and two-way mechanisms between state and society has not grown into a dense cluster of connections but has remained fairly thin and superficial. Indeed, collapse could be more readily anticipated in contexts where there has been a limited and somewhat artificial state presence 'in' society, Somalia or Chad, for example, than in others where the idea and reality of statehood has a long-standing background, as in Ethiopia and India. This would remain true even if ex-imperial Ethiopia, for example, fell apart at some point as a territorial entity. For the idea of 'state' and 'stateness' are likely to reassert themselves among several of the parts into which it might then fragment. Already, Eritrea's resurgence as a distinct political entity after 1991 has taken a very 'statist' form. Generally speaking, as the incidence of state collapse in recent years has been stronger in Africa than in Asia and other world regions, it seems reasonable to assume that this is connected with the existence of weaker state–society linkages in Africa than elsewhere.

In this connection, Zartman argues there is insufficient evidence to say that collapse results from inadequate or inadequately functioning institutions, that is, mal-adapted and mal-functioning 'Western-style' colonially derived state institutions. It is certainly true that some inconsistency between implanted institutions and their new contexts has been present in numerous situations, sometimes with major implications such as in India and South Asia generally. And indeed, maladapted as they have been, they have nonetheless often continued to 'function' and create new streams of interaction, resource management, and power structures. However, it may not so much be the mal-'functioning' of implanted institutions that has fuelled collapse but rather the extent of mismatch of novel institutions with their environment.

This would have allowed only few meaningful linkages between state and society to develop, thus leaving the state structure as a fairly artificial body hanging over society. Within the society concerned distinctive socio-political processes would evolve and possibly reassert themselves once the 'alien body' of the state system is abandoned. If in addition 'malfunctioning' in such instances also means arbitrary rule, enhancing people's insecurity, and engendering gross inequities in the access to resources, then a process leading towards ultimate collapse can easily accelerate, as in the Somali case.

The strand of writing which places particular emphasis on institutional failures and mismanagement as an explanation of state collapse is related to a good deal of donor critique which in recent years has been levelled at the performance of, in particular, African governments in terms of failures of 'governance'. Yet the ease and pace with which the 'good governance' discourse was embraced in donor circles hardly offers a tool for better understanding of different socio-political contexts to which state systems must try to relate, or why some may be failing at this.

Again, we should not generalize on the basis of only limited case-study material, as for instance Bayart et al. (1999) appear to do when they talk about the 'criminalization of African politics'. Even a demonstrable or increased incidence of criminalization in specific contexts cannot provide a valid basis for generalizations or for broadly depicting African politics in those terms. Nor can the occurrence of greed-driven

and hence basically criminal, rebel activity, witnessed in Sierra Leone and Liberia, provide sufficient ground to equate all rebel action in Africa with criminal activity as Collier (1999) suggests. It could be quite wrong to assume that rebel activity always starts out like a business enterprise (Berdal and Molone 2000). Again, there may be different layers of causality within one and the same context, requiring careful analysis that can reach below the surface. But while generalization about causal patterns is hazardous this is not to deny that factors identified in the general theories have played an important role in some particular cases.

## Key points

- State collapse is usually preceded by civil conflict of one kind or another, but civil conflict does not necessarily lead to state collapse.

- State collapse can occur more easily in situations where the state framework has a relatively thin presence in society than in contexts where state and society are strongly interwoven.

- 'Greed versus grievance' is too dichotomous a representation of realities and allows insufficient recognition of mutations occurring in the course of conflict.

- Generalizing about the causes of state collapse stimulates debate but tends to obscure sound analysis.

# Diverse trajectories

Short of, or beyond, some mega explanation pointing to changed global (pre-)conditions that have prompted an increased incidence of state collapse, it is important to identify to what extent different political and economic constellations have prompted different trajectories of collapse. Such an approach is akin to the way in which complex political emergencies have been distinguished from one another (Cliffe and Luckham 2000), and avoids starting out from a priori assumptions about the causes of state collapse. Put differently, there is no single 'recipe' for collapse or single path or set of determinants. At the same time, what evolves

clearly is not just random: recent examples suggest there are some recognizable and potentially recurrent patterns. Therefore it is reasonable to say that instances of state collapse, even if superficially similar, represent the provisional end result of different sets of dynamic processes, subject to different clusters of contextual variables and forces. Trying to chart out and categorize such different paths should therefore be a crucial step in any attempt to theorize about state collapse.

Yet it remains true that the present global context, where the major powers no longer have the same interest in maintaining inter-state balances of power, and by implication in maintaining states that they supported during the cold war—appears more prone to the incidence of state collapse than was previously the case, especially in Africa. Two years after 'September 11' the picture has not essentially changed in this regard, except that the chances of external intervention in existing state systems, possibly followed by their collapse, has evidently increased—witness the case of Iraq in 2003.

Generally, the rapidly changing global context, characterized by the drive towards economic liberalization and privatization, the pursuit of global market relations, the propagation of the rolling back of the state, the demanding role of the international financial institutions, and related features such as the global communications transformation, can certainly be viewed as offering a mega explanation of sorts. And the end of the cold war, together with the changed rationales of big power politics in the international arena and the new global conditions by which these have been accompanied, usually does figure as one 'general' explanatory cluster of variables.

Notwithstanding the presence of such a major change of (pre-)conditions it remains true that a common cause does not necessarily trigger common results. The kind of pattern that ensues will depend on more distinctive factors such as the structuring of political forces, societal divisions, resource endowments, and so on. In facing the forces of postcold war globalization, state systems with different fault lines in their social or economic structures exhibit contrasted patterns of fragmentation. It is important to explore such different contexts and possible trajectories, both for assessing the appropriateness of external responses, and for understanding new conflicts that might arise out of conflicting scenarios for political rebuilding.

When trying to identify different chain reactions to collapse a number of distinct patterns suggest themselves (see Box 11.1). The first four are more 'basic' in character, the last two conceivably more 'supplementary'.

In addition to these specific variants, we could think of states in which institutional failures to provide basic security in one or more respects (physical security, health, nutrition) have gone beyond a point of repair—for whatever specific reasons—thus invoking a state bankruptcy of sorts. This more general variant could figure as both a manifestation and determinant of collapse, the latter as deteriorating conditions become a factor in their own right.

It should also be understood that the above categorization does not imply strictly separate tracks. Rather, several of these dynamics could be operative at the same time, reinforcing one another. In this connection, one of the most important, and most difficult, distinctions to be made arises from mutations that sometimes set in. Even where rebel activity was born out of grievances based on ethnic inequalities, as in the DRC and Sierra Leone, for example, in due

---

## Box 11.1 Patterns of state failure and state collapse

- States in which the privatization of state assets and prerogatives of state rulers has become extreme, and in which there are deepening challenges to that rule from former associates as well as from various liberation fronts (Zaire/Congo under Mobutu, Haiti under Duvalier, Uganda under Amin, Somalia under Barre).

- States with a marked historical mismatch between the nature and orientation of state institutions and the socio-political processes and divisions within the society concerned (Somalia, Chad, Rwanda).

- States in which there are deepening fights over the control of strategic resources like diamonds, oil, and timber involving rebel groups and privatized armies, making state institutions irrelevant (Congo/DRC, Sierra Leone, Liberia, potentially Nigeria).

- States undergoing a major struggle over power and over the political and cultural orientation and organization of society (Cambodia, Afghanistan, potentially Sudan).

- States in which secession attempts escalate, potentially affecting the continuity of the state system as a whole (DRC, potentially Indonesia).

- Fragile states suddenly facing deteriorating economic conditions which seriously affect the livelihood of a large majority of the population, leading to a breakdown of state.

course it can still become transformed into coercive systems of primitive accumulation. The resulting pattern of development is therefore not necessarily strictly linear or singular. Furthermore, some patterns are conceivably more profound than others, and will require other facilitating or conditioning factors for their mobilization, for example the presence of vigorous social movements. Finally, again, we can never be certain until it has happened that any of these 'tracks' will result in collapse. A whole range of chance factors may in the end make all the difference between collapse and a state that simply lingers, or limps, on.

Mapping out different trajectories to collapse is important also for the choice of possible remedial or preventive action, and should take note of the mix of internal and external factors and actors involved. For instance, if the key problem in a given situation were identified as one of grossly malfunctioning institutions (as is often assumed), then presumably there could be a case for major institutional repair or overhaul. Of course that might leave unattended the real root causes of arbitrary rule, such as ethnic grievances or other conflicts responsible for the failing institutions in the first place. But if collapse has occurred or is threatening because of a state system's extreme vulnerability to changing, externally driven economic conditions, then obviously the focus for remedial action should reflect that. Again, if a basic mismatch between a country's state framework and societal structure lies at the root of collapse, then it may be more prudent to allow fresh departures to emerge out of that situation than expect the previous failing state structures to be reinstated. In other words, different routes for possible remedial or preventive action will be appropriate for different tracks leading to collapse. Mistakes in identifying the pattern of causality not only mean poor analysis but could give rise to unsuitable policy recommendations.

Unsurprisingly, several instances of collapse in recent years have been followed by international calls for restoration of 'order', sanctions, or even advocacy of some form of international trusteeship for certain situations. The latter was advocated for Sierra Leone, for example, and in a de facto way was implemented for a short while with the British military intervention there.

More generally, however, the option of intervention and international trusteeship has been advanced as a possible form of international action for wider clusters of countries and appears to have been under consideration in some multilateral forums, including the World Bank. In somewhat similar vein, there have been proposals for a 'de-certification' of certain categories of countries, a measure meant to exclude them from normal privileges and reciprocities among UN members. Such generalized responses are problematic, because they do not distinguish the merits or demerits of specific situations or how they have come about. Rather, they seem to be based on an assumption that the order which had previously existed—such as that under the erstwhile Sierra Leone government—was in itself legitimate but was derailed and destroyed at the hands of unlawful elements. As a hypothesis, such a reading of the route to collapse emphasizes institutional failures as a root cause, while as a remedy it recommends redressing proper institutional mechanisms and procedures, thus putting the state back into place. This is not necessarily wrong, but that still does not make it right, or sufficient. For it begs the question how those institutional mechanisms (that is, state structures) came to be undermined, and at the hands of what forces? Furthermore, although 'collapse' at one level looks synonymous with 'disorder', the most appropriate response may not be to try to restore the previous order. What is more, especially in the wake of September 11, external actors should beware of intervening prematurely and in ways that do not allow the country's own actors to play a central role in efforts at political reconstruction. In such cases, a situation of statelessness lasting some time should not automatically be viewed as problematic, but could allow much-needed reappraisal of alternative structures, and futures.

## Key points

- The lifting of cold war hegemonic structures laid various states open and vulnerable to new very challenging economic and political conditions.

- The routes towards remedial or preventive action may need to be as different as the tracks leading to state collapse, which severely reduces the room for standard strategies.

- External actors should refrain from massive interventions likely to create new internal-external dichotomies.

# Statelessness and the international context

'Statelessness' may follow for longer or shorter periods after state collapse. The international community obviously takes an interest in these situations but its response should not be a 'one size fits all' approach. The situation will vary dramatically from one context to another, and there are some instances, like East Timor at the height of crisis (2000), where a forceful and timely international presence is essential. It is also hard to imagine Afghanistan now and in the foreseeable future without a strong international presence. Yet in the longer run it is important that Afghans themselves regain control over their own affairs, in ways which will be most consistent with their societal and political divisions.

The implications of collapse and statelessness vis-à-vis the external environment seem full of contradictions, as can be illustrated with the example of Somalia. Over a ten-year period, during which major parts of Somali society behaved as if no useful purpose would be served by a return to the former unified Somali state, the UN and other international agencies, as well as foreign governments, held to the myth of the sovereignty of the former Somali state. They maintained working relations on the ground with a plurality of actors, while strenuously upholding the image of undivided Somali sovereignty. Meanwhile, Somaliland, the former British protectorate that had merged with Italian-controlled Somalia at independence in 1961, determined that it wanted to revert to its own, separate status at the collapse of the Somali state in 1991, thus (re-)declaring its independence. It has done so in view of the traumatic experiences to which it had been subjected following the merger. So far its calls for international recognition tabled with the UN have gone unheeded. By contrast, the UN and other international actors were quick to give their support to the government setup briefly in 2001 in Mogadishu, which claimed control over all of Somalia, even though the claims remain controversial in various regions. What explains such different responses?

First, there seems to be a sense of unease at the sight of blank spaces emerging on the world's maps. With the end of colonialism, all global territory was supposedly divided into states. This has become a bottom-line to the 'new world order', representing a new, prescriptive normalcy. There is now even an emerging, yet entirely unsubstantiated assumption that where there are no states, there might be 'terrorists'. By contrast, the idea that the ubiquity of states might no longer be so normal, seems frightening from the perspective of a world system that for its own existence has come to depend on the premise of normalcy of states.

More practically, there are other concerns: the international system needs mailboxes and addressees for each entity within its orbit. In that light, no constituent unit should be allowed to disappear or to go underground. But also, there must be a natural fear for precedents: if one weak state collapses and is allowed to get away with it, others might follow. More serious, and more difficult to resolve, is the fact that all countries, even the poorest and most vulnerable, have become tied to a whole web of treaties and international obligations through the sheer fact of their independent status and membership in the international order. Last but not least, if a collapsing state has incurred huge debts, who is to be held responsible for those debts? The idea of debtor countries one by one disappearing, dissolving, leaving no address whatsoever, must be an international banker's nightmare. Presumably, therefore, the myth of uninterrupted sovereignty is also necessary to ensure that some body or entity, with some kind of address, remains accountable for the debts and obligations of previous governments of the former state.

Looking at these issues in terms of sovereignty, two points demand attention. Sovereignty supposedly embodies a nation's ultimate self-determining powers over its own future, which is entrusted in conditional custody by its people to the state. In the case of collapsed states, however, it now appears that the international system, specifically the United Nations Security Council, is advancing itself as an alternative custodian, empowered to withhold sovereignty and to grant it to successor rulers when it considers that the appropriate moment has come.

Second, with reference to many of Africa's post-colonial states it has been argued that their survival as independent states would have come to a halt had it not been for the international recognition of their sovereignty (and the big powers' interests in propping it up) (Jackson 1990). This thesis tended to disregard the role of international actors themselves in narrowing the room for manoeuvre and the sovereign scope for policy initiatives and policy coordination by post-independence African governments. Nevertheless, sovereignty in this perspective could be viewed as a saving grace for otherwise failing or collapsing states. It would be ironic then, if having arrived at a point where collapse has run its full course and former constituent units see no more future for it, the international recognition of sovereignty were to hamper the exploration of alternative futures.

With collapse, therefore, new kinds of situations are arising: international recognition may no longer serve as a protective umbrella for weak regimes, but may become a potential stumbling bloc to fresh starts and rejuvenation by insisting on holding on to old territorial boundaries and political entities. This departs sharply from the idea of international recognition following the logic of internal evolution and paths of reconfiguration and state formation. Inevitably, therefore, this raises new questions about the scope for political restarts in situations where external recognition plays an increasingly decisive role.

If the incidence of state collapse and non-recognition of newly emerging entities were to increase, it is conceivable that earlier (pre-UN) patterns in international relations might be repeated once again, entailing recognition of 'states' by some other (neighbouring or like-minded) partners, but not necessarily by the system as a whole. This would add to a recent trend towards unilateral action on the international front in other respects, threatening the aspirations to universality for the United Nations and its institutions. The US invasion of Iraq, though strictly not belonging to the domain of 'state collapse', has brought this out dramatically. If the UN in the long run is to retain a central role in these matters, it needs to develop some degree of positive flexibility in this regard.

## International actors

As a result of the perceived challenges of failing states and instances of state collapse, many multilateral and bilateral aid agencies have in recent years set up their own programmes meant to respond to the complex political emergencies to which these give rise. A common objective is to try to be prepared for rapid and effective action. Significantly, these developments acquire a dynamic of their own, and ultimately can lead away from, rather than towards, developing capacities to design approaches more specific to the individual circumstances.

On the donor front, several features deserve attention. One is the tendency to search for common strategies, in part as a corrective to situations in which different external agencies were all doing their own thing, resulting in confusion. Second and closely related is a tendency to work towards set recipes, which can be deployed at once and in all situations, again in response to perceived urgencies and demands of effectiveness. Third, some authors and agencies are becoming less inhibited about suggesting the need to sideline the 'sovereignty' of some of the affected countries, proposing to have it temporarily replaced through a UN or some other mandate. Fourth, there is a trend among leading multilateral agencies to see post-conflict contexts as a suitable ground, and moment, to install market-friendly frameworks, thus seeing fresh starts as the moment for fresh designs of a particular kind.

All this creates a paradox. As external parties become increasingly prepared to intervene, with a view to re-creating political space in ways that promise accelerated political and economic liberalization, the chances of taking the distinctive features of specific situations into account or of leaving the initiative to internal actors will arguably diminish. At most there could be lip service to the idea that reconstruction at a national or regional scale requires some involvement of 'local' leadership, joint action, or whatever. A new field of discourse then presents itself, around the emerging 'politics of reconstruction', where multilateral agencies and other donors partly in competition amongst each other (though basically moving towards coordinated action) intervene and deprive local leaders of the power of self-determination for their society. Afghanistan today has all the necessary ingredients. Powerful tensions between political actors inside the country and influential external parties can easily deepen and sharpen in the process, and novel forms of domination emerge around the introduction of new frameworks of political and economic accountability and control.

## Key points

- The international system, theoretically based as it is on membership of all independent and sovereign states, has difficulty accepting the reality of statelessness. By insisting on the conservation of (former) state boundaries and the myth of enduring state sovereignty it blocks possible new departures in state formation.

- International actors increasingly search for common strategies and set recipes in response to situations of state collapse and civil conflict. This leaves less chance for situation-specific approaches and priorities and for the social leaderships of affected countries to have a decisive influence over the processes of reconstruction.

- The 'politics of reconstruction' is emerging as a pivotal field of academic interest as well as of international engagement.

- The possibility of powerful new tensions between domestic and influential external actors is one possible outcome of international intervention in situations of civil conflict and state collapse.

# Conclusions

State collapse can be understood in different ways and should be distinguished from state failure. Similarly the routes to state failure and collapse are many and complex. But what lies beyond collapse, and what lessons can be drawn from past experiences? Historically speaking, one would expect a new political order to surface from amidst the ruins of the old, possibly building on elements that had been suppressed or ignored. Connections between old and new can be extremely important in understanding the emergence and evolution of new political forms. In European history, state formation processes often restarted in new directions and in new constellations following the demise of a previous order. Today in various developing world settings it is important to recognize that the internal social and political actors and dynamics should play a central role in recreating order and some kind of 'normalcy'. That *might mean* fundamental political change in the direction of revising our existing political maps and atlases.

The chapter has also shown that in order to understand forms of state collapse, its causes and consequences, a tendency to excessive generalization should be avoided—a lesson applicable both to analysts and to external actors who are minded to get practically involved. We should all learn to appreciate the implications of contrasted contexts, different dynamics and different trajectories that may continue to play crucial roles, especially when investigating how societies can move on from state collapse to recovery. Responses should be sensitive to context and local trends, and must not start out from a priori positions.

Fresh start moments, almost by definition, are delicate. They may be full of promise and expectations of brighter futures, distanced from the past. At the same time, they are extremely fragile, as the conflicts and violence that were inherent in the processes of breakdown and collapse will still be alive in the memory, and could conceivably be reignited. Fresh starts therefore need sound understanding of the circumstances that gave rise to them, and careful handling by all concerned. Although external actors have become increasingly if selectively involved and can make an important contribution they should be aware of the risks of complicating the process if they expect *their* designs for new political futures and structures to play a primary role.

## QUESTIONS

**1**   What is the key defining element in the notion of state collapse?

**2**   How do state collapse and civil conflict relate to one another?

**3**   What kinds of developments may lead to the collapse of state structures?

**4**   What connections can be identified between processes of state collapse and state formation?

**5**   Why has there appeared to be an increase of the incidence of state collapse in the post-cold war era?

**6**   What role do international actors and the international community tend to play vis-à-vis collapsed states?

**7**   What are the pitfalls of generalizing about the causes of and external responses to instances of state collapse?

## GUIDE TO FURTHER READING

Addison, T. (ed.), *From Conflict to Recovery in Africa* (Oxford: Oxford University Press, 2003).

Bayart, Jean-François, Ellis, Stephen, and Hibou, Béatrice Hibou, *The Criminalization of the State in Africa* (Bloomington, Ind.: Indiana University Press/Oxford: James Currey, 1999).

Berdal, Mats, and Malone, David (eds.), *Greed and Grievance: Economic Agendas in Civil Wars* (Boulder, Colo.: Lynne Rienner, 2000).

Collier, Paul, Elliott, Lani, Hegre, Håvard, Hoeffler, Anke, Reynal-Querol, Marta, and Sambanis, Nicholas, *Breaking the Conflict Trap* (Washington: World Bank and Oxford University Press, 2003).

Jackson, Robert H., *Quasi-States: Sovereignty, International Relations and the Third World* (Cambridge: Cambridge University Press, 1990).

Reno, William, *Warlord Politics and African States* (Boulder, Colo.: Lynne Rienner, 1998).

Zartman, I. William (ed.), *Collapsed States: The Disintegration and Restoration of Legitimate Authority* (Boulder, Colo.: Lynne Rienner Publishers, 1995).

## WEB LINKS

**www.colorado.edu/conflict**   Comprehensive gateway to the website of the University of Colorado Conflict Resolution Consortium.

**www.prio.no**   The site of the International Peace Research Institute, Oslo.

**www.roape.org**   The site of the *Review of African Political Economy*, which publishes many articles about state collapse, state failure, and political violence in Africa.

 **COMPANION WEB SITE**

For additional material and resources, see the companion web site at:
**www.oup.com/uk/booksites/politics/**

# Democratization

*Peter Burnell*

## OVERVIEW

The late 1980s and early 1990s saw a 'wave' of change embracing political liberalization and democratization in Africa, Asia, and other developing areas. The completion of an almost worldwide process of democratization that began earlier in the 1980s with the widespread return to elected civilian governments in Latin America seemed imminent. This chapter explores democratization issues in a developing country context. It elucidates the concept and its relationship to democracy; summarizes recent trends; compares different understandings of democratic consolidation and explanations for successful transition to democracy. The relationship between democratization and development provides a central theme. Because these political changes take place at a time of increasing economic liberalization, globalization, and international democracy promotion, the implications these developments have for democratic self-determination of developing countries also merit investigation.

# Introduction

Democracy is an essentially contested concept. The long history of theorizing about its meaning provides few certainties about what 'democratization'—a relative newcomer to the vocabulary—really means. Clearly democratization refers to a process of change; but most writers conceive of it as a journey without end. Even in the longest established or 'mature' democracies there is scope for democratization. Scholars in the West, the United States in particular, have made the dominant contribution to the literature on democratization even though reflecting on political trends in Europe and the developing world. They have drawn little on the considerable experience of democracy in the Caribbean and countries like India; and few attempts have been made to compare contemporary democratization with its historical precursors.

A number of preliminary observations should be made here. Obviously democratization is not a new phenomenon. In a widely used metaphor Huntington characterized the extension of democracy beginning around 1974 as **democracy's 'third wave'**, the two earlier 'waves' in 1828–1926 and 1943–62 each being followed by a reverse wave. Huntington's influential book *The Third Wave* (1991) pre-dated the large number of more recent democratic experiments. And his periodization has been contested, such that the democratic breakthroughs occurring in developing countries from the late 1980s could also be characterized as a 'fourth wave'. 'Third wave' examples of democratization are, then, clearly not confined to developing countries; much attention has focused on southern Europe (Greece; Portugal; Spain) and post-communist countries in Central and Eastern Europe, a showcase of successful recent democratic transitions. Scholarly approaches analysing democratization reflect this wider universe of cases, although it was the abandonment of authoritarianism in Latin America that was responsible for some of the earliest most influential contributions (for example O'Donnell, Schmitter, and Whitehead 1986). Moreover like Argentina (returning to elected civilian rule in 1983) and Uruguay (military-controlled civilian government prevailed from 1973 to 1985), many former colonial states have in the last fifteen years or so been attempting not so much to democratize as to redemocratize, following earlier democratic failure(s). Thus Ghana in 1992 reintroduced democratic stability after successive earlier attempts to re-establish rule by elected civilian politicians failed, the military holding power in 1966–9, 1972–9, and 1981–92.

# Regime change, democracy, and democratization

There is a temptation to present democratization as a unilinear movement from political authoritarianism to democracy, which implies a simple dichotomy of regime types. There have been different kinds of authoritarian regime — absolute monarchs; personalist dictators; military-bureaucratic rule, *de jure* one-party states as in Zambia, 1973–91, and so on. Hence there is a range of different outcomes to authoritarian breakdown. The collapse of an authoritarian regime could be followed by protracted civil war (as in Angola and Mozambique after gaining independence), or 'warlordism' and the disintegration of the state, as happened in Somalia in the 1990s. Alternatively it could lead to a different kind of authoritarian regime or a diminished sub-type, for instance semi-authoritarian or one of its variants, '**competitive authoritarianism**'. In competitive authoritarian regimes, 'formal democratic institutions are widely viewed as the principal means of obtaining and exercising political authority. Incumbents violate those rules so often and to such an extent, however, that the regime fails to meet conventional minimum standards for democracy' (Levitsky and Way 2002: 52). Regime change could also lead to some other intermediate regime type or hybrid version of democracy—one of the many varieties Collier and Levitsky (1997) called 'democracy with adjectives', for instance proto, semi, quasi, limited, partial, pseudo, façade, and so on. The term 'low-intensity democracy'—'not even an approximation to actual western liberal democracy or present forms of bourgeois rule' (Gills et al. 1993: 8) has also caught on in the literature. In large countries, such as federal systems, regime variations and unevenness in democratization can occur across provinces or localities. But not unusually, although countries may be 'in transition' from an authoritarian regime, there is no clarity about what they are in transition to.

Democracy, from the Greek for rule by the people, has been called an inherently debatable and changeable idea. Even so, ideas resembling the model of polyarchical democracy (**polyarchy**) advanced by the American political scientist Robert Dahl in the 1970s, have dominated much of the democratization discourse, although challenged by writers like Gills et al. (1993) who prefer a more 'participatory progressive' idea of democracy. Polyarchy centres on two main pillars: public contestation and the right to participate.

Polyarchical democracy has been criticized for robbing democracy's content of actual political equality and, in the most minimalist versions, for putting the principle of contestation between ruling elites ahead of genuinely popular control of government or popular sovereignty. It is said to prioritize institutional arrangements and procedures over ends and ideals; moreover it fails to recognize the crucial political importance of socio-economic inequalities. So,

democratic models remain a continuing source of controversy. Nevertheless, **liberal democracy**, which is akin to polyarchy, remains the most commonly cited yardstick for judging the progress of democratization. This is generally believed to avoid the **fallacy of electoralism**. Diamond (1996), a prominent contributor to the literature, thus usefully distinguishes between liberal democracy, where there is extensive provision for political and civic pluralism as well as for individual and group freedoms, and mere 'electoral democracy' (even where elections appear 'free and fair'). In the latter civil freedoms are less prized and minority rights are insecure.

Freedom House is a New York-based non-profit organization that conducts annual evaluations of political rights and civil liberties everywhere in the world. It defines democracy, at minimum, as a political system in which people choose their authoritative leaders freely from among competing groups and individuals who are not chosen by the government. Freedom is the chance to act spontaneously in a variety of fields outside the control of government and other centres of potential domination. Democracies are judged either free or partly free, as measured along a seven-point scale (1–2.5 = free; 3–5 = partly free; 5.5–7 = not free).

Freedom House's approach has been criticized on a number of grounds. Nevertheless, its ratings are widely used for the purpose of discerning global trends in democratization and make comparisons cross-nationally and over time. They are convenient and accessible. For Diamond, Freedom House's 'free rating' is the best available indicator of liberal democracy.

---

## Box 12.1 **Dahl on democracy**

Citizens must have unimpaired opportunities to formulate their preferences, signify them and have them weighted equally. This requires certain institutional guarantees: freedom to form and join organisations; freedom of expression; right to vote; eligibility for public office; right of leaders to compete for support; alternative sources of information; free and fair elections; institutions for making government policies depend on votes and other expressions of preference.

(Dahl 1971)

## Trends

The data indicate that following a dramatic initial expansion of democracy after the onset of Huntington's third wave, which increased both the number and proportion of all states that could be termed democratic, the number of liberal democracies levelled off in the early 1990s. Of course some countries like Cuba, Vietnam, and Libya were never caught up in the tide; others actually moved against it, like the Gambia, where a military coup in 1994 interrupted the democracy that dated from independence (1965). Many of the newer democracies soon began to show signs of democratic erosion or 'hollowing out', settling on the form but less so on the substance of electoral democracy, although usually retaining multi-party-ism and elections. By the twenty-first century a trend towards **pseudo democracy** is as striking as the earlier trend toward democracy (Diamond 2002).

The 2002 Freedom House survey (Karatnycky 2003) claimed a new high-water mark in the number and proportion of democratically elected governments worldwide (121), but could identify only 86 free countries, with strong regional variations:

- Africa (53 countries): 9 free; 24 partly free; 20 not free. Twenty countries qualify as electoral democracies or better.
- Asia (39 countries): 18 free; 10 partly free; 11 not free. Twenty-four countries qualify as electoral democracies or better.
- Americas (35 countries): 23 free; 10 partly free; 2 (Cuba and Haiti) not free. Thirty-two countries qualify as electoral democracies or better.
- Middle East (14 countries excluding North Africa): 1 free (Israel); 3 partly free; 10 not free. Only Israel and Turkey are electoral democracies.

The 2003 survey (Karatnycky 2004: 92) showed little change, and made the point that freedom levels are significantly lower among the countries with annual per capita Gross National Income of less than $1,500, with only three out of twenty-nine countries having incomes below $300 being free. The data also show that low-income countries 'can establish democratic practices and respect for civil liberties rooted in the rule of law. Out of 128 countries with an annual GNI of $3,500 or less, 38 rate as Free in the survey.'

## Key points

- The dichotomy of authoritarian and democratic regimes is too simple: it ignores the variety of non/pre-democratic regime types and the different possible outcomes of political transition.
- As an idea democratization is beholden to the fact that the very meaning of democracy itself is contested.
- The recent progress of democratization in the developing world has been erratic and uneven; some countries are experiencing democratic decay.
- We should not exaggerate democratization's usefulness as an analytical framework for understanding the politics of all developing countries.

# Democratization as process

Conceptual distinctions between political liberalization, democratic transition, and democratic consolidation are commonplace, but do not imply a necessary let alone inevitable sequence of events. As a prelude to 'political opening', authoritarian breakdown can happen in different ways—gradual or sudden, violent or peaceful—and may range from moderate to absolute. Liberalization can become stalled or 'frozen' rather than lead on to democratization, as in Jordan. Conversely, largely free elections might be introduced without first establishing the rule of law, full executive accountability, and a flourishing civil society—or what has been called **democratization backwards**. It gives rise to what Zakaria (1997) dubbed 'illiberal democracy', citing Iran and President Fujimori's Peru as examples. But liberalization and democratic opening can also happen simultaneously, where authoritarian collapse is sudden and complete, as in South Africa's abolition of apartheid. They can also come together, where rulers who at first allowed some liberalization without intending to embrace democracy, lose control of the momentum and are overtaken by society's irresistible demands for fuller democratic opening.

Just as there can be political transition without transition to democracy so there can be democratic transition without democratic consolidation—the situation typical in many 'emerging' democracies. Similar claims can be made about democratic reversals.

Political liberalization has no firm definition but can refer to some combination of what has changed, the extent of the changes, and the means employed. A typical view is that it is a top-down process, made by political leaders who aim to maintain power for themselves and do not accept that institutionalized uncertainty regarding electoral outcomes should be the determining principle of who governs (and the possibility of alternation in office that implies). Liberalization advances political freedoms less than civil liberties. In contrast democratization introduces arrangements for competitive elections. A further distinction some analysts make is that democratization 'comes from below', and involves political, though not necessarily violent, struggle. But this unnecessarily precludes cases of negotiated or **pacted transition**, including where the elites involved in this have an intention to forestall a groundswell of popular sentiment seeking more radical change.

## Democratic consolidation

Whether conceived as a process or an end state, how do we recognize democratic consolidation? This question is far from settled. Answers range from those equating consolidation with longevity to those identifying it with democratic 'deepening'—qualitative improvements such as in the levels of participation or real political equality. However, Schedler (1998) observes that this latter approach invites an open and boundless definition. He recommends we restrict consolidation to two 'negative' notions: avoiding democratic breakdown and avoiding democratic erosion. Put differently, democratic consolidation refers to expectations of regime continuity—and to nothing else. A minimal definition like this maximizes the number of developing countries qualifying for democratic consolidation. More extravagant accounts that rest on 'democratic 'widening'—the incorporation of democratic principles in economic and social areas like the family and church—establish criteria that not even the developed countries satisfy. One solution is to reserve such claims for some idea of 'post-consolidation'. In practice the developments they refer to could proceed alongside democratic consolidation confined to the more specifically political domain. However, respect for the equality of the sexes

and the establishment of democracy in the home could be vital if women are to exercise full political rights.

More significant for democratic consolidation than a democracy's longevity is its ability to survive threats and withstand shocks—generated at home or abroad, and inclusive of political (e.g. an attempted military coup) and financial or economic shocks like the East Asian crisis, 1997. One thesis is that resilience is strengthened by progress in respect of democratic 'deepening'. However, we would not be able to know whether a democracy is consolidated—or that expectations of continuity are justified—until it has been so put to the test. Certainly a number of developing countries have persisted with (e.g. India) or have successfully reintroduced (e.g. Ghana) democracy against seemingly unfavourable odds. Yet to make that a criterion for consolidation seems biased against democracies privileged by more favourable circumstances.

A less romantic but more easily applied notion of consolidation is Huntington's (1991: 266–7) double turnover test. The test requires that a party that took office after a democratic election should relinquish office after losing a comparable election without seeking to resist or overturn the result. This would imply that Botswana, where the Botswana Democratic Party has yet to lose an election after thirty years of civilian government and peaceful electoral politics, is not a consolidated democracy. A more persuasive view sees consolidation as being achieved once democracy has become **the only game in town**. This requires an appropriate attitudinal shift, not just a temporary behavioural accommodation. The military, then, however reluctantly no longer think it appropriate to meddle in government. On that basis Venezuela, after 1958 one of Latin America's longest continuous democracies, failed the test in 2002, when the army briefly deposed the elected president, Hugo Chávez.

Democrats regard **legitimacy** as one of democracy's most distinctive and distinguished properties. For Diamond, consolidation is legitimation. Legitimacy is like reinforcing glue, helping ensure survival in the face of crises and shocks. Indeed, we could say the regime truly consolidates when it ceases to rely on 'performance legitimacy' (acceptance grounded on meeting society's wants or needs such as security and prosperity), and achieves 'intrinsic legitimacy'—grounded in acceptance of and respect for democracy's fundamental values and principles. 'Intrinsic legitimacy' shelters democracy against such failings as poor developmental performance. In a settled democracy discontent with the performance of government is exacted on the government, by peacefully removing it from office at the polls.

The conceptual baggage of transition and consolidation can be criticized for presenting too rigid a framework for analysing what in reality are likely to be multifaceted, multi-dimensional and multi-directional processes of political change. As Schedler has argued, in practice the 'tip over' point between transition and consolidation and their outer boundaries are blurred; elements of the two movements could overlap. In consequence it could be more insightful to liken democratization to variable geometry: some of democracy's ingredients could be moving in one direction (possibly at different speeds), others moving in the opposite direction (again at different speeds), and yet others standing still, all contemporaneously. To require evidence of progress on all fronts is too demanding for consolidation.

We can, then, move to a more nuanced evaluation of a country's democratic record. The concept of a democratic audit was pioneered by David Beetham. Building on a design for auditing democracy in Britain, Beetham and colleagues have produced a detailed *Handbook on Democracy Assessment* (2002), under the auspices of the Stockholm-based International Institute for Democracy and Electoral Assistance. Their assessment framework groups issues under four headings: citizenship, law, and rights; representative and accountable government; civil society and popular participation; and international dimensions. While guarded about converting qualitative evidence into quantitative scores and ranking countries on a single scale, they include an economic and social rights audit as essential to both the process and the outcome of democratic change. They also factor in the international constraints (drawing on the advice of consultant advisers from the South).

## Key points

- A minority of developing countries qualifies as liberal democracies and barely over half are electoral democracies, with marked regional variations.

- Democratic consolidation has been defined in different ways, with implications for which developing countries are thought to qualify.

- Democratization can be a slow and protracted affair whereas a democracy's deterioration or collapse may be swift.

- The idea of democracy assessment offers a potentially powerful new tool of comparative analysis and self-assessment.

# Explaining democratization

Explaining how democratization occurs and why it takes particular forms generates considerable debate. The same is true where democratization has gone into reverse or is simply absent. Drawing on the familiar terminology, explanations of consolidation can be expected to diverge from explanations of authoritarian collapse and democratic transition; similarly, the reasons that illuminate deconsolidation and stalled transition might differ and fail to explain the complete collapse of a democracy.

Explanations betray contrasting perspectives and schools of thought. For instance one approach emphasizes the impact of historical legacies (political, financial, economic, and other) and **path-dependence**. At its most elaborate path-dependence claims that the nature of the pre-existing regime and the mode used to change it influence the sequel and, ultimately, can determine a new democracy's chances of survival. This confirms why it is important to distinguish between types of authoritarian regime as well as to establish if there were any previous, failed attempts to democratize. For example in Chile the democratic transition from the military dictatorship of General Pinochet in 1990 respected the privileged position of the armed forces that was constitutionally enshrined in 1981. Critics claim this limited Chile's new democracy.

## Box 12.2 **Rustow's methodological propositions**

Although Rustow (1970: 346) advanced the following methodological propositions before Huntington's account of the 'third wave' they help make sense of recent democratic experiments in developing countries:

- The factors that keep a democracy stable may not be the ones that brought it into existence: explanations of democracy must distinguish between function and genesis.

- Correlation is not the same as causation: a genetic theory must concentrate on the latter.

- Not all causal links run from social and economic to political factors: the flow can be in both directions.

- Not all causal links run from beliefs and attitudes to action: the flow can be in both directions.

- The genesis of democracy need not be geographically uniform; there may be many roads to democracy.

- The genesis of democracy need not be temporally uniform: different factors may become crucial during successive phases.

- The genesis of democracy need not be socially uniform: even in the same place and time the attitudes that promote it may not be the same for politicians and common citizens.

(Rustow 1970: 346)

Like much of the theorizing in the democratization literature, path-dependence provides more valuable insights for some countries than for others.

One of the most widely accepted, and with notable exceptions like Taiwan, applicable, ideas is that national unity 'must precede all the other phases of democratization' (Rustow 1970: 351). By national unity Rustow meant 'the vast majority of citizens . . . must have no doubt or mental reservation as to which political community they belong to' (ibid.). Many developing countries lack this very simple background condition. Yet they may look to democracy as a means to manage or resolve inter-group conflicts. However, democratic advance may itself on occasions be responsible for increasing (violent) conflict in a country. It gives sub-national groups freedoms to demand increased self-determination for themselves (as in Indonesia), and may provoke vulnerable minorities to fear a tyranny by the majority or some other politically dominant group. Leaders like Kenya's President arap Moi fragmented the nation by manipulating and aggravating inter-communal rivalries as a strategy to divide opponents and win elections. The institutional forms a democracy takes could be an important determining factor, for example the electoral system.

More broadly, the literature explaining democratization can be distinguished into accounts emphasizing structure and accounts that dwell on agency. The first investigates the 'conditions' and even preconditions whereby democratic trends are variously enabled, facilitated, and actively promoted, or come to be frustrated. The second focuses on process, highlighting the role of actors and institutions. Institutions are so defined as to include rules, norms, expectations, and traditions, both formal and informal, and more concrete organizations like parliaments and parties. The first account is closest to reductionist interpretations of politics as a product of more deep-seated forces, notably forces located in economy and society. The second, 'new institutionalist' perspective, has a more contingent flavour and construes politics as relatively autonomous. March and Olsen (1984: 747) say new institutionalism is 'simply an argument that the organisation of political life makes a difference', being neither a theory nor a coherent critique of one. Accordingly democracy depends in part on the design of political institutions, not just the socio-economic conditions.

All things considered, then, democratization is best understood as a complex interaction that links structural constraints and opportunities to the shaping of contingent choice (Karl 1990). Neither 'underlying forces' nor voluntary agency by themselves fully illuminate what is happening or can unerringly predict where events will lead.

## Socio-economic conditions

Following a seminal article by S. M. Lipset in the *American Political Science Review* (1959) on 'Some Social Requisites Of Democracy: Economic Development and Political Legitimacy' (revisited in Lipset 1994), one school of thought maintains a positive relationship exists between, on the one side, the persistence of stable democracy or the chances of democratic consolidation and the levels of socio-economic modernization. 'Requisites' are not *pre*requisites or *pre*conditions, that is to say these conditions need not be established in advance; authoritarian breakdown and democratic transition can take place amid poverty and economic backwardness. Overall, the idea that material progress enhances the chances of extending democratization and experiencing democratic longevity is strongly supported by developing world evidence accumulated since Lipset's original enquiry, although the positive effects do seem to vary across aspects of performance and across regions. Thus Foweraker and Landman (2004) find the associations between development and the protection of political and civil liberties are less strong outside the advanced industrial countries.

Only relatively recently have social scientists begun to investigate seriously the possibility that development could be the dependent variable and treat democracy as the independent or 'causal' factor (see *Democratization's significance for development*, p. 178 below). But the idea that certain sorts of freedoms, notably economic freedoms, are beneficial to wealth creation goes back a long way, to Adam Smith (1723–90). But for many years after 1945 the dominant view was that developing countries faced a **cruel choice**. Either countries could do what was necessary to develop their economies, which means concentrating on saving and investing to expand the productive capital stock, or they could emulate the political systems of the West. The former probably requires government to take some unpopular decisions, like enforcing abstinence from current consumption. Authoritarian regimes that are well insulated from social pressures seemed best situated to this purpose. In contrast the structure of political incentives posed by competitive party politics appears biased towards raising popular expectations about public spending on welfare. Politicians running for office will promise 'jam today', at the expense of doing what is needful

for 'jam tomorrow'. In the long run economic ruin beckons—the experience of Argentina, where the International Monetary Fund's refusal to provide more support precipitated a massive financial crisis in December 2001.

The moral seemed to be that democracy is a luxury that poor countries can ill afford. After development, sustainable democracy becomes more viable—an option whose opportunity cost (the alternatives forgone) becomes more affordable. The term **wealth theory of democracy** captures the idea. The dramatic economic performance of East Asian 'tiger' economies like Taiwan and South Korea which only later experienced successful democratic transition appear to bear out the general theory. Critics, however, point to established democracies like Botswana, Mauritius (since independence, 1968) and Costa Rica (a democracy since 1899 with only brief interruptions in 1917 and 1948) to demonstrate there is no iron law. The first two democracies in particular have managed impressive development. Also, India (for over fifty years 'the world's largest democracy'), with an average annual income per capita still little over $US2,000 and when economic growth barely kept pace with population increase for several decades, shows that democracy can be maintained even where socio-economic conditions look unpropitious. More than half India's population live on the equivalent of less than $1 a day; and inequalities there are increasing as middle-class Indians have become more affluent. Nevertheless, in regard to much newer democracies we should still ask if there is a discernible threshold of development that makes the desired combination of development and sustained democracy a more assured possibility. And what is the lead-time before development's benefits impact on the prospects for democratic sustainability?

## The significance of development for democratization

There is much statistical evidence of a correlation between social and economic advance (depicted by what is happening to average incomes, poverty and inequality) and democratic durability. Przeworski et al. (1996) found that democracies can survive even in the poorest nations *if* they manage to generate development and reduce inequality while meeting certain other conditions. But what makes modernization and development significant for democratization? Is it primarily a matter of resources? Or of transforming attitudes, values, and patterns of behaviour? Or of the changing class structure that comes with capitalist development in particular? Or is it something to do with the consequences of development's tendency to integrate society into global structures and norms? Different theories emerge from concentrating on different aspects of development:

- Democratic institutions require substantial financial and economic resources, demand high levels of organizational commitment and public involvement that an affluent and well-educated society can most easily provide. Technological and economic progress improve the physical infrastructure of political communication.

- Social modernization erodes old values that inculcated deference to traditional authority and generates self-confidence; it inclines people to see themselves more as citizens than just subjects, so increasing demands for, and acceptance of, rational-legal authority. Pragmatic values sympathetic to the politics of compromise and consensus lying at the heart of the 'democratic way' supplant traditional non-negotiable values like exclusive ethnic loyalties that can frustrate national unity and produce violent disagreements. The attainment of material security for all is an opportunity for *homo politicus* to move centre stage. Closer integration into the global economy brings exposure to the liberal and democratic values already enjoyed in the outside world ('demonstration effect').

- There is a well-known aphorism 'no bourgeois, no democracy'. Development breaks the exclusive power of feudal landlords. Capitalist development creates a plurality of potential centres of power and influence independent of the state. A property-owning middle class has a vested interest in checking the arbitrary use of executive power, and has the economic means and know-how to organize pressure for the redistribution of power. There is a caveat, however. Necessary conditions are not sufficient conditions. Economic growth can produce wide economic inequalities that sustain inequalities of power. Middle-class elements will defend an illiberal or undemocratic regime if they believe it serves their interests, for instance by providing

stability. Thus, notwithstanding an average annual income per capita that is among the highest in the world Singapore is only 'partly free' in the Freedom House classification.

- Industrialization and urbanization make it possible for an organized working class to mobilize mass support to demand greater political rights and civil liberties for ordinary people, especially in response to the unequal distribution of the benefits of economic growth. Thus Rueschemeyer, Stephens, and Stephens (1992) reject the view that democracy is the creation of the bourgeoisie. They highlight the progressive role of the working class acting together with middle-class elements. Some larger developing countries have very sizeable manufacturing sectors. For example in Brazil the political base of President Luis da Silva lies in the labour movement. But in many countries the industrial base is still small; and in some it has been weakened by economic liberalization. For example Zambia's mineworkers who pushed for the return of multi-party democracy in 1991 are now much fewer in number: they are politically emasculated. Organized labour is a major weakness of civil society in many developing countries compared to its leading role in democratizing Western European countries.

## The ambivalent relationship of market economy and democratic polity

A frequent assumption is that the market constitutes a necessary but not sufficient condition of democracy: there have been authoritarian regimes with market economies but no examples of non-market democracies. In reality the relationship is more ambivalent. As Beetham (1997) explains, there are some negative effects associated with the virtues of the market, and even its positive points must be qualified (Box 12.3).

## Political culture

Ideas about the significance of political culture date from G. Almond and S. Verba's *The Civic Culture: Political Attitudes and Democracy in Five Nations* (1965). **Political culture** embodies the attitudes, beliefs, and

## Box 12.3 Positive and negative connections between democracy and the market

**Positive connections**

- The more extensive the state, the more difficult it is to subject to public accountability or societal control.

- The more that is at stake in elections, the greater the incentive for participants to compromise the process, or reject the outcome. Market freedoms and political freedoms are mutually supportive: both require the rule of law, and to ensure this for one is to ensure it for both.

- Sovereignty of consumer and voter both rest on same anti-paternalist principle.

- Market economy is necessary for long-term economic growth which assists durable democracy.

**Negative connections**

- Independence of the market from the state makes the economy difficult to subject to democratic control.

- Free market competition intensifies economic and social inequalities, which can translate into political inequality and so compromise democratic institutions.

- Market dispositions undermine the integrity of the democratic public sphere: market choices come to pre-empt political choices; the logic of private self-interest tends to colonize the public sphere.

(Beetham 1997)

---

values that are said to underlie a political system. For Almond and Verba a 'civic culture' supports democracy. After years during which some analysts argued the concept has no scientific validity, providing at best an explanation of last resort, political culture now features prominently in accounts of democratization. Sustainable democracy is said to require a special set of values such as tolerance, mutual respect, a willingness to trust in fellow citizens together with a healthy scepticism towards persons in authority, in addition to possessing basic knowledge and understanding of democracy's mechanics. The idea of **social capital** is a near relation.

However, there is disagreement over the main constituents of a democratic political culture and the relationships among constituents, their requisites, and how to take measurements. For instance it was once thought that the 'Protestant ethic' made famous by the German sociologist Max Weber was more closely adapted than Roman Catholicism or Confucianism to liberal democracy, yet evidence from many developing countries now makes that doubtful. Very significant for many countries is how far Islamic beliefs are compatible with a democratic culture. Views on this differ widely, in part depending on how Islamism is interpreted. The incompatibility of ideas of popular sovereignty and the sovereign power of God is problematic but not peculiar to Islam. And Singapore's Lee Kuan Yew's (elder statesman and

former Prime Minister) idea of specifically 'Asian values' contests the individualist presuppositions of Western liberal democracy, implying that the more collectivist consciousness found in some East Asian societies demands a different kind of political regime (see pp. 247–8 below).

If something like 'civic culture' is essential to democracy, is it a prerequisite or can it be allowed to develop later and, if so, what will encourage that to happen? This introduces the idea of civic education, instruction in democracy that goes well beyond 'voter education' in the procedure of secret ballots. It also gives rise to further questions about whose culture is most important for democratic sustainability, particularly in the early stages of democratization— the culture of the elite or the mass? One argument is that the primary threat to new democracies comes from the people in power, especially 'old generation' politicians who have taken on democratic pretensions to stay in power rather than out of conviction. They aspire to undermine the new democracy or hold back progress. The developing world contains many examples. In contrast, public attitude surveys carried out in emerging developing country democracies suggest widespread popular attachment to the idea of democracy, even alongside disenchantment with the elected leaders and dissatisfaction with the performance of democratic institutions.

# Institutional crafting

The agency of individual politicians is thought more likely to influence events at critical moments or 'turning points' such as an authoritarian collapse and the immediate aftermath than to determine democratic consolidation. This is the Mandela factor (after Nelson Mandela's benign role in South Africa). In the long haul other factors, including socio-economic ones, have greater bearing. But the design of political institutions—by contributors who often approach this as an opportunity to secure particularist and self-regarding political goals—can have important consequences for the overall distribution of political power, for how the democratic process operates and the democracy's sustainability. This applies, for instance, to constitutional engineering that aims at decentralizing power away from the centre, such as through federal structures and local government, or seeks guaranteed political representation for and legal protection of minorities (such as by adopting consensual, inclusionary decision-making processes rather than simple majoritarianism). On the one hand, formal organizational changes sometimes make little difference to the way things actually work, where inherited informal institutions or patterns of behaviour are impervious to change. On the other hand, institutional reforms including democratic innovations can acquire a degree of permanence once new constellations of vested interests build around them and construe further change as being to their disadvantage. Designing democracy in problematic surroundings, such as a long history of social conflict or very weak state structures, should take account of the possibility that there will be unintended consequences—what Bastian and Luckham in their review of war-torn societies are tempted to call an 'iron law of the perverse consequences of institutional design' (Bastian and Luckham 2003: 314).

Two sets of institutional concerns that have attracted special attention in new democracies are, first, the balance of power and mutual oversight among the executive, legislature, judiciary, and other constituents of a 'self-restraining state'; secondly, electoral systems and party systems. A self-restraining state embraces multiple institutional mechanisms for making government accountable (see Schedler, Diamond, and Plattner 1999). So, for instance

Linz (1990) has compared presidential systems unfavourably with parliamentary systems; and Mainwaring (1993) argues the combination of presidentialism and multi-partyism is especially prone to instability.

O'Donnell (1994) proposed the category **delegative democracy**, much cited in a Latin American context. It rests on the premise that whoever wins election to the presidency is thereby entitled to govern as they think fit—constrained only by the hard facts of existing power relations and a constitutionally limited term of office. The last is something many presidents have schemed to remove, Argentina's Menem and Malawi's Muluzi for instance. Electoral victors in delegative democracies may present themselves as being above political parties and organized interests; they aspire to be accountable to no one. Accountability has been called the linchpin of democratic control of government by the governed (Beetham et al. 2002: 45). O'Donnell makes the valuable distinction between vertical accountability, which makes government accountable to the ballot box and includes supervision by civil society as well as opposition parties, and horizontal accountability across a network of relatively autonomous institutions associated with the 'self-restraining state'. The judiciary's power to enforce the rule of law—even, and especially, against democratically elected governments—is significant in this context, as are bodies like the Auditor General, Ombudsman, Truth and Reconciliation Commissions, Human Rights Commissions, and Central Bank independence. Bodies like these have proliferated in developing countries. There comes a point at which democrats may be legitimately concerned about the power such unelected bodies wield, but in reality governments often obstruct their operational effectiveness such as by provided inadequate resources and exercising control over appointments. Anyway, horizontal accountability is usually weak in delegative democracies.

# Elections and parties

While we must not commit the fallacy of electoralism, the issue of how electoral systems structure political competition is an enduring subject especially relevant to new democracies. It has been said that in developing countries the problem of conducting free and fair elections is 'compounded by the intensity of politicization at an early stage in the democratization process' (Pastor 1999: 7–8). There is growing recognition of how important the organizational framework of electoral management and adminstration is to the quality of electoral democracy (and hence liberal democracy too)—considerations like the competence and impartiality of 'independent' Elections Commissions—which often seem defective. Bratton (1998) found the 'late founding' elections in Africa's new democracies were inferior to their predecessors; half the second-round elections after 1994 compared unfavourably with 1990–4. Pastor (1999: 16) claims 41 per cent of elections in Africa in 1989–99 were 'flawed', compared with 21 per cent in Asia and only 6 per cent in Latin America and the Caribbean. The question what makes elections free and fair is deceptively simple. But governments minded to rig the outcome usually take steps well before the formal campaign.

Although civil society has been credited with responsibility for bringing about authoritarian collapse in some countries, and theorists argue a vibrant civil society is essential to healthy democracy, there is a consensus that political parties are indispensable to liberal democracy and democratic consolidation. Certain functions vital for democracy and political order more generally and public policy specifically cannot easily be replicated by other actors, although where parties are weak and the party system under-institutionalized some tasks like representation may still be carried out by civic associations, social movements, and grass-roots organizations. A party system is defined by the number of parties and the relations between them, their relative size, and how much meaningful choice is presented to the electorate. At minimum an effective party system furnishes government; a competitive party system means there is some possibility of alternation in power. Among the older democracies parties are said to be in decline. In many emerging democracies the development of comparable organizations and the establishment of reasonably competitive party systems is proving to be a major challenge, particularly difficult in Africa, where deeply embedded neo-patrimonial and clientelistic patterns reduce the significance ascribed to party policy or programmatic performance (see Randall and Svåsand 2002).

## Key points

- Different dimensions and phases of democratic change require their own explanation.
- In the long run economic development may be one of the best guarantors of durable democracy especially if the benefits are widely distributed.
- Different understandings of how and why socio-economic development advances the democratic prospect resonate differently in different countries.
- The relationship of market-based or capitalist development to democratization is ambivalent.
- 'New institutional' perspectives on the process of political change complement economistic explanations of democratization's successes and failures.
- Establishing where democratic legitimacy comes from and its dynamics could be central to gauging the prospects for successful democratization.

# The international politics of democratization

A distinguishing feature of democratization in the last thirty years is the role played by external or international factors. The end of the cold war and collapse of Soviet power help explain the increased agitation for political reform in the developing world, although the return to democracy in Latin America was already well advanced. It is the interplay between internal and external factors that is often most significant. The respective influence exerted by the different factors will be specific to the kind of political changes under way (e.g. transition or consolidation), and their direction.

External influence can work in various ways, such as by example, persuasion, and direct intervention of a more or a less forceful nature. The influence exerted by developments in neighbouring countries and the region (democratization/de-democratization 'by contagion') should not be forgotten. Peer pressure from within the Organisation of American States to discourage attempts among members to change government by unconstitutional means has had partial success. Even so, much of the attention has focused on the role of the West, in particular the United States and European Union, which after 1990 expanded efforts to promote or 'internationalize' democracy, in several ways.

Two main approaches are to attach democratic, human rights, and governance conditions (also called 'conditionalities') to development aid or other concessions such as trade concessions, and to offer technical, financial, material, or symbolic support to democracy projects and programmes (i.e. democracy assistance). Aid **conditionality** means the benefits could be denied, withheld, terminated, or withdrawn in the event of non-compliance. The threat or application of such sanctions is sometimes called negative conditionality; the introduction of incentives (possibly offers of democracy assistance) sometimes called positive conditionality. But many examples question the effectiveness of such pressure. Determined leaders like Zimbabwe's President Mugabe or Myanmar's military rulers resist change even though society pays a price through the aid forgone. In 2003 the USA and its allies forced 'regime change' on Iraq, but democratic progress there will depend on a sense of ownership, which ultimately must come from within. The alternative—'donor democracies'—are likely to be short-lived.

The real motives behind democracy promotion efforts are probably mixed, not least because the agents include non-governmental and international organizations as well as states, and in foreign policy-making democracy promotion can conflict with higher priorities of national interest. However, one rationale for universalizing democratic systems that is influential emphasizes the positive consequences for development. Here then we need to reconsider the question of democratization's usefulness to development, raised earlier when discussing the socio-economic conditions of democratization.

---

## Box 12.4 **Democracy assistance objectives and modalities**

| Sector | Sector Goal | Type of Aid |
|---|---|---|
| Electoral process | Free and fair elections | Electoral aid |
| | Strong national parties | Party building |
| State Institutions | Democratic constitution | Constitutional assistance |
| | Independent, effective judiciary | Rule-of-law aid |
| | Competent, representative legislature | Legislative strengthening |
| | Responsive local goverment | Local government development |
| | Pro-democratic military | Civil-military relations |
| Civil Society | Active advocacy bodies | Building civil society organizations |
| | Politically educated citizenry | Civic education |
| | Strong, independent media | Media strengthening |
| | Strong, independent unions | Union building |

*Source*: Adapted from Carothers (1999: 88).

# Democratization's significance for development

The thinking behind the idea of a 'cruel choice' between democracy and development is no longer fashionable. Many examples show that authoritarian regimes—especially weak and fearful autocracies—can be self-serving and produce developmental failures, precisely because they are unaccountable and lack legitimacy. In contrast party-based government may offer a responsible approach to economic management in democracies because of the parties' calculation that over the long run reputation will impact on their electoral fortunes. Also, democratically elected governments possess the legitimacy to take tough but necessary economic decisions. Accountability makes the gross abuse of public resources less likely. Furthermore, the United Nations Development Programme argues that *human* **development** depends as much on whether poor people—assumed to be the majority—have political power as on their opportunities for economic progress. The UNDP's report (2002: v) claims too that democracies are better adapted than authoritarian regimes to handle domestic conflict in ways that do not damage the economy. By arguing that sustained poverty reduction requires equitable growth but also requires that poor people have political power, the possibility of a virtuous circle is implied. Democratic opening (*possibly* conditioned on certain socio-economic attainments) improves the outlook for human development by empowering people to exert pressure for an expansion of social and economic opportunities. That in turn makes democratic sustainability and democratic deepening more achievable.

Once again, however, a necessary condition is not a sufficient condition; thus the UNDP's Report acknowledges there is insufficient evidence to claim democracy actually causes economic growth; it does not *guarantee* equitable social and economic development either. The great variety of political regimes makes generalization about their economic performance very risky. The developing world's established democracies do not stand out in terms of tackling poverty, although those with strong party systems and an effective state organization appear to perform best (Moore and Putzel 1999: 4–8). Other influences might have an even more significant bearing on development, in particular poverty reduction, and on democratization. Deep and widespread poverty can persist in democracies (India for example) and inequalities can widen in developing countries undergoing democratization (as in Latin America).

# Globalization, democracy, and democratization

International influences exert both positive and negative effects on democratization. Even democracy assistance can be counter-productive if badly designed or hijacked by anti-democratic forces; for example ruling elites may use it to tap into nationalism or anti-Americanism, thereby mobilizing

---

## Box 12.5 **Three views on democracy and development**

- Democracy is too conservative a system of power. It has a bias towards consensus and accommodation that cannot promote the radical change in the system of wealth that is essential to establishing developmental momentum, especially in late developing societies. A truly developmental state needs to be insulated from society and may not be a democracy (Leftwich 2002).

- Developing countries differ from the West in that democratic contestants do not have to compromise with capitalists; instead they aim to capture power for themselves. This rent-seeking behaviour by politicians destroys the chances of development (Khan 2002).

- Powerlessness and poverty go together. Democratic models more expansive than the minimalist versions offer an emancipatory potential that would empower the poor and serve development, for example by attacking the corruption that benefits the privileged few (Grugel 2002).

    *Source*: Adapted from 'Debate: Democracy and Development', in *New Political Economy*, 7/2 (2002).

opposition to the foreigners' political agenda. This has happened in parts of the Middle East. Moreover Western powers still support undemocratic or illiberal regimes where they judge it important to key interests such as national security, as in President Musharraf's Pakistan and Saudi Arabia. In any case a plausible argument is that the West's unsystematic approach to promoting democracy and the spotlight it now places on democratic development in developing countries are really a sideshow, marginalized by globalization and its effects.

**Globalization** has been defined as 'processes whereby many social relations become relatively delinked from territorial geography, so that human lives are increasingly played out in the world as a single place' (Scholte 2001: 14–15). Globalization diminishes the value of conventional democratic models by making state-bound structures increasingly untenable, and this is said to be particularly true for many developing countries. In a globalizing world the human forces that most influence people's lives are increasingly transnational and supraterritorial, whereas democracy is historically rooted in and confined to the borders of the nation-state.

First, powerful agencies of global governance are shrinking the space available for national political self-determination. These agencies are not themselves democratically accountable and possess specialized technical knowledge of complex global issues that small poor countries and micro-states can only envy. By devaluing democracy's credibility these developments threaten to induce political apathy among citizens.

Secondly, the political space where self-rule remains an option is penetrated more and more by a variety of non-accountable external actors, who establish local branches or subsidiaries and form linkages and alliances that enable capture of the domestic policy and decision-making processes. Small and poor states with internal political weaknesses are the most vulnerable. Corporate bribery of politicians and officials is one example, but even some kinds of international assistance for 'good governance' may end up subverting democracy. The argument here is that such endeavours aim to implant the 'Washington consensus'. Governance reforms make it easier to monitor financial and economic performance, rendering governments more accountable to foreign creditors. In addition, experience in Latin America suggests

that, because elected governments have greater political legitimacy, they are better able to implement tough measures required as part of the obligations of international debt service and repayment. Western assistance to doctrinal development by new political parties and for civil society helps reinforce the overall message of economic neo-liberalism. Similarly it is argued that international democracy promotion seeks to control the reform process by limiting it to 'low intensity' democracy, thereby serving the interests of transnational capital.

However, there are several counter-arguments, not least that globalization's progress need not be uniformly adverse to democratization over time. The threat it poses may be more to some specific forms of democracy, or to certain countries only, rather than to democracy as such.

First, the international spread of democratic values is itself a part of globalization—hence we can speak of globalizing democracy. This process is furthered by the increased mobility of people, knowledge, and ideas that comes from revolutions in information technology, international communications, and transportation—highly visible signs of globalization. Globalization forces political openness, which threatens authoritarian regimes.

Second, if globalization is or can be made a more powerful force for economic progress and especially if development's benefits are shared more equitably, the prospects for stable democracy will increase.

Third, democracy is predicated on there being some measure of state power, if only to counter democracy's enemies at home and abroad. The wealth generated by globalization can finance state reconstruction and improved governance, thereby allowing weak states to become more responsive to societal demands.

Fourth, the UNDP *Report* (2002) calls for greater pluralism in respect of global decision-making, through enlarging the space for participation by non-state actors. The globalization of civil society ('global civil society') is already under way, and could recapture influence for the people even where familiar state institutions seem incapable. Global networks give support to local civic actors in their struggles to open up political space at home; local actors draw support from regional and global coalitions when endeavouring to stand up to such powerful international institutions as the World Bank. Civil society organizations themselves should be democratically organized and accountable (see Scholte 2001: 26–30).

Finally, there are projected schemes some more visionary than others pertaining to 'cosmopolitan democracy' (i.e. a 'democratic international order') and ideas for democratizing institutions of governance at levels reaching all the way from the local to the global and the United Nations. When accompanied by measures to empower such institutions vis-à-vis market forces that affect peoples' livelihoods, such proposals could rescue democracy's purposes.

## Key points

- The jury is still out on the potency of democratization to bring about the very socio-economic conditions that could be essential to its own survival.

- There are many different routes by which the international environment can influence democratization in developing countries: only some are supportive; some are unintentional, and their effects vary among countries.

- The West's capacity to determine sustainable democratic development through political conditionalities or democracy assistance should not be overestimated.

- From a democratization perspective, globalization invites us to think not only about how to make the political space more democratic but how to restore power to the political as well.

- Globalization has helped undermine some authoritarian regimes but might pose a longer-term threat to democracy.

# Conclusion

Key issues at the heart of debates about democratization in developing countries include: what is democratization and how much progress has there been? What explains democratic developments and the influence on future prospects? What are democratization's relationships to development? And how important are the international dimensions? This chapter has argued that democratization's meaning, like democracy itself, is contested. And while most developing countries have undergone political change over the last two decades or so, illustrated for example by a marked reduction in military regimes, the number of stable new liberal democracies is modest. In many countries competing analytical frameworks such as nation and state-building may offer more insights into their contemporary politics.

Attention is now turning away from explaining democratic transition ('transitology') and specifying the character and causes of democratic consolidation ('consolidology'), towards democracies' 'hazard rates' (the probability that they will decay or die) and the reasons why the momentum of political reform so often stalls. Our typology of regimes has been enriched by the proliferation of different forms of diminished authoritarianism ('authoritarianism with adjectives') and diminished democracy. There is a 'chicken and egg' conundrum of how to sort out democratization's many apparent requisites from its possible consequences. Thus it is important to establish how far economic circumstances and external forces over which governments might have little control determine democratization's fortunes, and how much is influenced by political choice and institutional initiatives. In the long run development appears to favour democracy, but there are reservations about the full effects of the market. Moreover, democratization could be essential to a sustained improvement in development, yet it offers no guarantee and in some places the impact might even be negative. A comprehensive assessment of the possibilities for democratic self-rule and of progress to date should take account of the international involvement in developing countries and globalization and their consequences.

## QUESTIONS

1   Why does democratization take different 'flight trajectories' in different developing countries?

2   How do we know which developing countries are experiencing democratic consolidation?

3   When assessing a country's democratic progress which of the following offers the most appropriate yardstick: its recent past; the people's expectations; comparable countries elsewhere; some international 'gold standard'?

4   Does democratization have any specific requisites or prerequisites?

5   How important is good institutional design to the democratic prospect, and what does it look like?

6   How can democratization help and how might it hinder development?

7   Should developing countries resist external involvement in bringing about and making democratic reform?

8   Why is globalization ambiguous towards democratic development?


## GUIDE TO FURTHER READING

Beetham, D., Bracking, S., Kearton, I., and Weir, S., *International IDEA Handbook on Democracy Assessment* (The Hague, London, New York: Kluwer Law International, 2002).

Burnell, P. (ed.), *Democratization through the Looking-Glass* (Manchester: Manchester University Press, 2003). Introduces multi-disciplinary perspectives on democratization and comparative analysis from the regions.

Carothers, T., *Aiding Democracy Abroad* (Washington: Brookings Institution, 1999). Critically assesses United States' democracy assistance.

'Debate: Democracy and Development', *New Political Economy*, 7/2 (2002): 269–81. This sets out contending perspectives on the relationship between democracy and development.

Diamond, L., *Developing Democracy: Towards Consolidation* (Baltimore and London: The Johns Hopkins University Press, 1999). An extensive survey and analysis from a leading analyst.

Diamond, L., 'Thinking about Hybrid Regimes', *Journal of Democracy*, 13/2 (2002): 21–35. Explores regime types that combine democratic and authoritarian elements.

Haynes, J., *Democracy in the Developing World. Africa, Asia, Latin America and the Middle East* (Oxford: Polity, 2001). Employs structured contingency to explain variations in democratic consolidation.

Huntington, S. P., *The Third Wave. Democratization in the Late Twentieth Century* (Norman, Okla., and London: University of Oklahoma Press, 1991).

O'Donnell, G., Schmitter, P., and Whitehead, L., *Transitions from Authoritarian Rule* (Baltimore: The Johns Hopkins University Press, 1986).

Rustow, D. A., 'Transitions to democracy', *Comparative Politics*, 2/3 (1970): 337–63.

United Nations Development Programme, *UNDP Human Development Report 2002. Deepening Democracy in a Fragmented World* (New York and Oxford: Oxford University Press, 2002).

*Democratization* (edited in the UK) and the *Journal of Democracy* (edited in the US) are two well-known journals. The first issue each year of the latter includes a digest of the latest annual Freedom House Survey.

## WEB LINKS

**www.democracy.stanford.edu**   The comparative democratization project led by Larry Diamond among others.

**www.cdi.anu.edu.au**   The site of the Centre for Democratic Institutions, Australian National University, useful for democracy developments in the Asia-Pacific region.

**www.ifes.org**   Presents information from the US-based International Foundation for Election Systems.

**www.idea.int**   The site of the multi-member International Institute for Democracy and Electoral Assistance (Stockholm) and its democracy promotion activities.

**www.ipu.org**   The site of the Inter-Parliamentary Union, on parliamentary democracy.

**www.ned.org**   The site of the Washington-based, non-governmental, National Endowment for Democracy, which among other things houses the International Forum for Democratic Studies.

**www.undp.org/governance**   Presents the work of the United Nations Development Programme on democratic governance.

 ## COMPANION WEB SITE

For additional material and resources, see the companion web site at:
**www.oup.com/uk/booksites/politics/**

# Part Four

# Policy issues

In this part several major policy domains in development are examined. The themes do not concern developing countries only; but in all the developing regions they represent notable challenges to both state and non-state actors at the present time. Our concern is not with 'development' per se or as a universal concept. Instead this part again has two main aims. **First** it aims to show how states like other major actors in the economy and society are confronted by certain key issues in development and face seemingly inescapable challenges. States in particular have to entertain large decisions that involve political risks and impose considerable administrative burdens, concerning such matters as economic development, welfare, the environment, and human rights. The **second** aim is to show the different ways in which governments and non-governmental actors determine their response, by comparing different strategies and their likely consequences. The relevance here of international influences on policy agendas and the formulation of policy and the exogenous stimuli and constraints shaping decisions and decision processes are regularly pointed out. The object is to reveal the process as well as substance of policy. What choices are open to developing countries, and just how much scope for exercising choice independently do they have? Does state action necessarily offer the most appropriate way forward? Does one size fit all, or can the political response embody distinct national and sub-national approaches to defining problems and devising solutions and their implementation?

# Development

*Tony Addison*

## OVERVIEW

This chapter discusses development policy objectives, noting how these have changed over the years, with a more explicit focus on poverty reduction coming to the fore recently. It also examines the relationship between economic growth and poverty reduction. The chapter then discusses how to achieve economic growth, starting with the caveat that growth must be environmentally sustainable, and moves on to the big question of the respective roles for the market mechanism and the state in allocating society's productive resources. The chapter then discusses how economic reform has been implemented, and the political difficulties that arise. It concludes that getting development policy right has the potential to lift millions out of poverty.

# Introduction

There are over 1 billion people living in extreme poverty today, defined as having less than one US$ per day to survive on (see Table 13.1). The situation in sub-Saharan Africa is especially desperate; nearly half of the population is poor and poverty has increased over the last decade. Some 799 million people, or 17 per cent of the population in developing countries, are undernourished, and in sub-Saharan Africa one-third of the population is undernourished, the largest of any developing region, and a percentage that is rising (World Bank 2003c: 6). Yet, set against this grim picture there has also been considerable progress, notably in East Asia where the percentage of people living in extreme poverty has been cut in half (from 30.5 per cent in 1990 to 15.6 per cent in 1999: see Table 13.1). Even in South Asia, which has the largest numbers of poor people of all the main regions (some 488 million), the percentage of people in poverty has fallen substantially over the last decade.

Looking at **economic growth** (the rate of growth in Gross Domestic Product (GDP) often presented on a per capita basis), sub-Saharan Africa has performed very badly for much of the period since 1980 (with notable exceptions such as Botswana and Mauritius). Many African countries today have a level of per capita GDP below that of 1980; GDP per capita is below the level of the 1960s in countries that have experienced civil war, for example Angola, the Democratic Republic of the Congo, and Liberia. In contrast, some East Asian countries have grown at rates that are historically unprecedented. Whereas it took the United Kingdom—the world's first industrial nation—fifty-four years to develop from a low per-capita income economy to a middle-income economy, it took Hong Kong, Singapore, and Taiwan only ten years to achieve middle-income status (estimates from Parente and Prescott 2000). China is presently growing at over 9 per cent a year. Latin America achieved steady if unspectacular growth in the period up to the late 1970s but then went into deep recession during the debt crisis of the 1980s (described by Latin Americans as the 'lost decade'). Latin America recovered in the 1990s, but the region has begun to falter again, with a spectacular economic collapse in Argentina which was the star reformer of the early to mid-1990s. Lastly, the Middle-East and North African countries raised their standard of living using their oil wealth, but have largely failed to achieve economic diversification and provide employment for their growing and young populations, while dictatorship

**Table 13.1** Extreme poverty, 1990–2015

| | People living on less than $US 1 a day (millions) | | | Share of people living on less than $US 1 a day (%) | | |
|---|---|---|---|---|---|---|
| | 1990 | 1999 | 2015 (forecast) | 1990 | 1999 | 2015 (forecast) |
| East Asia and Pacific | 486 | 279 | 80 | 30.5 | 15.6 | 3.9 |
| Excluding China | 110 | 57 | 7 | 24.2 | 10.6 | 1.1 |
| Europe and Central Asia | 6 | 24 | 7 | 1.4 | 5.1 | 1.4 |
| Latin America and Caribbean | 48 | 57 | 47 | 11.0 | 11.1 | 7.5 |
| Middle East and North Africa | 5 | 6 | 8 | 2.1 | 2.2 | 2.1 |
| South Asia | 506 | 488 | 264 | 45.0 | 36.6 | 15.7 |
| Sub-Saharan Africa | 241 | 315 | 404 | 47.4 | 49.0 | 46.0 |
| Total | 1,292 | 1,169 | 809 | 29.6 | 23.2 | 13.3 |
| Excluding China | 917 | 945 | 735 | 28.5 | 25.0 | 15.7 |

*Source*: World Bank (2003c: 5).

**Table 13.2** Economic growth, 1980–2001 (average annual % growth)

|  | 1980–90 | 1990–2001 |
|---|---|---|
| **Low income** | 4.5 | 3.4 |
| **Middle income** | 2.9 | 3.4 |
| Lower middle income | 4.0 | 3.7 |
| Upper middle income | 1.7 | 3.1 |
| **Low and middle income** | 3.2 | 3.4 |
| East Asia and Pacific | 7.5 | 7.5 |
| Europe and Central Asia | 2.1 | −1.0 |
| Latin America and the Caribbean | 1.7 | 3.2 |
| Middle East and North Africa | 2.0 | 3.0 |
| South Asia | 5.6 | 5.5 |
| Sub-Saharan Africa | 1.6 | 2.6 |
| **High income** | 3.3 | 2.5 |
| Europe EMU | 2.4 | 2.0 |

*Source*: World Bank (2003c: 188).

and war have driven such countries as Iraq down into the low-income country group.

In sum, the developing world today presents a very mixed picture: very fast growth and poverty reduction in much of Asia; slow or negative per capita GDP growth in sub-Saharan Africa combined with rising poverty; high economic volatility in Latin America;

and widespread stagnation in North Africa and the Middle East, despite often abundant natural resources.

What role has development policy played in these different outcomes? What policies are most important for accelerating development? Is the development past a guide to the development future? What lessons can we transfer across countries? As Nobel Laureate Robert Lucas says: 'the consequences for human welfare involved in questions like these are simply staggering. Once one starts to think about them, it is hard to think about anything else' (Lucas 1988). In fact the answers contained in ideas about development policy have changed over time. On some issues there is now considerable agreement about what needs to be done. But many issues remain deeply controversial, with starkly contrasting viewpoints.

## Key points

- Over 1 billion people live in extreme poverty, about one-sixth of the world's population.

- Poverty is falling in Asia, but remains high and increasing in sub-Saharan Africa.

- Developing countries show very mixed economic performance, with success in much of Asia, but poor performance in sub-Saharan Africa, and economic instability in Latin America.

# Defining development policy objectives

Much of today's debate is centred on poverty reduction as the primary objective for development policy (as can be seen when you look at the websites of the international agencies given at the end of this chapter). People differ as to how to define poverty: economists typically favour monetary measures, using data collected from household surveys of incomes and expenditures. If the household falls below a defined poverty line then it is classified as poor. However, not all countries have the data to define poverty in this way, so the $US1 per day measure is often used to calculate the global and regional aggregates.

Non-monetary measures of poverty are increasingly used as well—measures such as infant mortality, life expectancy, and literacy—and nearly everyone now accepts that poverty is a multi-dimensional phenomenon. This is evident in the **Millennium Development Goals (MDGs)** which were adopted by the world's leaders in the UN Millennium Declaration of September 2002, and these are now the guiding principles for the international development community (see Box 13.1).

In the early days of development policy, during the era of decolonization from the late 1940s through to

## Box 13.1 The Millennium Development Goals

### Goal 1: Eradicate extreme poverty and hunger

Target 1: Halve, between 1990 and 2015, the proportion of people whose income is less than US$1 a day

Target 2: Halve, between 1990 and 2015, the proportion of people who suffer from hunger

### Goal 2: Achieve universal primary education

Target 3: Ensure that, by 2015, children everywhere, boys and girls alike, will be able to complete a full course of primary schooling

### Goal 3: Promote gender equality and empower women

Target 4: Eliminate gender disparity in primary and secondary education, preferably by 2005 and in all levels of education no later than 2015

### Goal 4: Reduce child mortality

Target 5: Reduce by two-thirds, between 1990 and 2015, the under-five mortality rate

### Goal 5: Improve maternal health

Target 6: Reduce by three-quarters, between 1990 and 2015, the maternal mortality ratio

### Goal 6: Combat HIV/AIDS, malaria and other diseases

Target 7: Have halted by 2015 and begun to reverse the spread of HIV/AIDS

Target 8: Have halted by 2015 and begun to reverse the incidence of malaria and other major diseases

### Goal 7: Ensure environmental sustainability

Target 9: Integrate the principles of sustainable development into country policies and programmes and reverse the loss of environmental resources

Target 10: Halve by 2015 the proportion of people without sustainable access to safe drinking water

Target 11: Have achieved by 2020 a significant improvement in the lives of at least 100 million slum dwellers

### Goal 8: Develop a global partnership for development

Target 12: Develop further an open, rule-based, predictable, non-discriminatory trading and financial system (includes a commitment to good governance, development, and poverty reduction—both nationally and internationally)

Target 13: Address the special needs of the least developed countries (includes tariffs- and quota- free access for exports, enhanced program of debt relief for and cancellation of official bilateral debt, and more generous official development assistance for countries committed to poverty reduction).

Target 14: Address the special needs of land-locked countries and small-island developing states (through the Program of Action for the Sustainable Development of Small Island Developing States and 22nd General Assembly Provisions).

Target 15: Deal comprehensively with the debt problems of developing countries through national and international measures in order to make debt sustainable in the long term.

Target 16: In cooperation with developing countries, develop and implement strategies for decent and productive work for youth.

Target 17: In cooperation with pharmaceutical companies, provide access to affordable essential drugs in developing countries.

Target 18: In cooperation with the private sector, make available the benefits of new technologies, especially information and communication technologies.

(UNDP 2003: 1–3)

the 1960s, poverty reduction was often more implicit than explicit in development strategies. These tended to focus on raising GDP per capita (more loosely income per capita) by means of economic growth—it being assumed that poverty reduction would then follow, more or less, from growth. Early development thinkers emphasized raising output, in particular increasing overall labour productivity (output per person) by shifting labour from sectors where its productivity is low to sectors where it is high. This led to a concentration on industrialization which was seen as the dynamic sector, while for many policy-makers smallholder ('peasant') agriculture appeared to be hopelessly backward and unproductive (it could therefore release large amounts of labour for industry). Crudely put, industrialization and urbanization became synonymous with development in the minds of many policy-makers from the 1940s to the 1960s. This was reinforced by what appeared, at the time, to be the successful example of the Soviet Union which achieved large-scale industrialization from the 1930s onwards. Aid donors enthusiastically supported big infrastructure projects, especially when these benefited their own suppliers of capital equipment.

Income per capita is an *average* measure of a country's living standard, and there can be a wide *variation* around this mean. This variation—the inequality of income—exhibits substantial differences across countries (see Fig. 13.1), reflecting differences in the distribution of wealth (land, other property, and financial wealth) and **human capital** (peoples' skills and capabilities, which are partly a product of their education, and which make them more productive). The

differences in turn reflect country-specific histories of colonization, war, and policy decisions. South Africa's extreme inequality in income and wealth is a legacy of apartheid, for instance.

Quite apart from the ethical dimension and the possibility that high inequality can be socially destabilizing, economic growth will have a smaller benefit in reducing absolute poverty when a society starts from a position of high inequality. It is simply the case that the rich will gain more from any percentage point of GDP growth than the poor when the rich command substantial income and wealth to start with. A great deal of growth in economic output will be required before the labour market tightens and average wages start to rise. Put differently, high-inequality societies need to grow a lot faster to achieve the same amount of annual poverty reduction as low-inequality societies.

Calculating how much economic growth is needed to halve the proportion of the world's people in

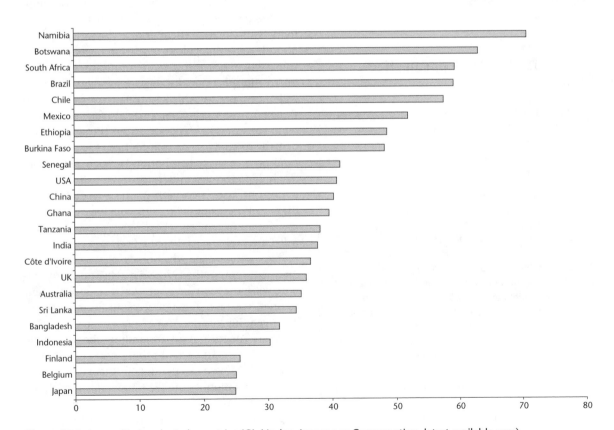

**Figure 13.1** Inequality in selected countries (Gini Index: Income or Consumption, latest available year)
*Source*: World Bank (2003c: 64–7).

poverty between 1990 and 2015 (MDG Goal 1) is very important. This has led to an often heated debate about how much growth reduces poverty (for differing perspectives see Shorrocks and van der Hoeven 2004). If we assume unchanged income inequality then, for the developing world as a whole, the United Nations Development Programme (UNDP) reckons that the poverty rate declines by 2 per cent for each 1 per cent increase in average per capita income (UNDP 2003: 67). On this score Africa performs badly. In 2002, only five of Africa's fifty-three countries achieved the 7 per cent annual growth estimated necessary to meet the MDG for reducing extreme poverty, with average growth being 3.2 per cent for sub-Saharan Africa (UNECA 2003). Forty-three countries achieved positive growth but below 7 per cent, and five saw a decline in GDP. The picture is bleakest in the conflict-affected countries such as the Democratic Republic of the Congo, Liberia, and the Sudan (see Box 13.2). And the spread of HIV/AIDS is also dramatically affecting MDG indicators, and undermining economies, especially in southern Africa which has a high incidence of the disease.

The assumption that as growth proceeds, income (and wealth) inequality remains unchanged is too simple. In practice, as economic growth proceeds some of the poor will begin to accumulate capital to invest in their livelihoods, buying more land, and using their own money to pay for their children's education—who will then obtain more remunerative occupations than their parents. But this will be a very tough challenge, with high vulnerability to setback; some will never get started at all, or will fall deeper into poverty, perhaps because of ill health.

So, countries need to protect and build the assets of the poor, particularly their human capital as well as the natural capital such as the soils, forests, and fisheries on which their livelihoods depend. Subsidizing primary education, basic health care, water, and sanitation will not only raise the **human development** of poor people but will also raise their productivity. This will help them diversify their livelihoods in both self-employment (e.g. from dependence on **subsistence** agriculture and into cash crops and micro-enterprises) and wage-employment (the poor will earn more as skilled workers than as unskilled workers). Asset *redistribution* may also be necessary to build the assets of the poor. Often this applies particularly to land and its transfer from the rich to the rural poor. Asset redistribution is much more challenging politically, and large-scale redistributions tend to be associated with political revolutions. In these ways, economic growth will start to become more pro-poor, and each percentage point of growth will deliver more poverty reduction.

This awareness of what holds poor people back came to the fore in the 1970s, in part because of disillusion with the outcomes of the first development decades. The high hopes of decolonization proved to be largely illusory in Africa; and poverty persisted in Latin America notwithstanding the economic growth. This led to a radicalization of the development debate with **dependency theory** much in vogue. In addition, by the 1970s there was much more evidence from academic research on the determinants of poverty and how poverty responds to economic and social change. This led to a reconsideration of the earlier view that smallholder agriculture was

## Box 13.2 **The development effects of conflict**

The period 1990–2000 saw nineteen major armed conflicts in Africa, ranging from civil wars to the 1998–2000 war between Eritrea and Ethiopia. Peace has been elusive, and the term 'post-conflict' is often a sad misnomer.

While achieving peace has received much attention, the nature of post-conflict recovery also merits close study. The end of war saves *lives*—including those of the poor who are often its main victims—but it may deliver hardly any improvement in *livelihoods*. War destroys the human and physical capital of the poor. It undermines the bonds of family and kinship, or **social capital**, central to the livelihoods of Africa's communities. These effects, together with the destruction of essential services and infrastructure, may so weaken the poor that they are unable to share in national recovery. Moreover, those who control the post-war state may be unable (or unwilling) to ensure that reconstruction benefits the majority. A narrow elite, sometimes including former **warlords**, may instead reap most of the gain; recovery's benefits will then be narrow rather than *broad based* in their distribution.

un-dynamic, and a new emphasis on the talents of poor people as farmers and micro-entrepreneurs. Development professionals began to see new ways of helping the poor to build their existing livelihoods. The World Bank, under its then President, Robert McNamara, began to move away from its traditional emphasis on lending to physical infrastructure and towards poverty reduction, particularly through agricultural development, the principal livelihood of the world's poor.

Note that a direct focus on poverty reduction has a sharper political dimension than a focus on growth in the development strategy. For a start, the poor may be poor because they have very little, if any, political voice. This is true of much of the rural poor in sub-Saharan Africa, for instance. This is seen in the way that development strategies have often ignored them or, perversely, taxed them (see Bates 1981). Politicians need to expend very little political capital when they talk about economic growth being 'like a tide that raises all boats'. But when it comes to spending public money, basic pro-poor services—especially those that serve the rural poor—are often left behind, after services that prioritize the needs of more vocal, and more effectively organized, non-poor groups (especially in urban political centres). A general bias against the rural areas and in favour of the urban areas (**urban bias**) was evident in much of post-independence Africa. Vocal and wealthy interests can effectively control the legislatures that determine the pattern of public spending and taxation (as in Central America). When economic crisis strikes, governments often let the burden of adjustment fall on the meagre services that do benefit the poor.

However, some governments do more for poor people than others, as is evident from the fact that among countries experiencing similar levels of per capita income there are some substantial differences in poverty. For instance while Niger and Tanzania have similar average incomes the former has twice the percentage of its population living on less than a dollar a day. At a higher average income level the same applies to Nigeria and Senegal, and at even higher average levels the same applies to Nicaragua and Vietnam: in each pairing a substantially lower proportion of the population in the latter country lives below the poverty line. Similarly in terms of human development, a country like Vietnam has a relatively favourable level for its average income, whereas a country like Zimbabwe performs worse than some other countries with comparable levels of economic development (UNDP 2003: 68). At least part of the variation is due to differences in governments' political commitment to poverty reduction. Also, even within countries, different regions often spend very different amounts on pro-poor services, reflecting the operation of local political factors: for instance in India, the state of Kerala has comparatively superior human development indicators.

In reality, the discussion of poverty strategies often amounts to producing 'wish lists'—long lists of everything that needs to be done for the poor, without much consideration of the cost. But how to finance the poverty reduction strategy is of critical importance, either through mobilizing more public money—requiring often difficult political decisions about taxation—or more external resources, including foreign aid. This in turn leads to often difficult decisions for the recipient government over how to deal with foreign aid donors and aid **conditionality**, as well as political difficulties for donors who want governments to use their aid more effectively for poverty reduction. This issue has come to a head with the formulation of **Poverty Reduction Strategy Papers** (PRSPs), many of which are inadequately linked to the fiscal policies of governments (or are too ambitious for the available resources) and will therefore be under-funded.

External capital flows, including foreign aid, can do much to assist poor countries. But many developing countries need to do more to mobilize additional domestic revenues to finance increased public spending if pro-poor development is to happen. This requires effective state organizations to mobilize the revenue and spend it wisely. It also requires economic growth to expand the tax base (sales taxes, income taxes, and capital gains taxes). But achieving economic growth poses its own problems.

## Key points

- Poverty reduction has become a more explicit objective of development policy, and economic growth is now seen as more of a means to an end, rather than a final objective in itself.

- The effectiveness of economic growth in achieving poverty reduction lies in understanding how poor people make their livelihoods and whether they share in economic growth, and how the revenues generated by growth are used.

- Effective states are necessary to achieve development objectives, particularly in providing pro-poor services and infrastructure.

# Achieving economic growth

Economic growth can occur in many ways; population growth adds to the stock of workers and, provided that they are productive, to output; labour productivity rises through the accumulation of capital equipment together with technical progress. The implications of growth for poverty reduction depend in part on how growth occurs; whether it involves expanding the output and income that the poor derive from self-employment or their opportunities for wage-employment, for example. The nature of growth also determines whether its environmental impact is benign or destructive. Agricultural output growth may result from a careful husbanding of 'natural capital' on which livelihoods depend, or these renewable resources may be depleted to levels that threaten their very existence. Although early development strategies ignored this dimension, how to achieve economic growth in a more environmentally sustainable way is now a major issue in itself (see Chapter 14).

# Markets and states

Most people agree that states have an important role to play in protecting property rights, providing law and order, and defending their citizens against external aggression. States can thereby reduce the **transactions costs** of market exchange. But the demands that these tasks place on states should not be underestimated.

However, beyond a core set of **public goods** such as defence, disagreement starts to open up about (a) the amount of physical infrastructure (like roads and water systems) and social-sector provision (such as education and health care) the state should provide, together with the scale of its subsidy to users of these services and (b) how far the state should intervene in the market mechanism (the operation of supply and demand).

In regard to infrastructure and social-sector provision in the context of poverty reduction, there is wide agreement on the need for investment in education and basic health care, but there are differences over the scale of subsidy that the state should provide. The latter is also governed by the resources available to the state from taxation, user fees, domestic borrowing, foreign borrowing, and foreign aid. The range of provision can vary from partially subsidizing basic services only, through to finely targeted pro-poor transfers, up to more generous subsidies at higher levels of service, and finally welfare states on the European model. Unless the state enjoys generous revenues from abundant natural resources such as oil or strong capital inflows, there will be some hard choices. Moreover the many organizational challenges should not be underestimated either.

For all these reasons, countries vary widely in their level of public spending as a share of GDP (Fig. 13.2). This is one dimension along which analysts measure

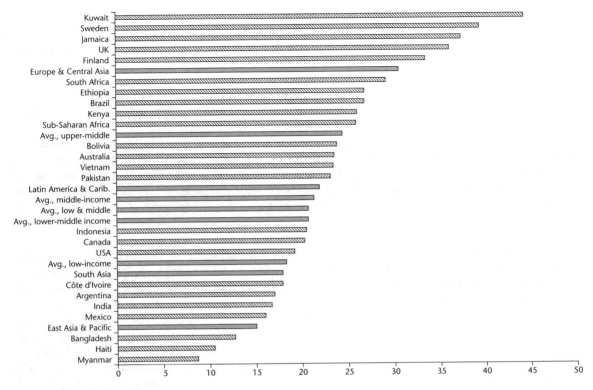

**Figure 13.2** Total public expenditure as % of GDP for country groups and selected countries, 2000

*Note*: Total public expenditure on central government activities, as defined in World Bank (2003c: 226–9).

the involvement of government in the economy. But it is not the only dimension: the second dimension is the extent of the state's intervention in markets through controls on prices, quantities traded, and the number and nature of participants (including the state itself as a supplier of goods and services). Much of the debate about development strategy can be reduced to differences in views about how far market mechanisms (the operation of supply and demand) yield socially desirable outcomes and therefore the virtue or otherwise of state action (where the definition of 'socially desirable' is also contested).

While nearly everyone is agreed on the need for poverty reduction, considerable disagreement centres on how well market mechanisms yield poverty reduction—or, indeed, whether markets sometimes work against poor people. On the other hand, some analysts favour state action to reduce income

inequality in addition to reducing poverty (i.e. to reduce the spread of incomes right across society, not just reducing the number of people living on less than $US 1 per day). Others are vehemently opposed to such egalitarian ideas, citing individual freedom, including the right to accumulate wealth (this is reflected in the traditional political debates of social democracy versus conservatism). The ability of market mechanisms to yield economic growth, and whether a higher (or lower) growth rate will result from state intervention in the market mechanism (and how different types of intervention increase or decrease the prospects for growth), likewise are controversial. Similarly, there is much debate on how far 'market-led' or 'state-led' development is compatible with, and supportive of, democratization and domestic political stability, as well as national security and national sovereignty.

People who are optimistic about the market's ability to produce their preferred set of socially desirable outcomes will favour a minimal state: one that provides protection for property rights together with public goods that the market either does not supply or under-supplies (defence is one example, transport infrastructure is another). In contrast, people who are pessimistic about the market mechanism's ability to deliver any or all of their chosen set of socially desirable outcomes will favour a more active state, but their conceptualization of what the state should do can show a very wide range. At one extreme is central planning (practised by the former Soviet Union) where society's productive factors are allocated according to a plan without reference to market prices, and where state ownership of enterprises and property prevails. At the other end of the scale of the active state, there is the 'European model' where continental European states provide very high levels of public goods, regulate the market 'in the public interest', but otherwise encourage a very vigorous private sector.

Clearly, views about the desirability of state action are not only driven by attitudes towards markets but also by views on the effectiveness of states in correcting 'undesirable' market outcomes. Views on state effectiveness have swung like a pendulum over the last fifty years. As countries came to independence, they built national planning apparatuses and wrote national plans. The Soviet Union's example was very influential in China, Cuba, and Vietnam and so was the state planning that even the capitalist economies introduced during the 1940s and many retained afterwards. However, by the late 1970s this confidence in the state's abilities was starting to erode, as growth slowed down, and often turned negative, thanks to a combination of policy failure—including the drain on the public purse of loss-making state-owned enterprises (SOEs)—together with major shocks arising from the first (1974) and second (1979) oil price hikes, and the associated world recessions.

The intellectual pendulum swung back (albeit with considerable resistance) towards the market mechanism in the 1980s, a movement reinforced by the International Monetary Fund and the World Bank and the conditionality they applied to their lending. This accelerated with the collapse of communism, and the start of the transition to market economies in Eastern Europe and the Soviet Union, and the emergence of the **Washington Consensus**.

These global changes influenced the climate of national debate within developing countries. In India, for example, the early 1990s saw a significant economic liberalization, as earlier ideas of planning and state ownership came under intense domestic criticism. However, later in the decade a reaction against market liberalization and privatization set in, and the intellectual pendulum began to swing back towards the state, owing to sharp increases in inequality, rising concern over liberalization's social effects, and the mismanagement of privatization. This was bound up in an intense debate about globalization (see Nayyar 2002). Economists increasingly recognized the importance of **institutions** to making the market mechanism work well for development and poverty reduction. The World Bank stepped back from its emphasis on the market alone and refocused attention on institutional development.

## Key points

- The economic role of the state is one of the central issues dividing opinion on development strategy.

- Views on the role of the state have changed over the years, with an early emphasis on state-led development being increasingly challenged by a market-liberal view, leading to widespread economic liberalization.

- Despite the roll-back of the state in many countries, the state still has many roles to play including the provision of public goods and the regulation of markets in the public interest.

# Trade policy as an instrument for development

For market liberals, developing countries that follow their **comparative advantage** will reap higher living standards from trading as much as possible with the developed countries (see Chapter 2). Their foreign exchange earnings will be used to finance imports of products in which they have a comparative *disadvantage*—those which are intensive in the use of capital equipment in their manufacture, where the developed countries will have the competitive edge, by virtue of their greater endowments of capital. The market liberal story of trade is one of mutual gains from trade for both the developing and the developed worlds, overturning the old mercantilist view of trade in the eighteenth century that saw one country's gain from trade as another's loss.

For market liberals comparative advantage is also the foundation of their view of how trade contributes to economic growth, through **outward-orientated** development. The growth in developing countries' labour-intensive exports will eventually bid up the price of labour (thereby contributing to poverty reduction). Capital-for-labour substitution will start to occur, and there is obviously much scope for government to subsidize education and training to create the skills that an export economy needs as it moves in this direction. Moreover the state has to protect the property rights of investors, ensure macro-economic stability, and provide public goods, particularly transport infrastructure. So even in market liberal accounts of economic performance, the state has a very important role to play. Countries that have successfully pursued this type of development strategy, Mauritius for instance, have possessed an active state with a clear sense of priorities.

Nevertheless, from the 1940s to the 1970s, many policy-makers saw the domestic market as the main motor for growth; in other words inward-orientated development was favoured over outward-orientated development. This was the era of import-substituting industrialization (see Chapter 2), which acquired its own momentum, for two reasons. First, governments derive revenue from tariffs which are both administratively and politically much easier to collect than indirect (sales) taxes or income taxes. Second, producers in

industries protected by tariffs and quotas earn more than in a free market. So it pays them to lobby for protection, either through the political system—supporting political parties that favour protection—or through **corruption**, in both cases sharing some of their profits with state actors, who may themselves form partnerships with private-sector actors to profit from controls. In addition, when imports are subject to quotas, the restrictions raise the domestic price of the import, creating an **economic rent** for any fortunate enough to possess the import licence. They too have an incentive to press for import quotas that benefit their businesses, and to lobby vigorously for the valuable licence.

So, although import protection may be introduced for the best of reasons, its critics argue that, once in place it generates powerful forces that overwhelm national development priorities. Eventually, trade policy comes to be driven by personal gain, not development priorities—with ever higher levels of protection undermining economic growth (thereby raising poverty). This view of the political economy of the **rent-seeking** society became highly influential in the World Bank's perspective from the early 1980s onwards.

The effects on policy-making, and therefore on economic performance, of lobbying and rent-seeking vary widely. They appear to have been worst in sub-Saharan Africa where the smallness of domestic markets, combined with extensive use of import quotas, led to very high domestic prices for import-substituting domestic manufactures. Sub-Saharan Africa's infant industries achieved little learning by so doing, and manufacturing has not achieved the expected growth. In India, there was much criticism of the so-called 'licence raj'—leading to economic liberalization in the early 1990s—but India's growth performance was respectable, if undramatic, prior to liberalization. Proponents of import protection as a positive force for development point to South Korea, where the planning mechanism effectively contained rent-seeking and where export subsidies offset the disincentive to export production inherent in import protection (see Box 2.2, p. 32 and Chapter 21*b*).

## Key points

• While the failure of many countries to achieve growth through import protection increased support for outward-orientated development, this too requires a well-designed strategy, particularly in creating new skills to sell in the global marketplace.

# Capital flows and economic reform

A major catalyst for economic policy change was the shocks experienced by the world economy in the 1970s and 1980s. But changes in the level and composition of international capital flows—foreign aid, commercial bank lending, and foreign direct investment—to developing countries have also been influential in inducing policy reform.

In the 1970s the non-oil-producing developing countries encountered serious macro-economic trouble with the first (1974) and second (1979) oil price shocks when the Organization of Petroleum Exporting Countries quadrupled the world price of oil. During this time the International Monetary Fund became very important in providing balance of payments support. Several of the oil exporters also borrowed heavily using their oil revenues as collateral, for example Nigeria, Mexico, and Venezuela and they developed serious macro-economic difficulties when the world oil price fell during the 1980s. All this brought about the debt crisis (see Chapter 3). However, it is worth noting that in East Asia, Malaysia, Singapore, South Korea, and Taiwan escaped largely unscathed and indeed maintained high growth during the 1980s and into the 1990s, until the Asian financial crisis of 1997–8. And although by the early 1980s South Korea was as highly indebted as some Latin American countries, by then its strong export economy was able to generate the foreign exchange necessary to maintain debt service. This brought home an important lesson: countries neglect export markets at their peril. Chinese policy-makers quickly learnt this lesson and China now has a significant share of global manufacturing exports. Some analysts believe China's success poses a problem for smaller developing countries also seeking to grow by means of increasing their share of world markets for relatively low-cost manufactured goods.

## Structural Adjustment

With so many of its client countries in deep distress, the World Bank was compelled to move beyond its traditional project lending and in the 1980s it started to provide balance of payments support through **Structural Adjustment Loans** (SALs). These carried such policy conditionalities as currency devaluation (to stimulate the supply of exports); the conversion of import quotas into import tariffs to reduce rent-seeking (and then tariff reduction in order to place more competitive pressure on inefficient infant industries); the removal (liberalization) of market controls in agriculture (to provide more incentives for farmers); and the reform of public expenditures and taxation (to shift more spending towards development priorities and to mobilize more public revenues to finance spending). IMF lending also carried policy conditionality, most notably targets for reducing the fiscal deficit and, relatedly, the growth in the money supply. The IMF's aims are to eliminate high inflation (and the associated loss of export competitiveness) which results from large fiscal deficits—deficits financed by monetary expansion—and to reduce the 'crowding out' of private investment which occurs when governments borrow heavily in domestic financial markets.

Although World Bank and IMF adjustment lending was intended to deal with the immediate macro-economic crises, it was also seen as a way of introducing greater efficiency into the economy. For, according to the **Washington consensus**, that required a reduced role for the state in the productive sectors (hence the start of privatization in the 1980s) as well as reduced controls (liberalization) on the private sector. Irrespective of the merits or otherwise of reform, most countries had little alternative but to sign up to the conditionality, since private capital flows slowed dramatically with the onset of the debt crisis in the 1980s, and official development flows became one of the few sources of external finance. This was especially true for the low-income countries: bilateral aid donors increasingly endorsed the Bank and Fund viewpoint, and linked their own aid programmes to acceptance of economic reform ('cross-conditionality'). In real terms the volume of aid fell, although since 2000 it has risen significantly.

Yet market liberalization has had very mixed results. Take the market for food staples, for example. This market is vital, for it affects farmers, who produce a surplus to sell, farmers who produce too little themselves and must buy food, rural wage-labourers, and urban households. If the state withdraws, partially or wholly, from buying, storing, transporting, and selling food then it has to be replaced by private entrepreneurs willing to undertake these tasks and bear the risks. But there is more profit to be made in supplying food to major urban centres than in marketing in remote and poor rural areas. Similarly, market liberalization in the manufacturing sector has had mixed effects. The rapid removal of import protection led to factory closures and the loss of jobs in many reforming countries. New jobs may eventually be created if export activities take over, but the necessary investment takes time to build. In the meantime, unemployment may rise sharply.

It is not therefore surprising that many people oppose market liberalization. Moreover, reform's effects are never clear cut. Many people will oppose reform (*ex ante*) fearing a loss, even if this isn't the case (*ex post*). Conversely, some people may gain a lot (for example those producing exports) but the gains may take time to become apparent. And it may be the case that most people gain from a particular reform, but each individual's gain is small, whereas a minority may lose, but their individual loss is very much larger. The incentive for the losers to organize to oppose the reform is therefore greater than the incentive of the winners to support the reform. Reform implementation may therefore stall even if, in aggregate, it benefits the majority. This is a good example of what Olson (2001) calls a collective action problem, which refers to the difficulties that arise in organizing a group of people to achieve a common objective.

Although it is highly controversial, market liberalization is straightforward in its implementation because the state simply withdraws, partially or wholly, from the market. But to be successfully implemented, some reforms require state capacity to be strengthened (see Chapters 9 and 10). This is especially true of revenue and public expenditure reforms. The state's capacity to mobilize tax and customs revenues and to then spend these resources effectively on pro-poor services and development infrastructure requires a capable and well-motivated government administration, at both central and local levels (the latter being especially important to improving local education and health, for example). However, the quality of civil services, together with their motivation, was in steep decline before reform began in many countries, especially in Africa where inflation eroded real wages in the public sector. Governments were therefore attempting to implement demanding changes with very limited institutional and human resources. At the same time they faced vocal opponents of public expenditure and taxation reforms. Reform breakdown and policy reversals have been common. Zambia, for example, has gone through a series of donor-supported adjustment programmes that largely failed to achieve progress, notwithstanding there being greater political commitment by the government to this in the 1990s than in earlier years.

The social impact of economic reform has generated considerable controversy since the early years of adjustment lending. The picture is complicated because reforms have both positive and negative implications for the poor. These vary across countries depending on economic structures (agrarian-based economies versus the semi-industrialized) and thus the means by which the poor participate in the market economy (as smallholders or wage-employees for example). The initial concentration of assets (particularly land) and incomes also determines much of the distribution of the benefits if reform does increase growth. The urban poor, as well as food-deficit rural households, suffer when devaluation raises the prices of imported food staples, especially if the devaluation is large and sudden. There is also a fierce debate on whether economic reform contributed to the breakdown of states and societies in countries like Sierra Leone and Somalia (see Chapter 11).

So-called 'second generation' reforms (privatization and financial reform, in particular) have been taking place since the 1990s in countries such as Ghana, Uganda, and Tanzania that began their first-generation reforms (devaluation and trade liberalization) in the 1980s. Implementation of second-generation reforms has often been problematic. For instance privatization has been non-transparent in many cases, thereby transferring valuable assets to the politically connected. Financial reform has been especially difficult. Asia's financial crisis, and Africa's bank failures, both highlight the need to build capacity for prudential supervision and regulation in central banks before major liberalization of financial controls. Tax reform and the construction of better systems of public expenditure management (both essential to not just more investment in development infrastructure but pro-poor services specifically) have stalled in many cases. All this illustrates the importance of building effective state capacities, to regulate the (financial) market in the public interest, and to achieve improvements in the public goods essential to a well-functioning market economy as well as poverty reduction.

## Key points

- Many countries are engaging in economic reform, driven by the failure of past development strategies, policy conditionality attached to development aid, and the need to attract private capital.
- Market liberalization is much easier to achieve than reforming the state to become more effective in achieving development.
- Reform may be opposed because it has large social costs, or because the losers from reform often have more incentive, and find it easier to organize themselves politically, than the winners from reform.

# Conclusions

There are issues on which there is considerable consensus, and issues where deep controversy remains. That development policy must have an explicit focus on poverty reduction is one of the main areas of consensus in today's development policy community. In contrast to the period up to the 1970s, when it was thought that economic growth would automatically deliver poverty reduction, it is now recognized that while growth can achieve some poverty reduction, pro-poor policies are necessary to maximize growth's benefits for the poor. Moreover, it is widely agreed that poverty reduction does not just entail higher incomes, but also improving human development indicators: poverty is a multi-dimensional concept. This implies improving the delivery of pro-poor services, particularly in basic health care, safe water and sanitation, and primary education, with a particular emphasis on delivery to rural areas (which contain high levels of poverty) and to women (see Chapter 7). Relatedly, it is widely agreed that the formation of human capital through better health and education is not only good for poverty reduction, but also contributes to economic growth, especially as countries attempt to move beyond exporting primary products to selling skill-intensive manufactures and services.

Compared to the 1940s and 1950s, when the first development strategies were set out, there is a greater recognition within the development community of the role of the market in driving development. This shift is somewhat grudging and reflects more the failure of state-led development in many (but certainly not all) countries rather than a large-scale intellectual conversion. Accompanying this has been a move away from heavy import protection and a greater awareness of value of exporting. Yet, many of the poorer countries find it difficult to achieve export success, especially outside their traditional primary products. They are highly vocal critics of rich country protectionism, especially in agriculture. There is much less support for the idea that the state should directly run manufacturing enterprises or farms, and a greater recognition of the private sector's strengths. However, there is much less consensus on whether utilities—power, water, transport infrastructure—should be in private or public ownership, although the fiscal crises of developing countries have driven many governments to privatize their state utilities. Finally, countries are now keener to attract private capital flows, in part because of the decline in official flows, but private flows remain concentrated on relatively few countries.

Getting development policy right has the potential to lift millions of people out of poverty and misery. But making the right policy choices is not just a technical matter. It requires careful political judgement about how to promote economic and social change in ways that stand the most chance of success.

## QUESTIONS

**1**  Why has East Asia achieved considerably faster economic growth than other developing regions, and are the lessons transferable to other developing regions?

**2**  Does economic growth maximize poverty reduction, and how does growth's potential to reduce poverty vary across developing countries?

**3**  Why do countries differ significantly in their level of public spending, and in their intervention in markets?

**4**  What should be the appropriate role for the state in development in developing countries?

**5**  What are the main elements of economic reform and what are the principal determinants of the ability of governments to achieve economic reform?

## GUIDE TO FURTHER READING

Addison, T., 'Economics', in P. Burnell (ed.), *Democratization through the Looking Glass* (Manchester: Manchester University Press, 2003). Examines how democracy affects economic performance, and contrasts democracy to autocracy in its development effects.

Amsden, A. H., *The Rise of the 'Rest': Challenges to the West from Late-Industrializing Economies* (Oxford: Oxford University Press, 2001). A comprehensive discussion of the East Asian success, and the role of the state in guiding the growth process.

Chang, H.-J., *Kicking Away the Ladder: Development Strategy in Historical Perspective* (London: Anthem Press, 2002). Contrasts the historical experiences of today's developed countries, and challenges the conventional wisdom on how development institutions are created.

Kanbur R., 'Economic Policy, Distribution and Poverty: The Nature of Disagreements', *World Development*, 29/6 (2001): 1083–94. A clear and balanced view of the contemporary poverty debate, and why people differ over growth's effects on poverty. Includes very useful comparisons between the differing viewpoints of the World Bank and non-governmental organizations on poverty.

Kirkpatrick, C., Clarke, R., and Polidano, C. (eds.), *Handbook on Development Policy and Management* (Cheltenham: Edward Elgar, 2002). Provides summaries of the main economic and political issues in development policy, including further discussion of many of the topics of this chapter.

Rodrik, D., *In Search of Prosperity: Analytic Narratives on Economic Growth* (Princeton: Princeton University Press, 2003). A good place to start on the causes of the different development outcomes of countries, and the role of development strategy in determining success.

Wade, R., *Governing the Market: Economic Theory and the Role of Government in East Asian Industrialization* (Princeton: Princeton University Press, 1990, repr. 2003 with a new introduction by the author). An authoritative assessment of how East Asia achieved its economic success, which challenges the market liberal view and emphasizes the role of the state.

## WEB LINKS

**www.developmentgateway.org**   An independent site that introduces the latest development research, with frequent updates of new research papers and breaking news in development.

**www.eldis.org**   Very easy to use site, with downloadable research papers, reports, and many links to other sites. It has a very useful section on how to use the web for development research, and the issues facing web users in developing countries with slow band width.

**www.ideaswebsite.org**   The website of the International Development Economics Associates, a network of heterodox economists, critical of the conventional wisdom on economic development.

**www.imf.org**   The IMF posts reports on its member countries, and agreements with governments (such as 'Letters of Intent') which spell out in detail economic reforms. The IMF's annual reports on the state of the world economy are also widely read.

**www.odi.org.uk**   The website of the Overseas Development Institute (UK), an independent think-tank on development issues. The ODI *Briefing Papers* provide authoritative insight into the latest development issues.

**www.undp.org**   The website of the United Nations Development Programme (UNDP) which is leading the UN's work on the Millennium Development Goals. The UNDP's annual *Human Development Report* can also be viewed at this site.

**www.unrisd.org**   The website of the United Nations Research Institute for Social Development (UNRISD). UNRISD focuses on the social dimensions of development, as well as development's political aspects.

**www.wider.unu.edu**   The website of the United Nations University's World Institute for Development Economics Research (UNU-WIDER). WIDER's *Discussion Paper* series offers a wide range of viewpoints on economic development issues, particularly in the areas of measuring poverty and the development effects of violent conflict.

**www.worldbank.org**   The website of the World Bank offers an enormous range of country material, particularly on poverty reduction, as well as many of the statistics (such as the *World Development Indicators*) used by the development community.

 **COMPANION WEB SITE**

For additional material and resources, see the companion web site at:
**www.oup.com/uk/booksites/politics/**

# Environment

*Peter Newell*

## OVERVIEW

This chapter explores how developing countries are managing the relationship between environment and development. Traditionally considered a threat to their economic development and prospects for growth, environmental issues have come to feature on policy agendas throughout the developing world. Driven by donors, public concern, and vocal environmental environments, responses to these issues have taken a number of different forms as they compete for 'policy space' with other pressing development concerns and are subject to changing thinking about the effectiveness of policy tools to tackle environmental problems. This chapter explores these issues, connecting global agendas to national policy processes, explaining differences and similarities between countries on these issues, and identifying patterns of continuity and change in the politics of environment in the developing world.

# Introduction

From an issue on the periphery of the policy agendas of most developing country governments, the environment has assumed an important and rising status on the national political agendas of states in Africa, Latin America, and Asia. This shift results from a combination of pressures from global institutions, donors, and active citizen movements, and has evolved alongside a growth in both scientific understanding about environmental problems and rising levels of public concern, often generated by environmental disasters.

Yet the status of the environment as an issue on developing country agendas is not secure. Environmental issues, in many areas of the world, are only loosely embedded within national policy processes, incoherently related to wider economic and social agendas and subject to displacement by issues which assume a greater priority for most countries. The theme of this chapter then is of continuity and change. Most countries are operating in a radically different policy context in which an increasingly globalized economy impacts more directly than ever before on the relationship between environment and development concerns. At the same time, environmental issues have been grafted onto existing policy agendas, national priorities, and decision-making processes that, in many cases, are characterized by bureaucratic inertia, organized opposition to reform, and reluctance to realign priorities.

The chapter is organized into four sections. The first part sketches the increasingly important global context for debates about environment and development and the links between them. Such links have been institutionalized through the growth of global bodies and areas of international environmental law produced through a series of UN negotiations. The second looks at policy processes at the national level; how these global agendas have been responded to and addressed at the national level. This means tackling questions about what is unique about policy processes in developing countries and what extra challenges are associated with tackling environmental problems in these settings. The third section looks at the range of tools and strategies that developing countries have adopted in order to combat environmental degradation. This includes discussion about the shifting roles of governments, market actors such as businesses and civil society in natural resource use management and protection. The final section assesses probable future directions of environmental politics in the developing world, pulling together these patterns of continuity and change.

## Key points

- The environment has assumed an important and rising status on the national political agendas of states in Africa, Latin America, and Asia.

- Yet the status of the environment as an issue on developing country agendas is not secure. It is often subject to displacement by issues which assume a greater priority for most countries.

- We can observe a process of continuity and change, in which environmental challenges are handled within existing national policy frameworks but where globalization has changed the relationship between environment and development.

# Global context

There is little agreement about what we mean by environmental issues and particularly about which issues are most deserving of an effective policy response. It is often assumed that differences of opinion on this issue fall along North–South lines, where developed countries are more concerned about global problems such as climate change and ozone depletion and conservation issues such as whaling and forest protection, while developing countries attach greater priority to rural issues such as desertification and soil erosion and urban environmental issues such as water pollution and air quality in cities. Even a cursory look at the politics of global negotiations on these issues suggests that these categorizations are at best only partially true.

First, we need to consider issues of causation and impact. Many of those people who contribute most to global environmental degradation are not those that will suffer its most adverse consequences. While climate change will have global impacts, wealthier countries are better placed to adapt to its adverse consequences. While the Netherlands can build sea defences against sea-level rise, Bangladesh will suffer serious flooding of low-lying agriculturally important areas. While Australians can use sun lotions to protect themselves from harmful UV rays that are stronger as a result of ozone depletion, many rural Chileans will not be able to afford the luxury.

Yet it is the developed world that contributes to global environmental problems to a proportionally much greater extent. For example 80 per cent of the world's climate-changing carbon dioxide is produced by less that 25 per cent of the world's population. Despite increasing efforts to integrate developing countries into the ozone negotiations, the key deals leading to the conclusion of the landmark Montreal Protocol in 1987 were negotiated between developed countries, principally the USA and EU. This reflected that the fact that, at that time, these countries were the largest contributors to the problem and were best placed technologically to find substitutes to ozone-depleting chemicals such as CFCs (Chlorofluorocarbons).

Secondly, the economic importance of natural resources to a country's economic development is a significant determinant of its position on a particular environmental policy problem, making it difficult for developing countries to form common policy positions. Brazil has traditionally resisted calls to view the Amazonian rainforests as part of the common heritage of humankind because of their strategic importance to the country's economic development. Many other developing countries, however, have called for this principle of **global stewardship** to apply to a range of common pool resources such as Antarctica and the deep sea-bed on the basis that

if those resources are to be exploited, it should be for the benefit of all and not just those that are in a position to exploit them. Similarly, while the Alliance of Small Island States (AOSIS), threatened by sea-level rise associated with global climate change, have strongly advocated controls on greenhouse gas emissions, the OPEC bloc whose economies are heavily dependent on the export of oil, have resisted such controls.

While some developing countries view environmental policy as an opportunity to secure additional aid and new forms of technology transfer, others feel threatened by agendas which seem to constrain their prospects for growth. While the G77 bloc of least-developed countries (formed at the UN after a meeting of UNCTAD in 1964, for the purpose of promoting the collective economic interest of 'Third World countries') has traditionally placed the responsibility for short-term action on climate change upon the North in the negotiations on the subject, many Latin American countries now see opportunities to earn much-needed revenue from participating in projects under the Clean Development Mechanism set up under the Kyoto Protocol concluded in 1997. Such projects entitle Northern countries to claim credits for paying for carbon 'sink' (carbon-absorbing) projects in heavily forested areas in Central and Southern America, for example.

Third, aside from areas where core national economic interests may be at stake, global environmental institutions have played a key role in shaping the national environmental policy agendas of many developing countries. Box 14.1 summarizes the mandates and key activities of some of the more prominent global environmental institutions.

It is their access to financial resources and the mandate they have to oversee the implementation of key global environmental accords, that allows these bodies to play this role. As Box 14.1 shows, the GEF has responsibility for overseeing the transfer of aid and technology transfer to developing countries in order to help them meet their obligations under the Rio agreements, for example on climate change and biodiversity conservation. The provision of aid and technology to developing countries to meet these commitments recognizes that these countries require assistance in making a contribution to global efforts to tackle forms of environmental degradation which

## Box 14.1  Key global environmental institutions

### United Nations Environment Programme

- Created following Stockholm conference on the Human Environment in 1972

- Initially conceived as clearing-house of environmental data and research and to set up demonstration projects

- No statute or charter to describe its function and role

- Governing Council of fifty-eight members elected by UN General Assembly on regional formula for three-year terms

- The council is mandated to promote cooperation on environmental issues; recommend appropriate policies

- Budget of only $100 million a year

- Depends on volunteer contributions from member countries for financing specific projects

- No structured system of dispute settlement

- Enforcement reliant on peer review and moral pressure

### Commission on Sustainable Development

- Inter-governmental body; members selected from UN

- Composed of fifty-three members elected for three-year terms

- Meets annually

- Reports to ECOSOC (Economic and Social Council) of UN

- Purpose: to review progress at international, regional, and national level in implementation of Rio ('Earth summit') agreements such as Agenda 21, the Rio Declaration, and The Forest Principles

- Means: provide policy guidance; promote dialogue; build partnerships with major groups

### Global Environment Facility

- Key financing body for actions on climate change, biodiversity loss, ozone depletion, land degradation, persistent organic compounds (POPs); new and additional grant and concessional funding for incremental costs for global benefits

- Three implementing agencies: UNEP, UNDP, World Bank

- World Bank administers facility on day-to-day basis and is trustee of the GEF trust fund

- Decisions made by consensus; where dispute, decisions made on double majority basis

they currently contribute very little to. Concern was expressed at the time of the UN Conference on Environment and Development in Rio that aid for the implementation of these international environmental agreements should be 'additional' to that which developing countries receive for other development purposes.

Increasingly, however, these institutions and the conventions they seek to enforce have sought to facilitate the integration of environmental and developmental concerns rather than see them as competing issues. There has been a clear shift towards addressing development concerns that can be traced from the Stockholm Conference on the Human Environment in 1972 onwards (see Box 14.2). This prepared the ground for the famous Brundtland report 'Our Common Future' (1987)—which first

coined the phrase **sustainable development**, defined as 'Development which meets the needs of the current generation without compromising the ability of future generations to meet their own needs'. The title of the Rio conference that followed five years later encapsulated the rhetorical integration of environmental and developmental objectives, namely the United Nations Conference on Environment and Development. Ten years on, the language of sustainable development was placed centrally in the naming of the follow-up to Rio, the 'World Summit on Sustainable Development' in Johannesburg in 2002.

Despite this rhetorical shift, many developing countries and activists have been critical of the way in which certain issues have been actively kept off the agenda of these summits. The Rio conference attracted criticism for not addressing issues such as

Box 14.2 **Chronology of environment and development on the international agenda**

**1972: Stockholm Conference on the Human Environment**

- Created UNEP

- Established key principles of responsible global environmental stewardship

- Set in train global scientific cooperation

**1980: Brandt Commission**

- North–South: A Programme for Survival

- Addressing North–South elements more clearly: trade, debt, energy, food

**1987: World Commission on Environment and Development**

- Our Common Future (Brundtland Report)

- Birth of a concept: Sustainable Development

**1992: UNCED**

- United Nations Framework Convention on Climate Change

- Convention on Biological Diversity

- Rio declaration

- Statement of Forest Principles

- Agenda 21

**2002: WSSD: Johannesburg**

- Agreement on water and sanitation (to halve the number of people without access to basic sanitation by 2015)

- Agreement on fisheries (plan to restore world's depleted stocks by 2015; create marine areas around the world by 2012)

debt, terms of trade, or the regulation of multinational companies, issues which some developing countries have sought to advance since the early 1970s, initially through the platform of the New International Economic Order. The US delegation to the conference fought hard to remove references to unsustainable levels of consumption in the Rio documents and concerns were raised during the WSSD (World Summit on Sustainable Development) at attempts to thwart the negotiation of a new convention on corporate accountability.

Rather than viewing environmental issues as stand-alone concerns, it is becoming increasingly clear that it is necessary to 'mainstream' environmental concerns into the activities of leading development actors. While the World Bank continues to draw fire for the environmental impact of some of its lending operations, as far back as 1987 it set up an environmental department and now insists on detailed environmental impact assessments of all its lending programmes. Also largely as a result of a vocal lobbying by environmental groups, the World Trade Organization has created a Committee on Trade and Environment which first met in 1995 to look at the relationship between environmental

standards and trade liberalization, though notably and controversially not the environmental impacts of trade. The emphasis has, therefore, been on defining the legitimate circumstances in which environmental and human health concerns can be invoked as exceptions to the normal obligations countries assume through membership of the WTO, rather than the ecological cost of transporting greater volumes of goods across ever larger distances, for example. For developing countries, one of the key concerns has been the growth in environmental standards that many fear will be used as barriers to trade and disguised forms of protectionism to protect Northern producers from competitive exports from the South. High-profile cases that have come before the WTO's Dispute Settlement Mechanism such as the notorious dolphin-tuna case have reflected this fear. In this case, the USA sought to ban yellow-fin tuna from Mexico on the grounds that the nets being used by the Mexican fishing industry to catch tuna fish were also killing dolphins.

This apparent integration of environmental issues into the policy practice of development actors has not just occurred at the inter-governmental level. One of the millennium development goals agreed by the Development Action Committee of the OECD is for all countries to have in place by the year 2005 a National Strategy for Sustainable Development (NSSD). Interestingly, country ownership is highlighted as a central component of an effective NSSD. Broad consultation to open up the debate and build consensus are seen as key for strategy formulation. This approach acknowledges that while sustainable development is a universal challenge, the practical response to it can only be defined nationally and locally according to different values and interests. A recent OECD report notes that a standardized blueprint approach should be avoided, and is at best irrelevant and at worst counter-productive (OECD 2001). Instead, working with existing approaches and institutional arrangements according to individual countries' needs, priorities, and available resources is preferable.

## Key points

- There is now a wide range of global environmental agreements which developing countries have signed and are in the process of implementing.

- Though development issues have gained a higher profile in global environmental summits and agreements, there is still some concern that Northern countries control the agenda.

- Countries' positions on these issues do not fall neatly along North–South lines, however, and key differences exist between developing countries on many high-profile global environmental issues.

- There has been a move towards mainstreaming environmental concerns into the lending practices of multilateral development agencies and into poverty reduction strategies.

# Environment and development: an uneasy relationship

The relationship between environment and development is not an easy one, and many conflicts are subsumed under the convenient banner of 'sustainable development' whose aims it is difficult for anyone to refute. The term has been used to describe all manner of projects and activities from large dams to controversial mining projects. Many have, therefore, questioned its value as an analytical concept, when it can be invoked so easily to justify 'business as usual' polluting activities. The term disguises conflicts over priorities between environment and development, gives few, if any, indications about which forms of development are sustainable, and is inevitably interpreted by different actors in different contexts to mean different things. Fundamental conflicts over the causes and appropriate solutions to environmental degradation persist. These include the debate about the extent to which population growth is a cause of environmental degradation. Malthusian (after the eighteenth-century thinker the Reverend Thomas Malthus) analysis of resource degradation, popular in certain strands of 1970s environmental

thinking (Ehrlich 1972), suggested that rapid increases in population were driving the planet towards ecological collapse. The influential 'limits of growth' report in 1972 of the Club of Rome suggested instead that unsustainable patterns of resource use would ultimately bring about ecological collapse because of the finite nature of the natural resource base upon which we all depend. Many developing countries and more radical environmental groups target over-consumption and affluence in Western societies, rather than population, as the key cause of the global environmental crisis.

Given this lack of consensus on the causes of environmental degradation, it is unsurprising that consensus eludes attempts to find appropriate solutions. Old conflicts in development over aid, trade, debt, and the role of technology get replayed through discussions about how to combat environmental degradation. Those believing that poverty leads people to use resources unsustainably have looked to ideas such as debt-for-nature swaps as a way out of this cycle; providing debt relief in exchange for commitments to preserve areas of forest, for example. Others have argued that increased patterns of trade interdependence have the effect of raising standards as developing country exporters seek access to lucrative Western markets that require higher environmental standards (Vogel 1997). Critiques of the effect of aid and technology transfer on developing countries that have existed in development for decades get rehearsed in environmental debates. It is claimed that the use of aid to extract environmental commitments amounts to 'eco-colonialism'. Technologies that are transferred as part of global environmental agreements, are often out of date and in reality serve both as a subsidy to Northern producers of technologies for which markets no longer exist and to entrench the dependency of developing countries on the North. In environmental terms, it is also argued that technology is no substitute for tough action aimed at reducing unsustainable patterns of production and consumption and that developed countries often prefer to transfer technologies to developing countries rather than take measures to address the source of environmental degradation in their own countries.

This then is the global historical and contemporary context that shapes the ways in which developing countries have been seeking to tackle environmental issues at the national level. The next section looks in more detail at the commonalities and differences in the ways developing countries have responded to these global environmental agendas while grappling with their own unique environmental problems and development needs.

## Key points

- The term sustainable development disguises conflicts over priorities between environment and development.

- There is no consensus on the social causes of environmental degradation.

# Policy processes

## Political diversity

It is impossible to make generalizations about environmental policy that would apply across the entire developing world. Though nearly all developing countries are involved in global negotiations on the issues raised above, the processes by which they translate those commitments into workable policies at the national level are very different. First, there is the issue of power. There is clearly a difference between a country like China or India with significant scope for independent action and power to assert their interests in global fora dealing with these issues and smaller and less powerful countries. This difference relates in part to the resources they can commit to participating in global processes which can be highly time and resource intensive. Environmental negotiations often take place in Geneva or New York and to participate effectively in them requires a large delegation with access to scientific and legal expertise. Developing countries are often only able to send one or two government representatives to these negotiations which are often run with parallel meetings that a small delegation cannot attend.

But it is also a function of the degree of power they wield in global economic terms and the extent to which they are aid-dependent. Countries such as Mali and Ethiopia are highly dependent on aid. In Mali's case the overwhelming majority of that aid comes from its former colonizer, France. Research programmes and policy priorities are therefore strongly affected by such bilateral financial ties. Countries such as Brazil, on the other hand, have a larger degree of discretion in determining policy positions and they can draw on greater economic weight in trade and industrial terms to advance their preferences on environmental issues.

Secondly, but related, are issues of capacity for the enforcement of policy. Many countries, such as India, have some of the most impressive legislative acts on environmental issues in the world. But lack of resources, training, and corruption of local pollution control officials often conspire to delay implementation. Sometimes the nature of the problem and the size of the country are the key constraints. For example, regulating the cultivation and trade in genetically modified (GM) seeds is almost impossible in a country the size of China and many instances of illegal growing of non-authorized seeds have been reported. Managing the transborder movement of GM seeds, as is required by the Cartagena Protocol on Biosafety (2000), presents many problems for developing countries where seed markets are often poorly regulated and even basic equipment with which to test shipments of seeds across borders is unavailable. Where countries have a strong economic and developmental incentive to ensure active compliance, extra steps may be taken. Kenya is keen to be seen as an attractive tourist location for wildlife safaris. Because tourism provides a large source of revenue, officials have gone to controversial lengths to tackle the problem of illegal poaching of elephants and rhinos for their ivory and horns, including shooting poachers and banning tribal groups from culling animals for food, even on their own ancestral lands.

Thirdly, the degree of importance that will be attached to environmental concerns, at the expense of broader development goals, will reflect the nature of democratic politics in the country. The strength of environmental groups in a country, pushing for new policy and acting as informal 'watchdogs' of compliance with environmental regulations will be determined by the degree of democratic space which exists within the country. Countries such as India and Mexico have strong traditions of active civil society engagement in environmental policy. India, for instance, hosts such globally recognized outfits as the Centre for Science and Environment and its more research-oriented counterpart, TERI (The Energy and Resources Institute) which are active in global policy debates as well as domestic agenda-setting. In Singapore and China, by contrast, the avenues for policy engagement are few and tightly restricted. The scope and effectiveness of environmental policy will also be shaped by the extent to which the interests of leading industries are affected by proposed interventions. Where policy directly impinges on the interests of a particularly powerful industry, policy reform is often stalled or environmental concerns are kept off the agenda altogether. The close ties between logging

companies and state officials that often have personal commercial stakes in the companies is an often-cited reason for the lack of progress to reverse unsustainable logging in South-East Asia (Dauvergne 1997).

The way governments formulate and implement policy also reflects the diversity in styles of environmental policy-making across the developing world. Each country has a unique history when it comes to its approach to regulation, the organization of its bureaucracy, and, as we have seen, the extent to which public participation in policy is encouraged. The Chinese government is able to act decisively and in a 'command-and-control' fashion to sanction industries failing to comply with pollution control regulations. In India, the Supreme Court has played a decisive role in moving environmental policy forward, often in controversial circumstances, setting strict and sometimes unrealistic targets for the phasing out of non-GNG (Compressed Natural Gas) vehicles in Delhi, for example, or instructing the eviction of thousands of small industries from the outskirts of Delhi because of the pollution their activities were generating.

Approaches to environmental policy also reflect the different ways in which knowledge, especially scientific knowledge, informs policy. Keeley and Scoones (2003: 5) show how, in the case of soils policy, international science is refracted through local processes: 'By shaping the way development problems are thought about, science influences the nature of networks and relationships between states, within and across bureaucracies and in relation to how alternative expertise is thought about'. Scientific knowledge does not provide a neutral and value-free guide to which environmental problems are the most serious or how they should be addressed. It is employed strategically by government officials to support their position within the bureaucracy, but can also change political practice and priorities by highlighting some areas of concern while ignoring others.

Given these factors, there is sometimes also a mismatch between the expectations contained in multilateral environmental agreements about the way in which commitments should be implemented and the realities of what is possible in many developing country settings. We have the problem of capacity where the resources and skills to oversee micro-level implementation of environmental regulations emanating from central government to meet global commitments are often lacking. In addition, many agreements, including the Cartagena Protocol on Biosafety, specify the process by which national environmental frameworks should be designed, for example to involve active public consultation and participation. While some developing countries have recently engaged with the policy process requirements of the World Bank/IMF **Poverty Reduction Strategy**, many are poorly placed to meaningfully set up elaborate participatory processes for deliberative and inclusive decision-making involving a cross-section of their societies. Democratic values are weakly embedded in many societies, and publics in many places remain sceptical of interaction with official bodies such that good global intentions may not translate well into local practice.

## Common challenges

Despite these differences in the policy positions and policy styles that developing countries have adopted, it is worth highlighting some common challenges that nearly all developing and of course many 'developed' countries face in the design and execution of environmental policy. First, we have already noted the scale of resources required to tackle environmental problems. Undertaking scientific research and monitoring the enforcement of pollution control places large resource demands on developing countries in particular. International environmental agreements create new demands of governments for more regulation, more monitoring, and an efficient and effective bureaucracy to oversee these, often across multiple levels of governance right down to the local level. Despite the availability of global funds to support some of these activities (see Box 14.1), it remains difficult even for larger developing countries to meet these expectations for many of the reasons mentioned above.

Secondly, in spite of the efforts of active environmental movements within developing countries, as well as globally, it remains true that *political constituencies with a strong preference for more effective environmental policy are weakly entrenched*. The issue is not only that the beneficiaries of environmental policies are not present in policy debates (future

generations) or not adequately represented (indigenous peoples, lower castes), but that political parties with strong commitments to environmental issues are not well developed in most parts of Asia, Africa, and Latin America. Conversely, the presence in Europe of Green parties has served to keep environmental issues on the agendas of the main parties.

This issue is not just one of party politics, but also of class. It has traditionally been the case in the West that wealthier social groups, predominantly the middle classes, are the strongest advocates of environmental protection measures and those most likely to belong to environmental interest groups such as World Wide Fund for Nature (WWF). While there is evidence that urban middle classes in larger developing countries such as Argentina and India are demanding consumer rights and have sought, for example, to get labelling for foods containing GMOs, in many developing countries rural environmental issues are often closely related to more controversial and intractable issues of land reform and rural livelihoods. Campesino (peasant-based) movements in Latin America often incorporate environmental issues into broader campaigning platforms for land redistribution and greater levels of compensation for the appropriation of their resources. Struggles to protect biological resources in India often get caught up in broader debates about access to genetic resources and whether foreign multinationals should be able to patent living organisms that derive from India. Explicitly framing their campaign in anti-colonial terms, activists opposed to biotechnology called on the company Monsanto to 'Quit India!' The ability of movements to use environmental issues to advance other agendas serves to entrench the suspicion that many governments have of environmental agendas.

Thirdly, we have to recognize the global economic pressures which all countries face but which developing countries face more acutely. Crushing debt burdens and the conditions attached to **Structural Adjustment Programmes** often create incentives for economic activities that are highly destructive of the environment. Export-led growth patterns which often require intensive use of land with heavy applications of chemical fertilizers, and the creation of export processing zones whose aim is to attract foreign capital to areas where labour is cheap and environmental standards are lower, provide examples.

Deteriorating terms of trade for timber, minerals, and agricultural produce also drive developing country economies, dependent on single commodities, to exploit that resource unsustainably. In the aftermath of the financial crisis in South-East Asia in the late 1990s, for example, timber producers increased exports to unsustainable levels to compensate for the losses they incurred from depreciating national currencies.

The broader issue is what has been termed the 'race to the bottom' in environmental standards as developing countries compete to lower environmental regulations in order to attract increasingly mobile investors. The evidence for this is mixed. However, there are many examples of regulatory reforms not being introduced or not implemented for fear of deterring investors. For example, in response to pressure from soybean exporters in the USA, the Chinese government delayed plans to introduce a series of restrictive biosafety measures. In other cases, lack of environmental regulation has been used as a comparative advantage to attract environmentally hazardous production of substances such as toxic wastes and asbestos that have been banned in the North. The desperation of many developing countries to attract investment on any terms clearly therefore both affects their ability to prioritize action on the environment and in certain situations will lead them to lower standards in order to attract mobile capital.

It is also the case that many developing countries have abundant natural resources which make them key locations for extractive industries. For years activists have berated the mining industry for its environmental pollution, human rights violations, and displacement of indigenous peoples. The oil industry too has been accused of double standards when it operates in developing countries. The activities of firms such as Shell in the Niger Delta, Nigeria and Texaco in Ecuador have attracted global attention as a result of activist exposure and high-profile legal actions against the companies. It is often the case that foreign companies get caught up in local disputes over access to land and conflicts between particular tribal groups or regions and the central government. In most cases, however, the strategic importance of the minerals and resources found in those countries means that companies are willing to endure the controversy and bad publicity, preferring instead

to launch public relations campaigns defending their actions, as well as invoking arguments about using their economic clout to press for social and environmental reforms in the country where they are operating.

It is also important, however, to differentiate between countries regarding the extent to which the 'greening' of business has taken place. It is now commonplace for larger companies based in the West to claim that their companies adopt the principles of sustainable development in their investment decision-making. Among globally connected industry associations in the developing world, such as the Makati Business Club in the Philippines or the Confederation of Indian Industry, this discourse is being picked up. However, it remains the case that many of the drivers of corporate environmental responsibility, including government incentives, civil society watchdogs, and consumer and investor pressure are currently underdeveloped in many parts of the developing world. It is almost certainly the case that firms within countries with strong trading ties to overseas markets where compliance with tougher environmental regulations is expected will have higher standards than firms in parts of sub-Saharan Africa, for example, that are more isolated from such global pressures.

Ironically, when developing countries have sought to implement high levels of environmental protection, they have faced criticism. There are many instances of developing countries being subject to intense pressure when their environmental regulations impinge upon exports from powerful developed countries. For example, on many recent occasions the USA has shown itself willing to use threats to withdraw aid or bring a case at the WTO against countries whose regulations on GMOs are alleged to be incompatible with their obligations under the trade body. No such cases have yet been brought before the WTO because countries such as Sri Lanka and Croatia, fearful of the economic consequences of not succumbing to the USA's demands, have backed down. These sorts of pressures clearly serve to restrict, however, the menu of policy options that developing countries can realistically chose from when deciding what course of action to take.

Fourthly, the underdevelopment of the scientific expertise that underpins environmental policy is a characteristic common to many developing countries. While there are many international scientific research programmes on environmental issues and many international environmental agreements have panels or rosters of experts associated with their activities, the representation of scientists from developing countries is often lacking. There have been initiatives from UNEP to try and address this problem by ensuring, for example, that a percentage of scientists on such bodies are from developing countries. But the problem endures, and the implication is that the policy and scientific agendas of Northern researchers and their policy networks attract greater attention and resources than issues and concerns that are more pertinent to the developing world. This criticism has been levelled at the work of GEF, for instance, for being more responsive to the agendas of Northern donors upon which it is dependent for funding than to the recipients of its capacity-building measures in the South. The World Bank (2000: 14) itself has conceded that its 'preference for big loans can easily distract regulators from confronting their communities' most critical pollution problems'.

## Key points

- The status of environmental issues on the national policy agendas of many developing countries is not secure and remains subject to displacement by other pressing development concerns.

- This is in spite of the fact that most developing countries are now intimately involved in the negotiation and implementation of international environmental agreements and in the design of 'National Strategies for Sustainable Development'.

- There are some important differences in priorities, policy autonomy, resources and capacity, policy styles, and the role of environmental and business groups in policy formulation and implementation across the developing world.

- There are, however, many common challenges that developing countries face when it comes to environmental policy: weaknesses in enforcement capacity; economic vulnerability, which means trade and aid leverage can be used to change policy; and an underdeveloped knowledge base from which to develop environmental policy.

# New policy instruments for environmental protection

We have already noted the different policy styles that developing countries around the world have employed in the design and implementation of environmental policy. It is also the case, however, that they have been affected by shifts in prevailing thinking about the most efficient and effective way to provide environmental goods without jeopardizing development progress. Strong developmental states are still willing and able to intervene forcibly to close down polluting industry; the important role of legal systems in driving environmental policy reform and in protecting the rights of citizens against their own government has also been noted.

Courts have been a key site for poorer groups to seek compensation for socially and environmentally destructive investments that have undermined their livelihoods. They have provided a venue to draw attention to grievances that have not been recognized elsewhere and, where successful, legal cases can uphold key rights to environmental information, to have environmental impact assessments undertaken in advance of large industrial projects or to contest the forced displacement that is associated with infrastructural projects such as dams. Legal cases have been brought in Brazil and India over the legality of the process by which the governments authorized the growing of GM crops, for example. In Nigeria numerous cases have been brought against the oil giant Shell, seeking compensation for damage to land caused by oil spillages from the company's pipelines in the Niger Delta. Companies exploiting lower health and environmental standards in developing countries, providing their workers with less protection than counterparts in the North, have ended up paying large out-of-court settlements to victims of industrial hazards.

Relying on legal remedies to tackle environmental problems is often inadequate, however. Often people resort to the law only after the pollution has occurred. There are also limits to how poorer groups can use the law to their benefit. Poorer communities that are often the frontline victims of industrial pollution frequently lack the financial resources to bring a case and lack the 'legal literacy' necessary to understand their rights under the law and how they can be realized. These problems of access are often compounded by long backlogs of cases, distrust in the independence of the legal system and the many legal barriers to successfully demonstrating cause and effect between a polluting activity and evidence of damage to human health or the environment.

State-based environmental regulation, in general, however, has been subject to sustained criticism from key development actors such as the World Bank on the grounds that it is excessively inflexible, inefficient, and often ineffective at delivering the change in behaviour that it intends. Increasingly, the preference is for the use of the market as a tool for incentivizing positive action and deterring polluting activities. Box 14.3 cites examples from a World Bank report on the role of communities, markets and governments in tackling pollution which makes the case for moving beyond a 'one size fits all' approach to pollution control.

Examples of pollution charging in China, Colombia, and the Philippines show that pollution from factories has been successfully reduced when steep, regular payments for emissions have been enforced. Familiar problems of tax collection and corruption may yet undermine the effectiveness of some such initiatives, but there can be little doubt that their increasing use indicates a shift in policy direction. Market tools such as labelling have also been accepted in many developing countries as a means by which to assure global buyers of the environmentally responsible way in which the product has been produced as well as to facilitate consumer choice. For example certification has been used in the fisheries and forestry sectors where the popular FSC scheme (Forestry Stewardship Council) is based in Oaxaca, Mexico.

Another general trend in environmental policy that is catching on in the developing world is the popularity of voluntary measures by industry. Codes of conduct among leading companies are now commonplace in the North and many of those firms investing overseas are insisting that their suppliers and partners adopt the same principles. The trend comes on the back of a rejection of the efficiency and effectiveness of central government 'command and control' policy measures imposed from above. But it also reflects the preference of firms to set their own standards appropriate to their own circumstances in a way which avoids state intervention. In the environmental context, environmental management systems such as ISO 14001 created by the International Organization for Standardization (ISO) are increasingly popular. While traditionally such standards have tended only to apply to larger firms that can afford the compliance costs and those seeking access to developed country markets, there is some evidence from countries like Mexico that even small and medium-sized enterprises are seeking ISO certification in order to serve as subcontractors for ISO-certified enterprises.

There are also sector-specific programmes such as 'Responsible Care' in the case of the chemical industry, which set up a programme to deflect criticism away from its track record in the USA and which has been adopted in countries like Mexico and Brazil. Garcia-Johnson (2000) describes this as 'exporting

---

> ## Box 14.3 **New ideas in pollution regulation**
>
> *National level economic reforms* (such as privatization, liberalizing trade, removing subsidies that support polluting activities): China, India, Brazil
>
> *Pollution charges*: China, Colombia, and Philippines
>
> *Pollution rating and systems of public disclosure*: Indonesia and Philippines
>
> *Public education* for pollution awareness leading to action plans negotiated between communities and companies: Mexico
>
> *Training in environmental management*: Mexico
>
> (World Bank 2000)

environmentalism'. It is clear then that global market pressures from buyers and consumers increasingly exercise as significant an influence on environmental policy practice in many parts of the developing world as the international agreements which governments sign up to.

As a reaction to the limitations of market-based and voluntary mechanisms, there has also been a growth in what has been termed **civil regulation** (Newell 2001): the increasing use of such tools as shareholder activism and boycotts, and the growth of groups like OilWatch based in Ecuador, are illustrative. New forms of engagement in constructing codes of conduct and building partnerships also come under the umbrella of civil regulation. While concern has been expressed that many of these tools are only available to well-resourced groups with good access to the media and in societies with strong traditions of free speech, there does seem to be evidence of these strategies being employed across the global South. Strategies of resistance and exposure of corporate wrongdoing date from colonial times, but there has also been a notable proliferation in groups across the entire spectrum, ranging from confrontation to collaboration. Many of these groups are also increasingly globally well connected, so that companies engaging in environmentally controversial activities in the developing world can also expect to face shareholder resolutions and embarrassing media publicity in their home countries. The Canadian company Tiomin, for example, has faced considerable pressure from activists in Canada over its proposed mining operations on Kenya's coast, working with local groups such as CoastWatch in Kenya.

It is unclear at this stage what the net effect of these forms of civil regulation will be on the environmental performance of investors in developing countries. The hope is that groups with the expertise and capabilities to plug gaps and weaknesses in systems of government pollution control and monitoring can play an important complementary role as informal regulators. Their very presence may encourage firms to respect the environmental standards of the countries in which they operate to a greater degree than if they were not there, and so help deter the exploitation of double standards by firms when they operate in developing countries. The extent to which groups will be allowed to perform this role will depend on the strength of civil society in a given setting and the extent to which its activities are tolerated or encouraged by the state. Issues of who the groups represent and who they are accountable to will also have to be faced if they are to be seen as legitimate actors in environmental policy. It will be important that such groups are not seen to deter much-needed investment but instead seek to attract investors that are more socially and environmentally responsible, and therefore more likely to bring long-term development gains to countries.

## Key points

- Many countries continue to use central government controlled 'command-and-control' environmental policy measures.

- There has been a shift, however, in thinking about how best to tackle environmental pollution towards the use of market instruments and voluntary approaches.

- Many companies in developing countries are seeking certification for their products in order to get access to Northern markets.

- In recent years there has been a trend towards informal industry regulation by civil society groups. The long-term impact of this form of civil-society-based regulation will vary by country and the extent to which such groups are able to address issues of their own accountability and representation.

# Futures

Attempting to predict the likely future of environmental policy in the developing or developed world with any degree of accuracy and precision is a fruitless endeavour. It is, however, possible to identify certain patterns of continuity and change. We have seen how many developing countries face common challenges in terms of how to reconcile pressing development needs with longer-term environmental goals. While countries have inevitably responded in different ways which reflect, among other things, their political systems, the nature of their economies, and the level of civil society engagement, we have seen similar problems of enforcement at the national level, constraints that arise from economic relationships of trade, aid, and debt, and conflicts between global, often Northern-determined environmental priorities and issues that appear to be more pressing at the local level.

Through global processes of negotiation, increasingly integrated supply chains, and globally interdependent trading patterns, we have seen how pressures come to be exerted on developing countries to design and implement environmental policies in ways which reflect the priorities of others. Shifts in thinking about environmental policy and what makes it more effective and efficient are transmitted through donor lending and the global reach of transnational companies. These are the sorts of pressure that bring about conformity and harmonization in environmental politics in the developing world.

But there is much that is subject to change, such as the fragile and often ephemeral status of environmental issues on the policy agendas of countries the world over. The status of such issues is as vulnerable to the state of the world economy as it is to the health of the planet. Government spending on environmental programmes notoriously goes down in times of recession, when other issues assume a higher profile. In recent times issues of regional and global security have risen rapidly on the agendas of many developing countries in the wake of the events of 'September 11'. Priorities shift according to global events as much as they reflect changes in domestic politics following changes of government. A realignment of donor priorities in the wake of these shifts may have a significant impact on resource allocations for environmental projects, or the extent to which some regions of the developing world come to be favoured over others on the basis of their strategic value to Western interests. Nevertheless, with or without donor support, developing countries face many environmental challenges of their own, including water pollution and urban air quality. It is often the human impact of these problems that attracts attention and acts as the driver for change. In developmental terms, the increasingly high human cost of environmental degradation exacts an economic price; costs to health systems increase, levels of disease increase, and an unhealthy workforce is an unproductive workforce. Despite increasing acknowledgement of the human and developmental case for tackling environmental degradation, stark trade-offs between environmentally damaging investment and no investment at all continue to force governments to put profit above people and planet. Global economic pressures from highly mobile companies and global economic institutions further load the dice towards investment and exports over the imperatives of sustainable development.

Sometimes, of course, environmental problems draw attention to themselves, and demand action from governments. Floods in Mozambique, droughts in Ethiopia, the intensity of which will increase as our climate changes, and other such crises prompt short-term emergency measures. Rarely, however, do they initiate deeper reflection about the causes of the crisis. Nevertheless, the increased incidence of such human-induced yet seemingly 'natural' events may, more than any other single factor, serve to focus the world's attention on the environmental consequences of current patterns of development and act as a catalyst to more radical action aimed at combating environmental degradation.

## Key points

- Developing countries face a range of often contradictory pressures from international institutions, market actors, and civil society regarding how to reconcile environmental protection with broader development goals.

- How they handle these challenges will be a function of many domestic political factors.

- This pattern of change will continue as national events shift priorities and the context in which environmental policy is made is continually altered by change in the global political economy.

- A key driver of policy responses will continue to be environmental disasters that focus public attention on the impacts of particular types of development. The challenge is to harness this concern towards longer-term change aimed at tackling the causes of environmental degradation rather than merely addressing some of the consequences.

## QUESTIONS

1   How effectively has a balance between environment and development been achieved on the international policy agenda?

2   How useful and practicable a concept is sustainable development?

3   What factors explain the different priorities that developing countries have attached to environmental issues?

4   Is there anything unique about environmental policy processes in the developing world?

5   How effectively have environmental issues been integrated within national development strategies?

6   What is the relationship between poverty and the environment?

7   How effective are the policy tools currently being used to tackle environmental degradation?

8   What political and economic changes might be required in order to reconcile environment and development issues more effectively in the future?

## GUIDE TO FURTHER READING

Adams, W. M., *Green Development: Environment and Sustainability in the Third World* (London: Routledge, 2nd ed., 2001). Provides a detailed history of the concept of sustainable development and the different ways in which it has been interpreted and applied in the mainstream and by its critics.

Barry, J., and Frankland, E. G., *International Encyclopedia of Environmental Politics* (London and New York: Routledge, 2002). This encyclopedia provides short summaries and guides to further reading on key issues from 'African environmental issues' to 'Water pollution' and just about everything in between.

Bryant, R. L., and Bailey, S., *Third World Political Ecology* (London: Routledge, 1997). Provides a useful actor-based introduction to the key forces shaping environmental politics in the developing world from business and multilateral institutions to NGOs and the role of the state.

Elliott, L., *The Global Politics of the Environment* (London: Macmillan, 1998). Wide-ranging textbook that covers not only the global environmental agenda but also issues of trade, debt, and aid which bring together environmental and development agendas.

Keeley, J., and Scoones, I., *Understanding Environmental Policy Processes: Cases from Africa* (London: Earthscan, 2003). Drawing on research in Ethiopia, Mali, and Zimbabwe, this book examine the links between knowledge, power, and politics in understanding how environmental issues come to be framed and the consequences of this for how they are acted upon.

Peets, R., and Watts, M., *Liberation Ecologies: Environment, Development and Social Movements* (London: Routledge, 1996). Explores the theoretical implications of the relationship between development, social movements, and the environment in the South. Draws this out through case studies on a range of environmental issues from countries including China, India, Zimbabwe, Ecuador, and Gambia.

## WEB LINKS

**www.ids.ac.uk** (Institute of Development Studies, University of Sussex, UK) By clicking on 'Environment Team' you can access the work of the IDS Environment Team on issues such as soil erosion, forests, water, biotechnology, and climate change as they relate to the developing world. Working papers can be downloaded for free. The IDS site also provides access to the Eldis gateway from where searches for information and studies on particular environmental issues in specific developing countries can be undertaken.

**www.iied.org** (International Institute of Environment and Development, London, UK). This contains details on latest research and publications produced by the institute on a range of environment and development issues.

**www.iisd.org** (The International Institute for Sustainable Development, Winnipeg Canada). Among other useful databanks this site gives access to the 'Earth Negotiations Bulletin', which provides updates on all the leading international environmental negotiations.

**www.cseindia.org** (Centre for Science and Environment, Delhi, India). Contains reports and details of campaigns on key environmental challenges facing India, though maintains a global focus too.

**www.twnside.org.sg** (Third World Network, Kuala Lumpur, Malaysia). Contains position papers, reports, and information updates from the network's members.

**www.itdg.org** (Intermediate Technology and Development Group, UK). Contains details on the organization, its project and research work, and reports and publications.

**www.unep.org** (United Nations Environment Programme, Nairobi, Kenya). A mine of information about global environmental issues and the negotiations aimed at tackling them.

**www.iucn.org** (International Union for the Conservation of Nature, Geneva, Switzerland). Reports, information, and detail on the world's leading conservation agency.

 ## COMPANION WEB SITE

For additional material and resources, see the companion web site at:
**www.oup.com/uk/booksites/politics/**

# 15

# Human rights

*Michael Freeman*

## OVERVIEW

The language of **human rights** is a pervasive feature of contemporary international politics, but it is not well understood. This chapter offers an analysis of the concept, a brief account of its history and a description of the **international human rights regime**. It proceeds to examine two persistent problems that arise in applying the concept to developing countries: the relations between human rights and development; the relations between the claim that the concept is universally valid and the realities of cultural difference around the world. The idea of human rights derives from historical problems of the West. It is necessary to consider its applicability to the problems of developing countries in a world constituted by great inequalities of political power and wealth.

# Introduction

The concept of human rights derives primarily from the United Nations Charter, which was adopted in 1945 immediately after the Second World War. The preamble to the Charter declares that the UN was determined to 'reaffirm faith in fundamental human rights, in the dignity and worth of the human person, in the equal rights of men and women, and of nations large and small'. In 1948, the General Assembly of the UN adopted the Universal Declaration of Human Rights, which sets out a list of human rights 'as a common standard of achievement for all peoples'. The list includes such civil and political rights as those to freedom from slavery, torture, arbitrary arrest, and detention, freedom of religion, expression, and association, and a number of economic and social rights, such as the rights to education and an adequate standard of living. These rights were intended to protect everyone from tyrannical governments like that of Nazi Germany, and from the economic misery that was thought to have facilitated the rise of fascism.

Although the countries of Latin America, Asia, and Africa formed the majority of those that produced the Declaration, many of the world's people lived at that time under colonial rule, and were thus excluded from this process. The concept of human rights was derived from a Western philosophical tradition, and was shaped mainly by European historical experience. Colonialism was itself condemned for its human rights violations, and, when worldwide decolonization brought many new states to the UN, the post-colonial states accepted human rights in principle, although their priorities differed from those of the West, emphasizing self-determination, development, economic and social rather than civil and political rights, and anti-racism.

Disagreements about which human rights should be legally binding led to the adoption of two UN human rights covenants in 1966: the International Covenant on Civil and Political Rights and the International Covenant on Economic, Social, and Cultural Rights. The UN's World Conference on Human Rights, held in Vienna in 1993, declared all human rights to be 'indivisible and interdependent'.

Now, each covenant has been ratified by about three-quarters of the UN's member states.

The UN has adopted several more specialized conventions (see Box 15.1). There are also regional human rights conventions, although these do not cover the whole world, especially the Middle East and Asia. The European Convention on Human Rights was signed in 1950; the American Convention on Human Rights in 1969; and the African Charter on Human and Peoples' Rights in 1981.

Many developing countries have poor human rights records. There are internal and external explanations of this. The internal explanations include poverty, ethnic tensions, and authoritarian government. Some of the internal problems of developing countries are legacies of colonialism. The external explanations include support for dictatorships by the great powers, especially during the cold war, and the global economic system, which many believe is

---

## Box 15.1 Universal and regional human rights regimes

The Universal Declaration of Human Rights 1948

The European Convention on Human Rights 1950

The International Covenant on Civil and Political Rights 1966

The International Covenant on Economic, Social, and Cultural Rights 1966

The International Convention on the Elimination of Racial Discrimination 1966

The American Convention on Human Rights 1969

The Convention on the Elimination of Discrimination against Women 1979

The African Charter on Human and Peoples' Rights 1981

The Convention against Torture 1984

The Convention on the Rights of the Child 1989

biased against developing countries, and thereby hinders their capacity to develop the institutions necessary to protect human rights. Since the end of the cold war, and the discrediting of the Soviet, state socialist model of development, **neo-liberalism**—the ideology of free markets—has dominated global economics. Whether neo-liberalism promotes respect for, or violation of human rights is highly controversial. The Universal Declaration's conception of human rights, however, presupposed effective states, and neo-liberalism tends to weaken states, and especially their capacity to protect social and economic rights, such as those to health, education, and freedom from poverty. The harmful effects of such policies disproportionately affect women and children.

Developing countries have been vulnerable both to military coups and to ethnic conflict. Both are attributable to legacies of colonialism, and both lead to serious human rights violations. While the dominant human rights discourse is highly *legalistic*, and emphasizes legal solutions to human rights problems, social scientists have recently revived the concept of **civil society** as a barrier to tyranny. Developing countries vary considerably in the strength of their civil societies, but some observers see civil society as the best hope both for development and the improvement of human rights protection. Human rights seem to require a balance between effective states and strong civil societies, which is difficult to achieve when resources are scarce.

In 1979 the authoritarian, Westernizing regime of the Shah was overthrown in Iran, and an Islamic republic established. This stimulated challenges to dominant conceptions of human rights from the perspectives of Islam and other non-Western cultures. In the mid-1990s government representatives and intellectuals from the economically successful countries of South-East and East Asia argued that human rights should be reinterpreted according to

'Asian values' in their societies. The critique of human rights from the standpoint of cultural diversity was thereby added to, and sometimes confused with, the critique from the standpoint of economic inequality.

## Key points

- The concept of human rights derives from the determination of the United Nations after the Second World War to oppose dictatorship and the social conditions that gave rise to dictatorship. It was embodied in the UN Charter (1945) and the Universal Declaration of Human Rights (1948).

- At that time many of the world's people lived under colonial rule, and were thus excluded from participating in the formulation of the UN's human rights concept. After decolonization, the new, postcolonial states accepted human rights in principle, but gave higher priority to development-related rights.

- In the decades after 1948 the UN developed a large body of international human rights law.

- Many developing countries have poor human rights records. This can be explained by internal factors, such as poverty, ethnic divisions, and authoritarian governments, and external factors, such as great-power rivalries and the effects of the global economy.

- Developing societies have been vulnerable to military coups and ethnic conflicts, both of which lead to serious human rights violations. Some see hope in the development of civil society, but this is difficult where resources are scarce.

- Many developing countries have challenged dominant interpretations of human rights by appealing to their own cultural traditions.

# The concept of human rights

**Human rights** are rights of a special kind. The concept of 'rights' is derived from that of 'right'. Right is distinguished from wrong, and all societies have standards of right and wrong. 'Right' is sometimes called 'objective', because it refers to a supposedly objective standard. Many people would say that the prohibition of murder is objectively right. 'Rights' are sometimes called 'subjective' because they 'belong' to individuals or groups who are the 'subjects' of rights. Thus subjective rights are **entitlements**, and differ from 'objective' concepts such as 'right' by emphasizing the just claims of the rights-holder. The idea of subjective rights is often said to be distinctively Western and relatively modern.

Human rights are commonly defined as the rights that everyone has simply because they are human. Philosophically, this is problematic, because it is not clear why anyone has rights because they are human. A theory of rights is needed to justify this belief. Legally, it is also problematic, because some human rights are attributed to particular kinds of human, such as children. Politically, human rights are those rights that have generally been recognized by governments. The Universal Declaration provides us with an authoritative list of human rights, but it is difficult to distinguish precisely between human rights, other rights, and other social values. It may, however, be important to do so, because people increasingly claim as their human rights what may not be human rights, or may not be rights at all, but social benefits or merely what people happen to want.

The two 1966 covenants distinguish between two categories of human rights: civil and political rights, on the one hand, and economic, social and cultural rights, on the other. Western governments tend to give priority to the first type, while developing countries tend to give priority to the second. The distinction itself is, however, controversial: the right to property, for example, is often regarded as a civil rather than an economic right, which seems absurd. The Vienna Declaration (1993) sought to overcome the distinction by proclaiming that all human rights are 'indivisible'. It is now also often said that there are three 'generations' of rights: the two types already mentioned constitute the first and second generations, while there is a third generation, consisting of 'solidarity' rights, such as the right to development. These distinctions are also controversial, both because the reference to 'generations' misrepresents the history of human rights, and because the meaning and value of third-generation human rights are questionable.

## A brief history

Some say that the concept of human rights is ancient, and found in all or most of the world's cultures. This claim usually confuses subjective rights with objective right. Notions such as justice or human dignity are found in many cultures. The idea of individual, subjective rights is more unusual and, consequently, more controversial.

Some scholars have argued that individual rights cannot be found before the late Middle Ages, and did not become politically important until the seventeenth century in England. The concept of *citizens' rights* is, however, found in ancient Greek and Roman thought. The modern concept of human rights derives from that of natural rights, which was developed in Europe in the late Middle Ages, and featured prominently in the political struggles of seventeenth-century England. Natural rights were derived from natural law, and were known by reason. This idea burst onto the stage of world politics with the American and French revolutions in the late eighteenth century. In the nineteenth century it fell out of favour, because it was thought to be unscientific and subversive of social order. The concept of human rights revives that of natural rights without necessarily endorsing the natural-law philosophy that underpinned it.

## Contemporary conceptions

The dominant conception of human rights today derives from its origins in Western **liberalism**, the philosophy that gives priority to individual freedom.

Human rights are the rights of individuals, and the individualism of the concept—its isolation of the human individual and the special value placed on that individual—is often said to be alien to non-Western cultures. It is not certain, however, that all human rights are individual rights. Both the 1966 covenants recognize that *peoples* have the right to self-determination. The right to development may be an individual or a collective right, or both. Western countries have a strongly individualistic conception of human rights, whereas developing countries have a more collectivistic conception.

## Key points

• Human rights are rights of a special kind. Rights are entitlements of individuals or groups, and differ from ideas of justice or human dignity. Human rights are either the rights everyone has because they are human or those generally recognized as such by governments or in international law.

• Distinctions are often made between civil and political rights, on the one hand, and economic, social, and cultural rights, on the other hand, and also among three generations of human rights. Theorists have criticized these distinctions as confused.

• Citizens' rights were recognized in ancient Greece and Rome, but human rights are modern, deriving from the late medieval idea of natural rights. This idea fell out of favour after the French Revolution because it was believed to be unscientific and subversive. It was revived by the UN as the concept of human rights.

• The dominant conception of human rights is controversial in developing countries because it is thought to express the Western philosophy of individualism.

# Human rights regimes

A **regime** is a set of rules and practices that regulate the conduct of actors in a specified field. Human rights regimes exist at international, regional, and national levels.

## The UN system

The **international human rights regime** consists of a large body of international law and a complex set of institutions to implement it. Chief among these institutions is the UN Commission on Human Rights, established 1945–7. Its members represent governments, and it has been criticized for political bias. Independent experts, however, work in various parts of the system. The Commission employs them as members of working groups or as rapporteurs on specific themes (such as torture) and countries. The members of the Sub-commission on the Promotion and Protection of Human Rights and of the committees that monitor the various treaties are also independent experts. **Non-governmental organizations** (NGOs)—consisting of citizen activists and experts—play an important role in providing information. It is difficult to evaluate the effectiveness of the international regime, but the consensus of scholars is that it is rather weak.

## Regional and national regimes

There are regional human rights regimes in Europe, the Americas, and Africa. The European is the most effective, and the African the least effective. Many scholars believe that the most important location for the protection of human rights is that of national law. The international regime is fairly effective in *promoting* human rights, but relatively ineffective in *implementing* them. Regional regimes are generally effective only if they are supervising relatively effective national regimes.

## Legal regimes and power politics

Developing countries frequently complain that the international human rights regime is a smokescreen behind which the powerful states of the West pursue their interests at the expense of the poorer states. There is undoubtedly truth in this charge, but many governments of developing countries have terrible human rights records, and this has in most cases probably hindered rather than promoted development. The powerful states of the West, and the UN itself, have been criticized both for not intervening to prevent human rights violations, as in the Rwandan genocide of 1994, and for intervening too forcefully or for dubious motives, as in Iraq in 2003.

## Key points

• The human rights conduct of states is regulated, with varying degrees of effectiveness, by legal and political regimes at international, regional, and national levels.

• The international human rights regime is a fairly effective promotional regime but a relatively ineffective implementation regime.

• Of the three regional regimes in Europe, the Americas, and Africa, the African is the least effective.

• Human rights can be promoted and fine-tuned at international and regional levels, but are best protected by national laws.

• The international human rights regimes are predominantly legal, and, behind them, international power politics dominates the human rights agenda, which for developing countries makes them matters of intense controversy.

# 'Human rights begin at breakfast'

There is a widely held view that developing countries must give development priority over human rights. The fundamental intuition underlying this view is that starving people cannot benefit from, say, the right to free speech, and that, without development, human rights are not possible, and perhaps not even desirable. 'Human rights begin at breakfast', Léopold Senghor, President of Sénégal, is supposed to have said. Various arguments support this position. It is claimed, for example, that human rights—especially economic and social rights—are simply too expensive for poor countries. It is also maintained that, especially in less developed countries with problematic ethnic divisions, human rights subvert social order and thus hinder development: the government of Singapore, for example, has often made this argument. Even if this is not so, free societies tend to divert resources from savings and investment to consumption, and this slows down long-term development. Empirically, the so-called Asian tigers—South Korea, Taiwan, Malaysia, and Singapore, in particular—are

cited as examples of successful economic development under authoritarian rule. The idea that human rights are *necessary* for development—an idea commonly promoted by the West—is thereby falsified. Most Western countries developed their economies and human rights over long periods of time, and generally recognized human rights only when they had sufficiently developed economies to support them. Developing countries are less favourably placed in the world economy, and there is a view that only authoritarian government can deliver rapid economic progress.

## Conceptions of development

'Development' is often assumed to mean economic development, and economic development is measured by per capita income. Recently, however, 'development' has been reconceptualized as 'human development', with emphasis on the quality of life.

This produces some striking results: African Americans, for example, have higher incomes but lower life expectancy than the Chinese (Sen 1999*a*: 21). The economic development of states is compatible with the misery of many people. The new conception of development sees 'human rights' and 'development' as *conceptually* overlapping. There is, for example, a human right to an adequate standard of living. If 'development' is defined in terms of the standard of living, then human rights and development are positively correlated *by definition*. The new conceptualization has had practical implications: the UN Development Programme, for example, has recently included the protection of human rights in its policies.

## Are human rights and development interdependent?

The Vienna Declaration asserted that human rights and development are 'interdependent'. Is this true?

The arguments that restrictions of human rights are either *necessary* or *sufficient* for development are not well supported by the evidence. The arguments often rely on very selective use of case studies, especially from East Asia. South Korea and Taiwan achieved rapid economic development under authoritarian governments, but both developed into liberal democracies. Singapore has also been economically successful with a so-called 'soft authoritarian' regime, which does not appear to be liberalizing. Other cases are ambiguous. Some Latin American countries—such as Pinochet's Chile—had some economic growth, but also some economic setbacks, under authoritarian rule, while China has achieved rapid economic growth combined with serious human rights violations in recent years. Authoritarian regimes can sometimes achieve rapid economic development. Most repressive regimes, however, have failed to deliver development. This suggests that violating human rights as such does not explain economic development. The causal connection between human rights violations and development has never been established. Some countries that have combined economic development with restrictions of civil and political rights—such as South Korea, Singapore, and China—have relatively good records with respect to economic

and social rights, such as education and health. Some development economists believe that investment in *education* is conducive to success in development.

The relations between development and human rights may well be mediated by other factors, including the economic strategies adopted by governmental elites and the country's security situation. Taiwan, South Korea, and Singapore all faced external and/or internal security threats that made authoritarian government more likely, if not strictly *necessary*, and all were able to locate themselves favourably within the global economic system.

Respect for human rights is, therefore, not generally *necessary* for economic development, and violation of human rights is certainly not *sufficient* for economic development. *Most countries that have persistently and seriously violated human rights have been unsuccessful in developing their economies.* The increasing political repression in Zimbabwe, for example, has been accompanied by economic collapse, and the former is certainly a cause of the latter. It is very difficult to generalize about the relations between development and human rights, however, and we should be very cautious about inferring policies for particular countries from generalizations, and, a fortiori, from the experience of selected countries. It does not follow from the fact that Singapore developed its economy with a fairly authoritarian government that Burkina Faso should follow its lead.

The relation between human rights and development is very complex and almost certainly strongly influenced by other factors specific to the individual countries. Attempts to establish statistical relations between human rights and development in large numbers of countries have produced inconclusive and sometimes apparently contradictory results. The famous Indian economist, Amartya Sen, has argued that the evidence suggests little correlation, positive or negative, between respect for civil and political rights and economic growth, and that the violation of such rights is not *necessary* to economic development. He reminds us that human rights have a value that is independent of development, in so far as we believe in 'the dignity and worth of the human person', and argues consequently that the available evidence is no barrier to the policy of pursuing development-with-human-rights (Sen 1999*b*). But if the relation between human rights and development is unclear, and developed states have far from perfect records in respecting human rights, then the most grave human-rights disasters of recent years—such as the tyranny of Idi Amin in Uganda (1972-8), the mass killings by the Khmer Rouge in Cambodia (1975-9), the terror regime of Saddam Hussein in Iraq (1979-2003), and the genocide in Rwanda (1994)—have taken place in developing countries. Why is this?

Developing countries are mostly poor, and are economically vulnerable to the power of rich states. This makes economic development difficult. Without economic development, the resources for implementing human rights are scarce. Paradoxically, where resources are not scarce (as in oil-producing countries, such as Nigeria, Saudi Arabia, Iraq, and Iran), the temptations of corruption and authoritarianism may also be great.

The achievement of independence from colonial rule, the ethos of the United Nations and world culture, and the spread of information and images through modern media of communication have raised expectations of economic progress among the peoples of the developing countries. The combination of these rising expectations and the persistent inability of governments to meet them have created widespread and intense social frustration, active opposition to governments, and consequent repression.

These problems are aggravated in many developing countries by ethnic divisions. Ethnic diversity does not necessarily lead to conflict and human rights violations. Colonial rulers often created the potential for conflict where it did not exist before: for example, the genocidal conflict between Hutus and Tutsis in Rwanda had significant colonial origins. In situations of scarcity and high expectations, however, ethnic divisions are difficult to manage, because ethnicity is a potent source of competition, and they can therefore lead to serious human rights violations.

Developing countries should not be seen simply as dependent victims of domination by rich states, international institutions, multinational corporations, or global capitalism. They have some autonomy, however limited, as the success of the Asian tigers demonstrates. Corrupt and incompetent government has contributed to the economic failures of many developing countries, and human rights violations are partly explained by the desire of powerful and corrupt rulers to remain in power. China, Indonesia, Iraq, Saudi Arabia, Nigeria, and Zimbabwe are only some of the developing countries in which power has been corrupting, and corruption is among the causes of human rights violations.

Finally, most developing countries lack traditions of human rights. They may have traditional cultures with morally admirable features, such as mutual solidarity, and they may also have active human rights organizations—which are found throughout much of Asia, Africa, and Latin America—and even individual 'human rights heroes' (such as Aung San Suu Kyi in Myanmar/Burma). But, in contrast with Europe, the value of human rights may not be deeply embedded in the *public culture* of the society. Even where the government has ratified international human rights treaties, and human rights are written into national constitutions, human rights may not be a strong feature of the political culture. It has been suggested, for example, that the military was able to mount successful coups and maintain repressive regimes in Latin America in the 1970s and 1980s partly because both the political right and the left had 'solidaristic' ideologies that allowed little place for individual rights (Roniger and Sznajder 1999).

The Vienna Declaration maintained that democracy, development, and human rights were interdependent. The relations between democracy and development are complex in ways that are similar to those between human rights and development. The relations between democracy and human rights are, however, less straightforward than they are often assumed to be. Democracy may be compatible with human rights partly *by definition*, because democracy may be defined in terms of such rights as those to freedom of expression, association, and political participation. There is also empirical evidence that democracies generally respect human rights better than authoritarian regimes do. Nevertheless, democracies can violate human rights in serious ways. The transition from authoritarian rule to democracy in several Latin American countries (for example, Brazil) has not diminished all kinds of human rights violations, and may have increased some kinds. The protection of human rights by legal institutions may run counter to the democratic will of the people. The human rights of suspected criminals, refugees, and ethnic and political minorities are particularly

---

## Box 15.2 Barriers to human rights implementation by developing countries

Most developing countries are poor, and cannot afford the full implementation of human rights.

- Most developing countries have little power in the global economic system, and are consequently vulnerable to the policies of powerful states and non-state actors that are often unfriendly to human rights.

- In the conditions of contemporary global culture and media of mass communication, where the expectations of many people in developing countries for economic progress are high, the inability of governments to meet those expectations stimulates protest and repression.

- Most developing countries have ethnic divisions that predispose to conflict in conditions of scarcity, and consequently to repression.

- Corrupt and incompetent government has been common in developing countries, and human rights are explained in part by the desire of corrupt rulers to remain in power.

- Many developing countries have had traditional cultures, wherein human rights enjoyed little place, and have developed a modern human rights culture only in a weak form.

---

vulnerable to democratic violations, in developed and developing countries. Finally, in developing countries with ethnic divisions and weak human rights traditions, the process of democratization itself may lead to serious human rights violations. Democratization played a role in ethnic conflict and genocide in Rwanda, for example. In both the Philippines and Indonesia, democratization has led to new forms of human rights violations, as space is made for ethnic demands that are met by repressive responses.

## Key points

- It is commonly argued that development should have priority over human rights, and that some restriction of human rights is necessary for development.

- Development may be defined as per capita income or alternatively as quality of life which makes development and human rights overlapping concepts.

- Some repressive regimes have produced rapid economic development, but most have not.

- No one has shown that violating human rights is necessary for economic development. It is likely that other factors are the major causes of economic development.

- Although the empirical relationship between human rights and development is not well understood, the available evidence suggests that it is weak; there are independent reasons for valuing human rights.

- Democracies generally respect human rights better than authoritarian regimes do, but democracies sometimes violate human rights, and human rights are intended to protect individuals from abuse of power by democratic, as well as non-democratic governments.

# Universalism and cultural diversity

The Preamble to the Universal Declaration of Human Rights refers to 'the equal and inalienable rights of all members of the human family', and the Declaration proclaims itself to be 'a common standard of achievement for all peoples'. Article 1 states that all human beings 'are born free and equal in dignity and rights'. The Vienna Declaration reaffirmed the universality of human rights: the belief that human rights belong to all human beings simply because they are human beings.

This universalism of human rights beliefs derives from the liberal Enlightenment doctrine of eighteenth-century Europe that the 'Rights of Man', as human rights were then called, were the rights of everyone, everywhere, at all times. This doctrine derived in turn from Christian teaching that there was only one God, and that the divine law applied to everyone, equally, everywhere, and at all times. One source of Christian philosophy was the Greco-Roman theory of natural law, which taught that all human beings formed a single moral community, governed by a common law that was known to human reason. The philosophical school of the Stoics was the proponent of pre-Christian, natural-law philosophy. The natural-law philosophical tradition that runs from the Stoics through medieval Christianity to Enlightenment liberalism and the contemporary concept of human rights forms a powerful, though controversial, component of Western, and to some extent global, culture.

## Cultural imperialism and cultural relativism

The belief that human rights are universal appears to conflict with the obvious cultural diversity of the world. Moral and political ideas, many people say, derive from culture, and different societies have different cultures. To impose human rights on everyone in the world is therefore intolerant, imperialistic, and unjustified. This moral logic may be supported by the *historical* claims that: (1) the concept of human rights is a Western concept; and (2) the West has a history of political, economic, and cultural imperialism that is not yet over. Some non-Western critics of human rights argue, not only that human rights is a concept alien to non-Western cultures, but its use by the West is part of a project of global political and economic domination. The 2003 war in Iraq might be cited as an example of the use of human rights to legitimate political expansionism.

This argument requires careful analysis. Much of the *moral* critique of human rights derives from the claim that it constitutes **cultural imperialism**, and relies on the intuition that imperialism is obviously wrong. If we ask *why* imperialism is wrong, however, we may say that it violates the *rights* of those who are

its victims. If we next ask *which* rights of the victims are violated by imperialism, the most common answer is **the right to self-determination**. At this point, the objection to moral universalism depends on a universal principle (the right to self-determination) and is therefore self-contradictory. If there is at least one universal right (the right to self-determination), there may also be others. It is difficult to argue that the right to self-determination is a universal right without accepting that the right not to be enslaved is also a universal right. This appeal to universalism does not necessarily justify the full list of rights in the Universal Declaration, but it does refute one common line of argument against universalism.

Another approach would be to reject all forms of universalism, and rely on the claim that all moral principles derive from *particular* cultures, particular cultures are *diverse*, some cultures reject at least some human rights principles (gender equality is a common example), and human rights are valid only within the culture of the modern West. On this view, there is a 'human rights culture'. But it is only one culture among many, and, because it derives from Western (secular) liberalism, it is not particularly appealing, still less *obligatory*, for those who, perhaps on the basis of their religious beliefs, subscribe to non-liberal moral and political codes.

This argument avoids the self-contradiction of the anti-imperialist approach, but at a considerable cost. The first difficulty is that the argument that all actual moral principles are justified by the cultures of which they form a part is another universal principle that cannot be used against universalism as such without self-contradiction. The next difficulty is that, if all principles are justified by their cultures, then imperialism would be justified by imperialistic cultures—a view which is anathema to critics of human rights universalism. They could argue that, according to the criteria of *their* culture, imperialism is wrong, but not show would-be imperialists why they should act according to these criteria. In practice, most critics of human rights universalism accept that racism is universally wrong, and cannot be justified by racist cultures like that of apartheid South Africa. A further difficulty with the 'culturalist' conception of morality is that actual cultures are complex, contested, and overlapping. There are, for examples, many schools of Islamic thought, there are disputes about the requirements of the religion, and Islamic ideas have mixed with other ideas in different ways in different societies. The idea of a homogeneous 'culture' that justifies particular moral ideas is a myth. The world is full of a great diversity of complex moral ideas, some of which cohere in different ways, with different degrees of uniformity and solidarity, into patterns which are themselves subject to change, in part as the result of interaction with other cultures.

These arguments do not themselves provide a justification of human rights. Only a justificatory theory of human rights could do that, and any such theory is likely to be controversial, not just between the West and the rest, but within Western thought, and even among human rights supporters. They also imply no disrespect for culture as such. Culture provides meaning, value, and guidance to human life, and there is a human right to participate in the cultural life of one's community. They do show that cultures are not *self-justifying*, and that we commit no logical nor moral error in subjecting actual cultures to critical scrutiny.

## The 'Asian values' debate

When the UN convened its world conference on human rights in Vienna in June 1993, a number of East Asian and South-East Asian countries—Japan, South Korea, Taiwan, Hong Kong, Malaysia, Singapore, and Indonesia—had achieved remarkably high rates of economic development. All had cultures markedly different from those of the West; all had been colonies of and/or been engaged in conflict with the West; and some had been criticized by the West for human rights violations. In the run-up to the Vienna conference, several governmental representatives and intellectuals of these countries called into question the universality of human rights, or at least the dominant interpretation of it, and defended an Asian approach to human rights.

The argument was at first puzzling. Asia contains almost all the world's major cultures. What *were* the Asian values that were supposed to justify an Asian approach to human rights? It soon became clear that 'Asia' meant East and South-East Asia. This clarification left many puzzles, however. Malaysia and Indonesia were predominantly Muslim countries, whereas China was officially communist and

atheistic. Could there be a greater cultural difference than that between Islam and communism? The 'Asian values' argument came mainly from two countries: Malaysia and Singapore: the first of these is mainly (though not exclusively) Muslim, and the second mainly (though not exclusively) ethnically Chinese. Japan was ambivalent, for it was undoubtedly Asian, but valued its alliance with the West and its membership of the international community. One of the leading proponents of 'Asian values'—Dr Mahathir Mohamad, Prime Minister of Malaysia—acknowledged that 'Asian values' were similar to *conservative* Western values: order, harmony, respect for authority. This made the concept of 'Asian values' clearer, but made the debate one between liberalism and conservatism, rather than between the West and Asia.

The 'Asian values' position was officially embodied in the Bangkok Declaration of Asian states in April 1993. This declaration reaffirmed the orthodox view that human rights were 'universal in nature', but went on to state that they must be considered in the context of an evolving process of international norm-setting, 'bearing in mind the significance of national and regional particularities and various historical, cultural and religious backgrounds'. Read literally, this statement is uncontroversial, for it would be foolish to interpret and implement human rights without 'bearing in mind' the significance of these cultural differences. The Vienna Declaration itself repeated the 'bearing in mind' statement, and this was generally interpreted as consistent with the universalist orthodoxy. However, more than 100 *Asian* non-governmental organizations produced an alternative Bangkok declaration that was universalist without qualification, and thus Bangkok 1993 produced two different Asian approaches to human rights.

Because some of the leading proponents of 'Asian values' had been accused of human rights violations, some human rights activists and scholars interpreted the doctrine as nothing more than an ideological attempt to justify authoritarian government. This may be partly true, but the issue produced an extensive debate among Asian and Western scholars, which sought to reconcile the core values of international human rights with respect for cultural traditions that are truly important for the diverse peoples of the world. The debate between the claims of human

## Box 15.3 'Asian values'

- 'The rights of the individual are certainly not in splendid isolation from those of the community. Excessive individual freedom leads to a decay in moral values and weakens the whole social fabric of nations. In the name of individual rights and freedoms, racial prejudices and animosities are resurfacing to the extent that we are witnessing the rise of new forms of racism and xenophobia, increasingly manifested in violence.' Statement by Datuk Abdullah Haji Ahmad Badawi, Minister of Foreign Affairs, Malaysia, Vienna, 18 June 1993.

- 'All cultures aspire to promote human dignity in their own ways. But the hard core of rights that [are] truly universal is perhaps smaller than we sometimes like to pretend. Most rights are still essentially contested concepts. There may be a general consensus. But this is coupled with continuing and, at least for the present, no less important conflicts of interpretation.' Statement by Wong Kan Seng, Minister for Foreign

Affairs of the Republic of Singapore, Vienna, 16 June 1993.

- 'If current Western policies of punishing authoritarian governments had been in force in the sixties and seventies, the spectacular economic growth of Taiwan and South Korea would have been cut off at its very inception by Western demands that the governments then in power be replaced by less authoritarian regimes. Instead, by allowing the authoritarian governments, which were fully committed to economic development, to run the full course, the West has brought about the very economic and social changes that have paved the way for the more open and participative societies that Taiwan and South Korea have become. The lessons from East Asia are clear. There are no short-cuts. It is necessary for a developing society to succeed *first* in economic development before it can attain the social and political freedoms found in the developed societies.' Mahbubani (1999).

rights and culture continues, because there are deeply embedded cultural practices in the world that are inconsistent with human rights standards.

## Key points

- Human rights are supposed to be universal. In view of the cultural diversity in the world, some say that they are Western, and that attempts to universalize them are imperialistic.

- The anti-imperialistic argument presupposes the universal right to self-determination and therefore fails as a critique of universal rights.

- The argument that all values are relative to culture is unconvincing because cultures are not self-justifying, and hardly anyone believes that anything done in the name of culture is justified.

- The concept of human rights includes the right to practise one's culture, and thus human rights and culture may be compatible. Some cultural practices may, however, violate human rights standards.

- The concept of Asian values has challenged the universality of human rights. This has been associated with Asian authoritarianism and East Asian economic success, but it raises valid questions about how human rights are best combined with deeply embedded cultures.

# The new political economy of human rights

Marxists have traditionally argued that human rights are 'bourgeois', and are either illusory, or, at best, formal, and conceal real inequalities of wealth and power. The inclusion of economic and social rights in

the list of human rights has been intended to meet this criticism, but it has not been successful, because (1) economic and social rights are relatively neglected in international politics compared with civil and political rights, and (2) great inequalities of wealth and power persist worldwide.

## Globalization

'Globalization' is a contested concept in social science. Global trade is ancient, and there is a dispute as to how it may have changed in recent times. However, whatever economic historians may say about global trends, it is obvious that we live in a dynamic, interrelated world that is changing rapidly in certain important respects. What is the impact of globalization on human rights?

Globalization has been opposed by a worldwide protest movement expressing diverse concerns, including world poverty, environmental degradation, and human rights. This has replaced, to a considerable extent, the earlier socialist movement opposing capitalism. The targets of this movement are primarily rich states, associations of rich states (such as the so-called G8), and multinational corporations (MNCs). The human rights movement has recently increased its concern about the role of MNCs in human rights violations, either directly (for example, by the employment of child labour) or in collaboration with repressive governments. Issues of globalization, development, the environment, and human rights have often come together as MNCs seek to develop natural resources in ways that damage the environment and local ways of life, and protests are met by governmental repression.

The relations between human rights and globalization are complex, however. The idea of human rights claims to be universal, and the human rights movement seeks global reach, and achieves it to some extent by global means of communication (email, internet, mobile phones). Meyer (1998) has conducted an empirical investigation into the impact of MNCs on human rights in developing countries, and concluded that there is a *positive* correlation between MNC investment in developing countries and human rights. He does not deny that some MNCs are involved in human rights violations in these countries. Other scholars, using different methods, have reached different conclusions (Smith, Bolyard, and Ippolito 1999). Globalizing, some say, increases inequality, drives the vulnerable to the margins of

survival, and thereby feeds religious and nationalist extremism. After the financial crisis in South-East Asia at the end of the 1990s, for example, the International Monetary Fund imposed strict conditions on Indonesia that led to ethnic and religious riots. On the other hand, it has been argued that neo-liberal globalization has tended to undermine the caste system in India, thereby emancipating the untouchables and advancing the cause of human rights (Sikand 2003: 112).

Global capitalism is a dynamic process that probably has positive and negative consequences for human rights. There is also a global economic regime—consisting of organizations such as the G8, the European Union, the North American Free Trade Agreement (NAFTA), the World Bank, the International Monetary Fund (IMF), and the World Trade Organization (WTO)—that regulates global capitalism and the economies of the developing countries. The World Bank and the IMF are powerful actors in the international economy, and have traditionally been unconcerned with human rights. Critics have alleged that their policies have often been very harmful to human rights, especially economic and social rights. The World Bank has recently opened up a dialogue with NGOs and independent experts on human rights, but it remains to be seen whether this will change its policies significantly. The WTO is also accused of working to the disadvantage of the developing countries (Pogge 2002: 17–19). The UN conception of human rights is a statist, social democratic idea, whereas the global economy, and the international financial institutions that are supposed to regulate it, are based on a neo-liberal ideology that prefers vibrant markets and weak states.

## Key points

- Marxists have traditionally criticized human rights because they are thought to disguise the inequalities of wealth and power inherent in capitalism.

- The critique of capitalism has recently been replaced by the anti-globalization movement that criticizes globalization on various grounds, including concern for human rights.

- There is no doubt that global capitalist institutions, such as multinational corporations, are quite frequently involved in human rights violations, but the general relations between global capitalism and human rights are not well understood, though almost certainly complex.

- The global economic regime that seeks to regulate global capitalism almost certainly has a major impact on human rights, but this is yet to be studied in detail.

# Conclusion

The concept of human rights became important in world politics only with the adoption of the United Nations Charter in 1945. Although it was derived from Western moral, legal, and political philosophy, it was declared to be universal. On the foundation of the UN Universal Declaration of Human Rights (1948) a large body of international human rights law has been elaborated. Most of this is legally binding on most states, and the principles of the Declaration have been reaffirmed by all UN members. Nevertheless, international procedures for implementing human rights are weak, human rights violations are common, and the concept of human rights is not universally accepted as culturally legitimate.

The leading issue raised by human rights in the developing countries is the relationship between development and human rights. This is a complex issue. There is more than one definition of 'development', and some definitions include human rights. There is, however, a widespread view that some restriction of human rights is a precondition of development, and that development should take priority over human rights. There is no doubt that some countries have achieved rapid rates of economic development while violating civil and political rights. However, most rights-violating countries have poor records of development. The relations between human rights and development are still not well understood, but the evidence suggests that, generally, factors other than human rights are more important in promoting or obstructing development. The case for violating human rights for the sake of development is therefore much weaker than it has often been thought to be. The view that human rights are necessary for economic development is, however, not well supported by the evidence. There are also strong reasons for respecting human rights independently of their relation to development.

Developing countries are generally poor, which makes it difficult to fund the implementation of human rights. They may not want to do so because their governments are corrupt and unconcerned with human rights. They may not be able to because external agents—for example, donor governments and/or international financial institutions—limit their capacity to do so by insisting on the reduction of state budgets.

The United Nations is right in seeing development and human rights as interdependent, not in the sense that each always helps the other, but in so far as improvements in each makes the achievement of the other easier. Crises of development are often accompanied by crises of human rights, as countries like Somalia, the Democratic Republic of Congo, and Liberia show. Development success is good news for human rights—as South Korea and Taiwan illustrate—although the interests of elites and local cultures may limit human rights achievements, as in Singapore.

The process of globalization has been associated with the assertion of cultural difference. This has meant that the claim that human rights are universal, although reaffirmed by UN member states in 1993, is constantly challenged. Some of these challenges express the interests of the powerful, who are reluctant to allow a voice to dissenters. Others raise difficult questions about legitimating universal principles in a culturally diverse world.

Arguments that the concept of human rights expresses the interests of the West or the rich are generally not convincing. Taking human rights seriously would benefit most the poorest and most oppressed. There is a danger, however, that Western states may discredit the concept by associating it with their own foreign policies motivated by their own interests. The cause of human rights will be damaged if it is, or is perceived to be, a new form of imperialism. Although human rights are now well established in great power politics, it may be that the best hope for their future lies with the increasing number of grass-roots movements in the developing countries.

## QUESTIONS

**1**  'The idea of human rights is the world's first truly global ideology'. Discuss.

**2**  What is the moral force of the idea of human rights?

**3**  Explain the chief characteristics of the international human rights regime.

**4**  Is the UN right to believe that human rights and development are interdependent?

**5**  Can human rights be universally valid in a world of deep cultural difference?

**6**  Is global capitalism on the whole good or bad for human rights?

**7**  What strategies provide the best hope for improving the protection of human rights in developing countries?

## GUIDE TO FURTHER READING

Bauer, J. R., and Bell, D. A., *The East Asian Challenge for Human Rights* (Cambridge: Cambridge University Press, 1999). The most interesting of several good collections of essays on 'Asian values'.

Brownlie, I., and Goodwin-Gill, G. S. (eds.), *Basic Documents on Human Rights*, 4th edn. (Oxford: Oxford University Press, 2002). An authoritative collection of international legal texts.

Donnelly, J., *Universal Human Rights in Theory and Practice*, 2nd edn. (Ithaca, NY: Cornell University Press, 2003). An excellent introduction to the international conception of human rights and the principal issues of human rights implementation.

Forsythe, D. P., *Human Rights in International Relations* (Cambridge: Cambridge University Press, 2000). An authoritative introduction to the topic.

Freeman, M. A. *Human Rights: An Interdisciplinary Perspective* (Cambridge: Polity, 2002). A comprehensive introduction for social science students and law students who want a non-legal approach.

Peters, J., and Wolper, A. (eds.), *Women's Rights, Human Rights: International Feminist Perspectives* (New York: Routledge, 1995). A good introduction to the large literature on women and human rights.

Pogge, T., *World Poverty and Human Rights* (Cambridge: Polity, 2002). A collection of philosophical essays on various aspects of development and human rights.

Risse, T., Ropp, S. C., and Sikkink, K., *The Power of Human Rights: International Norms and Domestic Change* (Cambridge: Cambridge University Press, 1999). A very interesting attempt to explain successes and failures of human rights implementation with several case studies of developing countries.

Sen, A., *Development as Freedom* (Oxford: Oxford University Press, 1999). A thought-provoking argument for the mutual relations between development and freedom.

## WEB LINKS

**www.unhchr.ch**   The website of the UN High Commissioner for Human Rights, which is the best way into the UN human rights system.

**www.bayefsky.com**   For which state has ratified which treaty, and much other information about the UN human rights treaty system.

**www.hri.ca/welcome.asp**   The website of Human Rights Internet, excellent, especially for information about NGOs.

**www.amnesty.org**   Amnesty International.

**http://shr.aaas.org/dhr/about.html**   The American Association for the Advancement of Science, Directory of Human Rights Resources on the Internet.

 ## COMPANION WEB SITE

For additional material and resources, see the companion web site at:
**www.oup.com/uk/booksites/politics/**

# Part Five

# Case studies

In this part we deploy a range of case studies to add 'thick description' to the 'thin description' provided by the wide selections of examples that have been cited in the discussions in the earlier Parts. There are two main aims. **First**, to illustrate in depth many of the larger themes that have been introduced and discussed in the earlier parts, by reference to countries chosen as cases for their capacity to reveal the complexity of the issues involved. Our **second** aim is to demonstrate the great diversity of experience through a combination of cases drawn from all the main developing regions, with some countries showing what might be considered positive developments or genuine achievements and others displaying more troublesome features. Basic data for socio-economic and political indicators for all these countries, with the exception of the Pacific islands where data is sparse and necessarily more fragmented (but see p. 333), can be found in Appendix 1 (p. 383).

The country cases themselves each tell their own story but the pairings supply evidence of some contrasting experiences. At the same time the evidence shows that often we must be qualified in our judgements. For instance although Indonesia might seem like a country where increasing fragmentation is to be expected, following the erosion of political authoritarianism there, the account given in Chapter 16 presents a more nuanced picture. In contrast South Africa's recent past is suggestive of a more unambiguously positive experience in nation-building. In Chapter 17 the complexities of civil society and its political implications are brought out in the cases of India and Saudi Arabia. In neither one is civil society found to be wholly passive or unequivocally vibrant; in both, there are elements of civil society that are a major source of political tension. In Chapter 18 Chile is offered as one example of the developing world's relatively rare strong states, that has delivered real development, although in recent years the picture has started to undergo significant change. By comparison the political disintegration of the DRC prompts questions about whether something like that was made inevitable by the circumstances of the country's colonial past and the violence of the early years of independence, or by the wider regional situation.

In Chapter 19 Nigeria exemplifies the point that while certain large developing countries can be powerful actors in their region and possess a considerable international profile, much will depend on the manner in which they are ruled internally. At the other end of the scale, the island states of the Pacific show that the old adage 'small is beautiful' is not unreservedly true. On the contrary, small and very small states can share many of the problems of their larger neighbours and moreover face distinctive challenges of their own. Regional networking is one obvious approach to a solution. In Chapter 20 Pakistan provides an example of a country experiencing repeated cycles of military intervention. Many have concluded that Pakistan cannot sustain a political system in which the armed forces do not play a major role; it appears to be stuck in the past. In contrast Mexico has made rapid strides forward, from 'electoral authoritarianism' to 'democratization by elections'. In the final chapter Guatemala is a good example of how underdevelopment, as an interrelated complex of social, economic, cultural, and especially political conditions, can be highly persistent and is difficult to change. South Korea, in comparison, is a success story in terms both of economic and social development and political transition. But it also illustrates that the political challenges of development are never completely resolved; even undoubted progress can give rise to new challenges (as South Korea and other cases like Mexico and Chile show).

All told, the chapters in this part demonstrate that to understand politics in the developing world a detailed historical knowledge acquired on a case-by-case basis forms an indispensable complement to the larger theorizing. This part should help us to decide which theoretical approaches offer the most insight into this or that particular case. And although the case studies are brought together in this part, readers are recommended to read the case study or studies that are most relevant to a big issue or theme immediately after studying the relevant chapter, or chapters, in earlier parts.

# Fragmentation or nation-building?

## Indonesia

*Richard Robison*

### OVERVIEW

This chapter explains how a powerful and pervasive system of centralized state authority was constructed in Indonesia between 1960 and 1998 and how various religious, regional, and social/political challenges were progressively eliminated or co-opted. It then examines how far this system of state power has unravelled over the past five years, as the Asian economic crisis and the fall of President Soeharto increased the possibilities for a vast, disorganized array of political, economic, religious, and regional interests to enter the political arena. Can Indonesia survive intact in the post-Soeharto era and will these new and fragmented interests be contained or accommodated in a new system of state power defined by political parties and parliaments? The chapter argues that the main threat to the integrity of Indonesia's national state does not come from regional, religious, or ethnic interests aimed at dismantling centralized or secular rule. It comes instead from the diffusion of state power and from new political operators and interests emerging in the context of decentralized money politics who seek merely to seize authority over revenues, patronage, and rents and to redistribute power and wealth within the old structures.

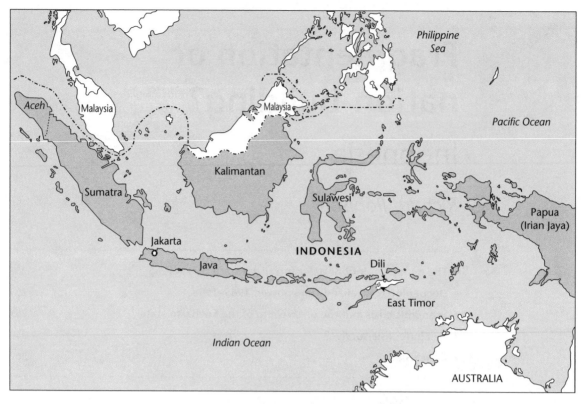

**INDONESIA**

---

### Box 16*a*.1 **Key dates in Indonesia's history**

| | |
|---|---|
| **1945** | Declaration of the Republican Constitution |
| **1949** | Formal end of colonial rule and establishment of the Republic |
| **1960** | President Soekarno formally declares the establishment of centralized rule by 'guided democracy' |
| **1965/6** | Overthrow of Soekarno regime by Soeharto and the elimination of the Communist Party of Indonesia |
| **1975** | Invasion of East Timor |
| **1997/8** | Indonesia's economy devastated by economic crisis, followed by fall of Soeharto |
| **1999** | First free parliamentary elections |
| **2000** | East Timor gains independence |

# The genesis of Indonesia's centralized state, 1949–1965

Indonesia proclaimed independence in 1945. Over 300 years of colonial rule by the Dutch imposed an increasingly effective system of central state authority on those diverse political, ethnic, and social entities that were to become the nation of Indonesia. A vast and complex central bureaucracy and legal system were established together with effective military control over the archipelago. Significantly, the forces dominating domestic political resistance to colonial rule in the twentieth century were also those aiming to create a strong, modern national state rather than promote backward-looking religious or regional interests. Nevertheless, the departure of the Dutch in 1949 meant the new state had to construct new institutions to embed national unity and mobilize new social alliances to support its authority.

Indonesia's new state began as a constitutional parliamentary democracy, but although all the major parties were committed to the integrity of the new nation a series of volatile and fragile governments rose and fell with great rapidity. In the process, the democratic formula began to frustrate the main forces supporting the development of a highly centralized secular power. These included President Soekarno himself, the main secular nationalist party, the officials of the state bureaucracy, and the military. Citing the need to achieve national unity and to build a national economy, Soekarno moved with the support of these groups to abandon democracy and nationalize the economy. By 1960 a new system of centralized authoritarian rule ('guided democracy') and state capitalism was in place (Feith 1962).

However, the creation of centralized authoritarian rule was not just about establishing order over democracy or national economic interests over the remnants of imperialism. In reality it was about power and the interests of the state and its officials and those beneficiaries of state favour and patronage. Thus, Soekarno immediately set about dismantling liberalism and establishing the authority of a state that was claimed to represent the common good above politics and vested interest. A new state philosophy, *pancasila*, proclaimed the organic nature of state power and effectively denied the legitimacy of political opposition. This was to be an effective political tool of Soeharto too in later years.

The rise of the new state was not without friction. Opponents had to be suppressed, including some groups assembled around various Islamic agendas. An extensive class of small-scale indigenous traders and manufacturers had been progressively destroyed, largely by the incursions of Chinese Indonesian business since the early twentieth century. Their resentment had taken a political form within the Sjarekat Islam, a movement with strong xenophobic and anti-Chinese sentiments that emerged through the 1920s and 1930s, wrapped firmly in appeals to Islam. Expecting protection and support from the new state in the 1950s, these Islamic petty business interests were disappointed, as the benefits of power, the trade monopolies, state bank credits, exchange rate policies, and government contracts were handed out to various party officials and family members, military commands, and Chinese business associates (Feith 1962).

With Islamic resentment of the new state also came the regional Islamic militia who were involved in the war of independence against the Dutch and were reluctant to hand over the territory to the republic in the 1950s. What was a dispute over authority and power soon became wrapped in appeals to religious resentment of the increasingly secular nature of the central state and to regional resentment of increasing central control over local affairs and the marginalization of local notables at the hands of central officials. In West Java, the Darul Islam waged a campaign against the republic that became caught up in demands for an Islamic state. Many of the leading figures in present-day Jemaah Islamiah, such as Abu Bakar Bashir, had their origins in this movement (International Crisis Group 2002). Other regional movements in Sulawesi and Sumatra also challenged the central state and appealed to broader Islamic resentments.

Although the military and the government had defeated these groups by the early 1960s, the regime continued to regard these xenophobic and right-wing elements of Islam as a threat. The Islamic party, Masjumi, was banned, and spokesmen calling for an Islamic state were strictly controlled, many of them fleeing to Malaysia and elsewhere in the 1980s where they were to fall, ironically, under the influence of more radical international Islamic movements.

Nevertheless the central authoritarian state remained vulnerable, plagued by a collapsing economy, rising inflation and debt, and internal struggles for power. These came to a head in 1965 with the fall of Soekarno and the seizure of power by the then General Soeharto. An accord was reached with Western powers to reschedule Indonesia's debts and undertake policy reforms that unlocked aid and loans and foreign investment. This did not usher in liberal market capitalism and democracy but enabled the regime to preside over economic growth and access to increasing revenues. Most important, the central contradiction of the regime was resolved with the violent elimination of the critical challenge of social radicalism posed by the Indonesian Communist Party (PKI). Not only did this confirm the pre-eminent position of the military but it attracted the support of the middle class, who had feared for their property and the existing social order.

## Key points

- Authoritarian rule replaced democracy a decade after independence.
- State capitalism triumphed over small, private Islamic-oriented trading and business interests with roots in the regions.
- Centralized state power was embedded in an alliance of the military, middle classes, and Western governments.

# Deepening centralized state power, 1965–1998

Studies of challenges to central national states often focus on the forces demanding devolution or independence, neglecting the fact that centralized states also have the backing of powerful interests and beneficiaries. No less than disintegrative movements, the pressures for integration have their social and economic bases. Understanding why centralized states are able to survive requires that these interests are uncovered and explained. Thus the period 1965–98 is an important one for Indonesia. The story is one of deepening and entrenching the institutions and alliances supporting centralized authoritarian rule, alongside an increasing repression or co-option of regional, religious, and reformist opponents.

Soeharto's regime, the so-called New Order, established a pervasive and efficient security apparatus, with broad powers of arrest and imprisonment. Tens of thousands of the remnants of the PKI were imprisoned and other former members and associates were denied employment. More reactionary populists of the Islamic right were also kept under tight control. As late as 1984, unrest in the port of Tanjung Priok was brutally suppressed. This had threatened a potentially dangerous linking of working-class resentment with Islamic political figures and disappointed former members of the regime.

There were also more sophisticated moves to co-opt people into the political apparatus of the regime and to disorganize civil society. Political activity was confined to organizations and institutions of the state, which established its own sanctioned political parties and front groups to monopolize legitimate political activity. Elections were highly orchestrated, resulting in massive government victories. By 1984, all civil organizations were also required to accept the principals of *pancasila*. This effectively proscribed any appeals to Islamic or liberal social agendas. So, no political activity was permitted outside the state, and prospective politicians were limited to operating within its parameters.

However, the regime also enjoyed an extensive base of political and social support, meaning that when the apparatus of authoritarian rule finally collapsed, the whole system of power did not disappear. At one level, the state was supported by the officials within its own vast apparatus: in the military, civil bureaucracy, judiciary and the courts, and in the state political party, Golkar. These officials were highly influential, being essential to the running of all the public services. At another level, most business interests established under the New Order were committed to its continued existence. Their business depended upon access to the monopolies, contracts, and concessions controlled by the state and upon alliances with powerful politicians and officials. The ending of this system and an opening to competitive markets fundamentally threatened them. Among the middle classes, too, the New Order attracted widespread support as well as some criticism. After all, the regime brought an era of unparalleled prosperity for them, despite extensive corruption. It

also protected them from the threat of reactionary populism of Islamic forces and from the radical populism of worker-based movements, and provided stability and order. Indonesia's middle-class dissidents were subjected to none of the violence and 'dirty wars' that have characterized relations between regimes and their middle-class critics elsewhere, in Latin America for instance (see Robison and Hadiz 2004).

## Key points

- An apparatus of repressive, 'emergency' authority was established, becoming a complex system of centralized ideological and corporatist rule.
- The centralized secular state was embedded in a social and political alliance of state officials, business and political entrepreneurs, and middle-class beneficiaries.

# Economic crisis and the unravelling of the Soeharto state

Economic crisis, the fall of Soeharto in 1998, and the collapse of the authoritarian state over which he presided for over three decades appeared to bring to an end one of the most successful episodes of centralized nation- and state-building of the twentieth century. Following the democratic reforms of 1999, power began to flow towards politicians, political parties, parliaments, and provincial governments, fuelling growing demands for a redistribution of power, revenue, and authority.

Asia's economic crisis was to have a devastating impact on Indonesia. The government was confident that attacks on the Indonesian currency by unregulated so-called 'hedge funds' in mid-1997 would not be successful, but they failed to account for the size of private corporate debt and the fact that much of it was unsecured. As a result, Indonesian businesspeople panicked and rushed to buy US dollars, forcing Indonesia's curency (the rupiah) into a free fall. International Monetary Fund (IMF) advice to float the currency, close down banks, and cut government

spending made the situation worse and the financial crisis soon turned into a deep economic and political crisis. Debt was largely located within the ranks of private investors and most of the large corporate groups soon found they were effectively insolvent, and forced to default. Indonesia's banks faced rising levels of non-performing loans, paralysing the whole financial system.

At one level, the cement of the regime itself, its ability to control the allocation of monopolies, contracts, and credit and to deliver these to those powerful politico-business families, was now being dismantled. The regime's support base began to fracture. At the same time, the regime's inability to stem the broader and accelerating economic decline eroded its popular credibility. Popular demonstrations against the regime, previously not allowed, now broke out on the streets of Jakarta and other cities. Anti-Soeharto sentiment became entangled with long-standing resentment of Chinese and power struggles within the regime itself. Anti-Chinese violence and the shooting of student demonstrators raised the temperature. Soeharto's closest supporters and the military itself now began to seek new alliances to preserve their power. By May 1998 Soeharto had resigned.

So pervasive and deep was the power Soeharto had concentrated in his own hands that his departure threatened to leave Indonesia with a political vacuum, threatening political chaos, economic collapse, and rule by extra-legal forces. The prospects for a widespread unravelling of power and order were real. In the event new political laws were passed, in 1999, that significantly changed the country's political architecture. Whereas the Soeharto regime tolerated only three state-controlled political parties and prohibited them from appealing to religious, social, or ideological agendas that departed from *pancasila*, the reforms now opened the way to diverse parties and ideologies with the exception of communism. Almost immediately, hundreds of parties were declared, although only thirty-eight eventually contested the 1999 general elections. Numerous Islamic parties were declared, including some hostile to the secularism of the entrenched ideals of the national state. The rise of Megawati Soekarnopoetri's (daughter of Indonesia's first president) Indonesian Democratic Party of Struggle, so recently repressed by the Soeharto regime, raised the spectre of more radical social policies and the possible entry of the poor and organized labour into politics. While the new parliament did not signal the dismantling of the centralized secular state it did, nevertheless, signal a shift from authoritarian rule to a system where political power was accumulated within electoral competition and parliamentary competition. This meant both the diffusion of power and the entry into the political arena of groups and interests previously marginalized. Politics was no longer confined within the state apparatus and those officials and families that controlled it. Now various political entre-

preneurs, wealthy families, and even gangsters fought over the spoils of power in national and regional parliaments. Government had reduced authority to impose law and ensure its policies were enforced.

Neo-liberal reformers had long dreamed of decentralization. It was thought that by breaking down centralized state power both civil society and markets would be given more breathing space. So it was no surprise that decentralization became one of the main demands for reform in the Letters of Intent signed between the government and the IMF after the economic crisis. Decentralization measures became central to the political reforms of 1999. Substantial administrative and revenue-collecting authority was transferred to provincial and sub-provincial governments, including notably resource royalties and taxes. This now made it worthwhile for various interests to enter the arena of local and regional politics, either to defend their privileges or to seek rents. For these local politicians, especially those in Indonesia's most resource-rich provinces and sub-provinces, there were real temptations to demand increasing levels of autonomy and press the pace and extent of decentralization (Hadiz 2003*b*).

## Key points

- The Asian financial crisis unravelled the economic authority of the state and its politico-business oligarchies.

- After 1999 a new system of parliamentary rule was created where parties became the new arenas of power

- The decentralization of administrative and fiscal authority and political power empowers provincial and sub-provincial government and politics.

# Will Indonesia survive?

Soeharto's successor, President Habibie, confronted the huge difficulties of managing an orderly transition to democratic rule while attempting to retain intact centralized state power and assuage the interests of the top politico-business families. New forces, formerly on

the margins of the state, began to seize control of the authority to allocate economic rents. At the same time, regional demands for independence re-emerged and Islamic radical groups, long suppressed under Soeharto, revived demands for an end to the secular state.

Ever since its invasion of East Timor in 1975 following the departure of Portuguese colonial power, Indonesia's government faced armed opposition within the province and persistent censure in world forums, especially as violence and human rights abuses mounted. After the fall of Soeharto the idea of granting some form of autonomy gained support even within the Indonesian military, apparently because they believed effective control could still be exercised through extensive pro-Indonesian militia. For reasons that are, even now, not entirely clear, Predident Habibie agreed in January 1999 to a referendum that would enable the population of East Timor to decide between autonomy under Indonesian rule or full independence. A United Nations-sponsored ballot (August 1999) overwhelmingly favoured independence. Widespread violence and panic followed, resulting in the deployment of UN troops in East Timor and the suppression of the militia. On 29 October, a formal transfer of sovereignty from Indonesia was agreed by Habibie's successor, President Wahid.

Does East Timor signal the beginning of a wider break-up of Indonesia, as other provinces see an opportunity to secede? East Timor was not the only province where there had been ongoing resistance to centralized rule. Although Papua had been incorporated into Indonesia following an Act of Free Choice in 1969, Indonesian rule met resistance there too; several independence movements emerged to periodically engage the military. On Indonesia's western flank, in the province of Aceh, resistance to the authority of Jakarta dates back to colonial times. Armed resistance under the Aceh Freedom Movement (GAM) has persisted since the mid-1970s, periodically resulting in intense confrontations with the Indonesian military.

Autonomy agreements were extended to both provinces in 2001, including the right to retain large percentages of locally generated revenues. Yet, in neither case has the central government shown any signs of acceding to independence. Unlike East Timor both provinces are part of the old Dutch East Indies. Also, both provinces contain enormous mineral and energy resources (copper and gold in Papua and gas in Aceh) that have been important to the national budget and to powerful public and private business interests. Since taking office in July 2001 President Megawati and her government have displayed impatience with secessionist demands and inclined more to military hardliners. The intensity of conflict in Aceh has increased. Martial law was declared in 2003. Yet, the demands for independence have not extended to Indonesia's other provinces. Various governors and local politicians occasionally raised the issue but more as a means of pressing for increased revenues and power from the central government. The decentralization laws of 1999 largely put a stop to this.

One of the important factors to emerge from the battles over regional autonomy is not so much the strength and determination of secessionist forces but the extent to which economic, political, and social elites in all regions have strong reasons to support the continuation of a central state. Nationalism retains its hold among Indonesians. Regional power-holders and elites have gained from decentralization but they are deeply integrated into the national state and power structures as well as social and cultural arenas, after four decades of authoritarian rule. Many powerful regional families now live in Jakarta and hold office in the national bureaucracy and government.

Although Soeharto's fall meant that forces long suppressed might now begin to organize, there has been no serious resurgence of radical Islam demanding an end to the secular state and a harder line towards Chinese and foreigners. There has been no descent into a world of reactionary populism under the banner of Islam. The main Islamic parties established to contest the 1999 elections were moderate parties long operating in the mainstream of Indonesian politics. Neither Wahid's party of conservative rural Muslims (PKB) nor the other main Muslim parties representing more urban and modernist Muslims have demanded an Islamic state or a radical review of the new democracy. In any case, they were able to capture only just over 30 per cent of seats in the new parliament. The larger number of smaller Islamic parties fared even worse. It was clear that most Indonesian Muslims want a fairly tolerant society, stable and open to the outside world.

Yet the more radical Islamic movements have had some impact, owing to the disarray and conflict that followed the fall of Soeharto. Returning from exile in Malaysia and Europe, many Islamic radicals re-established themselves in Indonesia, among them, Abu Bakar Bashir, who focused around a series of Islamic schools (peasantren). A series of radical organizations were formed that became involved in violence; among them Jemaah Islamiyah, as well as Laksar Jihad, Forum Studi Kajian Islam, KISDI, and Front Pembela Islam. Variously they became involved in the bombing of Christian schools and churches and public buildings like the Jakarta Stock Exchange. Armed Islamic groups were sent to defend local Muslims in various ethnic and political conflicts, in Ambon and Poso in Eastern Indonesia. Others attacked bars, nightclubs, and other places of 'sin'. Many such groups advocate an Islamic state and solidarity with radical Islamic movements. Links with international terrorist groups like *al-Qaeda* became apparent, culminating in the bomb attacks in Bali and Jakarta in 2002 and 2003 (ICG 2001; 2002). While reluctant to take a hard public line against Islamicist movements, the government has moved against those suspected of involvement in terrorism and this has provoked no violent mass demonstrations or sustained protest from within the ranks of most Muslim parties.

A remarkable fact is that that none of the main parties to emerge in the new democracy looked to regional secession, or the end of the secular state or radical social policies. Indeed, the new freedoms saw much the same players grabbing the political headlines as during the New Order. Nevertheless, democratization and decentralization have presented a fundamental threat to centralized state authority. For power is now constructed upon electoral victories, control of parliaments, and the formation of complex political alliances. With more players in the game, rents and power have to be distributed over a vast array of interests. In the process, it is more difficult to impose policy. One example is the uncontrolled free-for-all that has taken place in the forestry industry, as central government proves unable to prevent the unchecked plunder by powerful families and businesses, the military, local officials, and gangsters.

Decentralization has deepened this problem. Whereas the World Bank sees decentralization as potentially increasing the accountability and transparency of government, in Indonesia it has increased the numbers of people jostling to share the spoils of power. For example, investors now find a greater range of claims upon them, extending from regional and local taxes and royalties, tolls on trade across provincial boundaries, and demands for various extra-legal payments. This diffusion of central authority also extends into the political arena, where candidates for office must now assemble complex alliances that may include local notables, officials, military and police, business groups, as well as gangsters and criminals to support their bids for election (Hadiz 2003*a*). Nevertheless, these new political entrepreneurs do not challenge either the secular nature of the state or the retention of some core measure of central control. Ironically, their attempts to share out the spoils are effective only so long as there is enough central power to impose some measure of macro-economic stability and to concentrate core of revenues and budgetary expenditure.

## Key points

- Centralized state power has confronted but not been fundamentally challenged by regional separatism in Timor, Aceh, and Papua.

- The post-Soeharto years have seen the re-emergence of Islamic radicalism, ethnic and religious tension.

- The authority of the centralized state is being challenged by the decentralization of power and resources to regional and local governments, although the survival of central power is not yet in doubt.

# Conclusion

A substantial apparatus of central state authority remains deeply entrenched and resilient in Indonesia, not just because its vast military and state apparatus has survived but because it continues to be supported by extensive social and economic forces. The main threats to the Indonesian state are not, therefore, from regional secession movements or from Islamic challenges to the secular state. They come instead from the declining capacity of the central government itself to provide stable and effective rule and the rise of powerful local and regional politicians and officials and the informal groups surrounding them who are seizing more of the central authority for themselves. Central rule is, therefore, not threatened by disintegration and collapse so much as a progressive weakening and fragmentation of its authority, as more players enter the arena and its capacity to impose order declines.

## QUESTIONS

**1**  Why has the old Soeharto state not unravelled to a dramatic degree, and what forces and interests want the old system of centralized and secular state power to remain?

**2**  Is Indonesia really threatened by the secession of its regions?

**3**  With a population that is around 90 per cent Muslim, why is fundamentalist or radical Islam not a more major threat to centralized and secular state power in Indonesia?

**4**  Has decentralization opened the door to a more responsive, accountable, and democratic form of government or has it simply provided another arena for predatory interests and extra-democratic forces?

## GUIDE TO FURTHER READING

Bourchier, David, and Hadiz, Vedi R., *Indonesian Politics and Society: A Reader* (London: Routledge, 2003). An outstanding collection of primary sources on Indonesian political history.

Crouch, Harold, *The Army and Politics in Indonesia* (Ithaca, NY: Cornell University Press, 1978). A standard work by one of the closest observers of Indonesian politics.

Feith, H., *The Decline of Constitutional Democracy in Indonesia* (Ithaca, NY: Cornell University Press, 1962). A standard work on the earlier period.

Ramage, Douglas E., *Politics in Indonesia* (London: Routledge, 1995). A broad history of Islamic politics in Indonesia.

Robison, Richard, 'What Sort of Democracy', in Catarina Kinnvall and Kristina Jonsson (eds.), *Globalization and Democratization in Asia* (London and New York: Routledge, 2002), 92–113.

—— and Hadiz, Vedi R., *Reorganising Power in Indonesia: The Politics of Oligarchy in an Age of Markets* (London: Routledge, 2004). One of the most up-to-date studies of recent political developments.

Schwarz, Adam, *A Nation In Waiting: Indonesia's Search for Stability* (Sydney: Allen and Unwin, 1999). A highly readable volume that covers a vast swathe of Indonesia's economic and political history.

## WEB LINK

**www.crisisweb.org**   Site of the International Crisis Group, with pages on Indonesia as well as many other countries.

 **COMPANION WEB SITE**

For additional material and resources, see the companion web site at:
**www.oup.com/uk/booksites/politics/**

# Fragmentation or nation-building?

## South Africa

*Robert A. Schrire*

## OVERVIEW

If ever a country's history made it seem predestined to fail, South Africa would be such a country. From its creation in 1910 to the first democratic elections in 1994, South Africa was ruled by a white minority determined to maintain power and privileges irrespective of the costs to nation-building or other social groups. The interests of this minority were placed above those of over a dozen other ethnic and racial groups. Many discriminatory economic and political policies were implemented over several decades. In time the white regime began to meet the growing black challenge with increased ruthlessness, which frequently transcended even **apartheid** legality. Authoritarian white rule in turn created a powerful black response, increasing from the 1970s onwards. Few observers prior to 1990, then, believed in the possibility of relatively peaceful deracialization. Even fewer would have predicted that an ANC-controlled South Africa would be able to manage peacefully the massive historical cleavages, based upon class, ethnic, and racial interests. Yet with stunning speed, power was transferred from white to black hands. And far from collapsing, South Africa, a genuine democracy since 1994, has experienced uninterrupted economic growth and relative internal peace. This chapter explains this paradoxical outcome by exploring the historical legacy of apartheid, the nature of the armed struggle, the negotiation process, the complex question of identity, and the significant role of leadership in shaping nation-building in South Africa.

The author thanks his research assistant Paul Boughey for his valuable contribution and Anthony Butler for his useful comments.

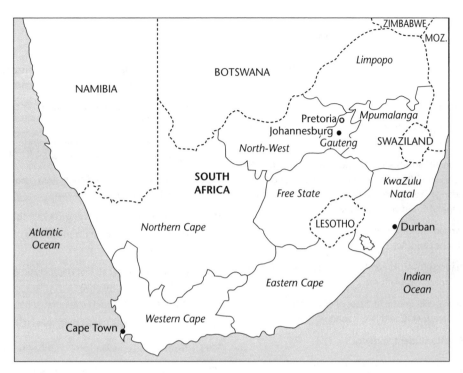

**SOUTH AFRICA**

# The historical legacy

The Union of South Africa, established in 1910, faced many problems, none more important than the issues of nationality and political rights. The Union constitution reflected a compromise between the different 'native' policies of the former colonies and in general represented a reduction in the limited black political rights exercised previously. English and Afrikaans-speaking whites competed fiercely for power up to the decisive victory of Afrikaner nationalism in 1948. The English, as a demographic minority, tended to advocate the politics of white unity while many Afrikaner leaders advocated the politics of exclusive Afrikaner nationalism. After 1948, the National Party (NP) representing Afrikaner nationalism was able to consolidate its political dominance, as white unity took precedence in response to growing pressures, from both the outside world and black South Africans, accelerating after the establishment of a republic in 1961. The key dilemma—never resolved—was to create a morally acceptable political framework, which did not endanger the Afrikaner's grasp of power. Meeting the political aspirations of the African majority was an intractable problem. The government's answer was the policy of grand apartheid, which constituted the African population as ten ethnic nations, each entitled to sovereign independence. Every African, irrespective of culture, birthplace, residence, or personal preferences, was assumed to be an immutable member of one of these ethnic communities. The ostensible aim of the policy was to create ten independent African nations, in which the Africans would have full citizenship rights. However, most of the homeland leaders, most notably KwaZulu's Mangosuthu Buthelezi, rejected the proposals, in part because of their normative vision of an undivided South Africa under democratic control, although some traditional leaders did accept the separatist paradigm, leading to the creation of four independent homelands.

## Box 16b.1  Key dates in South Africa's history

**1652** Dutch settlement under Jan van Riebeck at the Cape

**1795** First British occupation at the Cape

**1836** Beginning of the Great Trek by Afrikaners into the interior

**1910** Union of South Africa founded with merging of conquered Boer Republics of Transvaal and Orange Free State and the British Colonies of the Cape of Good Hope and Natal

**1912** African National Congress founded to resist Native Land Act

**1948** Nationalist-Afrikaner Party coalition wins election on apartheid platform

**1960** Sharpeville massacre. State of emergency declared. ANC and PAC banned

**1976** Soweto student uprisings

**1982** Period of tentative informal negotiations between the Apartheid government and ANC leaders, first in exile and then in prison begins

**1984** Mass black township uprisings begin. Government declares state of emergency

**1989** F. W. De Klerk becomes leaders of National Party

**1990** (February 2) Nelson Mandela released from prison

**1990** ANC and NP leaders meet to sign historic Groote Schuur Accord charting the way to negotiations

**1991** Congress for a Democratic South Africa (CODESA) begins

**1992** De Klerk wins a whites only referendum to approve negotiations with the ANC

**1992** (May) CODESA 2 convenes, then breaks down over deadlock in negotiations

**1993** (March) A new negotiating council convenes

(November) National Council adopts Interim Constitution.

**1994** (April) South Africa's first democratic election, ANC wins large majority

(May) Nelson Mandela inaugurated President

Government of National Unity takes (GNU) office

**1995** Truth and Reconciliation Commission formed

**1996** (May) Constitutional Assembly adopts final SA Constitution

**1997** National Party under F. W. de Klerk withdraws from GNU

**1999** South Africa's second democratic election. ANC again wins a large majority

**2004** ANC wins a two thirds majority in the third democratic election

## The struggle

The African National Congress (ANC) was founded in 1912 to oppose the land acts, which were designed to ensure that most of South Africa's land resources remained permanently in white hands. Until the 1950s it was marginal to the great dramas taking place in white politics. Its strategy of seeking allies in the white, coloured, and Indian communities and especially from the ranks of the South African Communist Party (SACP) had mixed results, and caused the government to view it increasingly as an enemy of the state; repression escalated, polarizing national politics even further. The Pan Africanist Congress (PAC) split from the ANC in 1958 and fierce competition for African support ensued, including mass protests, the burning of passes that restricted movement, and attempts to force the police to engage in mass arrests, culminating in 1960 in the Sharpeville 'massacre'. Both the ANC and PAC were banned (the SACP had already been proscribed) and went underground and began to plan an armed insurrection. Nelson Mandela was chosen by the ANC to organize an armed struggle. That said, the commitment to violence was taken only with great reluctance by a largely Christian leadership, and by the early 1960s the insurrection was smashed, and Mandela and other leaders either imprisoned or in exile. Peace returned to South Africa for another decade but the illusion was shattered in 1976 by another massacre, at Soweto, sparked in part by educational grievances. Violence and protests spread rapidly throughout the country forcing the government to declare yet another state of emergency, which this time proved to be less effective.

In 1983 new constitutional proposals by the government unexpectedly brought massively increased politicization and anger, leading the National Party to embark on modest reform initiatives for urban Africans, coloureds, and Indians. Widely resented by the black population, the proposals nevertheless opened up political space for public debate and greater participation. The United Democratic Front (UDF), formed in August 1983 to oppose the government's constitutional proposals, was a highly significant development for several reasons. It brought together a wide range of civil society groups into the political arena, supported by the ANC in exile. Its membership and leadership were drawn from all segments of the population: white, African, coloureds, and Indian, rural and urban, middle class and poor. The UDF was an important and successful experiment in non-racial political cooperation. The new tricameral system failed to gain legitimacy despite gaining the support of a whites-only referendum.

## Key points

- With the establishment of the Union of South Africa, Africans were formally excluded from access to political institutions, and Afrikaner nationalism became the dominant political force.

- The normative ideal of a democratic and non-racial South Africa remained overwhelmingly powerful to the majority of Africans.

- Armed struggle increasingly seemed inevitable, as African's political aspirations were continuously thwarted by apartheid and the creation of the homeland system.

- The clear rejection of African interests by the NP government brought about a new and significant degree of cooperation between moderate and conservative African leaders.

- The NP government increasingly had to react to protests through the use of state-sponsored violence, indicative in the handling of the 1976 student uprisings.

- Growing resentment and politicization throughout the 1980s, encapsulated by the creation of UDF, created the possibility of future non-racial cooperation.

# Negotiations

The factors favouring a negotiated outcome included national economic decline, white divisions, sanctions, and other global pressures, which had seriously dented growth and prosperity, increasing both unemployment and the tax burden especially on the white community. Three additional factors are of pivotal importance in understanding the transition. First, the government failed to restore 'normality' to South African society after the unrest resumed in the early 1980s. The country was far from being ungovernable but there seemed no end in sight to the turmoil in black areas, the industrial unrest, and the implosion in black education: a genuine stalemate existed. Secondly, once the negotiations began, there were very strong forces at work, which would make a failure to reach an accommodation very costly because it

would destroy the leaderships in both parties. White politics would at best have seen a move to the ultra-reactionary right and at worst a military takeover. In the ANC, failure would have ensured that the moderate leadership of Mandela and Mbeki would have been discredited. The country would have been plunged into escalating violence—consequences 'too dreadful to contemplate' in the words of former Prime Minister Vorster.

Finally and perhaps paradoxically, the negotiations once initiated did not take the form of white vs. black. Although there were racially exclusive splinter groups, including the fragmented Afrikaner right, the key players—the ANC and the NP—fielded multiracial delegations. The ANC, in partnership with the UDF and SACP, had a significant and influential non-African component including communist leader Joe Slovo. Similarly the NP led a heterogeneous grouping, which included conservative coloureds and African tribal leaders. Although the core of the historical conflict was the issue of political power and the consequent struggle between Afrikaner and African nationalism, the negotiations themselves involved teams of multiracial delegates seeking to determine the broad principles, which would regulate a post-apartheid South Africa.

The Convention for a Democratic South Africa (CODESA)-initiated formal discussions began in 1991.The following year De Klerk won a whites-only referendum on the reform policy which he interpreted as a mandate for legitimizing the final proposals. The alienation of the conservative Zulu Inkatha Freedom Party (IFP) and its leader Buthelezi, who threatened violence and the boycott of elections, was not easily defused. Despite challenges and setbacks along the way, in 1994 broad agreement was reached around the principles embodied in an interim constitution. After ad hoc arrangements were in place to ensure that the ruling NP did not use the advantages of incumbency to advance its cause, including an independent electoral commission, elections were held. All major groups and interests, including the white right and Zulu traditionalists, took part in the election. The newly elected parliament, acting as a constituent assembly, drew up a final constitution based upon the principles agreed to in the interim constitution, and in 1996 the final constitution was ratified both by the legislature and the Constitutional Court. The country's second general election in 1999 was thus the first election held in terms of a constitution and the results followed closely those of 1994.

## Key points

- Although not yet ungovernable, entrenched structural weaknesses in the South African economy, growing internal unrest, the changed regional context, and the hardening of international attitudes towards South Africa by her traditional allies resulted in a genuine stalemate.

- Realization by the leadership on both sides that failure to reach a negotiated compromise would ensure that South Africa would face a devastatingly violent future.

- Negotiations culminated in the multi-party elections of 1994, that included participation by groups on the margin of the political spectrum, the white right, and Zulu traditionalists.

# The new order: from apartheid to the rainbow nation

The emergence of a non-racial and democratic South Africa constituted a dramatic reversal of centuries of history which few had imagined possible. Perhaps the real South African miracle was not the successful negotiations but the transformation of the political discourse away from race and ethnicity. Both the dominant ANC and the NP espoused a vision for South Africa that transcended their historical race/ethnic constituencies. Although the core of ANC support came from the African population, the party was greatly influenced by the minority of coloureds and Indians and a few notable whites. Yet it is still surprising how rapidly the ideal of a non-racial and non-ethnic society captured the reform process. The initial leanings of the NP and the largely Zulu-based Inkatha Freedom Party towards a society in which ascriptive group rights were to be constitutionally entrenched were soon thrust aside. The negotiations produced, in Mandela's words, a 'normal democracy'. And Africanist proponents of an African-only state exercised even less influence on the deliberations.

South Africa is constitutionally a non-racial democracy but it has based itself upon a very liberal notion of nationality. The so-called rainbow nation has been built upon a rejection of the model of a nation conceptualized as a people united around one identity, language, and set of national symbols. To give institutional content to this vision, new institutions had to be created profoundly different from those existing in the former centralized and monocultural state. The foundation of a stable order has thus been based upon recognition both of a common nationality and of important diversities. Indeed the motto under the National Coat of Arms is 'Diverse People Unite'. The national anthem is composed of a combination of the old Afrikaner (South African) national anthem and a traditional African unity anthem. To give expression to the demographic diversity, the country has been divided into nine provinces, which reflect the historical continuities of history and ethnicity, which although not genuinely federal, does create a power structure outside the centre. Each province is headed by a premier and may draw up its own constitution. The divisive issue of the allocation of resources between provinces has been taken out of the political arena with the creation of a technocratic Financial and Fiscal Commission, which makes decisions on the basis of fixed criteria such as population and poverty levels. The country has eleven official languages with English the language of record. Each province may determine which languages will be used officially. The national parliament has two chambers—the popularly elected National Assembly, constituted on the basis of strict proportional representation, and the ninety-member National Council of Provinces in which each province has ten members including ex officio the premiers of all the provinces or their representatives.

A critical problem has been the issue of dealing with the past. Would perpetrators of human rights abuses face legal retribution? Would victims receive reparations? The political solution devised was to pass the Promotion of National Unity and Reconciliation Act, which created the Truth and Reconciliation Commission (TRC) to deal with these issues.

However, its attempts to be even-handed managed to antagonize almost all key parties including the ANC and NP. In that sense it may have succeeded by creating a consensus in favour of ignoring many of its findings! One could argue that this has liberated the polity to focus on issues of contemporary public policies. The resolution of amnesty and other contentious issues made it possible to adopt the interim constitution which mandated a government of national unity (GNU) to include the majority party and all other parties which received at least 10 per cent of the vote. In 1994, the GNU under President Mandela worked quite harmoniously for two years until De Klerk led a divided NP out of the coalition. After the 1999 elections, in which the ANC effectively won a two-thirds majority, it kept its coalition partner the IFP in the cabinet and indeed offered its leader the deputy presidency—which was declined. For elections, the strict system of proportional representation with no threshold ensures that even minor interests that can mobilize some support can be represented in parliament. The official language policy and the various associated statutory bodies dilute the implications of the reality of English-language dominance.

## Key points

- The 'real miracle' of South African transition is transformation of the political discourse from one based on race and ethnicity to one founded on a common national identity based on important diversities.

- An institutional framework was created to reflect the principle of inclusiveness, by creating a quasi-federal system, proportional representation, formal and informal power-sharing, all designed to ensure significant space and legitimacy for cultural and political minorities.

# Political transformation and nation-building

Had South Africa disintegrated into ethnic and racial conflicts, analysts would have had many explanations: the legacy of white domination, traditional ethnic animosities, high levels of inequality, and

many others. So, why has South Africa thus far confounded so many of the critics? In multi-ethnic societies, several types of conflicts may threaten to destroy the state. The most serious by far is directly related to the central issue of nation-building: whose country is it? What symbols and values should dominate? Indeed, who is a citizen of the state? Today the issue seems to have been decisively resolved in favour of a broad South Africanism. The two threats from Zulu and Afrikaner nationalists have been decisively defeated. There is no 'clash of civilizations' in South Africa; most of the population is predominantly Christian and Western-oriented in core value systems. Politics, then, revolves largely around issues of who gets what, when, and how. The issue of citizenship is illustrative. South Africa has been an independent state for almost a century, and even before Union in 1910 many of the provinces had lengthy experiences of centralized administration, producing a large measure of acceptance of an identity that transcended in part traditional ethnicities. The vast majority of Africans and coloureds became converts to Christianity. The emergence of a capitalist economy too created powerful integrating forces. All who resided legally in the country were accepted as South Africans—at least until the social engineering of the 1960s.

Then the NP policy of apartheid and ethnic mobilization created a powerful reaction in black politics against race and ethnicity and helped legitimize the demand for a non-ethnic and non-racial South Africa. The manipulation of ethnicity by whites produced exactly the outcome it was designed to prevent—an African population committed to the ideals of one nation. White racism did not create black racism and the only major black party with a race-based policy, the PAC, has been all but eliminated as both an electoral and political force. The racial/ethnic composition of the ANC leadership reflects its normative commitment to a united South Africa, and the vital importance of utilizing the skills of all sectors of the population in grappling with often intractable problems. Thus following the 1994 elections, the ANC's parliamentary delegation included 170 Africans, 40 whites, 23 Indians, and 19 coloureds. After the 1999 elections, the composition was 193 Africans, 31 whites, 27 coloureds, and 15 Indians. Racial minorities are strongly represented in executive positions in the party, parliament, and the government.

A second set of factors contributing to national unity and a decline in the politics of ethnic mobilization is the political arithmetic of race and ethnicity. If the salient divisions are seen to be African, white, coloured, and Indian, then the dominance of the African population (nearly 77 per cent) makes it unnecessary for an African-oriented party to emphasize race for political ends. Similarly parties with traditional support bases in the white, coloured, and Indian communities have a strong incentive to try to attract African support if they wish to play a major role in national politics. If, however, language and ethnicity are seen as constituting the prime elements of political identity, as the old NP used proudly to proclaim when it described South Africa as a nation of minorities, then the political arithmetic also contributes to nation-building. No political party with national aspirations can build a powerful constituency by mobilizing ethnicity, as the statistics in Table 16b.1 confirm.

The dynamics of the political economy reinforce the demographic implications. The core of South Africa's industrial wealth lies in the Gauteng Province, which includes Johannesburg, the largest city, and Pretoria, the executive capital. This area has the largest concentration of wealth and second largest population, and is the most ethnically mixed. The rise of large urban centres from the late nineteenth century weakened the ethnic allegiances of the new urban migrants and for the first time created a significant non-ethnic community. The economic heart of the country is thus national and has played an important role in integrating the country, not least through channelling revenues to the other provinces,

Table 16b.1 South African linguistic groups, 1996

| | Number (m.) | % |
|---|---|---|
| Zulu | 9.2 | 22.9 |
| Xhosa | 7.2 | 17.9 |
| Afrikaans[a] | 5.8 | 14.4 |
| Sepedi | 3.7 | 9.2 |
| English | 3.5 | 8.6 |
| Sesotho | 3.1 | 7.7 |
| Tsonga | 1.8 | 4.4 |
| Swazi | 1 | 2.5 |
| Venda | 0.88 | 2.2 |
| Ndebele | 0.58 | 1.5 |

[a] The most important components are 2.9 m coloured people and 2.6 m whites.

especially the impoverished rural homelands. The Western Cape, the second wealthiest region, similarly has no dominant ethnic community, with large populations of whites, coloureds, and Xhosas.

## Race and inequality

Although the most important aspect of nation-building is the presence or absence of competing nationalisms in a single territory, the relationship between ascriptive groups is also significant. Historically, race and class coincided to a significant degree and, of course, this was no accident but reflected deliberate colonial and white policies over many centuries. The claim that South Africa was divided into two nations—a poor black and an affluent white nation—rang true up to the end of the 1980s. However, this historical relationship is now being undermined through public policy especially, as ANC leaders recognized the urgent need to move away from a racialized economy. Labour legislation, increased social expenditures, the deracialization of educational institutions, affirmative action especially in the public sector, and black empowerment policies have all contributed. As a consequence there are now three nations: a wealthy white, a wealthy black, and an impoverished black nation. Although the poor constitute about half of the total, what is politically important is that the size of the wealthy black and white groups are about equal and trends confirm that black wealth will in time overtake white wealth. Race and class are becoming delinked.

However, the critical problem of a large black underclass remains, which the upward mobility of privileged blacks does not resolve. Indeed inequality within the black community, including African, has increased dramatically. For example, whereas in 1975 the top 20 per cent of African households income was eight times higher than the bottom 40 per cent, this had increased to thirty-one times higher in 1996 and

today may be forty times as great. Meanwhile vast inequalities between whites and Africans continue to exist: in 1995 whites earned more than seven times African incomes and five times coloured incomes, a reality which is unlikely to have changed significantly. A major cause of inequality is unemployment: at the beginning of 2003, 37 per cent of Africans, 22 per cent of coloureds, and only 7 per cent of whites were officially unemployed.

These inequalities produce two sets of political problems. Policy measures such as affirmative action and black empowerment risk alienating whites and provoking emigration and the export of capital. Given the inevitably slow rate of change, black frustration could express itself in mass protests, violence, and the growth of support for populist and radical parties and movements.

## Key points

- The history of the South African state, the political arithmetic of race and ethnicity, and the structure of SA's political economy, all help explain why there is neither a public demand for separate nationalities nor a set of elite-driven political strategies based upon ethnic/race mobilization.

- Historically, race and class have coincided in South Africa, dividing it into two nations. The emergence today of a rapidly expanding black middle class undermines this conception and is delinking race and inequality.

- Strategies to address historical inequalities have the potential to frustrate both blacks and whites and could ultimately threaten nation-building and political stability.

- A powerful ANC is a force for reconciliation and nationhood yet this very power constitutes a potential threat to a genuine democratic order should its power be threatened.

# Leadership, national identities, and the future

South Africa has developed a remarkable tradition since 1989 of resolving apparently intractable problems through often tough negotiations. Part of the explanation lies in a mix of both history and personalities, which produced such remarkable leaders as Mandela, Oliver Tambo, and De Klerk.

Mandela took office with the recognition that his advanced years made a one-term presidency probable. He made as his central mission the reconciliation between the former oppressors and the newly liberated. His larger-than-life personality and his message of one nation with many cultures gave the new democracy an encouraging beginning.

Mandela's successor, Thabo Mbeki, has faced a more difficult task. If symbolism could inspire the first democratic government, the second administration had to deliver. Mbeki himself and the ANC in general remain wedded to the Mandela paradigm of the 'rainbow nation' and Mbeki has repeatedly maintained that all who live in South Africa have a claim to being Africans. The ruling party remains wedded to the ideal of inclusivity. Personalities alone cannot explain the quality of leadership. Mandela and Mbeki came into power at a very favourable historical juncture. The implosion of Marxism and the failures of grand apartheid heralded the final discrediting of social engineering and macro planning. The lesson from elsewhere in post-colonial Africa was that ambitious state-led projects to create nations by destroying indigenous customs and traditions were doomed to failure. Key ANC leaders spent many years in exile and personally witnessed such failures.

In addition, the magnitude of the challenges of poverty, inequality, and HIV/AIDS was almost overwhelming. In a world of financial globalization and Western dominance, the new rules of the economic game are dominated by the imperative to encourage multinational corporations to invest in South Africa. South Africa's elites recognized very quickly that the absence of rapid economic development would doom the country to poverty and social unrest. Government leaders have thus frequently been forced to repress their own personal prejudices and racial/ethnic attitudes in order not to alienate important domestic and foreign economic players.

On almost every major issue with cultural implications, the government has compromised rather than asserted its authority, in areas from minority rights of Afrikaners to traditional authorities and ethnic symbols. Of course an ANC that is not threatened from the left or from Africanist forces can afford to be magnanimous. It has had the political space to adopt nation-building policies. It is impossible to predict how it would react to a genuine threat to its power base.

It is not inevitable that the South African miracle will continue. But the historical factors discussed above have created a common web of identities in which a transcendent South African identity is prominent. Survey research conducted by the Afrobarometer confirms this conclusion (Mattes 2002). Most South Africans have multiple identities, which do not threaten the fabric of society. When asked in 2000 which primary categories in addition to South African a representative sample identified with, the results were as follows: race 22 per cent; language 20 per cent; religion 16 per cent; class 14 per cent; partisan 1 per cent; continental 9 per cent; regional 0 per cent; nothing 3 per cent. All these identities coexist with national loyalties. When asked if they were proud to be called South Africans, the results in the affirmative were as follows: Asian 84 per cent; African 94; white 75 per cent.

## Key points

- Individual leadership has played a significant role in shaping the conception of a non-racial and democratic South Africa.

- The process of nation-building is ongoing.

# Conclusion

In contemporary South Africa no important political party is asking the critically destructive question 'whose country is this?' The struggle cry 'one settler one bullet' has disappeared from the debate. Historically the two major threats to nation-building have come from the Afrikaner right and Zulu traditionalists. The former has almost totally disintegrated despite occasional posturing by a few. Zulu alienation could yet pose a problem.

Class and nationality conflicts are not the same. There is clearly a possibility of a black populist party emerging from the poorest sections of the population. But although it might contain anti-white elements it would be unlikely to challenge the core identity of the South African nation. However, most observers believe that the future challenge to the ANC will come from the class-oriented trade union movement under the banner of the Congress of Trade Unions (COSATU) and the SACP.

South Africa's political leadership reflects the sophistication of the country's large 'first world' economic and administrative systems. A recognition of the mutual dependency of all ethnic and racial communities and its importance is perhaps the most powerful factor shaping elite policies and attitudes. South Africa continues to face major problems of race and class. Indeed almost all problems—from HIV to job creation—are exacerbated by high levels of inequality. The high levels of unemployment have also produced an explosion in crime, especially violent crimes such as armed robbery. This threatens all sectors of society, especially the poor. These unresolved issues could yet destroy growth prospects by discouraging investment. The lack of a strong parliamentary opposition poses a real danger to the quality of democracy and creates both the temptation and the opportunity for corruption and authoritarianism in the ruling party. However, these challenges should not be confused with the issue of nation-building. Whatever other problems South Africa faces, there is little debate over the definition of citizenship. The future debate will be over how this citizenship is to be given meaning.

## QUESTIONS

1   How important is the distinction between class and nationality conflicts with regards to nation-building in South Africa?

2   What key realities forced the ANC and the NP to begin the negotiation process?

3   What factors contributed to the decline of black vs. white conflict during the transition to a non-racial democracy in South Africa?

4   How important in relative terms were internal and external factors in contributing to the end of apartheid in South Africa?

5   What are the key features of nation-building in South Africa?

6   How does the nature of the democratic system in post-apartheid South Africa relate to the principles of nation-building?

7   What are the implications of class and race coinciding in South Africa for the future of nation-building?

8   Name the key factors that have ensured that ethnic identity has not been the primary tool for mobilizing popular support in post-apartheid South Africa.

**9** Discuss how South Africa's handling of the vexed question of national identity has implications for other entrenched conflicts such as those in the Middle East.

## GUIDE TO FURTHER READING

*African Nation Congress 49th Annual Conference 1994*, 'From Resistance to Reconstruction and Nation-Building'—Secretary General's Report (Bloemfontein, 1994).

Baines, G., 'The Rainbow Nation?: Multiculturalism and Nation-Building in Post-Apartheid South Africa, Paper presented at a Conference entitled *Multicultural citizenship in the new South Africa*, IDASA, Cape Town, 1997.

Butler, A., *Contemporary South African Politics* (Basingstoke: Palgrave, 2004). An introduction to emerging patterns of economic, social, and political life in South Africa with reference also to its place in the regional and wider environment.

Giliomee, H., and Schlemmer, L., *From Apartheid to Nation Building* (Cape Town: Oxford University Press, 1989). Analysis of the roots of apartheid and of the possibilities for conflict-resolution in South Africa as seen from the vantage of the late 1980s, before the system reached the point of collapse.

Ishikawa, K., *Nation building and Development Assistance in Africa: Different but Equal?* (New York: St Martins Press, 1999).

Lodge, T., *Politics in South Africa; From Mandela to Mbeki* (Cape Town: David Philip, 2002 and Bloomington, Ind.: Indiana University Press, 2003). Contains thirteen detailed essays on contemporary politics starting with Mandela presidency.

Simkins, C., *The Prisoners of Tradition and the Politics of Nation Building* (Johannesburg: South African Institute of Race Relations, 1988).

Southall, R. (ed.), *Opposition and Democracy in South Africa* (London: Frank Cass, 2001). A substantial collection on the political parties and party system—past, present, and future prospects.

Terreblanche, S., *A History of Inequality in South Africa 1652–2002* (Pietermartizburg: University of Natal Press, 2004). Historical examination of the economic exploitation of the indigenous peoples by settler groups. Argues that society in South Africa is more unequal now than ever, with social democracy offering a more appropriate solution than 'neo-liberal democratic capitalism'.

## WEB LINKS

**www.nedlac.org.za**   The National Economic Development and Labour Council—'South Africa's primary institute for social dialogue'.

**www.idasa.org.za**   The Institute for Democracy in South Africa (Cape Town), an independent, non-profit, public interest organization.

**www.mg.co.za**   The *Mail* and *Guardian* online.

**www.gov.za**   The official website of the South African government.

**www.anc.org.za**   The website of the African National Congress.

**www.hsrc.org.za**   The site of the Human Sciences Research Council, Pretoria.

 ## COMPANION WEB SITE

For additional material and resources, see the companion web site at:
**www.oup.com/uk/booksites/politics/**

# 17a

# Civil society: active or passive?

## India

*Rob Jenkins*

## OVERVIEW

This chapter examines civil society in the 'world's largest democracy'. Unlike most developing countries, India has maintained a democratic political system since emerging from colonial rule—a feat often attributed to the vibrancy of its civil society. After outlining some of the salient features of India's recent political history, this chapter examines: (1) controversies surrounding the size and composition of India's civil society; (2) issues relating to regional variations in the nature of associational life; (3) the question of whether states can help to spur the development of civil society; and (4) problems in understanding the contribution of civil society to improved governance, including consideration of civil society's darker side.

**INDIA**

# Introduction

The Indian National Congress, the premier organization in the struggle for independence from British rule, was formed in 1885 by a group of English-educated lawyers and professionals. It was not until the 1920s, under the leadership of Mohandas K. Gandhi, that 'Congress' became a mass movement capable of pressing the colonial authorities for greater self-rule. This was also the period when, largely through Congress-related efforts, India's **civil society** began to flourish. The process was aided by the mobilizing efforts associated with the pre-independence elections to legislative councils. India's constitution of 1950 outlined the functions of its political institutions, including the division of powers between the

## Box 17a.1 **Key dates in the history of independent India**

**1947** 'Partition' of colonial India creates two independent states, India and Pakistan; more than a million people killed in accompanying Hindu–Muslim riots; Jawaharlal Nehru (of the Indian National Congress) becomes first Prime Minister

**1950** Constitution ratified, confirming India as federal, democratic, secular, and committed to social justice

**1967** Fourth General Election: under Prime Minister Indira Gandhi Congress loses power in several states

**1975–9** Mrs Gandhi's national 'Emergency' (1975–7); widespread protest action leads to electoral defeat for Mrs Gandhi (1977) and India's first non-Congress central government (1977–9)

**1984** Mrs Gandhi assassinated by Sikh bodyguards; her son, Rajiv, becomes Prime Minister

**1991** Rajiv Gandhi assassinated by Sri Lankan Tamil separatists; new Congress government of P.V. Narasimha Rao initiates economic liberalization programme

**1992** Destruction of Babri Mosque by Hindu nationalist militants

**1998** BJP assumes national power (in coalition); following year, BJP receives fresh electoral mandate (also in coalition)

**2002–3** After a train carrying Hindus is burnt, thousands of Muslims are killed in Gujarat, with suspected state complicity

**2004** Voters replace BJP-led coalition government with coalition headed by Congress

central and provincial tiers of its federal system. The constitution contained the usual liberal protections that make civil society possible (freedom of speech, of assembly, and so forth). But India's civil society was also shaped by other legal provisions, such as the 'reservation' of roughly one-fifth of parliamentary constituencies for members of the so-called Scheduled Castes and Scheduled Tribes. Within the **Hindu caste system**, a complex and ancient though evolving system of social stratification in which people's caste status is determined at birth, Scheduled Castes (now often referred to as Dalits) were marginalized and regarded as almost subhuman 'untouchables'. The mainly forest-dwelling Scheduled Tribes were similarly regarded as beyond the pale of civilized life.

Congress dominated the first twenty years of post-Independence politics. Its stranglehold over state-level (i.e. provincial) power was broken only at the 1967 general elections. Another decade elapsed before Congress first lost power at the national level in the 1977 general elections. By the late 1980s, not only was unchallenged Congress dominance a thing of the past; so was control over electoral politics by the richer, more powerful and better-educated groups in the Hindu social order—the so-called upper castes. Increasingly, parties appealed to members of the

lower castes, particularly those just above the Scheduled Castes in the hierarchy, often recruiting a greater number of candidates from these communities. Parties constructed around lower-caste identity also emerged. From the late 1980s, regional parties—those confined mainly to a single state—began increasing their share of the vote.

To these trends, the 1990s added two others of great significance. The first was the ascendancy of the Hindu nationalist Bharatiya Janata Party (BJP). The BJP's primary pledges were to tear down the Babri Mosque in the north Indian town of Ayodhya (accomplished by BJP-affiliated militants in 1992), and to abolish legal provisions that permitted religious minorities to follow different sets of social practices concerning marriage, divorce, and other matters. The BJP began the 1990s as a pariah party with which almost no other mainstream grouping would ally; by 1998 it was leading the national coalition government. The BJP was aided by the 'regionalization' of party politics, through which single-state parties emerged as significant electoral players. In several states, regional parties proved more than willing to ally with the BJP in order to defeat their long-time local rival—the Congress. The BJP—which polling data have consistently shown as more popular among richer and higher-caste voters—also benefited from a backlash against the political assertiveness of traditionally subordinated groups among the lower castes.

The second key trend of the 1990s was the shift from a state-dominated economic policy framework to one giving greater scope to market signals. The programme of economic liberalization undertaken by a Congress government in 1991, but continued by successive governments from the left and the right, has unfolded much more gradually than similar reforms in other developing countries. But while much controversy remains concerning the impact of India's reforms, particularly on the poor, by the twenty-first century India's role in the world economy (and in international economic diplomacy) had clearly increased.

## Key points

- India's civil society first emerged with nationalist and electoral mobilization by Congress.
- Congress dominance was increasingly challenged from the late 1960s.
- The BJP's rise during the 1990s coincided with the regionalization of party politics.
- Since 1991 there has been significant economic liberalization.

# Size and composition of India's civil society

Whatever its shortcomings, India's democratic system is known, even to those without detailed knowledge of the country, as a site of lively political contestation, with all manner of civic groups endlessly aligning and realigning with one another on every conceivable issue—from how to reform affirmative action provisions in government employment, to the appropriate nuclear doctrine for a country in India's geostrategic position. Even during periods when India's democratic institutions were undergoing decay, observers (within and outside India) have always had great faith in the ability of India's vast and varied civil society to take up some of the slack (Kothari 1984).

It will therefore surprise many people to learn that considerable controversy has recently surfaced over whether India's civil society is so impressively diverse and prolific after all. In *Democracy Without Associations*, Chhibber (1999) turned conventional wisdom on its head, arguing that India's civil society was characterized by relatively small size and thin substance. The dearth of civic associations, Chhibber maintained, caused India's political parties to mobilize people on the basis of caste, sect, ethnicity, or linguistic group. In a vicious circle, the politicization of these 'ascriptive identities'—groupings to which people belong by birth, rather than by

choice—further shrank the space available for non-partisan civil society.

## The role of ascriptive identity

The claim that India's associational life was weak drew intense criticism. Particularly targeted was Chhibber's apparent insistence that 'informal' associations—those in which there are no office-bearers or codified rules—did not qualify for inclusion within a narrow definition of civil society. There is a long-standing argument over whether ethnicity-based organizations—such as **caste associations**, religious brotherhoods, and groups that seek to politicize linguistic identity—should be considered part of Indian civil society. But Chhibber's critics felt he had gone too far in the restrictive direction. One otherwise positive reviewer asked: 'is focusing on formal associations a reasonable indicator of the presence of solidarities between the family and the state' (Sethi 1999: 94)? In another review, the co-author of a key 1960s text that challenged the assumption that organizations had to be either modern or traditional (Rudolph and Rudolph 1967), argued that Chhibber was defining civil society too narrowly: 'Caste associations are anomalous; they are intentional associations, hybrids that combine voluntary with ascriptive characteristics' (Rudolph 2003).

These associations exemplify 'the modernity of tradition': in order to advance the interests of traditional caste groups, they sought access to modern means of social mobility and political influence. Caste associations, such as those representing various segments of the Jat community in north India, have done this by establishing scholarship programmes and student hostels, promoting internal reforms of the community's social practices (particularly around gender relations) and demanding representation in government service. Jat and other caste associations sometimes endorse candidates or parties at election time. But even when they do not, they are engaged in modern politics. In fact, contesting elections can alter the structure and meaning of caste itself—modernizing it, one could say. For instance, the geographical and social boundaries of a caste often broaden considerably as associations seek to increase their numbers, the currency of electoral democracy. Divisions among the various sections of what came to be known as the Maratha 'caste cluster' in western India are papered over in the name of constructing a more encompassing political identity for the group (Lele 1990).

Rudolph's main point, however, concerned the broader characterization of India's civil society: '[i]f caste associations, demand groups, issue and movement politics, and nongovernment organisations are taken into account, India could be "read" as having a pervasive and extraordinarily active associational life, perhaps one of the most participatory in the world' (Rudolph 2003). Even if Chhibber's critics are largely right on the question of civil society's vibrancy—their case looks extremely strong on certain methodological points—Chhibber has still provided a valuable service by directing attention towards places where civil society's size or importance has been overstated, or where it is looking frayed around the edges. For foreigners who come into contact with elements of India's civil society it sometimes seems bigger than it actually is; there is a tendency to be impressed by the absolute numbers of associations involved, and the amount of noise they generate in English-language media, and to forget how unimpressive these numbers are given India's huge population. This is true of the trade union sector, for instance. Organized labour only exists in the outermost layer of Indian economic

activity. Three per cent is a common figure cited as the proportion of the population that belongs to a union. And yet, even here caution is warranted. Many labour organizations are unregistered, and though this means they are less capable of obtaining full legal recognition, it also means that there may be more associational activity taking place in various hidden parts of India's vast hinterland than the statistics indicate.

As for civil society's frayed edges, Varshney (2004), among others, observes that, whatever its merits, India's civil society may be living on borrowed time. Many associations exist in theory, but are shells of their former selves, lacking organizational substance. In some regions, the better part of local civil society consists of associations founded during the movement for independence. This is an institutional inheritance from an earlier era of organization-building. It consists of many functional organizations affiliated with the Congress movement—women's leagues, student federations, and so forth, not to mention cooperatives of various sorts, many of which are so highly compromised by government interference that they appear, in fact, to constitute good examples of the weak civil society perceived by Chhibber.

## Regional variations in civil society

In addition, both the strength and effectiveness of civil society vary from state to state. The southern state of Kerala, for instance, is a land of civic bounty: there one can find reading clubs, cinema clubs, drama clubs, alongside the more familiar actors such as trade unions (Kerala's strong Marxist political tradition has ensured this), business associations, and so forth. In the eastern state of Orissa, on the other hand, civil society is extremely weak, and in some areas non-existent.

The memberships (and conceptual horizons) of most associations do not, generally, extend beyond state borders. Katzenstein et al. (2001: 245) argue that 'issue-based Indian social movements have remained substantially limited to the regions within which they operate . . . even when the issues and interests they represent are national in their relevance'. There are good reasons for even functional associations (let alone 'movement' groups) to confine their work within the boundaries of their 'home' state. First, the sheer size of most states—in population terms alone—is usually sufficient to occupy the efforts of civic groups that deal intensively with public authorities. Second, in India's federal system states form a powerful tier of government. State governments make many important policy decisions, particularly in the era of economic liberalization. Third, most Indian parties are geared to the state level: they would prefer control over a state government to even the most senior cabinet positions in New Delhi, short of the prime ministership. Fourth, since India's federal system is organized along linguistic lines, there are natural barriers to the spread of many associational forms. Kerala's literature societies, for instance, find it hard to break out of their provincial boundaries. Associated cultural differences between states (not least the existence of distinct regional caste systems) further reinforce the federally segmented nature of associational life. Despite all these constraints, civil society's largely state-specific nature is undergoing profound change: the proliferation of national and international media (including the internet) has brought 'national organizing' within the grasp of an increasing number of associations.

The difficulty of pinning down the implications of these trends for the development of civil society is exemplified by the ambiguous impact of the so-called 'regionalization' of Indian politics alluded to earlier. Because political contestation is increasingly between single-state parties, one might expect a corresponding regionalization of civil society. There is some evidence of this: state-level units of national trade union federations are increasingly going their own way—or at least acting more autonomously (vis-à-vis their national leaderships) than in the past. However, over

the past decade, these same regional parties have joined with national parties of the left and the right to form coalition governments in New Delhi. This has made regional parties key actors on the national political stage. Again, it would not be surprising to find civil society mirroring this crucial political trend, with national-level ministers from, say, Andhra Pradesh's Telugu Desam Party providing a much needed point of access to central government agencies for Andhra Pradesh-based civic groups. There is some anecdotal evidence to support this claim, but it requires systematic empirical study. If true, such a trend would represent a major shift from past practice. The state-wise organization of India's civil society has often impeded the emergence of effective national lobbies on controversial policy matters—notably agriculture. In the 1980s, an alliance was formed among farmers' organizations from Karnataka, Maharashtra, and Uttar Pradesh; it collapsed when each group became focused on events in its respective home state.

## Key points

- The reputed vibrancy of India's civil society has recently been questioned.

- One issue is whether associations based on ascriptive identity should count as part of civil society.

- Many of the civil society organizations formed during the independence movement are moribund.

- India's federal system means that the nature and effectiveness of civil society varies between states, which also tends to impede activism across state boundaries.

# State fostering of civil society

While state-wise variations in the texture of civil society clearly exist, the *reasons* for these differences are much debated. For instance, while some attribute Kerala's diversified civil society to its high literacy rate, the nature of the Keralan state's interaction with

civil society can also be seen to breed further civic associationalism. The People's Plan Campaign (PPC), a radical programme of democratic decentralization, was established by the state's Left Democratic Front coalition in the mid-1990s. The newly introduced system of political representation (and development planning) did not just create more state bureaucracy; it also catalysed a huge flowering of civil society. Whether entities such as 'user committees', 'women's groups', and 'neighbourhood groups'—voluntary associations that under the People's Plan *had* to be formed in order to obtain certain state benefits—qualify as bona fide manifestations of civil society is almost as long-standing a debate as the question of how to classify ethnic associations. Clearly, many such associations do spring up merely to obtain a specific benefit, and have no substantive influence over state functioning. Indeed, many get 'captured' by syndicates of 'contractors', the politically connected people—sometimes politicians themselves—who obtain contracts for development works. But there are indications that at least some of Kerala's 'state-fostered' associations have gone on to seek improvements in systems and procedures of governance (Isaac 2000).

Readers might be surprised that it is considered legitimate in India for state policy to be explicitly geared towards creating civil society groups; the two sides of the state-civic divide are usually conceived of as autonomous and separate. But two factors—one related to India, the other more general—make this less unusual. First, as we have seen, India's nationalist movement was a hothouse of association-forming activism. This introduced into India's liberal political culture the idea that civil society need not spring up organically. The 'fostering' of civil society, whether by parties or the state (and the Congress, as a bridging institution, straddled the two), became an accepted route through which new associational forms could emerge. The second relevant factor is the influence of aid agencies, which as a result of their work in developing countries where the public sphere is less fertile than in India, are accustomed to funding programmes that, by design, try to create civil society organizations that could improve accountability (Jenkins 2001).

## Key points

- One reason for variation between states is the role of state governments in fostering civil society.
- Opinions differ on whether state-fostered associations should qualify for inclusion within civil society.

# Civil society and the promotion of better governance

Despite these hopes, the Indian case demonstrates that the role of civil society in promoting better governance is ambiguous at best. This can be illustrated with examples of civil society groups that have sought to combat corruption and tried to prevent communal violence.

Chandhoke (2003: 184) argues that 'legal and bureaucratic languages . . . even as they penetrate civil society, are embedded in the power of the state'. The language, and indeed practice, of legal-bureaucratic rationality has become a much more prominent focal point for the actions of certain civil-society actors in India. It has long been the operating idiom of the professionalized sector of civil society—for instance non-governmental organizations (NGOs), the policy advocates working in obscure areas of technical competence—but only during the past decade has the 'mass movement' sector of civil society fully embraced the language *and* practices of legal-bureaucratic rationality.

The rise of public-interest litigation in India has arguably triggered an interest by social movements in adopting, almost mimicking, legal processes. This has taken the form of procedurally complex public hearings—of which the approach taken by Mazdoor Kisan Shakti Sangathan (MKSS), detailed below, is but one version. People's hearings are held where voluntary groups feel compelled to substitute for authorities that fail to provide information or consult with citizens, especially on controversial infrastructure projects deemed likely to have damaging environmental impacts, such as the Enron power project in Maharashtra. The logistics of collecting evidence, both for one-off civil society-led hearings as well as for the researching of *faux*-official 'status reports' on incidents of police violence, are formidable and represent a 'legalization' of social action. Instead of demanding an inquiry, these civic groups conduct inquiries themselves, and if sufficiently successful in conveying their evidence to a larger constituency, can be in a strong position to demand inclusion in state investigations.

Civil society activism geared towards combating corruption tends to produce organizational hybrids—not in the sense of sharing modern and traditional characteristics, but in so far as they expand beyond their conventional roles. Rather than merely mobilizing voters *during* elections, and pressing governments to live up to their campaign promises *between* elections—that is, providing vertical accountability—many civic associations have insinuated themselves into *horizontal* channels of accountability, which traditionally involve state agencies (auditors, ombudsmen, judiciaries) monitoring other branches of the state (executive ministries, parastatal organizations). By combining their conventional role within vertical channels of accountability with participation in horizontal channels of accountability (from which non-governmental actors were once completely excluded), some civic associations have undergone a process of hybridization (Goetz and Jenkins 2004).

Based in the state of Rajasthan, the Mazdoor Kisan Shakti Sangathan (MKSS), or Workers' and Farmers' Power Organization, embodies this trend. The MKSS immediately presents the question of categorization. Is it a movement, as its leaders claim? Ironically, this claim is both bolstered and undermined by the MKSS's participation in the National Alliance of People's Movements (NAPM)—a 'movement' group, as its name suggests, but also an increasingly organized force in mainstream, institutionalized Indian politics. Is the MKSS a union? The 'Worker' part refers to day-labourers on employment-creation schemes, so it qualifies in one sense, but does not engage in the kind of collective bargaining conventionally recognized as trade unionism. Is it a party? Not really, but it has run, sometimes successfully, a few candidates in village elections.

Regardless of how it is classified, the MKSS's great innovation has been to use financial information from government documents as the catalyst for a participatory auditing exercise. This involves ordinary villagers cross-checking information from official files against what has actually been constructed by public works programmes on the ground. Part of the process is questioning workers on employment schemes to see how much they were actually paid, a sum that is almost always less than what financial records showed officials to have claimed on their behalf from the state exchequer. By exposing these discrepancies, in public, and based on people's own energies and testimonies, some corrupt officials and local notables have been forced to apologize and return stolen funds—major if isolated victories. A minor deterrent effect has been felt in some localities close to where the MKSS is active (Jenkins and Goetz 1999).

But the odds against long-term impact are huge. This may be partly why the MKSS has branched out into at least two other areas of work. First, it has sought to make use of new rules requiring candidates to declare their financial assets and whether they have criminal records. During state-level elections in 2003, the MKSS and other civic groups publicized this information in a form accessible to voters (Khera 2004). Second, the MKSS has participated in public-interest litigation against government agencies that have failed to use public grain stocks to alleviate famine in various parts of India. This has involved monitoring activities in coordination with commissioners appointed by the Supreme Court to obtain evidence of government compliance and non-compliance. Such state–civil society partnerships are often criticized for neutralizing civil society. But in this case there appears to be a genuine difference in the *quality* of the partnership: the litigants, MKSS among them, are engaged as active demanders of accountability, driving the advancement of rights, rather than as subcontractors delivering public services.

The role of civil society in communal relations is another area where the lines between traditional and modern, and between state and civil society, are blurred. It is also an area in which we are reminded of the distinction between civil and uncivil forms of associationalism. On the one hand, civil society organizations and the state seem—in some instances—excessively intertwined. In 2002-3, the state of Gujarat suffered India's worst communal rioting since partition. Thousands of Muslims lost their lives, and tens of thousands lost their homes. A pivotal player in these events was the 'voluntary sector' organization, the Rashtriya Swayamsevak Sangh (RSS), or National Volunteers' Association, which is the ideological core of the Hindu nationalist movement, the then ruling BJP being its political expression. The RSS's presence within organs of the state administration—among elite civil servants, the police, paramilitary units—was a crucial influence on the grisly outcome.

On the other hand, one of the few mechanisms that appear to have been effective at combating communal violence is something very similar, in terms of breaching the state–civil society divide. Varshney (2004: 206) has argued that under certain circumstances, in order to prevent communal violence, 'Civil society organizations, for all practical purposes, become the ears and arms of the state'. While this may sound sinister, Varshney is in fact referring to a positive version of state–civil society partnership with a proven ability to tackle small, localized communal flare-ups before they erupt into widespread violence.

Varshney's study of civil society and communal violence in Kerala and Uttar Pradesh (UP) addresses the question of why UP suffered so much Hindu–Muslim violence, compared to Kerala, which during the early part of the twentieth century had been a communal tinderbox. The conventional wisdom has interpreted the statistical correlation between state-wide levels of illiteracy and the propensity towards communal rioting as implying a causal relationship. Fewer illiterates in Kerala, in other words, means fewer chances to manipulate communal passions. Varshney suggests that states are the *wrong unit of analysis* for this particular problem. Communal violence is a local (primarily urban) phenomenon, and when data on development and communal violence are aggregated at the city or town level (instead of at the state level), the correlation between social high literacy and communal peace disappears. What *does* correlate, inversely, with lower levels of communal violence is the degree of local civil society organizing that spans the Hindu–Muslim divide—that is, the existence of *inter*-communal associations that can act as an unofficial institution for defusing disputes and preventing escalation into full-scale rioting.

## Key points

- Evidence that civil society organizations improve governance is ambiguous.
- The MKSS's efforts to combat corruption provides a good illustration.
- Some civil society organizations foment communal violence but other cross-communal organizations may contain it.

# Conclusion

The complex nature of India's associational life has spurred debates about its size and composition, its regional variations, its relations with the state, and its capacity to improve governance. The difficulty of resolving these issues demonstrates both the protean nature of India's civil society in particular, and the ambiguity of concepts used to analyse civil society more generally. Indian civil society challenges conventional analytical categories separating modern and traditional identities, civil and uncivil expressions of the associational impulse, and vertical and horizontal forms of accountability. India's civil society tends to revise and reconstitute itself with remarkable frequency. Though the exact nature of the impact is unclear, it is hard to deny that this process is being affected by **globalization**. Many Indian civic organizations have received a boost from their connections abroad—largely through transnational social networks connecting members of the Indian diaspora. In some cases, such linkages illustrate other trends discussed in this chapter. For instance, the reportedly large role played by overseas

Indians in fund-raising for the Vishwa Hindu Parishad (or World Hindu Council), another RSS-linked group, suggests not only that India has not bucked the worldwide trend towards mobilizing so-called traditional identities through modern means, but also that its civic associations are unafraid of deploying *un*civil methods to obtain their objectives.

## QUESTIONS

1 What can India's civil society teach us about the relationship between 'traditional' and 'modern' forms of politics?

2 What measures could be used to assess the *health* of India's civil society?

3 Do all federal systems give rise to state-wise variations in the texture of civil society to the degree found in India?

4 Under what conditions might state–civil society partnership be likely to result in improved governance, and under what conditions might it make matters worse?

5 What might be some of the constraints on civil society's capacity to curb corruption?

## GUIDE TO FURTHER READING

Chandhoke, N., *The Conceits of Civil Society* (Delhi: Oxford University Press, 2003). Uses the case of India to advance theoretically informed arguments about the way in which the idea of civil society has been deployed in much contemporary scholarship.

Jaffrelot, C., *India's Silent Revolution: The Rise of the Lower Castes in North India* (London: Hurst and Co., 2003). Sensitively analyses the emergence of socially marginalized groups into the mainstream of party politics, a process both reflecting and profoundly influencing the nature and development of India's civil society.

Jeffrey, R., *India's Newspaper Revolution: Capitalism, Politics and the Indian-Language Press, 1977–99* (Delhi: Oxford University Press, 2000). Charts, in fascinating detail, both encouraging and disturbing trends in the development of one of the key elements of any functioning civil society—the press.

Mahajan, G., 'Civil Society and Its Avatars: What Happened to Freedom and Democracy', *Economic and Political Weekly*, 15–21 May 1999 (available at **www.epw.org.in**). Excellent account of the relationship between thinking about civil society in the West and in India.

Sainath, P., *Everybody Loves a Good Drought: Stories from India's Poorest Districts* (New Delhi: Penguin, 1996). An excellent collection of reportage on the plight of India's most vulnerable citizens, showing both their need for strong associations to represent their interests and how sometimes oppressive forms of civil society contribute to the problem.

Varshney, A., *Ethnic Conflict and Civic Life: Hindus and Muslims in India* (New Haven: Yale University Press, 2002). Combines statistical sophistication and conceptual rigour to examine the role of *some* forms of civil society in defusing communal conflict.

## WEB LINKS

**www.pucl.org**   The site of the People's Union for Civil Liberties, an Indian civil society organization that campaigns for human rights.

**http://sarn.ssrc.org**   The site of the South Asia Research Network set up by the South Asia programme of the independent, international Social Science Research Council based in Washington, DC, United States.

**www.indiastat.com**   An extensive site of social, economic, and political data on India.

**http://parliamentofindia.nic.in**   The site of India's parliament.

**www.hinduonline.com**   The on-line version of *The Hindu*, a leading English-Language daily newspaper.

 **COMPANION WEB SITE**

For additional material and resources, see the companion web site at:
**www.oup.com/uk/booksites/politics/**

# Civil society: active or passive?

## Saudi Arabia

*David Pool*

## OVERVIEW

This chapter examines the emergence of the Saudi state from a tribally based stateless society to a kingdom with rulers drawn from the Saud family. The twin pillars of dynastic legitimacy are Islam and oil. Both pillars have consequences for the limited character of civil society. Since the late 1970s there have been stirrings of civil society and political opposition. Two political tendencies have emerged: liberal reformist and conservative Islamist. Underpinning these new dynamics have been increasing diversification of Saudi society, a decline in oil revenues in the 1980s and reactions to Saudi Arabia's alignment with the USA. Buffeted by these competing pressures, the ruling family has pursued policies balancing between them with uneven results for the evolution of civil society.

**SAUDI ARABIA**

---

### Box 17*b*.1  **Key dates in Saudi Arabia's history**

| | | | |
|---|---|---|---|
| 1774 | Oath of Dhiriyya between Saud and Muhammad Abd al-Wahhab | 1974 | Oil revenues quadruple |
| 1902 | Abd al-Aziz ibn Saud took Riyadh | 1975 | Khalid succeeds |
| 1926 | Abd al-Aziz proclaimed king of Hijaz and Sultan of Najd | 1979 | Seizure of Holy Mosque in Mecca |
| 1932 | Establishment of kingdom of Saudi Arabia | 1982 | Fahd succeeds |
| 1938 | Beginning of exploitation of oil | 1985 | Abdallah effective ruler as crown prince following Fahd's stroke |
| 1953 | Saud son of Abd al-Aziz succeeds | 1990–1 | War over Iraqi occupation of Kuwait |
| 1964 | Saud deposed. Faisal succeeds | 1993 | Consultative Council established |

# Introduction

Civil society and civil society organizations have played a limited role in Saudi Arabia's political development. The character of civil society has been shaped by the interrelationship between dynastic rule of the House of Saud and the twin pillars of dynastic legitimacy: Islam and oil. Whereas the link between the ruling Saud family and a strict version of Islam pre-date the establishment of the state, the impact of oil on Saudi society and politics is more recent. In the contemporary period there has been a complicated interplay between state, government,

Islamic politics, and the economic and social impact of oil revenues. These multiple factors are layered into the relationship between Saudi Arabia and the United States and have resulted in indications of a more active civil society, albeit a mix of the clandestine and unstructured. The emergence of two different tendencies (liberal-reformist and Islamic orthodox) have resulted in the monarchy attempting to balance between the two with uneven consequences for the emergence of an active civil society.

# The historical context of state-building

## From stateless society to the subordination of society

Saudi Arabia is exceptional among developing countries in that it was never colonized. External control was limited to military garrisons of the Ottoman Empire during the nineteenth century. It was not geared to the extraction of natural resources and did not generate the phenomena usually associated with colonialism: a colonial bureaucracy, the expansion of education, and a modern educated class to staff the indigenous institutions of colonial rule. There was no anti-colonial nationalist movement built on the social strata usually involved in nationalist activity: students, the intelligentsia, and merchants. Civil society was little changed by external intervention and for the most part retained the classic form of a stateless society embedded in kinship structures of tribe and clan.

Prior to the establishment of the state, Saudi Arabian society had two main forms of social organization: pastoral tribes located in the desert interior and the settled population of the oases and coastal areas. There was no central authority and inter- and intra-tribal disputes, changing tribal alliances and conflicts with enclaves of the settled population, were endemic. It was not through consensus on Islam nor through acceptance

of the rule of the Saud family that Saudi Arabia was unified but through force and conquest.

Islamic legitimation for the House of Saud originated with the alliance of Muhammad bin Saud, a local ruler from the interior village of Dhiriyya, and Muhammad bin Abd al-Wahhab, an Islamic preacher. It was symbolized by the oath to return to true Islam sworn between the two in 1744 and cemented by marriages between the two families that have continued until today. The alliance added a new Islamic dimension to conflicts as some tribes and tribal segments were incorporated into the *ikhwan* (the brethren)— the followers of Abd al-Wahhab. Tribal conflicts and the waxing and waning of tribal ascendancies continued for more than a hundred years until, at the beginning of the twentieth century, Abd al-Aziz bin Saud (known as Ibn Saud) began extending his conquests through war and Wahhabi doctrines. The *ikhwan* were sent among the tribes and tribal settlements were established based on common Islamic practice rather than kinship solidarity. The combination of Saud warrior leadership and the brethren's religious passion provided the dynamic for the establishment of the kingdom of Saudi Arabia in 1932.

With a new central power in the peninsular, marked by naming the state after the conquering family, and an Islamic ideology focused on enforcing religious conformity, segmentary tribal conflicts were contained as tribal leaders and tribes became subordinated to or associated with the centre. One means to achieve this was the practice of marrying Saud males to the daughters of prominent tribal families. The main opposition to the emergent state was a rebellion by a segment of the *ikhwan*. This was a protest against Abd al-Aziz ibn Saud's links to Christian Britain, the influx of new technologies of motor transport, telephone, and wireless, and the gradual territorial delineation of the Saudi state, whose new borders cut off certain tribes from their traditional wells. More importantly, it presaged the tensions between dynastic power and Wahhabi doctrines that emerged in the late twentieth century. The growth of oil revenues through the 1950s presented the ruling family with the material means to reinforce its power and authority and provide patronage as a means of incorporating dissident tribes and the conquered peripheries under Saud rule and Wahhabi principles. Oil revenues also permitted the gradual establishment of a state bureaucracy, increasing numbers of salaried officials and the growth of budgetary allocations for socio-economic development and educational expansion. A small working class emerged in the eastern oil-producing area and urban centres grew from villages and oases. Such social differentiation, however, took place in the context of strictly enforced conformity to Wahhabi principles. As a result, other than a network of chambers of commerce, social and economic development did not generate an organized civil society.

## Islam

The Islamic underpinnings of authority and legitimacy in Saudi Arabia provided both constraints on civil society organizations and justification for them. Contradictorily, it was in the fuzzy interstices between state and religion that Islam provided some justification for organizations with a degree of independence from the state. One institution difficult to categorize as either a civil society or state organization is the *ulema*. It is a body consisting of those educated in Islam and *sharia* (Islamic law) with the function of ensuring the implementation of Islamic precepts and thus has some characteristics of a corporate non-state organization linking together the local mosque preacher and the highest legal authority. However, given the role of

Islamic law as state law there is a fusion between state and religion at the highest level of *ulema* positions.

The Wahhabi message was based on the unity of God and opposed to the idolatrous accretions of saint worship found among mystical Islamic orders, the practices of the minority Shia community and general lax behaviour. With the establishment of the kingdom, Islam became the basis of the state, state institutions, and law. Saudi publications stress that the holy Koran is the constitution and *sharia* the determinant of personal and public behaviour. The judicial system was unified under the Hanbali school of law, the strictest of the four Islamic legal schools. The duty of the ruler, and basis of his legitimacy, was to ensure implementation of Islamic principles. There was no space for political parties or mechanism for expressing group interests outside of Islam. The *ulema* had a critical voice in decision-making given the absence of a formal constitution and a secular legal system. Clergy dominated key institutions—the Council of Higher Ulema, the High Judicial Council, and the Council of Grievances. The Committee for the Condemnation of Vice and Recommendation of Virtue policed moral conduct, ensuring proper Islamic behaviour, including female modesty. There was, then, an officially prescribed set of principles for both social and political values and behaviour.

Civil society in Saudi Arabia is constrained by a framework that stresses the promotion of the fulfilment of Islamic duties. In so far as civil society is understood to grow from a diverse range of social interests formulated in associations autonomous from the state, this Islamic framework provides limited scope for organized civil society based on factors other than religion. Although Islam in Saudi Arabia lacks anything like the structure of a church, in some respects the *ulema* are the only institution with a degree of autonomy from the state and accepted as a channel between society, government, and state. The centrality of Islam also provides scope for Islamic charitable organizations.

## The house of Saud

The Saud family played an important role in the tribal politics of the Najd interior from the eighteenth century onward. Originating from a small settlement north of Riyadh, the contemporary capital, the family expanded its control from Najd to the current borders of the Saudi kingdom and can look back on a continuous if sporadic role in the history of the peninsular. After thirty years of expansion and conquest, Ibn Saud took control of the Hijaz, with its holy towns of Mecca and Medina in 1925, declared himself King of Hijaz and Sultan of Najd and its Dependencies in 1926, and in 1932 proclaimed himself as first king of Saudi Arabia.

Since founding the state the Saud family has embedded itself in government and administration, invariably holding key positions like defence, foreign affairs, security, and provincial governorships. Other members are spread through important ambassadorships, the military and security establishment, and government commissions. Ibn Saud had scores of wives and descendants and when collateral family branches are added it is estimated that male family members number around ten thousand, all recipients of government stipends. It is an extended family of such proportion that recruitment from it into official positions is not difficult.

Reinforcing the official view of Islamic legitimacy there is an additional emphasis on two concepts: *shura* and *majlis*. *Shura* refers to consultation between the people and the ruler, although the more traditional practice is consultation with the *ulema*. *Majlis*, traditionally the tribal forum for male elders, has evolved into an institution for consultation between ruler and ruled and in practice a forum for airing grievances and the delivery of petitions. The latter process has been undermined by the growth of bureaucracy.

The framework of Islamic principles in Saudi Arabia and the family's pivotal historic role did not necessarily ensure **legitimacy** for family-dominated government and administration and its key role in the economy. An index of the symbiotic relationship between power and wealth are the land grants by Ibn Saud and his successors to Saud family members and advisers that became a source of enrichment with the massive increase in property prices after 1974 during the construction boom. The presence of such large numbers in important public positions, the allocation to them of stipends from public funds, and, in the 1970s, the increasing number involved in influence peddling and brokering state contracts illustrate the tension between family political power and the autonomy of governmental institutions.

---

### Box 17b.2 Saudi Arabian oil revenues ($, unadjusted for inflation)

| | | | |
|---|---|---|---|
| 1965 | 655m. | 1979 | 70bn. |
| 1973 | 4bn. | 1985 | 20bn. |
| 1974 | 23bn. | 2000 | 70bn. |

---

Of particular significance was the involvement of princes in the racket of commissions for state contracts and weapons procurement. In so far as the role of the family was legitimated by Islam, the extravagant palaces, reports and rumours of corruption, and un-Islamic behaviour in the fleshpots and casinos of Europe by some family members reflected badly on the Islamic pillar of legitimacy. Though the population of Saudi Arabia generally benefited from the oil boom, members of the House of Saud were the major beneficiaries and particularly well placed to profit through kinship connections to those members of the family in key decision-making positions.

## Oil and the rentier state

The role of oil revenues provides another competing and parallel explanation to that of Islam for Saud autocracy, the relative stability of dynastic power and the weakness of civil society. The theory of the **rentier state** defines a state like Saudi Arabia and accounts for a particular pattern of politics and social organization. In brief, a rentier state exists where the bulk of its revenues derive from external sources, akin to renting oil fields in return for income. In 1973–4 oil revenues quadrupled and have provided between 70 and 90 per cent of government revenues. Several political and social consequences are seen to follow from oil rent. Firstly, external rent accrues to the state and provides it with a high degree of autonomy from society. The major function of the state is the allocation of revenues to society. This allocative process is distinct from a state whose citizens are involved in producing goods and resources generated from taxing production. Secondly, citizens of a rentier state develop a 'rentier mentality'. Bureaucratic employment, welfare, medical care, and education are all provided through the state's allocation of oil revenues. Very few citizens are involved in the production of oil and taxation is minimal. In so far as the state does not tax its citizens they make no claims on the state. Those involved in most of the productive work are non-citizen migrant workers on short-term work contracts, dependent on Saudi citizen employers for their residence permits and are marginal members of Saudi society. The political implications of rentier state theory are that civil society is relatively passive; it lacks any imperative to challenge the authorities allocating the oil revenues; and opposition movements and demands for democratic reform and governmental accountability are unlikely to emerge. These implications have been concretized by the official prohibition against political parties and forms of social organization like trade unions and women's movements that might develop as a consequence of social diversification.

Saudi Arabian society, however, has not proved so passive. Demonstrations and protests have occurred sporadically, demonstrate a degree of civil organization, and reflect a disquiet at the lack of political and social change. These occurrences suggest the existence of a skeletal and clandestine civil society. Calls for reform and the emergence of clandestine groups using violent means are indicative of a polarization in Saudi society along two axes: liberal reform and a return to Wahhabi orthodoxy. That these political trends have emerged while Saudi Arabia has remained *by definition* a rentier state, albeit one in receipt of declining revenues, raises serious doubts about the value of rentier state theory for explaining state–society relations.

Dependence on oil revenues makes Saudi Arabia vulnerable to changes in the demand for and price of oil. The collapse of oil prices in the 1980s resulted in declining oil revenues, leading to cuts in government spending, pressure on the private sector to expand its employment of school and university graduates, and encouragement to family firms to become public companies. The retreat of the state as the dominant force in economic development might have significant implications for civil society, particularly in terms of greater autonomy of business and commerce from government. There would certainly appear to be a linkage between expenditure cuts, with a decline in per capita income and increasing youth unemployment, and the emergence of a more activist civil society.

## Key points

- The Saud family is at the apex of politics and the king at the apex of the family.
- Islam provides legitimacy for the monarchy and provides constraints against the development of civil society.
- Saudi Arabia is a rentier state: oil revenues strengthen the state and limit the development of civil society.
- Allocation of oil revenues legitimates the ruling family but results in a more diversified society.
- By definition Saudi Arabia has remained a rentier state but opposition has emerged as oil revenues and per capita income declined.

# Opposition, the rentier state, and Islam

One political implication of the rentier state is that civil society and opposition to government are unlikely to emerge given the material well-being of those who have all the privileges of citizenship. An analysis of the occurrence and character of opposition, therefore, is a means of assessing the utility of the rentier state explanation of Saudi society and state–society relations. Given the secret nature of Saudi politics the analysis of opposition must necessarily be somewhat

interpretative. It is, however, possible to link sporadic eruptions of protest to broad social and political trends. In the case of Saudi Arabia, it is becoming clear that stirrings of civil society activism are a consequence of the role of ideas in mobilizing civil society even if catalysts have been declining oil revenues and shrinking per capita income, on the one hand, and Saudi foreign policy on the other.

> ### Box 17b.3 *Shura* response to civil society demands
>
> 'passing over the demands of civil society could lead to our falling into the abyss . . . The Saudi citizen needs to have his basic rights and freedom of expression guaranteed . . . and his role in social and political participation strengthened, so he can feel part of an inclusive order.'
>
> (Mohammad Ibrahim al-Helwa, Member of the Consultative Council, December 2003)

## Liberalization protests

From the early 1990s, there have been increasing calls for liberalization of the political system. In January 2003 formal reform proposals were presented to Crown Prince Abdallah in 'A Strategic Vision for the Present and Future' (Dekmejian 2003). While accepting the monarchy and invoking Islamic precepts, the document called for the separation of powers, introduction of popular representation and participation, and a framework for establishing civil society organizations. The signatories, educated, professional middle-class, and male, reflected the social change of the previous three decades. They signed as individuals and there was no organizational imprimatur, indicative of the loose and limited nature of civil society. It was followed by a National Forum for Dialogue attended by liberal and moderate Islamist reformers and sanctioned by the Saud family. Popular support for reform was signalled later in the year with an unprecedented public demonstration demanding freedom of expression. In recognition of pressures for liberal reform the government introduced a *Shura* (Consultative) Council and has committed itself to holding the first elections in the kingdom in 2004, although these will be limited to municipal councils.

## The case of women

An examination of the role and position of women provides a useful case study. Female rates of economic participation are low and officially sanctioned prohibitions against women range from dress codes to driving cars. Justifications for this are that Islam determines the obligations of women, gives priority to their role within the family (al-Farsy 1990: 135) and demands modest behaviour. Priority is given to the strict Islamic principle rather than economic imperatives. However there is a tension between the women's low participation in the workforce and the need to import foreign labour with its perceived potential to undermine the traditional Islamic values.

One aspect of social change has been the expansion of educational opportunities of which women have been significant beneficiaries. Educational development also provides an index of the growth of the educated middle class, the usual candidates for civil society organizers. Total enrolment in secondary education in 1969 was 16,000. Of these 2,000 were girls. By 1986 there were almost 200,000 secondary-school students including 85,000 girls and 15,000 university graduates half of which were female. By the mid-1980s female participation rates in employment showed an increase among the younger generation: about 9 per cent for women in their twenties and 3 per cent for those in their forties. The issue of women's role in society and participation in the economy is controversial, linked to questions of liberalization and equality. The issue dramatically surfaced into politics in 1991 when a large group of educated women, defying the prohibition against women drivers, got behind the wheels of their cars and drove into the centre of Riyadh to the horror of the religious authorities. The women were publicly vilified as akin to prostitutes. The incident was indicative not only of the growing demands of educated Saudi women for equality and liberalization but also of an informal organizational network of women who were willing to take significant political action. In order to placate conservative Islamic circles the government introduced restrictions on women's travel abroad. Balancing these restrictions, the government also took a reformist tack by introducing an appointed *Shura* Council.

## Islamic protests and opposition

Contrasting with liberalization protests have been protests within a Wahhabi and neo-Wahhabi Islamist tradition. They have ranged from the takeover of the

Holy Mosque of Mecca in 1979, to mosque sermons opposed to the US presence in Saudi Arabia in 1990 and the more recent bombings apparently linked to Bin Laden's al-Qaeda movement. While Islam has provided legitimacy for the House of Saud, it has also provided a basis for opposition. This contradiction places the *ulema* in a difficult and ambiguous position: is it an organization that reflects the Islamic values of important segments of civil society, an institution subordinated to the state authorities, or a corporate social group independent of both state authorities and society?

The first serious Islamist eruption occurred in 1979 when Juhayman Utaibi, a religious studies student, and hundreds of followers seized the Mecca mosque, one of the holiest of Islamic sites. His opposition to the ruling family was grounded in religious principles and Saudi history. He rejected the ruling family's legitimacy on the grounds that they did not follow the Koran and the Sunna. He was also critical of Ibn Saud's subordination of the *ikhwan* and called for the *ulema* to oppose the House of Saud. His letters also included attacks on the alliance with the Christians, a clear reference to the West. Juhayman and his group and supporters represented a modern return to past principles and early Saudi Muslim society. The higher *ulema* rejected Juhayman's appeal to oppose the Saud family and supported the authorities with a **fatwa** (religious edict) permitting use of force to expel the rebels from the mosque. In doing so the *ulema* aligned itself with the state authorities rather than with a protest movement rooted in old Saudi society.

When the Iraqi army invaded and occupied Kuwait in 1990 Saudi Arabia was placed in a dilemma over whether to accede to US requests for a military presence to free Kuwait of Iraqi forces or to oppose a Western military intervention against a Muslim state. Consequent on the arrival of US forces a vigorous campaign against the foreign military presence was conducted by mosque preachers who distributed their sermons through cassettes.

Following the high *ulema* sanctioning the presence of foreign forces in Saudi Arabia, a 'Memorandum of Advice' was issued in September 1992 signed by 107 *ulema*, an indication of the existence of an autonomous section of the *ulema*. Among other things the Memorandum called for greater supervision over the state and government policy by a

---

> ### Box 17*b*.4 **Koran citation**
>
> 'When kings enter a city, they cause it to be corrupt, turning its honourable people into a humiliated people.'
>
> (Koran, chapter 27, verse 43 cited in the Memorandum of Advice, September 1992)

---

religious review body, a religious supreme court, and the invalidation of laws contradictory to *sharia*. A starker challenge to the ruling family was the anti-monarchy citation of chapter 27, verse 43 of the Koran. Making an implicit link between corruption and the ruling family, it also called for those who had gained wealth illegally, regardless of rank, to be punished (Cordesman 2002). Indicative of the need for Islamic legitimacy the authorities purged those who did not denounce the Memorandum from the Supreme Council of Senior Ulema. An additional response was the restriction on charitable fund-raising without government authorization, a measure weakly enforced within Saudi Arabia and impossible to enforce on groups outside.

In so far as church groups and church leaders in the West can be considered a part of civil society, so too could the Saudi *ulema*. Though fragmented with regard to their relationship to the state authorities, *ulema* networks could be viewed as informally organized expressions of civil society. The compliance of some of the leading *ulema* with state policy has brought forth non-*ulema* groups inspired by Islam like the Committee for the Defence of Legitimate Rights. That was established by the physicist Muhammad al-Masari in 1993 and fused together religious demands with democratic positions. Its adherents were subsequently arrested or fled into exile.

## Key Points

- Two poles of reformism opposition have emerged in Saudi Arabia despite its rentier character.
- Both are suggestive of the growth of civil society even if it is not formally organized.

- Liberal reformists advocate reform of the political system but maintenance of monarchy.
- Islamists and members of the *ulema* have called for strengthening the role of Islam and the *ulema*.

- The Saud family attempts to balance between the two poles of opposition.

# Foreign policy and dissent

Saudi foreign policy, and especially the US–Saudi relationship, has been a catalyst for Islamist opposition. Saudi Arabia's long-standing informal alliance with the USA has been reflected in both its foreign policy and its oil supply and pricing policies. Most arms purchased by Saudi Arabia were from the USA and accompanying them was a significant growth in American military personnel as advisers and technicians. There have, however, been persistent tensions arising from its ties to the USA and the latter's policies in the Middle East, particularly support for Israel and Israel's occupation of Palestine. The cold war mitigated the tensions in that Saudi Arabia's alignment with the West was against the atheistic communist East.

There were serious domestic repercussions of Saudi Arabia's foreign policy following the Iranian Revolution of 1978–9, the Soviet invasion of Afghanistan in 1980, and the Iraqi invasion of Kuwait in 1990. The establishment of the Shii Iranian Islamic Republic brought demonstrations by the downtrodden Saudi Shii community, possibly inspired seizure of the Mecca mosque, and tacitly challenged the Islamic legitimacy of monarchy in Saudi Arabia. The Soviet presence in Afghanistan, an Islamic country, resulted in organized Islamic resistance within Saudi Arabia providing money and arms and, more importantly, encouraging Saudi citizens to enlist. In the longer term, Saudi Arabia's involvement in Afghanistan lay behind the subsequent emergence of the most violent and organized opposition to the Saudi regime. Osama bin Laden, from a prominent Saudi family and key recruiter of young Saudis to the Afghan resistance, built the al-Qaeda movement and radicalized its members against the West, in their

language the Jews and Christians. Ultimately, the Saudi monarchy became a target because of its ties to the West, dramatically symbolized by its permission for the Western military presence in the kingdom for the offensive against the Iraqi army occupying Kuwait. Although organized abroad, the appeal of al-Qaeda has domestic roots in Saudi Arabia and could be considered the tip of a politicized network of clandestine civil society groups. Concerted attacks against US interests in Saudi Arabia and the wider region culminated in the '9/11' attacks. Most of those involved were Saudi citizens and subsequent investigation has made clear that funding from Saudi charities had played a significant role in the growth of al-Qaeda and its political and military activities. Islamic charitable organizations were the only civil society organizations permitted by the state. Since then the government has expanded its supervisory and regulatory role over charities after strong US pressure. Extremist Islamist supporters of al-Qaeda consider these developments a mark of the subordination of Saudi Arabia to US interests.

## Key points

- The US–Saudi relationship has generated internal opposition.
- Saudi state support for Afghan resistance and participation of Saudis gave rise to a clandestine and violent internal opposition linked to al-Qaeda.
- In reaction Saudi government has extended state control over charitable organizations, the only active civil society organizations.

# Conclusion

The development of civil society in Saudi Arabia has been a faltering process. The establishment of the Saudi state resulted in the subordination of autonomous tribal units to an autocratic monarchy drawn from the Saud family, whose members were politically, socially, and economically highly privileged. The monarchical system was underpinned by a moral and religious legitimacy provided by the centrality given to Islam and the *ulema*. In addition, massive increase in oil revenues and the family's control over their allocation have buttressed the power of both state and dynasty over society. As a consequence civil society and civil society organizations have played a limited role in Saudi Arabia's political development until recent decades.

Concurrent with declining state and personal income, the increasing differentiation of society and regional developments in the Middle East, the traditional position of the ruling family has been challenged. Caught in a vortex of social change and political challenges, the monarchy has sought to balance new forces represented by the emergence of a liberal reformist trend, and older forces represented by the *ulema* and civilian movements inspired by an anti-Western Islam. In the past, elements of emergent civil society like the inchoate women's protest movement have been curtailed in the name of balance. On the other hand, emergence of a violent and clandestine Islamist movement linked to al-Qaeda benefited the forces of reform, with the government introducing the appointed Consultative Assembly and proposing local elections. Although the future of civil society might seem brighter than before, it is likely to remain vulnerable to government strategies to balance competing domestic forces, fluctuations in oil income, and regional political events.

## QUESTIONS

1  How does the character of Islam in Saudi Arabia shape civil society and constrain the emergence of civil society organizations?

2  Does the theory of the rentier state account for the weakness of civil society?

3  Can the *ulema* be considered a part of civil society?

4  Why and how does the Saud king seek a balance between Islamic and liberal reformist protests?

5  What has been the impact of Saudi foreign policy on domestic politics?

## GUIDE TO FURTHER READING

Al-Farsy, F., *Modernity and Tradition: the Saudi Equation* (London: Kegan Paul International, 1990). Reflects the official view of Saudi society and politics.

Cordesman, A. H., *Saudi Arabia Enters the 21st Century* (Washington: Center for Strategic and International Studies, 2002). Clear analysis of opposition, Islam and Saudi government reaction to '9/11'.

Dekmejian, R., 'Saudi Arabia's Consultative Council', *Middle East Journal*, 52/2 (1998): 204–18. Discussion of the origins, membership and functions of the Consultative Council.

Dekmejian, R., 'The Liberal Impulse in Saudi Arabia', *Middle East Journal*, 57/3 (2003): 400–13. Interesting synthesis of the liberalizing tendency.

Luciani, G., 'Allocation vs. Production States: A Theoretical Statement', in G. Luciani (ed.), *The Arab State* (Los Angels: UCLA Press, 1992), 65–84. Clear statement of rentier state theory.

McLoughlin, L., *Ibn Saud: Founder of a Kingdom* (Basingstoke: Macmillan, 1993) Good introduction to the founder of the modern dynasty and the process of state formation.

Yamani, M., *Changed Identities: The Challenge of the New Generation in Saudi Arabia* (London: Royal Institute of International Affairs, 2000). Overview of attitudes of young Saudis; extensive illustrative quotes span the political and social spectrum.

## WEB LINKS

**www.saudinf.com**   website of the Saudi Ministry of Culture and Information.

**www.eia.doe.gov/emeu/cabs/saudi.html**   Detailed up-date of the country's oil industry.

**www.iad.org**   The religion of Islam home page.

**lcweb2.loc.gov/frd/cs/satoc.html**   Saudi Arabia profile by US Library of Congress Federal Research Division offers wealth of social, economic, and political data.

 ## COMPANION WEB SITE

For additional material and resources, see the companion web site at:
**www.oup.com/uk/booksites/politics/**

# 18a

# Strong state, weak state
## Chile

*Peter Siavelis*

## OVERVIEW

Unlike many Latin American countries, Chile established a strong, influential state early in the twentieth century. This resulted from the confluence of several variables, including the gradual expansion of suffrage, the early development of a tacit agreement concerning the appropriate role of the state, and the growth of effective political institutions. Consequently the Chilean state was central in promoting development and industrialization, in providing social welfare benefits, and while doing so, also ensuring government propriety. However, Chile's military dictatorship (1973–90) undertook to transform the state, with mixed results. While the Chilean state is more powerful and influential than most in the developing world, the policies of the dictatorship undermined it in some areas where it had traditionally been successful.

**CHILE**

---

### 18a.1  Key dates in Chile's history

**1810**   Chile declares independence; first *junta* created

**1814–17**   Temporary re-establishment of Spanish authority by re-conquest

**1817**   General José de San Martín and Chilean independence hero Bernardo O'Higgins defeat the Spanish at Chacabuco

**1890–1**   Civil War between supporters of President José Manuel Balmaceda and congressional forces

**1925**   New constitution approved and promulgated

**1938–41**   Anti-fascist Popular Front rule; creation of CORFO

**1970**   First popularly elected Marxist in the world, Socialist Salvador Allende, assumes the presidency

**1973**   Military coup led by Army General Augusto Pinochet

**1980**   Pinochet's constitution approved in a plebiscite of questionable propriety

**1988**   Pinochet loses plebiscite in bid for eight more years in power

**1990**   Freely elected, Christian Democratic Patrico Aylwin assumes the presidency, leading the *Concertación* coalition

**2000**   Socialist Ricardo Lagos assumes the presidency

# Introduction

Chile is unique among developing countries for having established a powerful and influential state early in the twentieth century. Chile successfully pursued a model of state-led development, mediated by strong democratic political institutions, including a powerful congress and an institutionalized party system. The state also effectively engaged in redistributive policies to create an early social welfare system at the time rivalled only by Uruguay in Latin America. All this it achieved while maintaining one of the least corrupt political systems in the world.

This chapter analyses the rise and transformation of the powerful Chilean state as an outlier in the developing world. It begins by exploring the role of the state in Latin America, explaining the origins of the strong Chilean state, and highlighting the interaction of historical, sociological, and political variables that contributed to its growth and perseverance. It then presents evidence of the strength of the Chilean state in the areas of development, social policy, and **corruption** prevention. An examination of the crisis of the state and the seventeen-year dictatorship of Augusto Pinochet (1973–90) follows.

It concludes with an analysis of the legacy of the dictatorship's policies today, and what can be learned from the rise and transformation of the Chilean state. In essence, while Chile had (and still has) one of the strongest, most effective states in the developing world, this chapter argues that the military's efforts to transform Chile's economic and political systems also undermined the state in areas where traditionally it had been effective.

## Key points

- Unlike most developing countries, Chile had a strong state and incorrupt, effective political institutions from the early twentieth century.

- The state assumed an early role in development and industrialization, social welfare provision, and in assuring cleanliness in government.

- While Chile still has a strong state, many policies under Pinochet's dictatorship reduced its traditional effectiveness.

# The Latin American state in historical perspective

Analysing the state is central to understanding contemporary Latin American politics. With the collapse of the region's export economies after 1929, a new development model grew from the realization of Latin America's dependence on exports and sensitivity to international price fluctuations for the primary goods on which most countries depended for income. Policymakers sought to reduce this dependency by turning inward to develop domestic economies, a policy later known as **import substituting industrialization** (ISI) (see Chapter 2). Given scarce private investment capital, the state necessarily became the primary motor of

ISI, and in most cases, a principal owner of the commanding heights of Latin American economies. This developmental orientation is only one facet of growing state involvement during this period. Along with it came the growth of welfare states, large bureaucracies, and extensive state regulatory frameworks (some more efficient than others). Thus, by the 1970s most of Latin America was characterized by what Cavarrozzi (1992) termed a 'state-centred matrix', where citizens looked to the state as an important actor in most aspects of daily life and as a central agent of development, industrialization, and redistribution.

The debt crisis of the 1980s coupled with deeper problems with the ISI model led to a profound rethinking of the role of the state. Governments, many led by authoritarian regimes, initiated comprehensive programmes of neo-liberal economic reform as a response to economic crisis, adopting market-based solutions to public problems. These reforms involved the removal of capital controls, dropping trade barriers, and most relevantly here, a deep restructuring of the state, including privatization of state-owned industries, dramatic cuts in state employment, and the scaling back of national social safety nets.

Following a widespread process of democratic transition, most governments in Latin America are now focusing on ways to transform the **developmentalist state** into an effective arbiter of market democracy, and to dislodge it from a central role in politics and social provision. In essence, for many Latin Americans the distribution of social welfare benefits and state employment provided crucial legitimizing political connections for the democratic system as a whole. Many of these connections have been severed by the widespread reform of states in the region. The major future challenge for Latin American states is to balance this tradition of extensive state involvement with streamlined states, maintaining capacity where the state has traditionally been effective and transforming the areas where it has not. The Chilean case illustrates this challenge.

## Key points

- The state has been a central actor in the development of Latin American economies and societies.

- As a result of the Great Depression, Latin American states developed the strategy of Import Substituting Industrialization to reduce dependency.

- By 1970, in most Latin American countries the state was the central agent of development, industrialization, and redistribution.

- Authoritarian regimes of the 1970s and 1980s partly resulted from the crisis of the ISI model, and most sought to roll back the state and introduce free market policies.

- Democratic governments that emerged in the 1990s are struggling to define the state's role, seeking both to scale it back and maintain a strong regulatory framework for market democracy.

# Explaining the origins of the strong Chilean state

Latin American states have historically varied in their influence and success. Where the state could effectively project its influence and legitimize its authority in national life, state-led development projects and national bureaucracies were most successful. The Chilean state accomplished these tasks, setting it apart from many developing countries. It is difficult to single out the key explanatory variables. Some theorists tie this success to the contextual features of the Chilean political system and concrete historical events. For example, Valenzuela (1989: 178–87) argues that the country's early consolidation of a strong national identity, the establishment of political authority and agreement on the rules of the game, coupled with gradual suffrage expansion, helped create a state with a good deal of legitimacy. This legitimacy, rare in Latin American comparative perspective, enabled the state to pursue its developmental, industrial, and social-welfare policy goals without the level of contestation that existed elsewhere in the region.

Concrete political and social agreements also built on this strong foundation to consolidate the legitimacy of the state, and, in particular, contributed to the early acceptance of what Chilean historians call the *estado de compromiso* or the **compromise state**. This was a tacit agreement among all significant social actors accepting both formal democracy and the desirability of an active developmentalist, welfare state. Despite its success, Chilean democracy very early on was characterized by deep divisions and disagreements. However, no one social class was able effectively to dominate the others, at least politically. As a result of this impasse, elites and the middle class agreed to accept a developmental, reformist state and the gradual electoral incorporation of new groups within the context of the compromise state. Eventually the working class was also included. At the same time, to placate the oligarchy this model also involved a tacit agreement not fundamentally to challenge property relations or land tenure patterns, an issue that will painfully resurface later (Oxhorn 1995: 44). The compromise state was the defining model of social relations until the 1970s. The middle class was at the centre of this compromise, and its values were reflected in the acceptance and, indeed, encouragement of the expansion of the activist state.

Finally, respect for legality and the rule of law in Chile was accompanied by functional and effective democratic institutions, which provided fertile ground for the development of a strong and relatively efficient state. Despite the profound crisis of the military coup in 1973, for most of its modern history Chile was a country where the president was legally limited in his powers, the Congress was an effective agent of representation, and the judiciary was independent and defended the rule of law. Just as important, a strong and effective multi-party system served as the political wiring of this entire system. Though often polarized and fractionalized, the party system was composed of parties with strong roots in society and a tradition of resolving conflict peacefully through consensus-building. Without these basic contextual features, it would have been quite difficult for such a strong state to emerge, and for it to function as effectively as it did for so many years.

## Key points

- States have been central to economic and social development in Latin American countries, though with varying levels of success. Those able to project their legitimate authority have been most successful.

- Suggested explanations for the Chilean state's relative success include optimal timing and sequencing of political events, the *estado de compromiso*, and early establishment of an incorrupt bureaucracy.

- The Chilean state's success is based on the combination of these three variables, and the elites' ability to build upon them to construct legitimate political institutions through negotiation and compromise.

# Development, social welfare, corruption, and success of the Chilean state

While the strength and influence of the Chilean state was evident in many areas, three stand out: development and industrialization; social welfare policy; corruption prevention.

## The developmentalist state and industrialization

Most accounts of Chilean history trace the origins of a strong state to President Diego Portales's so called Autocratic Republic (1830–70). Though Portales is in large measure responsible for establishing strong, stable government, the modern activist Chilean state emerges with the challenge of managing income from Chile's expanding nitrate revenues in the late nineteenth and early twentieth centuries. A new middle class emerged, composed of those tied to import–export trade and management of nitrate production. Revenues flowed into state coffers, underwriting the expansion of the bureaucracy and fantastic growth in state employment (Oxhorn 1995: 43).

The power of the state also grew as a political response to social change. In the early 1920s the middle and lower classes for the first time rebelled against the overwhelming power of Chile's landed oligarchy. President Arturo Alessandri was the inheritor of this electoral revolution, and for the first time in 1920 a president was elected who was perceived as a representative of the common people. He proposed extensive social and labour legislation. The truth was that Alessandri understood the inevitability of working-class participation and thought it more expedient to co-opt it than resist it. Even so, he proposed state control of banks, insurance companies, and underscored the importance of the state assuming a role in ensuring monetary stability and social security (Gil 1966: 57). Alessandri, facing conservative opposition and military pressure, eventually was forced to resign with his legislative package left incomplete. Still, his administration placed these issues on the agenda in a serious way for the first time.

The key milestone in establishing the developmentalist state was setting up CORFO (The Chilean Development Corporation) in 1939. CORFO's many roots included the Great Depression crisis, the dramatic loss of revenue resulting from the discovery of synthetic nitrates, and the realization of Chile's dependence on foreign markets for survival. CORFO definitively established a role for the state as the primary agent of industrialization. With an independent governing board composed of government, business, and labour representatives, the goal of this semi-autonomous agency was to promote development through direct financing of industry and/or encouragement of private–public partnerships. Besides aiding development of small industries, CORFO led the way in establishing major infrastructure, often in collaboration with international capital. Its most successful projects were establishing the Chilean Steel Industry, building basic infrastructure in utilities, and the expansion and modernization of metallurgy, Chile's major industry. However, CORFO also helped to launch Chile's cellulose, paper, and forestry enterprises (see Gil 1966: 139).

Several factors conspired to give CORFO widespread ideological support during the period of the *estado de compromiso*. While parties of the centre and left backed state intervention to spur the country's development, the right also supported CORFO for reasons of economic nationalism. Chile's unitary government also contributed to CORFO's

developmentalist mission. Santiago-based elites across the ideological spectrum have traditionally had something of a colonial attitude towards the remote north and south, advocating intervention by central authorities to ensure Chile's 'complete' national development.

Public-sector growth in Chile was remarkable in subsequent years. Public-sector investment accounted for 40 per cent of total investment by the mid-1940s and public employment doubled between 1930 and 1949 (Loveman 2001: 199). The Chilean developmentalist state reached its zenith in the 1970s. By 1970, only Cuba exceeded Chile in the measure of state involvement in the economy (Oxhorn 1995: 41). The state controlled over 50 per cent of credit and employed 13 per cent of the economically active population, as the state bureaucracy expanded to staff the many new institutions and regulatory agencies associated with the developmentalist state (Valenzuela 1978: 13).

## The social welfare state

Along with assuming an increasing role in encouraging development, the Chilean government established a far-reaching, redistributive welfare state aimed at providing a minimum level of social security, education, and health care for all citizens (Kurtz 2002: 293–4). Chileans' inability to cope with continuous economic instability and inflation elicited constant demands for state intervention to assure the well-being of citizens. The first Alessandri administration (1920–4) set down the basic model for modern social welfare policy. Reacting to the crisis of the 1930s governments created a series of public and, like CORFO, 'semi-autonomous' agencies to provide public housing, school construction, and social security, significantly expanding the size of the state and the scope of its activities (Loveman 2001: 199). The Popular Front administrations (1938–52) again expanded the country's welfare state. These policies, in turn, strengthened the burgeoning middle class, who continued to expect and demand expansion of the state into new areas of social provision.

The pace of welfare state expansion quickened in ensuing years; combined spending for health and social services was over one-fifth of the national budget by the mid-1960s. The growth in popularity of the left, domestically and internationally, coupled with working-class mobilization, lent growing urgency to the need for social reform and poverty alleviation. While often fragmented, difficult to understand, and internally stratified, the social welfare system that developed from the early 1900s up to 1973 was characterized by very broad coverage in comparative Latin American terms. By 1970, a medical professional was in attendance at 80 per cent of births, and a similar percentage of children received regular medical attention and a minimum level of basic nutrition. Of the eligible population 70 per cent had some formal affiliation with the country's social welfare system, and a similar percentage was covered by the *Servicio Nacional de Salud* (National Health Service). In the same year, 84 per cent of the school age population was enrolled in primary education, 38 per cent in secondary education, and 8 per cent of the age appropriate population was enrolled in some form of postsecondary or university education (Racysnski 1999: 126; Gil 1966: 81).

Though Socialist president Salvador Allende (1970–3) proposed a series of new social policies, significant movement towards further reform was stymied by the political and economic instability of the time. With the assumption of the military government in 1973, Chile's large-scale social welfare system was largely privatized.

## The state and corruption

Historically, Chile belied the image of the corrupt Latin American state. Indeed, even today, Chile ranks number 17 (1 being the least corrupt) in the world on Transparency International's corruption perception index—only one position behind the United States (Transparency International 2003). This tradition of clean government was created and maintained through an effective relationship between Congress and the state bureaucracy, the existence of an independent auditing agency known as the *Contraloría*, and a tradition of independent courts.

To avoid corruption, states must effectively deliver services, ensuring accountability, impartiality, and oversight in their delivery. Citizen demands in Chile were traditionally routed through the National

Congress, with citizens directly approaching legislators or their local agents in the provinces. Congress members, acting as citizen advocates, effectively navigated Chile's complex bureaucracy and extracted concrete benefits for constituents from a system with minimal resources (Valenzuela 1977). This was not the corrupt system of **patron–client relations** so typical of Latin America. Rather, it was accompanied by strong oversight bodies, a professionalized bureaucracy and a system of informal internal monitoring within political parties, who also wanted to steer clear of charges of impropriety.

The principal oversight body was the *Contraloría General de la República* (Comptroller General), an independent agency with a director appointed by the president for life. When created in 1927, it was charged with simply overseeing public accounts. However, by 1970, presidents had so expanded its power that it became the main oversight institution charged with assuring legality in government writ large. It oversaw all public accounts, judged the constitutionality of executive decrees, investigated charges of malfeasance, and assumed a crucial role in almost every facet of Chilean public administration. It was feared and respected at every level of government from the president to town councillors (Gil 1966: 97–9; Valenzuela 1978: 14–16).

Finally, the judiciary, at least before the military government, had a long tradition of independence, and the necessary legal acumen to navigate Chile's effective, yet highly complicated legal code. Seniority, impartiality, and meritocracy reigned within Chilean courts, and presidents could only choose judicial candidates from lists submitted by the courts themselves. This combination of practices, norms, and institutions (both formal and informal) provided the basis on which a strong state could be built.

## Key points

- Three areas in which the Chilean state was particularly influential include development and industrialization, social welfare provision, and corruption prevention.
- The semi-autonomous CORFO was the central agent of Chile's developmentalist state.

- The developmentalist goals of the Chilean state were backed by most social groups and parties.
- President Alessandri (1920–4) founded Chile's welfare state, which gradually expanded to provide basic housing, education, health care, and social security for most Chileans by 1970.
- Chile remains among the least corrupt states in the world, with government propriety guaranteed by a network of oversight institutions, notably the *Contraloría General de la República*.

# The crisis of the Chilean state

Chile's long-standing democratic government experienced a deep crisis in 1973, bringing with it a crisis of the state. Inaugurated in 1970 as the first freely elected Marxist leader in the world, President Salvador Allende aimed to expand one of Latin America's largest, most activist states. Ensuing economic and political instability plunged the country into a deep crisis. In 1973 Army Commander-in-Chief, Augusto Pinochet Ugarte, staged a violent military coup aided by the country's other armed forces and the US Central Intelligence Agency. In the years following, thousands were killed, arrested, tortured, or 'disappeared'. Pinochet blamed the country's polarized party system, its venal politicians, and, eventually, its large state for the crisis of Chilean democracy. Pinochet embarked on a concerted effort to transform the political system, especially targeting the state.

Though it is convenient to tie the coup to the threat Allende posed to economic elites and the very real subversion of the US government, its roots also lie in deeper economic and political changes. By the 1970s the crisis of state-led development was evident in Chile as in Latin America generally. While Chile's developmentalist state successfully laid the groundwork for industrial development, deepening of the ISI project came up against serious obstacles. Chile's high tariff and non-tariff barriers and paternalistic state nurtured inefficiency. But it also lacked a sufficient domestic market to support the ISI model. Finally, despite the state's central role in development, the ISI model failed to eliminate Chile's dependence on foreign sources of capital, credit, and industrial inputs (Loveman 2001: 200).

The crisis of the ISI state also directly challenged the financial and social bases of the *estado de compromiso*. This pattern of social relations ceased to be economically sustainable. In addition, the growth of the left and working class challenged the major assumptions on which this model was based, as Allende's election vividly illustrated. Leftist parties began to ask deeper, more revolutionary questions concerning unequal landownership, foreign domination of the economy, and the persistent poverty that the social welfare system had failed to ameliorate. For the first time since the 1920s both left and right questioned the fundamental assumptions and tacit agreements of the *estado de compromiso*. These questions and the struggles they elicited plunged the country into crisis, whose violent resolution fundamentally transformed the Chilean state.

## Key points

- While US intervention and domestic political crisis were immediate causes of the Pinochet's 1973 coup, a more fundamental cause was the crisis of the ISI state.
- For the first time, the bases of the *estado de compromiso* were questioned, leading to a reassessment of the role of the Chilean state.

# The Pinochet dictatorship and its legacy

It is paradoxical that this comparatively successful state was the very target of the military government. Pinochet partly blamed Chile's pronounced statism for the political and economic ills of the early 1970s. His government transformed the state's role in economic, political, and social life, building a new model of state–society relations based on neo-liberal capitalism.

First, it privatized the commanding heights of the Chilean economy, except for the all-important copper industry. Between 1974 and 1989, over 550 state-owned industries were privatized, and ownership became concentrated in a few large conglomerates. State employment was drastically reduced, from 8.4 per cent of the labour force in 1976 to 3.7 per cent by the end of Pinochet's dictatorship (Martínez and Díaz 1996: 121). While in 1970 the state accounted for 40.6 per cent of GNP, it was 29.5 per cent by 1985 and 21.6 per cent by 1992 (Siavelis 2000: 79). The economy underwent a radical opening with dramatic reductions in tariffs and foreign investment controls. Second, state-provided social services were significantly rolled back with the privatization of the National Health Service, the social security system, and important pieces of the primary and secondary education system.

In October 1988 Pinochet was defeated in a plebiscite on his continued rule, and a presidential election followed in December 1989. In 1990 Chile returned to elected civilian rule and Pinochet stood down from the presidency. Nonetheless, he remained Commander-in-Chief of the Armed Forces until early 1998, when he assumed a position as senator for life, both provisions guaranteed by the 1980 constitution. However, Pinochet was prevented from effectively assuming his seat by his October 1998 arrest in London on charges of human rights abuses, and the fallout and stream of court cases that his arrest provoked in Chile. And though the state has continued to be more influential and effective than in other parts of Latin America, its role in economic and political life is less than before Pinochet. In addition, the process of state reformulation has created longer-term difficulties not often recognized by supporters of a minimal state. First, state transformation disarticulated traditional

modes of interest representation. Traditionally for many Chileans, interactions with the bureaucracy and with members of Congress in search of state services provided the only direct connection between citizen and state. These interactions gave the redistributive state a good deal of legitimacy, thereby encouraging democratic participation. Today, Chileans are more likely to interact with a private pension administration firm as a consumer than with the state as citizen. This model may be more efficient but still signifies diminished interactions with the state, depriving it of one traditional source of legitimacy.

Second, the 1980 constitution, drafted under Pinochet, that governs Chile today, has weakened the representative capacity of Congress, and severely limits legislators' ability to engage in traditional forms of interest representation (Siavelis 2000: 191–217). The electoral system limits party representation. This combined with outright restrictions on Congress's ability to legislate in areas related to social policy has undermined the power of traditional constituencies, the legislature's influence, and, to some extent, the legitimacy of the political system (see Kurtz 2002: 301). Reforms restricting the power of labour and changes in the pension system exacerbate this problem, resulting in further 'disarticulation of what had formerly been exceedingly powerful beneficiary coalitions' (Kurtz 2002: 303). Thus, the weakening of democratic institutions has also undermined the framework which traditionally supported Chile's strong state.

Finally, in recent years corruption has grown in Chile. There have been very visible cases of alleged wrongdoing both by elected officials and bureaucrats. Charges of impropriety against legislators and high-ranking members of the ruling coalition have included accusations of favouritism in the awarding of contracts and public offices. While one cannot definitively attribute growing corruption to the transformation of the state, its smaller size has reduced its reach and regulatory capacity. Moreover, much of the probity of the Chilean political system was tied to the self-regulation of parties and pressure exerted by powerful political actors, who have been marginalized from the political arena given the strong limits to representation established by the Pinochet constitution. This too has exacted a cost on traditional forms of assuring accountability, probity, and clean government.

## Key points

- Despite the Chilean state's relative success, Pinochet and his aides targeted it as one cause of the crisis of democracy in Chile.

- The Pinochet government radically reduced the state and scaled back its developmental and welfare role.

- Although Pinochet stood down and Chile became a democracy in 1990, his legacy endures, especially in the 1980 constitution.

- Though the state is still influential, Pinochet's policies have undermined some of its traditional strengths; the 1980 constitution weakens representative institutions, and recently corruption has grown.

# Conclusion: lessons from the rise and transformation of the Chilean state

Despite the negative legacies of the dictatorship, the Chilean state was, and is, one of the most effective in the developing world. Three valuable lessons can be drawn from this distinctive case. First, it is apparent that conceptions of a strong state have changed in recent years. Though the interventionist states of the ISI period helped establish a basic infrastructure in many countries, they are now seen as a less effective model for the developing world. There has been an intellectual and practical shift away from the interventionist-developmentalist model of the ISI state towards one where its role is limited to the enforcement of property rights, ensuring the rule of law, and encouraging managerial and administrative efficiency.

Second, the Chilean case nonetheless shows that in the period of early national development, the state can play a crucial role in establishing basic infrastructure, social cohesion, and a standard of administrative efficiency. Though the Chilean state eventually exceeded its limits and capacity, contributing to the crisis of democracy, early on it provided the foundation upon which the success of the contemporary state still rests.

Third, the Chilean case also provides lessons for state reformers who see the simple shrinking of the state as a reform panacea. While supporters of the minimalist state laud Chile's transformations as a model for other countries, we see that the movement towards a minimal state also brings with it some potential problems. In this sense, the central challenge for developing world states is to consider carefully alternative patterns of state transformation in an effort to reform the state, while preserving the positive legacies of successful state action, and allowing the state to continue to do what it does well.

## QUESTIONS

1　How was the Chilean state of the early and mid-twentieth century different from those of other countries in the developing world?

2　What is the 'state-centered matrix' and how is it significant to the development of Latin American states?

3　Outline the reasons why Chile was able to develop a strong and influential state.

4　What is the *estado de compromiso* and why was it significant to the development of Chile's strong state?

5　Describe the elements of the Chilean political system which provided for a relatively clean and incorrupt political system.

6　How did the Pinochet government transform the Chilean state?

## GUIDE TO FURTHER READING

Bradford, Colin, *Redefining the State in Latin America* (Paris: OECD, 1994). A collected volume dealing with the restructuring of Latin American states. Theoretical chapters are complemented by several that deal with particular social groups and their relation to the state.

Geddes, Barbara, *Politicians' Dilemma: Building State Capacity in Latin America* (Berkeley: University of California Press, 1994). Analyses the dilemma politicians face in building state capacity, where they have incentives to cultivate a competent state but at the same time face temptations to engage in favouritism and corruption.

Gil, Federico, *The Political System of Chile* (Boston: Houghton Mifflin, 1996). The standard text on Chile's pre-authoritarian political and institutional framework.

Grindle, Merilee, *Challenging the State: Crisis and Innovation in Latin America and Africa* (Cambridge: Cambridge University Press, 1996). A comparative analysis of Kenya and Mexico with broader implications for the role of the state, and particularly how periods of crisis can compel leaders to successfully build more efficient state institutions.

Loveman, Brian, *Chile: The Legacy of Hispanic Capitalism* (New York: Oxford University Press, 2001). One of the most authoritative accounts of Chilean history from the Spanish Conquest to the democratic transition of the 1990s and beyond.

Martínez, Javier, and Díaz Alvaro, *Chile: The Great Transformation* (Geneva: UNRISD, 1996). A comprehensive and balanced account of how the military regime transformed Chile's political economy.

Oxhorn, Phillip, *Organizing Civil Society* (University Park, Pa.: Pennsylvania State University Press, 1995). A fieldwork-based analysis of the role of popular organizations among the urban poor and their ability to remain organized in the face of the onslaught of the military regime.

Siavelis, Peter, *The President and Congress in Postauthoritarian Chile: Institutional Constraints to Democratic Consolidation* (University Park, Pa.: Pennsylvania State University Press, 2000). An analysis of executive-legislative relations in post-authoritarian Chile, and the surprising success of democratic governments despite the country's non-democratic and awkward institutional framework.

Valenzuela, Arturo, *The Breakdown of Democratic Regimes: Chile* (Baltimore: Johns Hopkins University Press, 1978). The best analysis of the political dynamics of the breakdown of Chile's democratic regime in 1973.

Vellinga, Menno (ed.), *The Changing Role of the State in Latin America* (Boulder, Colo.: Westview Press, 1998. Analyses the role of the state in different facets of economic and political life, plus case studies from a number of Latin American countries.

## WEB LINKS

**www.presidencia.cl**   Chile's presidential website (English transl. available).

**www.gobiernodechile.cl**   The official site of the Chilean government.

**www.bcentral.cl/esp**   Site of Banco de Chile.

 **COMPANION WEB SITE**

For additional material and resources, see the companion web site at:
**www.oup.com/uk/booksites/politics/**

# Strong state, weak state

## The Democratic Republic of Congo

*Thomas M. Callaghy and Marton T. Markovits*

## OVERVIEW

This chapter examines the Zaire/Democratic Republic of Congo (DRC) as an example of the politics of state decay, from the 1970s to the 1990s. The case exemplifies the particular difficulties in building and maintaining an effective and coherent state in Africa. It demonstrates the results of state collapse in Zaire and illustrates the potential impact of state fragility and failure on the international borders of the state. It argues that even though borders are often presumed to be permanent, their nature is actually contingent; that a strong relationship exists between the internal complexion of a state and its external shape; and that there are murky links between the gradual processes of decay, and sudden, unexpected transformation.

**ZAIRE**

---

## Box18*b*.1  Key events in Congolese history to 1965

**1876**   King Leopold II convenes first meeting of Brussels International Geographical Conference

**1879–84**   Henry Morton Stanley establishes trading stations and acquires territory in Congo River basin for King Leopold

**1884–5**   United States becomes first country to recognize King Leopold's claims to Congo. Berlin West Africa Conference is held to ensure free trade in the Congo, free navigation of the Niger River, and to agree on the rules of future annexation of land in Africa

**1931**   Major revolt by Pende people against economic conditions imposed by the colonial state and concession companies

**1946**   Insurrection, resistance, and workers' strikes throughout country

**1948–54**   Series of initiatives are started by Belgians to give nominal rights to small group of Congolese *évolués*

**1955**   King Baudouin of Belgium visits Congo to hear *évolués*' demands

**1957**   Kasavuba and Abako party win municipal elections in Kinshasa

**1959**   Mass uprisings in Kinshasa call for independence. Belgian government says it will consider Congolese demands for freedom.

**1960**   Congolese Independence and collapse of central authority

**1963–4**   Katangan secession ends. Tshombe forced into exile. Popular rebellions occur throughout Congo against ineffective administration in Kinshasa. Foreign-led military operation launched against nationalist, Lumumba-inspired opposition. Tshombe returns from Spain and designated new Prime Minister

**1965**   Mobutu takes power for the final time in his second coup

# Introduction

For more than a decade, Central Africa, especially its Great Lakes region, has been a crucible for tragic conflict and dramatic change. It has experienced genocide in Rwanda; a Tutsi invasion of Rwanda by a Uganda-supported army that successfully overthrew the Hutu government in July 1994; and the flight of that government and its army, as well as large numbers of Hutu people, into Zaire. From these events erupted a totally unexpected civil war in Zaire in 1996, which occurred with the vigorous backing of several regional powers and resulted in the collapse of the brutal and ineffective regime of Africa's longest-ruling dictator, Mobutu Sese Seko (1965–97). A little more than a year later, fighting began anew; this time the conflict was to overthrow the new government of President Laurent Kabila in the capital, Kinshasa, of what had been renamed the Democratic Republic of Congo (DRC). African states intervened on both sides of the war, exacerbating the situation. These recent events highlight the culmination of post-colonial politics in the DRC, one of the most complex **failing states** on the continent. It is important to understand how a unique set of historical inheritances contributed to the context of collapse, civil war, **warlordism**, and interstate conflict, present in Central Africa today.

# Historical context: political, economic, and cultural repression

## King Leopold and the Congo Free State

The area that is today's DRC was recognized as the personal domain of King Leopold of Belgium at the close of the Berlin West Africa Conference on 26 February 1885. The Congo occupying an area eighty times the size of Belgium, was the only colony in Africa that belonged to an individual. The economy in Leopold's 'Congo Free State' was based on the extraction of raw resources, mainly rubber and ivory, and was supported by forced labour. Harsh measures were used to make people farm the rubber that grew wild in the Congo, and which could be sold on the world market in support of burgeoning industries. Land was appropriated and quotas implemented to ensure profits for Leopold. If quotas were not met, kidnapping, hostage-taking, rape, torture, mutilation, arson, and murder were used to terrorize the population. These acts were perpetrated both by European station agents who were posted throughout the colony and by African employees of the colonial state.

This system of exploitation and extraction had tremendously deleterious effects on the population of the Congo. Hochschild (1998: 233) has estimated that the death toll during Leopold's twenty-four years of rule was approximately ten million people, caused by murder, starvation, exhaustion, and disease. The plunder and exportation of its most precious commodities for the benefit of the few is a central theme throughout Congolese history. This type of exchange dominated the colonial economy under both King Leopold, and the Belgians, as well as the post-colonial economy during the reign of Mobutu Sese Seku.

## The Belgian Congo

International pressure for reform forced the Belgian government to assume control of the Congo Free State in 1908. Though it was neither interested in, nor prepared to administer a colony, the apparatus that Leopold had built was expanded and deepened economically, politically, and culturally under the Belgians.

## Box 18*b*.2  King Leopold's legacy

It follows from the fact of inheritance that Belgium inherited, not only a colony, but a colony possessed of a certain structure. The elements of that structure were a sparse and battered customary society; a vast territory which had not been properly administered; a system of direct economic exploitation, or an unfettered variant of the concessionaire system, and as a consequence at a further remove, abuse and atrocity.

(Anstey 1966: 261)

Economically, the Belgians capitalized on the network of private business monopolies created under Leopold to extract raw materials from the Congo. Corporations were ceded huge tracts of land laden with valuable mineral resources and allowed to develop the wealth in them using whatever means necessary. The colonial economy had devastating consequences for the Congolese people. Peasant life was disrupted because subsistence-level agriculture was forcibly changed to focus on the large-scale exportation of raw materials. Local artisans and merchants were marginalized thanks to the trading monopolies of the concession companies, and policies designed to shield them from all African competition. The colonial political apparatus corrupted local systems of rule by co-opting elites and indirectly integrating them into the state apparatus. Often, the local chiefs served as middlemen for the concessionaires as a way to maintain positions of nominal privilege in the colonial hierarchy. In this way, the former basis of authority was disrupted. Other African agents ensured that people paid taxes, worked on public projects, grew particular crops for export, served in the local military and police force, and provided labour for the colonial development machine.

The colonial state also worked to suppress the Congolese people culturally, since local culture was seen to be a source of resistance. This was accomplished through varying types of restrictions, both legal and unwritten, that divided the society into categories based on race and ethnicity. Africans were barred from certain areas, prevented from buying and selling land, and forced to live in segregated areas, with different labour laws. Africans were not able to use the same public facilities as the Europeans and there was an unofficial prohibition against interracial sex, though it only applied to African men and European women. Africans were barred entry to most elements of colonial society. Late in the period of Belgian colonial rule, however, some African merchants were given minor opportunities for advancement. It is one of the ironies of colonialism that many in the initial group of *évolués* (the evolved ones) became leaders of the Congolese independence movement.

## The struggle for the flag 1960–1965

The Congo won its independence on 30 June 1960. Patrice Lumumba was its first prime minister and Joseph Kasavuba its first president. Lumumba was the first person—and remains the only person—to receive a national mandate via elections in the Congo. The first five years after independence were marked by chaotic events that pushed the country to the brink of collapse. In all, five crises challenged the sovereignty of the Congo, disrupted its internal transition to indigenous rule, and adversely effected its political and economic development.

The first of these occurred a few days after independence when the regular soldiers of the Congolese army, the *Force Publique*, mutinied on 5 July 1960. The army was composed entirely of Congolese soldiers, but the officer corps remained Belgian. The regular soldiers were unhappy with this fact, as well as the lack of pay increases and promotions after independence. In response to the soldiers' demands, Lumumba called for the resignation of the army's Belgian commander, promoted everyone one rank, and renamed the *Force Publique* the Congolese National Army. He appointed two former Congolese soldiers to senior posts. Victor Lundula became General and Commander-in-Chief, and Joseph Mobutu, Colonel and Chief of Staff. Yet Lundula proved underqualified to manage a modern, national army and Mobutu would soon betray Lumumba by involvement in his assassination.

Before this calamity, however, there were two important secession attempts in the south-east of the country. The first began directly on heels of the Force Publique mutiny when Katanga, led by Moises

Tshombe, declared its independence on 10 July 1960. The second attempt occurred nearly a month later when Albert Kalonji announced the secession of South Kasai. The secession in mineral-rich Katanga was supported by Belgium, Britain, South Africa, and the United States as a means to destabilize Lumumba's new government, while securing exclusive access to the wealth in the region. In South Kasai, inter-ethnic conflict between two prominent groups, the Lulua and the Baluba, served to further destabilize nearly one-third of the new country while presenting overwhelming problems for the new government in Kinshasa.

Almost a month after the South Kasai secession, the Congo faced constitutional crisis. On 5 September 1960, Kasavuba dismissed Lumumba, holding him responsible for the conflict between the Lulua and Baluba. Since Lumumba's party held the most seats in parliament, Kasavuba lacked authority to remove him from office. In response, Lumumba asked Kasavuba to relinquish the presidency; Kasavuba refused. The legitimacy of the constitution was in doubt since neither man would step down. One week later, Mobutu intervened and politically 'neutralized' both men, claiming he intended to establish peace and stability. In reality, Western allies felt that Mobutu was more moderate and easier to control than Lumumba, and encouraged him to take power. It was Lumumba's strong nationalist desire for a unified Congo, free from outside interference, that made him look dangerous to those with major economic and political interests at stake.

The final crisis was the assassination of Lumumba in January 1961. The plot to kill him was facilitated by Mobutu, the Belgians, the USA, and his enemies in Katanga. It was only a matter of time before Mobutu took power again in a second coup on 24 November 1965; he remained in power until 1997. Out of chaos, order came to the vast new state under Mobutu, but the political form of his regime sowed the seeds of its eventual collapse.

## Key points

- Relations between the Congo and the West began when the Portuguese landed on the Congolese coast in 1482. The slave trade dominated these relations for nearly four centuries.

- King Leopold of Belgium staked claim to the Congo during the **scramble for Africa** in 1884–5. A system of forced labour, severe repression, and the exploitation of its most precious commodities characterized Leopold's reign.

- King Leopold's Congo Free State became the Belgian Congo in 1908. The colonial state apparatus was further extended and exploitation and repression intensified.

- The Congo won independence in 1960 in a nationalist struggle led by Patrice Lumumba, who became the first prime minister.

- The early independence period was characterized by cumulative crises, involving both competing domestic actors and several Western nations.

# Zaire as a failing state

Zaire under Mobutu represents a dramatic case of state collapse, but it is not unique in this regard. (see Chapter 11). There are several reasons, some internal and some external that must be examined to explain state collapse. In the case of Zaire, external factors include its colonial legacy, the cold war, and its position in the international economy. Internally, there is the failure of its ruler to foster economic development, permit mass political participation, and maintain basic order.

There are several models of the state with which the Mobutu regime may be compared: neo-Marxist, corporatist, absolutist, **patrimonial**, **neo-patrimonial**, liberal, and **developmental** (Clark 1998). Ultimately, however, Zaire was a classic example of an unproductive **extractive state**. It has also been called a 'kleptocratic', or 'vampire' or 'pirate' state. All are synonyms to describe what Villalón and Huxtable (1998: 13) have called a state that 'has been elaborated and has served primarily as an instrument for extracting mineral or other natural resources to the benefit of those who control it'. Zaire under Mobutu was an archetype of the extractive state, in which forcible removal of the national wealth became an end in itself, and occurred at the country's expense. There was a complete disconnection of the state from civil society, which became largely irrelevant to any functioning of the state. This dynamic led to state fragility, diminishing legitimacy and capacity, and finally collapse.

## The politics of Mobutu

Racked by multiple crises of order and identity in the 1960s, Zaire became a highly personalized state, ruled for over thirty years by a presidential monarch—Mobutu Sese Seko. His authoritarian regime was quietly failing for much of its existence as he tried to maintain control of his vast and mineral-rich country. The state under Mobutu was simultaneously soft, yet highly coercive. Corruption so permeated the system that the state was slowly hollowed out. The economy actually started to collapse in the middle 1970s, and the survival tactics of the informal economy spread. Control of the state was maintained for so long only by virtue of three mechanisms: a 'national' army of occupation, repeated rescue efforts by outside international powers, and Mobutu's astute statecraft. He created a legitimating doctrine that was a *mélange* of disparate, but initially believable ingredients—he was the father who saved the nation from chaos in the 1960s by bringing order, dignity, and development. Powerful customary notions of patrimonial authority, dignity, arbitrariness, grandeur, display, and the occult underpinned his authority.

---

### Box 18b.3 Important quotes (Congo/DRC)

I would like to make out of our little Belgium, with its six million people, the capital of an immense empire. The Netherlands, Spain, Portugal, are in a state of decadence and their colonies will one day or another come on to the market.

(King Leopold, as quoted in Hochschild 1998:167).

The country's unity is not in danger. This is the most durable achievement of my political career. Everybody will have to learn a lesson in this war: the Zairians are welded together by their national feeling.

(Mobutu Sese Seko in an interview with B. Grill, 'Zaïre: Mobutu Rules Out Giving in to Foreign Order to Resign', *Hamburg Die Zeit*, 25 April 1997)

There was not Zaïre before me, and there will be no Zaïre after me. (Ibid)

Resign; you have no more power; you have failed, and it's finished.

(Laurent Kabila in Lynne Duke, 'Stability and Democracy at Stake in Mobutu-Kabila Battle of Wills', *Washington Post*, 20 April 1997)

We are talking about changing the head of state, but we have no state.

(Francesca Bomboko, Zairian political analyst in 'Upheaval in Zaire to Go On Indefinitely', Reuters, 21 April 1997)

In the case of Zaïre, there must be democratic elections at regular intervals, press freedom and perhaps a beginning of the formation of a broad coalition government including all parties. Elections must be conveniently held, but there must first be a state to do so. There are certain state pillars, which are indispensable for the holding of elections, and such structures do not seem to exist today. I am talking of the army, the police, the justice system, and the civil service. This requires some time, so I would advise a two or three-year period. Elections must be organized with all seriousness to avoid elections, which cause more unrest than peace.

(Ugandan President Yoweri Museveni on Radio France Internationale 1997)

First of all, I'd say America is a nation, a strong nation, because it has stayed a united nation, since the last 200 years. I don't see why the Congo today must be a nation that everybody, or anybody, for that matter, should start thinking of dividing it.

(President Joseph Kabila, Interview with Ray Suarez on *The Newshour* with Jim Lehrer, 1 February 2002)

An external support system was shrewdly maintained and exploited, founded on the geopolitical perceptions and perversions of the Cold war and the manipulation of 'national' and regional power rivalries.

The peak of Mobutu's power was reached in the late 1970s, but even then his regime had to be rescued twice from attacks, in 1977 and 1978, by military forces of the failed 1960s secession in Katanga. In the early 1980s efforts to undermine the dominant monarchical doctrine began to make headway as an internal opposition coalesced around a former Mobutu official, Etienne Thsisekedi, a Luba from the Kasai region. This process was aided by five important factors. First, by opposition from the only major actor that could challenge the state in Zaire—the Catholic Church; second, by indigenous religious movements; third, by the safety net of the informal economy as it responded to the collapsing formal economy; fourth, by a massive foreign debt problem, and finally, by failed efforts at economic reform, shepherded by the International Monetary Fund and the World Bank. These factors together resulted in growing de facto regional autonomy, and a strengthening culture of opposition, both of which challenged the notions of

personal power that had been constructed around Mobutu for decades.

A watershed was reached in 1990 when Mobutu was forced by internal and external pressures to announce that he would begin to democratize Zaire, a process he thought he could control. By this point, however, the political opposition had managed to change the way the battle for political dominance was being contested, and there was thus more political space for the opposition to challenge the Mobutu regime. For six years, Mobutu managed to manipulate the process that was to bring democracy to Zaire. He prevented both major changes to the rules of the political game while maintaining his position and that of his ruling elite at the top of the regime, but the mechanism that he had used to maintain legitimacy and authority was badly weakened.

## Key points

- Mobutu Sese Seko ruled Zaire as his personal monarchy for over thirty years, but the role of the state that he built was purely extractive, which ultimately lead to its demise, and his overthrow.

# Zaire/DRC in the Central African cauldron: decomposition and reshaping

## The end of Mobutu

In early October 1996, a rebellion of the Banyamulenge and other enemies of Mobutu began in the eastern province of South Kivu. This armed mobilization was sparked because the Banyamulenge, a community of 300,000 Congolese Tutsi, were given one week to leave Zaire or face extermination. The Banyamulenge revolt was an opportunity for both Rwanda and Uganda to confront Mobutu, who had done little to meet their earlier demands for security along the border that they share with Zaire. In early November, Laurent Kabila, was identified as the leader of the rebel group—the 'Alliance des forces démocratiques pour la libération du Congo-Zaire' (AFDL). This group systematically advanced west and

swept across the country before taking Kinshasa on 17 May 1997. Kabila changed the country's name to the 'Democratic Republic of Congo' and named himself president. Mobutu, had already fled the capital and died soon after.

Kabila banned all political parties and promised elections and full democracy after a transitional period for state reconstruction The honeymoon he enjoyed quickly evaporated when it became apparent that he was consolidating power and seeking to establish political legitimacy in ways that were frighteningly similar to Mobutu. He issued a broad and vague one-page constitutional decree for a 'Third Republic' that allocated almost total power to himself. He lost friends on all fronts, without losing any enemies. Many believed that his regional partners were Kabila's major pillars of support, but Rwanda and Uganda quickly lost faith in him as an effective and trust-worthy political successor to Mobutu. This situation was further compounded by Kabila's serious domestic legitimacy problems because of the perception that Tutsi leaders and other foreigners put him in power.

Most significantly, Kabila made no effort to honour the mantle of legitimacy afforded by a National Conference that had been so central in Mobutu's attempts to maintain control of the political process near the end of his regime. It proved to be a critical lost opportunity. Kabila responded to his dilemma by moving relatives and members of his own clan, ethnic group (Balubakati), and region (Shaba), into key positions within the new government. At the same time, he began to ease Tutsi and Rwandan political and military officials out. This proved a delicate and dangerous game with unclear political pay-off in Kabila's efforts to foster legitimacy and fill the political vacuum left after Mobutu.

# Regional transformation

The Rwandans and Ugandans ultimately decided to overthrow Kabila's government because of his failure to live up to his promises and the prospect of his losing the little effective control over the Congo that he still maintained. In July 1998, Kabila handed General Paul Kagame, the new Tutsi President of Rwanda the excuse he needed for invasion by ordering all remaining Rwandan soldiers to leave the Congo and generally harassing the Tutsi in eastern Congo. Having no effective army, Kabila turned to his southern neighbours who proved willing to help him despite his failure to live up to earlier promises. Zimbabwean President Robert Mugabe sent planes and soldiers, while the Angolans eventually entered the Congo at several strategic points, trapping advancing Tutsi forces, and former Mobutu troops who had joined them, between the Angolan forces and Kinshasa. The Rwandans overreached themselves

---

## Box 18b.4 Recent chronology of peace and conflict in the DRC

**16 April 2002** Peace talks in South Africa in which government signs power-sharing deal with Ugandan-backed rebels, under which MLC leader would be Prime Minister. Rwandan-backed RCD rebels reject deal.

**30 July** Joseph Kabila and Rwandan President Kagame sign peace deal under which Rwanda will withdraw troops from east and DRC will disarm and arrest Rwandan Hutu gunmen blamed for killing Tutsi minority in Rwanda's 1994 genocide.

**6 September** Kabila and Uganda's President Museveni sign peace accord under which Ugandan troops will leave DRC.

**17 December** All parties to Inter-Congolese Dialogue (government and main rebel groups) sign comprehensive peace agreement in South Africa. Agreement calls for installation of transitional government in early 2003 in which rebels and members of political opposition would hold high-level positions in an interim government.

**2 April 2003** Kabila signs new constitution, under which an interim government will rule for two years, pending elections. Delegates also adopt a constitution drawn up at talks a month earlier.

**May** Last Ugandan troops allegedly leave eastern Congo as reports emerge of bloody clashes between rival militias in Bunia area, in the Ituri region. Thousands of civilians seek asylum in Uganda. UN warns of possible genocide unless peacekeeping force deployed.

**30 May** UN Security Council authorizes French-led 1,400-strong peacekeeping force for Bunia. French to stay until relieved by UN force.

**17 July** Kabila names transitional government to lead DRC until democratic elections. Four vice-presidents sworn in, including leaders of two main rebel movements. Inaugurates power-sharing government with very uncertain outcome.

and seriously underestimated the willingness of Kabila's other neighbours to assist him.

Despite the signing of peace accords by all the key actors involved in Lusaka, Zambia, in July 1999, the fighting continued, and at least eight African countries were directly involved to varying degrees. The rebels continued to gain ground slowly, but competing factions emerged on both the rebel political and military fronts. The two main rebel factions, the Rassemblement congolaise de la démocratie (RCD) and the Mouvement pour la libération du Congo (MLC), held different portions of territory in the east, which led to the possibility of multiple de facto states within the borders of the Congo. In short, much of the eastern Congo degenerated into complex forms of warlordism and extraction that will be very difficult to eliminate. Sporadic fighting continued for another six months until the surprise assassination of Kabila by one of his bodyguards on 16 January 2001. Major-General Joseph Kabila, son of the slain president, was immediately chosen by government leaders to succeed his father. By late 2003, despite formal peace and an incipient government of national unity, the Congo remained a failed state in chaos, with terrible consequences for its long-suffering population. Over three million people had died since the beginning of the first round of the war in 1996, and more were dying every day from violence and neglect despite a small United Nations 'peacekeeping' force and the intense efforts of international NGOs.

## Key points

- Laurent Kabila was unsuccessful in his attempts to rebuild, reconfigure, or reconstitute the Congo after Mobutu.

- Major external and newly invigorated internal actors, especially warlords and their foreign supporters, moved into the resulting political vacuum, to renew conflict and war amidst state collapse.

- The civil war in the former Zaire opened the possibility of moving and recreating national boundaries considered immutable since the late nineteenth century.

# Conclusion

This case demonstrates three things: first, although national boundaries are normally presumed to be permanent, their nature is actually contingent on a number of factors. The gap between the behaviour of Central African actors and international norms that militate against border modification and the creation of new states is aptly demonstrated by the case of the Congo. Second, the case provides sufficient evidence to conclude that there is a strong relationship between the internal complexion of a state and its external shape. States tend 'to revert to type' under conditions of extreme insecurity. This makes productive rebuilding and reconstitution of a failing state much more difficult, while simultaneously allowing for the possibility of border contestation and change. At the same time, these relationships underscore the importance of regional and international agents and processes. In this example, state failure has fostered the emergence of a truly competitive state system in Central Africa. Third, the case highlights the often shadowy connections between gradual processes of political metamorphosis and the onset of sudden transformation. Here can be seen the relationship between the processes of state failure and the classic statecraft needs of state building, along with the opportunity and ability to act boldly in violation of reputed regional and international norms.

Finally, while Zaire might be an exceptional case, it is apparent that in much of Africa severe contradictions exist between reality and any alternative conception of reality. It remains unclear whether a new generation of African leaders and post-cold war powers will find a mutually acceptable path or whether African regimes can be satisfactorily reconstituted without the disruption of borders. If it becomes clear that new political structures threaten the interests of powerful, already militarized, domestic, and regional groups, pressure to alter boundaries will increase significantly. Powerful external actors will undoubtedly also attempt to influence the outcome of political and economic development processes in Africa.

In important cases, major world powers will try to foster reconstitution without any change in national boundaries and attempt to use their own norms to encourage their preferred outcomes. These norms are not fully consistent with one another, however and can lead to ambiguous and conflicting foreign policies and unintended consequences. The Western vision of the simultaneous spread of democracy and market economies has created internal tensions that are exposed by exceedingly difficult and intractable African realities (Callaghy and Ravenhill 1993).

## QUESTIONS

1   What impact did colonialism have on the Congo?

2   Were there any positive consequences of colonial rule?

3   What were the primary causes of state collapse in the Mobutu regime?

4   Why wasn't Kabila able to rebuild and reconstitute the state?

5   What are the requirements for the DRC to enjoy political stability and economic progress in the future?

## GUIDE TO FURTHER READING

Clark, J. F. (ed.), *The African Stakes of the Congo War* (New York: Palgrave MacMillan, 2002). A fine volume with contributions from informed scholars on the Congo that provides a wealth of information on important aspects of the recent conflict in the DRC.

Hochschild, A., *King Leopold's Ghost: A Story of Greed, Terror and Heroism in Colonial Africa* (Boston and New York: Houghton Mifflin, 1998). A well-researched history of how Leopold acquired his African kingdom and the drive that sought reform in the Congo Free State.

Nzongola-Ntalaja, G., *The Congo From Leopold to Kabila: A People's History* (London and New York: Zed Books, 2002). A well done and up-to-date modern history of the politics that have shaped the Congo and its drive for independence and democracy.

O'Leary, B., Lustick I., and Callaghy, T. (eds.), *Right-sizing the State: The Politics of Moving Borders* (Oxford: Oxford University Press, 2001). A comparison of cases where 'less is really more'— institutional design including state contraction as a response to domestic instability and conflict.

van de Walle, N. *African Economies and the Politics of Permanent Crisis, 1979–1999* (Cambridge: Cambridge University Press, 2001). An insightful account.

Thompson A., *An Introduction to African Politics* (London and New York: Routledge, 2000). A nice primer on African politics, contemporary history, and economics.

Villalón, L., and Huxtable, P. (eds.), *The African State at a Critical Juncture: Between Disintegration and Reconfiguration* (Boulder, Colo.: Lynne Rienner, 1998). Focuses on the widespread changes in the African state in the early 1990s.

Zartman, W. (ed.), *Collapsed States: The Disintegration and Restoration of Legitimate Authority* (Boulder, Colo.: Lynne Rienner, 1995). Important analysis of the causes and characteristics of state collapse in Africa.

## WEB LINKS

**www.congo-pages.org**    Provides a virtual tour of the DRC with pictures on different topics from all over the country.

**www.crisisweb.org**    The International Crisis Group (ICG) is an independent, non-profit, multinational organization, with over ninety staff members on five continents, working through field-based analysis and high-level advocacy to prevent and resolve deadly conflict.

**www.sas.upenn.edu/African_Studies/Country_Specific/Zaïre.html**    Website at the African Studies Center at the University of Pennsylvania, which provides access to important sites concerning all aspects of the DRC.

**www.sul.stanford.edu/depts/ssrg/africa/Zaïre.html**    An annotated guide to internet resources on the DRC.

**www.worldrevolution.org/Projects/WebGuide/SpecialGuide.asp?Topic = congo+war** Provides a good overview of recent conflicts in Central Africa and the attendant human rights situation through reports and publications by advocacy NGOs, as well as links to other relevant websites.

 **COMPANION WEB SITE**

For additional material and resources, see the companion web site at:
**www.oup.com/uk/booksites/politics/**

# 19a

# From regional power to microstates
## Nigeria

*Stephen Wright*

## OVERVIEW

Since independence from Britain in 1960, Nigeria has struggled to maintain stability in the face of significant ethnic, regional, and religious divisions. Military governments have ruled the country for all but ten years, although there is hope that the civilian government of President Olusegun Obasanjo, elected to office in 1999 and again in 2003, is consolidating democracy in the country. Despite this instability, Nigeria has promoted a forceful foreign policy, and has often championed African causes globally. This strong external policy has been shaped by Nigeria's demographic size as Africa's largest country, as well as by its very significant petroleum exports, but probably its influence cannot be maintained without a strengthening of democracy internally.

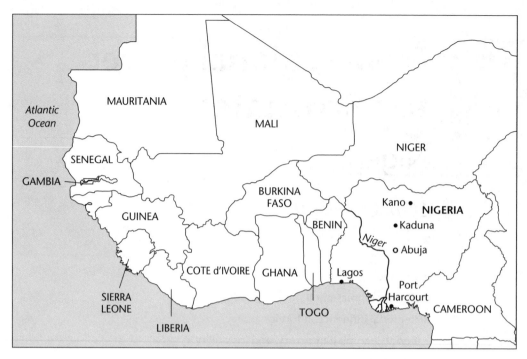

**NIGERIA**

---

## Box 19a.1 **Key dates in Nigeria's history**

**1914**   Britain pulls together various territories into the colony of Nigeria

**1960**   Independence from Britain

**1966**   Two military coups end the first civilian republic

**1967**   The start of the three-year civil war over Biafran secession

**1976**   Murtala Muhammed assassinated, and Olusegun Obasanjo takes over as military head of state, supervising a transition to civilian rule

**1979**   Second civilian republic inaugurated, under President Shehu Shagari

**1983**   Military coup on New Year's Eve ushers in sixteen years of military rule

**1985**   Ibrahim Babangida takes over in palace coup, and postpones multiple attempts to return to civilian government

**1993**   Moshood Abiola wins the presidency, but elections annulled by Babangida; later that year Sani Abacha seizes power in a coup

**1999**   Following the death of Abacha in 1998, a new transition is undertaken which elects Obasanjo to the presidency, and a new civilian republic begins

**2003**   Obasanjo re-elected for a further term amid allegations of electoral irregularities

# Introduction

The West African state of Nigeria offers an interesting case study of a country that has significant regional, and at times global, influence, and yet has struggled since its independence from Britain in 1960 with chronic political instability, resulting in the longest period of unbroken civilian rule being less than six years. Prior to colonial rule, the territory that was to become Nigeria consisted of numerous empires, and these were gradually absorbed into three administrative regions by the British. In turn, these regions were amalgamated into the colony of Nigeria in 1914, though each maintained a strong degree of identity and separation. Tensions between the three regions deepened in the 1950s, as ethnicity became a critical political issue in the jostling for power in a post-independent Nigeria. The inability to manage ethnic tensions has been a constant feature and has significantly contributed to the country's instability.

## Instability

The British installed a parliamentary democracy in Nigeria prior to their departure in 1960, but the system could not function effectively in the highly combative political environment. The first of many military *coups d'état* took place in January 1966, sweeping the civilians from office. A second coup later in the year slid the country towards a brutal civil war between 1967 and 1970, and civilian government was not allowed to return again until 1979. Despite efforts to ease ethnic and religious tensions, notably by breaking up the three powerful administrative regions into smaller units—eventually ending up with thirty-six internal states—instability remained high. The civilian government installed in 1979 barely lasted four years before the military swept back, and a despotic era of military rule lasted until 1999, when the current civilian government of President Olusegun Obasanjo (himself a former military head of state) was elected to office. His re-election in 2003 was considered a hopeful sign of a maturing democratic system.

## Regional power

Nigeria's regional prominence stems largely from two key factors: population and petroleum. Ethnicity politicizes the census process and makes an accurate headcount problematic, but the population is estimated to be around 120 million, a fraction under one-sixth of the continent's total population, and places the country as the world's tenth largest. Nigeria is by far the most populated country in West Africa, surpassing the next largest of Ghana and Côte d'Ivoire at 19 and 16 million respectively. Geological good fortune enabled Nigeria to be a prominent producer and exporter of oil and gas, making Nigeria's the largest economy in the region, and one of the largest in Africa. Currently, Nigeria stands as the world's fourteenth largest producer of oil, and the seventh largest in the Organization of Petroleum Exporting Countries (OPEC), almost on a par with Kuwait. Since its founding in 1975, Nigeria has been the leading member of the Economic Community of West African States (ECOWAS), and has often taken up leadership causes on behalf of the continent as a whole. Its demographic and economic prowess has assured close foreign policy linkages with countries outside Africa, notably the United States, Britain, and the European Union as a whole.

## Key points

- British colonization created a 'new' country of Nigeria, whose people had lived separately prior to colonial rule.
- Nigeria's population is the largest in Africa.
- Nigeria is the leading country in the fifteen-member Economic Community of West African States (ECOWAS), and its influence is based on population size and oil revenues.

# The economics of oil

## Transformation of the economy

At independence in 1960, agriculture dominated the economy. Climatic conditions had led the British to oversee the export production of single crops for each region—groundnuts in the north, palm oil in the south-east, and cocoa in the south-west. Oil production, focused in the fields of south-eastern Nigeria, began in earnest in the 1960s and proved to be a contributing factor in the country's civil war. Once peace was attained, oil production accelerated rapidly, contributing to an economic boom in the 1970s, helped significantly by soaring prices after 1973. Agriculture quickly lost its prominence as oil revenues contributed more than 90 per cent of export revenues, a figure which has remained fairly constant ever since. Massive development schemes were started, including dams, roads, airports, universities, and hospitals, but some of these projects were of more political significance than economic benefit.

The combination of oil wealth and a large consumer population led to considerable foreign investment. By the end of the 1970s, Nigeria was widely touted as the 'champion' of Africa, both in diplomatic and economic terms, and utilized this status to pursue important foreign policy initiatives, notably working for the 'liberation' of Zimbabwe and South Africa, and attempting to represent the views of developing countries in their call for a transformed global political economy.

## Elusive development

The hopes and ambitions of the 1970s were undermined after 1980 by a series of events. The most important of these was the glut of oil in world markets, which contributed to the collapse of Nigerian revenues. An economy distorted by the oil bonanza was in turn further dislocated by the rapid bust of the market. Development projects quickly became expensive white elephants, and import dependence racked up large national debt. Oil revenues had not only been squandered, but had been siphoned off to corrupt civilian and military elites, taking tens of billions of dollars out of the development process. The governments of the 1980s, civilian and military, were forced to relinquish their outspoken role in world politics and take up the very different challenge of seeking structural adjustment funding and debt support from the World Bank and International Monetary Fund.

The 1990s was arguably the most difficult decade in Nigeria's political and economic development. Continuing low oil revenues served to debilitate social and human development, and indicators such as infant mortality (78 deaths per 1,000 births) and life expectancy (average of 52 years) worsened as the new millennium opened. Infrastructure and transport crumbled, despite efforts at privatization and liberalization of critical sectors. External debt rose to its current level of $34 billion, the largest in Africa. Compounding the problem was the country's military leader between 1993 and 1998, General Sani Abacha, whose brutal rule led to Nigeria's ostracism from most international bodies.

The election of Obasanjo in 1999 helped to stabilize the economic environment. His attempt to crack down on corruption brought some limited success, though corruption remains endemic. Since 1999, Obasanjo has been able to engage the international financial community, and gained agreements on debt-rescheduling as well as helping to facilitate large investment inflows into the oil and gas sectors. As global demand for oil picks up, Nigeria is aiming to increase oil production from its current 2.1 million barrels a day (b/d) to 4 million b/d by 2010, with new reserves being found regularly. If the country is successful, then this revenue will provide another opportunity to promote economic and social development, hopefully with better results than previously.

## Key points

- The mainstay of the Nigerian economy is oil, accounting for more than 90 per cent of export revenue and 20 per cent of GDP.

- Following the collapse of the oil market in the early 1980s, Nigeria has struggled to maintain development projects, and has been forced to seek loans and debt-rescheduling from the international financial institutions.

- The early 2000s has witnessed a slight upturn in economic conditions, partly helped by the presence of a civilian government.

# Regional influence in foreign policy

Although there are differences of opinion over the extent of Nigeria's influence in the international arena, it is evident that the country exerts considerable influence in the West African region, and has an important role to play in many African issues, often representing the views of the continent on the world stage. The factors shaping this role are fairly evident. Nigeria's population size, market potential, military capability, oil and gas revenues, and OPEC membership provide important resources for the projection of influence. Conversely, most of its neighbours are very small and lack the demographic and economic resources to be all but reactive and relatively passive in the foreign policy arena. Neighbours such as Sierra Leone and Liberia have come close to being failed states, and tend to contribute little in the regional arena except in terms of mischief making.

Nigeria's foreign policy objectives are fairly typical of a developing state, although successive governments have had confidence to pursue them with more vigour than most. In the early years after independence, foreign policy was more muted, and in the economic arena followed a pro-Western bias. However, this did not prevent active espousal of policies favouring non-alignment and African development. The civil war opened new horizons, as the USA and Britain were lukewarm in their support of the Nigerian federal government, and the Soviet Union became a new partner in foreign policy. The country's armed forces mushroomed to over 200,000, and provided further leverage in foreign policy (they have since reduced to less than half of the figure, but still are a considerable force in the region). Perhaps the biggest shift in policy came in 1975, when the more radical government of General Murtala Muhammed refused to tow the Western line on Angolan independence, and came out in support of the Marxist faction struggling for power. Following the decline in oil revenue starting in the early 1980s, Nigeria's ability to influence policy outcomes was lessened, although the country continued to pursue policies championing African causes. This continuity was strengthened by a vibrant group of institutions such as the Nigerian Institute for International Affairs, universities, and the media, openly debating the country's foreign policy objectives.

## West Africa

The West African region has been the most important focus of foreign policy, although this has often been an unsympathetic arena for Nigerian endeavours. All of its neighbours are former French colonies, and the residual linkages of *la francophonie* have at times undermined Nigerian initiatives in the region. Many neighbours, along with France, were supportive of Biafran secession during the civil war, and these divisions were only slowly healed through Nigerian largesse. In 1975, Nigeria's lead in diplomacy with Benin brought about ECOWAS as an attempt to check French influence in the region, and the organization over its thirty years of life has attempted to improve trade and movement of people across its fifteen members. Official trade figures have remained low, as vital trade partners are in Europe, but unofficial (illegal) trade has flourished, with the porosity of the Nigerian borders being an important element of this trade. The role of Nigeria in the region's trade is important, either way.

Nigeria has a significant role in all ECOWAS policy areas, and has been vital in peacekeeping efforts in the region, notably in the long-standing civil wars in Liberia and Sierra Leone (ECOWAS Monitoring

Group, or ECOMOG) by providing at least a third of the total troops on average. The United Nations and Western states have been keen to support Nigeria as a West African peacekeeper. Nigerian troops have also often been present in UN peacekeeping missions, both in Africa and beyond (such as Burma, Lebanon, and Yugoslavia). In another example, when the civilian government in Equatorial Guinea was overthrown by the country's military in July 2003, it was expected that Nigeria would play a leading role in negotiations between the factions. Such a dynamic role is not always supported by everyone in the region, and complaints about Nigeria's 'regional hegemony' are heard.

## African champion

Nigerian governments have often taken on the role of African champion, promoting causes on behalf of the continent. During the 1960s and 1970s, these focused upon non-alignment, African independence, liberation in southern Africa, and economic rights. In 1973, for example, the Gowon administration was a leader of the New International Economic Order as well as in negotiations leading to the agreement signed in 1975 between the European Union and the African, Caribbean, and Pacific (ACP) States, which led to the first of four Lomé Conventions. At the end of that decade, significant diplomatic pressure was exerted to help with Zimbabwean independence and the release of Nelson Mandela from jail. It is difficult to quantify the importance of such pressure, or say how much it contributed to success, but there was a widespread expectation that Nigeria's foreign policy actions were credible. After 1980, as economic problems weakened Nigerian leverage, the country's role in the global arena was less certain.

During the 1990s, its position as Africa's proclaimed champion was undermined by several factors. First, the achievement of majority rule by South Africa meant that Nigeria's somewhat unchallenged 'leadership' of the continent was now rivalled by a stronger economic power in South Africa, whose GDP is three times larger than Nigeria's. Second, whereas Nelson Mandela was, and remains, an icon to the world, the despotic military leaders in Nigeria left the country increasingly isolated in the global arena. Nigeria's isolation peaked during the mid-1990s when minor sanctions were imposed upon the country by the Western powers, and Nigeria was suspended from the Commonwealth. Third, the failure to democratize until 1999 and the obvious frailty of democracy in the country, along with the continuing linkage of some Nigerian citizens to criminal gangs and the drug trade, served to undermine the legitimacy of the country to lead.

The new era opened up by the election of Obasanjo in 1999 helped to restore some credibility, and also repaired frayed relations with the United States, the European Union, and the international financial institutions. Massive investment in the oil and gas sectors picked up, although they had not really been affected much during the 1990s—and the Obasanjo government helped to restore the country's battered image. Nigeria played an important role in helping to establish the New Economic Partnership for Africa's Development (NEPAD) in the early 2000s, a major development initiative for the continent in partnership with the UN and industrialized countries. Its hosting of the Commonwealth Heads of Government (CHOGM) meeting in Abuja in December 2003 symbolized the country's return to good grace and status.

## Key points

- Nigerian governments in the 1970s were extremely active in promoting foreign policy objectives on behalf of the African continent.

- Nigeria championed the African, Caribbean, and Pacific (ACP) group of countries during negotiations leading to the Lomé Convention in 1975.

- In recent years, Nigeria's attempts to lead African opinion have been somewhat undermined by South Africa, with which some tensions have been witnessed.

# Social change, democracy, and instability

## Social fabric

Nigeria is made up of a complex mosaic of ethnic, regional, and religious identities, all of which have served at some time or other to undermine the country's stability. British colonialism forged together a country of disparate people, and also helped to create a heightened sense of ethnic identity and competition. The three regions—north, west, and east—of colonial Nigeria contained a single dominant ethnic group in each—Hausa, Yoruba, and Igbo respectively—who increasingly viewed politics as a battle for resources between the ethnic groups. The fledgling federal state at independence could not contain this animosity, and the early experiment was brought to a close in the 1966 military coup. Tensions between three powerful ethnic groups, while still a valid factor in the country's instability, form only a part of the story. Minority ethnic groups, particularly from the centre of the country, who form an important element of the armed forces, and from the country's oil belt have increasingly become a major factor in politics. Superimposed upon this ethnic tension is religion. Again, a rough division sees the country divided into a Muslim north and a Christian south, although the reality is much more complex. Religious differences have become increasingly politicized since the 1980s, and the establishment of *Sharia* (or Islamic) law in several northern states in the late 1990s exacerbated an already tense situation. Religious riots killing hundreds at a time are now commonplace, and provide a problem that no Nigerian government has been able to puzzle out.

It is probably fair to say that Nigeria's political elites, both civilian and military, have failed the country. Politics is based upon patrimonial inclinations, where access to political office normally translates into corrupt access to the nation's wealth. Massive corruption has undermined development efforts and continues to flourish. Even though the country is one of the continent's wealthiest countries, social development has remained poor, as money often does not make its way into productive usage. The most obvious example of this skewed development can be seen in the oil-producing areas of the Niger River delta. Potentially the wealthiest of all the regions, the people inhabiting the delta, such as the Ogoni and Ijaw peoples, have the lowest indicators of social development, and the environmental degradation of the region is staggering. This has led to massive social protests over the past decade, but these have consistently been met with brutal force from the federal government, often with the connivance of the oil corporations.

## Institutions and parties

Since 1960, Nigeria has had just under thirty years of military government, four different constitutions and republics, both parliamentary and presidential forms of government, at least eight governments overthrown by the military, and numerous different sets of political parties. The internal federal structure has evolved from three regions to thirty-six states in an effort to undermine the strength of regional and ethnic politics (and to offer more politicians the opportunity to extract wealth). In this environment of experimentation and instability, it is little surprise that democratic institutions and structures of government have been unable to establish themselves.

At independence, Nigeria was bestowed the **Westminster model** of government. This failed to contain the conflicts between government and 'opposition', which were themselves exacerbated by the power struggle between fledgling federal government and established ethnically driven regional governments. With hindsight, this system perhaps only effectively operated for two or three years, but it lingered until the 1966 military coup. Military governments ruled for all but four years between 1966 and 1999, and ranged considerably in capability and probity. Political parties were proscribed during much of military rule, and little progress was made in solving the social, ethnic, and religious problems facing the country. The civilian Second Republic (1979–83) was, like the first, dominated by northern power groups, and fizzled out in extreme corruption, ethnic bias, and electoral fraud before being swept from office on New Year's Eve 1983. This republic was very much fashioned upon the American presidential model, with an executive president, a Senate, and a House of Representatives. This political model is perhaps better suited to Nigerian political life, and was adopted for the Fourth Republic in 1999.

The 1990s proved to be the darkest period of political development, as the federal government became the personal plaything of one leader, Sani Abacha. In elections for the Third Republic in 1993, results pointed to a win by Chief Moshood Abiola, a Yoruba Muslim businessman. Alarmed at the possible consequences, the military government under Ibrahim Babangida—perhaps prompted by Abacha as the powerful minister of defence—annulled the elections and transferred power to a military and civilian coalition that lasted a few months before being overthrown by Abacha. When Abiola returned from exile in 1994, he was detained by Abacha, and eventually died in prison. Plans for a return to civilian government were repeatedly postponed, as civilian political leaders were hand-picked and dropped by Abacha. By 1998, Abacha had manipulated the political process to the extent that he was the sole presidential candidate of all five parties allowed by his regime. Upon his surprise death (assassination?), yet another political transition was started, and again a new slate of political parties created. The success of Obasanjo, a former military head of state, indicates the residual power of military leaders in the political process. In 2003, the presidential election was contested by two former military leaders, Obasanjo and Muhammadu Buhari, with a third, Babangida, biding his time for the 2007 elections. Elections have always been manipulated by incumbents, and the 2003 elections were no exception.

## Civil society

Despite long periods of oppressive rule, civil society groups have remained active and strong. The media have been outspoken during even the darkest times, and have helped to maintain a healthy dialogue about national and local policies. The universities have also played a strong role in voicing opinions about governments and policies, and student protests are a common feature. Similarly trade unions have been relatively well organized and not afraid to take action when their interests were threatened, and judges strove to maintain their independence. During the Abacha administration, repression of these groups was at its maximum, but many of them fought back against the regime, often from exile. Human rights and democracy organizations flourished, and worked with external groups to maintain pressure upon the regime. Unfortunately, these groups were often divided upon ethnic lines, but nevertheless were an important indication of the strength and vitality of civilian society, resisting blatant oppression. Prominent Nigerian writers such as Chinua Achebe, Ken Saro-Wiwa, and Wole Soyinka, were also important in maintaining pressure upon the corrupt regimes.

With such a vibrant civil society, one perhaps might expect significant advances in the political arena in terms of good governance and accountability. Unfortunately, to date, this has not transpired, and observers hope for more in the second Obasanjo administration.

## Key points

- The military has played a dominant role in the political history of Nigeria.

- Significant political experimentation with institutions and structures of government has occurred, but little has proved effective in containing societal strains brought about by ethnic, regional, and religious cleavages.

- Civil society groups have maintained a consistently strong role in Nigerian political life, despite many years of military rule, and even through the harshest period of the Abacha regime in the 1990s.

- The re-election of Obasanjo in 2003 is lending hope to the idea that the cycle of military rule has been broken, though Obasanjo's government is under fire for delivering very little to the average Nigerian and for not clamping down on corruption.

# Conclusion

Probably the best way to describe Nigeria is as a country of unfulfilled promise. Despite its demographic size and economic potential, the country has been dogged by numerous political and social problems. It has scored modest foreign policy successes, and continues to wield some influence, but even in this area the country has perhaps punched below its weight. Certainly, significant problems remain to be solved in its political development. However, Nigeria does provide an example of a country which can pursue a fairly dynamic foreign policy even with serious domestic instability.

So how should we view Nigeria? In terms of a positive outlook, Nigeria still remains a strong state with viable potential. Unlike some of its neighbours, the federal government exerts considerable power internally, and the country's borders remain relatively secure. The re-election of Obasanjo in 2003 provides optimism that the country has finally turned away from military government, and may be moving closer to some resolution of its political development problems. A buoyant oil economy, and continuing large flows of foreign investment into this sector, indicate that the economic profile can remain strong,

thereby shoring up the country's foreign policy importance.

Conversely, it is possible to pull together a number of negative factors that create a more pessimistic forecast. Instability and corruption remain endemic, with fraud being an important element of the 2003 elections. Ethnic and religious intolerance and violence is on the increase, with the government showing little capability to change that course. Talk of secession by different groups also increasingly fills the political airwaves. Continuing violence and labour unrest in the critical oilfields spell serious problems for Western oil companies. All these factors could continue to weaken Nigeria's foreign policy stature vis-à-vis South Africa's.

Which Nigeria do we see? On the one hand, many of these problems are not new, and Nigeria has weathered them quite effectively to date. On the other hand, there appears to be little if any progress over four decades in solving these endemic issues. Nigeria is often seen as a bellwether for other countries across the continent, and so how it develops over the coming years is of vital importance to the West African region if not the continent as a whole.

## QUESTIONS

1   What was the legacy of British colonization on the independent state of Nigeria?

2   How significant are ethnicity, religion, and regionalism in shaping domestic politics and society?

3   Has oil been detrimental to Nigerian economic development?

4   What factors enabled Nigeria to be influential in foreign policy, particularly within the West African region?

5   Why has democracy been elusive in Nigeria?

6   What is the importance of ECOWAS to Nigeria, and vice versa?

## GUIDE TO FURTHER READING

Diamond, L., Kirk-Greene, A., and Oyediran, O., *Transition without End: Nigerian Politics and Civil Society under Babangida* (Boulder, Colo.: Lynne Rienner, 1997). Examines the Babaginda regime and the problems of civilian transition.

Falola, T., *The History of Nigeria* (Westport, Conn.: Greenwood Press, 1999). An overview of the historical development of Nigeria, and the legacies of history faced today.

Ihonvbere, J., and Shaw, T., *Illusions of Power: Nigeria in Transition* (Trenton, NJ: Africa World Press, 1998). A political economy account of Nigerian development, offering a critique of more traditional perspectives on Nigeria.

King, M., *Basic Currents of Nigerian Foreign Policy* (Washington: Howard University Press, 1996). Offers an overview of the main themes of foreign policy, along with an account of major activities and policies.

Maier, K., *This House has Fallen: Midnight in Nigeria* (New York: Public Affairs, 2000). A more informal account of the political and social demise of Nigeria during the 1990s.

Osaghae, E., *Crippled Giant: Nigeria since Independence* (Bloomington, Ind.: Indiana University Press, 1998). An overview of Nigerian political and economic development since independence.

Soyinka, W., *The Open Sore of a Continent: A Personal Narrative of the Nigerian Crisis* (New York: Oxford University Press, 1996). The Nobel laureate's bitter account of the failings of the Abacha regime.

Wright, S., *Nigeria: Struggle for Stability and Status* (Boulder, Colo.: Westview Press, 1998). An analysis of Nigeria since independence, focusing upon domestic instability and efforts to promote a strong external policy.

## WEB LINKS

www.nigeriainfonet.com

www.nigeria.com

**www.ngrguardiannews.com** *Guardian* (Lagos) newspaper.

**www.vanguardngr.com** The site of Vanguard news media (Nigeria).

**www.nigeria.indymedia.org** Nigeria's independent media centre.

 ## COMPANION WEB SITE

For additional material and resources, see the companion web site at:
**www.oup.com/uk/booksites/politics/**

# From regional power to microstates

## The island states of the Pacific

*Mark Otter*

## OVERVIEW

The island states of the Pacific are extraordinarily diverse in terms of ethnicity, history, and economic, social, and political development. Yet they share common issues of smallness, isolation from major markets, and a relative detachment from the major political issues of the modern world. They struggle to have their voices heard in international forums, such as the World Trade Organization (WTO), and, for them, the modern globalized economy seems of little relevance. While their situation is not unique, Pacific island states are interesting examples of all developing states who share similar circumstances.

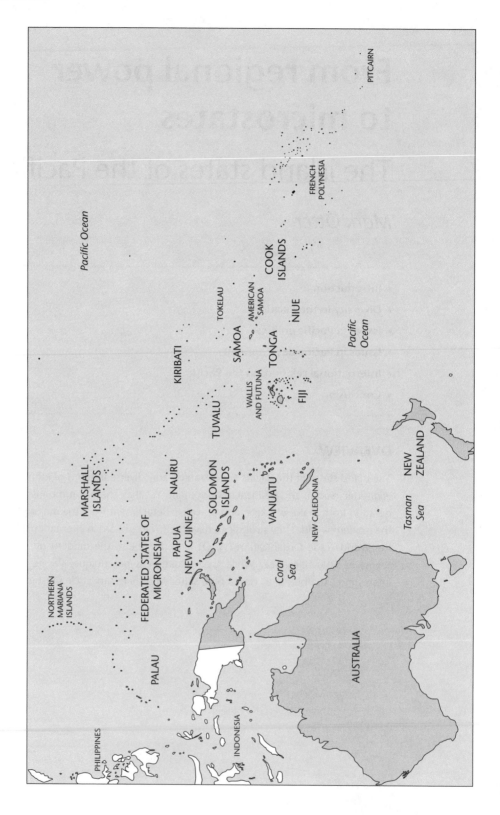

THE ISLAND STATES OF THE PACIFIC

**Table 19*b*.1** Islands in the Pacific: colonial heritage and system of government

| Country | Former colonial authority | Constitutional status/Form of government | Year of independence |
|---|---|---|---|
| American Samoa | — | Territory of the United States | — |
| Cook Islands | New Zealand | Constitutional monarchy with a parliamentary system and the British monarch as Head of State | 1964 (in association with NZ) |
| Federated States of Micronesia (FSM) | United States | Federal republic in a presidential system | 1986 (in association with the US) |
| Fiji Islands | British colony | Republic in a parliamentary system and a non-executive presidency | 1970 |
| French Polynesia | — | Territory of France | — |
| Guam | — | Territory of the United States | — |
| Kiribati | British colony (formerly the Gilbert Islands) | Republic in a parliamentary system with an executive presidency | 1976 |
| Marshall Islands | United States | Republic in a combined parliamentary/presidential system | 1986 (in association with the US) |
| Nauru | Australia–UN Trusteeship (Germany before WWI) | Republic in a parliamentary system with an executive presidency | 1968 |
| New Caledonia | — | Territory of France | — |
| Niue | New Zealand | Constitutional monarchy with a parliamentary system and the British monarch as Head of State | 1974 (in association with NZ) |
| Northern Marianas | — | Commonwealth of the United States | — |
| Palau | United States | Republic in a presidential system | 1995 (in association with the US) |
| Papua New Guinea | Australia—Papua an Australian territory, New Guinea a UN Trusteeship, (Germany before WWI) | Constitutional monarchy with a parliamentary system and the British monarch as Head of State | 1975 |
| Samoa (called Western Samoa until 1997) | New Zealand–UN Trusteeship (Germany before WWI) | Constitutional monarchy with a parliamentary system and an indigenous monarch as Head of State | 1962 |
| Solomon Islands | British Protectorate | Constitutional monarchy with a parliamentary system and the British monarch as Head of State | 1978 |
| Tonga | Special protectorate status with Britain | Monarchy with an indigenous monarch as Head of State | 1970 |
| Tuvalu | Britain (formerly the Ellice Islands) | Constitutional monarchy with a parliamentary system and the British monarch as Head of State | 1978 |
| Vanuatu | Britain and France (formerly the condominium of the New Hebrides) | Republic in a parliamentary system and a non-executive president | 1980 |
| Wallis and Futuna | — | Territory of France | — |

*Note*: Territories not listed by virtue of their extremely small size or incorporation into larger states include Tokelau (an incorporated territory of New Zealand), Pitcairn (a British colony), Norfolk Island (external territory of Australia), Hawaii (a US state), Easter Island/Rapanui (province of Chile), Galapagos (province of Ecuador), Torres Strait islands (part of the Australian state of Queensland), and the Indonesian province of Papua (formerly West Papua or Irian Jaya).

# Introduction

The 'picture postcard' image of the Pacific is far from reality. There is certainly some crystal clear water and there are still many pristine beaches, but tropical forests are being depleted by unscrupulous loggers, rivers are being polluted by mining operations, some once-plentiful fish and other species are at serious risk and rising sea levels threaten the physical existence of some small, low-lying island countries. In a number of Pacific states, income levels and education and health standards are falling and corruption, money politics, and ethnic violence are on the increase. The weak nature of some Pacific states puts their very political existence at risk. The Pacific is no longer, if it ever was, pacific.

The island states of the Pacific are not immune from the political and economic pressures of the modern world but they struggle to come to terms with global political concepts like democratization, and have difficulty in taking advantage of a globalized economy. As politically diverse as they are, no Pacific country has yet satisfactorily integrated Western forms of governance and law inherited from former colonial powers with traditional political and legal norms. As economically diverse as they are, no Pacific country has the capacity to trade its way out of its development dilemma.

What, if anything, marks the island states of the Pacific from the rest of the developing world? To a large extent, nothing—they have comparable income, education, and health indicators to many other developing countries and similar economic, political, and environmental vulnerabilities. In common with other small states, they lack political and economic clout in international forums. Like other isolated island states, they suffer from remoteness from major international markets. As with many tropical countries, Pacific island states are susceptible to frequent and devastating natural disasters. To study the island states of the Pacific, therefore, is to study many of the general issues confronting the developing world. But the Pacific also has unique cultures and environments which make its states worthy of special consideration.

## Key points

- The island states of the Pacific are beautiful, their peoples largely maintain a close relationship with their natural environment and there are, generally speaking, an abundance of natural resources.
- But they are not immune from political violence, economic stagnation, social ills, and irrelevance in international forums.
- Pacific island states are not unique in the developing world but they are good representations of the problems facing other small and isolated developing states.

# Diversity in the Pacific

In all, there are some twenty island states in the Pacific—fourteen of which are sovereign independent states. While the term 'South Pacific' is still in common usage, a number of states (mainly former US territories) lie to the north of the equator. The official, and more accurate, practice is, therefore, simply to use the term 'Pacific', as in, for example, the Pacific Islands Forum (which used to be called the South Pacific Forum).

All the states were colonized in one constitutional form or other, and at one stage or other, by Britain, France, Germany, the United States, Australia, or New Zealand. Most of the remaining non-independent territories are governed, directly or indirectly, by France or the United States. Table 19b.1 shows the colonial history of Pacific states together with their current constitutional status and form of government.

The diversity of colonial and constitutional heritage in the Pacific is matched by the diversity of its population. Only one country, Papua New Guinea, has more than one million people—another 5 million people are distributed among all the other island states. So Pacific populations are small, but they vary considerably in size (see Table 19b.2 for details). Ethnically, the region can be broadly divided into three groups:

*Melanesia*—Papua New Guinea, Solomon Islands, Vanuatu (whose people are called ni-Vanuatu), New Caledonia, and the Fiji Islands. There are also majority Melanesian populations in the Indonesian province of Papua (the western half of the island of New Guinea) and the Australian islands of the Torres Strait (between the northern tip of mainland Australia and the island of New Guinea).

*Polynesia*—Samoa (the independent state of Samoa as well as American Samoa), Tonga, French Polynesia, Wallis and Futuna, Tuvalu, Cook Islands and Nuie. There are also significant Polynesian minorities in Hawaii, New Zealand (both indigenous Maori and Pacific island migrants), and parts of Fiji, Solomon Islands, and Papua New Guinea.

*Micronesia*—Kiribati (pronounced *Kiribas*, whose people are called i-Kiribati), Nauru, Marshall Islands, the Federated States of Micronesia, Palau, Northern Marianas, and Guam.

Pacific island countries also vary considerably in their natural resource endowments—Papua New Guinea, Solomon Islands, and New Caledonia, for example, have large reserves of timber and minerals. Some island states have enormous sea areas (Kiribati is the best example with an EEZ—exclusive economic zone—very much larger than its land area) and have access to large stocks of fish, particularly tuna. Some Pacific states (such as Fiji, Cook Islands, and Vanuatu) have vigorous tourism industries which provide large contributions to their national income and employment. Other states (like Tuvalu and Niue), by virtue of their very small size, lack of resources, and distances from major markets struggle to meet the economic needs of their populations.

Development indicators for Pacific island states also show a widely varied picture. Table 19b.2 shows, for example, that there are huge differences in adult literacy between Vanuatu and Kiribati. Palau and Papua New Guinea have large disparities in incomes

**Table 19b.2** Islands States of the Pacific: selected development indicators

| | Population (1998 est.) | GDP/capita (US$) | Life expectancy at birth | Adult literacy (%) | Women in parliament (%) |
|---|---|---|---|---|---|
| Cook Islands | 16,500 | 4,947 | 73 | 93 | — |
| Federated States of Micronesia (FSM) | 114,000 | 1,973 | 68 | 81 | 0 |
| Fiji Islands | 798,000 | 2,061 | 69 | 93 | 5.7 |
| Kiribati | 85,000 | 430 | 62 | 100 | 4.8 |
| Marshall Islands | 61,000 | 1,830 | 65 | 91 | 3.0 |
| Nauru | 11,500 | 3,450 | 57 | 95 | 0 |
| Niue | 2,100 | 3,714 | 74 | 98 | — |
| Palau | 18,500 | 6,280 | 69 | 98 | 0 |
| Papua New Guinea | 4.4 million | 563 | 57 | 64 | 0.9 |
| Samoa | 175,000 | 1,465 | 69.5 | 98 | 6.1 |
| Solomon Islands | 418,000 | 614 | 68.7 | 76.6 | 0 |
| Tonga | 98,000 | 1,406 | 68.1 | 99 | 0 |
| Tuvalu | 11,000 | 1,157 | 67 | 98 | 0 |
| Vanuatu | 183,000 | 1,058 | 68.3 | 34 | 1.9 |

*Sources*: United Nations Development Programme (1999) and United Nations Development Programme (2003).

## Box 19b.1  Solomon Islands—a failing state?

Solomon Islands is at the crossroads of its history. Civil unrest between ethnic groups broke out in late 1997 and there was a coup in June 2000. Violence, and the ensuing tension and social mistrust have devastated the economy and bankrupted the government. Water, power, and sanitation services are seldom delivered; most health and education facilities lay idle. Incompetence, mismanagement, and corruption among many politicians and public officials have led many observers to believe that Solomon Islands has failed as a state.

Most Pacific island countries are weak, but Solomon Islands is the first to approach the brink of irrelevance. It is weak also because the institutions and processes of the state are largely imposed Western institutions lacking a sense of local ownership. Many Solomon Islanders consider that modern government and its participants are self-serving and without the interests of the people at heart.

Along with inappropriate structures, processes, and institutions of government, the focus of development

planning in Solomon Islands since independence has been on economic growth, primarily through developing natural resource export industries. Economic development was concentrated on a few large-scale industries (mainly logging, palm oil, and fisheries), it was over-centralized in the capital and its surrounding areas, and it was dominated by the political elite who were largely self-serving and incompetent. Economic management models better suited to a small fragile developing country were ignored in favour of high profile, quick-earning projects, most of which then failed.

The Solomon Islands government has been unable or unwilling to bring to justice the remaining warring militias, who have resorted to crime and intimidation to achieve their ends, and to control the police force. In July 2003, an international intervention force, led by Australia and including New Zealand, Papua New Guinea, Fiji, Vanuatu, Tonga, and Samoa, saw foreign troops, police, and public administrators attempt to bring Solomon Islands back into some semblance of order.

(Gross Domestic Product per capita). Some Pacific island states like Samoa and Tonga display good economic management and human resource development policies and practices resulting in relatively large numbers of well-educated people. But many Samoans and Tongans are unable to find employment at home and migrate to developed countries, particularly New Zealand, Australia, and the United States. Overseas remittances for Samoa and Tonga make up large proportions of their national income. Other Pacific island states manage their economies less well.

While it is true that large-scale violence and civil unrest have remained absent from most Pacific countries, the past two decades have shown a disturbingly un-pacific trend. There were two coups in Fiji in 1987 and another in 2000. The year 2000 also saw a coup in Solomon Islands and the region's second civil war (see Box 19b.1 for details). There was a civil war on the island of Bougainville in Papua New Guinea from 1989 to 1997. Lawlessness elsewhere in Papua New Guinea is a major concern which has serious impacts on the economy, social harmony, and governance.

There has also been political violence in Vanuatu and a politically motivated murder in Samoa.

Politically, most Pacific states have adopted—or adapted—Western styles of governance. Those with a British (or Australian or New Zealand) colonial heritage have generally adopted the parliamentary system. Those with a US colonial history generally have presidential systems. In some cases (Nauru, Kiribati), there is a mixture of both. There is mostly a good record of free and fair elections in the Pacific, with little election-related violence (Papua New Guinea is an exception). There have been relatively frequent changes of government and no serious attempt by a losing government to cling onto power—all measures of institutionalized democracy. Tonga, which has an absolute monarchy, is exceptional.

While this heritage of democratic institutions and practices may have contributed to social harmony in many parts of the Pacific, in others there is evidence of an alienation of Western political institutions from traditional political and legal systems. This is thought to be one of the problems leading up to the civil unrest in Fiji, Papua New Guinea, and Solomon Islands.

## Key points

- There is enormous geographic, ethnic, developmental, historical, and political diversity in the Pacific.

- While it might be possible to make some generalizations, there are just as many exceptions.

# Issues in Pacific politics

Notwithstanding the great diversity among Pacific island states, some fundamental issues are more or less common.

## Poor governance

A failing in many Pacific island states and most pronounced in the Melanesian countries is in the lack of knowledge, experience, and competence to formulate and implement sound public policy. This is a crucial component of good governance, necessary for the success of development programmes and for the maintenance of the state itself. There are cases of governments taking stopgap action in managing their financial and economic affairs, such as increasing debt levels and seeking additional external funds, sometimes from unscrupulous countries, organizations, and individuals. Governments have often failed to address underlying structural problems, to make essential reforms in management competence or to fight corruption.

## Incompatibility between modern and traditional governance

The weakness of many Pacific island governments relates to the fact that, for many people, the national government—or even the state itself—has less relevance than traditional or customary forms of political organization. The customary history of many of the states is one of primary association with the clan, the family, the village, or a particular island instead of the state, which is often seen as a colonial imposition. Indeed, many Pacific island states owe their existence under modern international law to the meanderings of early European explorers and territorial deals among colonial powers.

This does not necessarily mean that democracy is a foreign concept there. In most Pacific societies there are traditions of participation in decision-making in one form or other, although perhaps not with the same attention to the detail of equality across genders, ages, and racial groups as one would expect to see in modern Western liberal political systems. Among modern, educated Pacific islanders, however, there are strong feelings of exclusion and demands for greater participation in political processes. Systems and structures of government need to adjust to these dynamics.

## Key points

- Poor governance prevents many Pacific island states from realizing equitable and fair distribution of the fruits of development.

- An incompatibility between modern and traditional political systems has generated conflict in some cases.

# Issues in Pacific development

There are three terms commonly, but erroneously, used by those attempting to explain the development 'problem' in the Pacific. All go some way towards an explanation but all are also deficient and inadequate. The Pacific is more complex than any of these terms and in its modern existence is a mixture of universal and customary values.

First, the 'Pacific Paradox', a term coined by the World Bank in 1993, describes a situation in which there are large endowments of natural resources and generous receipts of foreign aid, but little economic, social, and political development to show for it. It is also a dilemma for aid donors and others working in Pacific development. A second, more dated, concept is 'subsistence affluence', which describes a situation where all the components of a happy and satisfying life exist without needing to participate in the modern economy. And yet another concept is 'Pacific Way', a term coined in the 1970s to describe distribution and consumption as opposed to savings and investment, extensive kinship networks versus individualism and the nuclear family, and a low priority given for work in the formal economy and measurable output.

The specific issues are the familiar ones of health, education, environment, and trade. Health concerns for the Pacific are HIV/AIDS and other transferable diseases, malaria, and such medical conditions of the 'modern world' as cardio-vascular diseases. Some countries have efficient and extensive decentralized primary health care systems. Others struggle to cope. And as Table 19b.2 shows, education levels vary widely among Pacific island countries. There are varying levels of school attendance and gender discrepancies.

Many parts of the Pacific have high degrees of ecosystem and species diversity, extraordinarily high levels of endemicity (where species are found nowhere else in the world) and high levels of economic and cultural dependence on the natural environment. Environmental concerns for Pacific islanders include climate change and global warming, especially as they relate to rising sea levels (some low-lying atoll countries are at risk of completely disappearing), over-exploitation of natural resources (including through corrupt governance practices), and susceptibility to natural disasters.

Finally, there is a general inability to integrate with the global economy because of low economies of scale, lack of comparative advantage, high transportation costs, and low levels of skill and education.

## Key points

- Simplistic or idealistic concepts of the Pacific are not helpful in developing a realistic understanding of modern problems.

- Environmental degradation may put economic well-being and the very existence of some Pacific island states at risk.

- A globalized economy is largely irrelevant to Pacific island states.

# International relations in the Pacific

Relations among Pacific island states—and between them and the region's two developed countries, Australia and New Zealand—have been conducted bilaterally and regionally. The predominant political institution in the region is the Pacific Islands Forum, which is an annual gathering of Pacific heads of government and administered by a permanent secretariat (called the Forum Secretariat), based in Suva, Fiji (see Box 19b.2 for details of other regional organizations). Most Pacific island states are also members of the Commonwealth of Nations, which takes a special interest in small island states (see Sutton 2001), and of the United Nations and its specialized agencies, where they are members of the

## Box 19b.2 Pacific regional institutions

*The Pacific Islands Forum* (known as the South Pacific Forum prior to 2000) is the region's principal political institution. The Forum brings together the independent and self-governing states of the Pacific in an annual leaders' summit. The Pacific Islands Forum is serviced by the *Forum Secretariat*, based in Suva, Fiji.

*The Pacific Community* (formerly known as the South Pacific Commission) is a non-political organization delivering development assistance to the territories and countries of the region. The Pacific Community is serviced by the Secretariat of the Pacific Community (SPC), based in Noumea, New Caledonia.

*The Forum Fisheries Agency* (FFA), based in Honiara, Solomon Islands, enables its members to maximize sustained benefits from the conservation and sustainable use of their fisheries resources.

*The South Pacific Regional Environment Programme* (SPREP), based in Apia, Samoa, promotes regional cooperation in environmental matters.

*The South Pacific Applied Geoscience Commission* (SOPAC), based in Suva, Fiji, assists members to assess, explore, and develop their mineral and other non-living resources.

*The Pacific Islands Development Program* (PIDP) of the East-West Center at the University of Hawaii, conducts specific research and training activities as directed by the annual Pacific Islands Conference of Leaders.

*The Tourism Council of the South Pacific* (TCSP), based in Suva, Fiji, promotes tourism development on a regional basis.

*The University of the South Pacific* (USP) is the Pacific's only regional university. Its main campus is in Suva, Fiji, and there are other campuses in Port Vila, Vanuatu, and Apia, Samoa. Most member countries have university centres, classrooms, and libraries.

Cooperation and collaboration is promoted through *the Council of Regional Organisations in the Pacific* (CROP), comprising the heads of the above organizations and chaired by the Secretary General of the Forum Secretariat.

---

Small Islands Developing States (SIDS) Network. Generally speaking, small island states struggle with making their presence felt on the international stage. Nowhere is this more apparent than in international trade negotiations, such as in the World Trade Organization (WTO).

There was considerable elation among a new band of energetic Pacific leaders when their countries achieved independence mostly during the 1960s and 1970s. That was also a time of heightened cold war tensions between the United States and the Soviet Union. Many Pacific leaders were adventurous in their newfound political freedoms and some made diplomatic advances to the Soviet Union, Libya, and Cuba.

Recognition of which government has rightful authority over China has been another international political issue dividing the Pacific for some years. Most island states recognize the People's Republic of China (Beijing) while others (particularly Solomon Islands and Nauru) have recognized the Republic of China (Taiwan). In Solomon Islands' case, Taiwan has rewarded their recognition by funding a large-scale compensation payments programme in the wake of the civil unrest—what many would class as 'chequebook' diplomacy.

Similarly, the majority of Pacific island countries have declared their exclusive economic zones as whale sanctuaries (in Polynesian Pacific especially, there is a strong cultural significance attached to whales). But one of the world's two remaining whaling nations, Japan, has used its aid programme to influence two Pacific countries (Solomon Islands and Kiribati) to vote against declaring the entire Pacific as a whale sanctuary.

Australia and, to a lesser extent, New Zealand are recognized unofficially as the 'mini super powers' of the Pacific. Both countries, but especially Australia, carry the major share of the foreign aid burden to the region and both provide the closest markets for Pacific trade. Australian and New Zealand commercial interests dominate foreign economic activity in most of the Pacific (with the exception of the former US territories). Other notable aid donors are the European Union (which has largely subsumed the aid programme of the United Kingdom), Japan, and the United States. The most important multilateral donor is the United

Nations Development Programme (UNDP), followed by the World Bank and the Asian Development Bank.

As most island countries of the Pacific do not have military forces (the only ones that do are Papua New Guinea, Fiji, and Tonga), responsibility for security matters falls largely to Australia and New Zealand. Security in the region has taken on an added importance since the terrorist attacks on the United States of September 2001 and, more locally, the Bali bombing of October 2002. A 2003 report by an Australian government-supported think tank, the Australian Strategic Policy Institute—called *Our Failing Neighbours: Australia and the Future of Solomon Islands*—linked money-laundering, international criminal activity, people-smuggling, biosecurity issues—and terrorism—to the domestic problems of Solomon Islands. The robust intervention by Australian-led troops and police to restore order in the Solomon Islands in July 2003 was, at least in part, a result of that report. While this intervention has been widely welcomed and has been successful, it has had its critics.

## Key points

- There is a history of Pacific island states being manipulated by larger world powers to further their own political agendas.
- Pacific regional organizations try to provide the international political voice that individual small islands states cannot.

# Conclusion

The fundamental political, economic, and social issues relating to Pacific island states are a function of their pre-colonial and colonial history, their economic endowments, their isolation from major markets, and their susceptibility to natural and human-induced environmental disasters. Because of their small size, they are relatively unimportant on the world political and economic stage and suffer from a lack of voice in major international forums. As such, they share many similarities with other small, developing, isolated island states. They can be seen as good examples of all these characteristics rather than being unique in themselves.

Some Pacific islanders claim that politics is 'white-man's business' and is therefore alien to their culture. However, perhaps what is needed in the Pacific is more politics—where people make more input into issues affecting their own well-being; in other words, democracy. On the economic front, more attention needs to be made to people-centred development (which might be termed economic democracy) instead of large-scale, capital-intensive, elite-oriented schemes. Regionalism and finding common ground with groups of small island states elsewhere in the world are strategies to reap improvements for the Pacific.

While in a globalizing world no country can exist or interact with others in a vacuum, the island states of the Pacific are largely immune from the desperate poverty experienced in some parts of Africa and South Asia. Poverty is definitely on the increase in the Pacific, however. And social problems associated with economic disadvantage and civil strife are more prevalent, including domestic violence, child abuse, increases in prostitution and sexually transmitted diseases. Nevertheless, so long as populations remain relatively small, economies are managed well and violence kept in check, good livings can still be had in most parts of the Pacific.

## QUESTIONS

**1**   Are political issues in the small Pacific islands any different in nature to those elsewhere in the developing world?

**2**   Are more aid and more trade the answer to Pacific islands states' development problems?

**3**   To what extent are developed countries responsible for the deteriorating political and economic conditions in the Pacific?

**4**   What is an appropriate policy response to the relationship between the environment and development in small states like those in the Pacific?

## GUIDE TO FURTHER READING

Crocombe, Ron, *The South Pacific* (Suva: The University of the South Pacific, 2001). Survey of the diversity and problems as well as the achievements of the region including parts of the North Pacific.

Crowards, Tom, 'Defining the Category of "Small" States', *Journal of International Development*, 14/2 (2002): 143–79. A conceptual review plus classification of all the world's 'small states'.

Lal, Brij V., and Fortune, Kate (eds.), *The Pacific Islands: An Encyclopedia* (Honolulu: University of Hawaii Press, 2002). A large and informative reference work.

Sutton, Paul, 'Small States and the Commonwealth', *Commonwealth & Comparative Politics*, 39/3 (2001): 75–94. Comparative political examination of a range of small states belonging to the Commonwealth, by an expert on the Caribbean.

World Bank, *Pacific Island Economies: Building a Resilient Economic Base for the Twenty-First Century* (Washington: World Bank, 1995).

## WEB LINKS

**www.forumsec.org.fj**   The site of the Pacific Islands Forum.

**www.spc.org.nc**   The site of the Secretariat of the Pacific Community.

**http://pidp.eastwestcenter.org/pidp**   The site of the Pacific Islands Development Program.

 **COMPANION WEB SITE**

For additional material and resources, see the companion web site at:
**www.oup.com/uk/booksites/politics/**

# Military in politics versus democratic advance

## Pakistan

*David Taylor*

## OVERVIEW

Since its creation in 1947 Pakistan has struggled to develop a system of sustainable democratic government, and for more than half its history the country has been under either military or quasi-military rule. From 1999 on, the country has been ruled by General Pervez Musharraf. This is in stark contrast to India, despite sharing the same colonial background. Ironically, the reintroduction of military rule has usually been welcomed in Pakistan as a relief from the factional disputes among the civilian political leaders and accompanying high levels of **corruption**. This chapter explains how and why the military continues to be central to the political process in Pakistan.

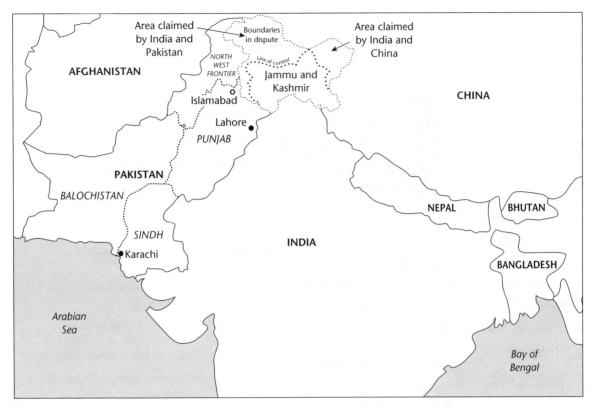

PAKISTAN

# Introduction: from independence to state breakup in 1971

Pakistan's military forces (principally the army, which numerically and politically has always been the key player) have dominated the country for most of its history since independence. This has meant not only political power but the pre-emption of a substantial share of economic resources. According to official figures, around 4.6 per cent of Gross Domestic Product (much more than in comparable countries such as India, Bangladesh, or Indonesia) is devoted to military expenditure, and other than debt-servicing military expenditure is the largest item in the national budget. The army is 550,000 strong, and many more depend on the army directly or indirectly for employment. Internationally, the image of Pakistan as a 'garrison state', although acceptable at times to the USA,

has often created difficulties, for example the country's suspension from the Commonwealth after the 1999 military coup until 2004.

The dominance of the military in Pakistan has been explained in different ways. Some note the way Pakistan inherited a strong army from the colonial state; others see it as an aspect of a social order still dominated by landowning groups. The two arguments come together in the fact that the army is recruited very heavily from the Punjab—the most populous of the country's four provinces and with a strong representation of landlord politicians, although the officer corps is increasingly coming from more middle-class families. Punjab's political leaders have tended to identify the interests of their

## Box 20a.1  Key dates in Pakistan's history

| | |
|---|---|
| **14 August 1947** | Pakistan independence |
| **11 September 1948** | Independence leader Mohammad Jinnah dies |
| **February 1954** | Pakistan joins a US-led military alliance (also known as the Baghdad Pact and later as CENTO) |
| **March 1956** | First constitution passed (but never fully implemented) |
| **October 1958** | General Ayub Khan carries out first military coup |
| **February 1960** | Ayub Khan elected president through indirect election |
| **March 1961** | Muslim Family Laws Ordinance |
| **March 1962** | New constitution passed |
| **September 1965** | Indecisive war with India |
| **March 1969** | Military coup led by General Yahya Khan deposes Ayub Khan |
| **December 1970** | Elections give absolute majority to East Pakistan-based Awami League |
| **December 1971** | Indian intervention brings about defeat of Pakistan army and separation of Bangladesh |
| **January 1972** | Zulfikar Ali Bhutto becomes president (later prime minister) |
| **April 1977** | General election returns Bhutto to power but opposition launches agitation claiming the results were rigged |
| **July 1977** | Military coup led by General Zia-ul Haq |
| **April 1979** | Bhutto executed |
| **December 1984** | Referendum gives Zia the basis to become president |
| **February/ November 1985** | Elections held sweeping constitutional amendments strengthen Zia's discretionary power |
| **August 1988** | Zia killed when his plane is blown up |
| **November 1988** | Elections return Benazir Bhutto to power |
| **October 1999** | Military coup led by General Pervez Musharraf topples government of Nawaz Sharif |
| **April 2002** | Referendum makes Musharraf president |
| **October 2002** | Elections bring to power the Pakistan Muslim League (Q), a party sympathetic to Musharraf |
| **December 2003** | Political deal between Musharraf and opposition elements leads to parliamentary approval for constitutional changes |

own province with those of Pakistan. Regional and international factors are also important, with Pakistan's long-running conflict with India over Kashmir and the cold war both influential. While Pakistan's efforts to define its identity as a Muslim state may not be directly linked to the dominance of the military, there is undoubtedly a connection. General Zia in particular, who held power for much of the 1980s, tried to merge the role of the army chief with that of a legitimate ruler of a Muslim country.

Pakistan inherited its state structures from the colonial period. At that time, the army was kept in reserve for use in emergencies (as, for example, in Amritsar in 1919 when an army commander perpetrated the Jallianwala Bagh massacre). Except for the North-West Frontier, where constant skirmishing took place between specially assigned and trained army units and local tribesmen, national security was hardly an issue, until the Second World War brought Japanese forces to the frontiers of India. On the other hand, Indian troops were regularly used outside India in pursuit of imperial objectives. The Indian army was a distinct entity from the British army, and most of its recruits came from a limited number of districts in the Punjab and the North-West Frontier Province. British colonial policy was designed to encourage this recruitment and maintain the soldiers' loyalty to the state, for example by generous treatment in the allocation of land and through the racially based classification of Indians into martial and non-martial groups.

When British India became independent in 1947, and was simultaneously divided into the two successor states of India and Pakistan, the armed forces were similarly divided. Pakistan got more than its proportionate share of soldiers. It also inherited a social structure in which control of land and of the people who worked the land was the single most important basis of political power. This was challenged by the arrival of large numbers of refugees from India. Those who were not Punjabi for the most part moved to Karachi, the initial capital, where they formed the core of the new state bureaucracy and the professions.

At first the unchallenged authority wielded by Muhammad Ali Jinnah, who had led the Pakistan movement from its inception, kept tensions between provinces and between locals and newcomers in check. However, after his death in 1948 the country lacked political leadership of national standing. While popular leaders emerged in the Eastern wing of the country (now Bangladesh), in the west (from where the army was recruited), provincial politicians battled for local control with little regard to national issues.

At the same time as Pakistan was facing difficulties in establishing stable structures of government, there was a belief that India's leaders had agreed to the partition of British India grudgingly and would miss no opportunity to sabotage its new neighbour. The distrust soon found a focus in the conflict over the princely state of Jammu and Kashmir. With a Hindu ruler and a powerful Hindu minority dominating the upper ranks of the bureaucracy, but with an overall Muslim majority, the Maharaja, Hari Singh, prevaricated over which new state to affiliate to. A 'tribal invasion' from the Pakistan side triggered an ultimatum from India that help to repel the invaders would only be forthcoming if he signed an instrument of accession to India. War ensued between India and Pakistan, until a truce under United Nations auspices was negotiated in August 1948. These events consolidated the army's position at the forefront of Pakistani society.

The weakness of Pakistan's political institutions and perceived need for security against a more powerful India meant the army as an institution became increasingly important in Pakistan's public life and took on a prominent political role. The first Pakistani Commander-in-Chief of the army, General Ayub Khan, became minister of defence for a period in 1954 and played a key role in bringing Pakistan into the US-led military alliance system that was constructed in Asia in the early 1950s. A complementary development was the assertion of the role of the bureaucracy as a guardian of the state in the absence of strong national leadership and in the face of challenges to the dominance of the established social order, in particular of the Punjab. While not identical, the social base of the army and the bureaucracy overlapped, and their perceptions of Pakistan were similar.

Under the constitution that had been adopted in 1956, Pakistan's first parliamentary elections were due in 1958. It seemed likely that they would bring to power H. S. Suhrawardy, a leader from East Bengal. However Suhrawardy was suspect both for the fact that the locus of power would shift from the west and for his populist rhetoric. Matters were pre-empted by a constitutional coup (October 1958), whereby the president declared martial law. Shortly after, Ayub Khan assumed political control. Ayub Khan was anxious to ensure his own formal legitimacy in terms of Pakistan's legal institutions, and was able to obtain a judgement from the Supreme Court authorizing his rule. He also conducted a campaign against the political leaders he had displaced. Hundreds of politicians were disqualified from further political activity, on the grounds of corruption. This was complemented by an analysis of the situation which seemed to draw both on colonial assumptions and on some of the contemporary thinking in the USA about economic and political development. Pakistan was seen as a society which needed leadership and guidance from the top if it was to move along a trajectory towards healthy national development. With considerable help and advice from the USA, with whom Pakistan now engaged in military alliance, the government initiated a programme of industrialization based on expanding the textile industry, underpinned by ample production of good-quality cotton.

Ayub Khan initiated what was called the Basic Democracies system. Elections, in the first instance on a non-party basis, were held for local councils. Those elected, around 80,000 in number, were termed basic democrats and elected the tier above them in a pyramid which culminated in the National Assembly. They also formed an electoral college for the presidency, and in 1960 Ayub Khan was duly elected president. This enabled him to dispense with martial law and to formulate a new constitution for the country—duly brought into effect in 1962. This defined Pakistan as a progressive Muslim state, pursuing policies that reflected a dynamic interpretation of religious values. In line with this, Ayub Khan's government in 1961 issued the Family Laws Ordinance which introduced reforms in the area of marriage and divorce, significantly improving the rights of women.

Ayub Khan decided that the re-establishment of political parties would provide a safety valve, and further that he should place himself at the head of one of them, which would attract many of the local leaders who had dominated rural politics in the past. The calculation was that his own prestige as president, command of the state machinery, and controls over the mass media, and distribution of **patronage** through the government would secure his political base, allowing him to preside over a modernizing society allied to the West, particularly the USA. In 1964 the system was put to the test in fresh elections under the basic democracies system. While in West Pakistan the strategy broadly worked, the feelings of alienation in East Pakistan—there since the very beginning—produced a show of support for the Awami League. In the presidential elections that followed, opposition parties in both wings of the country rallied behind Miss Fatima Jinnah, sister of Pakistan's founder. She obtained a majority of basic democrat votes in the east and a total of 37 per cent overall.

Following Indian Prime Minister Nehru's death in 1964 Ayub Khan launched an audacious plan to seize control of Kashmir. The plan backfired and led to all-out war with India in September 1965. Although a ceasefire was quickly arranged through the UN, growing discontent paved the way for the then army chief, General Yahya Khan, to displace Ayub Khan in March 1960 and declare a fresh period of martial rule. He promised direct parliamentary elections but also announced that when the new National Assembly met to frame a new constitution it would have to

work within a certain set of assumptions embodied in what was called the Legal Framework Order. These emphasized the integrity of Pakistan and were clearly designed to head off East Pakistan's demands for autonomy. However, East Pakistan's demographic majority was reflected in the distribution of seats; the province voted overwhelmingly for the Awami League, led by Sheikh Mujibur Rahman. Zulfikar Ali Bhutto, a former protégé of Ayub Khan who had established his own Pakistan People's Party (PPP) in 1967, won convincingly in the west but on a smaller scale. Sheikh Mujibur Rahman's insistence on his right to the prime ministership and on his power to write a constitution which would give full autonomy to the east was rejected by the army and West Pakistan's politicians, and in March 1971 the army deployed force to assert the authority of the (West) Pakistan state. Indian intervention led to a decisive military defeat for Pakistan, providing the circumstances for Bhutto to take over in the west.

## Key points

- Pakistan has been dominated by the army since its creation in 1947. Social and political factors, as well as the cold war context, have contributed to this situation.

- Pakistan's state structures derive from the colonial period; the colonial army was recruited heavily from the areas of British India that became Pakistan in 1947.

- Because conflict with India, especially over Kashmir, has fostered insecurity, the army has been able to place its needs and requirements at the centre of political life.

- Ayub Khan, Pakistan's first military ruler following the 1958 coup, attempted to develop an alternative political structure based on mobilization of rural leadership.

- The unsuccessful 1965 war with India ultimately led to Ayub Khan's downfall. The failure of his successor, General Yahya Khan, over Bangladesh led to his displacement by Zulfikar Ali Bhutto.

# Unstable government: 1971–1999

The Bhutto era represented an attempt at a politics of **populism**, but by using the apparatus of the state to achieve his ends Bhutto remained caught within its folds. The army as an institution remained a central actor, being used in 1974 to put down an internal rising in the province of Balochistan. The personalization of power by Bhutto alienated many army officers. In 1977 he faced a political crisis largely of his own making when he was accused by the opposition parties of rigging elections. Following three months of continuous agitation in the main cities, the army, headed by General Zia-ul Haq (whom Bhutto had promoted ahead of more senior generals in the belief that he had no political ambitions) intervened and called for fresh elections.

But Bhutto's evident popularity among his supporters persuaded General Zia to have him rearrested and the elections postponed. Bhutto was arraigned on murder charges and executed in April 1979. At the same time, Zia began to take steps to reconstruct Pakistan's institutions in a generally Islamic direction, with the support of a growing number of officers who were taking a prominent role in helping those Afghan forces that were fighting against the Soviet-backed government in Kabul during the 1980s. Other officers too held the civilian politicians in general, and the PPP in particular, in contempt, and had no difficulty with the continuation of military rule.

During the early 1980s, Zia pressed ahead with the Islamization of the country's institutions on several fronts, for example changes to the banking system to eliminate the payment of interest. In practice this also meant strengthening his own role as president. In 1985 he felt strong enough to end the period of direct martial rule, reintroducing a heavily modified constitution which gave the president sweeping discretionary powers, including the right to dismiss the prime minister and dissolve the National Assembly. This had been preceded by a referendum which was widely regarded as bogus but which enabled him to claim a five-year term as president. Elections held under the new constitution on a non-party basis then allowed the choice of a traditional landlord politician, Mohammad Khan Junejo, as the prime minister.

Nearly three years later, Zia exercised his power to dismiss the prime minister, claiming that Islamization was proceeding too slowly. Zia seemed set to continue to rule through a civilian façade but with strong presidential powers retained by himself, but in August 1988 he was killed by a bomb planted on his plane.

After Zia's death the elections brought back to power the PPP under Bhutto's daughter Benazir, and she alternated in office with the other major civilian political leader, Nawaz Sharif, whose power base lay in the Punjab. In eleven years there were four elections but throughout effective power was in fact shared between the political leadership, the army, and sections of the civilian bureaucracy. This uneasy arrangement produced constant difficulty. In 1993, a deadlock between the president, Ghulam Ishaq Khan, a former senior civil servant who had been close to Zia, and the then prime minister Nawaz Sharif, was eventually resolved through the intervention of the army chief, who insisted that both resign prior to new elections to be held under a neutral caretaker prime minister. Nawaz Sharif returned to power in 1997, and succeeded in amending the constitution to restrict the powers of the president, which had been abused by both Ghulam Ishaq Khan and his successor. He also appeared to be asserting his authority over the army. In 1998 he appointed as the new army chief General Pervez Musharraf, who was born in India and came to Pakistan as a refugee at independence. Musharraf reasserted the right of the army to take part in policy-making, by unilaterally embarking on a military adventure in Kashmir in 1999. The fighting—the most intense since 1971—was brought to an end through US diplomatic pressure and without any gains by Pakistan. This left the army and the government deeply suspicious of each other. In October General Musharraf launched a military coup to prevent his own dismissal.

## Key points

- Bhutto's failed attempt at populist politics, bypassing the military, triggered a coup by General Zia-ul Haq in 1977 and his own execution in 1979.

- Zia's political strategy relied heavily on presenting himself and the army as the guardians of Pakistan's Islamic goals: he retained sweeping powers as head of state but in 1985 introduced changes to the Constitution enabling restoration of the political process.
- Following Zia's assassination, the period 1988 to 1999 saw unstable civilian governments alternating between the PPP and Pakistan Muslim League, with the army and the bureaucracy continuing to exercise power behind the scenes.
- A failed military adventure over Kashmir in 1999 ultimately generated a further military coup led by General Pervez Musharraf.

# General Musharraf's rule since 1999

Coming after a period of instability, Musharraf began with substantial popular support. He promised action against the more notoriously corrupt politicians and bureaucrats and seemed in tune with the aspirations of many of Pakistan's urban population for a more liberal lifestyle. Relations with India remained cool; in 2002 the two countries again came close to war. At the time of the events of '9/11' he instantly decided to swing Pakistan behind the US stance on terrorism, and, subsequently, Pakistan has provided facilities for the USA in their actions in Afghanistan against the Taliban and al-Qaeda, notwithstanding criticism from some sections of the population.

Musharraf lost ground in 2002 with an ill-judged decision to hold a referendum to make himself president. The referendum was seen as manipulated and lacking legitimacy. Again in an echo of previous military rulers' strategies, Musharraf also increased devolution of administration to the local level and matched it with non-party elections to local councils. Elections later in 2002 were fought on a party basis, but the leaders of the two main parties were unable to participate directly and strong official backing was given to a faction of the Muslim League that broke away from Nawaz Sharif's party. In advance of the elections Musharraf introduced the Legal Framework Order (LFO) (echoing Yahya Khan's innovation), which strengthened the power of the president and sought to establish a National Security Council, where the military chiefs would have representation. The constitutional status of the LFO was unclear, and for the whole of 2003 the opposition brought the National Assembly to an effective halt over the issue, questioning Musharraf's entitlement to remain as army chief while also posing as a civilian president. At the beginning of 2004 a deal was struck with the main Islamist parties to allow an amended LFO to be adopted, but, given Musharraf's own liberal leanings, this was a tactical deal (for the Islamists the quid pro quo was a clear run for their government in the North-West Frontier Province) and served only to heighten the contradictions in his efforts to remain above civilian politics.

Musharraf presides over a deeply divided society. Two major attempts on his life in December 2003, almost certainly by Islamist elements opposed to his support for the USA and war on the Taliban and al-Qaeda, quite possibly had support from dissident elements in the army. And liberal opinion that had not been averse to his intervention in 1999 felt that he had betrayed them, by reverting to the failed strategies of his predecessors. Ironically, his main support comes from the 'time-servers' and local political bosses who were responsible in the past for blocking progressive and consistent policies of social and political reform. Externally, he enjoys the unstinted political and financial support of the USA, although the latter clearly sees India as the regional power of the future. In an about-turn at the beginning of 2004, Musharraf set in motion fresh talks with India over Kashmir, partly in response to pressure from the international community, and perhaps partly in the hope that a break-through would win back much of the civilian electorate.

## Key points

- Musharraf enjoyed substantial support for his coup, seen as promising relief from corrupt and incompetent civilian governments.

- Musharraf responded to '9/11' by giving full support to the USA, although this was unpopular with some sections of the population.
- Like his predecessors, Musharraf sought to discredit existing political leaders and build a party loyal to himself; he amended the constitution to increase his discretionary powers as president.
- Musharraf enjoys less popular support than in 1999.

# Conclusion

Zia was in power for eleven years, Ayub Khan for over ten. Musharraf seems intent on a similarly extended stretch in power. Each of the three military rulers have differed in social background and personal agenda, yet each turned out to follow similar strategies to stay in power. Rather than trying to rule in a wholly despotic and arbitrary manner, they have all sought to ground themselves in Pakistan's history and institutions. Yet in the first phase of power, each tried hard to discredit their predecessors, not just as individuals but as representatives of a political class which had failed the country.

This in a way is hardly surprising, as each period of military rule in fact laid the foundations for the next. A discourse on politics has developed which is shared not just by the military but to some degree by many other sections of society. Politics is envisaged as an aspect of the 'feudal' phase of Pakistani history. To break its hold and to usher in a new phase (the precise lineaments of which have been specific to each leader), the army may need to intervene to help the process along. The 'ordinary' Pakistani is a key figure in this discourse, and is brought into politics through carefully tailored institutions from which party politics are excluded, at least on the surface. At the same time, politicians are seen as people who may for their own selfish reasons betray Pakistan's key national interests, particularly over Kashmir.

While the army leadership projects itself as the guardian of the national interest, it is often seen by others as just as concerned with its own interests. Army officers are often appointed to senior administrative positions after retirement and are given preferential treatment in many different areas, most significantly perhaps the allocation of prime rural and urban land. A further issue is the extent to which the army is committed to preserving the existing social structure. The officer corps has been drawn by and large from the social elite and there has been little desire to challenge the status quo, either in terms of property ownership or the power of the central government versus the provinces. This may, however, be changing in respect to religious issues. Partly in consequence of the Zia period, Islamist ideas appeal to some sections of the army, and with recent world developments post '9/11' and post the invasion of Iraq these are likely to have gained greater resonance. The possibility of a coup within the army (as against the pattern to date where all four coups have been carried out by the army as an institution) cannot be ruled out.

Repeated cycles of military intervention have led both the army and many civilians to a belief that Pakistan cannot sustain a political system that does not give a major role to the armed forces. Turkey is often cited as a parallel example. The weakness of civil society and of the civilian political process and the special security needs not only of Pakistan itself but of the Muslim world more generally are seen as justifications for this view. This point of view is held particularly strongly in the Punjab, while in the other three provinces, especially Sindh and Balochistan, there is less willingness to accept a permanent role for the army. However, until there has been a lengthy spell of civilian rule under a prime minister who has the skills to wean the army away from its current set of assumptions without provoking a backlash, the present situation is likely to continue.

## QUESTIONS

1   What policies did the colonial state pursue that prepared the way for recurrent military intervention in politics after independence?

2   To what extent was the cold war a factor in facilitating the dominance of the army in Pakistan?

3   What analysis do army leaders make of Pakistan's politics and how do they see their own role within it?

4   Compare and contrast the political strategies of Generals Ayub Khan, Zia-ul Haq, and Pervez Musharraf.

5   What have been the consequences for Pakistani society of prolonged periods of military dominance?

## GUIDE TO FURTHER READING

Ali, T., *Can Pakistan Survive? The Death of a State* (Harmondsworth: Penguin Books, 1983). Highly critical analysis by a leading journalist and political activist.

Cloughley, B., *A History of the Pakistan Army—Wars and Insurrections* (Karachi: Oxford University Press Pakistan, 2000). A history of the army that details its role at various stages of Pakistan's history. The author has known many of the key personalities involved.

Cohen, S. P., *The Pakistan Army* (Karachi: Oxford University Press, 2002). Based on extensive interactions with the Pakistan army's leadership, this carefully documented analysis of the history and development of the army is coupled with a discussion of its political attitudes.

Dewey, C., 'The Rural Roots of Pakistani Militarism' in A. Low (ed.) *The Political Inheritance of Pakistan* (Basingstoke: Macmillan, 1999), 255–83.

Jaffrelot, C. (ed.), *A History of Pakistan and its Origins* (London: Anthem Press, 2002). An up-to-date collection on different aspects of Pakistan's history and social structure. The contributions by the editor are especially valuable.

Jalal, A., *State of Martial Rule: The Origins of Pakistan's Political Economy of Defence* (Cambridge: Cambridge University Press, 1990). A detailed study of the process by which the Pakistan army became central to the Pakistan state. The author locates internal processes within the general cold war context.

Rizvi, Hasan-Askari, *The Military and Politics in Pakistan* (Lahore: Progressive Publishers, 1986). Detailed study of civil-military relations by a leading Pakistani scholar.

Talbot, I., *Pakistan: A Modern History* (London: Christopher Hurst, 1998). The most reliable of recent histories of the country. Talbot has a strong sense of the provincial roots of contemporary Pakistan.

## WEB LINKS

**http://countrystudies.us/Pakistan**   A detailed US-based compilation of information on the history, economy, society, and politics of Pakistan.

**www.sacw.net**   The South Asia Citizens Web is an independent space that provides exchanges of information between and about citizen initiatives in South Asia.

 **COMPANION WEB SITE**

For additional material and resources, see the companion web site at:
**www.oup.com/uk/booksites/politics/**

# 20b

# Military in politics versus democratic advance

## Mexico

*Andreas Schedler*

## OVERVIEW

With a population close to 100 million, a vast and heterogeneous territory, an extended common border with the United States, and an enormously rich cultural heritage, Mexico is too important to be ignored. Traditionally classified as part of Mesoamerica, with the enactment of the North American Free Trade Agreement with the USA and Canada in 1994 Mexico was formally admitted into North America. In 2000, the victory of conservative opposition candidate Vicente Fox in Mexico's presidential election sealed the end of more than seven decades of uninterrupted single-party rule. For most of the twentieth century, the country was ruled by a broadly inclusive hegemonic party seeking to ratify its monopoly hold on power through controlled, non-competitive elections at all levels. In contrast to much of the literature, this chapter presents Mexico's post-revolutionary political system not as a regime *sui generis*—a unique, idiosyncratic form of authoritarianism—but rather as prototypical case of 'electoral authoritarianism' (see Box 20*b*.2). Similarly, it interprets the country's recent trajectory of regime change not as a transition *sui generis*—as a unique, idiosyncratic path of democratization—but instead as a prototypical case of 'democratization by elections'.

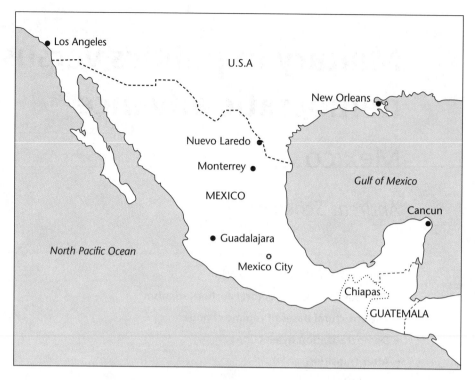

**MEXICO**

---

## Box 20b.1 Key dates in Mexico's history

| | |
|---|---|
| **1810–21** | War of Independence against Spain |
| **1846–48** | War between Mexico and the United States |
| **1857** | New republican constitution |
| **1876–1910** | Presidency of Porfirio Díaz |
| **1910–20** | Mexican Revolution |
| **1917** | New constitution (still in force) |
| **1929** | Foundation of the National Revolutionary Party, later changed to PRI |
| **1934–40** | Land redistribution, social reforms, and oil nationalization under President Lázaro Cárdenas |
| **1982** | Debt crisis |
| **1988** | 'Earthquake election': unprecedented competitiveness at a presidential election. The official candidate obtains a bare majority of valid votes; the opposition charges fraud |
| **1990** | Foundation of the Federal Electoral Institute (IFE). |
| **1994** | North American Free Trade Agreement; Zapatista rebellion |
| **1996** | The 'definitive' electoral reform. |
| **1997** | Divided government: in mid-term legislative elections, the PRI loses its absolute majority in the Chamber of Deputies |
| **2000** | Conservative opposition candidate Vicente Fox Quesada wins the presidency |
| **2003** | Divided government continued: the PRI comes victorious out of mid-term legislative elections, rendering President Fox a 'lame duck' |

# From independence to revolution

As Mexico reached independence from Spain after a decade of war in 1821, it faced the triple challenge of redefining its political regime, constructing a modern state, and laying the foundations of a capitalist economy. Failure in establishing a regime—in institutionalizing accepted rules of access to power and exercise of power—precluded success in building a state and developing a market. In its first thirty years of political independence, the country fell prey to the vicissitudes of **caudillismo**. Between 1821 and 1850, the country was (nominally) ruled by fifty different governments, most of them delivered by military rebellions. Internal instability was matched by external vulnerability. In the war against the United States (1846-8), Mexico lost around half its territory. At home, civilian politics was increasingly driven by the major cleavage common to most of nineteenth-century Latin America: conflict between conservatives and liberals. Conservatives sought to protect the inherited political, economic, and cultural power of the Catholic Church. Liberals strove to limit it and to create an autonomous sphere of secular politics.

The developmental dictatorship under Porfirio Díaz (1876-1910), while harshly repressive, brought an unprecedented measure of stability and institutional modernization. Having taken power by a coup, General Díaz proceeded to set up an early variant of electoral authoritarianism. Regular (indirect) presidential elections confirmed his continuity in power by acclamation. Regular legislative contests between extremely personalized and fragmented political parties produced mostly weak, even if nominally representative, legislatures. At the same time, something like a modern state started to take shape, with a central government, a national military, and a professional bureaucracy extending its reach to the country's periphery. In addition, foreign investment aided by public infrastructure (railroads) enabled some incipient, dependent industrialization through the development of an extractive enclave economy.

The Mexican Revolution (1910-20) is customarily explained as a response to the growing impoverishment of the rural masses. Its first impulse, however, was entirely political. After three decades of **electoral authoritarianism**, liberal reformer Francisco I. Madero demanded democratic elections (*sufragio efectivo*) and alternation in power (*no-reelección*). In the 1911 (indirect) elections, he won the presidency with 99.3 per cent of total votes. (He was murdered two years later in a military coup.) The ensuing civil war is commonly described as the first social revolution of the twentieth century, and about 1.4 million people out of a total population of 15.2 million lost their lives.

The revolutionary Constitution, enacted in 1917 and still in force today, enshrined a mixture of political liberalism and social reformism. It copied almost the full set of political institutions from the US Constitution: presidential government, federalism, bicameralism, and plurality elections at all levels. In addition, it limited the scope of the market economy by reserving 'strategic sectors' to the state while stipulating extensive social rights for peasants and workers. Ironically, under the one-party hegemony that emerged after the revolution, the constitution proved ineffective in its procedural as well as in its substantive aspects. It worked neither as an effective institutional constraint on politics nor as an effective policy programme.

---

### Box 20b.2 **Electoral authoritarianism**

Electoral autocracies display a nominal adherence to the principle of democratic rule, while subverting democracy in practice. Particularly, they hold regular multi-party elections, yet constrain and subvert them so deeply as to render them instruments not of democracy, but of authoritarian rule. Modern examples are the presidencies of Fujimori (Peru), Mugabe (Zimbabwe), and Soeharto (Indonesia).

---

## Key points

- During much of the nineteenth century, Mexico's difficulties in institutionalizing a political regime frustrated its efforts at state-building and economic development.

- The revolutionary 1917 Constitution established a liberal division of power, while locking in substantive policies in the fields of public education, labour rights, and control over national resources.

# The foundations of electoral authoritarianism

Post-revolutionary politics continued to be disorderly and violent. The bullet, alongside the ballot, enjoyed acceptance as a valid currency for gaining and losing public office. Violent protest, military rebellion, and the physical elimination of adversaries remained common. But regular elections took place at all levels, though nothing resembling a structured party system existed. Political parties were ephemeral collections of followers around local notables or military leaders. Politics remained a game of elite competition mediated by force, not by formal institutions.

The crisis of presidential succession in 1928 marked a turning point. After the assassination of president elect Alvaro Obregón in July, outgoing president Plutarco Elías Calles (1924–8) announced his intention to institutionalize the revolutionary government. In spring 1929, he founded the National Revolutionary Party (PRN) as an umbrella organization of all revolutionary leaders, factions, and parties.

## Twin institutionalization

The PRN was to pacify electoral disputes by providing a transparent mechanism of electoral coordination: it would select winning candidates from among the 'revolutionary family', reward their followers, and crush their opponents. In the beginning, the PRN still worked as a party federation battling against the centrifugal logic of its local members. By the mid-1930s, however, it was able to centralize candidate selection by dissolving its local party members and prohibiting the immediate re-election of deputies. Within five years, what was initially a loose alliance of local factions established itself as a centralized hegemonic party that was to rule Mexico for the rest of the century.

Before quitting power peacefully in the 2000 presidential elections, the successor party of the PRN, the Institutional Revolutionary Party (PRI), was the longest-reigning political party in the world. It had clearly excelled in fulfilling its original mission of pacifying and stabilizing the country. How did the PRI achieve this extraordinary success in party and regime institutionalization? Like all institutions, it had to accomplish two basic objectives: 'stability' and 'value' (Huntington 1968). The former is a matter of expectations, the latter one of evaluations. People had to know that the PRI was there to stay; that the revolutionary game it played was 'the only game in town'. But they had to value it, too. One-party hegemony had to appear as a fact of life as well as moral achievement.

## The institutional infrastructure

Over seven decades, the PRI sustained an authoritarian regime that looked as exceptional as its longevity. Scholars commonly described it as a civilian, inclusive, corporatist, and hyper-presidential authoritarian regime held together by a pragmatic, patronage-based state party. In essence, Mexico's 'authoritarianism with adjectives' rested upon three institutional pillars: a hierarchical state party, state corporatism, and electoral gate-keeping.

On the first, the hegemonic party operated as a big 'linkage mechanism' that turned the Mexican state into a unitary hierarchical organization. By controlling all branches and levels of government, the hegemonic party effectively cancelled the constitutional distribution of state power. It annulled the 'horizontal' division of power between the executive, legislative, and judicial branches as well as the 'vertical' division of power between central government, federal states, and municipalities. No political opposition, no checks and balances. The fusion between state and party granted almost unlimited 'meta-constitutional' powers to the president. He was the carrier of sovereignty, the temporal monarch, the 'supreme patron', who sat at the peak of an immense clientelist pyramid that was the Mexican state.

The state in turn controlled civil society, not so much through repression as by co-opting and corrupting potential dissidents and opponents. After all, it was supposed to be an inclusive, integrative enterprise, an institutional roof large enough to accommodate the whole revolutionary family. The party patronized, and at the same time domesticated, labour unions, peasant organizations, and popular movements by incorporating them into tightly controlled corporatist arrangements. It kept business people content with subsidies, market protection, and informal access to power. Through a mixture of material incentives and political constraints it kept the mass media quiet. Finally, the Catholic Church was persuaded to observe its constitutional mandate of keeping out of politics by reminders of the possible alternative: oppression by the state of religious institutions, as in the 1920s.

The state also controlled elections, which were held frequently. Unlike other electoral autocracies such as Taiwan until the 1980s, the PRI regime did not allow intra-party competition (within the ruling party) in the electoral arena. Instead, it admitted organized competition by opposition parties, albeit under (adverse) conditions not of their own making. From 1946, the organization of elections was under central control, which granted the government manifold opportunities to manipulate the process. Electoral autocracies like the PRI regime reproduce and legitimate themselves on the basis of periodic elections that show some measure of pluralism but fall short of minimum democratic standards. In such regimes, multi-party elections are not embedded in the 'surrounding freedoms' essential to liberal democracy. Instead, they are constrained through a variety of authoritarian controls. The violations of liberal-democratic norms may be manifold (see Schedler 2002b), and post-revolutionary Mexico had nearly all of them in place: limitations of civil and political liberties, restrictions on party and candidate registration, discriminatory rules of representation, electoral fraud, corruption, and coercion, as well as an uneven playing field, with the incumbent enjoying close to monopolistic access to media and campaign resources.

## The ideological infrastructure

Following Sartori (1976), scholars commonly portray Mexico's post-revolutionary regime as 'pragmatic' authoritarianism. True, the PRI did not institute a mobilizational dictatorship that tried to coerce its subjects into ideological uniformity. It accepted some measure of economic and civil liberties, including religious freedom, encouraged political opposition parties to its left and right (as long as they remained harmless), and accommodated considerable programmatic diversity within the party. The relative tolerance of pluralism, however, should not be mistaken for the absence of ideology. Its 'revolutionary nationalism' was not an empty box.

Actually, the PRI was admirably successful in creating what Antonio Gramsci called cultural 'hegemony'. The state party defined the lasting coordinates of national identity—the national history, national foes and heroes, national symbols, rituals, and holidays, and, last but not least, the promise of progress and justice under the name of 'revolutionary nationalism'. The official party effectively managed to turn its ideology—a combination of liberalism, nationalism, and the corporative defence of the welfare state—into the foundations of national 'political correctness'. Even today, the language and ideology of 'revolutionary nationalism' continues to constrain Mexican politics. It still sets the terms of public debate in numerous policy spheres, such as the management of natural resources, public education, and foreign policy.

## Key points

- Post-revolutionary Mexico developed an electoral authoritarian regime held together by a hegemonic party, the PRI.

- The party commandeered the state as well as civil society. Through its centralized control of elections, it acted as the sole gatekeeper to public office.

- The PRI did not exercise its power 'naked' but draped in 'national-revolutionary' ideology. Non-democratic rule lived off popular legitimacy.

# The structural bases of regime change

The relationship between economic development and political democracy has been subject to intense debate (see Chapter 12). But although for long a democratic under-achiever Mexico seems to confirm the systematic association between socio-economic and political modernization.

## Societal transformation

Not unlike Porfirio Díaz—even if less personalistic, repressive, and exclusionary—the PRI established its own version of developmental dictatorship. Especially during the 'Mexican miracle' between 1940 and 1970, it achieved steady rates of economic growth and expanding public services. Notwithstanding the economic crises that irrupted at each presidential succession from 1976 to 1994, seven decades of modernizing authoritarian rule by the PRI produced profound societal transformations. Mexico at the end of the revolution was a country dramatically different from Mexico at the end of hegemonic party rule. For example, in 1930, Mexico's population stood at 16.5 million, the annual per capita income stood at US$166 (in 1960 terms), 70.2 per cent of the workforce was employed in agriculture, 68.8 per cent of Mexicans lived in villages with less than 2.500 inhabitants, and the illiteracy rate among the population of age 10 and higher was 61.5 per cent. In 1995, by contrast, the population had jumped to 93.7 million, annual per capita income reached US$2,790 (current), primary sector employment was only 22.3 per cent, urbanization 74 per cent, and illiteracy down to 10.6 per cent (figures from Banco de México, Instituto Nacional de Estadística, Geografía e Informática and World Bank). Nevertheless, about half of the population still counts as poor, and the country displays one of the most unequal income distributions in the world, similar to South Africa under **apartheid**. Still, the structural transformation from poor and rural to middle-income and urban was bound to create strong pressures for democratization. The widening gap between socio-economic and political modernization was difficult to sustain. Societal pluralism could not be contained within the confinements of a single party. In addition, the structural dissociation between a hegemonic party and a complex society was deepened by dramatic performance failure, economic mismanagement, and crisis.

## Economic crises

After 1970, a mixture of structural disequilibria and systematic mismanagement pushed Mexico into periodic economic recessions. Each presidential succession from 1976 to 1994 was marked by economic crisis. The oil boom and external debt first postponed, and then aggravated, the big crash of 1982. In 1983, per capita GDP fell 4.2 per cent, annual inflation reached 80.5 per cent, and real minimum wages plummeted by 25.2 per cent (Banco de México). Popular discontent skyrocketed.

In retrospect, the debt crisis of the early 1980s was the starting point of democratization. There was nothing inevitable about it, however. Neither structural incongruence nor cyclical stress translate smoothly and automatically into democratizing progress. During the 1970s and 1980s, the talk of the day was about *crisis*—a situation of change and anxiety, without any clear sense of where the country was heading. Anything seemed possible, including a return to the violence of the past. It was only in the late 1980s that this diffuse sense of alarm receded. Actors and analysts started talking about democratic *transition*. And they started playing the game of transition—the game of peaceful, incremental political democratization.

## Key points

- Socio-economic modernization created multiple pressures for democratization.
- Cycles of economic crisis sapped the regime's legitimacy.

# Democratization by elections

Under electoral autocracies like the PRI regime, elections are not 'instruments of democracy' (Powell 2000) but battlefields of democratization. Unlike democratic elections, manipulated elections unfold as 'two-level games' in which parties compete for votes at the same time as they struggle over basic rules. Electoral competition goes hand in hand with institutional conflict. Democratization 'by elections' ensues when opposition parties succeed at both levels, when they manage to undermine both pillars of authoritarian rule: its popular support as well as its anti-democratic institutions (Schedler 2002*a*). Mexico's emergent opposition parties—the right-wing National Action Party (PAN), a tenacious regime opponent since the late 1940s, and the left-wing Party of the Democratic Revolution (PRD), founded in 1989—were able to start just such a self-reinforcing spiral of rising competitiveness and democratic reform. As they turned into serious contenders, they were able to remove successive layers of authoritarian control, in five negotiated electoral reforms following 1987.

## Electoral competition

Historic turnout figures indicate the hegemonic party's capacity for electoral mobilization was modest. Its official election results, by contrast, were impressive. Until 1982, all Mexican revolutionary and post-revolutionary presidents were elected by acclamation (except for 1946 and 1952 when they faced relatively popular splinter candidates). Plurality elections practically prevented opposition parties from winning legislative seats until the early 1960s. In 1963, the PRI introduced some element of proportional representation to keep the PAN in the electoral game, but without jeopardizing its two-thirds majority—a condition to enact constitutional changes.

In the wake of the 1982 debt crisis, however, the unbroken (and unbreakable) hegemony began to crumble. First, the PAN started to win, and to defend its victories in a series of post-electoral confrontations, at the municipal and state level in northern Mexico. Then, in the 1988 presidential election, the performance of PRI dissident Cuauhtémoc Cárdenas shattered the image of PRI invincibility at the national level. His followers continue to think he had actually won the contest, only being denied victory by blatant electoral fraud. Afterwards, opposition parties conquered more and more sites of subnational power, at the same time as they strengthened their presence in the bicameral national legislature.

Until the early 1980s, opposition parties succeeded in winning only occasional municipal elections; by the year 2000, opposition mayors governed more than half of Mexico's total population. Until 1989, opposition forces had not won any gubernatorial contests; by mid-2000 they controlled eleven of the thirty-one federal states. In 1988, the official party was stripped of its comfortable two-thirds majority in the Chamber of Deputies. In 1997, it lost its absolute majority, too, inaugurating an unprecedented period of divided government. Until 1988, no opposition candidate was elected to the Senate. In the 1997 senatorial elections, the PRI lost its two-thirds majority there, and in 2000 it fell below the 50 per cent threshold. Finally, in 2000 PAN candidate Vicente Fox won the real big prize in Mexican politics—the presidency.

## Electoral reform

The rising competitiveness of the party system made possible (and was made possible by) profound changes in the institutions of electoral governance. Today, vote-rigging and the state control of elections belong to the past. Within less than a decade, Mexico effectively remodelled its electoral institutions. The electoral reforms, negotiated under the pressure of hundreds of local post-electoral conflicts, and enacted in 1990, 1993, 1994, and culminating in 1996, added up to a veritable institutional revolution within the (self-denominated) regime of the institutional revolution.

The new electoral system rested upon three institutional columns: a new independent election body, the judicialization of conflict resolution, and comprehensive oversight by parties. Consonant with an international trend, Mexican parties decided to delegate the organization of elections to a permanent and independent election management body, the Federal Electoral Institute (IFE), founded in 1990. Electoral reformers have also set up a new system for the judicial resolution of election disputes: the Electoral Tribunal of the Judicial Power of the Federation (TEPJF) now has the last say in all electoral disputes, national as well as subnational. Finally, parties have institutionalized a 'panoptic regime' of surveillance that allows them to monitor closely the entire electoral process step by step. Their vigilant presence goes far beyond the deployment of representatives on voting day. They are legally entitled to oversee (and actively committed to overseeing) the organization of elections at every phase, from voter registration to vote counting.

## Outside the electoral arena

While political parties are the lead actors in democratization by elections, they have to be responsive to shocks and actors outside the electoral arena. Given the civilian nature of the Mexican regime, political actors have not had to worry much about the military, but nevertheless faced a complex configuration of other domestic and international players.

Business people—for long supportive of electoral authoritarianism—began to disown the PRI after 1982. Economic crisis and nationalization of the banks taught them authoritarian discretion was bad for business. Democratic checks and balances promised more secure private property rights and sound macro-economic management. By contrast, organized labour remained bound into PRI corporatism even as individual workers and dissident unions grew

autonomous. Until recently, the PRI could count as well on the 'green vote' of the rural poor. In 1994, the armed uprising by the Zapatistas in the southern state of Chiapas forced political parties to the negotiation table, playing out a recurrent irony of history: the threat of violence acting as a midwife of democratizing consensus.

Undoubtedly, international factors carried weight as well. Timing mattered: if the 1988 elections had been held just one year later, after the surprising success of Solidarity in Poland, its outcome might have been different. And geography mattered too. Poor Mexico, Porfirio Díaz is often cited as saying, so far from God and so close to the USA. Historically, very much like the Mexican middle class, the USA had always been more interested in Mexican stability than democracy. It started to distance itself from the PRI to the extent that the party lost its ability to guarantee the country's political and economic stability. The North American Free Trade Agreement (NAFTA), in force since 1994, did little to promote democracy directly. But by locking in liberal market reforms it made Mexican economic policies immune to democratic alternation in power. Democracy, rendered conservative in this way, stopped frightening economic liberals in Washington and in Mexico City.

## Key points

- Mexico's democratic advance resulted from the interplay between increasing inter-party competition and democratizing reform.
- Since its last mayor electoral reform in 1996, the country may be considered an electoral democracy.
- The North American Free Trade Agreement constrains the macro-economic policies of future democratic governments.

# After transition

Often, after the excitement of transition, political boredom and disenchantment set in. At latest with the 2000 alternation in power, Mexico has turned into a 'normal' Latin American democracy. For the

first time in a century, its political cycle is swinging in tune with the broad regional trend. With the country's political 'normalization' come the 'normal' challenges associated with a democracy operating in the context of a weak state and an unequal society.

## Dating regime change

Electoral autocracies often move within an ambiguous 'gray zone' (Carothers 2002) that makes them difficult to classify. Unless they collapse (like Serbia and Peru in 2000), it is often hard to tell when exactly they cross the threshold to democracy. Accordingly, throughout its democratic transition, the status of the Mexican regime was deeply contested. Until today, actually, many actors and observers continue to debate the extent of the regime change. Yet, the 2000 alternation in power may be taken as a plausible indicator confirming the advent of democracy. According to Przeworski et al. (2000: 24), when a long-ruling party suffers defeat at the polls, the regime should be classified 'as democratic for the entire period this party was in power under the same rules' (2000: 24). Under that rule, Mexico should be considered democratic since its last democratizing reform of 1996.

## Democratic consolidation

Alternation in power in 2000 marked the symbolic end of the democratic transition by giving a convincing demonstration of democracy at work. At the same time, it signalled that democratic consolidation had been accomplished, too. Not all democracies are born fragile. Not all democratic transitions lead to protracted processes of consolidation. Because of the comprehensiveness and inclusiveness of the 1996 democratic pact, the country accomplished the consolidation of its democracy at the same time as it completed its transition to democracy. Mexico's new democracy is not free of uncivic protest and political violence, nor is it immune to recurrent inter-party controversies over the authorities of electoral governance. Yet, democracy has come to stay. Its dense calendar of non-concurrent local elections, tri-annual legislative elections, and overall, overshadowing everything, the presidential elections at six-year intervals, keep Mexican politicians, very much like their counterparts in longer established democracies, in a state of permanent electoral campaign. Clearly,

all political parties in contemporary Mexico accept democracy as '**the only game in town**' (Linz and Stepan 1996).

## What kind of democracy?

In 2000, for the first time ever, Freedom House classified Mexico as an 'electoral democracy'. This could be misleading if it implies that democratizing progress had been limited to the electoral arena. True enough, struggles for democratization have revolved around the conduct of elections. Yet, as political actors were rebuilding the electoral arena they transformed other spheres of politics as well. Constructing new rules of *access* to power as well as new realities of inter-party competition had profound implications for the *exercise* of power as well.

The mere introduction of opposition at all levels changed the political system without the need to change its constitutional underpinnings. The rise of opposition parties to multiple sites of state power reinvigorated constitutional checks and balances that had lain dormant. Thanks to the new pluralism of the party system, the constitutional division of power, once a formality, is now meaningful reality. Today both the legislature and the judiciary impose tangible limits on the executive, and federalism is no longer hollow. Both state and municipal governments are real sites of power. A host of autonomous administrative, regulatory, and jurisprudential bodies complement the classic division of power, for instance, the Federal Electoral Institute, the National Commission for Human Rights, and the Federal Institute for Access to Public Information. Contemporary Mexico may not be a fully liberal democracy, but it is not a purely minimal democracy either. Given the dense web of formal and political constraints officeholders face, the country cannot be described as an '**illiberal**' or '**delegative**' democracy.

That said, there is considerable scope for democratic deepening. The rule of law is incomplete and fragile, much closer to the tyranny of bureaucracy than to formal justice. Above all, the realm of criminal law continues to form a theatre of tragic corruption and injustice, procedural as well as substantive, a persistent, encompassing threat to the integrity of private life. The extractive capacities of the state are weak, too, its claim to a monopoly of physical violence contested. Deep poverty for many and socio-economic inequality betray the democratic promise of equal participation in public life. The prohibition of immediate re-election of legislators and majors renders electoral accountability ineffective. Corruption is widespread and too many politicians seem to lack any sense of republican self-restraint. Citizen participation is shallow, discontent runs deep. Political incompetence, partisan infighting, and the constitutional fragmentation of power block urgent policy reforms. Of course, democracy never is the solution to all problems. It is an institutional framework for seeking solutions and resolving conflicts in a peaceful way. Yet democratizing democracy is clearly one of the big assignments of Mexico's fledgling democratic regime.

## Key points

- Mexico may be regarded a consolidated democracy. No extremist parties threaten the democratic system.

- Mexican democracy faces the twin challenge of socio-economic development and democratic deepening.

# Conclusion

After traumatic experiences of instability and violence, followed by seven decades of authoritarian stability, Mexico has finally found a way of reconciling political stability and democracy. Regular elections at national and sub-national levels provided the 'Archimedean point' to lift the authoritarian regime out of its hinges. Incremental electoral reforms made possible the rise of genuine opposition parties, and vice versa. In addition, the advent of democratic multi-party competition transformed the overall nature of politics by activating the constitutional division of power between branches and levels of government.

The democratic advances of the past two decades are beyond dispute, and they are generally appreciated. Still, a growing sense exists among the Mexican public that its fledgling democracy is floating adrift. Multiple performance failures, the poverty of public debate, legislative deadlock, and corruption scandals fuel public cynicism. True, democratization often leads to democratic disenchantment. New democracies tend to be disappointing democracies. Yet cynicism as well as complacency put democracy at risk. To secure the democratic advances of the past, citizens and politicians will have to push for further democratic advances in the future.

## QUESTIONS

1 How did post-independence Mexico meet the challenge of regime building?

2 How should the Mexican Revolution be characterized?

3 Compare the institutional foundations of Mexico's post-revolutionary authoritarianism and its ideological bases.

4 Why did socio-economic changes create pressures for democratization?

5 How did the Mexican transition progress, and what were its main distinguishing characteristics?

6 What kind of democracy is Mexico today and what main challenges does it face?

## GUIDE TO FURTHER READING

Casar, M. A., and I. Marván (eds.), *Gobernar sin Mayoría: México 1867–1997* (Mexico City: Taurus and CIDE, 2002). An insightful series of studies on historical and sub-national experiences of divided government.

Eisenstadt, T., *Courting Democracy in Mexico: Party Strategies and Electoral Institutions* (Cambridge: Cambridge University Press, 2003). A comprehensive study of the judicialization of post-electoral conflicts in the 1990s.

Elizondo, C., and B. Nacif (eds.), *Lecturas sobre el cambio político en México* (Mexico City: Fondo de Cultura Económica, 2003). A fine collection of essays on political change in Mexico.

Forment, C. A., *Democracy in Latin America, 1760–1900: Civic Selfhood and Public Life in Mexico and Peru* (Chicago: University of Chicago Press, 2003). An in-depth study of civil society in pre-revolutionary Mexico.

Garrido, L. J., *El Partido de la Revolución Institucionalizada: La formación del nuevo Estado (1928–45)* (Mexico City: Siglo XXI, 1982). A detailed history of the hegemonic party.

Lawson, C. H., *Building the Fourth Estate: Democratization and the Rise of a Free Press in Mexico* (Berkeley: University of California Press, 2002). A systematic study of media opening and democratization.

Levy, D. C., and K. Bruhn, with E. Zebadúa, *Mexico: The Struggle for Democratic Development* (Berkeley: University of California Press, 2001). Broad introduction into Mexican politics.

Lujambio, A., *El poder compartido: Un ensayo sobre la democratización mexicana* (Mexico City: Oceano, 2000). A concise reconstruction of opposition advances at all levels of state power in the 1990s.

Schedler, A., 'From Electoral Authoritarianism to Democratic Consolidation', in R. Crandall, G. Paz, and R. Roett (eds.), *Mexico's Democracy at Work: Political and Economic Dynamics* (Boulder, Colo., and London: Lynne Rienner, 2004), 9–37. An overview of democratic transition and consolidation with a synthesis of electoral reforms 1977–96.

Weldon, J. A., 'The Political Sources of Presidencialismo in Mexico', in S. Mainwaring and M. S. Shugart (eds.), *Presidentialism and Democracy in Latin America* (Cambridge: Cambridge University Press, 1997), 225–58. Much-cited analysis of the partisan foundations of Mexico's 'hyperpresidentialism'.

## WEB LINKS

**www.directorio.gob.mx**   Web Directory of the Mexican Government, includes links to ministries, legislatures, courts, sub-national governments, embassies, media, and universities.

**www.gob.mx**   Citizen Portal of the Federal Government contains legal and other information across a wide range of policy fields.

**www.ife.org.mx**   Federal Electoral Institute (IFE).

**www.trife.gob.mx**   Federal Electoral Tribunal (TEPJF).

**www.ifai.org.mx**   Federal Institute for Access to Public Information (IFAI).

**www.unam.mx**   National Autonomous University (UNAM).

**www.banxico.org.mx**   Banco de México (Central Bank).

**www.laneta.apc.org**   LaNeta—'alternative' civil society information.

 ## COMPANION WEB SITE

For additional material and resources, see the companion web site at:
**www.oup.com/uk/booksites/politics/**

# 21a

# Underdevelopment and development

## Guatemala

*Rachel Sieder*

## OVERVIEW

This study examines Guatemala as a persistent case of underdevelopment, defining development in terms of social, economic, cultural, and political rights. The principal features of underdevelopment in contemporary Guatemala are described. The account analyses historical patterns of state formation and economic development before examining the attempts to reverse historical trends and 'engineer development' represented by the 1996 peace agreement. The final section signals the main contemporary causes of the country's persistent underdevelopment: a **patrimonialist** and **predatory state** linked in turn to the strength and conservatism of the private sector, the weakness of the party system, and the continuing influence of the armed forces.

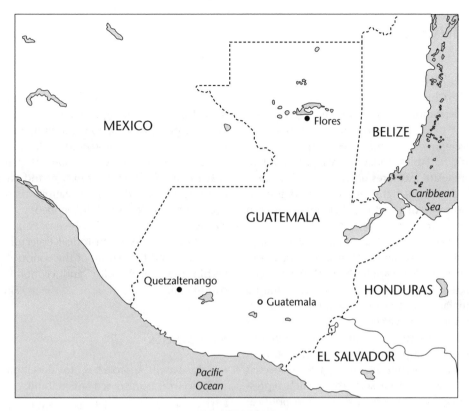

**GUATEMALA**

---

## Box 21a.1  Key dates in Guatemala's history

**1944**  Forced labour abolished, universal male suffrage introduced

**1952**  Agrarian reform law approved

**1954**  Democratically elected government of Jacobo Arbenz overthrown in CIA-backed coup

**1960**  First guerrilla insurgency

**1978–83**  Height of counter-insurgency war. 100,000 civilians killed or disappeared 1981–3

**1984–5**  Military oversee guided transition to elected, civilian government

**1990**  Oslo Accord between government and URNG establishes framework for national peace negotiations

**1993**  Attempted executive coup by President Serrano fails

**1994–6**  UN mediates peace process. Agreements reached on human rights, indigenous rights and identity, resettlement of displaced populations, clarification of human rights violations, agricultural modernization, and reform of the military and the state

**1996**  Final peace settlement signed

**1999**  United Nations Truth Commission finds Guatemalan state guilty of acts of genocide during armed conflict. Recommends prosecutions

**1999**  Frente Repúblicano Guatemalteco (FRG), led by former dictator Rios Montt, wins presidential elections

# Introduction

The influence of rights-based approaches to development (see also Chapter 15) in recent years has ensured that our understanding of 'development' and under-development' has become more holistic. Where previously development was measured simply in terms of economic variables, today assessments tend to include composite measures of the socio-economic, cultural, and political rights enjoyed by its inhabitants, and the extent to which their inclusion and well-being is secured.

Standard socio-economic indicators of development include poverty, access to health, education, and employment. These are both absolute and relative: the extent of equality or inequality, including gender and racial and ethnic equality, is thus an important indicator. Other important indicators include the extent to which the human rights of individuals and groups, including cultural rights of ethnic minorities and minority groups, are respected and protected and **citizen security**—which represents the threats to the public, social, and political order posed by rising common crime and public fear of crime. Lastly development should include political indicators: specifically the existence of democratic and participatory forms of governance, and accountable and efficient state institutions.

Undoubtedly there is increasing agreement on how to measure development and underdevelopment. However, explaining why some countries are less developed than others remains a highly complex and contested enterprise. Many argue that the very terms 'development' and 'underdevelopment' are culturally loaded and carry an implicit and problematic notion of poor countries somehow 'catching up'—or failing to catch up—with advanced industrial societies. Explanations of underdevelopment have tended either to ignore the role of history and international political economy (modernization theory) or to overemphasize the same (dependency theory). But clearly the interactions between a range of factors, including the specific historical trajectories of state formation and the nature of the country's insertion within the global polity and economy, must be considered.

## Key points

- Rights-based approaches to development have replaced measures based on economic growth alone.

- 'Development' includes the extent to which social, economic, political, and cultural rights are enjoyed by a country's inhabitants.

- Development is both absolute and relative: equality within society is an important measure.

- Patterns of state formation and the international political economy are central to explaining different countries' levels of development and underdevelopment.

# Guatemala: poverty and multiple inequalities

Guatemala can be characterized as a country with persistent underdevelopment. Rates of poverty and inequality are amongst the highest in Latin America and the Caribbean. It ranks worst in the region—and amongst the worst in the world—for malnutrition (World Bank 2003*b*). Gini indices for consumption and income for Guatemala are 48 and 57 respectively, making Guatemala one of the most unequal countries in Latin America, itself the most unequal region in the world. In other words, the population is characterized by a large, poor, low-income majority and a small, high-income minority. The percentage of Guatemala's population living in poverty (that is, on less than two US dollars a day) stood at 56 per cent (some 6.4 million people) in 2000, with some 16 per cent of the population living in extreme poverty—that is, with income insufficient to meet their minimum daily calorific requirements (World Bank 2003*b*).

## Ethnic, regional, and gender inequality

Economic differences between different regions of the country and ethnic groups are huge. According to World Bank figures for 2000, while Guatemala's twenty-three indigenous groups represented 43 per cent of the population (a conservative estimate), they accounted for 58 per cent of the poor and 72 per cent of the extreme poor. Almost three-quarters of indigenous people live in poverty, as compared with 41 per cent for non-indigenous. The predominantly rural indigenous areas of the country have the worst conditions of poverty, health, education, and land shortages. Government spending on welfare provision is lower in rural areas. The rate of rural poverty in 1998 was nearly three times that of the urban areas (77 per cent to 29 per cent) and four times that of the capital, Guatemala City. The rural rate of extreme poverty (40 per cent) was nearly six times the urban rate (7 per cent). Poverty also disproportionately affects children—in 2000 some 68 per cent of children under 6 (about 1.7 million) and 63 per cent of young people under 18 (about 3.8 million) were poor (World Bank 2003*b*).

Guatemala is classified as a middle-income country, but has a long history of low social spending. This is partly accounted for by historically low rates of tax collection: Guatemala's tax coefficient of 7.7 per cent of GDP in 1998—the lowest in Latin America—contrasts with 18.3 per cent in Chile. Total public spending on education and health in 2000 was only 3.6 per cent of GDP, even though social spending improved somewhat during the late 1990s. Guatemala's rate of illiteracy (31 per cent in 2000) is third only to Haiti and Nicaragua in the entire region. The legacy of gender and ethnic discrimination is evident in literacy statistics: in 1989 a staggering 82 per cent of indigenous women were illiterate. By 2000 it was 62 per cent, but indigenous women still lagged far behind their non-indigenous counterparts: overall female illiteracy rates stood at 39 per cent (World Bank 2003*b*).

## Health and education

Poverty and low educational achievement are directly correlated—very few poor children continue education through to secondary level. Child labour is a main cause of absenteeism and high school drop-out rates. The number of children working increased from 28.6 per cent in 1994 to 36.7 per cent in 1999. Rural school drop-out rates are over twice as high as urban rates and girls attend school at lower rates than boys. Health spending per capita in 1998 put Guatemala at $155, ahead only of Haiti and well below Nicaragua ($266) and Honduras ($210)—both poorer than Guatemala. This is reflected in life expectancy—Guatemalans live an average of 65 years, compared with 70 for Latin America and the Caribbean. Both infant and maternal mortality rates are exceptionally high: only Bolivia and Haiti perform worse. Indicators are improving, but more slowly than elsewhere. Moreover, health services tend to be concentrated in the capital, serving primarily the tiny proportion of the population with health insurance.

## Economic growth and under-employment

For much of its recent history, Guatemala has enjoyed relative macro-economic stability and reasonable growth—an annual average of 3.9 per cent from the 1950s through the 1990s. External debt-servicing pressures have been moderate (the ratio of public debt to GDP stood at 17.6 per cent in 2000). The economy suffered in the 1980s because of intensification of the civil war (which began in 1960) and a deteriorating international economic environment, but revived in the 1990s. Nonetheless, with one of the highest population growth rates in the region (around 2.6 per cent per annum) per capita growth rates were significantly lower (and even negative during the 1980s), averaging 1.3 per cent annually over the past fifty years. Economic development has not generated sufficient low-skilled jobs to absorb the poor. Consequently between 700,000 and one million Guatemalans are forced to migrate for seasonal harvest work. Working conditions for migrant workers are extremely tough; they are often paid less than the minimum wage and have little or no access to health and educational facilities. In recent years the structural crisis of coffee and sugar markets (two of Guatemala's main agro-exports) has drastically reduced national and regional employment opportunities for migrant workers and the numbers of those attempting to reach the USA as illegal migrants increased. Poor families increasingly rely on dollar remittances from family members working in the USA.

## Democratic disenchantment

Like most of Latin America, Guatemala is now formally a democracy. However, while respect for political and human rights has undoubtedly improved compared to the 1980s these rights are still far from secure and democracy remains fragile. Since restoration of electoral rule in 1986 elections have become freer and fairer and an increasingly broad spectrum of political opinion has been represented at the polls, particularly following the successful conclusion of a negotiated settlement to the armed conflict in December 1996. During the 1990s decentralization and electoral reforms increased opportunities for citizen participation in municipal government.

Yet Guatemalans' levels of political participation and faith in the institutions of government are low compared to other countries in the region. Voter turnout is comparatively poor (Sieder et al. 2002: 30), and regional public opinion surveys such as the Latin-Barometer regularly find that Guatemalans have some of the lowest regard for democratic norms in the region. One explanation could be corruption,

endemic both at national and local level. Another is citizen insecurity: Guatemala has one of the highest homicide rates in the region and extremely high levels of so-called common, especially violent, crime. Crime and gender-based violence are a common occurrence for many citizens, particularly the poor. The judicial system is weak, impunity is routine, and those responsible for criminal acts are rarely prosecuted. Respect for indigenous peoples' rights was a cornerstone of the peace accords (see below) but despite some advances, progress has been extremely slow. For most Guatemalans democracy clearly has yet to deliver.

## Key points

- Guatemala has among the highest rates of poverty and inequality in Latin American and Caribbean.

- In 2001 56 per cent of the population lacked sufficient income to meet their minimum subsistence requirements.

- Indigenous people, rural inhabitants, women, and children are amongst the poorest and most disadvantaged sectors of the population.

- Despite relative macro-economic stability, tax collection and social spending rates over the last three decades have been low.

- A return to electoral democracy occurred in 1986, but citizen disenchantment with democratic performance is high.

# Patterns of state formation

Guatemala's economic fortunes were built on agro-exports and based on a highly exploitative form of rural capitalism, which in turn was reflected in authoritarian and exclusive forms of politics and development. The dispossession of indigenous people from their historic lands began with colonization in the sixteenth century and accelerated during the late nineteenth-century coffee boom. New laws were introduced to stimulate coffee production and

agro-exports, and inequality of access to land grew rapidly. Colonial forms of labour coercion were replaced by such mechanisms as forced indebtedness and vagrancy laws, which remained on the statute books until the mid-twentieth century. The capitalist planter class in Guatemala relied on forced wage-labour, becoming increasingly dependent on the coercive power of the central state, dominated by the armed forces, to ensure its supply of workers. Economic downturns necessitated repression by the military to quell wage demands and ensure profitability margins. Ruling elites did not view the poor and particularly the indigenous as citizens, but rather as subjects to be disciplined, controlled, and 'civilized'. The richest families traced their descent to European settlers and viewed themselves as 'white'; indeed in the early twentieth century many still held *certificados de raza*—documents that supposedly proved they had no Indian blood. Race and class discrimination were mutually reinforcing and underpinned the economic system.

## The cold war: reform reversed

Between 1944 and 1954 reformist governments were elected, following a coup by junior military officers. The administration of Juan José Arévalo (1944–51) introduced universal male suffrage, abolished forced labour and indentured servitude, and sponsored progressive labour and social security legislation. The more radical government of Jacobo Arbenz (1952–4) introduced an agrarian reform law in an effort to stimulate agricultural production and address rural poverty. However, the expropriation of large, under-utilized estates and their distribution to landless peasants angered both rich landowners and the US-based United Fruit Company, one of the largest landowners in Guatemala. United Fruit conspired with US President Eisenhower's administration and elements of Guatemala's armed forces to overthrow the reformers, accusing the Arbenz government of communist sympathies. In 1954 Guatemala gained the dubious distinction of being the second country subject to a CIA-sponsored 'cold war coup' (Iran being the first in 1953). Following the overthrow of Arbenz the agrarian reform was reversed and peasant organizers persecuted. The Guatemalan armed forces received significant support from the USA within the regional framework of counter-insurgency training. The state became increasingly dominated by the military, who by the 1970s had become powerful economic actors in their own right. Espousing a virulent anti-communism, the private sector relied on the army to repress workers' demands for improved wages or better working conditions. Delegating the business of government to the military, they nonetheless exercised a permanent veto on social reform. Regular

elections took place but the spectrum was confined to transient centre-right and right-wing parties who invariably fielded military officers as presidential candidates. Participation was low and levels of political violence and intimidation high.

## Insurgency, counter-insurgency, and genocide

Such acute socio-economic and political exclusion contributed to the emergence of a guerrilla insurgency in the 1960s. This was brutally repressed by the army. State violence increased throughout the 1970s targeting trade unionists, social activists, and reformist politicians, reaching a peak in the early 1980s when de facto military regimes fought an all-out war against the civilian population to stamp out a second guerrilla insurgency. This involved hundreds of army-led massacres, 'scorched earth' measures, forced displacement of thousands of Guatemalans, mandatory paramilitary 'civil patrols' for all indigenous men in the countryside, and the militarization of the entire state apparatus; it constituted one of the most extreme cases of state repression in twentieth-century Latin America. In total during thirty-six years of armed conflict some 200,000 people were killed (2 per cent of the 1980 population), nearly a quarter of whom 'disappeared'. Another million were displaced, either internally or into Mexico. In 1999 the United Nations found that the Guatemalan state was responsible for over 90 per cent of gross human rights violations documented throughout the armed conflict and was guilty of acts of **genocide** against the indigenous population between 1981 and 1983. This massive destruction of human and social capital had significant negative consequences for Guatemala's development prospects.

## Electoral democracy and peace negotiations

In the mid-1980s the military returned the country to civilian rule in a 'guided transition' to democracy designed to improve the country's standing before the international community, while perpetuating effective control by the armed forces over national affairs. The return to elected government, encouraged by US President Reagan's administration, permitted restoration of US military aid—suspended since 1978 by US President Carter in protest at human rights violations. Presidential elections held in 1985 were won by the centre-right Christian Democrat party; a new constitution was adopted in 1986. Yet political parties remained weak and fragmented, the influence of the military was undiminished, and state-perpetrated political repression of political opponents and trade union and human rights activists continued. In 1993 gridlock between executive and congress led President Jorge Serrano to attempt a 'self-coup', closing down congress and dismissing the Supreme Court. Serrano was thwarted by a combination of popular mobilization and opposition from the domestic private sector, the international community, and sectors of the armed forces, representing an important step in the strengthening of Guatemala's weak democracy.

The armed conflict was not resolved until December 1996, when the pro-business sector government of President Alvaro Arzú signed a definitive peace settlement with the insurgent Unidad Revolucionaria Nacional Guatemalteca (URNG), bringing nine years of stop-start peace talks to a successful conclusion. The international community exerted considerable pressure to secure a settlement: the final phase of the negotiations was overseen by the United Nations, and after 1994 an on-site UN mission (Misión de las Naciones Unidas en Guatemala, MINUGUA) was charged with verification and supervision of the peace accords. Through its sponsorship of the peace settlement the international community became highly involved in attempts to kick-start development in Guatemala.

## Key points

- Guatemala's republican history is characterized by authoritarian rule, coercive rural capitalism, and racist discrimination.

- A reformist democratic regime was overthrown in 1954 at the height of the cold war by a US-backed military coup.

- In response to guerrilla challenges, the armed forces militarized the state and used extreme violence against the civilian population.

- The country returned to elected civilian government in 1986, but the military continued to dominate politics and repress opponents.

- Thirty-six years of civil war finally ended with a UN-sponsored negotiated settlement in 1996.

# The peace accords: a turning point?

The peace accords aimed not only to formally end the armed conflict, but also to reverse the country's historically exclusionary pattern of development. They comprised thirteen separate accords, involving four main areas:

- Resettlement of displaced populations, reincorporation of former guerrillas, and reconciliation regarding past violations of human rights.

- An integrated programme for human development, which mandated a 50 per cent increase over five years in health and education spending.

- Goals for productive and sustainable development, including market-led reform of the agricultural sector.

- Modernization of the democratic state, including reduction in the role of the armed forces, strengthening the rule of law and increasing **civil society** participation, particularly in implementing the accords themselves.

Three cross-cutting elements were emphasized: the rights of indigenous communities, commitments regarding the rights and position of women, and greater social participation. The international community pledged more than $3.2 billion in aid—over 60 per cent as grants to implement the accords. The agreements also contained a commitment to reform taxation and increase revenues from 8 per cent to 12 per cent of GDP by 2000.

## Lack of domestic commitment

The peace accords constituted important achievements in their own right, but implementation was slow and uneven. Given the country's violent past and history of socio-economic and ethnic and gender exclusion, meeting the comprehensive goals of the peace settlement was bound to be challenging. However lack of commitment by key domestic actors further constrained prospects for success. While the international community and civil society organizations backed the agreements, the commitment of the main political parties, the military, and the private sector to the settlement was weak. The powerful and conservative private sector staunchly defended its privileges, despite the more progressive stance of certain reformist elements within the business community. During the negotiating process the private sector association CACIF (*Comité de Asociaciones Comerciales, Industriales y Financieras*)—dominated by large landowners—steadfastly vetoed attempts at land reform, insisting on the sanctity of private property. In the wake of the settlement CACIF successfully blocked far-reaching fiscal reform or tax reforms, especially any increase in direct taxes.

## Implementation: a mixed record

Other aspects of the peace settlement were more successful. The guerrillas (all but decimated as a military force by the violence of the early 1980s) were reincorporated into civilian life—the ceasefire was not breached and the URNG became a political party. Displaced and returned refugee populations were resettled, though many complained of being allocated poor land and of insufficient access to credit. A UN-led truth commission was completed in 1999, a major achievement that signalled army responsibility for gross violations of human rights and recommended legal prosecutions. Yet, despite the efforts of human rights organizations to secure justice, impunity remains the norm. Attacks have occurred against organizations and indigenous communities trying to secure exhumations of mass graves and bring perpetrators to trial. Spending on health and education did increase and a number of important structural reforms were implemented, particularly in education. How-

ever, this has not yet had an appreciable impact on social indicators. Social spending was supposed to be redirected towards the poorer regions, but the record has been mixed. The global economic downturn in 2000–1 combined with the global fall in agro-export prices severely hampered even the limited development plans for the rural sector set out in the peace accords. The rural poor continue to lack access to land. In some cases large landowners made a healthy profit from the peace funds provided by the international community by selling unproductive lands at inflated prices to the national peace fund. Landless peasants settled on these lands found they were unable to feed themselves and saddled with debt repayment obligations they could not meet.

## A patrimonialist state

In addition to private sector intransigence, the failure to modernize the state and the weakness of democratic institutions provide clues to Guatemala's continuing underdevelopment. The internationally prescribed formula of institutional strengthening and 'civil society strengthening' contained in the peace accords failed to transform an exclusive, patrimonialist state into a developmental state. This reflects the balance of political forces and inherent difficulty of changing historically entrenched patterns. The nature of Guatemala's party system is both cause and effect of the patrimonialist state. Guatemalan parties tend to be dominated by *caudillo* figures—charismatic strongmen who build **patronage** networks in order to command powerful personal loyalties—and are subject to continuous division and fragmentation. Many are little more than electoral alliances of convenience. Party discipline is weak and **clientelism** rife. Although a number of centre-left parties, including the URNG, have gained ground since 1995, their share of the vote remains limited and the parties themselves far from consolidated.

## Military power

The armed forces largely retained their power following the peace settlement. In contrast to neighbouring El Salvador, the armed challenge from the guerrilla forces in Guatemala was negligible and the leverage of the USA over the armed forces limited. Troop numbers were reduced during the late 1990s, but the military budget increased, directly contravening the peace accords. Commitments to reform military intelligence services remain unfulfilled. While efforts to consolidate a civilian police force have advanced, the police remains weak and under-funded and the army has again been employed in public security functions. In addition to the slowness of institutional reform of the armed forces, more sinister manifestations of military power are evident. Serving and former military officers form part of a network of so-called 'parallel powers' which has influence within the highest spheres of government. These mafia-style networks are implicated in corruption scandals, organized crime, and maintaining impunity for those guilty of gross violations of human rights.

## Weak civil society

Civil society organizations have become more vocal advocates of government transparency and accountability in recent years, but face adverse conditions. Violence and intimidation against rights activists continue and popular awareness of the historically high costs of dissent means that Guatemalan civil society remains comparatively weak. Indigenous Mayan organizations gained a national presence after the early 1990s and have advanced important national and local development initiatives, but their influence has recently declined. According to the framework for peace negotiations, all reforms to the constitution had to be approved by congress and then passed by a majority in a national referendum. A poll held in May 1999 (with a turnout of less than 20 per cent) rejected a package of constitutional reforms which included the official recognition of Guatemala as a multicultural and multi-ethnic nation-state. Elements of the private sector campaigned vociferously against recognition of indigenous peoples' rights, arguing it would lead to 'reverse discrimination' and **'balkanization'** of the country. Unlike other Latin American countries with large indigenous populations—for example Bolivia or Ecuador—multicultural reforms of the Guatemalan state have been relatively limited to date.

## State–civil society conflict

Despite some decentralization and greater involvement of non-governmental organizations (NGOs) in delivery of public services during the 1990s, state–civil society relations remain conflictive. Whilst in some cases more participatory local government has been strengthened, in others local administration is characterized by corruption and clientelism. Instead of working with the state, civil society organizations often go *around* the state in an effort to secure their demands. For example, echoing what has been called the 'boomerang effect', human rights organizations work through transnational networks to persuade foreign governments and donors to put pressure on the Guatemalan state to meet its human rights obligations.

After winning elections in November 1999 the Frente Republicano Guatemalteco (FRG), led by former military dictator Ríos Montt, did little to strengthen democratic mechanisms. Instead the party manipulated state institutions for its own political and economic advantage, in the process sidelining the traditional landowning elite and favouring a new clientele of regionally based party loyalists and former military officers. Despite the party's **populist** discourse, appealing to impoverished peasants to stand up to the 'oligarchy', accusations of government corruption, kickbacks, and clientelism mounted and confrontation between government and civil society groups increased. In 2003 the FRG stacked the Constitutional Court to secure Rios Montt's presidential candidacy, further weakening the constitutional order and the rule of law (according to the 1986 constitution anyone who has participated in a coup or attempted coup is prohibited from presidential office). Rios Montt himself was indicted by the UN truth commission for crimes of genocide. Guatemalan human rights organizations are currently seeking his prosecution before the courts. The FRG's electoral victory represented a historic displacement of the Guatemalan private sector, which had controlled the presidency since the return to electoral democracy in 1986, and relations between the government and CACIF have been especially acrimonious since 1999, particularly regarding fiscal reform and corruption. In the medium term this may encourage the private sector to develop more effective political parties, form broader electoral alliances, and work to strengthen the accountability of state institutions, but at present such changes remain a remote possibility.

## Key points

- The 1996 peace accords set out a programme aiming to reverse exclusionary development and improve social participation, especially of women and indigenous peoples.
- The accords were backed by the international community and civil society groups, but the commitment of the armed forces, private sector, and political parties to the settlement was low.

- Some progress on implementation has been made, but targets have not been met. Private sector resistance to raising fiscal revenues remains high.
- Key factors impeding emergence of a developmental state include opportunist, clientelist, and fragmented political parties, a powerful and autonomous military and relatively weak civil society.
- Confrontational party politics and the rise of organized crime and 'parallel powers' pose serious threats to Guatemalan democracy and obstacles to development.

# Conclusions

Guatemala is a 'predatory' rather than a developmental state. The US-supported derailing of the reformist administration of Jacobo Arbenz produced one of the most violent and authoritarian regimes in the region. The state lacked autonomy and was effectively colonized by powerful private interests to the detriment of the majority of the population. During the cold war it was supported by the regional superpower under the aegis of anti-communism. Despite transition to electoral rule two decades ago, such predatory tendencies have not disappeared—indeed many now point to the increasingly mafia-style operation of the Guatemalan state.

The peace process of the 1990s provided an important space for reorienting historically exclusionary patterns of development. However, without the political commitment of the most powerful domestic actors, international pressure and the support of civil society organizations were unable to secure such a shift. Guatemala today is a weak and illiberal democracy—the population may enjoy suffrage or political rights, but civil rights are not enforced and the rule of law is routinely flouted by powerful actors within and outside government. Historical patterns of ethnic and economic exclusion combined with the legacy of extreme levels of state violence against the civilian population mean that citizen participation is relatively weak. The strength and conservatism of the private sector, its historic reliance on the armed forces, and the systematic persecution of the left and centre-left has engendered a particularly weak and venal political class and party system constituting another impediment to development. More progressive elements secured a foothold during the 1990s, but they face powerful opposition and have yet to consolidate effective parties capable of winning elections.

Finally, long-term structural factors have not favoured the Guatemalan economy. Historically reliant on a particularly exploitative form of rural capitalism, the private sector has largely failed to adapt to new global conditions despite the relative decline of traditional agro-exports. The historic lack of investment in human capital is a serious impediment to future economic development. And as in most of Latin America, adherence to neo-liberal orthodoxies of the international financial institutions has proved singularly incapable of generating greater development and equality.

## QUESTIONS

1   What factors, domestic and external, have led to Guatemala's persistent underdevelopment?

2   How important is the historical legacy of a country in explaining its underdevelopment?

3   What can the international community do to support development efforts in a country like Guatemala?

4   What is the relationship between political democracy and development in the case of Guatemala?

## GUIDE TO FURTHER READING

Chase-Dunn, C., Jonas, S., and Amaro, N. (eds.), *Globalization on the Ground: Postbellum Guatemalan Democracy and Development* (Lanham, Md: Rowman and Littlefield, 2001). Considers prospects and problems for democracy and development after the civil war.

Jonas, S., *Of Centaurs and Doves: Guatemala's Peace Process* (Boulder, Colo., and London: Westview Press, 2000). A comprehensive overview of the peace process and of contemporary Guatemalan politics.

REMHI, *Guatemala: Never Again! Recovery of Historical Memory Project. The Official Report of the Human Rights Office, Archdiocese of Guatemala* (London: Catholic Institute of International Relations/ Latin American Bureau, 1999). Based on testimonies from thousands of victims of Guatemala's dirty war.

Schirmer, J., *The Guatemalan Military Project: A Violence Called Democracy* (Philadelphia: University of Pennsylvania Press, 1998). Analyses the military's role in Guatemala's fragile transition to democracy.

Sieder, R. (ed.), *Guatemala After the Peace Accords* (London: Institute of Latin American Studies, 1998). Academics and practitioners consider the challenges following the peace agreements.

—— Thomas, M., Vickers, J., and Spence, J., *Who Governs? Guatemala Five Years After the Peace Accords* (Washington: Hemisphere Initiatives/ Washington Office on Latin America, 2002). Reports on the progress of the peace settlement after five years.

## WEB LINKS

www.undp.org/hdr2003/indicator/cty_f_GTM.html    UNDP Human Development Indicators for 2003.

http://wbln0018.worldbank.org/LAC/LACInfoClient.nsf/Date/By+Author_Country/EEBA795 E0F22768D85256CE700772165?OpenDocument    World Bank Guatemala Poverty Assessment (2003).

 ## COMPANION WEB SITE

For additional material and resources, see the companion web site at:
www.oup.com/uk/booksites/politics/

# Underdevelopment and development

## South Korea

*Peter Ferdinand*

## OVERVIEW

This chapter concentrates on the role of the state in directing and leading development in the Republic of Korea since the end of the Korean war in 1953. It falls into five parts, beginning with four legacies from recent Korean history that favoured success. The second part identifies key institutions of Korea's developmental state, most notably the Economic Planning Board and a bureaucracy with 'embedded autonomy' from societal pressures. The third part assesses the success of Korea's development policies: land reform, industrialization that from the mid-1960s was increasingly export-led, and investment in education. The fourth part examines the transition to democracy, since 1987. The final part identifies new challenges for South Korea in a world of increasing globalization, especially the need to transcend the previously successful developmental state model, increasing pressures on the state to provide welfare services, and problems of corruption and democratic consolidation.

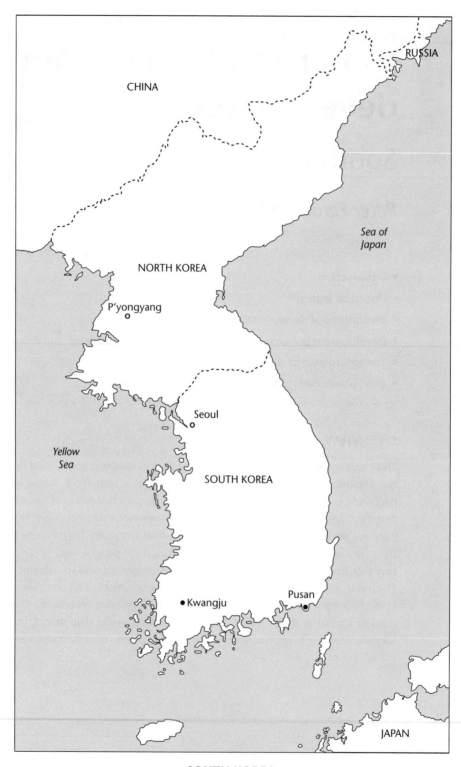

**SOUTH KOREA**

# Introduction

In 1945 the Korean peninsula was freed from Japanese colonial rule by the USA and the Soviet Union. It was divided into two states—one communist in the north and one capitalist in the south. In 1950 North Korea (the Democratic People's Republic of Korea, or DPRK) invaded the south (Republic of Korea, or ROK). In three years over one million people died as a result of the conflict, and it left per capita income in the south, approximately US $67 per year (in 1996 dollars), among the lowest in the world. By 2001 that figure had risen to around US $9,400. In 1995 it became only the second Asian state after Japan and the first former colony anywhere to be admitted to the Organization for Economic Cooperation and Development (OECD). By 2002, too, according to the International Telecommunications Union, 58.2 per cent of the South Korean population had access to the Internet, the highest figure in Asia and the fourth highest in the world, fractionally higher even than in the USA.

## Key points

- On all conventional measures South Korea's record of development since the early 1950s is highly impressive.

---

**Box 21*b*.1 Key dates in modern Korea's history**

| 1910 | Colonized by Japan |
|---|---|
| 1945 | Creation of two separate independent Korean states in the north and the south |
| 1950–3 | Korean war |
| 1961 | General Park Chung Hee seizes power in South Korea |
| 1980 | Kwangju massacre |
| 1987 | Democracy re-emerges as President Roh Tae Woo allies with former oppositionist Kim Young Sam to form the Democratic Liberal Party and rule through it |
| 1992 | Kim Young Sam becomes the first civilian president since 1961 |
| 1997 | Asian financial crisis and Kim Dae Jung is elected president |

---

# Historical legacies

Four legacies from before 1953 contributed to the drive for national economic development, especially after 1961: social traditions; the traditional 'vortex' of centralization; the impact of Japanese colonialism, partition, and civil war; South Koreans' perception of their place in the East Asian region and the world.

First, South Korea has the distinct advantage of being ethnically homogeneous. Although the civil war generated millions of refugees and separated family units across the new border, creating long-lasting hatreds and fears, there has been no contestation of the right to exist of a Korean state. No significant group in society wanted to leave. Thus Korea met Rustow's first criterion for a viable democracy: 'The vast majority of citizens in a democracy-to-be must have no doubt or mental reservations as to which political community they belong to' (Rustow 1970: 350). The only unresolved business was: which Korean state should represent the whole of the Korean nation?

Also, over the centuries Confucianism became the dominant ideology of social organization. Large numbers of Koreans are Buddhists or Christians, but principles of Confucian social organization are deeply embedded in Korean society. These respect a hierarchy of relationships within the family, where everyone knows their obligations towards everyone else, as the basis for a well-ordered society. The patriarchal head of the family was entitled to absolute respect. So too was the emperor or ruler. Filial piety—the devotion of the son to the father—was the core relationship. The word for 'state' (*guk'ka*) in Korean is an amalgam of 'nation' and 'family', as it is in Chinese. And within both the family and the state the ideal condition was the absence of strife. Deference and subservience were regarded as positive qualities for the sake of harmony.

Second, an early analysis of South Korean politics identified a 'vortex' of centralization as the dominant dynamic determining Korean political development into the modern era. This meant two things: the dominance of the court (in imperial times) and the capital over the rest of a country of villages; a lack of intermediate social organizations. Traditionally Korea was polarized between rulers and the mass of society. There was weak horizontal organization (Henderson 1968). Korea experienced centripetal rather than centrifugal forces.

Third, colonialism launched Korean modernization and development. Until the twentieth century the Korean peninsula—the 'hermit kingdom'—was a poor backwater, largely ignored by its neighbours. After 1910, Japanese colonialism introduced a wider set of regional relations and industrialization in the north, but in consequence the Japanese occupied all the important managerial and administrative posts. Nevertheless a small middle class of Korean entrepreneurs emerged. After 1945 they laid the foundation for Korea's indigenous industrialization drive in the south. In the north they were repressed; and almost all industrial sites were devastated during the civil war. What remained was the experience of organizing factories Japanese-style—intellectual capital that turned to rebuilding the country, after 1953. At the same time the colonial experience generated a very powerful sense of patriotism among Koreans, both in the north and the south. The injustices that had been inflicted by the Japanese—their treatment as inferiors—created a strong unifying factor.

Fourth, a hunger to remake the country after the civil war underlay the development drive in both north and south, where both were conscious of the immense size of their near neighbours and respective superpower protectors. In the DPRK it spawned the '*juche* ideology'—the principle of national self-reliance—propagated by Kim Il Sung, from the early 1960s. North Korea was allied to both the Soviet Union and China but never joined the Warsaw Pact or Comecon. In the ROK the mistrust was more muted, but calls for neutralism and resentment over the US troops stationed in the country persisted.

## Key points

- A unique combination of four distinct historical legacies has exercised a powerful influence on South Korea's distinctive developmental success over the last fifty years

# Institutions of development

South Korea's government was determined to pursue industrialization vigorously, for security's sake as much as prosperity.

Politics in South Korea was dominated by the military up until the 1990s, even though Rhee Syngman (Korean family names come first), its first president, was a civilian. His regime was widely perceived to be corrupt. When he claimed victory in fraudulent elections in 1960 the military refused to repress widespread demonstrations. The liberal government under Chang Myon that took over was soon paralysed by polarization between the authorities and students demonstrating on the streets. In 1961 General Park Chung Hee staged a coup, and from then until 1992 the generals dominated government, presenting themselves as guardians of the nation and order, committed to making the nation 'rich and strong'. General Park declared, 'It is an undeniable fact that the people in Asia today fear starvation and poverty more than the oppressive duties thrust upon them by totalitarianism . . . In other words, the Asian peoples want to obtain economic equality first and build a more equitable political machinery afterward' (in Jones and Sakong 1980: 43).

General Park laid the basis for what has subsequently been termed a **'developmental state'**. Its main features have been described as: (*a*) a nationalist agenda; (*b*) state direction of finance for priority development projects; (*c*) an effective and technocratic bureaucracy; (*d*) the state and business are partners; (*e*) authoritarianism; (*f*) favourable international circumstances. (Woo-Cumings 1999: 1–31). The major development decisions were formulated by the Economic Planning Board (EPB), founded in 1961. For the next fifteen years the economy grew faster than 'planned'.

A key factor was the state's **'embedded autonomy'** (Evans 1995): aimed at developing capitalist enterprises, the state was insulated from excessive pressure of those interests. The military's political domination helped. During the 1960s and 1970s a solid, merit-based bureaucracy was created, replacing the political appointees of the 1950s. This was accompanied by, in Myrdal's terms, a 'hardening' of the state's structures and operating practices. Myrdal (1968: i. 66–7) said that in **'soft' states** policies are often not enforced, if they are enacted at all, whereas in 'hard' states 'the success of planning for development requires a readiness to place obligations on people in all social strata to a much greater extent . . . [and] requires . . . rigorous enforcement of obligations, in which compulsion plays a strategic role'. The Korean military reacted against the ineffectiveness of the Rhee and Chang Myon regimes, and relied on trusted businessmen. Some had established companies under the Japanese. Others took advantage of the new opportunities created by a shortage economy that ran on permits and licences. They were able to accumulate business empires, the most successful building *chaebols*— business groups or conglomerates.

The *chaebols* were family-based companies with cross-holdings of shares in subsidiaries. They benefited from government favouritism; financing remained the preserve of state banks. General Park was able to direct the nation's economy and initiate industrial projects by summoning the thirty top business leaders for meetings within one room; cartels were encouraged to form and compete among themselves. Individual *chaebols* were compensated for government-induced financial losses (Lee 1997). A few families grew exceedingly rich and were also widely resented (Eckert 1990). In 1989 the Ministry of

**Table 21*b*.1** South Korea's average annual growth of Gross Domestic Product (%)

| 1950–9 | 1960–9 | 1970–9 | 1980–9 | 1990–2000 |
|--------|--------|--------|--------|-----------|
| 5 | 8.5 | 9.5 | 9.4 | 5.7 |

*Source*: World Bank, *World Development Report* (various years).

Finance estimated that in each of the ten largest *chaebols* the main family held roughly 50 per cent of all the shares, whether directly or through cross-holdings (Janelli 1993: 84). The relationship between the regime and leading *chaebols* was one of both mutual support and vulnerability, with the balance of power gradually tipping towards the *chaebols*, although government kept control of financial resources, thereby stunting the development of an independent financial sector. Debt/asset ratios of *chaebols* soared, but few, if any, thought about the likely consequences until the financial crisis of 1997. The government also tightly controlled the labour unions; memories of the civil war and military service, and fear of communist infiltration were justifying pretexts (Janelli 1993).

Korea followed Japan in concentrating upon full employment policies to raise welfare, rather than introduce a welfare state for which there was no popular demand, in part because of the Confucian tradition of family obligations. Large construction and infrastructure policies rather than welfare programmes were used to stimulate economic activity when the business cycle turned downwards.

According to the World Bank average annual per capital GNI growth between 1960 and 1995 was around 7.5 per cent (see Table 21*b*.1).

## Key points

- An intensive period of economic development and industrialization between 1961 and 1979 created a powerful business sector but also solidified business dependence upon the state.

- From the early 1980s onwards successive administrations tried to shift support towards small and medium-sized businesses but were stymied by the entrenched power of the *chaebols*, upon whom the government became increasingly dependent to deliver national prosperity.

# Development policies

In 1953 the economy was still overwhelmingly agricultural. The first task was land reform, to introduce greater fairness into the size of landholdings and free up capital and workers for industrialization. In the first period of development the second priority was rebuilding the country—a nationalist project, whose execution created rents for businessmen who supported the government.

The government also strongly encouraged large-scale savings, by imposing punitive taxes on expensive consumer imports, and periodically mobilized the media to urge people to be 'patriotic' in their spending. The results were impressive (see Table 21*b*.2), and the savings were channelled towards government-determined investment priorities.

Initially the government pursued **import-substitution industrialization**, as much for reasons of national security as for the prevailing orthodoxy of development economics. In 1965, however, the government was forced to change strategy, as the USA reduced its aid to Korea in response to increasing expenditure on the Vietnam war. Korea reacted by concentrating more upon exports, with the blessing of the USA and increasing access to world markets. The selective targeting of industries for national development succeeded handsomely, and by the early 1970s the government was sufficiently confident to introduce a policy to develop Heavy and Chemical Industries (HCI). That was subsequently undermined by the oil price shocks. Fortunately for Korea, Japan's revaluation of the yen, brought about by pressure from the G7 leaders of the main industrial countries in 1985, created new export opportunities, leading to a doubling of exports to the USA between 1985 and 1988. Also, Korean corporations were now able to tap international financial markets for investments.

The government's commitment to education also had considerable long-term economic significance. Literacy was virtually eliminated by 1963; by 1978 the proportion of secondary-school-age pupils actually in school was higher than in Singapore, Argentina, Mexico, Turkey, or India. By the 1990s the proportion of students in higher education was higher than in Japan and as can be seen from Table 21*b*.3, dramatically higher than in some other still-developing countries. Amsden (1989: 219) remarked, 'Korea, therefore, is both a general case of a well-educated late industrializing country and a special case of an exceptionally well-educated one.'

As Korean industry began to catch up with technologically more sophisticated international competitors, it also began to distance itself from government direction. The *chaebols*, now frequently obtaining cheaper funds abroad than from the government, increasingly began to talk of 'economic democracy'—autonomy from state interference. The outstanding success of their economic contribution and South Korea's development strategy overall is clearly demonstrated by the contrast with North Korea and Burma—which pursued quite different development policies.

Like North Korea, which before the civil war was more industrialized than South Korea, Burma (Myanmar) was traumatized by violent conflict during the Second World War. In 1950 Burma's population approximated to South Korea's and enjoyed

**Table 21*b*.2** Gross Domestic Savings as a percentage of South Korea's growing GDP

| 1960 | 1970 | 1980 | 1990 | 1999 |
|------|------|------|------|------|
| 2 | 16.2 | 20.8 | 36.1 | 34 |

*Sources*: World Bank, *World Development Report* (various years).

**Table 21*b*.3** Enrolment rates in higher education (%)

| | 1970 | 1980 | 1990 | 1997 |
|---|------|------|------|------|
| Guatemala | 3 | 8 | 8 | 8 (1996) |
| India | 5 | 5 | 6 | 7 (1996) |
| Indonesia | 3 | 4 | 9 | 11 |
| Myanmar | 2 | 5 | 4 | 5 |
| S. Korea | 7 | 15 | 39 | 68 (1994) |

*Source*: UNESCO (1999).

**Table 21b.4** Comparative development of South Korea, North Korea, and Burma

| | Burma | | North Korea | | South Korea | |
|---|---|---|---|---|---|---|
| | 1960 | 2002 | 1960 | 2002 | 1960 | 2002 |
| Population (millions) | 22.3 | 42.2 | 10.5 | 22.2 | 25 | 48.3 |
| Life expectancy (years) | 44 | 55.4 | | 71.3 | 54 | 74.9 |
| Urban percentage of total population | 17 | 23[a] | 29 | 58.5[b] | 28 | 77.6[b] |
| GDP per capita (US $)[c] | 59 | 1,500 | | 1,000 | 133 | 19,400 |
| Share of GDP in per cent from | | | | | | |
| Agriculture | 33 | 42[d] | | 30[d] | 40 | 4 |
| Industry | 12 | 17[d] | | 32[d] | 19 | 42 |
| Services | 55 | 41[d] | | 37[d] | 41 | 54 |
| Share of workforce (in per cent) | | | | | | |
| Agriculture | | 65[e] | | 36 | 62 | 10 |
| Industry | | 10[e] | | 64 | 7.2 | 22 |
| Services | | 25[e] | | | 30.8 | 69 |
| Export/GDP ratio (in per cent) | 17.1 | 0.42[e] | | | 0.86 | 35.6 |

[a] 1983 (the latest available figure).
[b] 1995.
[c] Figures for 1960 GDP are in current prices, whilst those for 2002 are in Purchasing Power Parity terms.
[d] 2000 estimate   [e] 1999 estimate.

*Sources*: B. R. Mitchell, *International Historical Statistics—Africa, Asia and Oceania 1750–1988* (Basingstoke, Macmillan, 2nd edn., 1995); World Bank, *World Development Report* (Oxford: OUP, various years); *CIA World Factbook 2002;* UNCTAD, *Handbook of International Trade and Development Statistics, 1969* (Geneva, 1969); *UN Demographic Yearbook* (New York: UN, various years); ILO, *Yearbook of Labour Statistics 1966* (Geneva: ILO, 1966); IMF, *International Financial Statistics Yearbook 2000* (Washington: IMF 2001).

a comparable level of development. The Burmese people accepted military leadership so as to preserve independence, while its leaders determined on a low profile in international affairs so as to avoid renewed colonial or neo-colonial entanglement. Burma is ethnically more diverse, but both North Korea and Burma share a socialist orientation, and, like North Korea's *juche* the 'Burmese road to socialism' minimized contact with the world economic system. South Korea's economic performance has been vastly superior to both. While Burma remains predominantly an agricultural society with the structure of the labour force still very similar to that of South Korea in 1960, and whilst North Korea is predominantly an industrial country, the distribution of South Korea's workforce now more closely resembles the post-industrial societies of the West. But perhaps the most striking feature of South Korea's development is its high degree of income equality. The Gini coefficient for income inequality was 0.312 in 1985 and fell as low as 0.283 in 1997 on the verge of the Asian financial crisis. That crisis led to increased inequality and by summer 2003 it had risen to 0.329—still impressive by international standards.

## Key points

• South Korea's adoption of a state-led strategy for development has been outstandingly successful especially by comparison with near neighbours who pursued more socialist and inward-looking policies.

# The emergence of democracy

During the 1990s Korea turned into a functioning multi-party democracy, which withstood the Asian financial crisis of 1997–8 without any attempt by the military to regain control. In elections in 1997 power changed hands from one party to another for the first time, and peacefully, allowing Kim Dae Jung, a veteran oppositionist to the military's rule, to become president.

Thus Korea's growing prosperity was followed by democratization, seeming to bear out theories that suggest a sequential process or link between the two. The political reform can be attributed in part to pressure from the labour movement and students, followed by white-collar workers, in part to increased pressure from the US administration, and in part due to a greater willingness of later military leaders to make compromises.

Until the late 1980s it was commonly said of Korea (and other countries in the region) that democracy was an alien, Western concept. There was no example of a Confucian society practising democracy. The military leaders of the country played upon the fear of communism and subversion from the north. The USA tolerated military dictatorship, unwilling to risk collapse. The memory of wartime devastation concentrated public opinion on rebuilding the country. Yet the military leaders never abolished the national legislature, and they tried to enhance their own legitimacy by organizing their own party and winning elections.

Such was the country's economic development in the 1980s that in 1988 GDP exceeded $US3,000 per capita—the threshold beyond which for Huntington (1996b: 7–8) military coups scarcely succeed. Even in 1980 the overwhelming majority of the population said they felt 'middle class' (Choi 1997: 106), although still heavily dependent on state largesse. There was no permanently active civil society counterposed to the state—something that only began to appear in the 1990s, as much a consequence of democratization as a cause.

However, the owners of *chaebols* were becoming restive about state control. They no longer automatically deferred to government direction. They felt better equipped than government bureaucrats to determine development strategy. As Moon puts it, the relationship was becoming increasingly 'unruly' (Moon 1994). Yet the main catalysts for change were workers and students. The labour unions saw democracy as essential to asserting their members' interests, after decades of repression. And although students benefited from the massive expansion of the education system made in response to Confucian values and the needs of a more technologically advanced economy, they were less deferential to their elders than previous generations. There were also far more of them. By the late 1980s there were 1.4 million university students; in 1960, when students brought the short-lived Chang Myon government to power, there were only 101,000. Repression by the riot police and the army alienated parents, especially middle-class ones. And organized religion became a more potent factor in democratization. Christianity attracted many more believers among the newly urbanized. By the mid-1980s roughly a quarter of the population had converted to Christianity. Both Protestant and Catholic churches openly challenged the military leaders and became the chief forum for political protest in the early 1980s.

The first crisis came in 1980. Students in Kwangju city took to the streets to show solidarity with striking industrial workers. The riot police reacted with force, leading to at least 240 deaths. The regime survived the crisis, but as the eyes of the world fixed on Korea and its preparations to host the 1988 Olympic Games, a new crisis emerged. For in 1987 General Park Chung Hee provoked widespread public anger and street protests by nominating General Roh Tae Woo as the next president. White-collar workers also joined in. The decision needed ratification by general election, but the regime failed to win an overall majority, and the opposition was divided. Although the precedent of direct presidential rule was an option, the regime wanted more sympathetic treatment from the international media, especially in the USA. President Reagan specifically telephoned President Park to warn against bloodletting. So the authorities embarked upon protracted secret negotiations, at the end of which Roh Tae Woo agreed with the leader of the largest opposition party, Kim Young Sam, to form a new party with the understanding that Kim would become the next president after Roh. They called the new merged party the Democratic Liberal Party, deliberately echoing the name of the Liberal Democratic Party that had ruled Japan for over thirty years. They hoped to inaugurate a similar period of conservative, ruling-party dominance.

The 1990s saw democratic consolidation. The military did withdraw from politics. Kim Young Sam replaced Roh Tae Woo as president as planned, and launched an anti-corruption campaign. Military officers were accused of misappropriating public funds, which harmed the image of the armed forces. And then Kim launched prosecutions against the two preceding presidents, Chun Doo Hwan and Roh Tae Woo, on grounds that included massive corruption and responsibility for the Kwangju massacre. Both were sentenced to long prison terms.

To break the tradition of over-centralization Kim introduced elected institutions for local government, which in turn provided opportunities for the parties to extend their activities and provide additional posts to reward party members. But because political habits change slowly, this increase in elected officials also increased the amount 'needed' to achieve 'favourable' decisions. More traditional exchanges of services between patrons and clients became monetized. Businessmen complained that democracy increased the costs of corruption. So while remaining a comparatively 'hard' state, democracy made it somewhat softer.

In 1995 Kim led Korea into the OECD, which many pro-democracy activists had long advocated as a means to strengthen the democratic basis of politics, as well as entrench a more market-oriented approach to economic management. Nevertheless Kim's term of office ended in ignominy; the hopes of creating a hegemonic ruling party were dashed, and Kim Dae Jung replaced Kim Young Sam. He in turn promised to deepen democracy and root out corruption. He guided Korea's responses to the Asian financial crisis that engulfed the country in 1997–8, but then his term of office ended ignominiously too, with two sons arrested on charges of corruption.

By 2003 Korean politics was beginning to undergo a generational transformation, as leaders who had dominated the opposition movement for thirty years left the scene. The new president, Roh Moo Hyun, also from Kim Dae Jung's party, was in his fifties and offered electors a fresh start. He appointed other newcomers to national office. But whether they could also provide skilful leadership remains to be seen. For within nine months of his election he resigned from the party, after his plans for reform were obstructed. And yet another presidential aide was accused of soliciting bribes from *chaebols*.

## Key points

- Economic development reconfigured social forces and gradually constrained military rule. Then a changing external environment acted as a key catalyst in South Korea's transition to democracy.

- Democratic consolidation has yet to witness a marked decrease in high-level corruption.

# Conclusion: emerging problems

South Korea has come a long way since 1953. It is now a moderately prosperous and economically developed country with an apparently consolidated democracy. In the process the Korean perception of Confucianism has been modified. Many old values persist, for instance family life as the basis of social organization. But in Korea the new Confucian ethic has incorporated dimensions that promote patriotism and prosperity; it can assimilate Western values such as individualism, material success, and pragmatism. It has also accommodated itself to democracy. Thus while traditional values continue to shape society they are themselves reshaped by development. Korea now seems qualitatively different from both the Korea of 1945 and much of the developing world. Yet the country does face substantial new challenges. Most of them stem from globalization.

The most significant economic challenge concerns the reform of the developmental state model that served Korea so well until 1997. Korea is moving towards a more market-based system of economic management. The expectation is that the state will move increasingly towards a regulator rather than director of economic activity. There will also be strengthened property rights. This does not mean, however, at least for a long time, that Korea will have anything like an Anglo-American liberal type of macro-economic management. Instead it will be closer to the 'coordinated market economy' found in parts of Western Europe, but the state will still be needed to play a key active role. The crucial task of transferring greater allocative responsibility to the financial sector away from the state still awaits financial restructuring, for many banks became insolvent following the regional financial crisis. The state has learnt that it can no longer afford to provide the ultimate guarantees. But for the present the only solutions are for the state to restructure the main banks' capital reserves or allow banks to be taken over by foreign banks. A combination of these two is most likely. Anyway, without the pressure arising from the Asian financial crisis of 1997–8 it is questionable whether the Korean state would have had the resolution to pursue reform.

A second economic challenge is to restructure the *chaebols*. Some have been allowed to go bankrupt. Others have undergone major restructuring. The complex cross-shareholdings between companies within the same group have been unwound. Popular opinion in Korea is very reluctant to see their prime economic assets disposed to foreigners. There is greater pressure on the Korean government diplomatically to distance itself more from the USA. Yet compared to most other countries in the region Korea now has the reputation of a greater willingness to tolerate foreign capital. The distinctive pattern of state-driven Korean industrialization from the 1960s to the 1990s seems no longer viable. A new, outward-looking, generation of political and business leaders, many of them educated abroad, are coming forward.

A third challenge concerns the provision of welfare, where until 1997 the Korean state spent relatively little. It thought that supporting industrial and agricultural production would generate the income to support the needy, and relied upon the family for distribution. The financial crisis has changed all that. Unemployment rose to 8.8 per cent in February 1999, with only 11 per cent of those laid off entitled to unemployment benefit. This is no longer politically sustainable. Korean officials are looking to Europe for ideas on ways of combining state welfare provision with economic regeneration.

Then there are expressly political challenges. Earlier concerns about the centralizing 'vortex' of Korean politics have largely been solved. Yet the predominance of the capital, Seoul, has grown in another way: its population is now over 10 million—a quarter of all citizens, compared to only 7 per cent in 1949. Also, collective action remains a problem. Economic development has contributed social differentiation and middle-level, horizontal, social organization, but civil society is still relatively underdeveloped, which is a weakness for democracy. Purposeful social cooperation in Korea still partly rests upon state integration, as only around a third of the populace have a strong sense of both a communal identity and civic obligation to others. Most crucially, this constrains the establishment of durable party institutions. Although the general principles of democracy are now well accepted, the main parties are still dominated by individual leaders. Korea is not unique in this respect, but it is certainly unusual in that the main parties change their names before each presidential election. In a post-cold war world there are great difficulties in formulating ideological platforms that can win mass appeal even in long-established democracies. But ironically it is pushing Korea in the direction of 'catch-all' political parties with charismatic, or at least media-oriented, leaders such as are found in the USA.

Lastly the problem of political corruption persists (Ferdinand 2003). During the 1990s there was a widespread perception that democracy had actually exacerbated the problem. Democratization multiplied the number of government decision-makers who could or needed to be bribed. According to the surveys of Transparency International South Korea was ranked twenty-seventh out of forty-one countries in 1995 and fiftieth out of 133 countries in 2003 (first place being least corrupt), with almost identical raw scores. In one sense this is a globalization issue, for such rankings affect foreign investors' perception of the business climate and willingness to invest in a country.

But it is also a domestic political problem. As long as Korean politicians are expected to perform social roles of giving gifts on constituents' family occasions when their official salaries are insufficient, this problem will persist.

## QUESTIONS

**1** How important a constraint on economic and political development was traditional culture in South Korea? Is it still?

**2** What were the main features of Korea's developmental state?

**3** Why did the military play such a prominent part in Korean government up to the 1990s, and why does it not do so now?

**4** Why and in what ways did business leaders disentangle themselves from government domination?

**5** How do you explain the emergence of democracy in Korea, and is it well consolidated?

**6** Are the challenges facing Korea in the years ahead more similar to those facing developing countries or those of the developed world?

## GUIDE TO FURTHER READING

Amsden, Alice H., *Asia's Next Giant: South Korea and Late Industrialization* (Oxford: Oxford University Press, 1989). Examines how and why Korea got prices 'wrong' and yet achieved dramatic economic growth.

Choi, Sang-Yong (ed.), *Democracy in Korea: Its Ideals and Realities* (Seoul: Korean Political Science Association, 1997). Contains a stimulating and wide-ranging set of views on democratization in Korea.

Eckert, Carter J., 'The South Korean Bourgeoisie: A Class in Search of Hegemony', *Journal of Korean Studies*, 7 (1990): 115–48. Outlines the rise of the families owning *chaebols*.

Evans, Peter, *Embedded Autonomy: States and Industrial Transformation* (Princeton: Princeton University Press, 1995). Focuses on a key element of the developmental state.

Henderson, Gregory, *Korea: the Politics of the Vortex* (Cambridge, Mass.: Harvard University Press, 1968). A very influential early attempt to theorize politics in Korea.

Janelli, Robert L., *Making Capitalism* (Stanford, Calif.: Stanford University Press, 1993). The internal life of a Korean *chaebol* based on extended fieldwork.

Jones, Leroy P., and Il, Sakong, *Government, Business and Entrepreneurship in Economic Development: the Korean Case* (Cambridge, Mass.: Harvard University Press, 1980). A revealing early account of the key role of government in Korean development.

Lee, Yeon-ho, *The State, Society and Big Business in South Korea* (London and New York: Routledge, 1997). A very good account of this key relationship.

Myrdal, Gunner, *Asian Drama: an Enquiry into the Poverty of Nations* (Harmondsworth: Penguin, 1968). A very influential analysis.

Shin, Doh C., *Mass Politics and Culture in Democratizing Korea* (Cambridge: Cambridge University Press, 1999) The best single account of the emergence of Korea's democracy.

Woo-Cumings, Meredith (ed.), *The Developmental State* (Ithaca, NY, and London: Cornell University Press, 1999). Outlines the basic principles and their realization in various countries around the world.

## WEB LINKS

**www.korea.net**   The South Korean government's official homepage.

**www.kdi.re.kr**   Korean Development Institute.

**www.koreaherald.co.kr/index.asp**   The *Korean Herald* (Seoul).

 **COMPANION WEB SITE**

For additional material and resources, see the companion web site at:
**www.oup.com/uk/booksites/politics/**

# Appendix 1  Case study countries: basic indicators

| | Population million 2001 | Annual population growth 1990–2001, % | GNI 2001, $ billion, PPP | GNI per capita 2001, PPP | GDP: average annual % growth 1990–2001 | % of population on less than $1 a day | GINI index | HDI (value), 2001 | Political rights 2002 | Civil liberties 2002 |
|---|---|---|---|---|---|---|---|---|---|---|
| Chile | 15.4 | 1.5 | 145 | 9420 | 6.4 | <2 | 56.7 | 0.831 | 2 | 1 |
| Congo, DR | 52.4 | 3.1 | N/A | N/A | −0.1 | N/A | N/A | 0.363 | 6 | 6 |
| Guatemala | 11.7 | 2.6 | 45 | 3850 | 4.1 | 10 | 55.8 | 0.652 | 4 | 4 |
| India | 1033 | 1.8 | 2530 | 2450 | 5.9 | 44.2 | 37.8 | 0.590 | 2 | 3 |
| Indonesia | 213.6 | 1.6 | 628 | 2940 | 3.8 | 12.9 | 31.7 | 0.682 | 3 | 4 |
| Mexico | 99.4 | 1.6 | 872 | 8770 | 3.1 | 15.9 | 53.1 | 0.800 | 2 | 2 |
| Nigeria | 129.9 | 2.7 | 108 | 830 | 2.8 | 70.2 | 50.6 | 0.463 | 4 | 4 |
| Pakistan | 141.5 | 2.5 | 271 | 1920 | 3.7 | 31.0 | 31.2 | 0.499 | 6 | 5 |
| Saudi Arabia | 21.4 | 2.8 | 236 | 11390* | 1.5 | N/A | N/A | 0.769 | 7 | 7 |
| South Africa | 48.2 | 1.9 | 411 | 9510 | 2.1 | 11.5 | 59.3 | 0.684 | 1 | 2 |
| South Korea | 47.6 | 1.0 | 863 | 18110 | 5.7 | <2 | 31.6 | 0.879 | 2 | 2 |

*Notes*: GDP (Gross Domestic Product), GNI (Gross National Income), PPP (purchasing power parity), GINI index value 0 = perfect equality and 1 = perfect inequality in distribution of income or consumption; HDI (Human Development Index), a composite of education, longevity and GDP per capita; N/A = not available; political rights and civil liberties on scale 1 (most free)–7 (least free); * figure for most recent year available. For data on Pacific island states see p. 333 in Chapter 19b.

*Sources*: United Nations Development Programme, *Human Development Report 2003* (column 8); World Bank, *World Development Report 2003* (columns 1–7); Freedom House, *30th Anniversary Freedom House Survey*, 2003 (columns 9, 10).

# Appendix 2  Regional inter-governmental organizations in the developing world

Different institutional forms and structures are represented among the more noteworthy regional inter-governmental organizations in the developing world. The organizations each have their own individual aims and objectives. And while progress towards realizing the stated purposes has varied considerably, the further development of regional cooperation and integration is the kind of initiative that the developing countries themselves can make. It is increasingly seen as an appropriate response to globalization.

## Africa

African Union (2002, formerly Organization of African Unity, 1963): originally to promote the unity and solidarity of the African states.

Economic Community of West African States (ECOWAS) (1975): the largest regional economic community in West Africa, aims to promote cooperation and integration leading to a common market and monetary union.

Central American Common Market (1960): to set up a common market.

Central African Customs and Economic Union (1966): to promote the establishment of a regional common market Common Market for Eastern and Southern Africa

(COMESA) replaced the African Preferential Trade Area for Eastern and Southern Africa (established by treaty in 1981) in 1994, with the aim initially of finalizing a free trade area. With 22 members the largest regional economic community in Africa.

Monetary and Economic Community of Central Africa: formerly the Central African Customs and Economic Union established in 1964, aims to promote a common market.

Southern African Customs Union; negotiated in 1969 but with its origins in the nineteenth century this union of South Africa, Botswana, Lesotho, Swaziland, and Namibia shares customs revenue in line with a negotiated formula.

Southern African Development Community (formerly Southern African Development Coordination Conference, 1980) (SADC): to promote economic integration and strengthen regional solidarity, peace, and security.

## Americas

Andean Community of Nations (formerly Andean Pact, 1969): to promote balanced, harmonious development through economic integration.

Association of Caribbean States (ACS) (1994): to promote economic integration.

Caribbean Community and Common Market (CARICOM) (1973): to promote economic integration and development.

Central American Common Market (CACM) (1960, collapsed 1969 and reinstated 1991): to establish a common market.

Common Market of the South (Southern Cone) (MERCOSUR) (1991): to establish a regional common market.

Free Trade Area of the Americas: negotiations on establishing a common market to include all the countries lying between Alaska and Cape Horn with the single exception of Cuba are due to conclude in 2005—a deadline considered by many to be optimistic.

Latin American Economic System (SELA) (1975): to promote intraregional cooperation on economic and social matters.

North American Free Trade Agreement (NAFTA) (1992): to create a free trade and economic integration zone comprising Mexico, the United States, and Canada.

Organization of American States (OAS) (1948, with origins in 1890 as the International Union of American Republics): to promote an order of peace, justice, and solidarity among the American states; includes Canada and the United States, but Cuban participation excluded since 1962.

Organization of Eastern Caribbean States (OECS) (1981): to increase cooperation in foreign relations and promote measures leading to deeper sub-regional integration.

## Asia

Asia-Pacific Economic Cooperation (APEC) (1989): to provide a forum for discussion on a broad range of economic issues and to promote multilateral cooperation.

Association of Southeast Asian Nations (ASEAN) (1967): to accelerate development through trade liberalization in the region and promote collaboration and mutual assistance in industrial development. In 2003 ASEAN's ten members agreed to forge a common market by 2020; India signed an agreement to establish an Indo-Asean free trade area by 2012. Some of the members urge the development of a 'security community' dimension too.

## Middle East

Arab Maghreb Union (1989): to promote political coordination, cooperation, and complementarity across various fields.

Cooperation Council for the Arab States of the Gulf (Gulf Cooperation Council) (1981): to strengthen cooperation and unity including on military and security issues.

Gulf Cooperation Council (1981) to promote regional cooperation in economic, social, political, and military affairs.

League of Arab States (the Arab League) (1945): to strengthen relations among member states by coordinating policies and mediating disputes.

Organization of the Islamic Conference (1969): to promote Islamic solidarity and cooperation in economic, social, cultural, and political affairs.

South Asian Association for Regional Cooperation (SAARC) (1985): to promote economic, social and cultural cooperation.

## Other

Africa-Caribbean-Pacific (ACP) grouping of 78 states in a special development cooperation relationship with the European Union, dating from Yaoundé Convention (1969) and its successor the Lomé Conventions.

The Commonwealth (a voluntary association stemming from Britain's imperial past, formalized in 1931): over 54 developing and developed nations, to promote respect, encourage equal trust and friendship, and common prosperity.

Non-Aligned Movement (1961): to promote a transition from the old world order based on domination to a new world order based on freedom, equality, and social justice and the well-being of all.

Organization of Arab Petroleum Exporting Countries (1968): to promote cooperation in the petroleum industry.

Organization of the Petroleum Exporting Countries (OPEC) (1960): to coordinate and unify petroleum policies of member countries and determine the best means of safeguarding their interests. The developed world's oil producers, Russia and Mexico are not members.

Pacific Islands Forum (1971): (originally south pacific forum) aims to enhance economic and social well-being of the peoples of the South Pacific through cooperation between the 16 member governments including Australia and New Zealand and with international organizations.

Pacific Community (formerly South Pacific Commission, 1947): to promote regional cooperation in economic and social matters.

United Nations Conference on Trade and Development (UNCTAD) (1964): inclusive of all UN members, aims to promote trade for the economic benefit of developing countries and formulate and implement policies to that end.

# Glossary

**Apartheid** an Afrikaans word meaning separateness, in South Africa expressed as the official government policy of racial segregation, between 1948 and 1989

**ascriptive identities** groupings to which people belong by birth rather than by choice

**autonomy of politics/political autonomy** the extent to which politics as a level or sphere of social life is determined by economic and/or social/cultural dimensions of society or is able independently to impact on those dimensions

**balkanization** referring to the breaking up of a region or country into small territorial units, often as a means to 'divide and rule'

**caste associations** organizations to represent the interests of a caste group or cluster of closely related caste groups

**caudillismo** historically referring to the organization of political life in parts of Latin America by local 'strongmen' (*caudillos*) competing for power and its spoils

**chaebols** the family-based business groups or conglomerates, many of them with cross-ownership, that have been South Korea's primary source of capital accumulation

**christian democracy** the application of Christian precepts to electoral politics

**citizen security** reflecting the threats to public, social, and political order posed by crime and fear of crime

**civic national identities** involving unity among citizens of an autonomous state

**civil regulation** in the environmental arena referring to a range of activities undertaken by civil society actors aimed at creating new frameworks of expectation and obligation for companies

**civil society** a term highly contested, and concerning the realm of voluntary citizen associations that exists between the family and the state, enjoying independence of the latter, and seeking to influence public policy without aspirations to public office. **Modern civil society** comprises formal, professionalized non-governmental organizations typical of the late twentieth century; **traditional civil society** is organized more informally, and may follow patterns with deep and enduring roots in history and society

**clash of civilizations** referring to Samuel P. Huntington's prediction that after the end of the cold war international conflicts would increasingly have cultural characteristics, most notably setting the Christian 'West' against the mostly Muslim, mostly Arab 'East'

**clientelism** referring to the exchange of specific services or resources (usually publicly funded) between individuals in return for political support such as votes, and essentially a relationship between unequals

**collapsed state** *see* **state collapse**

**comparative advantage** the economic theory that countries should specialize in the production and export of those goods and services they have a *relative* cost advantage in producing compared to other countries

**competitive authoritarianism** a kind of 'illiberal democracy' where formal democratic institutions are widely viewed as the principal source of political authority but rulers violate the rules so strikingly that the regime fails to meet conventional minimum standards of democracy

**compromise state (*estado de compromiso*)** in Chile referring to a tacit agreement among all significant social actors accepting both formal democracy and the desirability of an active developmentalist, welfare state

**conditionality** referring to the attachment of policy and or other conditions to offers of financial and other assistance, with the possibility of aid sanctions for non-compliance

**corruption** involving the private use of public office and resources and generally considered illegal

**cruel choice** Jagdish Bhagwati's term for the dilemma he believed faced developing countries: either concentrate on economic development, or emulate the political systems of the West

**cultural imperialism** the domination of vulnerable peoples by the culture of economically and politically powerful societies

**delegative democracy** according to Guillermo O'Donnell, resting on the premise that whoever wins election to the presidency is thereby entitled to govern as they think fit, constrained only by the hard facts of existing power relations and a constitutionally limited term of office

**democratic peace theory** the claim that democracies do not go to war with one another

**democratization backwards** describing situations where largely free elections are introduced in advance of such basic institutions of the modern state as the rule of law, full executive accountability, and a flourishing civil society

**dependency theory** an argument that the weak structural position of developing countries in the international capitalist system influences important variables in their political life as well as explains their failure to achieve stronger development

**deprivation** according to Fraser (1997) 'being denied an adequate material standard of living'

**despotic power** the power to control and suppress (as Michael Mann has called it) as opposed to **infrastructural power**, the power to penetrate and transform society

**developing world** a term conventionally referring to the predominantly post-colonial regions of Africa, Asia, Latin America and the Caribbean, and the Middle East, perceived to be poorer, less economically advanced, and less 'modern' than the developed world

**development administration** a field of study aimed at providing an understanding of administrative performance in the specific economic and cultural contexts of poor, non-Western societies

**developmental state** according to Adrian Leftwich, concentrating sufficient power, autonomy, and capacity at the centre to bring about explicit developmental objectives, whether by encouraging the conditions and direction of economic growth or by organizing it directly. The hallmarks include a competent bureaucracy and the insulation of state institutions from special interests in society, in other words, the state enjoys **embedded autonomy**. While there are significant differences among the cases commonly cited as examples of the development state, the most successful examples in East Asia have tended to be authoritarian

**discourse theory** an interpretative approach closely associated with Michel Foucault that analyses power in terms of the dominant discourses, or chains of meaning, which shape understanding and behaviour

**eco-colonialism** an argument that the imposition of environmental conditions on financial and economic support for developing countries restricts their development

**economic growth** the rate of growth in a country's national output or income, usually measured by its Gross Domestic Product (GDP) or Gross National Product (GNP) and often presented on a per capita basis

**economic marginalization** 'being confined to undesirable or poorly paid work' (Fraser 1997)

**economic rents** incomes derived from the possession of a valuable licence or permit, particularly for the import of foreign goods

**electoral authoritarianism/autocracy** where elections are an instrument of authoritarian rule, an alternative to both democracy and naked repression

**embedded autonomy** according to Peter Evans characterized by the relative facility of the developmental state to transcend sectional interests in society, providing a sound basis for pursuing national industrial transformation

**entitlements** justified rights or claims belonging to individuals or groups

**equality of outcome** an approach that aims to make people equal whatever their original differences

**establishmentarianism** legal recognition of one church as the only established church, as in Britain

**ethnic identities** socially constructed identities that follow when people self-consciously distinguish themselves from others on the basis of perceived common descent and/or shared culture. Many but not all such identities are politicized

**ethnic morphology** refers to the form and structure of groups

**ethnonational identities** defining the nation in ethnic terms, attaining unity through the merger of ethnic and national identities, and demanding autonomy for ethnic nations

**ethnopolitical identities** those ethnic identities that have been politicized, that is, made politically relevant

**evaluation research** research into the outcomes of programme intervention or policy change

**exploitation** in Fraser's (1997) words, 'having the fruits of one's labour appropriated for the benefit of others'

**extents of freedom** in Sen's terminology, the capabilities or the *freedom* to achieve whatever functionings an individual happens to value

**extractive state** the idea that the extraction of the nation's (natural resource) wealth for the benefit of its rulers become the primary goal of the ruler(s)

**failing state** a state that is failing in respect of some or all of its functions without yet having reached the stage of 'collapse'

**fallacy of electoralism** privileging electoral contestation as if that were a sufficient condition for democracy to exist

**fatwa** a religious edict issued by an Islamic leader

**feminism** comprising recognition and action on women's common bonds and inequalities between men and women

**gender** referring to ideas about male and female and the relations between them as social constructions rather than the product of biological determinants only

**genocide** referring to deliberate extermination of a social group selected on grounds of culture, ethnicity, or race

**Gini coefficieint** a commonly used measure of inequality (household income or consumption)—the higher the figure, the more unequal the distribution

**global stewardship** referring to resources that are said to be part of the common heritage of humankind and should be managed for the benefit of all

**globalization** a highly contested term, defined in different ways that range from increasing global economic integration, in particular international trade, to processes whereby many social relations become relatively delinked from territorial geography and human lives are increasingly played out in the world as a single place

**globalization theory** focusing on a process of accelerated communication and economic integration which transcends national boundaries and increasingly incorporates all parts of the world into a single social system

**Heavily Indebted Poor Countries Initiative (HIPC)** arranged by the World Bank and International Monetary Fund has the objective of bringing the countries' debt burden to sustainable levels, subject to satisfactory policy performance, so as to ensure that adjustment and reform efforts are not put at risk by continued high debt and debt service burdens

**Hindu caste system** a complex and ancient though evolving system of social stratification in which people's caste status is determined at birth

**human capital** referring to the knowledge, skills, and capabilities of individuals

**human development** according to the United Nations Development Programme, about freedom, well-being and dignity of people everywhere; the UNDP's human development index measures longevity, educational attainment, and standard of living

**human rights** either the rights everyone has because they are human or those generally recognized as such by governments or in international law

***Ikhwan*** the brethren, religious followers of *Wahhabism*

**illiberal democracy** Fareed Zakaria's term for polities where governments are elected but have little respect for constitutional liberalism—the rule of law, separation of powers, and such basic liberties as speech, assembly, religion, and property

**import-substituting industrialization (ISI)** referring to the economic strategy of protecting the growth of manufacturing industry by reserving the home market for domestic producers ('infant industries'), through introducing barriers to imports

**informal economy** referring to employment and wealth creation that is not captured by the official data, offering opportunities for people who are unable to participate in the formal economy; governments find it difficult to regulate and tax the informal sector

**informal labour** paid work outside official regulations

**institutions** collections of (broadly) agreed norms, rules, procedures, practices, and routines, either formally established or written down and embodied in organizations or as informal understandings embedded in culture

**international human rights regime** a large body of international law and a complex set of institutions to implement it

***juche*** the principle of national self-reliance propagated by leader Kim Il Sung for North Korea

**La francophonie** to the former French colonies

**legitimacy** a psychological relationship between the governed and their governors, which engenders a belief that the state's leaders and institutions have a right to exercise political authority over the rest of society.

**liberal democracy** embodying a combination of political rights and civil liberties which go beyond **electoral democracy's** more limited attachment to civil freedoms and minority rights

**liberalism** a political philosophy that gives priority to individual freedom.

**liberation theology** a radical ideology, developed in Latin America in the 1960s, that demanded greater social and economic justice for the poor in the name of Christian values and beliefs

**mainstreaming** in the context of gender and environment, infusing public policies with a gender or environmental focus

***majlis*** a traditional tribal forum for male elders and has evolved into an institution for consultation between ruler and ruled (Saudi Arabia)

**Millenium Development Goals (MDGs)** established by the United Nations Millenium Declaration (September 2000) in the following eight areas: eradicate extreme poverty and hunger; achieve universal primary education; promote gender equality and empower women; reduce child mortality; improve maternal health; combat HIV/AIDS, malaria, and other diseases; ensure environmental sustainability; develop a global partnership for development

**modernization** referring to a complex set of changes in culture, society, and economy characterized by urbanization, industrialization, and in some cases secularization although one response to it may be religious revival

**modernization revisionism** a critique of **modernization theory**, centred on its oversimplified notions of tradition, modernity, and their interrelationship

**multinational ethnic identities** defining the nation in terms of several ethnic identities contained within citizenship and political interaction in an autonomous state

**national identities** inherently political, emphasizing the autonomy and unity of the nation as an actual or potential political unit

**nation-building** referring to building a sense of national belonging and unity

**natural capital** comprising nature's free goods and services

**neo-liberalism** stressing the role of the market in resource allocation and a correspondingly reduced role for the state, together with integration into the global economy. Aspects of the neo-liberal agenda are exhibited in the **Washington consensus** associated with the Bretton Woods institutions

**neo-patrimonialism** combining patrimonialism and legal-rational bureaucratic rule, which gives formal recognition to the distinction between the public and the private

**new institutional economics (NIE)** an approach that focuses on the way society's institutions affect economic performance

**New International Economic Order** comprising a set of reform proposals for the international financial and trading systems, to help the economic development of the developing countries, first proposed at a summit meeting of the Non-Aligned Movement (1973) and incorporated in a Declaration of the UN General Assembly in 1974

**new protectionism** referring to the measures of developed countries to reserve their domestic markets for home producers by means of non-tariff barriers such as imposing environmental standards

**newly (or new) industrialized(izing) countries (NICs)** referring to those developing countries primarily but not exclusively in East Asia (there also sometimes called 'dragon' or 'tiger' economies) that experienced dramatic industrialization soonest after 1945

**non-governmental organizations (NGOs)** organizations that operate in civil society and are not part of government or the state (although sometimes dependent, in part, on government for funding)

**official development assistance (ODA)** comprising resources transferred on concessional terms with the promotion of the economic development and welfare of the developing countries as the main objective

**only game in town** when applied to a perception that democratic elections are a permanent institution, often said to mark out democratic consolidation

**ontological equality** the assumption that all people are born equal

**Orientalism** referring to Edward Said's influential account (1978) of Western dominance of the East and how images of the Orient (the 'other') helped define the West as its contrasting image

**outward-oriented development** looking to the global economy as a driving force for economic growth, through the creation of a favourable policy environment for exports

**overpopulation** referring to birth rates that exceed death rates, producing growth that is difficult to sustain with the given resource base

**pacted transition** where transition to democracy comes about by agreement among political elites integral to the precursor regime

**pancasila** the official ideology of Soeharto's Indonesia, enjoining belief in a supreme being, humanitarianism, national unity, consensus democracy, and social justice

**path dependence** claiming that where you come from and, possibly, the method of change, significantly influence the destination that is attained

**patriarchy** referring to the ideology and institutions of male rule, male domination, and female subordination

**patrimonialism** treating the state as the personal patrimony or property of the ruler (hence patrimonialist state), and all power relations between ruler and ruled are personal relations

**patronage** the politically motivated distribution of favours, intended to create and maintain political support among groups

**patron–client relations** connecting **patronage** and **clientelism**

**political culture** embracing the attitudes, beliefs, and values that are said to underlie a political system

**political development** understood in the 1960s as a process of political change associated with increasing equality, political system capability, and differentiation of political roles and structures

**politicide** referring to extermination of political enemies

**politics** on a narrow understanding a kind of activity associated with the process of government, and in modern settings also linked with the 'public' sphere. On a broader understanding it is about 'power' relations and struggles not necessarily confined to the process of government or restricted to the public domain

**politics of order** a critique of political development theory which focused on the need for strong government and political order

**polyarchy** Robert Dahl's influential idea of democracy that rests on the two pillars of public contestation and the right to participate

**populism** a political ideology or approach that claims to be in the interests of 'the people'

**post-colonial state** a predominantly Marxist term for states in the developing world

**post-structuralism** sometimes also referred to as post-modernism, a broad philosophical approach that questions the epistemological foundations of 'rational' enlightenment thinking

**poverty reduction strategy (papers) (PRSPs)** referring to a requirement of the Bretton Woods institutions that governments seeking financial assistance and in particular debt relief display a policy process to arrive at pro-poor policies, after consulting with civil society

**predatory state** close to the idea of an **extractive state**, one that exploits the people for the benefit of the rulers and holds back development

**pronatalism** referring to policies or values that motivate high birth rates

**proxy wars** conflicts carried out on behalf of, and supported by, the great powers, as was often the case in developing areas during the cold war era

**pseudo-democracy** existing where there is not a sufficiently fair arena of electoral contestation to allow the ruling party to be turned out of power

**public goods** goods like defence that if supplied to anybody are necessarily supplied to everybody, and in consequence the market is unlikely to provide them in sufficient quantity

**rational choice theory** a deductive approach that argues from the premise that in making choices individual political actors behave rationally in terms of the objectives they pursue. The quest for individual utility maximization is assumed to be paramount

**regime** a set of rules and practices that regulate the conduct of actors in a specified field (as distinct from political regime understood as a system of government)

**religio-politics** political activity with religious dimensions

**religious fundamentalism** a disputed term applied most often to groups of Islamic, Hindu, and Christian worshippers who place strong emphasis on a return to their faith's fundamentals and resistance to secularization, often through political means

**rentier state** a state whose revenues take the form primarily of rents from a resource like oil rather than from taxing the subjects, which gives it high autonomy from society and can moderate the citizens' demands for democratically accountable government

**rent-seeking** referring to the pursuit of gains (**economic rents**) to be derived from control over scarce goods or services—a scarcity that might be artificially created for the purpose

**right to self-determination** the claimed right of a distinct group of people to determine their own political, economic, and cultural destinies

**scramble for Africa** a name given to the late nineteenth-century territorial expansion of European powers in Africa, leading to the Congress of Berlin (1884–5) which formally adopted the division of the new colonies and protectorates

**secularization** the gradual diminution of the influence of religion on public affairs. Liberal secularism advocates separation of church and state, with the second power being dominant and no one religion having official priority

**Sharia law** or Islamic religious law, incorporated to varying degrees in the legal systems of states with large Islamic populations

**shura** an Islamic term used for consultation between the people and the ruler

**social capital** referring to social networks, norms, and trust, that enable participants to function more effectively in pursuing a common goal. Arguably high levels are valuable both for political and economic cooperation

**social movements** loose networks or informal organizations that come about in response to an issue, crisis, or concern and seek to influence social and other public policy such as environmental policy often through using direct action

**societal collapse** occurring where the fabric of linkages and feedback mechanisms between state and society and within society are irreparably ruptured

**soft state** Gunnar Myrdal's term for states with low enforcement capacity such as those with lax bureaucracy and corruption

**state collapse** occurring where a functioning state system ceases to exist

**state failure** indicating a less than complete collapse of the state system

**state–church relations** the interactions in a country between the state and the leading religious organization(s)

**stateless societies** societies which do not have a state but may still enjoy a measure of social and economic order

**status** a quality of social honour or a lack of it, which is mainly conditioned as well as expressed through a specific style of life

**structural adjustment programmes (SAPS)** designed to shift economic policy and management in the direction of the **Washington consensus**, sometimes leading to more narrowly focused sectoral adjustment programmes, and often associated with **structural adjustment loans** (SALS) from the Bretton Woods institutions and other aid donors

**subsistence economy** referring to activity outside the cash economy for barter or home use

**sustainable development** a disputed term, which was defined by the Brundtland Report (1987) as development which meets the needs of the current generation without compromising the ability of future generations to meet their own needs

**third wave of democracy** Samuel P. Huntington's term for democratization in the late twentieth century

**transaction costs** the costs of doing business in a market economy, including the cost of finding market information as well as the costs incurred when parties to a contract do not keep to their agreement

**ulema** Islamic clergy or body consisting of those educated in Islam and *sharia* (Islamic law) with the function of ensuring the implementation of Islamic precepts

**underdevelopment** or lack of development, according to dependency theory, which is a consequence of capitalist development elsewhere

**unequal exchange** the idea that international trade between developed and developing countries is an instrument whereby the former exploit the latter and capture the greater part of the benefits

**unsecularization** meaning a global religious revitalization

**urban bias** bias in public policy and spending against the rural areas in favour of urban areas or urban-based interests, due to their greater political influence

**warlords** powerful regional figures possessing coercive powers, inside a country

**Washington consensus** the term applied (by John Williamson, in 1989) to a package of liberalizing economic and financial policy reforms deemed essential if Latin America (and subsequently other parts of the developing world) are to escape debt and rejuvenate their economic performance. The term quickly became attached to the policy approach in the 1990s of the Bretton Woods Institutions especially, namely the International Monetary Fund and World Bank. The central elements are fiscal discipline, reorientation of public expenditures, tax reform, financial liberalization, openness to foreign direct investment, privatization, deregulation, and secure property rights (see Williamson 2003)

**weak states** according to Joel Migdal, states lacking the capability to penetrate society fully, regulate social relations, extract and distribute resources, or implement policies and plans

**wealth theory of democracy** claiming that the prospects for stable democracy are significantly influenced by economic and socio-economic development

**Westminster model** referring to the institutional arrangement of parliamentary government bequeathed by Britain to many of its former colonies

**women's machinery** units within government such as women's bureaux, commissions of women, ministries of women, and women's desks

**women's policy interests** referring to official decisions or practices in which women have a special stake because of need, discrimination, or lack of equality

# References

Acharya, Amitav (1999). 'Developing Countries and the Emerging World Order', in L. Fawcett and Y. Sayigh (eds.), *The Third World Beyond the Cold War*. Oxford: Oxford University Press, 78–98.

Addison, T. (ed.) (2003). *From Conflict to Recovery in Africa*. Oxford: Oxford University Press for UNU-WIDER.

Adelman, I., and Morris, C. (1973). *Economic Growth and Equity in Developing Countries*. Stanford, Calif.: Stanford University Press.

Alavi, H. (1979). 'The State in Post-Colonial Societies', in H. Goulbourne (ed.), *Politics and the State in the Third World*. London: Macmillan, 38–69.

Al-Farsy, F. (1990). *Modernity and Tradition: The Saudi Equation*. London: Kegan Paul International.

Allison, R., and Williams, P. (1990). *Superpower Competition and Crisis Prevention in the Third World*. Cambridge: Cambridge University Press.

Almond, G. (1987). 'The Development of Political Development', in M. Weiner and S. P. Huntington (eds.), *Understanding Political Development*. New York: Harper Collins, 437–90.

—— and Coleman, J. (eds.) (1960). *The Politics of the Developing Areas*. Princeton: Princeton University Press.

—— and Powell, B. (1966; 1987). *Comparative Politics: A Developmental Approach*. Boston: Little, Brown.

Amsden, Alice H. (1989). *Asia's Next Giant: South Korea and Late Industrialization*. Oxford: Oxford University Press.

Anderson, B. (1991). *Imagined Communities: Reflections on the Origin and Spread of Nationalism*, rev. edn. London: Verso.

Anstey, Roger (1966). *King Leopold's Legacy: the Congo under Belgian Rule 1908–1960*. London: Oxford University Press.

Barton, J. R. (1997). *A Political Geography of Latin America*. London: Routledge.

Bastian, S., and Luckham, R. (eds.) (2003). *Can Democracy Be Designed? The Politics of Institutional Choice in Conflict-Torn Societies*. London: Zed.

Bates, R. (1981). *States and Markets in Tropical Africa: The Political Basis of Agricultural Policy*. Berkeley: University of California Press.

Bauer, P. T. (1981). *Equality, the Third World and Economic Delusion*. London: Methuen.

Bayart, J.-F. (1993). *The State in Africa. The Politics of the Belly*. London: Longman.

Bayart, Jean-François, Ellis, Stephen, and Hibou, Béatrice (1999). *The Criminalization of the State in Africa*. Bloomington, Ind.: Indiana University Press/Oxford: James Currey.

Baylis, J., and S. Smith (2001). *The Globalization of World Politics*, 2nd edn. Oxford: Oxford University Press.

Beetham, D. (1997). 'Market Economy and Democratic Polity'. *Democratization*, 4/1: 76–93.

Beetham, D., Bracking, S., Kearton, I., and Weir, S. (2002). *International IDEA Handbook on Democracy Assessment*. The Hague, London, New York: Kluwer Law International.

Bello, W. F. (1999). *Dark Victory: The U.S., Structural Adjustment, and Global Poverty*. London: Pluto.

Berger, M. (1994). 'The End of the "Third World"?' *Third World Quarterly*, 15/2: 257–75.

—— (ed.) (2004). 'After the Third World?', special issue of *Third World Quarterly*, 25/1.

Berman, B. (1998). 'Ethnicity, Patronage and the African State: The Politics of Uncivil Nationalism'. *African Affairs*, 97/388: 35–341.

Béteille, A. (ed.) (1969). *Social Inequality*. Harmondsworth: Penguin.

Billig, M. (1995). *Banal Nationalism*. London: Sage.

Boserup, E. (1989). *Women's Role in Economic Development*, new edn. London: Earthscan.

BP (2003). *BP Statistical Review of World Energy 2003*, available at **www.bp.com**

Bratton, M. (1998). 'Second Elections in Africa'. *Journal of Democracy*, 9/3: 51–66.

—— and van de Walle, N. (1997). *Democratic Experiments in Africa*. Cambridge: Cambridge University Press.

Bräutigam, D. (1996). 'State Capacity and Effective Governance', in B. Ndulu and N. van de Walle (eds.), *Agenda for Africa's Economic Renewal*. Oxford: Transaction Publishers, 81–108.

BRIDGE Development—Gender (2003). *Gender and Budgets*. Brighton: Institute of Development Studies, University of Sussex.

Burnell, P. (ed.) (2003). *Democratization Through the Looking-Glass*. Manchester: Manchester University Press.

—— and Calvert, P. (eds.) (1999). *The Resilience of Democracy. Persistent Practice, Durable Idea*. London: Frank Cass.

Cain P. J., and Hopkins, A. G. (2002). *British Imperialism: 1688–2000*, 2nd edn. Harlow: Longman.

Callaghy T., and Ravenhill, J. (eds.) (1993). *Hemmed In: Responses to Africa's Economic Decline*. New York: Columbia University Press.

Calvert, P., and Calvert, S. (2001). *Politics and Society in the Third World*, 2nd edn. Harlow: Pearson Education.

Cammack, P. (1997). *Capitalism and Democracy in the Third World: The Doctrine for Political Development*. Leicester: Leicester University Press.

—— Pool, D., and Tordoff, W. (1993). *Third World Politics. A Comparative Introduction*. Basingstoke: Macmillan.

Cardoso, F. H. (1973). 'Associated Dependent Development: Theoretical and Practical Implications', in A. Stepan (ed.), *Authoritarian Brazil*. New Haven: Yale University Press, 142–76.

—— and Faletto, E. (1979). *Dependency and Development in Latin America*. Berkeley: University of California Press.

Carothers, T. (1999). *Aiding Democracy Abroad*. Washington: Brookings Institution.

—— (2002). 'The End of the Transition Paradigm'. *Journal of Democracy* 13/1: 5–21.

Casanova, J. (1994). *Public Religions in the Modern World*. Chicago and London: University of Chicago Press.

Cavarozzi, Marcelo (1992). 'Beyond Transitions to Democracy in Latin America', *Journal of Latin American Studies*, 24/3: 665–84.

Chabal, P., and Daloz, J. (1999). *Africa Works* (Oxford: James Currey).

Chandhoke, N. (2003). *The Conceits of Civil Society*. Delhi: Oxford University Press.

Chaney, Elsa. M., and Castro, Mary G. (eds.) (1989). *Muchachas No More: Household Workers in Latin America and the Caribbean*. Philadelphia: Temple University Press.

Chang, H. (2002). *Kicking Away the Ladder*. London: Anthem Press.

Chatterjee, P., and Finger, M. (1994). *The Earth Brokers: Power, Politics and World Development*. London: Routledge.

Chenery, H., et al. (1974). *Redistribution with Growth*. New York: Oxford University Press.

Chhibber, P. (1999). *Democracy without Associations: Transformation of the Party System and Social Cleavages in India*. Ann Arbor: University of Michigan Press.

Choi, Sang-Yong (ed.)(1997). *Democracy in Korea: Its Ideals and Realities*. Seoul: Korean Political Science Association.

Chossudovsky, M. (1996). *The Globalization of Poverty: Impacts of IMF and World Bank Reforms*. London: Zed.

Claes, D. H. (2001). *The Politics of Oil-Producer Cooperation*. Boulder, Colo.: Westview Press.

Clague, C., et al. (eds.) (1997). *Institutions and Economic Development. Growth and Governance in Less-Developed and Post-Socialist Countries*. Baltimore: Johns Hopkins University Press.

—— Keefer, P., Knack, S., and Olson, M. (1997). 'Institutions and Economic Performance', in Clague et al. (1997), 67–90.

Clapham, C. (2002). 'The Challenge to the State in a Globalized World'. *Development and Change*, 33/5: 775–95.

Clark J. (1998). 'The Nature and Evolution of the State in Zaïre'. *Studies in Comparative International Development*, 32/4: 3–23.

Clark, C., and Chan, S. (1994). 'The Developmental Roles of the State: Moving Beyond the Developmental State in Conceptualising Asian Political Economies'. *Governance*, 7/4: 332–59.

Cliffe, Lionel, and Luckham, Robin (2000). 'What Happens to the State in Conflict?: Political Analysis as a Tool for Planning Humanitarian Assistance'. *Disasters*, 24/4: 291–313.

Collier, D., and Levitsky, S. (1997). 'Democracy with Adjectives'. *World Politics*, 49: 430–51.

Cordesman, A. H. (2002). *Saudi Arabia Enters the Twentieth Century*. Washington: Center for Strategic and International Studies.

Coulon, C. (1983). *Les Musulmans et le Pouvoir en Afrique Noire*. Paris: Karthala.

Craig, A. L., and Cornelius, W. A. (1995). 'Mexico', in A. Mainwaring and T. R. Scully (eds.), *Building Democratic Institutions*. Stanford, Calif.: University of California Press, 249–97.

Croucher, S. L. (2003). 'Perpetual Imagining: Nationhood in a Global Era'. *International Studies Review*, 5: 1–24.

Cumings, B. (ed.) (1999). *The Developmental State*. Ithaca, NY: Cornell University Press, 276–305.

Dahl, R. (1971). *Polyarchy: Participation and Opposition*. New Haven and London: Yale University Press.

Dauvergne, P. (1997). *Shadows in the Forest: Japan and the Politics of Timber in SouthEast Asia*. Cambridge, Mass.: MIT Press.

de Tocqueville, A. (2000). *Democracy in America*. Chicago and London: University of Chicago Press.

Dekmejian, R. (2003). 'The Liberal Impulse in Saudi Arabia'. *Middle East Journal*, 57/3: 400–13.

Diamond, Larry (1994). 'Toward Democratic Consolidation'. *Journal of Democracy*, 5/3: 4–17.

—— (1996). (ed.) 'Is the Third Wave Over?' *Journal of Democracy*, 7/3: 20–37.

—— (1999). *Developing Democracy: Towards Consolidation*. Baltimore: Johns Hopkins University Press.

—— (2002). 'Thinking About Hybrid Regimes'. *Journal of Democracy*, 13/2: 21–35.

Dicken, P. (2003). *Global Shift: Reshaping the Global Economic Map in the 21st Century*. London: Sage.

Dickson, A. K. (1997). *Development and International Relations: A Critical Introduction*. Cambridge: Polity.

Doornbos, Martin (2002). 'Somalia: Alternative Scenarios for Political Reconstruction'. *African Affairs*, 101: 93–107.

Dorr, S. (1993). 'Democratization in the Middle East', in R. Slater, B. Schutz, and S. Dorr (eds.), *Global Transformation and the Third World*. Boulder, Colo.: Lynne Rienner, 131–57.

Dunn R. M., and Mutti, J. H. (2000). *International Economics*, 5th edn. London: Routledge.

Easton, D. (1965). *A Systems Analysis of Political Life*. New York: Wiley.

Eckert, Carter J. (1990). 'The South Korean Bourgeoisie: A Class in Search of Hegemony'. *Journal of Korean Studies*, 7: 115–48.

Edison, H. (2003). 'Testing the Links. How Strong are the Links between Institutional Quality and Economic Performance?' *Finance and Development*, 40/2: 35–7.

Ehrlich, P. (1972). *The Population Bomb*. London: Pan/Ballantine.

Elliot, L. (1993). 'Fundamentalists Prepare for Holy War in Nigeria', *Guardian*, 14 April.

Emmanuel, A. (1972). *Unequal Exchange: A Study of the Imperialism of Trade*. New York: Monthly Review Press.

Eriksen, T. H. (1993). *Ethnicity and Nationalism: Anthropological Perspectives*. London: Pluto Press.

Evans, P. (1995). *Embedded Autonomy: States and Industrial Transformation*. Princeton: Princeton University Press.

Fawcett , L., and Sayigh, Y. (eds.) (1999). *The Third World Beyond the Cold War: Continuity and Change*. Oxford: Oxford University Press.

Fearon, J. D. (2003). 'Ethnic and Cultural Diversity by Country'. *Journal of Economic Growth*, 8: 195–222.

Feith, H. (1962). *The Decline of Constitutional Democracy in Indonesia*. Ithaca, NY: Cornell University Press.

Ferdinand, Peter (2003). 'Party Funding and Political Corruption in East Asia: The Cases of Japan, South Korea and Taiwan', in International IDEA, *Funding of Political Parties and Election Campaigns*. Stockholm: International Institute for Democracy and Electoral Assistance, 55–69.

Ferguson, N. (2003). *Empire: How Britain Made the Modern World*. London: Allen Lane.

Fields, G. S. (1980). *Poverty, Inequality and Development*. Cambridge: Cambridge University Press.

Foster-Carter, A. (1978). 'The Modes of Production Controversy'. *New Left Review*, 177: 47–77.

Foweraker, J., and Landman, T. (2004). 'Economic Development and Democracy Revisited: Why Dependency Theory is Not Yet Dead'. *Democratization*, 11/1: 1–20.

Frank, A. G. (1969). *Capitalism and Underdevelopment in Latin America: Historical Studies of Chile and Brazil*. New York: Monthly Review Press.

—— (1971). *The Sociology of Development and the Underdevelopment of Sociology*. London: Pluto Press.

Fraser, N. (1997). *Justice Interruptus, Critical Reflections on the 'Postsocialist' Condition*. London: Routledge.

Fukuyama, F. (1992). *The End of History and the Last Man*. Harmondsworth: Penguin.

Garcia-Johnson, R. (2000). *Exporting Environmentalism: U.S Chemical Corporations in Brazil and Mexico*. Cambridge, Mass.: MIT Press.

Garnett, H., Koenen-Grant, J., and Reilly, C. (1997). 'Managing Policy Formulation and Implementation in Zambia's Democratic Transition'. *Public Administration and Development*, 17/1: 77–91.

Gil, Federico (1966). *The Political System of Chile*. Boston: Houghton Mifflin.

Gill, S. (1995). 'Globalization, Market Civilization and Disciplinary Neoliberalism'. *Millennium*, 24/3: 399–424.

—— (2003). *Power and Resistance in the New World Order*. Basingstoke: Palgrave.

Gills, B., Rocamora, J., and Wilson, R. (1993). 'Low Intensity Democracy', in B. Gills, J. Rocamora, and R. Wilson (eds.), *Low Intensity Democracy. Political Power in the New World Order*. London and Boulder, Colo.: Pluto Press, 3–34.

Goetz, A. M., and Jenkins, R. (2004). *Reinventing Accountability: Making Democracy Work for the Poor*. Basingstoke: Palgrave/Macmillan.

Gramsci, A. (1992). *Prison Notebooks*. New York: Columbia University Press.

Grindle, M. S. (1996). *Challenging the State. Crisis and Innovation in Latin America and Africa*. Cambridge: Cambridge University Press.

Grugel, J. (2002). 'Conservative Elites and State Incapacities'. *New Political Economy*, 7/2: 277–9.

Gurr, T. R. (1993). *Minorities at Risk: A Global View of Ethnopolitical Conflicts*. Washington: United States Institute of Peace Press.

—— (2000). *Peoples Versus States: Minorities at Risk in the New Century*. Washington: United States Institute of Peace Press.

Hadiz, Vedi R. (2003a). 'Power and Politics in North Sumatra: The Uncompleted Reformasi', in E. Aspinall and G. Fealey (eds.), *Local Power and Politics in Indonesia: Democratisation and Decentralisation*. Singapore: Australian National University and Institute of Southeast Asian Studies, 119–2003.

—— (2003b). 'Decentralisation and Democracy in Indonesia: A Critique of Neo-Institutional Perspectives'. Working Papers Series No. 47, May 2003, Southeast Asian Research Centre, City University of Hong Kong.

Hallencreutz, C., and Westerlund, D. (1996). 'Anti-secularist Policies of Religion', in D. Westerlund (ed.), *Questioning the Secular State. The Worldwide Resurgence of Religion in Politics*. London: Hurst.

Halliday, F. (1989). *Cold War, Third World: An Essay on Soviet-US Relations*. London: Hutchinson.

—— (2002). *Two Hours that Shook the World: September 11, 2001, Causes and Consequences*. London: Saqi.

Harff, B. (2003). 'No Lessons Learned from the Holocaust? Assessing Risks of Genocide and Political Mass Murder since 1955'. *American Political Science Review*, 97/1: 57–73.

Hawes, G., and Liu, H. (1993). 'Explaining the Dynamics of the Southeast Asian Political Economy'. *World Politics*, 45/4: 629–60.

Haynes, J. (1993). *Religion in Third World Politics*. Buckingham: Open University Press.

—— (1996). *Religion and Politics in Africa*. London: Zed Books.

Hegel, G. (1942). *Philosophy of Right*. Trans. with notes T. M. Knox. Oxford: Clarendon Press.

Held, D., McGrew, A., Goldblatt, D., and Perraton, J. (1999). *Global Transformations*. Cambridge: Polity Press.

Hellman, J. S., Jones, G., and Kaufmann, D. (2000). ' "Seize the State, Seize the Day". State Capture, Corruption and Influence in Transition'. World Bank Policy Research Working Paper 2444. Washington: World Bank Institute, World Bank.

Henderson, Gregory (1968). *Korea: the Politics of the Vortex*. Cambridge, Mass.: Harvard University Press.

Herbst, J. (2000). *States and Power in Africa*. Princeton: Princeton University Press.

Herring, R. J. (1979). 'Zulfikar Ali Bhuto and the "Eradication of Feudalism" in Pakistan'. *Comparative Studies in Society and History*, 21/4: 519–57.

Heywood, P. (1997). 'Political Corruption: Problems and Perspectives'. *Political Studies*, 45/3: 417–35.

Higgott, R. A. (1983). *Political Development Theory*. London and Canberra: Croom Helm.

Hilderbrand, M. E., and Grindle, M. S. (1997). 'Building Sustainable Capacity in the Public Sector. What Can be Done?', in M. S. Grindle (ed.), *Getting Good Government. Capacity Building in the Public Sectors of Developing Countries*. Cambridge, Mass.: Harvard Institute for International Development.

Hirschman, D. (1993). 'Institutional Development in the Era of Economic Policy Reform: Concerns, Contradictions and Illustrations from Malawi'. *Public Administration and Development*, 13/2: 113–28.

Hirst, P., and Thompson, G. (1996). *Globalization in Question*. Cambridge: Polity Press.

Hochschild, A. (1998). *King Leopold's Ghost: A Story of Greed, Terror and Heroism in Colonial Africa*. Boston and New York: Houghton Mifflin.

Horowitz, D. (1985). *Ethnic Groups in Conflict*. Berkeley: University of California Press.

Hough, J. F. (1986). *The Struggle for the Third World: Soviet Debates and American Options*. Washington: Brookings.

Hunt, D. (1989). *Economic Theories of Development*. Hemel Hempstead: Harvester Wheatsheaf.

Huntington, S. P. (1968). *Political Order in Changing Societies*. New Haven: Yale University Press.

—— (1971). 'The Change to Change'. *Comparative Politics*, 3/3: 283–332.

—— (1991). *The Third Wave. Democratization in the Late Twentieth Century*. Norman, Okla., and London: University of Oklahoma Press.

—— (1993). 'The Clash of Civilizations?' *Foreign Affairs*, 72/3: 22–49.

—— (1996a). *The Clash of Civilizations and the Remaking of World Order*. New York: Simon and Schuster.

—— (1996b). 'Democracy for the Long Haul'. *Journal of Democracy*, 7/2: 3–14.

Hutchinson, J., and Smith, A. D. (1994) (eds.) *Nationalism*. Oxford: Oxford University Press.

Ibrahim, Y. (1992). 'Islamic Plans for Algeria on Display'. *New York Times*, 7 January.

International Crisis Group (2001). *Indonesia: Violence and Radical Muslims*, at **www.crisisweb.org**

—— (2002). *Al Qaeda in Southeast Asia: The Case of the 'Ngruki Network' in Indonesia*, at **www.crisisweb.org**

International Energy Agency (2003). *Key World Energy Statistics 2003*, available at **www.iae.org**

Isaac, T. M. T., with Franke, R. W. (2000). *Local Democracy and Development: People's Campaign for Decentralized Planning in Kerala*. New Delhi: LeftWord Books.

Jackson, R. H. (1987). 'Quasi-states, Dual regimes and Neoclassical Theory: International Jurisprudence and the Third World'. *International Organization*, 41/4: 519–49.

—— (1990). *Quasi-States: Sovereignty, International Relations and the Third World*. Cambridge: Cambridge University Press.

—— and Rosberg, C. (1982). 'Why Africa's Weak States Persist: The Empirical and the Juridical in Statehood'. *World Politics*, 35/1: 1–24.

Janelli, Robert L. (1993). *Making Capitalism*. Stanford, Calif.: Stanford University Press.

Jenkins, R. (2001). 'Mistaking Governance for Politics: Foreign Aid, Democracy and the Construction of Civil Society', in Sudipta Kaviraj and Sunil Khilnani (eds.), *Civil Society: History and Possibilities*. Cambridge: Cambridge University Press, 250–68.

—— and Goetz, A. M. (1999). 'Accounts and Accountability: Theoretical Implications of the Right-to-Information Movement in India'. *Third World Quarterly*, 20/ 3: 603–22.

Jenks, R. (1975). *Inequality*. Harmondsworth: Penguin.

Johnson, C. (1982). *MITI and the Japanese Miracle. The Growth of Industrial Policy 1925–1975*. Stanford, Calif.: Stanford University Press.

Jones, Leroy P., and Il, Sakong (1980). *Government, Business and Entrepreneurship in Economic Development: the Korean Case*. Cambridge, Mass.: Harvard University Press.

Karatnycky, A. (2003). 'The 30th Anniversary Freedom House Survey'. *Journal of Democracy*, 14/1: 100–13.

—— (2004). 'The 2003 Freedom House Survey. National Income and Liberty'. *Journal of Democracy*, 15/1: 82–93.

Karl, T. L. (1990). 'Dilemmas of Democratization in Latin America'. *Comparative Politics*, 23/1: 1–21.

Katzenstein, M., Kothari, S., and Mehta, U. (2001). 'Social Movement Politics in India: Institutions, Interests and Identities', in A. Kohli (ed.), *The Success of India's Democracy*. Cambridge: Cambridge University Press, 242–69.

Kaul, M. (1997). 'The New Public Administration: Management Innovations in Government'. *Public Administration and Development*, 17/1: 13–26.

Keeley, J., and Scoones, I. (2003). *Understanding Environmental Policy Processes: Cases from Africa*. London: Earthscan.

Khan, M. H. (2002). 'Fundamental Tensions in the Democratic Compromise'. *New Political Economy*, 7/2: 276–7.

Khera, R. (2004). 'Monitoring Disclosures', *Seminar* 534 (February): 51–8.

Klitgaard, R. (1997). 'Cleaning Up and Invigorating the Civil Service'. *Public Administration and Development*, 17/5: 487–509.

Knack, S., and Keefer, P. (1995). 'Institutions and Economic Performance: Cross-Country Tests Using Alternative Institutional Measures'. *Economics and Politics*, 7/3: 207–27.

Kothari, R. (1984). 'The Non-Party Political Process'. *Economic and Political Weekly* (Mumbai) (4 February): 216–24.

Kurtz, Marcus (2002). 'Understanding the Third World Welfare State After Neoliberalism'. *Comparative Politics*, 34/3: 293–313.

Kuznets, S. (1955). 'Economic Growth and Income Inequality'. *American Economic Review*, 45: 1–28.

Lee, Yeon-ho (1997). *The State, Society and Big Business in South Korea*. London and New York: Routledge.

Leftwich, A. (1993). 'Governance, Democracy and Development in the Third World'. *Third World Quarterly*, 14/3: 603–24.

—— (1995). 'Bringing Politics Back in: Towards a Model of the Developmental State'. *The Journal of Development Studies*, 31/3: 400–27.

—— (2000). *States of Development. On the Primacy of Politics in Development*. Cambridge: Polity Press.

—— (2002). 'A Contradiction in the Politics of Economics'. *New Political Economy*, 7/2: 269–73.

Lele, J. (1990). 'Caste, Class and Dominance: Political Mobilization in Maharashtra', in F. Frankel and M. S. A. Rao (eds.), *Dominance and State Power in Modern India: Decline of a Social Order*, vol. ii. Delhi: Oxford University Press, 115–211.

Levitsky, S., and Way, L. A. (2002). 'The Rise of Competitive Authoritarianism'. *Journal of Democracy*, 13/2: 51–65.

Linz, J. J. (1990). 'The Perils of Presidentialism'. *Journal of Democracy*, 1/1: 51–69.

—— and A. Stepan (1996). *Problems of Democratic Transition and Consolidation: Southern Europe, South America, and Post-Communist Europe*. Baltimore: Johns Hopkins University Press.

Lipset, S. M. (1994). 'The Social Requisites of Democracy Revisited'. *American Sociological Review*, 53/1: 1–22.

Loveman, Brian (2001). *Chile: The Legacy of Hispanic Capitalism*. New York: Oxford University Press.

Lucas, R. E., Jr. (1988). 'On the Mechanics of Economic Development'. *Journal of Monetary Economics*, 22/1: 3–42.

McGrew, A. (1992). ' A Global Society?', in S. Hall, D. Held, and A. McGrew (eds.), *Modernity and Its Future*. Cambridge: Polity Press, 62–102.

McMichael, P. (2000). *Development and Social Change: A Global Perspective*, 2nd edn. London: Sage.

Mahbubani, K. (1999). 'An Asian Perspective on Human Rights', in P. Van Ness (ed.), *Debating Human Rights: Critical Essays from the United States and Asia*. London: Routledge.

Mainwaring, S. (1993). 'Presidentialism, Multipartism and Democracy. The Difficult Combination'. *Comparative Political Studies*, 26/2: 198–228.

Mair, P. (1996). 'Comparative Politics: An Overview', in R. E. Goodin and H. Klingemann, *A New Handbook of Political Science*. Oxford: Oxford University Press, 309–35.

Mandel, J. R. (2003). *Globalization and the Poor*. Cambridge: Cambridge University Press.

Mann, M. (1986). *The Sources of Social Power*, Vol. i. Cambridge: Cambridge University Press.

Manor, J. (ed.) (1991). *Rethinking Third World Politics*. London: Longman.

March, J., and Olsen, J. (1984). 'The New Institutionalism: Organisational Factors in Political Life'. *American Political Science Review*, 78/3: 734–49.

—— (1989). *Rediscovering Institutions. The Organizational Basis of Politics*. New York and London: Free Press.

Martínez, J., and Díaz, A. *Chile: The Great Transformation*. Geneva: UNRISD, 1996.

Marty, Martin E., and Appleby, R. Scott, 'Introduction' (1993), in Marty and Scott Appleby (eds.), *Fundamentalism and the State. Remaking Polities, Economies, and Militance*. Chicago: University of Chicago Press.

Marx, K. (1970). *The German Ideology*. London: Lawrence and Wishart.

Mattes, R. (2002). 'Uniquely African', in S. Burgers (ed.), *South African Tribes*. Cape Town: David Philip.

Mazrui, Ali A. (1995). 'The African State as a Political Refugee: Institutional Collapse and Human Displacement'. *International Journal of Refugee Law*, 7: 21–36.

Merrill, D. (1994). 'The United States and the Rise of the Third World', in G. Martel (ed.), *American Foreign Relations Reconsidered, 1890–1993*. London: Routledge, 166–86.

Mesbahi, M. (ed.) (1994). *Russia and the Third World in the Post-Soviet Era*. Gainesville, Fla.: University Press of Florida.

Meyer, W. H. (1998). *Human Rights and International Political Economy in Third World Nations*. Westport, Conn.: Praeger.

Migdal, J. S. (1988a). 'Strong States, Weak States: Power and Accommodation', in M. Weiner and S. P. Huntington (eds.), *Understanding Political Development*. Boston: Little, Brown, 391–429.

—— (1988b). *Strong Societies and Weak States. State–Society Relations and State Capabilities in the Third World*. Princeton: Princeton University Press.

—— (1994). 'The State in Society: An Approach to Struggles for Domination', in J. S. Migdal, A. Kohli, and V. Shue (eds.), *State Power and Social Forces. Domination and Transformation in the Third World*. Cambridge: Cambridge University Press, 7–34.

—— (1996). 'Integration and Disintegration: An Approach to Society Formation', in L. van de Goor, K. Rupesinghe, and P. Scarione (eds.), *Between Development and Destruction. An Enquiry into the Causes of Conflict in Post-Colonial States*. London: Macmillan, 91–106.

Mihevc, J. (1995). *The Market Tells Them So: The World Bank and Economic Fundamentalism in Africa*. London: Zed.

Moon, Chung-in (1994). 'Changing Patterns of Business-Government Relations in South Korea', in Andrew MacIntyre (ed.), *Business and Government in Industrialising Asia*. Sydney: Allen and Unwin, 142–66.

—— and Prasad, R. (1994). 'Beyond the Developmental State: Networks, Politics and Institutions'. *Governance*, 7/4: 360–86.

Moore, M. (2000). 'Political Underdevelopment', paper presented to 10th Anniversary of the Institute of Development Studies Conference, September 7–8. See also at **www.ids.ac.uk/ids/govern**.

—— and Putzel, J. (1999). *Politics and Poverty: A Background Paper for the World Development Report 2000/1*. **www.worldbank.org/poverty/wdrpoverty/dfid**

Mozaffar, S. (1995). 'The Institutional Logic of Ethnic Politics: A Prolegomenon', in H. Glickman (ed.), *Ethnic Conflict and Democratization in Africa*. Atlanta: African Studies Association Press, 34–69.

—— Scarritt, J. R., and Galaich, G. (2003). 'Electoral Institutions, Ethnopolitical Cleavages, and Party Systems in Africa's Emerging Democracies'. *American Political Science Review*, 97/3: 379–90.

Myrdal, Gunner (1968). *Asian Drama: an Enquiry into the Poverty of Nations*. Harmondsworth: Penguin.

—— (1971). *The Challenge of World Poverty*. Harmondsworth: Penguin.

Nabli, M. K., and Nugent, J. B. (1989). 'The New Institutional Economics and its Applicability to Development'. *World Development*, 17/9: 1333–47.

Nayyar, D. (ed.) (2002). *Governing Globalization: Issues and Institutions*. Oxford: Oxford University Press for UNU-WIDER.

Nelson, J. M. (1990). 'Conclusions', in J. M. Nelson (ed.), *Economic Crisis and Policy Choice. The Politics of Adjustment in the Third World*. Princeton: Princeton University Press, 321–61.

Neuman S. G. (ed.) (1998). *International Relations Theory and the Third World*. Basingstoke: Macmillan.

Newell, P. (2001). 'Environmental NGOs, TNCs and the Question of Governance', in D. Stevis and V. Assetto (eds.), *The International Political Economy of the Environment: Critical Perspectives*. Boulder, Colo.: Lynne Rienner, 85–107.

Nixson, F. (2001). *Development Economics*, 2nd edn. Oxford: Heinemann.

North, D. (1989). 'Institutions and Economic Growth: an Historical Introduction'. *World Development*, 17/9: 1319–32.

—— (1990). *Institutions, Institutional Change and Economic Performance*. Cambridge: Cambridge University Press.

Nzomo, Maria, and Staudt, Kathleen (1994). 'Man-made Political Machinery in Kenya: Political Space for Women?', in Barbara J. Nelson and Najama Chowdhury (eds.), *Women and Politics Worldwide*. New Haven: Yale University Press, 415–35.

O'Donnell, G. (1994). 'Delegative Democracy'. *Journal of Democracy*, 5/1: 55–69.

—— (1996). 'Illusions about Consolidation'. *Journal of Democracy*, 7/2, 151–9.

—— Schmitter, P., and Whitehead, L. (1986). *Transitions from Authoritarian Rule*. Baltimore: Johns Hopkins University Press.

Olowu, B. (1999). Redesigning African Civil Service Reforms'. *Journal of Modern African Studies*, 37/1: 1–23.

Olson, M. (2001). *Power and Prosperity: Outgrowing Communist and Capitalist Dictatorships*, New York: Basic Books.

Onis, Z. (1991). 'The Logic of the Developmental State'. *Comparative Politics*, 24/1: 109–26.

Organisation for Economic Cooperation and Development (2001). *Strategies for Sustainable Development: Practical guidance for development cooperation*. Paris: OECD.

Ottaway, M. (2003). *Democracy Challenged. The Rise of Semi-Authoritarianism*. Washington: Carnegie Endowment for International Peace.

—— and Carothers, T. (2000). *Funding Virtue: Civil Society Aid and Democracy Promotion*. Washington: Carnegie Endowment for International Peace.

—— and Chung, T. (1999). 'Debating Democracy Assistance: Toward a New Paradigm'. *Journal of Democracy*, 10/4: 99–113.

Oxfam (2001). *Eight Broken Promises: Why the WTO isn't Working for the World's Poor*, Oxfam Briefing Paper 9. Oxford.

Oxhorn, Phillip (1995). *Organizing Civil Society*. University Park, Pa.: Pennsylvania State University Press.

Parente, S. L., and Prescott, E. C. (2000). *Barriers to Riches*. Cambridge, Mass.: MIT Press.

Parry, J. H. (1966). *The Spanish Seaborne Empire*. London: Hutchinson.

Parsons, T. (1960). *Structure and Process in Modern Societies*. Glencoe: Free Press.

Pastor, R. (1999). 'The Role of Electoral Administration in Democratic Transitions: Implications for Policy and Research'. *Democratization*, 6/4: 1–27.

Pempel, T. J. (1999). 'The Developmental Regime in a changing World Economy', in M. Woo-Cumings (ed.), *The Developmental State*. Ithaca, NY: Cornell University Press, 137–81.

Pogge, T. (2002). *World Poverty and Human Rights*. Cambridge: Polity Press.

Porter, B. (1996). *The Lion's Share: A Short History of British Imperialism 1850–1995*, 3rd. edn. London: Longman.

Powell, G.B. (2000). *Elections as Instruments of Democracy: Majoritarian and Proportional Visions*. New Haven: Yale University Press.

Przeworski, A., Alvarez, M., Cheibub, J., and Limongi, F. (1996). 'What Makes Democracies Endure?' *Journal of Democracy*, 7/1: 39–55.

—— Alvarez, M.E., Cheibub, J.A., and Limongi, F. (2000). *Democracy and Development: Political Institutions and Well-Being in the World, 1950–1990*. Cambridge: Cambridge University Press.

Putnam, R. (1993). *Making Democracy Work: Civic Traditions in Modern Italy*. Princeton: Princeton University Press.

Pye, L. W. (1966). *Aspects of Political Development*. Boston: Little, Brown.

Racysnski, Dagmar (1999). 'Políticas sociales en los años noventa en Chile: Balance y desafío', in Paul Drake and Iván Jaksic (eds.), *El modelo chileno: Democracia y desarrollo en los noventa*. Santiago: LOM Ediciones, 125–54.

Rai, S. M. (ed.) (2003). *Mainstreaming Gender, Democratizing the State? Institutional Mechanisms for the Advancement of Women*. Manchester and New York: Manchester University Press.

Ram-Prasad, C. (1993). 'Hindutva Ideology Extracting the Fundamentals'. *Contemporary South Asia*, 2/3, 285–309.

Randall, V., and Svåsand, L. (2002). 'Political Parties and Democratic Consolidation in Africa'. *Democratization*, 9/3: 30–52.

Rawls, J. (1971). *A Theory of Justice*. Oxford: Oxford University Press.

Reno, William (1998). *Warlord Politics and African States*. Boulder, Colo.: Lynne Rienner.

—— (2000). 'Shadow States and the Political Economy of Civil Wars', in M. Berdal and D. Malone (eds.), *Greed and Grievance. Economic Agendas in Civil Wars*. Boulder, Colo.: Lynne Rienner, 43–68.

Richards, Paul (1996). *Fighting for the Rainforest: War, Youth and Resources in Sierra Leone*, Oxford: James Currey.

Robison, Richard, and Vedi R. Hadiz (2004). *Reorganising Power in Indonesia: The Politics of Oligarchy in an Age of Markets*. London: Routledge.

Roniger, L., and Sznajder, M. (1999). *The Legacy of Human-Rights Violations in the Southern Cone: Argentina, Chile, and Uruguay*. Oxford: Oxford University Press.

Rose-Ackerman, S. (1999). *Corruption and Government. Causes, Consequences and Reform*. Cambridge: Cambridge University Press.

Rudolph, L. I. (2003). Review of Pradeep Chhibber, *Democracy without Associations. Comparative Political Studies*, 36/ 9: 1115–9.

—— and Rudolph, S. H. (1967). *The Modernity of Tradition: Political Development in India*. Chicago: University of Chicago Press.

Rueschemeyer, D., Stephens, E. H., and Stephens, J. D. (1992). *Capitalist Democracy and Development*. Cambridge: Polity Press.

Rustow, Dankwart (1970). 'Transitions to Democracy: Toward a Dynamic Model'. *Comparative Politics*, 2/3: 337–63.

Said, E. W. (1995). *Orientalism*. Harmondsworth: Penguin.

Sandbrook, R. (1986). 'The State and Economic Stagnation in Tropical Africa'. *World Development*, 14/3: 319–32.

Sartori, G. (1976). *Parties and Party Systems: A Framework for Analysis*. Cambridge: Cambridge University Press.

Scarritt, J. R., and Mozaffar, S. (1999). 'The Specification of Ethnic Cleavages and Ethnopolitical Groups for the Analysis of Democratic Competition in Contemporary Africa'. *Nationalism and Ethnic Politics*, 5/1: 82–117.

—— (2003). 'Why Do Multi-ethnic Parties Predominate in Africa and Ethnic Parties Do not'. Unpublished paper.

Schedler, A. (1998). ' What is Democratic Consolidation?' *Journal of Democracy*, 9/2: 91–107.

—— (2002a). 'The Nested Game of Democratization by Elections'. *International Political Science Review*, 23/1: 103–22.

—— (2002b). 'Elections Without Democracy: The Menu of Manipulation'. *Journal of Democracy*, 13/2: 36–50.

—— Diamond, L., and Plattner, M. (eds.) (1999). *The Self-Restraining State*. Boulder, Colo.: Lynne Rienner.

Schneider, B. R. (1999). 'The *Desarrollista* State in Brazil and Mexico', in M. Woo-Cummings (ed.), *The Developmental State*. Ithaca, NY, and London: Cornell University Press, 276–305.

Scholte, J. A. (2001). 'The Globalization of World Politics', in J. Baylis and S. Smith (eds.), *The Globalization of World Politics*. 2nd ed. Oxford and New York: Oxford University Press, 13–32.

Sen, A. (1990). 'More Than 100 Million Women are Missing'. *New York Review of Books*, 20 December.

—— (1992). *Inequality Reexamined*. Oxford: Oxford University Press.

—— (1999a). *Development as Freedom*. Oxford: Oxford University Press.

—— (1999b). 'Human Rights and Economic Achievements', in J. R. Bauer and D. A. Bell (eds.), *The East Asian Challenge for Human Rights*. Cambridge: Cambridge University Press, 88–99.

Sethi, H. (1999). Review of Pradeep Chhibber, *Democracy without Associations, Seminar* 480 (August): 90–4.

Shearman and Williams, P. (eds.) (1988). *The Superpowers, Central America and the Middle East*. London: Brassey's Defence.

Shin, Doh C. (1999). *Mass Politics and Culture in Democratizing Korea*. Cambridge University Press: Cambridge.

Shorrocks, T., and van der Hoeven, R. (eds.) (2004). *Growth, Inequality, and Poverty: Prospects for Pro-Poor Economic Development*. Oxford: Oxford University Press for UNU-WIDER.

Siavelis, Peter (2000). *The President and Congress in Postauthoritarian Chile: Institutional Constraints to Democratic Consolidation*. University Park, Pa.: Pennsylvania State University Press.

Sieder, R., Thomas, M., Vickers, G., and Spence, J. (2002). *Who Governs? Guatemala Five Years After the Peace Accords*. Washington: Hemisphere Initiatives/Washington Office on Latin America.

Sikand, Y. (2003). 'Response to Shiva', in M. J. Gibney (ed.), *Globalizing Rights*. Oxford: Oxford University Press, 109–14.

Silverman, S. F. (1977). 'Patronage and Community–Nation Relationships in Central Italy', in S. Schmidt, J. C. Scott, C. Landé, and L. Guasti (eds.), *Friends, Followers and Factions*. Berkeley: University of California Press, 293–304.

Sklair, L. (1991). *Sociology of the Global System*. London: Prentice-Hall.

Smith, A. D. (1995). *Nations and Nationalism in a Global Era*. Cambridge: Polity Press.

Smith, D. (1990). 'Limits of Religious Resurgence', in E. Sahliyeh (ed.), *Religious Resurgence and Politics in the Contemporary World*. Albany, NY: State University of New York Press.

Smith, J., Bolyard, M., and Ippolito, A. (1999). 'Human Rights and the Global Economy: A Response to Meyer'. *Human Rights Quarterly*, 21/1: 207–19.

Smith, T. (1979). 'The Underdevelopment of Development Literature: The Case of Dependency Theory'. *World Politics*, 31/2: 247–88.

Snyder, Jack (2000). *From Voting to Violence: Democratization and Nationalist Conflict*. New York: Norton.

Staudt, K. (1997). *Women, International Development and Politics: The Bureaucratic Mire*. 2nd edn. Philadelphia: Temple University Press.

—— (1998). *Policy, Politics and Gender: Women Gaining Ground*. West Hartford, Conn.: Kumarian Press.

—— and Coronado, I. (2002*). Fronteras No Mas: Toward Social Justice at the U.S.–Mexico Border*. New York: Palgrave USA.

Stiglitz, J. (2002). *Globalization and its Discontents*. London: Allen Lane.

Sutton, P. (2001). 'Small States and the Commonwealth'. *Commonwealth and Comparative Politics*, 39/3: 75–94.

Swatuk, L. A., and Shaw, T. M. (1994). *The South at the End of the Twentieth Century*. New York: St Martin's Press.

Tarrow, S. (1998). *Power in Movement. Social Movements and Contentious Politics*. 2nd edn. Cambridge: Cambridge University Press.

Tawney, R. H. (1952). *Inequality*. London: Allen and Unwin.

Thomas, C. (2000). *Global Governance, Development and Human Security: The Challenge of Poverty and Inequality*. London: Pluto.

Todaro, M., and Smith, S. (2003). *Economic Development*, 8th edn. Boston: Addison Wesley.

Toye, J. (1987). *Dilemmas of Development*. Oxford: Blackwell.

Transparency International (2002). *Corruption Perceptions Index*. Online. **www.transparency.org/cpi/2002/cpi2002.en.html**

Turner, M., and Hulme, D. (1997). *Governance, Administration and Development. Making the State Work*. London: Macmillan.

UNCTAD (2001). *World Investment Report 2001*. New York and Geneva: United Nations.

—— (2003). *Economic Development in Africa. Trade Performance and Commodity Dependence*. New York and Geneva: United Nations.

UNECA (2003). *Economic Report on Africa 2003*: *Accelerating the Pace of Development*. Addis Ababa: United Nations Economic Commission for Africa. Available at: **www.uneca.org/era2003/**

UNESCO (1999). *UNESCO Statistical Yearbook*. Paris: UNESCO.

United Nations Development Programme (1995) *Human Development Report*. New York: Oxford University Press.

—— (1999). *UNDP Pacific Human Development Report 1999*. Suva: UNDP Fiji Office.

—— (2002). *UNDP Human Development Report 2002. Deepening Democracy in a Fragmented World*. New York and Oxford: Oxford University Press.

—— (2003). *UNDP Human Development Report*. New York and Oxford: Oxford University Press.

Valenzuela, A. (1977). *Political Brokers in Chile: Local Government in a Centralized Polity*. Durham, NC: Duke University Press.

—— (1978). *The Breakdown of Democratic Regimes: Chile*. Baltimore: Johns Hopkins University Press.

—— (1989). 'Chile: Origins, Consolidation, and Breakdown of a Democratic Regime', in Larry Diamond, Juan J. Linz, and Alfred Stepan (eds.), *Democracy in Developing Countries: Latin America*. Baltimore: Johns Hopkins University Press.

Varshney, A. (2003). 'Nationalism, Ethnic Conflict, and Rationality'. *Perspectives on Politics*, 1/1: 85–99.

—— (2004). 'States or Cities? Studying Hindu-Muslim Violence', in R. Jenkins (ed.), *Regional Reflections: Comparing Politics Across India's States*. Delhi: Oxford University Press, 177–218.

Verba, S. (1965). *The Civic Culture: Political Attitudes and Democracy in Five Nations*. Boston: Little, Brown.

Villalón, L., and Huxtable, P. (eds.) (1998). *The African State at a Critical Juncture: Between Disintegration and Reconfiguration*. Boulder, Colo.: Lynne Rienner.

Vogel, D. (1997). *Trading Up: Consumer and Environmental Regulation in the Global Economy*. 2nd edn. Cambridge, Mass.: Harvard University Press.

Wallerstein, I. (1974). *The Modern World System*, vol. i. London: Academic Press.

—— (1979). 'The Rise and Future Demise of the World Capitalist System: Concepts for Comparative Analysis', in I. Wallerstein, *The Capitalist World-Economy*. Cambridge: Cambridge University Press, 1–36.

Weber, Max (1964). *The Theory of Social and Economic Organization*, ed. by Talcott Parsons. New York: Free Press.

—— (1970). H. H. Gerth and C. Wright Mills (eds.), *From Max Weber: Essays in Sociology*. London: Routledge.

Weiss, J. (2002). *Industrialisation and Globalisation: Theory and Evidence from Developing Countries*. London: Routledge.

Weiss, L., and Hobson, J. M. (1995). *States and Economic Development*. Cambridge: Polity Press.

Weldon, S. L. (2002). *Protest, Policy, and the Problem of Violence Against Women: A Cross-National Comparison*. Pittsburgh: University of Pittsburgh Press.

White, G. (1984). 'Developmental States and Socialist Industrialization in the Third World'. *Journal of Development Studies*, 21/1: 97–120.

—— (1998). 'Constructing a Democratic, Developmental State', in M. Robinson and G. White (eds.), *The Democratic Developmental State. Politics and Institutional Design*. Oxford: Oxford University Press, 17–51.

Wickham C. R. (2002). *Mobilizing Islam: Religion, Activism, and Political Change in Egypt*. New York: Columbia University Press.

Williamson, J. (2003). 'From Reform Agenda to Damaged Brand Name'. *Finance and Development*, 40/3: 10–13.

Woo-Cumings, Meredith (ed.) (1999). *The Developmental State*. Ithaca, NY, and London: Cornell University Press.

Woodhead, L., and Heelas, P. (eds.) (2000). *Religions in Modern Times*. Oxford: Blackwell.

World Bank (1990). *World Development Report 1990*. Washington: World Bank

—— (1991). World *Development Report 1991. The Challenge of Development*. New York: Oxford University Press.

—— (1997). *World Development Report 1997. The State in a Changing World*. New York: Oxford University Press.

—— (1999). *World Development Report 1999/2000: Entering the 21st Century*. Oxford: Oxford University Press, and available at **www.econ.worldbank.org.**

—— (2000). *Greening Industry: New Roles for Communities, Markets and Governments*. Washington: World Bank.

—— (2001). *World Development Report 2001*. Washington: World Bank.

—— (2002). *World Development Indicators 2002*. Washington: World Bank.

—— (2003*a*). *Global Development Finance 2003*, available at **www.worldbank.org/prospects/gdf2003**

—— (2003*b*). *Guapa: Guatemala Poverty Assessment*. Washington: World Bank.

—— (2003*c*). *World Development Indicators 2003*. Washington: World Bank.

World Commission on Environment and Development (1987). *Our Common Future*. Oxford: Oxford University Press.

Young, C. (1976). *The Politics of Cultural Pluralism*. Madison: University of Wisconsin Press.

—— (1994). *The African Colonial State in Comparative Perspective*. New Haven: Yale University Press.

—— (2001). 'Nationalism and Ethnic Conflict in Africa', in M. Guibernau and J. Hutchinson (eds.), *Understanding Nationalism*. Cambridge: Polity Press, 164–81.

Zakaria, F. (1997). 'The Rise of Illiberal Democracy'. *Foreign Affairs*, 76/6: 22–43.

Zartman, I. William (ed.) (1995). *Collapsed States: The Disintegration and Restoration of Legitimate Authority*. Boulder, Colo.: Lynne Rienner.

# Index